OXFORD SCHOOL ATLAS

Prepared by
the Cartographic Department
of the Clarendon Press

under the general editorship of
D. P. BICKMORE and F. C. COUZENS

THIRD EDITION

OXFORD UNIVERSITY PRESS

Oxford University Press, Walton Street, Oxford OX2 6DP

OXFORD NEW YORK TORONTO

DELHI BOMBAY CALCUTTA MADRAS KARACHI

PETALING JAYA SINGAPORE HONG KONG TOKYO

NAIROBI DAR ES SALAAM CAPE TOWN

MELBOURNE AUCKLAND

and associated companies in

BEIRUT BERLIN IBADAN NICOSIA

Oxford is a trade mark of Oxford University Press

First Edition 1955
Second Edition 1958
Third Edition 1960
Reprinted 1963, 1964
Reprinted with revision 1967, 1968, 1969, 1970, 1971
Reprinted and metricated 1973
Reprinted with revision 1974, 1976, 1977, 1978
Reprinted with further revision 1981
Reprinted 1982, 1983, 1985

THE MAPS & GAZETTEER HAVE BEEN

COMPILED, DRAWN & PHOTOGRAPHED BY THE

CARTOGRAPHIC DEPARTMENT OF THE CLARENDON PRESS

PRINTED IN HONG KONG

CONTENTS

Map scales are given in Representative Fractions. Here they are abbreviated to 2 points of a million.

Notes on the National Grid . . . iv

GAZETTEER OF THE BRITISH ISLES . v-xi

GREAT BRITAIN & IRELAND

	Scale	Page		Scale	Page
Roman Britain	*1: 4·75*	xii	S.E. England	*1: 1·00*	6-7
Population	*1: 4·75*	1	S.W. England	*1: 1·00*	8-9
Rainfall	*1: 4·75*	2	Wales & Midlands	*1: 1·00*	10-11
Land Use	*1: 4·75*	3	N. England	*1: 1·00*	12-13
Physical	*1: 4·75*	4	S. Scotland	*1: 1·00*	14-15
Geology	*1: 4·75*	5	N. Scotland	*1: 1·00*	16-17
			Ireland	*1: 1·25*	18-19

EUROPE

	Scale	Page		Scale	Page
Physical	*1: 19·0*	22	Europe & the Mediterranean	*1: 12·50*	20-21
Climate	*1: 19·0*	23	Spain & Portugal	*1: 6·30*	25
Population & Communications	*1: 19·0*	24	France-Poland	*1: 6·30*	26-27
			France	*1: 3·15*	28-29
			Italy & the Balkans	*1: 6·30*	30-31
			Germany & the Alps	*1: 3·15*	32-33
			Scandinavia	*1: 6·30*	34-35

ASIA

	Scale	Page		Scale	Page
Population & Communications	*1: 44·00*	36-37	U.S.S.R.	*1: 25·00*	42-43
Physical	*1: 44·00*	38-39	Western U.S.S.R.	*1: 12·50*	44-45
Vegetation	*1: 44·00*	40-41	Middle East, Pakistan & India	*1: 19·00*	46-47
			Middle East	*1: 12·50*	48-49
			Far East	*1: 19·00*	50-51
			India & Pakistan	*1: 12·50*	52
			China	*1: 12·50*	53
			Japan	*1: 6·30*	54

OCEANIA

	Scale	Page		Scale	Page
Population & Communications	*1: 44·00*	56	New Zealand	*1: 6·30*	55
Vegetation	*1: 44·00*	57	Australasia	*1: 22·00*	58-59
Physical	*1: 44·00*	57	Eastern Australia	*1: 6·30*	60-61

AFRICA

	Scale	Page		Scale	Page
Population & Communications	*1: 44·00*	62-63	N. Africa	*1: 19·00*	66-67
Physical	*1: 44·00*	64	Africa	*1: 12·50*	68-69
Vegetation	*1: 44·00*	65	East Africa	*1: 19·00*	70-71

NORTH & SOUTH AMERICA

	Scale	Page		Scale	Page
Population & Communications	*1: 44·00*	72-73	Canada	*1: 19·00*	78-79
Physical	*1: 44·00*	74-75	S. Canada & U.S.A.	*1: 12·50*	80-81
Vegetation	*1: 44·00*	76-77	U.S.A. & Central America	*1: 19·00*	82-83
			Great Lakes	*1: 6·30*	84-85
			S. America (North)	*1: 19·00*	86-87
			S. America (South)	*1: 19·00*	88-89

	Scale	Page		Scale	Page
Atlantic Ocean	*1: 63·00*	90	Pacific Ocean	*1: 63·00*	92-93
The Antarctic	*1: 25·00*	91			

WORLD

Physical . . . 94
Build . . . 95
Vegetation . . . 96
Rainfall . . . 97
Climate . . . 98-99
Soils . . . 100
Agriculture . . . 101
Economic Maps—Wheat; Maize & Rice; Cattle; Pigs & Sheep; Petroleum; Coal; Thermal Electricity; Hydro-Electricity; Iron Ore, Steel; Copper, Tin & Bauxite; Lead & Zinc; Shipbuilding; Motor Vehicles; Cotton Lint & CottonYarn; Wool Yarn . . . 102-109
Population . . . 110-111
Countries of the World . . . 112-113
Air Routes . . . 114-115
Selected World Geographical Name Changes from 1945 . . . 116-117
GAZETTEER OF THE WORLD . . . 118-130
Appendix to the Gazetteer . . . 131
Abbreviations . . . 132

To get the best out of this atlas note well these points

A LEGEND is found on each map. It is the "Highway Code" of the atlas and you will be in danger of misunderstanding the maps if you do not use the legend and know it almost by heart.

THE SCALE of a map is one of the most vital pieces of information about it. Make sure you have read it (from the title panel) before looking at the map. It is given as the ratio of the distance between two points, measured *on the map*, to the distance between the same two points, measured *on the ground*. For example 1:1 000 000 means that 1 cm on the map *represents* 1 000 000 cm (10 km) on the ground; it can equally well be expressed as 1 inch on the map *represents* 1 000 000 inches (approximately 16 miles) on the ground. Or 1: 6 300 000 means that 1 inch on the map *represents* 6 300 000 inches (approximately 100 miles) on the ground. For this reason, the scale ratio is known as the *representative fraction*, or R.F. You will find that many of the scales are the same or easily related.

THE GRATICULE of a map is the framework of lines of latitude and longitude on which the map is built. On nearly all the maps we have shown the graticule at every 5°, so that you can find the same "5° squares" of country on maps of different scales and projections. The different shapes of these "squares" reflect the different projections that have been used. Notice that the name of the projection is shown at the lower left corner of each map.

THE ARRANGEMENT of the atlas and the sequence of the maps is shown at the very front of the book. Study this page carefully and often, or you may find that you are not using the map you really need. Remember that you can find out a great deal more about a place by consulting several of the maps; population and vegetation maps, for example, as well as the general map.

THE FIRST MAPS are of Britain. With the help of the National Grid you will easily be able to relate these maps at 1:100,000 to the Ordnance Survey maps of your home district, e.g. at 1:50,000 or 1 cm to 0.5 km. But to do this you must read the notes about the National Grid below.

COLOURS. Notice that the same colours have been used to show the same things throughout the atlas. A tint of green or brown on a physical map means the same altitude anywhere in the world.

GAZETTEER. Often you will be able to find a place more quickly by looking it up in one or other of the two Gazetteers. Notice that there is one Gazetteer for the British Isles and another for the rest of the world. Positions are shown in Great Britain by the grid; in Ireland by letter and number; and the rest of the world by Latitude and Longitude to the nearest degree.

OTHER ATLASES. To know more about an area look it up in a bigger atlas. We have designed this atlas to lead on to the New Oxford Atlas and the Oxford Economic Atlas of the World.

METRICATION :- Distance, altitude, temperature, etc. are given in metric values and, where appropriate, imperial units are given as well.

The National Grid

(as used on pp. 6–17, and in the Gazetteer of the British Isles)

The National Grid is a network of imaginary lines covering Great Britain and beginning in the sea off Land's End. These lines are numbered in metres, first to the east, and then to the north.

Grid references in the Gazetteer, e.g. **'ST 36'**, are made up of three elements:

1. The first letter (**'S'** in the example). The diagram shows how the letters **'S'**, **'T'**, **'N'**, and **'H'** fall in relation to England, Wales, and Scotland.

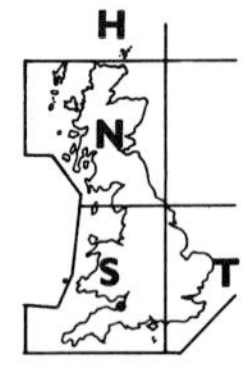

2. The second letter (**'T'** in the example). The second diagram shows how each big square is divided into twenty-five 'second-letter' squares, each being 100 × 100 kilometres.

3. The Figures. Each of these 100-kilometre squares is subdivided by lines running at 10-kilometre intervals. Distance is calculated from the south-west corner of the square, first to the east (eastings) then to the north (northings). The diagram shows the position **36** approximately.

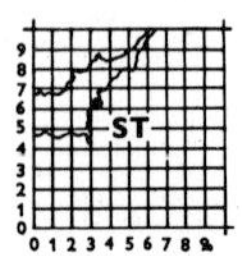

To define the position more exactly the 10-kilometre squares may be further subdivided into 1-kilometre squares. The two eastings distances—**32**—are given first; followed by the two northings distances—**61**—to produce the 'four-figure reference' **ST 3261**.

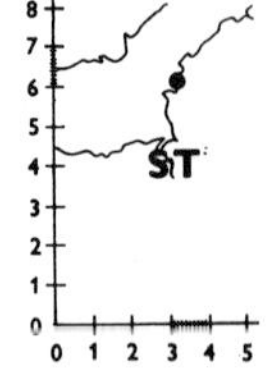

With larger-scale maps - 1:50,000 (1 cm to 0.5 km) - the process of subdivision goes further and 'six' or even 'eight figure references' are used to indicate positions more precisely.

(1 kilometre = 0·62 mile, and 1 mile = 1·61 kilometres)

The National Grid is used in this Atlas with the sanction of the Director General, Ordnance Survey, and of H.M. Stationery Office

GAZETTEER OF THE BRITISH ISLES

Local Government Reorganisation (England & Wales 1974, Scotland 1975):

Names are gazetteered to the pre-existing counties. The maps on pp6-17 show both the old and new county boundaries.

ABBEYFEALE — BRENTWOOD

Name	Page	Ref.
Abbeyfeale: Lim.	19	C3
Abbey Hd.: Kirkc.	15	NX74
Abbotsbury: Dorset	9	SY58
Abbotsford: Rox.	15	NT53
Aberayron: Card.	10	SN46
Abercarn: Mon.	10	ST29
Aberchirder: Banff.	17	NJ65
Aberdare: Glam.	10	SO00
Aberdaron: Caer.	10	SH12
ABERDEEN: Co., Scotland	17	NJ90
*Aberdovey: Card.	10	SN69
Aberfeldy: Perth.	17	NN84
Abergavenny: Mon.	10	SO21
Abergele: Denb.	10	SH97
Abernethy: Perth.	15	NO11
Abersychan: Mon.	10	SO20
Abertillery: Mon.	10	SO20
Aberystwyth: Card.	10	SN58
Abingdon: Berks	11	SU49
Aboyne: Aber.	17	NO59
Accrington: Lancs	13	SD72
Achill: i. & head, Mayo	18	A6
Achnashellach For.: Ross & Crom.	16	NH04
A. Chralaig: mt., Ross & Crom.	16	NH11
A Chruach: mt., Perth.	16	NN35
Acle: Norf.	6	TG41
Add: r.	14	NR89
Adur: r.	7	TQ12
Adwick le Street: Yorks	13	SE50
Aeron: r.	10	SN65
Affric: r.	16	NH11
Agnew's Hill: Antrim	18	K8
Aherlow: r.	19	E3
Ailsa Craig: i., Ayr	14	NX09
Ainsdale: Lancs	12	SD31
Aintree: Lancs	12	SJ39
Aird, The: Inv.	17	NH54
Airdrie: Lan.	15	NS76
Aire: r., Yorks	13	SE62
Aith: Shet. Is.	17	HU35
Alaw: r.	10	SH38
Alcester: War	11	SP05
Alchester: Oxon	11	SP52
Aldborough: Yorks	13	SE46
Alde: r.	6	TM36
Aldeburgh: Suff.	6	TM45
Alderley Edge: Ches.	11	SJ87
Aldermaston: Berks	9	SU56
Alderney: i., Chan. Is.	9	Inset
Aldershot: Hants	7	SU85
Aled. r.	10	SH96
Ale Water: r.	15	NT41
Alexandria: Dunb.	14	NS38
Alford: Lincs	6	TF47
Alfreton: Derby	11	SK45
Alham: r.	9	ST63
Allen: r., Corn.	8	SX07
Allen: r., Dorset	9	SU00
Allen: r., Northumb.	13	NY86
Allen, L.: Rosc./Leit.	18	E7
Allendale Town: Northumb.	13	NY85
Allen Water: r.	15	NN70
Allerston Forest: Yorks	13	SE88
Alloa: Clack.	15	NS89
Almond: r., Perth.	15	NN92
Almond: r., W. Loth.	15	NT07
Almondbury: Yorks	13	SE11
Aln: r.	15	NU11
Alne: r.	11	SP16
Alness: r.	17	NH67
Alnwick: Northumb.	15	NU11
Alsager: Ches.	11	SJ75
Alston: Cumb.	13	NY74
Alt: r.	12	SD30
Althorp: Northants	11	SP66
Alton: Hants	7	SU73
Altrincham: Ches.	11	SJ78
Alun: r.	10	SJ26
Alva: Clack.	15	NS89
Alvie: Inv.	17	NH80
Alwen Res.: Denb.	10	SH95
Alyth: Perth.	15	NO24
Amble: Northumb.	15	NU20
Ambleside: Westmor.	12	NY30
Amersham: Bucks	7	SU99
Amlwch: Anglesey	10	SH49
Amman: r.	10	SS61
Ammanford: Carm.	10	SN61
Ampleforth: Yorks	13	SE57
Ampthill: Beds	7	TL03
Ancholme, r.	13	SE97
An Clachan: c., Islay	14	NR27
An Cuaidh: Ross & Crom.	16	NG78
Andover: Hants	9	SU34
ANGLESEY: Co., Wales	10	SH47
ANGUS, Co., Scot.	17	NO46
Anker: r.	11	SP39
Annan: & r., Dumf.	15	NY16
Annandale: Dumf.	15	NY09
Annet: i., Scilly Is.	8	SV80
Annfield Plain: Dur.	13	NZ15
Annick Water: r.	14	NS34
Anstruther: Fife	15	NO50
An Teallach: mt., Ross & Crom.	16	NH08
ANTRIM: Co., N. Ireland	18	J8
Antrim Mts.	18	J9
An Uaimh: Meath	18	H6
Appin: Argyll	16	NM95
Appleby: Westmor.	12	NY62
Applecross: & for., Ross & Crom.	16	NG74
Appledore: Devon.	8	SS43
Aran Fawddwy: Mer.	10	SH82
Aran I.: Don.	18	D8
Aran Is.: Gal.	19	B5
Aray: r.	14	NN01
Arbor Low: Derby.	11	SK16
Arbroath: Angus	15	NO64
Arbury: War	11	SP38
Ardee: Louth	18	H6
Ardersier: Inv.	17	NH75
Ardgour: Argyll	16	NM96
Ardivochar Pt.: S. Uist	16	NF74
Ardlamont Pt.: Bute.	14	NS06
Ardle: r.	17	NO15
Ardmolich: Inv.	16	NM77
Ardmore Point: Islay	14	NR45
Ardmore Point: Mull	14	NM45
Ardnamurchan: Argyll	16	NM56
Ardnave Point: Islay	14	NR27
Ardoch: Perth.	15	NN80
Ardpatrick Pt.: Argyll	14	NR75
Ardrossan: Ayr.	14	NS24
Ards Peninsula: Down	18	L7
ARGYLL: Co., Scotland	14	—
Arisaig: Inv.	16	NM88
Arkengarthdale: Yorks	13	NY90
Arkleton Hill: Dumf.	15	NY49
Arklow: Wick.	19	J4
Armadale: W. Loth.	15	NS96
Armadale Bay: Skye	16	NG60
ARMAGH: Co., N. Ireland	18	H7
Arnisdale: Inv.	16	NG81
Aros: r.	14	NM54
Arran: i., Bute.	14	NR93
Arrow, Lough: Sligo	18	E7
Arrow, r.	10	SO35
Artro: r.	10	SH62
Arun: r.	7	TQ02
Arundel: Sussex	7	TQ00
Ascot: Berks	7	SU96
Ash: r.	7	TL31
Ashbourne: Derby.	11	SK14
Ashburton: Devon.	8	SX77
Ashby de la Zouch: Leics.	11	SK31
Ashdown Forest: Sussex	7	TQ43
Ashford: Kent	7	TR04
Ashington: Northumb.	15	NZ28
Ashridge: Herts	11	SP91
Ashton in Makerfield: Lancs	12	SJ59
Ashton under Lyne: Lancs	13	SJ99
Askival: mt., Rhum	16	NM39
Askrigg: Yorks	13	SD99
Atherstone: War	11	SP39
Atherton: Lancs	12	SD60
Athlone: Westmeath	18	F5
Athy: Kild.	19	H4
Attingham Park: Salop	11	SJ50
Attleborough: Norf.	6	TM09
Auchterarder: Perth.	15	NN91
Auchtermuchty: Fife	15	NO21
Aughrim: Wick.	19	J4
Aultbea: Ross & Crom.	16	NG88
Aust: Glos.	9	ST58
Avan: r.	10	SS89
Avebury: Wilts.	9	SU06
Aviemore: Inv.	17	NH81
Avoca: & r., Wick.	19	J4
Avon: r., Banff	17	NJ11
Avon: r., Devon.	8	SX75
Avon: r., Glos	9	ST66
Avon: r., Stirl.	15	NS97
Avon: r., War.	11	SP04
Avon: r., Wilts.	9	SU12
Avonmouth: Glos	9	ST57
Avon Water: r.	14	NS64
Awbeg: r.	19	D3
Axbridge: Som.	9	ST45
Axe: r., Dorset	9	ST30
Axe Edge: Derby	13	SK06
Axminster: Devon.	9	SY29
Aylesbury: Bucks	7	SP81
Aylsham: Norf.	6	TG12
Ayr: Ayr	14	NS32
Ayr: r.	14	NS62
AYRSHIRE: Scot.	14	NS—
Babbacombe Bay: Devon.	9	SX97
Bacup: Lancs	13	SD82
Badenoch: Inv.	17	NN68
Bagenalstown: Carlow	19	H4
Baggy Pt.: Devon.	8	SS44
Bagh nam Faoileann: N/S. Uist	16	NF84
Baildon: Yorks	13	SE13
Baile Atha Cliath: Dublin	19	J5
Bain: r., Lincs	13	TF26
Bain: r., Yorks	13	SD98
Bakewell: Derby	13	SK26
Bala: & L., Mer.	10	SH93
Balbriggan: Dublin	18	J6
Balcary Pt.: Kirkc.	15	NX84
Balder: r.	13	NY81
Baldock: Herts	7	TL23
Balemartine: Tiree	14	NL94
Baleshare: Uist	16	NF76
Ballachulish Ferry: Inv.	16	NN05
Ballaghaderreen: Rosc.	18	D6
Ballantrae: Ayr.	14	NX08
Ballater: Aber.	17	NO39
Ballina: Mayo	18	C7
Ballinasloe: Gal.	19	E5
Ballinrobe: Mayo	18	C6
Ballycastle: Antrim	18	J9
Ballyclare: Antrim	18	J8
Ballydavid Head: Kerry	19	Inset
Ballyhaunis: Mayo	18	D6
Ballyheige Bay: Kerry	19	B3
Ballyhoura Hills: Ireland	19	E3
Ballymena: Antrim	18	J8
Ballymoney: Antrim	18	H9
Ballynahinch: Down	18	K7
Ballyshannon: Don.	18	E8
Ballyteige Bay: Wex.	19	H3
Balmoral Castle: Aberdeen	17	NO29
Balmoral Forest: Aberdeen	17	NO28
Balnagown: r.	17	NH77
Baltimore: Cork	19	C1
Bamburgh: Northumb.	15	NU13
Bampton: Devon.	8	SS92
Bampton: Oxon.	11	SP30
Banbridge: Down	18	J7
Banbury: Oxon.	11	SP44
Banchory: Kinc.	17	NO79
Bandon: & r., Cork	19	D2
BANFF: Co., Scot.	17	NJ66
Bangor: Caer.	10	SH57
Bangor: Down	18	K8
Bann: r., Down	18	J7
Bann: r., N. Ireland	18	H9
Bann: r., Wex.	19	J4
Bannockburn: Stirl.	15	NS89
Bantry: & bay, Cork	19	C2
Banwy: r.	10	SJ00
Bardsey: i., Caer.	10	SH12
Bargoed: Glam.	10	SO10
Barking: Essex	7	TQ48
Barle: r.	8	SS83
Barmouth: Mer.	10	SH61
Barnard Castle: Durham	13	NZ01
Barnet: Herts	7	TQ29
Barnoldswick: Yorks	13	SD84
Barnsley: Yorks	13	SE30
Barnstaple: & bay, Devon	8	SS53
Barra: i., Inv.	16	NF60
Barra Hd.: Berneray	16	NL57
Barrhead: Renf.	14	NS55
Barrow: r.	19	H4
Barrowford: Lancs	13	SD83
Barrow in Furness: Lancs	12	SD16
Barr Water: r.	14	NR63
Barry: Glam.	10	ST16
Barshill: Dumf.	15	NY08
Barton upon Humber: Yorks	13	TA02
Barvas: r., Lewis	16	NB34
Basildon: Essex	7	TQ78
Basingstoke: Hants.	7	SU65
Bassenthwaite L.: Cumb.	12	NY22
Bass Rock: Firth of Forth	15	NT68
Bath: Som.	11	ST76
Bathgate: W. Loth.	15	NS96
Batley: Yorks	13	SE22
Battle: Sussex	7	TQ71
Battock, Mt.: Angus	17	NO58
Bawtry: Yorks	13	SK69
Bayfordbury: Herts	7	TL31
Beachy Head: Sussex	7	TV59
Beacon Hill: Rad.	10	SO17
Beaconsfield: Bucks	11	SU99
Beadnell Bay: Northumb.	15	NU22
Beaminster: Dorset	9	ST40
Beane: r.	7	TL22
Beaulieu: Hants	9	SU30
Beauly: r., Inv.	17	NH54
Beaumaris: Anglesey	10	SH67
Bebington: Ches.	10	SJ38
Beccles: Suff.	6	TM49
Beckenham: Kent	7	TQ36
Bedale: Yorks	13	SE28
Bedford: Beds	7	TL04
BEDFORDSHIRE: England	7	TL—
Bedgebury Park: Kent	7	TQ73
Bedlington: Northumb.	15	NZ28
Bedwas: Mon.	10	ST18
Beela: r.	12	SD58
Beer Head: Devon	9	SY28
Beeston: Ches.	11	SJ55
Beeston: Notts	11	SK53
Beg, Lough: N. Irel.	18	J8
Beinn a'Bhuird: Aber.	17	NO09
Beinn A'Chuallaich: Perth.	17	NN66
Beinn A'Ghlo: Perth.	17	NN97
Beinn an Tuirc: Argyll.	14	NR73
Beinn Bhàn: R. & Crom.	16	NG84
Beinn Bhàn: Inv.	16	NN18
Beinn Bheigeir: Islay	14	NR45
Beinn Bheula: Argyll	14	NS19
Beinn Bhreac: Jura.	14	NR59
Beinn Bhreac: Skye	16	NG25
Beinn Bhuidhe: Argyll	14	NN21
Beinn Dearg: Perth.	17	NN87
Beinn Dearg: R. & Crom.	16	NH28
Beinn Dhorain: Sutherland.	17	NC91
Beinn Dorain: Argyll	14	NN33
Beinn Edra: Skye	16	NG46
Beinn Eighe: R. & Crom.	16	NG96
Beinn Fhada: R. & Crom.	16	NH01
Beinn Heasgarnich: Perth	14	NN43
Beinn Ime: Argyll	14	NN20
Beinn Iutharn Mhòr: Perth	17	NO07
Beinn Laoigh: Perth.	14	NN22
Beinn Mhòr: Lewis.	16	NB20
Beinn nam Bad Mor: Caith.	17	NC95
Beinn na Sreine: Mull	14	NM43
Beinn Stumanadh: Sutherland.	17	NC64
Beinn Tharsuinn: R. & Crom.	17	NH67
Beinn Udlamain: Inv.	17	NN57
Beith: Ayr	14	NS35
Belcoo: Ferm.	18	F7
Belfast: & L., N. Irel.	18	K8
Belford: Northumb.	15	NU13
Bell Crags: Northumb.	15	NY77
Belleek: Ferm.	18	E7
Bellingham: Northumb.	15	NY88
Belmullet: Mayo	18	B7
Belper: Derby.	11	SK34
Belturbet: Cavan	18	G7
Belvoir Castle: Leics.	11	SK83
Bembridge: I. of Wight	7	SZ68
Ben Aigan: Banff	17	NJ34
Ben Alder: Inv.	17	NN47
Benbane Head: Antrim	18	J9
Ben Barvas: Lewis	16	NB33
Benbecula: i., Inv.	16	NF85
Benbradagh: Lon.	18	H8
Ben Bragar: Lewis	16	NB24
Ben Chonzie: Perth.	15	NN73
Ben Cruachan: Argyll	14	NN03
Benderloch: Argyll	14	NM93
Benenden: Kent	7	TQ83
Beneraird: Ayr.	14	NX17
Ben Griam More: Sutherland.	17	NC83
Ben Hee: Suther.	17	NC43
Ben Hiant: Argyll	16	NM56
Ben Hope: Suther.	17	NC45
Ben Horn: Suther.	17	NC80
Ben Klibreck: Suther.	17	NC63
Ben Lawers: Perth.	14	NN64
Ben Ledi: Perth.	14	NN50
Ben Lomond: Stirl.	14	NN30
Ben Loyal: Suther.	17	NC54
Ben Macdhui: Aber.	17	NN99
Ben More: Mull.	14	NM53
Ben More: Perth.	14	NN42
Ben More Assynt: Suther.	16	NC32
Benmore Head: Antrim.	18	J9
Bennane Hd.: Ayr	14	NX08
Bennan Hd.: Bute.	14	NR92
Ben Nevis: Inv.	16	NN17
Ben Resipol: Argyll.	16	NM76
Ben Rinnes: Banff	17	NJ23
Ben Sgriol: Inv.	16	NG81
Ben Stack: Suther.	16	NC24
Ben Starav: Argyll	14	NN14
Ben Venue: Perth.	14	NN40
Ben Vorlich: Dunb.	14	NN21
Ben Vorlich: Perth.	14	NN61
Ben Vrackie: Perth.	17	NN96
Benwee Head: Mayo	18	B7
Ben Wyvis: R. & Crom.	17	NH46
Bere Alston: Devon	8	SX46
Bere I.: Cork	19	B2
Berkeley: Glos	11	ST69
Berkhamsted: Herts	9	SP90
BERKSHIRE: Eng.	7	SU—
Berkshire Downs	7	SU47
Berneray: i., Inv.	16	NL58
Berneray: i., Inv.	16	NF98
Berriedale Water: r., Caith.	17	ND03
Berrow Flats: Som.	9	ST25
Berry Head: Devon.	9	SX95
Bertraghboy Bay: Galway	19	B5
BERWICKSHIRE: Scotland	15	NT—
Berwick upon Tweed: Northumb.	15	NT95
Berwyn: mts., Mer.	10	SJ03
Bessbrook: Armagh	18	J7
Bessy Bell: mt., Tyr.	18	G8
Bethesda: Caer	10	SH66
Bettws-y-coed: Caer.	10	SH75
Beult: r.	7	TQ84
Beverley: Yorks	13	TA03
Bewcastle Fells: Cumb.	15	NY58
Bewdley: Worcs	11	SO77
Bexhill: Sussex	7	TQ70
Bibury: Glos	11	SP10
Bicester: Oxon.	11	SP52
Biddulph: Staffs	11	SJ85
Bidean nam Bian: Argyll	16	NN15
Bideford: & bay, Devon	8	SS42
Bigbury: & bay, Devon	8	SX64
Biggar: Lan.	15	NT03
Biggin Hill: Kent	7	TQ45
Biggleswade: Beds	7	TL14
Billericay: Essex	7	TQ69
Billingham: Dur.	13	NZ42
Bill of Portland: Dorset	9	SY66
Bilston: Staffs	11	SO99
Binevenagh: mt., Antrim	18	H9
Bingham: Notts.	11	SK73
Bingley: Yorks	13	SE13
Binnein Mor: Inv.	16	NN26
Birkenhead: Ches.	12	SJ39
Birmingham: War	11	SP08
Birnam: Perth.	15	NO04
Birr: Offaly	19	F5
Birstall: Yorks	13	SE22
Birtley: Dur.	13	NZ25
Bishop Auckland: Durham	13	NZ22
Bishop Rock: Scilly Is.	8	SV80
Bishop's Castle: Salop	10	SO38
Bishop's Lydeard: Somerset	9	ST12
Bishop's Stortford: Herts	7	TL42
Bishop's Waltham: Hants	7	SU51
Blackadder Water	15	NT74
Blackburn: Lancs	12	SD62
Blackbushe: airport, Hants	9	SU85
Black Combe: Cumb	12	SD18
Blackcraig Hill: Ayr	14	NS60
Black Down: Sussex	7	SU92
Blackdown Hills: Somerset	9	ST11
Black Edge: Derby	13	SK07
Black Esk: r.	15	NY29
Black Hd.: Clare	19	C5
Black Hd.: Corn.	8	SW71
Black Hill: Ches.	13	SE00
Black Hill: Dur.	13	NZ05
Blackhope Scar: Scotland	15	NT34
Black Isle: R. & Crom.	17	NH66
Blackmoor: Corn.	8	SX05
Blackmoor Vale: Dorset	9	ST71
Black Mount: Argyll	14	NN24
Black Mountains: Breck.	10	SO22
Blackpool: Lancs	12	SD33
Blacksod Bay: Mayo	18	A7
Blackstairs: mts., Carlow	19	H4
Blackwater: r., Essex	7	TL81
Blackwater: r., Hants	7	SU85
Blackwater: r., Meath	18	H6
Black Water: r., Perth.	15	NO15
Blackwater: r., Wat.	19	E3
Bladnoch: r.	12	NX36
Blaenau-Ffestiniog: Mer.	10	SH74
Blaenau Morgannwg: Glam.	10	SN90
Blaenavon: Mon.	10	SO20
Blair, Mt.: Perth.	17	NO16
Blair Atholl: Perth.	17	NN86
Blairgowrie: Perth.	15	NO14
Blakeney: Glos	11	SO60
Blakeney Pt.: Norf.	6	TG04
Blanchland: Northumb.	13	NY95
Blandford Forum: Dorset	9	ST80
Blane Water: r.	14	NS58
Blarney: Cork	19	D2
Blaydon: Dur.	15	NZ16
Bleakow Hill: Derby.	13	SK19
Blenheim Palace: Oxon.	11	SP41
Bletchley: Bucks	11	SP83
Blithe: r.	11	SK03
Bloody Foreland: Donegal	18	E9
Bloxham: Oxon.	11	SP43
Blue Stack Mts.: Donegal	18	E8
Blyth: Northumb.	15	NZ38
Blyth: r., Norf.	6	TM47
Blyth: r., Northumb.	15	NZ27
Blythe: r.	11	SP17
Boat of Garten: Inv.	17	NH91
Boderg, L.: Rosc./Leit.	18	F6
Bodmin: Corn.	8	SX06
Bodmin Moor: Corn.	8	SX17
Bodnant: Denb.	10	SH87
Boggeragh Mts.: Cork	19	D3
Bognor Regis: Sussex	7	SZ99
Bog of Allen: Offaly	19	G5
Bogrie Hill: Dumf.	15	NX78
Bollington: Ches.	11	SJ97
Bolsover: Derby.	13	SK47
Bolt Head: Devon.	8	SX73
Bolton: Lancs	13	SD70
Bolton Abbey: Yorks.	13	SE05
Bolt Tail: Devon.	8	SX63
Bolus Head: Kerry	19	Inset
Bo'ness: W. Loth.	15	NT08
Bootle: Lancs	12	SJ39
Boreray: i., Inv.	16	NF88
Borgie: r.	17	NC65
Boroughbridge: Yorks	13	SE36
Borth: Card.	10	SN68
Borthwick Water: r.	15	NT30
Boscastle: Corn.	8	SX09
Boston: Lincs	6	TF34
Bosworth Field: Leics.	11	SK40
Botesdale: Suff.	6	TM07
Botley: Hants	7	SU51
Boulsworth Hill: Lancs	13	SD93
Bourne: Lincs	6	TF02
Bourne: r.	9	SU31
Bournemouth: Hants	9	SZ09
Bournville: War	11	SP08
Bourton on the Water: Glos	11	SP12
Bovey: r.	8	SX78
Bovey Tracey: Devon	8	SX87
Bowmore: Islay.	14	NR35
Bowness: Westmor	12	SD49
Box Hill: Surrey	7	TQ15
Boyne: r.	18	J6
Brackley: Northants	11	SP53
Bracknell: Berks	7	SU86
Bradfield: Berks	11	SU67
Bradford: Yorks	13	SE13
Bradford-on-Avon: Wilts	9	ST86
Brading: I. of Wight	7	SZ68
Bradninch: Devon.	8	SS90
Bradnor Hill: Here.	10	SO25
Braemar: Aber.	17	NO19
Braeriagh: mt., Scotland	17	NN99
Braes of Angus	17	NO45
Brain: r.	7	TL72
Braint: r.	12	SH46
Braintree: Essex	7	TL72
Bramhall: Ches.	11	SJ88
Brampton: Cumb.	15	NY56
Bran: r.	16	NH25
Brandon: Suff.	6	TL78
Brandon Bay: Kerry	19	A3
Brandon Mt.: Kerry	19	A3
Brant: r.	13	SK96
Bray: & hd., Wick.	19	J5
Bray: r.	8	SS63
Bray Head: Kerry	19	Inset
Breadalbane: Perth.	14	NN54
Breaksea Point: Glam.	10	ST06
Breamish: r.	15	NT91
Brechin: Angus	17	NO66
Breckland: Norf.	6	TL79
BRECKNOCKSHIRE: Wales	10	SN/SO
Brecon: & beacons, Breck.	10	SO02
Brecqhou: i., Chan. Is.	9	Inset
Brede: r.	7	TQ81
Bredon Hill: Worcs.	11	SO93
Breidden Hill: Montg.	10	SJ21
Brendon Hills: Som.	8	SS93
Brentford: Middx.	7	TQ17
Brentwood: Essex	7	TQ59

* See Page 131

BRESSAY — DINAS HEAD

Page Ref.
Bressay: i., Shet. Is.. 17 HU54
Brett: r. 7 TL95
Bridgend: Glam. 10 SS97
Bridge of Allan:
Stirl. 15 NS79
Bridgnorth: Salop 11 SO79
Bridgwater: Som. 9 ST23
Bridlington: Yorks. 13 TA16
Bridport: Dorset 9 SY49
Brierfield: Lancs 13 SD83
Brierley Hill: Staffs. 11 SO98
Brigg: Lincs. 6 TA00
Brighouse: Yorks 13 SE12
Brightlingsea: Essex 7 TM01
Brighton: Sussex 7 TQ30
Brims Ness: Caith.. 17 ND07
Bristol: England 9 ST57
Bristol Channel. 8 SS/ST
Brit: r. 9 SY49
Briton Ferry: Glam. 10 SS79
Brixham: Devon 8 SX95
Broad Bay: Lewis 16 NB53
Broad Cairn: Scot. 17 NO28
Broadford: Skye 16 NG62
Broad Haven: Mayo 18 B7
Broad Law: mt.,
Scotland 15 NT12
Broadstairs: Kent 7 TR36
Broadway:Worcs 11 SP03
Brock: r. 12 SD53
Brodick: Bute 14 NS03
Bromley: Kent 7 TQ46
Bromsgrove:Worcs 11 SO97
Bromyard: Here. 11 SO65
Brora: & r., Suther. 17 NC90
Broseley: Salop. 11 SJ60
Brosna: r. 19 F5
Brotton: Yorks. 13 NZ61
Brough:Westmor. 13 NY71
Brough Head:
Ork. Is.. 17 HY22
Broughton in
Furness: Lancs. 12 SD28
Brown Cow Hill:
Aber. 17 NJ20
Browney: r.. 13 NZ24
Brownhills: Staffs 11 SK00
Brownsea I.: Dorset 9 SZ08
Brown Willy: mt.,
Corn. 8 SX18
Brue: r. 9 ST44
Bruernish Pt.: Barra 16 NF70
Bruton: Som. 9 ST63
Bryanston: Dorset 9 ST80
Bryher: Scilly Is. 8 SV81
Bryn Brawd: mt.,
Card. 10 SN65
Brynmawr: Mon. 10 SO11
Buchan: Aber. 17 NJ95
Buchan Ness: Aber. 17 NK14
Buck, The: mt.,
Scotland 17 NJ42
Buckden Pike: mt.,
Yorks 15 SD97
Buckfastleigh:
Devon 8 SX76
Buckhaven: Fife 15 NT39
Buckie: Banff 17 NJ46
Buckingham: Bucks. 11 SP63
BUCKINGHAMSHIRE:
England 7 SP—
Buckland Abbey:
Devon 8 SX46
Buckley: Flint. 10 SJ26
Buddon Ness:
Angus 15 NO53
Bude: & bay, Corn. 8 SS20
Budleigh Salterton:
Devon 9 SY08
Builth Wells: Breck. 10 SO05
Bull Bay: Anglesey 10 SH49
Pull Pt.: Devon. 8 SS44
Buncrana: Don. 18 G9
Bundoran: Don. 18 E7
Bungay: Suff. 6 TM38
Buntingford: Herts 7 TL32
Bure: r. 6 TG41
Burford: Oxon. 11 SP21
Burgess Hill: Sussex 7 TQ31
Burghead: Moray 17 NJ16
Burgh le Marsh:
Lincs 6 TF56
Burghley House:
Northants 11 TF00
Burhou: i., Chan. Is. 9 Inset
Buriton: Hants. 7 SU72
Burn: r. 13 SE17
Burnham Flats:
North Sea 6 TF75
Burnham Market:
Norf. 6 TF84
Burnham-on-
Crouch: Essex. 7 TQ99
Burnham on Sea:
Som. 9 ST34
Burnley: Lancs 13 SD83
Burnswark: Dumf. 15 NY17
Burntisland: Fife 15 NT28
Burrow Head:Wig. 14 NX43
Burry Holms: Glam. 8 SS49
Burry Port: Carm. 10 SN40
Burslem: Staffs 11 SJ84
Burton: Westmor. 12 SD57
Burton Latimer:
Northants 11 SP97
Burtonport: Don. 18 E8
Burton upon Trent:
Staffs 11 SK22
Burtonwood: Lancs 12 SJ59
Bury: Lancs. 13 SD81
Bury St. Edmunds:
Suff. 6 TL86
Bush: r. 18 H9
Bushey: Herts 7 TQ19
BUTESHIRE:
Scotland 14 NR/NS
Bute Sound 14 NS05
Butser Hill: Hants 7 SU72
Buttermere: Cumb. 12 NY11
Butt of Lewis 16 NB56

Page Ref.
Buxey: Essex 7 TM10
Buxton: Derby. 13 SK07

Cadbury Castle:
Som. 9 ST62
Cader Idris: mt.,
Mer. 10 SH71
Caerleon: Mon.. 10 ST39
*Caernarvon: Caer.. 10 SH46
CAERNARVONSHIRE:
Wales 10 SH—
Caerphilly: Glam. 10 ST18
Caha Mts.:
Cork/Kerry 19 B2
Caher: Tip. 19 F3
Caher I.: Mayo 18 A6
Cahersiveen: Kerry 19 A2
Cahore Point: Wex. 19 J4
Cain: r. 10 SJ12
Cairngorm Mts.:
Scotland 17 NH90
Cairnharrow: Kirkc. 14 NX55
Cairn Pat: Wig. 12 NX05
Cairnsmore: Kirkc. 14 NX59
Cairnsmore of Fleet:
Kirkc. 14 NX56
Cairn Table:
Ayr./Lan. 14 NS72
Cairn Toul: Aber. 17 NN99
Cairn Water: r.. 15 NX88
Caistor: Lincs 6 TA10
CAITHNESS: Co.,
Scotland 17 ND14
Calder: r. 13 SE02
Caldew: r. 12 NY34
Caldy I.: Pemb.. 10 SS19
Cale: r. 9 ST72
Calf of Man: I. of Man 12 SC16
Calgary Bay: Argyll 15 NM35
Calgary Point: Coll 16 NM15
Caliach Point: Argyll 16 NM35
Callan: Kilk. 19 G4
Callander: Perth. 14 NN60
Callievar Hill: Aber. 17 NJ51
Callington: Corn. 8 SX36
Calne: Wilts. 9 ST97
Calshot Castle:
Hants 7 SU40
Cam: r. 6 TL57
Camberley: Surrey. 7 SU85
Camborne: Corn. 8 SW64
Cambrian Mts.:
Wales 10 —
Cambridge: Cambs. 6 TL45
CAMBRIDGESHIRE:
England 6 TL—
Camel: r. 8 SX07
Camelford: Corn. 8 SX18
Cam Loch: Suther.. 16 NC21
Camoge: r. 19 D4
Campbeltown:
Argyll 14 NR72
Campsie Fells: Stirl. 14 NS68
Can.: r. 7 TL61
Canisp Assynt: mt.,
Suther. 16 NC21
Canna: i., Inv. 16 NG20
Cannich: r. 16 NH23
Cannock: Staffs. 11 SJ90
Canterbury: Kent 7 TR15
Canvey I.: Essex 7 TQ78
Capel Curig: Caer.. 10 SH75
Capel Garmon:
Denb. 10 SH85
Cara: i., Argyll 14 NR64
Cardiff: Glam. 10 ST17
Cardigan: Card. 10 SN14
Cardigan Bay: Card. 10 SN—
Cardigan I.: Card. 10 SN15
CARDIGANSHIRE:
Wales 10 SN—
Carey: r. 8 SX39
Carisbrooke: I. of
Wight 7 SZ48
Carlingford L.: Irel. 18 J7
Carlisle: Cumb. 12 NY35
CARLOW: Co., R.
of Ireland 19 H4
Carluke: Lan. 15 NS85
Carmarthen: Carm. 10 SN42
CARMARTHENSHIRE:
Wales 10 SN—
Carmel Head:
Anglesey 10 SH29
Càrn Bàn: Inv. 17 NH60
Càrn Coire na h-
Easgainn: Inv. 17 NH71
Càrn Easgann Bàna:
Inv. 17 NH40
Carnedd Dafydd:
Caer. 10 SH66
Carnedd Llywelyn:
Caer. 10 SH66
Carnedd Wen:
Montg. 10 SH90
Carnedd y Filiast:
Wales 10 SH84
Càrn Eige:
Ross & Crom. 16 NH12
Carnforth: Lancs 12 SD47
Càrn Glas-Choire:
Inv. 17 NH82
Càrn Mairg: Perth 17 NN65
Càrn Mòr: Banff. 17 NJ21
Càrn na Caim:
Inv./Perth.. 17 NN68
Càrn na Loine:
Moray. 17 NJ03
Càrn na Saobhaidhe:
Inv. 17 NH61
Carnoustie: Angus. 15 NO53
Carnsore Point:
Wex. 19 J3
Carra, L.: Mayo. 18 C6
Carrauntuohil: mt.,
Kerry 19 B3
Carreg Ddu: Caer.. 10 SH24
Carregwasted Pt.:
Pemb. 10 SM94
Carrick: Ayr. 14 NX39

Page Ref.
Carrickfergus:
Antrim. 18 K8
Carrickmacross:
Monaghan 18 H6
Carrick on Shannon:
Leit. 18 E6
Carrick-on-Suir: Tip. 19 G3
Carron: r.,
Ross & Crom. 16 NG94
Carron: r.
Ross & Crom. 17 NH59
Carron: r., Stirl. 15 NS78
Carrowmore Lake:
Mayo 18 B7
Carse of Forth:
Stirl. 14 NS79
Carse of Gowrie:
Perth. 15 NO22
Carshalton: Surrey. 7 TQ26
Carstairs Junc.: Lan. 15 NS94
Carter Bar:
Eng./Scot. 15 NT60
Cartmel: Lancs 12 SD37
Cary: r. 9 ST42
Cashel: Tip. 19 F4
Casquet Banks:
Chan. Is. 9 Inset
Casquets: i.,
Chan. Is. 9 Inset
Cassley: r. 17 NC41
Castell Carreg
Cennen: Carm. 10 SN62
Castlebar: Mayo 18 C6
Castlebay: Barra 16 NL69
Castleblaney:
Monaghan 18 H7
Castle Cary: Som. 9 ST63
Castlederg: Tyr. 18 F8
Castle Douglas:
Kirkc. 14 NX76
Castleford: Yorks 13 SE42
Castleisland: Kerry 19 C3
Castle Loch:Wig. 12 NX25
Castle of Mey:
Caith. 17 ND27
Castlepollard:
Westmeath 18 G6
Castlerea: Rosc. 18 E6
Castleton: Derby. 13 SK18
Castletown: I. of M. 12 SC26
Catcleugh: L.,
Northumb. 15 NT70
Caterham: Surrey 7 TQ35
Cat Law: Angus. 17 NO36
Catterick Camp:
Yorks 13 SE19
Cauldcleuch Head:
Rox. 15 NT40
CAVAN: Co.,
R. of Ireland 18 G6
Cawdor: Nairn. 17 NH85
Cawood: Yorks. 13 SE53
Ceannanus Mór:
Meath 18 H6
Ceann Riobha:
Argyll. 14 NR38
Cefni r. 10 SH47
Ceiriog: r. 10 SJ23
Ceirw: r. 10 SH94
Cemaes Bay:
Anglesey 10 SH39
Cemaes Head:
Pemb. 10 SN15
Ceri: r. 10 SN34
Cerne: r. 9 SY69
Cerne Abbas:
Dorset 9 ST60
Chagford: Devon 8 SX78
Chalgrove: Oxon 9 SU69
Chanctonbury Ring:
Sussex 7 TQ11
Channel Islands. 9 Inset
Chapel Cross:
Dumf. 15 NY27
Chapel en le Frith:
Derby. 13 SK08
Char: r. 9 SY49
Chard: Dorset 9 ST30
Charlbury: Oxon 11 SP31
Charlestown of
Aberlour: Banff. 17 NJ24
Charleville: Cork 19 D3
Charnwood Forest:
Leics. 11 SK41
Charterhouse:
Surrey 7 SU94
Chater: r. 11 SK90
Chatham: Kent. 7 TQ76
Chat Moss: Lancs 12 SJ79
Chatsworth House:
Derby. 13 SK27
Chatteris: Cambs. 6 TL38
Cheadle: Ches. 13 SJ88
Cheadle: Staffs 11 SK04
Cheddar: & gorge,
Som. 9 ST45
Chedworth: Glos. 11 SP01
Chelmer: r.. 7 TL62
Chelmsford: Essex 7 TL70
Chelsea: London 7 TQ27
Cheltenham: Glos.. 11 SO92
Chepstow: Mon. 11 ST59
Chequers: Bucks. 11 SP80
Chertsey: Surrey 7 TQ06
Cherwell: r. 9 SP52
Chesham: Bucks. 7 SP90
CHESHIRE: Eng. 11 SJ—
Cheshunt: Herts 7 TL30
Chesil Beach:
Dorset 9 SY58
Chess: r. 7 SU99
Chester: Ches. 11 SJ46
Chesterfield:
Derby. 13 SK37
Chester le Street:
Dur. 13 NZ25
Chesters:
Northumb. 15 NY97
Chesters: Rox. 15 NT61
Chet: r. 6 TG20

Page Ref.
Cheviot, The: mt.,
Northumb. 15 NT92
Cheviot Hills:
Eng./Scot. 15 NT70
Chew: res. & r.. 9 ST57
Chichester: Sussex. 7 SU80
Chigwell: Essex 7 TQ49
Chiltern Hills: Bucks 11 SU—
Chippenham: Wilts. 9 ST97
Chipping Campden:
Glos. 11 SP13
Chipping Norton:
Oxon 11 SP32
Chipping Ongar:
Essex 7 TL50
Chipping Sodbury:
Glos. 11 ST78
Chislehurst: Kent 7 TQ47
Chorley: Lancs 12 SD51
Christchurch:
Hants 9 SZ19
Christ's Hospital:
Sussex 7 TQ12
Chudleigh: Devon 8 SX87
Chulmleigh: Devon. 8 SS61
Church Stretton:
Salop 11 SO49
Churn: r. 9 SU09
Churnet: r. 13 SK04
Chwefru: r.. 10 SN95
Cilfaesty Hill:
Montg. 10 SO18
Cinderford: Glos. 11 SO61
Cirencester: Glos. 11 SP00
Clach Leathad:
Argyll. 14 NN24
CLACKMANNAN:
Co., Scotland 15 NS99
Clacton on Sea:
Essex 7 TM11
Claerwen: r. 10 SN86
Claggain Bay: Islay 14 NR45
Clara: Offaly 19 F5
Clare: Suff. 7 TL74
CLARE: Co., R. of
Ireland 19 D4
Clare: r. 18 D6
Clare I.: Mayo 18 A6
Claremorris: Mayo. 18 C6
Clatteringshaws
Loch: Kirkc. 14 NX57
Claw: r. 8 SX39
Clay Cross: Derby. 13 SK36
Clay Head:
I. of Man 12 SC47
Clayton: Yorks. 13 SE13
Clear, Cape: Cork 19 B1
Clear I.: Cork 19 C1
Cleator Moor:
Cumb. 12 NY01
Cleckheaton: Yorks 13 SE12
Clee Hills: Salop 11 SO58
Cleethorpes: Lincs. 6 TA30
Clent Hills: Worcs. 11 SO97
Cleobury Mortimer:
Salop 11 SO67
Cletwr: r. 10 SN44
Clevedon: Som. 9 ST47
Cleveland: Yorks 13 NZ61
Cleveland Hills:
Yorks 13 NZ60
Cleveleys: Lancs 12 SD34
Clew Bay: Mayo 18 B6
Clifden: Gal. 18 A5
Cliffs of Moher:
Clare 19 C4
Clifton Gorge:
Bristol 9 ST57
Clisham: mt., Harris 16 NB10
Clitheroe: Lancs 13 SD74
Clogher Head:
Louth 18 J6
Clonakilty: Cork 19 D2
Clondalkin: Dublin 19 J5
Clones: Monaghan 18 G7
Clonmel: Tip. 19 F3
Clontarf: Dublin 19 J5
Clovelly: Devon. 8 SS32
Clun: r. 10 SO38
Clun Forest: Salop 10 SO28
Clunie Water: r. 17 NO18
Clwyd: r. 10 SJ15
Clwydian Range:
Wales 10 SJ16
Clyde: r. 14 NS37
Clydebank: Dunb. 14 NS47
Clydesdale: Lanark. 15 NS84
Clyst: r.. 8 SY09
Clywedog: r., Denb. 10 SJ05
Clywedog: r.,
Montg. 10 SN89
Cnoc Moy: mt.,
Argyll. 14 NR61
Coalbrookdale:
Salop 11 SJ60
Coalisland: Tyr. 18 H8
Coalville: Leics. 11 SK41
Coatbridge: Lan. 14 NS76
Coatham: Yorks 13 NZ52
Cobh: Cork. 19 E2
Cockenzie: E. Loth. 15 NT47
Cockermouth:
Cumb. 12 NY13
Cock of Arran:
Bute. 14 NR95
Cod's Head: Cork 19 A2
Coggeshall: Essex 7 TL82
Colchester: Essex 7 TM02
Cold Fell: Cumb. 12 NY65
Coldstream: Ber. 15 NT83
Cole: r. 11 SU18
Coleford: Glos.. 11 SO51
Coleshill: War.. 11 SP18
Coll: i., Argyll.. 16 NM15
Collinstown:
Dublin 18 J5
Coln: r. 9 SP10
Colne: Lancs 13 SD83
Colne: r. 7 TL92
Colne Point: Essex. 7 TM11

Page Ref.
Colonsay: i., Argyll. 14 NR39
Colt Hill: Dumf. 14 NX69
Colwyn Bay: Denb. 10 SH87
Colyton: Devon 9 SY29
Comber: Down 18 K8
Comeragh Mts.:
Wat. 19 F3
Compton Wynyates:
War. 11 SP34
Cona: r. 16 NM97
Congleton: Ches. 11 SJ86
Conisbrough: Yorks 13 SK59
Coniston: Lancs 12 SD39
Conistone Moor:
Yorks 13 SE07
Coniston Water:
Lancs 12 SD39
Conn, L.: Mayo. 18 C7
Connah's Quay:
Flint. 10 SJ26
Connaught: Prov.,
Ireland 18/19 —
Connemara: Gal. 18 B5
Consett: Dur. 13 NZ15
Constantine Bay:
Corn. 8 SW87
*Conway: & bay,
Caer. 10 SH77
*Conway: r. 10 SH85
Cookstown: Tyr. 18 H8
Coomacarren:
Kerry 19 A2
Cootehill: Cavan 18 G7
Coppins: Bucks. 7 TQ08
Coquet: r., & dale,
Northumb. 15 NZ19
Corbridge:
Northumb. 15 NY96
Corby: Northants 11 SP88
Corfe Castle:
Dorset 9 SY98
CORK: Co., R. of
Ireland 19 E2
Cork Harbour:
Cork 19 E2
CORNWALL: Co.,
England 8 SW/SX
Cornwall, Cape:
Corn. 8 SW33
Corran: Argyll.. 16 NN06
Correen Hills:
Aber. 17 NJ52
Corrib, L.: Gal.. 19 C5
Corse Hill: Lanark. 14 NS64
Corserine: Kirkc. 14 NX48
Corsham: Wilts. 9 ST87
Corve: r., Salop 11 SO58
Corwen: Mer. 10 SJ04
Cosham: Hants. 7 SU60
Cotehele: Corn. 8 SX46
Cothi: r. 10 SN63
Cotswolds: Glos. 11 ST/SP
Cottingham: Yorks 13 TA03
Coul Point: Islay 14 NR16
Coulsdon: Surrey 7 TQ35
Coupar Angus:
Perth. 15 NO23
Courtmacsherry
Bay: Cork 19 D2
Coventry: War. 11 SP37
Cover: r. 13 SE07
Covesea Skerries:
Moray 17 NJ17
Cowal: Argyll. 14 NS09
Cowbridge: Glam. 10 SS97
Cowdenbeath: Fife. 15 NT19
Cowdray Park:
Sussex 7 SU92
Cowes: I. of Wight. 7 SZ49
Cowie Water: r. 17 NO88
Cowley: Oxon 11 SP50
Craigmore: Bute. 14 NS16
Crail: Fife 15 NO60
Crailing: Rox. 15 NT62
Crake: r. 12 SD28
Cranborne Chase:
Dorset 9 ST91
Cranbrook: Kent 7 TQ73
Cranleigh: Surrey 7 TQ03
Cranwell: Lincs. 6 TF04
Crathie: Aber. 17 NO29
Craven: Yorks 13 SD95
Craven Arms:
Salop 11 SO48
Crawley: Sussex 7 TQ23
Creach Bheinn:
Argyll. 14 NN04
Creag Meagaidh:
Inv. 17 NN48
Creag Riadhach na
Graidhe: Suther. 17 NC62
Crediton: Devon 8 SS80
Cree: r. 14 NX37
Creran: r. 16 NN05
Creswell: Notts 11 SK57
Crewe: Ches. 11 SJ65
Crewkerne: Som. 9 ST40
Crianlarich: Perth.. 14 NN32
Criccieth: Caer. 10 SH43
Cricklade: Wilts. 11 SU09
Crieff: Perth. 15 NN82
Criffell: mt., Kirkc. 15 NX96
Croagh Patrick:
Mayo 18 B6
Croglin Water: r. 12 NY64
Cromalt Hills:
Suther.. 16 NC20
Cromarty:
Ross & Crom. 17 NH76
Cromarty Firth:
Ross & Crom. 17 NH66
Cromer: Norf. 6 TG24
Crook: Dur. 13 NZ13
Crookston Castle:
Lan.. 14 NS56
Crosby: Lancs 12 SJ39
Cross Fell: Cumb. 12 NY63
Cross Hill: Tyr.. 18 F8
Crossraguel Abbey:
Ayr. 14 NS20

Page Ref.
Crouch: r. 7 TQ89
Crowland: Lincs. 6 TF21
Crowle: Lincs. 6 SE71
Crowlin Is.:
Ross & Crom.. 16 NG63
Croydon: Surrey 7 TQ36
Cruden Bay: Aber.. 17 NK03
Cuckfield: Sussex 7 TQ32
Cuckmere: r. 7 TQ50
Cudworth: Yorks 13 SE30
Cuilcagh: Cavan 18 F7
Cuillin Hills: Skye 16 NG42
Culbin Wood:
Moray 17 NH96
Cullen: Banff. 17 NJ56
Culin, L.: Mayo. 18 C6
Culloden Moor: Inv. 17 NH74
Cullompton: Devon 8 ST00
Culm: r. 9 ST01
Cul Mòr:
Ross & Crom.. 16 NC11
Culross: Fife 15 NS98
Culter Fell: Lan. 15 NT02
Culvain: mt., Inv. 16 NN08
Culzean Castle:
Ayr. 14 NS21
CUMBERLAND:
Co., England 12 NY—
Cumnock: Ayr.. 14 NS51
Cumnor: Berks. 11 SP40
Cunningham: Ayr.. 14 NS34
Cupar: Fife 15 NO31
Curragh, The: Kild. 19 H5
Currane, L.: Kerry. 19 A2
Curraun Penin.:
Mayo 18 B6
Cushat Law:
Northumb. 15 NT91
Cushendun: Antrim 18 J9
Cutra, L.: Gal. 19 D5
Cwmbran: Mon. 10 ST29
Cynin: r. 10 SN21
Cynon: r. 10 SN90
Cywyn: r. 10 SN32

Dacre: Cumb. 12 NY42
Dagenham: Essex 7 TQ58
Dalbeattie: Kirkc. 15 NX86
Dalcross: Inv. 17 NH75
Dalkeith: Midloth. 15 NT36
Dalkey: Dublin. 19 J5
Dallas: Moray 17 NJ15
Dalmally: Argyll. 14 NN12
Dalton in Furness:
Lancs 12 SD27
Dalwhat Water: r.. 14 NX79
Dalwhinnie: Inv. 17 NN68
Dan, L.: Wick. 19 J5
Dane: r. 13 SJ86
Darent: r. 7 TQ56
Darlaston: Staffs 11 SO99
Darlington: Dur. 13 NZ21
Dart: r. 8 SX76
Dartford: Kent. 7 TQ57
Dartington: Devon 8 SX76
Dartmoor: Devon 8 SX68
Dartmouth: Devon 8 SX85
Darton: Yorks 13 SE31
Darvel: Ayr. 14 NS53
Darwen: r. 12 SD62
Daventry:
Northants 11 SP56
Davington: Dumf. 15 NT20
Dawley: Salop 11 SJ60
Dawlish: Devon 8 SX97
Deal: Kent 7 TR35
Dean Water: r.. 15 NO34
Dearne: r. 13 SE40
Deben: r. 6 TM26
Debenham: Suff. 6 TM16
Deddington: Oxon. 11 SP43
Dee: r., Aber. 17 NJ90
Dee: r., Ches. 10 SJ36
Dee: r., Kirkc. 14 NX75
Dee: r., Yorks 13 SD68
Deeps, The: Shet. Is. 17 HU33
Deer: r.. 8 SS30
Deeside: Aber.. 17 NO69
Denbigh: Denb. 10 SJ06
DENBIGHSHIRE:
Wales 10 SH/SJ
Denby Dale: Yorks. 13 SE20
Denge Marsh: Kent 7 TR01
Denny: Stirl. 15 NS88
Derby: Derby. 11 SK33
DERBYSHIRE:
England 11 SK—
Derg. L.: Don. 18 F8
Derg. L.:
R. of Ireland 19 E4
Derravaragh, L.:
Westmeath 18 G6
Derrynasaggart Mts.:
Kerry/Cork 19 C2
Derryveagh Mts.:
Don. 18 E8
Derwent: r., Cumb. 12 NY03
Derwent: r., Derby 13 SK26
Derwent: r. Dur. 13 NY94
Derwent: r., Yorks 13 SE76
Derwent Water:
Cumb. 12 NY22
Desborough:
Northants 11 SP88
Deveron: r., Banff.. 17 NJ64
Devilsbit: mt., Tip. 19 F4
Devil's Bridge:
Card. 10 SN77
Devil's Dyke:
Cambs. 6 TL66
Devils Water: r. 13 NY95
Devizes: Wilts.. 9 SU06
Devon: r. 15 NS99
Devonport: Devon. 8 SX45
DEVONSHIRE:
England 8 SS/SX
Dewsbury: Yorks 13 SE22
Didcot: Berks 11 SU59
Dighty Water: r. 15 NO33
Dinas Head: Pemb.. 10 SN04

* See Page 131

Page Ref.
Dingle: Kerry 19 A3
Dingwall: Ross & Crom. 17 NH55
Dionard: r. 16 NC35
Diss: Norf. 6 TM18
Ditchling Beacon: Sussex 7 TQ31
Ditsworthy Warren: Devon 8 SX56
Divis: mt., Antrim 18 J8
Dizzard Pt.: Corn. 8 SX19
Dochart: r. 14 NN53
Dodman Pt.: Corn. 8 SX03
Dodworth: Yorks 13 SE30
Dolgarrog: Caer. 10 SH76
Dolgelley: Mer. 10 SH71
Dollar: Clack. 15 NS99
Dollar Law: Peeb. 15 NT12
Don: r., Aber. 17 NJ81
Don: r., Yorks 11 SK49
Donaghadee: Down 18 K8
Doncaster: Yorks 13 SE50
Donegal: Don. 18 E8
DONEGAL: Co., R. of Ireland 18 E8
Donegal Bay: Don. 18 E8
Donington: Lincs 6 TF23
Doolsh: mt., Tyr. 18 F8
Doon: r. 14 NS40
Dorback Burn: r. 17 NJ04
Dorchester: Dorset 9 SY69
Dorchester: Oxon 11 SU59
Dore: r. 11 SO43
Dorking: Surrey 7 TQ15
Dorn: r. 11 SP42
Dornoch: Suther. 17 NH88
DORSET: Co., England 9 SY—
Douglas: I. of Man 12 SC37
Douglas: r. 12 SD41
Douglas Water: r., Lan. 15 NS83
Doulus Head: Kerry 19 Inset
Doune: Perth. 14 NN70
Doune Hill: Dunb. 14 NS29
Dounreay, Lower: Caith. 17 NC96
Dove: r., Derby. 11 SK22
Dove: r., Suffolk 6 TM17
Dove: r., Yorks. 13 SE69
Dovedale: Staffs/Derby. 11 SK15
Dover: Kent 7 TR34
Dovestone Tor: Derby. 13 SK18
DOWN: Co., N. Ireland 18 J7
Downe House: Kent 7 TQ46
Downham Market: Norf. 6 TF60
Downpatrick: Down 18 K7
Downpatrick Head: Mayo 18 C7
Downs, The: roadstead 7 TR45
Downside School: Som. 9 ST65
Drogheda: Louth 18 J6
Droichead Nua: Kild. 19 H5
Droitwich: Worcs. 11 SO96
Dromore: Down 18 J7
Dronfield: Derby 13 SK37
Druim Fada: Inv. 16 NN08
Drummond Hill: Perth. 15 NN74
Drumnadrochit: Inv. 17 NH53
Drumshanbo: Leit. 18 E7
Dryburgh Abbey: Rox. 15 NT53
Dryfe Water: r. 15 NY18
Drygarn Fawr: Breck. 10 SN85
Duart Point: Mull 14 NM73
Dubh Artach: i., Argyll. 14 NM10
Dubh Eilean: i., Argyll. 14 NR38
DUBLIN: Co., R. of Ireland 19 J5
Dublin Bay: Dublin 19 J5
Duchray Water: r. 14 NN40
Duddon: r. 12 SD29
Dudley: Worcs. 11 SO99
Dufftown: Banff. 17 NJ33
Dukeries, The: Eng. 13 SK67
Dulais: r. 10 SN70
Dulnan: r. 17 NH82
Dulverton: Som. 8 SS92
Dumbarton: Dunb. 14 NS47
Dumfries: Dumf. 15 NX97
DUMFRIESSHIRE: Scotland 15NX/NY
Dunaff Head: Don. 18 F9
Dunbar: E. Loth. 15 NT67
DUNBARTON: Co., Scotland 14 NS—
Dunbeath Water: r. 17 ND13
Dunblane: Perth. 15 NN70
Duncannon: Wex. 19 H3
Duncansby Head: Caith. 17 ND47
Dundalk: Louth 18 J6
Dundee: Angus 15 NO43
Dundonald: Ayr. 14 NS33
Dundonald: Down 18 K8
Dundrum Bay: Down 18 K7
Dunfermline: Fife 15 NT08
Dungannon: Tyr. 18 H7
Dungarvan: Wat. 19 F3
Dungeness: Kent 7 TR01
Dunkeld: Perth. 15 NO04
Dunkery Beacon: Som. 8 SS84
Dun Laoghaire: Dublin 19 J5
Dunmanway: Cork 19 C2
Dunmurry: Antrim 18 J8
Dunnet Hd.: Caith. 17 ND17
Dunoon: Argyll. 14 NS17
Dun Rig: Peeb./Selk. 15 NT23
Dunrobin Castle: Suther. 17 NC80
Duns: Ber. 15 NT75
Dunscore: Dumf. 15 NX88
Dunstable: Beds 7 TL02
Dunstaffnage Castle: Argyll. 14 NM83
Dunster: Som. 8 SS94
Dunvegan: Skye 16 NG24
Dunvegan Head: Skye 16 NG15
DURHAM: Co., England 13 NZ24
Durinish: Skye 16 NG24
Durlston Head: Dorset 9 SZ07
Dursey: i., Cork 19 A2
Dursley: Glos. 11 ST79
Dwyfor: r. 10 SH44
Dyce: Aber. 17 NJ81
Dyfi: r. 10 SN79
Dyke: r. 17 NC84
Dysart: Fife 15 NT39
Dysynni: r. 10 SH60

Ealing: Middx. 7 TQ17
Earby: Yorks 13 SD94
Earlestown: Lancs 12 SJ59
Earls Colne: Essex 7 TL82
Earlsferry: Fife 15 NT49
East Allen: r. 13 NY85
Earn's Heugh: Ber. 15 NT96
Easdale: i., Argyll. 14 NM71
Easingwold: Yorks 13 SE56
Eask, L.: Don. 18 E8
Eastbourne: Sussex 7 TV69
East Dereham: Norf. 6 TF91
Eastern Cleddau: r. 10 SN01
Easter Ross Ross & Crom. 17 NH48
East Fen: Lincs 13 TF45
East Grinstead: Sussex 7 TQ33
Eastham: Ches. 12 SJ38
East Ham: Essex 7 TQ48
East Harling: Norf. 6 TL98
East Ilsley: Berks 11 SU48
East Kilbride: Lan. 14 NS65
Eastleigh: Hants 7 SU41
East Linton: E. Loth. 15 NT57
East Loch Roag: Lewis 16 NB14
East Loch Tarbert: Harris 16 NG19
East Looe: Corn. 8 SX25
EAST LOTHIAN: Co., Scotland 15 NT—
East Neuk of Fife: Fife 15 NO50
East Retford: Notts 13 SK78
East Riding: Admin. Co., Yorks. 13 SE/TA
East Stour: r. 7 TR03
East Suffolk: Admin. Co., Suff. 6 TM26
East Sussex: Admin. Co., Sussex 7 TQ62
Eau: r. 13 SK99
Eaval: mt., N. Uist 16 NF86
Ebble: r. 9 SU02
Ebbw: r. 9 ST19
Ebbw Vale: Mon. 10 SO10
Eccles: Lancs 13 SJ79
Eccleshall: Staffs 11 SJ82
Eckford: Rox. 15 NT72
Eckington: Derby. 13 SK47
Eday: i., Ork. Is. 17 HY53
Eddleston Water: r. 15 NT25
Eddrachillis Bay: Suther. 16 NC13
Eddystone Rocks: England 8 SX33
Eden: r., Cumb. 12 NY54
Eden: r., Fife 15 NO21
Eden: r., Kent 7 TQ44
Eden: r., Mer. 10 SH72
Edenbridge: Kent 7 TQ44
Edenderry: Offaly 19 G5
Edenside: Cumb. 12 NY53
Edgbaston: War. 11 SP08
Edgehill: War. 11 SP34
Edgware: Middx. 7 TQ19
Edgworth: Lancs 13 SD71
Edinburgh: Midloth. 15 NT27
Edmonton: Middx. 7 TQ39
Eggardon Hill: Dorset 9 SY59
Egham: Surrey 7 TQ07
Eglingham: Northumb. 15 NU11
Egremont: Cumb. 12 NY01
Ehen: r. 12 NY00
Eigg: i., Inv. 16 NM48
Eilean an Roin Mor: i., Suther. 16 NC15
Eilean Donnan: Ross & Crom. 16 NG82
Eilean Mòr: i., Coll. 16 NM26
Eilean nan Ròn: Argyll. 14 NR38
Eilean nan Ròn: i., Suther. 17 NC66
Eilean Shona: i., Inv. 16 NM67
Eilean Trodday: i., Inv. 16 NG47
Elan: r. 10 SN87
Elford: Staffs 11 SK11
Elgin: Moray 17 NJ26
Elie: Fife 15 NO40
Elland: Yorks 13 SE12
Ellen: r. 12 NY03
Ellesmere: Salop 11 SJ33
Ellesmere Port: Ches. 11 SJ47
Elliott's Pike: mt., Northumb. 15 NY58
Ellon: Aber. 17 NJ93
Elmdon Heath: War. 11 SP18
Elwy: r. 12 SH97
Ely: Cambs. 6 TL58
Ely: r. 8 ST08
Emsworth: Hants 7 SU70
Enard Bay: Suther. 16 NC01
Enborne: r. 7 SU56
Enfield: Middx. 7 TQ39
English Channel 8/9 —
Ennell, L.: Westmeath 18 G5
Ennerdale Bridge: Cumb. 12 NY01
Ennis: Clare 19 D4
Enniscorthy: Wex. 19 H4
Enniskillen: Ferm. 18 F7
Ennistimon: Clare 19 C4
Enrick: r. 17 NH42
Ensay: i., Inv. 16 NF98
Eorsa: i., Argyll. 14 NM43
Epping: Essex 7 TL40
Epsom: Surrey 7 TQ26
Epworth: Lincs 6 SE70
Erch: r. 10 SH34
Erewash: r. 6 SK44
Ericht: r. 15 NO14
Eriskay: i., Inv. 16 NF81
Erith: Kent 7 TQ57
Erlestoke: Wilts. 9 ST95
Erme: r. 8 SX66
Errigal: mt., Don. 18 E9
Erris Head: Mayo 18 A7
Esher: Surrey 7 TQ16
Esk: r., Cumb. 12 SD19
Esk: r., Dumf./Cumb. 15 NY37
Esk: r., Midloth. 15 NT36
Esk: r., Yorks 13 NZ70
Eskdale: Dumf. 15 NY29
Eskdale Green: Cumb. 12 NY10
ESSEX: Co., Eng. 7 TL—
Etive: r. 14 NN14
Eton: & coll., Berks. 7 SU97
Ettrick: & r., Dumf. 15 NT21
Ettrick Forest: Midloth. 15 NT32
Ettrick Pen: mt., Scotland 15 NT10
Ettrick Water: r. 15 NT31
Euchan Water: r. 15 NS70
Evelix: r. 17 NH79
Evenlode: r. 11 SP22
Evesham: Worcs 11 SP04
Ewenny: r. 10 SS97
Ewenny Priory: Glam. 10 SS97
Ewes Water: r. 15 NY39
Exe: r. 8 SX99
Exeter: Devon 8 SX99
Exmoor: Som. 8 SS74
Exmouth: Devon 8 SY08
Eye: Suff. 6 TM17
Eyemouth: Ber. 15 NT96
Eye Peninsula: Lewis 16 NB53
Eye Water: r. 15 NT86

Fairford: Glos 11 SP10
Fair Hd.: Antrim 18 J9
Fair Isle: Shet Is. 17 HZ27
Fakenham: Norf. 6 TF93
Fal: r. 8 SW94
Fala: E. Loth. 15 NT46
Falkirk: Stirl. 15 NS88
Falkland: Fife 15 NO20
Falloch: r. 14 NN32
Falmouth: & bay, Corn. 8 SW83
Fanad Head: Don. 18 F9
Faraid Hd.: Suther. 17 NC37
Fareham: Hants 7 SU50
Faringdon: Berks 11 SU29
Farland Hd.: Ayr. 14 NS14
Farnborough: Hants 7 SU85
Farne Is.: Northumb. 15 NU23
Farnham: Surrey 7 SU84
Farrar: r. 16 NH33
Farsley: Yorks 13 SE23
Fashven: mt., Suther. 16 NC36
Fastnet Rock: Cork 19 B1
Faversham: Kent 7 TR06
Fawley: Hants 7 SU40
Feeagh, L.: Mayo 18 B6
Felixstowe: Suff. 7 TM33
Fell of Fleet: Kirkc. 14 NX57
Felsted: Essex 7 TL62
Fenny Stratford: Bucks 11 SP83
Fens, The: East Anglia 6 TL41
Fergus: r. 19 D4
FERMANAGH: Co., N. Ireland 18 F7
Fermoy: Cork 19 E3
Fetlar: i., Shet. Is. 17 HU69
Ffestiniog: Mer. 10 SH74
Fforest Fawr: Breck. 10 SN81
FIFE: Kingdom of, Scotland 15 NT/NO
Fife Ness: Fife 15 NO60
Filey: Yorks. 13 TA18
Filton: Glos. 9 ST67
Finaghy: Antrim 18 K8
Finchley: Middx. 7 TQ29
Findhorn: r. 17 NH83
Findon Ness: Kinc. 17 NO99
Finedon: Northants 11 SP97
Fingal's Cave: Argyll. 14 NM33
Finn: r. 18 F8
Finnart: Dunb. 14 NS29
Fintona: Tyr. 18 G7
Fionn Loch: Ross & Crom. 16 NG97
Fire Beacon Point: Corn. 8 SX19
Firth of Clyde: Scot. 14 NS16
Firth of Forth: Scot. 15 NT49
Firth of Lorne: Scot. 14 NM72
Firth of Tay: Scot. 15 NO32
Fishguard: & bay, Pemb. 10 SM93
Five Sisters: mt., Ross & Crom. 16 NG91
Flamborough Head: Yorks 13 TA27
Flatford Mill: Suff. 7 TM03
Flat Holm: i., Som. 9 ST26
Fleet: Hants 7 SU85
Fleet: r. 17 NC70
Fleetwood: Lancs 12 SD34
Flint: Flint. 10 SJ27
FLINTSHIRE: Wales 10 SJ—
Flodden Field: Northumb. 15 NT83
Fochabers: Moray 17 NJ35
Foel-fras: Caer. 10 SH66
Foel-Wen: mt., Denb. 10 SJ13
Foinaven: mt., Suther. 16 NC35
Folkestone: Kent 7 TR23
Font: r. 15 NZ09
Fordingbridge: Hants 9 SU11
Foreland: I. of Wight 7 SZ68
Foreland Pt.: Devon 8 SS75
Forest of Arden: War. 11 SP17
Forest of Atholl: Perth. 17 NN77
Forest of Bere: Hants 7 SU61
Forest of Bowland: England 12 SD65
Forest of Dean: Glos. 11 SO60
Forest of Harris: Harris 16 NB01
Forest of Knaresborough: Yorks 13 SE25
Forest ef Rossendale: Lancs 13 SD82
Forest Ridge: Sussex 7 TQ62
Forfar: Angus 15 NO45
Formartine: Aber. 17 NJ82
Formby: Lancs 12 SD20
Formby Pt.: Lancs 12 SD20
Forres: Moray 17 NJ05
Fort Augustus: Inv. 16 NH30
Forth: r. 14 NS69
Forth Bridge: Scot. 15 NT17
Fortrose: Ross & Crom. 17 NH75
Fort William: Inv. 16 NN17
Foss: r., Yorks 13 SE66
Fossebridge: Glos. 11 SP01
Fotheringhay: Northants 6 TL09
Foula: i., Shet. Is. 17 HT93
Foulness: i., Essex 7 TR09
Foulness: r., Yorks. 13 SE83
Foulness Pt.: Essex 7 TR09
Fountains Abbey: Yorks 13 SE26
Fowey: & r., Corn. 8 SX15
Foyers: Inv. 17 NH42
Foyle: r. 18 G8
Foyle, L.: Ireland 18 G9
Foynes: Lim. 19 C4
Framlingham: Suff. 6 TM26
Fraserburgh: Aber. 17 NJ96
Freshwater: I. of Wight 7 SZ38
Frinton: Essex 7 TM21
Frome: Som. 9 ST74
Frome: r., Dorset 9 SY69
Frome: r., Glos. 11 SO90
Frome: r., Here. 11 SO64
Frome: r., Som. 9 ST74
Fuday: i., Inv. 16 NF70
Furness Abbey: Lancs 12 SD27
Furness Fells: Lancs 12 SD29
Fylde: Lancs 12 SD33
Fyne: r. 14 NN21

Gade: r. 7 TL00
Gaick Forest: Inv. 17 NN78
Gainsborough: Lincs 6 SK89
Gairloch: Ross & Crom. 16 NG87
Gairn: r. 17 NJ20
Galashiels: Selk. 15 NT43
Gala Water: r. 15 NT44
Gallan Head: Lewis 16 NB03
Galley Head: Cork 19 D2
Galloway: Scotland 14 NX—
Galston: Ayr. 14 NS53
Galtee Mts.: Lim./Tip. 19 E3
Galtymore: mt., Lim. 19 E3
GALWAY: Co., R. of Ireland 19 C5
Gam: r. 10 SH90
Gara, L.: Sligo/Rosc. 18 E6
Gare Loch: Dunb. 14 NS28
Garno: r. 10 SO09
Garroch Hd.: Bute 14 NS05
Garron Pt.: Antrim. 18 K9
Garron Pt.: Kinc. 17 NO98
Garry: r. 17 NN76
Garstang: Lancs 12 SD44
Gartan, L.: Don. 18 F9
Garvellachs: is., Argyll. 14 NM61
Gatehouse of Fleet: Kirkc. 14 NX55
Gateshead: Dur. 15 NZ26
Gatwick: airport, Surrey 7 TQ24
Geal Chàrn: Inv. 17 NJ01
Geal-chàrn Mòr: Inv. 17 NH81
Geldie Burn: r. 17 NN98
Gelt: r. 12 NY55
Georgemas: Caith. 17 ND15
Gerrards Cross: Bucks 7 TQ08
Giant's Causeway: Antrim 18 H9
Gigha: i., Argyll. 14 NR65
Gill, L.: Sligo/Leit. 18 E7
Gillingham: Dorset 9 ST82
Gillingham: Kent 7 TQ76
Gipping: r. 6 TM05
Girdle Ness: Kinc. 17 NJ90
Girton: Cambs. 6 TL46
Girvan: Ayr. 14 NX19
Glamis: Angus 15 NO34
GLAMORGAN: Co., Wales 10 SS/ST
Glasgow: Lan. 14 NS56
Glas Maol: Angus 17 NO17
Glass: r. 16 NH33
Glastonbury: Som. 9 ST43
Glaven: r. 6 TG03
Glen: r. 6 TF11
Glen Affric: Inv. 16 NH12
Glen Almond: Perth. 15 NN83
Glen Artney: Perth. 14 NN71
Glenaruddery Mts.: Kerry 19 C3
Glen Avon: Banff. 17 NJ10
Glen Cannich: Inv. 16 NH23
Glen Cassley: Suther. 17 NC41
Glen Clova: Angus 17 NO37
Glen Coe: Argyll. 16 NN15
Glendalough: Wick. 19 J5
Glen Dochart: Perth. 14 NN53
Gleneagles: Perth. 15 NN91
Glen Esk: Angus 17 NO57
Glenfinnan: Inv. 16 NM98
Glen Garry: Inv. 16 NN19
Glenkens, The: Kirkc. 14 NX58
Glen Lednock: Perth. 15 NN72
Glen Lyon: Perth. 14 NN64
Glen More: Inv. 17 NH—
Glen Moriston: Inv. 16 NH31
Glen Nevis: Inv. 16 NN16
Glen of Aherlow: Tip. 19 E3
Glen Orchy: Argyll. 14 NN23
Glen Orrin: Ross & Crom. 16 NH34
Glenrothes: Fife 15 NO20
Glen Roy: Inv. 16 NN38
Glen Spean: Inv. 16 NN37
Glen Tarbert: Argyll. 16 NM85
Glenties: Don. 18 E8
Glen Trool: Kirkc. 14 NX47
Glen Urquhart: Inv. 17 NH43
Gleouraich: Inv. 16 NH00
Glossop: Derby. 13 SK09
Gloucester: Glos. 11 SO81
GLOUCESTERSHIRE: England 11 SO—
Glyder Fawr: Caer. 10 SH65
Glyme: r. 11 SP32
Glyndebourne: Sussex 7 TQ41
Goat Fell: Arran 14 NR94
Godalming: Surrey 7 SU94
Godmanchester: Hunts 6 TL27
Gog Magog Hills: Cambs. 6 TL45
Gola I.: Don. 18 E9
Golcar: Yorks 13 SE01
Golspie: Suther. 17 NH89
Gomersal: Yorks 13 SE22
Goodwin Sands. 7 TR45
Goodwood House: Sussex 7 SU80
Goole: Yorks 13 SE72
Goonhilly Downs: Corn. 8 SW72
Gordonstoun: Moray 17 NJ16
Gorey: Wex. 19 J4
Goring Gap: Berks/Oxon 11 SU58
Gort: Gal. 19 D5
Gorumna I.: Gal. 19 B5
Gosforth: Northumb. 15 NZ26
Gosport: Hants 7 SZ69
Gourock: Renf. 14 NS27
Gower: penin., Glam. 10 SS58
Gowna, L.: Long./Cavan 18 F6
Gowy: r. 12 SJ56
Graiguenamanagh: Kilk. 19 H4
Grampian Highlands: Scotland 17 NN/NO
Grand Havre: Chan. Is. 9 Inset
Graney, L.: Clare 19 D4
Grange: Lancs 12 SD47
Grangemouth: Stirl. 15 NS98
Grangetown: Yorks 13 NZ52
Grantham: Lincs. 6 SK93
Grantown-on-Spey: Moray 17 NJ02
Grasmere: Westmor. 12 NY30
Grassholm I.: Pemb. 8 SM50
Grassington: Yorks 13 SE06
Grass Pt.: Argyll. 14 NM73
Gravesend: Kent 7 TQ67
Grays Thurrock: Essex 7 TQ67
Great Badmington: Glos. 11 ST88
Great Bernera: Lewis 16 NB13
Great Blasket: i., Kerry 19 Inset
Great Cumbrae I.: Bute 14 NS15
Great Driffield: Yorks 13 TA05
Great Dunmow: Essex 7 TL62
Great Eau: r. 13 TF58
Great Gable: mt., Cumb. 12 NY21
Great Haldon: Devon 8 SX98
Great Harwood: Lancs 12 SD73
Great Mew Stone: Devon 8 SX54
Great Mis Tor: Devon 8 SX57
Great Ormes Head: Caer. 10 SH78
Great Russel: Chan. Is. 9 Inset
Great Torrington: Devon 8 SS41
Great Whernside: mt., Yorks 13 SE07
Great Yarmouth: Norf. 6 TG50
Greenlaw: Ber. 15 NT74
Greenock: Renf. 14 NS27
Greenore: Louth 18 J7
Greenore Pt.: Wex. 19 J3
Greenstone Pt.: Ross & Crom. 16 NG89
Greenwich: London 7 TQ37
Greian Hd.: Barra 16 NF60
Greta: r., Cumb. 12 NY22
Greta: r., Yorks 13 SD77
Gretna Green: Dumf. 15 NY36
Greystones: Wick. 19 J5
Gribbin Hd.: Corn. 8 SX14
Grime's Graves: Norf. 6 TL88
Griminish Point: N. Uist 16 NF77
Grimsby: Lincs 6 TA20
Grimsetter: Ork. Is. 17 HY41
Grimspound: Devon 8 SX78
Grosnez, C.: Jersey 9 Inset
Grove: Berks 11 SU49
Grovely Ridge: Wilts. 9 ST93
Guernsey: i., Chan. Is. 9 Inset
Guildford: Surrey 7 TQ05
Guisborough: Yorks 13 NZ61
Guiseley: Yorks 13 SE14
Gulland Rock: Corn. 8 SW87
Gullane: E. Loth. 15 NT48
Gurnard's Head: Corn. 8 SW43
Gwash: r. 11 SK90
Gwaun: r. 10 SN03
Gweebarra: r. 18 E8
Gweebarra B.: Don. 18 E8
Gweedore: Don. 18 E9
Gwennap Hd.: Corn. 8 SW32
Gwili: r. 10 SN42
Gwydderig: r. 8 SN73
Gwyrfai: r. 10 SH45
Gypsey Race: r. 13 TA07

Hackney: London 7 TQ38
Haddington: E. Loth. 15 NT57
Haddon Hall: Derby. 11 SK26
Hadleigh: Suff. 7 TM04
Hadrian's Wall: Cumb./Northumb. 15 NY66
Haileybury College: Herts 7 TL31
Hailsham: Sussex 7 TQ50
Hale: Ches. 13 SJ78
Halesowen: Worcs. 11 SO98
Halesworth: Suff. 6 TM37
Halifax: Yorks 13 SE02
Halkyn: mt., Flint. 10 SJ17
Halladale: r. 17 NC85
Halstead: Essex 7 TL83
Haltwhistle: Northumb. 15 NY76
Hamble: Hants 7 SU40
Hambledon: Hants. 7 SU61
Hambledon Hill: Dorset 9 ST81
Hambleton Hills: Yorks 13 SE58
Hamilton: Lan. 14 NS75
HAMPSHIRE: Eng. 9 SU—
Hampshire Downs. 9 SU55
Hampstead: London 7 TQ28
Hampton Court: Middx. 7 TQ16
Handa I.: Suther. 16 NC14
Hanley: Staffs 11 SJ84
Hardwick Hall: Derby. 13 SK46
Harewood: Yorks 13 SE34
Harlech: Mer. 10 SH53
Harleston: Norf. 6 TM28
Harlow: Essex 7 TL41
Harpenden: Herts 7 TL11
Harper's Brook: r. 6 SP98
Harrington: Cumb. 12 NX92
Harris: i., Inv. 16 NG19
Harrogate: Yorks 13 SE35
Harrow: Middx. 7 TQ18
Hart Burn: r. 15 NZ08
Hart Fell: Dumf. 15 NT11
Hartland: Devon 8 SS22
Hartlepool: Dur. 13 NZ53
Harwell: Berks 11 SU48
Harwich: Essex 7 TM23

Page Ref.
Haslemere: Surrey 7 SU93
Haslingden: Lancs 13 SD72
Hastings: Sussex 7 TQ81
Hatfield: Herts 7 TL20
Hatfield Broad Oak: Essex 7 TL51
Hatherleigh: Devon 8 SS50
Havant: Hants 7 SU70
Haverfordwest: Pemb. 10 SM91
Havergate I.: Suff. 7 TM44
Haverhill: Suff. 7 TL64
Hawes: Yorks 13 SD88
Hawes Water: Westmor. 12 NY41
Hawick: Rox. 15 NT51
Hawkshead: Lancs 12 SD39
Haworth: Yorks 13 SE03
Haydock: Lancs 12 SJ59
Hayle: & r., Corn. 8 SW53
Hayling I.: Hants 7 SU70
Hay-on-Wye: Here. 10 SO24
Haywards Heath: Sussex 7 TQ32
Hazel Grove: Ches. 13 SJ98
Headingley: Yorks 13 SE23
Heads of Ayr: Ayr. 14 NS21
Heanor: Derby. 11 SK44
Heart Law: Midloth. 15 NT76
Hebden Bridge: Yorks 13 SD92
Hebrides: Sea of 16 NL NG
Hecla: mt., S. Uist 16 NF83
Hedon: Yorks 13 TA12
Helensburgh: Dunb. 14 NS28
Hell's Mouth: Caer. 10 SH22
Helmsdale: & r., Suther. 17 ND01
Helmsley: Yorks 13 SE68
Helston: Corn. 8 SW62
Helvellyn: Cumb. 12 NY31
Helvick Head: Wat. 19 F3
Hemel Hempstead: Herts 7 TL00
Hendon: Middx. 7 TQ28
Henley in Arden: War. 11 SP16
Henley-on-Thames: Oxon 7 SU78
Hereford: Here. 11 SO54
HEREFORDSHIRE: England 11 SO—
Herefordshire Beacon 11 SO73
Herm: i., Chan. Is. 9 Inset
Herma Ness: Shet. Is. 17 HP61
Hermitage Castle: Rox. 15 NY49
Herne Bay: Kent 7 TR16
Herstmonceux: Sussex 7 TQ61
Hertford: Herts 7 TL31
HERTFORDSHIRE: England 7 TL—
Hessle: Yorks 13 TA02
Hetton le Hole: Dur. 13 NZ34
Hexham: Northumb. 15 NY96
Heysham: Lancs 12 SD46
Heywood: Lancs 13 SD81
Hickling Broad: Norf. 6 TG42
Higham Ferrers: Northants 11 SP96
High Bentham: Yorks 12 SD66
Highbridge: Som. 9 ST34
High Edge: Derby. 13 SK06
High Seat: mt., Westmor. 13 NY80
High Street: mt., Westmor. 12 NY41
High Willhays: mt., Devon 8 SX58
Highworth: Wilts. 11 SU29
High Wycombe: Bucks 7 SU89
Hill of Fare: Aber. 17 NJ60
Hill of Stake: Renf. 14 NS26
Hillsborough: Down 18 J7
Hills of Cromdale: Banff. 17 NJ12
Hilpsford Pt.: Lancs 12 SD26
Hinckley: Leics. 11 SP49
Hindhead: Surrey 7 SU93
Hindley: Lancs 12 SD60
Hingham: Norf. 6 TG00
Hitchin: Herts 7 TL12
Hodder: r. 12 SD64
Hoddesdon: Herts 7 TL30
Hoghton Tower: Lancs 13 SD62
Hogs Back: Surrey 7 SU94
Holbeach: Lincs. 6 TF32
Holderness: penin., Yorks 13 TA—
Holkham Hall: Norf. 6 TF84
Holland: Admin. Co., Lincs. 6 TF32
Holland Fen: Lincs. 6 TF24
Hollesley Bay: Suff. 7 TM34
Holme: r. 13 SE10
Holmesdale: Surrey 7 TQ24
Holmfirth: Yorks 13 SE10
Holsworthy: Devon 8 SS30
Holt: Norf. 6 TG03
Holtye House: Sussex 7 TQ43
Holyhead: Anglesey 10 SH28
Holy I.: Anglesey 10 SH27
Holy I.: Bute 14 NS03
Holy I.: Northumb. 15 NU14
Holywell: Flint. 10 SJ17
Holywood: Down 18 K8
Holywood: Dumf. 15 NX98
Honddu: r. 10 SO32
Honiton: Devon. 9 ST10
Hook Head: Wex. 19 H3

Page Ref.
Hopes, The: E. Loth. 15 NT56
Horbury: Yorks 13 SE21
Horncastle: Lincs. 6 TF26
Horn Hd.: Don. 18 F9
Hornsea: Yorks 13 TA24
Horsey Mere: Norf. 6 TG42
Horsforth: Yorks 13 SE23
Horsham: Sussex 7 TQ13
Horwich: Lancs 12 SD61
Hott Hill: Rox. 15 NT41
Houghton le Spring: Dur. 13 NZ35
Hounslow: Middx. 7 TQ17
Housesteads: Northumb. 15 NY76
Hove: Sussex 7 TQ20
Howardian Hills: Yorks 13 SE57
Howden: Yorks 13 SE72
Howe of Fife 15 NO41
Howe of the Mearns: Kinc. 17 NO67
Hownam Law: Rox. 15 NT72
Howth: Dublin 18 J5
Howtown: Westmor. 12 NY41
Hoy: i., Ork. Is. 17 ND29
Hoylake: Ches. 12 SJ28
Hoyland Nether: Yorks 13 SE30
Hucknall Torkard: Notts. 11 SK54
Huddersfield: Yorks 13 SE11
Hughenden Manor: Bucks 7 SU89
Hugh Town: Scilly Is. 8 SV91
Hull: see Kingston, upon Hull
Hull: r. 13 TA04
Hulme End: Staffs. 11 SK15
Humber: r. 13 TA21
Hungerford: Berks. 9 SU36
Hunmanby: Yorks 13 TA07
Hunterston: Ayr. 14 NS26
Huntingdon: Hunts 6 TL27
HUNTINGDONSHIRE: England 6 TL—
Huntly: Aber. 17 NJ53
Hurn: airport, Hants 9 SZ19
Hurstpierpoint: Sussex 7 TQ21
Hyde: Ches. 13 SJ99
Hythe: Kent 7 TR13

Iarconnaught: Gal. 19 C9
Idle: r. 11 SK79
Idrigill Point: Skye 16 NG23
Ilford: Essex 7 TQ48
Ilfracombe: Devon 8 SS54
Ilkeston: Derby. 11 SK44
Ilkley: Yorks 13 SE14
Ilminster: Som. 9 ST31
Immingham: Lincs 6 TA11
Inchcape: rock, Scotland 15 NO72
Inchkeith: i., Scot. 15 NT28
Inchmarnock: i., Bute 14 NS06
Ingatestone: Essex 7 TQ69
Ingleborough: mt., Yorks 13 SD77
Inglewood Forest: Cumb. 12 NY44
Inishark: i., Gal. 18 A6
Inishbofin: i., Don. 18 E9
Inishbofin: i., Gal. 18 A6
Inisheer: i., Aran Is. 19 B5
Inishkea: is., Mayo 18 A7
Inishmaan: i., Aran Is. 19 B5
Inishmore: i., Aran Is. 19 B5
Inishmurray: i., Sligo 18 D7
Inishowen Hd: Don. 18 H9
Inishowen Penin: Don. 18 G9
Inishtrahull: i., Don. 18 G9
Inishturk: is., Irel. 18 A6
Inkpen Beacon: Berks 9 SU36
Inner Hebrides: Scotland 16 NM—
Inner Sound: Inv. 16 NG64
Inny: r., Corn. 8 SX37
Inny: r., Kerry 19 A2
Instow: Devon 8 SS43
Inveran: Suther. 17 NH59
Inveraray: Argyll. 14 NN00
Inverbervie: Kinc. 17 NO87
Inver Dalavil: bay, Skye 16 NG50
Inverdruie: Inv. 17 NH91
Inverewe: Ross & Crom. 16 NG88
Invergarry: Inv. 16 NH30
Invergordon: Ross & Crom. 17 NH76
Inverkeithing: Fife 15 NT18
Inverliever Forest: Perth. 14 NM91
INVERNESS: Co., Scotland 17 NH64
Inverurie: Aber. 17 NJ72
Iona: i., Argyll. 14 NM22
Ipswich: Suff. 7 TM14
Ireland: Repub. of 18/19 —
Irfon: r. 10 SN84
Irish Sea 18/19 —
Irlam: Lancs. 13 SJ79
Iron-Bridge: Salop 11 SJ60
Irt: r. 12 SD09
Irthing: r. 13 NY66
Irthlingborough: Northants 11 SP97
Irvine: Ayr. 14 NS33
Irvine: r. 14 NS33
Irvinestown: Ferm. 18 F7

Page Ref.
Irwell: r. 13 SJ89
Ise: r. 6 SP88
Isla: r., Angus 15 NO13
Isla: r., Banff. 17 NJ45
Island Magee: Antrim 18 K8
Island of Bute: Bute 14 NS06
Island of Danna: Argyll. 14 NR67
Island of Skye: Inv. 16 NG—
Islay: i., Argyll 14 NR36
Isle: r. 9 ST32
Isle Martin: Ross & Crom. 16 NH09
Isle of Athelney: Som. 9 ST32
Isle of Axholme: Lincs 6 SE70
*Isle of Ely: Cambs. 6 TL49
Isle of Ewe: Ross & Crom. 16 NG88
Isle of Man: Irish Sea 12 SC38
Isle of May: Fife 15 NT69
Isle of Oxney: Kent 7 TQ92
Isle of Purbeck: Dorset 9 SY98
Isle of Sheppey: Kent 7 TQ96
Isle of Thanet: Kent 7 TR36
Isle of Walney: Lancs 12 SD16
Isle of Wight: Hants 7 SZ48
Itchen: r., Hants 9 SU53
Itchen: r., War. 11 SP45
Ithon: r. 10 SO06
Ivel: r. 7 TL13
Ivybridge: Devon 8 SX65

Jarlshof: Shet. Is. 17 HU30
Jarrow: Dur. 15 NZ36
Jedburgh: Rox. 15 NT62
Jed Water: r. 15 NT61
Jersey: i., Chan. Is. 9 Inset
Jethou: i., Chan. Is. 9 Inset
John o'Groat's House: Caith. 17 ND37
Johnstone: Renf. 14 NS46
Joyce's Country: Gal. 18 B6
Jura: i., Argyll. 14 NR58
Jurby Head: I. of Man 12 SC39

Kaimes Hill: Midloth. 15 NT16
Kale Water: r. 15 NT71
Kanturk: Cork 19 D3
Keady: Armagh 18 H7
Kebock Head: Lewis 16 NB41
Keen, Mt.: Angus 17 NO48
Keeper Hill: Tip. 19 E4
Keighley: Yorks 13 SE04
Keith: Banff. 17 NJ45
Kells: Kilk. 19 G4
Kells: Meath 18 H6
Kelso: Rox. 15 NT73
Keltie Water: r. 14 NN61
Kempston: Beds 7 TL04
Kendal: Westmor. 12 SD59
Kenilworth: War. 11 SP27
Kenmare: & r., Kerry 19 B2
Kennet: r. 9 SU16
Kennett: r. 6 TL66
KENT: Co., Eng. 7TQ TR
Kent: r. 12 NY40
Kerloch: mt., Kinc. 17 NO68
Kerrera: i., Argyll. 14 NM82
KERRY: Co., R. of Ireland 19 B3
Kerry Head: Kerry 19 B3
Kesteven: Admin. Co., Lincs 6SK TA
Keswick: Cumb. 12 NY22
Kettering: Northants 11 SP87
Key, L.: Rosc. 18 E7
Keynsham: Som. 9 ST66
Kidderminster: Worcs 11 SO87
Kidlington: Oxon 11 SP41
Kidsgrove: Staffs 11 SJ85
Kidwelly: Carm. 10 SN40
Kilbrannan Sound: Scotland 14 NR83
Kilconnell: Gal. 19 E5
KILDARE: Co., R. of Ireland 19 H5
Kilkee: Clare 19 B4
Kilkeel: Down 18 J7
KILKENNY: Co., R. of Ireland 19 G4
Kilkieran Bay: Gal. 19 B5
Killala: & bay, Mayo 18 C7
Killamarsh: Derby. 13 SK48
Killarney: Kerry 19 C3
Killary Harbour: Ireland 18 B6
Killebegs: Don. 18 E8
Killegray: i., Inv. 16 NF98
Killin: Perth. 14 NN53
Killiney: Dublin 19 J5
Killyleagh: Down 18 K7
Kilmacolm: Renf. 14 NS36
Kilmallock: Lim. 19 D3
Kilmarnock: Ayr 14 NS43
Kilmore: Argyll. 14 NM82
Kilmory: Rhum 16 NG30
Kilninver: Argyll. 14 NM82
Kiloran Bay: Colonsay 14 NR39
Kilpatrick Hills: Dunb. 14 NS47
Kilrea: Lon. 18 H8
Kilrenny: Fife 15 NO50
Kilrush: Clare 19 C4
Kilsyth: Stirl. 14 NS77
Kilsyth Hills: Stirl. 14 NS68
Kilwinning: Ayr. 14 NS34

Page Ref.
Kilworth Mts.: Cork 19 E3
Kimbolton: Hunts 6 TL06
Kimmeridge: Dorset 9 SY97
KINCARDINE: Co., Scotland 17 NO—
Kincardine: Fife. 15 NS98
Kinder Scout: Derby. 13 SK08
Kingairloch: Argyll. 16 NM85
Kinghorn: Fife 15 NT28
Kingie: r. 16 NN09
Kings: r. 19 F4
Kingsbridge: Devon. 8 SX74
Kingsclere: Hants 7 SU55
King's Lynn: Norf. 6 TF62
King's Seat: mt., Angus 15 NO23
Kingston upon Hull: Yorks 13 TA02
Kingston-upon-Thames: Surrey 7 TQ16
Kingstown: Dublin. 19 J5
Kingswear: Devon. 8 SX85
Kington: Here. 10 SO25
Kingussie: Inv. 17 NH70
King Water: r. 12 NY56
King William's Coll.: I. of Man 12 SC26
Kinloch: Rhum 16 NM49
Kinlochbervie: Suther. 16 NC25
Kinlochewe: Ross & Crom. 16 NH06
Kinlochleven: Inv. 16 NN16
Kinloch Rannoch: Perth. 17 NN65
Kinnairds Head: Aber. 17 NK06
Kinnel Water: r. 15 NY09
KINROSS: & Co., Scotland 15 NO10
Kinsale: Cork 19 D2
Kintail: Inv. 16 NG91
Kintore: Aber. 17 NJ71
Kintyre: Argyll. 14 NR73
Kippure: mt., Irel. 19 J5
Kirkburton: Yorks. 13 SE11
Kirkby in Ashfield: Notts 11 SK55
Kirkby Lonsdale: Westmor. 12 SD67
Kirby Moorside: Yorks 13 SE68
Kirkby Stephen: Westmor. 13 NY70
Kirkcaldy: Fife 15 NT29
KIRKCUDBRIGHT: Stewartry of, Scot. 14 NX—
Kirkcudbright: Kirkc. 14 NX65
Kirkham: Lancs. 12 SD43
Kirkintilloch: Dunb. 14 NS67
Kirkland Hill: Dumf. 14 NS71
Kirkoswald: Cumb. 12 NY54
Kirkwall: Ork. Is. 17 HY41
Kirriemuir: Angus 17 NO35
Kirtle Water: r. 15 NY27
Kirton in Lindsey: Lincs 6 SK99
Knaik: r. 15 NN81
Knapdale: Argyll 14 NR77
Knaresborough: Yorks 13 SE35
Knighton: Rad. 10 SO27
Knockadoon Hd: Cork 19 F2
Knockanteagal: Benbecula 16 NF75
Knockboy: mt., Irel. 19 C2
Knockfin Heights: Scotland 17 NC93
Knock Hill: Banff. 17 NJ55
Knockmealdown Mts.: Ireland 19 F3
Knottingley: Yorks 13 SE52
Knowlton Circles: Dorset 9 SU01
Knoydart: Inv. 16 NG80
Knutsford: Ches. 11 SJ77
Kyle: Ayr 14 NS52
Kyleakin: Skye 16 NG72
Kyle of Durness: Suther. 16 NC36
Kyle of Lochalsh: Ross & Crom. 16 NG72
Kyle of Tongue: Suther. 17 NC55
Kylesku Ferry: Suther. 16 NC23
Kyles of Bute: Bute. 14 NS07
Kym: r. 6 TL16

Ladder Hills: Banff. 17 NJ21
Ladhar Bheinn: Inv. 16 NG80
Ladybank: Fife 15 NO31
Lady Isle: Ayr 14 NS22
Laggan Bay: Islay 14 NR25
Laich o' Moray: Moray 17 NJ16
Lairg: Suther. 17 NC50
Lake District: Cumb. Westmor. 12 NY12
Lamachan Hill: Kirkc. 14 NX47
Lambay I.: Dublin 18 J5
Lambourn: & r., Berks 11 SU37
Lambourn Downs: Berks 9 SU38
Lamb's Head: Kerry 19 A2
Lamlash: Bute 14 NS03
Lammermuir: Ber. 15 NT75
Lammermuir Hills: E. Loth. 15 NT66
Lampeter: Card. 10 SN54
LANARK: Co., Scotland 15 NS84
LANCASHIRE: England 12 SD54

Page Ref.
Lancaster: Lancs 12 SD46
Lancing College: Sussex 7 TQ10
Land's End: Corn. 8 SW32
Langdales: Westmor. 12 NY30
Langholm: Dumf. 15 NY38
Langport: Som. 9 ST42
Langstrothdale Chase: Lancs 13 SD87
LAOIGHIS: Co., R. of Ireland 19 G5
Largs: Ayr 14 NS25
Lark: r. 6 TL77
Larne: Antrim 18 K8
Larriston Fells: Rox. 15 NY59
Lasswade: Midloth. 15 NT36
Lauder: Ber. 15 NT54
Lauderdale: Ber. 15 NT54
Launceston: Corn. 8 SX38
Laurencekirk: Kinc. 17 NO77
Lavenham: Suff. 7 TL94
Laxey: & bay, I. of Man 12 SC48
Laxton: Notts 13 SK76
Lea: r., Essex 7 TL30
Leach: r. 11 SP10
Leadon: r. 11 SO72
Leam: r. 11 SP56
Leamington Spa: War. 11 SP36
Leane, L.: Kerry 19 B3
Leannan: r. 18 F8
Leatherhead: Surrey 7 TQ15
Lechlade: Glos 11 SU29
Ledbury: Here. 11 SO73
Lee: r. 19 D2
Leeds: Yorks 13 SE33
Leek: Staffs 11 SJ95
Leen: r. 11 SK54
Leicester: Leics. 11 SK50
LEICESTERSHIRE: England 11 SK—
Leigh: Lancs 12 SJ69
Leighton Buzzard: Beds 9 SP92
LEINSTER: Prov., R. of Ireland 18/19 —
Leinster, Mt.: Carlow Wex. 19 H4
Leintwardine: Here. 11 SO47
Leiston: Suff. 6 TM46
Leith: Midloth. 15 NT27
Leith Hill: Surrey 7 TQ14
LEITRIM: Co., R. of Ireland 18 E7
Len: r. 7 TQ85
Lene, L.: Westmeath 18 G6
Lennox: Stirl. 14 NS49
Lennox Hills: Scot. 14 NS68
Lennoxtown: Stirl. 14 NS67
Leominster: Here. 11 SO45
Leri: r. 10 SN68
Lerwick: Shet Is. 17 HU44
Les Ecrehou: is., Chan. Is. 9 Inset
Leslie: Fife 15 NO20
Letchworth: Herts. 7 TL23
Letterkenny: Don. 18 F8
Lettermore I.: Gal. 19 B5
Leven: & r., Fife. 15 NO30
Leven: r., Yorks 13 NZ40
Lew: r. 8 SS50
Lewes: Sussex 7 TQ41
Lewis: i., Ross & Crom. 16 NB23
Lewisham: London 7 TQ37
Leyburn: Yorks 13 SE19
Leyland: Lancs 12 SD52
Liathach: Ross & Crom. 16 NG95
Lichfield: Staffs 11 SK10
Liddel Water: r. 15 NY48
Liddesdale: Rox. 15 NY58
Liffey: r. 19 H5
Ligger Bay: Corn. 8 SW75
Limavady: Lon. 18 H9
LIMERICK: Co., R. of Ireland 19 D4
Limerick Junction: Tip. 19 E4
Lincoln: Lincs 6 SK97
Lincoln Heath: Lincs 6 SK98
Lincoln Marsh: Lincs 6 TF—
LINCOLNSHIRE: England 6 TF—
Lincoln Wolds: Lincs 6 TF—
Lindsey: Admin. Co., Lincs 6 TF19
Ling: r. 16 NG93
Linlithgow: W. Loth. 15 NT07
Linney Hd.: Pemb. 10 SR89
Linslade: Bucks. 7 SP92
Lisburn: Antrim 18 J8
Liscannor Bay: Clare 19 C4
Liskeard: Corn. 8 SX26
Lismore: Wat. 19 F3
Lismore I.: Argyll 14 NM84
Listowel: Kerry 19 C3
Little Colonsay: i., Argyll 14 NM33
Little Cumbrae I.: Bute. 14 NS15
Little Dart: r. 8 SS71
Littlehampton: Sussex 7 TQ00
Little Loch Broom: Ross & Crom. 16 NH09
Little Minch, The: Scotland 16 NG16
Little Ouse: r. 6 TL68
Little Ross: Kirkc. 14 NX64
Little Sark: Chan. Is. 9 Inset
Little Stour: r. 7 TR15

Page Ref.
Little Walsingham: Norf. 6 TF93
Liverpool: & bay, Lancs 12 SJ39
Lizard, The: Corn. 8 SW71
Lizard Point: Corn. 8 SW61
Llanbedr: Mer. 10 SH52
Llandaff: Glam. 10 ST17
Llanddewi-Ystradenny: Rad. 10 SO16
Llandilo: Carm. 10 SN62
Llandovery: Carm. 10 SN73
Llandrindod Wells: Rad. 10 SO06
Llandudno: Caer. 10 SH78
Llanegryn: Mer. 10 SH60
*Llanelli: Carm. 10 SN50
Llanfairfechan: Caer. 10 SH67
Llanfyllin: Montg. 10 SJ11
Llangefni: Anglesey 10 SH47
Llangollen: Denb. 10 SJ24
Llanidloes: Montg. 10 SN98
Llanrhidian Sands: Glam. 10 SS49
Llanrwst: Denb. 10 SH76
Llanthony Abbey: Mon. 10 SO22
Llanwern: Mon. 9 ST49
Llanwrtyd Wells: Breck. 10 SN84
Lleyn: penin., Caer. 10 SH23
Lliw: r., Glam. 10 SN60
Lliw: r., Mer. 10 SH83
Llynfi: r. 10 SO13
Loanhead: Midloth. 15 NT26
Lochaber: Inv. 16 NN19
Loch a' Chroisg: Suther. 16 NH15
Loch Affric: Inv. 16 NH12
Loch Alsh: Ross & Crom. 16 NG82
Lochan Fada: Ross & Crom. 16 NH07
Loch Ard: Perth. 14 NN40
Loch Arkaig: Inv. 16 NN09
Lochar Water: r. 15 NY07
Loch Assynt: Suther. 16 NC22
Loch Awe: Argyll 14 NM91
Lochay: r. 14 NN53
Loch Ba: Mull 14 NM53
Loch Boisdale: S. Uist. 16 NF71
Loch Bracadale: Skye 16 NG23
Loch Brittle: Skye 16 NG31
Loch Broom: Ross & Crom. 16 NH19
Loch Brora: Suther. 17 NC80
Loch Buie: Mull 14 NM62
Loch Calder: Caith. 17 ND06
Loch Caolisport: Argyll 14 NR77
Loch Carron: Ross & Crom. 16 NG93
Loch Cluanie: Inv. 16 NH10
Loch Creran: Argyll 14 NM94
Loch Dee: Kirkc. 14 NX47
Loch Doine: Perth. 14 NN41
Loch Doon: Ayr 14 NX49
Loch Duich: Ross & Crom. 16 NG92
Loch Dun Seilcheig: Inv. 17 NH63
Loch Dunvegan: Skye 16 NG25
Loch Earn: Perth. 14 NN62
Loch Eck: Argyll 14 NS19
Loch Fil: Inv. Argyll 16 NN07
Loch Eishort: Skye 16 NG61
Loch Eriboll: Suther. 16 NC46
Loch Ericht: Inv./Perth. 17 NN57
Loch Erisort: Lewis 16 NB32
Loch Etive: Argyll 14 NN03
Loch Ewe: Ross & Crom. 16 NG88
Loch Eynort: Skye 16 NG32
Loch Eynort: S. Uist 16 NF82
Loch Fannich: Ross & Crom. 16 NH26
Loch Fleet: Suther. 17 NH79
Loch Frisa: Mull 14 NM44
Loch Fyne: Argyll 14 NR99
Loch Gairloch: Ross & Crom. 16 NG77
Loch Garry: Inv. 16 NH20
Lochgelly: Fife 15 NT19
Lochgilphead: Argyll 14 NR88
Loch Glass: Ross & Crom. 17 NH57
Loch Glencoul: Suther. 16 NC23
Loch Goil: Argyll 14 NS19
Loch Harport: Skye 16 NG33
Loch Hope: Suther. 17 NC45
Loch Hourn: Inv. 16 NG80
Loch Inchard: Suther. 16 NC25
Lochinch Castle: Wig. 14 NX16
Loch Indaal: Islay 14 NR25
Lochindorb: L., Moray 17 NH93
Lochinver: Suther. 16 NC02
Loch Katrine: Perth. 14 NN40
Loch Kishorn: Skye 16 NG83
Loch Laggan: Inv. 17 NN48
Loch Laxford: Suther. 16 NC15
Loch Leven: Kinr. 15 NO10
Loch Leven: Inv./Argyll 16 NN16
Loch Linnhe: Argyll 14 NM95
Loch Lochy: Inv. 16 NN29
Loch Lomond: Scot. 14 NS39
Loch Long: Scot. 14 NS29
Loch Loyal: Suther. 17 NC64

* See Page 131

Page Ref.

- Loch Luichart: Ross & Crom. 16 NH36
- Lochmaben: Dumf. 15 NY08
- Loch Maree: Ross & Crom. 16 NG97
- Loch Merkland: Suther. 16 NC33
- Loch Mhor: Inv. 17 NH51
- Loch Moidart: Inv. 16 NM67
- Loch Monar: Ross & Crom. 16 NH14
- Loch Morar: Inv. 16 NM79
- Loch More: Suther. 17 NC33
- Loch Morie: Ross & Crom. 17 NH57
- Loch Muick: Aber. 17 NO28
- Loch Mullardoch: Inv. 16 NH23
- Lochnagar: Aber. 17 NO28
- Loch Na Keal: Mull 14 NM53
- Loch nan Clar: Suther. 17 NC73
- Loch na Sheallag: Ross & Crom 16 NH08
- Loch Naver: Suther. 17 NC63
- Loch Ness: Inv. 17 NH52
- Loch Nevis: Inv. 16 NM79
- Loch of Stenness: Ork. Is. 17 HY21
- Loch of Strathbeg: Aber. 17 NK05
- Loch Ossian: Inv. 14 NN36
- Loch Pooltiel: Skye 16 NG15
- Loch Quoich: Inv. 16 NH00
- Loch Rannoch: Perth. 17 NN55
- Loch Resort: Lewis 16 NB01
- Loch Rimsdale: Suther. 17 NC73
- Loch Roag: Lewis 16 NB13
- Loch Ryan: Wig. 14 NX06
- Loch Scavaig: Skye 16 NG41
- Loch Scridain: Mull 14 NM42
- Loch Shiel: Inv./Argyll 16 NM87
- Loch Shin: Suther. 17 NC41
- Loch Snizort: Skye 16 NG35
- Loch Striven: Argyll 14 NS07
- Loch Sunart: Argyll 14 NM76
- Loch Sween: Argyll 14 NR78
- Loch Tarbert: Jura 14 NR58
- Loch Tay: Perth. 14 NN63
- Loch Teacuis: Argyll 14 NM65
- Loch Torridon: Ross & Crom. 16 NG76
- Loch Treig: Inv. 16 NN37
- Loch Tuath: Mull 14 NM44
- Loch Urigill: Suther. 16 NC21
- Loch Watten: Caith. 17 ND25
- Lochy: r. 16 NN18
- Lockerbie: Dumf. 15 NY18
- Loddon: Norf. 6 TM39
- Loftus: Yorks 13 NZ71
- Lomond Hills: Scot. 15 NO20
- LONDON: Co. & town, England 7 TQ—
- LONDONDERRY: Co., N. Ireland 18 G8
- Longa I.: Ross & Crom. 16 NG77
- Long Barrow: Glam. 8 SS58
- Long Crag: Northumb. 15 NU00
- Long Eaton: Notts 11 SK43
- LONGFORD: Co., R. of Ireland 18 F6
- Longleat Park: Wilts. 9 ST84
- Long Mountain: Salop. 10 SJ20
- Long Mynd, The: Salop 11 SO49
- Longridge: Lancs 12 SD63
- Long Sutton: Lincs. 6 TF42
- Longton: Staffs 11 SJ94
- Longtown: Cumb. 15 NY36
- Looe I.: Corn. 8 SX25
- Loop Head: Clare 19 B4
- Lorne: Argyll 14 NN03
- Lossie: r. 17 NJ15
- Lossiemouth: Moray 17 NJ27
- Lostwithiel: Corn. 8 SX15
- Loughborough: Leics. 11 SK51
- Loughor: r., Glam. 10 SN50
- Loughrea: Gal. 19 D5
- Loughros More Bay: Don. 18 D8
- Louth: Lincs 6 TF38
- LOUTH: Co., R. of Ireland 18 J6
- Lower Dounreay: Caith. 17 NC96
- Lower Lough Erne: Ferm. 18 F7
- Lowestoft: Suff. 6 TM59
- Low Moor: Yorks 13 SE12
- Lowther College: Flint. 10 SH97
- Lowther Hills: Scot. 15 NS90
- Loy: r. 16 NN08
- Lucan: Dublin 19 J5
- Luce Bay: Wig. 14 NX24
- Ludlow: Salop 11 SO57
- Lugar Water: r. 14 NS52
- Lugg: r. 10 SO36
- Lugnaquillia: mt., Wick. 19 J4
- Luing: i., Argyll 14 NM71
- Lunan Bay: Angus 15 NO75
- Lunan Water: r. 15 NO65
- Lundy I.: Devon 8 SS14
- Lune: r., Lancs 12 SD56
- Lune: r., Yorks 13 NY82
- Lunga: i., Argyll 14 NM70
- Lurgan: Armagh 18 J7
- Luss: Dunb. 14 NS39
- Luton: Beds. 7 TL02
- Lutterworth: Leics. 11 SP58
- Luxulyan: Corn. 8 SX05
- Lydd: Kent 7 TR02
- Lydney: Glos 11 SO60
- Lyme Bay: Dorset 9 SY38
- Lyme Hall: Ches. 13 SJ98
- Lyme Regis: Dorset 9 SY39
- Lymington: Hants 7 SZ39
- Lymm: Ches. 11 SJ68
- Lympne: Kent 7 TR13
- Lynas, Point: Anglesey 10 SH49
- Lyndhurst: Hants 9 SU30
- Lyne: r. 12 NY46
- Lynher: r. 8 SX36
- Lynmouth: Devon. 8 SS74
- Lynton: Devon. 8 SS74
- Lyon: r. 14 NN54
- Lytham: Lancs 12 SD32

- Maamturk Mts.: Gal. 18 B6
- Mablethorpe: Lincs 6 TF58
- McArthur's Hd.: Islay 14 NR45
- Macclesfield: Ches. 11 SJ97
- Macduff: Banff 17 NJ76
- Macgillycuddy's Reeks: Kerry 19 B2
- Machars, The: Wig. 14 NX35
- Machrihanish: Argyll 14 NR62
- Machynlleth: Montg. 10 SH70
- Macleod's Tables: mt., Skye 16 NG24
- Macnean, Lough: Ferm. 18 F7
- Macroom: Cork 19 D2
- Maentwrog: Mer. 10 SH64
- Maesteg: Glam. 10 SS89
- Maghera: Lon. 18 H8
- Magherafelt: Lon. 18 H8
- Maiden Castle: Dorset 9 SY68
- Maidenhead: Berks 7 SU88
- Maiden Newton: Dorset 9 SY59
- Maidens, rocks, Antrim 18 K8
- Maidstone: Kent 7 TQ75
- Maigue: r. 19 D4
- Main: r., Antrim 18 J8
- Mainland: i., Ork. Is. 17 HY31
- Mainland: i., Shet. Is. 17 HU—
- Malahide: Dublin 18 J5
- Maldon: Essex 7 TL80
- Malin Head: Don. 18 G9
- Malinmore Head: Don. 18 D8
- Mallaig: Inv. 16 NM69
- Mallow: Cork 19 D3
- Malmesbury: Wilts. 11 ST98
- Maltby: Yorks 13 SK59
- Malton: Yorks 13 SE77
- Malvern: Worcs 11 SO74
- Malvern Hills: Eng. 11 SO74
- Mamble: Worcs 11 SO67
- Mamore Forest: Inv. 16 NN16
- Manacles, The: Corn. 8 SW82
- Manchester: Lancs 13 SJ89
- Mangerton Mt.: Kerry 19 C2
- Mangotsfield: Glos 9 ST67
- Manningtree: Essex 7 TM13
- Manorbier: Pemb 10 SS09
- Manor Water: r. 15 NT23
- Mansfield: Notts 13 SK56
- Mansfield Woodhouse: Notts 13 SK56
- Maplin Sands: Essex 7 TR08
- Mar: Aber. 17 NJ50
- Marazion: Corn. 8 SW53
- March: Cambs. 6 TL49
- Mar Forest: Aber. 17 NO09
- Margam: Glam. 10 SS88
- Margate: Kent 7 TR37
- Margery Hill: Yorks 13 SK19
- Market Deeping: Lincs 6 TF11
- Market Drayton: Salop 11 SJ63
- Market Harborough: Leics. 11 SP78
- Market Rasen: Lincs 6 TF18
- Market Warsop: Notts 13 SK56
- Market Weighton: Yorks 13 SE84
- Markinch: Fife 15 NO20
- Marlborough: Wilts. 9 SU16
- Marlow: Bucks 7 SU88
- Marple: Ches. 13 SJ98
- Marsh, The: Glos 11 ST58
- Marsh, The: Lincs 6 TF42
- Marshfield: Glos 9 ST77
- Marston Moor: Yorks 12 SE55
- Marteg: r. 10 SN97
- Martock: Som. 9 ST41
- Maryborough: Laoighis 19 G5
- Maryport: Cumb. 12 NY03
- Masham: Yorks 13 SE28
- Masham Moor: Yorks 13 SE07
- Mask, Lough: Mayo 18 C6
- Matlock: Derby 11 SK36
- Matlock Bath: Derby 11 SK25
- Maughold Head: I. of Man 12 SC49
- Maun: r. 13 SK56
- Maxwelltown: Kirkc. 15 NX97
- Mayar: mt., Angus 17 NO27
- Maybole: Ayr 14 NS31
- MAYO: Co., R. of Ireland 18 C6
- Mealasta I.: Lewis 16 NA92
- Mealfuarvonie: mt., Inv. 16 NH42
- Meall Dubh: mt. Inv. 16 NH20
- Meall Meadhonach: mt., Suther. 17 NC46
- Meall nan Caoraich: Perth 15 NN93
- Meall nan Con: Argyll 16 NM56
- Mease: r. 11 SK21
- MEATH: Co., R. of Ireland 18 H6
- Meaul: mt., Kirkc. 14 NX59
- Medbourne: Leics. 11 SP79
- Meden: r. 11 SK66
- Medway: r. 7 TQ64
- Meese: r. 11 SJ72
- Meig: r. 16 NH35
- Meikle Millyea: mt., Kirkc. 14 NX58
- Melbourne: Derby 11 SK32
- Melksham: Wilts. 9 ST96
- Melrose: Rox. 15 NT53
- Meltham: Yorks 13 SE01
- Melton Mowbray: Leics. 11 SK71
- Melvin, Lough: Leit/Ferm. 18 E7
- Menai Bridge: Anglesey 10 SH57
- Mendip Hills: Som. 9 ST55
- Meon: r. 7 SU62
- Mere: Wilts. 9 ST83
- MERIONETHSHIRE Wales 10 SH—
- Merrick: Kirkc. 14 NX48
- Merse: dist., Ber. 15 NT74
- Mersea Island: Essex 7 TM01
- Mersey: r. 11 SJ68
- Merthyr Tydfil: Glam. 10 SO00
- Methwold: Norf. 6 TL79
- Mevagissey: Corn. 8 SX04
- Mew I.: Down 18 K8
- Mew Stone: Devon. 8 SX94
- Mexborough: Yorks 13 SK49
- Mickle Fell: Yorks 13 NY82
- Middleham: Yorks 13 SE18
- Middlesbrough: Yorks 13 NZ42
- *MIDDLESEX: Co., England 7 TQ28
- Middlesmoor: Yorks 13 SE07
- Middleton: Cork 19 E2
- Middleton: Lancs 12 SD80
- Middle Tongue: mt., Yorks/Lancs 13 SD88
- Middleton in Teesdale: Dur. 13 NY92
- Middlewich: Ches. 11 SJ76
- Midhurst: Sussex 7 SU82
- MIDLOTHIAN: Co., Scotland 15 NT—
- Milborne Port: Som. 9 ST61
- Mildenhall: Suff. 6 TL77
- Milford Haven: Pemb 10 SM90
- Milk Hill: Wilts. 9 SU16
- Miller's Dale: Derby 13 SK17
- Milleur Point: Wig. 14 NX07
- Millom: Cumb. 12 SD18
- Milngavie: Dunb. 14 NS57
- Milnrow: Lancs 13 SD91
- Milton Regis: Kent. 7 TQ96
- Miltownmalbay: Clare 19 C4
- Milverton: Som. 9 ST12
- Minchinhampton: Glos 11 SO80
- Minehead: Som. 8 SS94
- Mine Head: Wat. 19 F2
- Minginish: Skye 16 NG42
- Mingulay: Inv. 16 NL58
- Misbourne: r. 7 TQ08
- Mitcham: Surrey 7 TQ26
- Mitcheldean: Glos. 11 SO61
- Mitchelstown: Cork 19 E3
- Mizen Head: Cork 19 B1
- Mizen Head: Wick. 19 J4
- Moate: Westmeath 19 F5
- Modbury: Devon. 8 SX65
- Moel Fferna: mt., Mer. 10 SJ13
- Moelfre: mt., Carm. 10 SN33
- Moelfre: mt. Montg. 10 SN89
- Moel Hebog: mt., Caer. 10 SH54
- Moel Seisiog: Denb. 10 SH85
- Moel Siabod: mt. Caer. 10 SH75
- Moffat: & r., Dumf. 15 NT00
- Moidart: Inv. 16 NM77
- Mold: Flint. 10 SJ26
- Mole: r., Som. 8 SS61
- Mole: r., Surrey 7 TQ15
- Monadhliath Mts.: Inv. 17 NH71
- MONAGHAN: Co., R. of Ireland 18 H7
- Monavullagh Mts.: Wat. 19 F3
- Money Head: Wig. 14 NX04
- Monifieth: Angus 15 NO53
- Monkstone Point: Pemb. 10 SN10
- Monkton Combe: Som. 9 ST76
- MONMOUTH: Co., England 11 SO51
- Monnow: r. 11 SO42
- Montacute: Som. 9 ST41
- Montgomery: Montg. 10 SO29
- MONTGOMERYSHIRE: Wales 10 —
- Montrose: Angus 17 NO75
- Moorfoot Hills: Midloth. 15 NT35
- Moors, The: Wig. 14 NX26
- Morar: Inv. 16 NM78
- Moray Firth: Scot. 17NH/NJ
- MORAYSHIRE: Scotland 17 NJ15
- Morda: r. 10 SJ32
- Morecambe: Lancs 12 SD46
- Moretonhampstead: Devon. 8 SX78
- Moreton in Marsh: Glos 11 SP23
- Morley: Yorks 13 SE22
- Morpeth: Northumb. 15 NZ28
- Morte Bay: Devon. 8 SS44
- Morte Pt.: Devon. 8 SS44
- Morven: mt., Caith. 17 ND02
- Morven: mt., Aber. 17 NJ30
- Morvern: Argyll 16 NM75
- Mossley: Lancs 13 SD90
- Mostyn: Flint. 12 SJ18
- Mote of Urr: Kirkc. 15 NX86
- Motherwell: Lan. 15 NS75
- Mountain Ash: Glam 10 ST09
- Mountmellick: Laoighis 19 G5
- Mount's Bay: Corn. 8 SW52
- Mountsorrel: Leics. 11 SK51
- Mourne Mts.: Down 18 J7
- Mousehole: Corn. 8 SW42
- Moville: Don. 18 G9
- Moy: r. 18 C7
- Much Wenlock: Salop 11 SO69
- Muck: i., Inv. 16 NM47
- Muckish: mt., Don. 18 E9
- Muckle Roe: Shet. Is. 17 HU36
- Muick: r. 17 NO39
- Muine Bheag: Carl. 19 H4
- Muirneag: Lewis 16 NB44
- Mull: i., Argyll 14 NM63
- Mullaghareirk Mts.: Ireland 19 C3
- Mullaghcarn: mt., Tyr. 18 G8
- Mullet Penin: Mayo 18 A7
- Mull Hd.: Ork. Is. 17 HY55
- Mullingar: Westmeath 18 G6
- Mullion I.: Corn. 8 SW61
- Mull of Galloway: Wig. 12 NX13
- Mull of Kintyre: Argyll 14 NR50
- Mull of Logan: Wig. 14 NX04
- Mull of Oa: Argyll 14 NR24
- Mumbles Hd.: Glam. 10 SS68
- Muncaster Castle: Cumb. 12 SD19
- Munster: Prov., R. of Ireland 19 —
- Munster: r. 19 G4
- Muntervary Hd.: Cork 19 B2
- Musselburgh: Midloth. 15 NT37
- Mutton I.: Clare 19 B4
- Mynydd Bach: Card. 10 SN66
- Mynydd Bwlch-y-Groes: Breck. 10 SN83
- Mynydd Du: Carm. 10 SN71
- Mynydd Eppynt: Breck. 10 SN94
- Mynydd Hiraethog: Denb. 10 SH95
- Mynydd Pencarreg: Carm. 10 SN54
- Mynydd Prescelly: Pemb. 10 SN13

- Naas: Kild. 19 H5
- Nadder: r. 9 SU03
- Nagles Mts.: Cork 19 D3
- Nailsworth: Glos 9 ST89
- Nairn: Nairn 17 NH85
- Nairn: r. 17 NH74
- NAIRNSHIRE: Scot. 17 NH84
- Nantwich: Ches. 11 SJ65
- Nar: r. 6 TF71
- Narberth: Pemb. 10 SN11
- Naseby: Northants 11 SP67
- Nash Point: Glam. 10 SS96
- Navan: Meath 18 H6
- Nave I.: Argyll 14 NR27
- Naver: r. 17 NC74
- Naworth Castle: Cumb. 15 NY56
- Nayland: Suff. 7 TL93
- Naze, The: Essex 7 TM22
- Neagh, L.: N. Irel. 18 J8
- Neath: & r., Glam. 10 SS79
- Needham Market: Suff. 6 TM05
- Needles, The: I. of Wight. 7 SZ28
- Nefern: r. 10 SN13
- Nelson: Lancs 13 SD83
- Nenagh: & r., Tip. 19 E4
- Nene: r., Hunts 6 TL08
- Nene: r., Norf. TF42
- Nephin: mt., Mayo. 18 C7
- Nephin Beg Range: Mayo 18 B7
- Ness: dist., Lewis 16 NB56
- Neston: Ches. 10 SJ27
- Nether Wallop: Hants. 9 SU33
- Nevin: Caer. 10 SH34
- New Alresford: Hants 7 SU53
- Newark upon Trent: Notts 11 SK75
- Newbiggin by the Sea: Northumb. 15 NZ38
- Newborough: Anglesey 10 SH46
- Newbridge: Kild. 19 H5
- New Brighton: Ches. 10 SJ39
- New Buckenham: Norf. 6 TM09
- Newburgh: Fife 15 NO21
- Newburn: Northumb. 15 NZ16
- Newbury: Berks 9 SU46
- Newcastle: Down 18 K7
- Newcastle: Lim. 19 C3
- Newcastle Emlyn: Carm. 10 SN34
- Newcastle under Lyme: Staffs 11 SJ84
- Newcastle upon Tyne: Northumb. 15 NZ26
- Newent: Glos. 11 SO72
- New Forest: Hants. 9 SU20
- New Galloway: Kirkc. 14 NX67
- Newhaven: Sussex 7 TQ40
- New Holland: Yorks 13 TA02
- New Hunstanton: Norf. 6 TF64
- Newmarket: Suff. 6 TL66
- New Mills: Derby. 13 SK08
- Newmilns: Ayr. 14 NS53
- Newnham: Glos 11 SO61
- Newport: Fife 15 NO42
- Newport: I. of Wight. 7 SZ48
- Newport: Mon. 10 ST38
- Newport: Salop 11 SJ71
- Newport Pagnell: Bucks 11 SP84
- New Quay: Card. 10 SN35
- Newquay: Corn. 8 SW86
- New Romney: Kent 7 TR02
- New Ross: Wex. 19 H3
- Newry: Armagh/Down 18 J7
- Newstead Abbey: Notts 6 SK55
- Newton Abbot: Devon. 8 SX87
- Newton-le-Willows: Lancs 12 SJ59
- Newton Stewart: Wig. 14 NX46
- Newtown: Montg. 10 SO19
- Newtownards: Down 18 K8
- Newtownbreda: Down 18 K8
- Newtown Forbes: Long. 18 F6
- Neyland: Pemb. 10 SM90
- Nidd: r. 13 SE35
- Nidderdale: Yorks 13 SE16
- Nith: r. 15 NX97
- Nithsdale: Dumf. 15 NX99
- Noe: r. 13 SK18
- Noirmont Point: Jersey 9 Inset
- Nore: r. 19 H3
- NORFOLK: Co., England 6 TF/TG
- Norfolk Broads: Norf. 6 TG31
- Normanton: Yorks 13 SE32
- Northallerton: Yorks 13 SE39
- Northampton: Northants 11 SP76
- NORTHAMPTONSHIRE: England 11 SP—
- Northampton Uplands: Northants 11 SP56
- North Beck: r. 6 TF14
- North Berwick: E. Loth. 15 NT58
- North Carr Beacon: Fife 15 NO71
- North Channel: N. Irel./Eng. 18 K9
- North Dorset Downs 9 ST60
- North Downs: Kent 7TQ/TR
- Northern Ireland 18 —
- North Esk: r. 17 NO57
- North Foreland: Kent 7 TR46
- North Minch: Scot. 16 NB—
- North Riding: Admin. Co., Yorks. 13 SD/SE
- North Ronaldsay: i. & firth, Ork. Is. 17 HY75
- North Sound: Gal. 19 B5
- North Sound, The: Ork. Is. 17 HY54
- North Tawton: Devon. 8 SS60
- North Tyne: r. 15 NY78
- North Uist: i., Inv. 16 NF87
- NORTHUMBERLAND: Co., England 15 —
- North Walsham: Norf. 6 TG23
- North West Highlands 16NH/NC
- Northwich: Ches. 11 SJ67
- North Yorks. Moors 13SE/NZ
- Norwich: Norf. 6 TG20
- Noss Hd.: Caith. 17 ND35
- Nottingham: Notts 11 SK54
- NOTTINGHAMSHIRE: England 11 SK—
- Nuneaton: War. 11 SP39
- Nutt's Corner: Antrim 18 J8

- Oa, The: Islay 14 NR34
- Oakengates: Salop 11 SJ71
- Oakham: Rut. 11 SK80
- Oban: Argyll 14 NM83
- Ochil Hills: Perth. 15NN/NO
- Ock: r. 9 SU39
- Odiham: Hants. 7 SU75
- OFFALY: Co., R. of Ireland 19 F5
- Offa's Dyke Path: Wales 10 SO/SJ
- Ogwen: r. 10 SH66
- Oh Me Edge: Northumb. 15 NY69
- Okehampton: Devon. 8 SX59
- Oldany I.: Suther. 16 NC03
- Old Bolingbroke: Lincs 13 TF36
- Oldbury: Worcs 11 SO98
- Oldbury Camp: Wilts. 9 SU06
- Oldham: Lancs 13 SD90
- Old Head of Kinsale: Cork 19 D2
- Old Howe: r. 13 TA15
- Oldmeldrum: Aber. 17 NJ82
- Old Nene: r. 6 TL39
- Old Sarum: Wilts. 9 SU13
- Ollerton: Notts 13 SK66
- Olney: Bucks 11 SP85
- Omagh: Tyr. 18 G8
- Onny: r. 10 SO38
- Orchy: r. 14 NN23
- Ore: r. 15 NT29
- Orford: Suff. 7 TM45
- Orford Ness: Suff. 7 TM44
- Orkney Islands: & Co., Scotland 17 Inset
- Ormskirk: Lancs 12 SD40
- Oronsay, i., Argyll 14 NR38
- Orpington: Kent 7 TQ46
- Orrin: r. 16 NH34
- Orwell: r. 7 TM14
- Osborne: I. of Wight. 7 SZ59
- Ossett: Yorks 13 SE22
- Oswestry: Salop 10 SJ22
- Otley: Yorks 13 SE24
- Ot Moor: Oxon. 11 SP51
- Otter: r. 9 SY09
- Otter Rock: Islay 14 NR33
- Ottery: r. 8 SX38
- Ottery St. Mary: Devon. 9 SY09
- Oughter, L.: Cavan 18 G7
- Oughtmore: mt., Tyr. 18 H8
- Oundle: Northants 6 TL08
- Ouse: r., Bucks 11 SP53
- Ouse: r., Norf. 6 TF60
- Ouse: r., Sussex 7 TQ41
- Ouse: r., Yorks. 13 SE62
- Outer Hebrides: Scotland 16NF/NA
- Ouzel: r. 6 SP92
- Overton: Flint 11 SJ34
- Owel, L.: Westmeath 18 G6
- Oxborough Hall: Norf. 6 TF70
- Oxford: Oxon. 11 SP50
- OXFORDSHIRE: England 11 SP—
- Ox Mountains: Sligo 18 D7
- Oykell: r. 16 NC30
- Oyster Haven: Cork 19 E2

- Pabbay: i., Inv. 16 NF88
- Pabbay: i., Inv. 16 NL68
- Padiham: Lancs 13 SD73
- Padstow: Corn. 8 SW97
- Paignton: Devon. 8 SX86
- Painswick: Glos 11 SO80
- Paisley: Renf. 14 NS46
- Pangbourne: Berks 7 SU67
- Pant: r. 7 TL63
- Papa Stour: i., Shet. Is. 17 HU16
- Papa Westray: Ork. Is. 17 HY55
- Paps, The: Kerry 19 C3
- Park: dist., Lewis 16 NB31
- Park Head: Corn. 8 SW87
- Parrett: r. 9 ST33
- Parsonstown: see Birr
- Partry Mts.: Mayo 18 C6
- Passage de la Déroute: England/France 9 Inset
- Pass of Brander: Argyll 14 NN02
- Pass of Killiecrankie: Perth. 17 NN96
- Pateley Bridge: Yorks 13 SE16
- Patrington: Yorks 13 TA32
- Pawlaw Pike: Dur. 13 NZ03
- Peacehaven: Sussex 7 TQ40
- Peak District: Derby 13 SK18
- Peebles: Peeb. 15 NT24
- PEEBLESSHIRE: Scotland 15 NT—
- Peel: I. of Man 12 SC28
- Peel Fell: mt., Eng./Scot. 15 NT60
- Pegwell Bay: Kent 7 TR36
- Pembroke: Pemb. 10 SM90
- PEMBROKESHIRE: Wales 10SM/SN
- Penarth: Glam. 10 ST17
- Pen Brush: Pemb 10 SM83
- Penbwchdy: Pemb 10 SM83
- Penclegyr: Pemb 10 SM83
- Pendle Hill: Lancs 13 SD84
- Penicuik: Midloth. 15 NT25
- Penistone: Yorks 13 SE20
- Penk: r. 11 SJ91
- Penmaen-Mawr: Caer. 10 SH77
- Pennines: range, England 15 —
- Pennine Way 13SD/NY
- Penrhyn Mawr: Anglesey 10 SH27

*See Page 131

PENRITH — STALBRIDGE

Page Ref.
Penrith: Cumb. 12 NY53
Penryn: Corn. 8 SW73
Pentire Point: Corn. 8 SW98
Pentland Firth: Scot. 17 ND48
Pentland Hills: Scot. 15 NT15
Pentland Skerries: Caith. 17 ND47
Penwith: penin., Corn. 8 SW43
Pen-y-Ghent: Yorks 13 SD87
Penzance: Corn. 8 SW43
Perran Bay: Corn. 8 SW75
Perranporth: Corn. 8 SW75
Perry: r. 10 SJ32
Pershore: Worcs 11 SO94
Perth: Perth. 15 NO12
PERTHSHIRE: Scotland 15NN/NO
Peterborough: Northants 6 TL19
Peterhead: Aber. 17 NK14
Peter Hill: Aber. 17 NO58
Peterlee: Dur. 13 NZ44
Petersfield: Hants 7 SU72
Petworth: Sussex 7 SU92
Pevensey: Sussex 7 TQ60
Peveril Castle: Derby 13 SK18
Pewsey: Wilts. 9 SU15
Pickering: Yorks 13 SE78
Pickhill: Yorks 13 SE38
Piddle or Trent: r. 9 SY79
Pike Rigg: Northumb. 13 NY75
Pint Stoup, The: Angus 15 NO64
Pitlochry: Perth. 17 NN95
Pittenweem: Fife 15 NO50
Pladda: i., Bute. 14 NS01
Plas Newydd: Denb. 10 SJ24
Plockton: Ross & Crom. 16 NG83
Plym: r. 8 SX56
Plymouth: Devon. 8 SX45
Plympton: Devon. 8 SX55
Plymlimon Fawr: Card. 10 SN78
Pocklington: Yorks 13 SE84
Point Lynas: Anglesey 10 SH49
Point of Ardnamurchan: Argyll 16 NM46
Point of Ayre: I. of Man 12 NX40
Point of Knap: Argyll 14 NR67
Point of Stoer: Suther. 16 NC03
Polden Hills: Som. 9 ST43
Pollaphuca Res.: Wick. 19 H5
Polmaddie: Ayr 14 NX39
Polperro: Corn. 8 SX25
Pontefract: Yorks 13 SE42
Pontypool: Mon. 10 SO20
Pontypridd: Glam. 10 ST09
Poole: & bay, Dorset 9 SZ09
Porlock: & bay, Som. 8 SS84
Portadown: Armagh 18 J7
Portaferry: Down 18 K7
Port Ann: Argyll 14 NR98
Port Appin: Argyll 14 NM94
Portarlington: Laoighis 19 G5
Port Dinorwic: Caer. 10 SH56
Port Ellen: Islay 14 NR34
Port Erin: I. of Man 12 SC16
Port Errol: Aber. 17 NK03
Porth: Glam. 10 ST09
Port-Eynon Pt.: Glam. 10 SS48
Port Glasgow: Renf. 14 NS37
Porthcawl: Glam. 10 SS87
Porth Neigwl: Caer. 10 SH22
Port Isaac: Corn. 8 SW98
Portishead: Som. 9 ST47
Portlaoighise: Laoighis 19 G5
Portland Bill: Dorset 9 SY66
Portmadoc: Caer. 10 SH53
Portobello: Midloth. 15 NT37
Portree: Skye 16 NG44
Portrush: Antrim 18 H9
Portsmouth: Hants 7 SU60
Portsoy: Banff 17 NJ56
Portstewart: Lon. 18 H9
Port Sunlight: Ches. 10 SJ38
Port Talbot: Glam. 10 SS79
Portumna: Gal. 19 E5
Post Rocks: Islay 14 NR47
Potton: Beds 7 TL24
Poulter: r. 11 SK67
Poulton le Fylde: Lancs 12 SD33
Powis Castle: Montg. 10 SJ20
Prawle Pt.: Devon. 8 SX73
Preesall: Lancs 12 SD34
Prestatyn: Flint. 10 SJ08
Presteigne: Rad. 10 SO36
Preston: Lancs 12 SD52
Prestonpans: E. Loth. 15 NT37
Prestwich: Lancs 13 SD80
Prestwick: Ayr 14 NS32
Priest I.: Ross & Crom. 16 NB90
Princes Risborough: Bucks 7 SP80
Princetown: Devon. 8 SX57
Prudhoe: Northumb. 15 NZ06
Prysor: r. 10 SH63
Pudsey: Yorks 13 SE23
Puffin I.: Anglesey 10 SH68
Puffin I.: Kerry 19 Inset
Pwllheli: Caer. 10 SH33

Page Ref.
Quantock Hills: Som. 9 ST13
Queenborough: Kent 7 TQ97
Queensberry: Dumf. 15 NX99
Queensferry: W. Loth. 15 NT17
Quinag: mt., Suther. 16 NC22
Quinnish Pt.: Mull 14 NM45
Quirang: mt., Skye 16 NG46

Raasay: i., Inv. 16 NG54
Raby Castle: Dur. 13 NZ12
Race of Alderney: Chan. Is. 9 Inset
Radcliffe: Lancs. 13 SD70
Radley: Berks 11 SU59
Radnor Forest 10 SO26
RADNORSHIRE: Wales 10 SO—
Radstock: Som. 9 ST65
Rafford: Moray. 17 NJ05
Ragstone Ridge: Kent 7 TQ55
Rainhill: Lancs 12 SJ49
Rame Head: Corn. 8 SX44
Ramor, L.: Cavan 18 G6
Ramsbottom: Lancs 13 SD71
Ramsey: Hunts 6 TL28
Ramsey: I. of Man 12 SC49
Ramsey I.: Pemb 10 SM72
Ramsgate: Kent 7 TR36
Randalstown: Antrim 18 J8
Rannoch Moor: Perth. 14 NN35
Rathdrum: Wick. 19 J4
Rathfriland: Down 18 J7
Rathlin: i., Antrim 18 J9
Rathluirc: Cork 19 D3
Rathmullan: Don. 18 F9
Rattray: Perth. 15 NO14
Rattray Hd.: Aber. 17 NK15
Raunds: Northants 11 SP97
Ravenglass: Cumb. 12 SD09
Rawmarsh: Yorks 13 SK49
Rawtenstall: Lancs 13 SD82
Ray: r., Oxon. 11 SP62
Ray: r., Wilts. 9 SU19
Rayleigh: Essex 7 TQ89
Raynham Park: Norf. 6 TF82
Rea: r., Salop 10 SJ30
Rea: r., Worcs 11 SP08
Reading: Berks 7 SU77
Redcar: Yorks 13 NZ62
Redditch: Worcs 11 SP06
Redesdale: Northumb. 15 NY89
Redhill: Surrey 7 TQ25
Red Hills: Skye 16 NG52
Redlake: r. 10 SO37
Redruth: Corn. 8 SW74
Red Wharf Bay: Anglesey 10 SH58
Ree, L.: R. of Irel. 18 F6
Reepham: Norf. 6 TG12
Reeth: Yorks 13 SE09
Reigate: Surrey 7 TQ25
RENFREW: Co., Scotland 14 NS56
Renvyle: Gal. 18 B6
Repton: Derby. 11 SK32
Rey Cross: Yorks 13 NY91
Rhayader: Rad. 10 SN96
Rheidol: r. 10 SN67
Rheola Forest: Glam. 10 SN80
Rhinns, The: Wig. 14 NX05
Rhinns of Islay: Islay 14 NR25
Rhinns of Kells: Kirkc. 14 NX48
Rhinns Pt.: Islay 14 NR15
Rhinog Fawr: Mer. 10 SH62
Rhiw: r. 10 SJ10
Rhobell Fawr: Mer. 10 SH72
Rhondda: Glam. 10 SS99
Rhoose: Glam. 10 ST06
Rhu Coigach: Ross & Crom. 16 NB91
Rhuddlan: Flint. 10 SJ07
Rhum: i., Inv. 16 NM39
Rhyl: Flint. 10 SJ08
Rhymney: Mon. 10 SO10
Rhymney: r. 10 ST28
Rib: r. 7 TL32
Ribble: r. 13 SD63
Ribblesdale: Yorks 13 SD85
Richborough: Kent 7 TR36
Richmond: Surrey 7 TQ17
Richmond: Yorks 13 NZ10
Rickmansworth: Herts 7 TQ09
Ridlees Cairn: Northumb. 15 NT80
Rievaulx Abbey: Yorks 13 SE58
Rineanna (Shannon Airport): Clare 19 D4
Ringway: airport, Ches. 13 SJ88
Ringwood: Hants 9 SU10
Ripley: Derby. 11 SK45
Ripley: Yorks 13 SE26
Ripon: Yorks 13 SE37
Risca: Mon. 10 ST29
Rishton: Lancs 12 SD73
Risley: Lancs 12 SJ69
Roan Fell: Scotland 15 NY49
Roaringwater Bay: Cork 19 B1
Rochdale: Lancs 13 SD91
Rochester: Kent 7 TQ76
Rochford: Essex 7 TQ89
Rockingham: Northants 11 SP89
Rodel: Harris 16 NG08

Page Ref.
Roden: r. 11 SJ53
Roding: r. 7 TL50
Rodings, The: Essex 7 TL51
Rogan's Seat: Yorks 13 NY90
Roineval: mt., Skye 16 NG43
Rois-Bheinn: Inv. 16 NM77
Rollright Stones: Oxon. 11 SP23
Roman: r. 7 TL92
Rombalds Moor: Yorks 13 SE04
Romford: Essex 7 TQ58
Romney Marsh: Kent 7 TR03
Romsey: Hants 7 SU32
Rona: i., Inv. 16 NG65
Ronaldsway: I. of Man 12 SC26
Ronas Hill: Shet. Is. 17 HU38
Ronay: i., Argyll 16 NF95
Rosapenna: Don. 18 F9
ROSCOMMON: Co., R. of Ireland 18 E6
Roscrea: Tip. 19 F4
Rosehearty: Aber. 17 NJ96
Rosemullion Hd.: Corn. 8 SW82
Rossall School: Lancs 12 SD34
ROSS & CROMARTY: Co., Scotland 16 NH—
Rosses, The: Don. 18 E8
Rosslare Harbour: Wex. 19 J3
Ross of Mull: Mull 14 NM31
Ross-on-Wye: Here. 11 SO62
Rothbury: & forest, Northumb. 15 NU00
Rother: r., E. Sussex 7 TQ82
Rother: r., W. Sussex 7 SU82
Rother: r., Yorks 13 SK48
Rotherham: Yorks 13 SK49
Rothes: Moray 17 NJ24
Rothesay: Bute. 14 NS06
Rothwell: Northants 11 SP88
Rothwell: Yorks 13 SE32
Roughty: r. 19 B2
Round Hill: Yorks 13 SE15
Rousay: i., Ork. Is. 17 HY43
ROXBURGH: Co., Scotland 15 NT63
Roy: r. 16 NN39
Royal Leamington Spa see Leamington Spa
Royal Tunbridge Wells see Tunbridge Wells
Royston: Herts. 7 TL34
Royston: Yorks. 13 SE31
Rubha Ardvule: c., S. Uist 16 NF73
Rubha Dubh: c., Tiree. 14 NM04
Rubh' a' Geodha: c., Argyll 14 NR49
Rubha Hunish: c., Skye 16 NG47
Rubh' a' Mhàil: c., Argyll 14 NR47
Rubha nan Leacan: c., Islay 14 NR34
Rubh' an Dùnain: c., Skye 16 NG31
Rubha Réidh: c., Ross & Crom. 16 NG79
Rubha Shamhnan Insir: c., Rhum 16 NG30
Ruel: r. 14 NS09
Rue Point: I. of Man 12 NX40
Rugby: War. 11 SP57
Rugeley: Staffs 11 SK01
Ruislip: Middx. 7 TQ08
Runcorn: Ches. 11 SJ58
Runnymede: Surrey 7 SU97
Rush: Dublin 18 J6
Rushden: Northants 11 SP96
Rutherglen: Lan. 14 NS66
Ruthin: Denb. 10 SJ15
Ruthven: Perth. 15 NO24
RUTLAND: Co., England 11 SK90
Ryde: I. of Wight 7 SZ59
Rye: & bay, Sussex. 7 TQ92
Rye: r. 13 SE58
Ryton: r. 13 SK68

Saddle, The: mt., Inv./Ross & Crom. 16 NG91
Saddleback: mt., Cumb. 12 NY32
Saffron Walden: Essex 7 TL53
St. Abb's Head: Ber. 15 NT96
St. Agnes: & head, Corn. 8 SW75
St. Albans: Herts 7 TL10
St. Alban's Head: Dorset 9 SY97
St. Andrews: Fife 15 NO51
St. Anne's on the Sea: Lancs 12 SD32
St. Anns Hd.: Pemb. 10 SM80
St. Asaph: Flint. 10 SJ07
St. Aubin: Jersey 9 Inset
St. Austell: Corn. 8 SX05
St. Bees: Cumb. 12 NX91
St. Blazey: Corn. 8 SX05
St. Boswells: Rox. 15 NT63
St. Bride's Bay: Pemb. 10 SM71
St. Catherine's Hill: Hants 7 SU42
St. Catherine's Pt.: I. of Wight. 7 SZ47
St. Columb Major: Corn. 8 SW96
St. David's: Pemb. 10 SM72
St. Fagan's Castle: Glam. 10 ST17

Page Ref.
St. Finan's Bay: Kerry 19 Inset
St. George's Chan. 19 J3
St. George's: i., Corn. 8 SX25
St. Germans: Corn. 8 SX35
St. Govan's Head: Pemb 10 SR99
St. Helens: Lancs 12 SJ59
St. Helier: Jersey 9 Inset
St. Ives: Corn. 8 SW54
St. Ives: Hunts 6 TL37
St. John's Chapel: Dur. 13 NY83
St. John's Pt.: Don. 18 E8
St. John's Pt.: Down 18 K7
St. Just: Corn. 8 SW33
St. Leonards: Sussex 7 TQ80
St. Leonard's For.: Sussex 7 TQ13
St. Magnus Bay: Shet. Is. 17 HU26
St. Margaret's Hope: Ork. Is. 17 ND49
St. Martin's: i., Scilly Is. 8 SV91
St. Martin's Point: Guernsey 9 Inset
St. Mary's: Scilly Is. 8 SV91
St. Mary's L.: Selk. 15 NT22
St. Mawes: Corn. 8 SW83
St. Michael's Mt.: Corn. 8 SW53
St. Neots: Hunts 6 TL16
St. Ninian's Cave: Wig. 14 NX43
St. Peter Port: Guernsey 9 Inset
St. Peter's: Jersey 9 Inset
St. Tudwal's Is.: Caer. 10 SH32
Salcey Forest: Northants 11 SP85
Salcombe: Devon 8 SX73
Sale: Ches. 13 SJ79
Salford: Lancs 13 SJ79
Salisbury: Wilts 9 SU13
Salisbury Plain: Wilts 9 ST/SU
Sally Gap: Wick. 19 J5
Saltash: Corn. 8 SX45
Saltburn by the Sea: Yorks 13 NZ62
Saltcoats: Ayr 14 NS24
Saltee Is.: Wex. 19 H3
Salthouse Broad: Norf. 6 TG04
Sanda: i., Argyll 14 NR70
Sanday: i., Inv. 16 NG20
Sanday: i., Ork. Is. 17 HY74
Sandbach: Ches. 11 SJ76
Sand Bay: Som. 9 ST36
Sandgate: Kent. 7 TR23
Sandhurst: Berks 7 SU86
Sandlings, The: Suff. 7 TM35
Sandness: Shet. Is. 17 HU15
Sandown: I. of W. 7 SZ58
Sandray: i., Inv. 16 NL69
Sandringham: Norf. 6 TF62
Sandwich: Kent 7 TR35
Sanquhar: Dumf. 15 NS71
Sark: i., Chan. Is. 9 Inset
Sark: r. 15 NY37
Savernake Forest: Wilts. 9 SU26
Sawbridgeworth: Herts 7 TL41
Sawdde: r. 10 SN72
Sawel Mt.: N. Irel. 18 G8
Saxmundham: Suff. 6 TM36
Sca Fell: Cumb. 12 NY20
Scalpay: i., Harris 16 NG29
Scalpay: i., Skye 16 NG63
Scapa Flow: Ork. Is. 17 HY40
Scar: r. 14 NS70
Scarba: i., Argyll 14 NM60
Scarborough: Yorks 13 TA08
Scariff I.: Kerry. 19 A2
Scarp: i., Inv. 16 NA91
Schiehallion: mt., Perth. 17 NN75
Schole Bank: Chan. Is. 9 Inset
Schull: Cork 19 B2
Scilly Is. 8 SV—
Scolt Hd.: Norf. 6 TF84
Scrabster: Caith. 17 ND17
Scunthorpe: Lincs 6 SE81
Scurdie Ness: Angus 17 NO75
Scurrival Pt.: Barra 16 NF60
Seaford: Sussex. 7 TV49
Seaham Harbour: Dur. 13 NZ44
Seana Bhraigh: Ross & Crom. 16 NH28
Sea of the Hebrides: Scotland 16NL/NF
Seascale: Cumb. 12 NY00
Seaton: Devon 9 SY29
Sedbergh: Yorks 12 SD69
Sedgefield: Dur. 13 NZ32
Sedgemoor: Som. 9 ST33
Seil: i., Argyll 14 NM71
Selborne: Hants 7 SU73
Selby: Yorks 13 SE63
Selker B.: Cumb. 12 SD08
SELKIRK: Co., Scot. 15 NT42
Sellafield: Cumb. 12 NY00
Selsey Bill: Sussex 7 SZ89
Sence: r. 11 SK60
Seph: r. 13 SE59
Settle: Yorks 13 SD86
Seven: r. 13 SE78
Seven Heads: Cork 19 D2
Sevenoaks: Kent 7 TQ55
Severn: r. 11 SO82
Sgarbh Breac: mt., Islay 14 NR47
Sgreadan Hill: Argyll 14 NR72

Page Ref.
Sgùman Còinntich: mt., R. & Crom. 16 NG93
Sgùrr a' Chaorachain: Ross & Crom. 16 NH04
Sgùrr a' Choire Ghlais: Inv. 16 NH24
Sgùrr a' Mhaoraich: Inv. 16 NG90
Sgùrr a' Mhuilinn: Ross & Crom. 16 NH25
Sgùrr Bàn: Ross & Crom. 16 NH07
Sgùrr Mòr: Ross & Crom. 16 NH27
Sgùrr na Ciche: Inv. 16 NM99
Sgùrr na Lapaich: Inv. 16 NH13
Sgùrr Ruadh: Ross & Crom. 16 NG95
Shaftesbury: Dorset 9 ST82
Shanklin: I. of Wight. 7 SZ58
Shannon: r. 19 D4
Shannon Airport (Rineanna): Clare 19 D4
Shap: & fells, Westmor. 12 NY51
Shapinsay: i., Ork. Is. 17 HY51
Sharpnose Points: Corn. 8 SS21
Shaw: Lancs. 13 SD90
Sheaf: r. 13 SK28
Sheelin, L.: R. of Irel. 18 G6
Sheep Haven: Don. 18 F9
Sheep I.: Argyll. 14 NR70
Sheep I.: Pemb 10 SM80
Sheep's Head: Cork 19 B2
Sheerness: Kent 7 TQ97
Shee Water: r. 17 NO16
Sheffield: Yorks 13 SK38
Shefford: Beds 7 TL13
Sheffry Hills: Mayo. 18 B6
Shehy Mts.: Cork 19 C2
Shelf: Yorks 13 SE12
Shepshed: Leics. 11 SK41
Shepton Mallet: Som. 9 ST64
Sherborne: Dorset. 9 ST61
Sherburn in Elmet: Yorks 13 SE43
Sheringham: Norf. 6 TG14
Sherkin I.: Cork 19 C1
Sherwood Forest: Notts 11 SK55
Shetland Is.: Scot. 17 Inset
Shiant Is.: Ross & Crom. 16 NG49
Shifnal: Salop 11 SJ70
Shildon: Dur. 13 NZ22
Shipley: Yorks 13 SE13
Shipston on Stour: War 11 SP24
Shira: r. 14 NN11
Shoeburyness: Essex 7 TQ98
Shoreham-by-Sea: Sussex 7 TQ20
Shotton: Flint. 10 SJ36
Shrewsbury: Salop. 11 SJ41
Severn Tunnel 11 ST58
Shrivenham: Berks. 11 SU28
SHROPSHIRE Eng. 11 SO/SJ
Shuna: i., Argyll 14 NM70
Shuna: i., Argyll 14 NM94
Sidcup: Kent 7 TQ47
Sidlaw Hills: Angus/Perth. 15 NO34
Sidmouth: Devon. 9 SY18
Sighty Crag: Cumb./Northumb. 15 NY68
Silchester: Hants 7 SU66
Silloth: Cumb. 12 NY15
Silsden: Yorks 13 SE04
Silvermine Mts.: Tip. 19 E4
Silverstone: Northants 11 SP64
Silverton: Devon. 8 SS90
Sinclair's B.: Caith. 17 ND35
Sion Mills: Tyr. 18 G8
Sittingbourne: Kent 7 TQ96
Sizewell: Suffolk 6 TM46
Skara Brae: Ork. Is. 17 HY21
Skegness: Lincs 6 TF56
Skellig Rocks: Kerry 19 Inset
Skelton: Yorks 13 NZ61
Skerries: Dublin 18 J6
Skerryvore: i., Hebrides 14 NL82
Skibbereen: Cork 19 C2
Skiddaw: mt., Cumb. 12 NY22
Skipness Point: Argyll 14 NR95
Skipton: Yorks 13 SD95
Skirfare: r. 13 SD97
Skokholm I.: Pemb. 10 SM70
Skomer I.: Pemb 10 SM70
Skye: i., Inv. 16 NG—
Slaithwaite: Yorks 13 SE01
Slaney: r. 19 H4
Slea: r. 6 TF04
Sleaford: Lincs 6 TF04
Slea Head: Kerry 19 Inset
Sleat: Skye 16 NG60
Sliabh Gaoil: Argyll 14 NR87
Slieve Anierin: Leit. 18 F7
Sleive Aughty: Gal. 19 E5
Slieve Beagh: Ferm. 18 G7
Slieve Bernagh: Clare 19 D4
Slieve Bloom: Laoighis 19 F5
Slieve Car: Mayo 18 B7
Slieve Donard: Down 18 K7
Slieve Elva: Clare 19 C5
Slievefelim: Lim. 19 E4

Page Ref.
Slieve Gallion: Lon. 18 H8
Slieve Gamph: Sligo 18 D7
Slieve Gullion: Armagh 18 J7
Slieve Mish: Kerry 19 B3
Slieve Miskish: Cork 19 B2
Slieve More: Mayo 18 A7
Slievenaman: Tip. 19 F3
Slieve Rushen: Cavan/Ferm. 18 F7
Slieve Snaght: Don. 18 G9
Sligachan Inn: Skye 16 NG42
SLIGO: Co., R. of Ireland 18 D7
Sligo Bay 18 D7
Slioch: mt., Ross & Crom. 16 NH06
Slough: Bucks 7 SU97
Slyne Head: Gal. 19 A5
Smethwick: Staffs 11 SP08
Snaefell: I. of Man 12 SC38
Snaith: Yorks 13 SE62
Snowdon: Caer. 10 SH65
Soa I.: Mull 14 NM21
Soar: r. 11 SK42
Soay: i., Skye 16 NG41
Soham: Cambs. 6 TL57
*Soke of Peterborough: Admin. Co., Northants 6 TF10
Solent, The: chan., Hants 9 SZ49
Solfach (Solva): r. 10 SM82
Solihull: War 11 SP17
Solva: Pemb 10 SM82
Solway Firth: Eng./Scot. 15 NY05
SOMERSET: Co., England 9 ST—
Somerton: Som. 9 ST42
Sound of Arisaig: Inv. 16 NM68
Sound of Barra: Outer Hebr. 16 NF71
Sound of Canna: Inv. 16 NG30
Sound of Eigg: Inv. 16 NM48
Sound of Gigha: Argyll 14 NR64
Sound of Harris: Harris 16 NF98
Sound of Islay: Argyll 14 NR46
Sound of Jura: Argyll 14 NR68
Sound of Monach: Outer Hebr. 16 NF76
Sound of Mull: Argyll 14 NM64
Sound of Raasay: Inv. 16 NG55
Sound of Rhum: Inv. 16 NM49
Sound of Shiant: Lewis 16 NG39
Sound of Sleat: Inv. 16 NG70
Southall: Middx. 7 TQ18
Southam: War. 11 SP46
Southampton: Hants 7 SU41
South Bank: Yorks. 13 NZ52
South Barrule: I. of Man 12 SC27
Southborough: Kent 7 TQ54
South Cave: Yorks. 13 SE93
South Dorset Downs 9 SY69
South Downs: Sussex 7SU/TQ
Southend-on-Sea: Essex 7 TQ88
Southerness Point: Kirkc. 12 NX95
Southern Uplands 14/15 —
South Esk: r. 17 NO55
South Foreland: Kent 7 TR34
South Hams: Devon 8 SX65
South Lee: mt., N. Uist. 16 NF96
South Molton: Devon. 8 SS72
Southport: Lancs 12 SD31
South Ronaldsay: i., Ork. Is. 17 ND48
South Shields: Dur. 15 NZ36
South Sound: Clare 19 C5
South Tyne: r. 12 NY65
South Uist: i., Inv. 16 NF73
Southwell: Notts 11 SK75
Southwick: Dur. 12 NZ35
Southwold: Suff. 6 TM57
Sow: r. 11 SJ82
Sowe: r. 11 SP37
Sowerby Bridge: Yorks 13 SE02
Spalding: Lincs 6 TF22
Spean Bridge: Inv. 16 NN28
Speke: Lancs 12 SJ48
Spennymoor: Dur. 13 NZ23
Sperrin Mts.: N. Ireland 18 H8
Spey: r. & bay, Moray. 17 NJ35
Spilsby: Lincs 6 TF46
Spithead: Hants 9 SZ69
Spofforth: Yorks 13 SE35
Sprint: r. 12 NY50
Spurn Head: Yorks 13 TA41
Stackpole Head: Pemb 10 SR99
Stack Rocks: Pemb. 10 SM81
Stacks Mts.: Kerry 19 B3
Staffa: i., Argyll. 14 NM33
Stafford: Staffs 11 SJ92
STAFFORDSHIRE: England 11 SJ/SK
Staines: Middx. 11 TQ07
Stainmore: Westmor./Yorks 13 NY91
Stalbridge: Dorset. 9 ST71

* See Page 131

Page Ref.
Stalham: Norf. 6 TG32
Stalybridge: Ches. 13 SJ99
Stamford: Lincs 6 TF00
Stamford Bridge: Yorks 13 SE75
Stanhope Dur. 13 NY93
Stanley: Dur. 13 NZ15
Stanley: Yorks 13 SE32
Stanton Moor: Derby. 11 SK26
Start Bay: Devon. 8 SX84
Start Point: Devon. 8 SX83
Start Point: Ork. Is. 17 HY74
Staveley: Derby. 13 SK47
Staverton: Glos 11 SO82
Steep Holme: i., Som. 9 ST25
Steeping: r. 6 TF46
Stenhousemuir: Stirl. 15 NS88
Stevenage: Herts 7 TL22
Stewarton: Ayr 14 NS44
Steyning: Sussex 7 TQ11
Stiffkey: r. 6 TF94
Stilton: Hunts 6 TL18
Stinchar: r. 14 NX29
STIRLING: Co., Scotland 14 NS79
Stob a Choin: mt., Perth. 14 NN41
Stockbridge: Hants 7 SU33
Stockport: Ches. 13 SJ89
Stocksbridge: Yorks 13 SK29
Stockton on Tees: Dur. 13 NZ41
Stoke on Trent: Staffs 11 SJ84
Stoke Point: Devon 8 SX54
Stokesay: Salop. 11 SO48
Stokesley: Yorks 13 NZ50
Stone: Staffs 11 SJ83
Stonefield: Argyll 14 NR87
Stonehaven: Kinc. 17 NO88
Stonehenge: Wilts. 9 SU14
Stonehouse: Lan. 15 NS74
Stonybreck: Fair Isle 17 HZ27
Stonyhurst College: Lancs 12 SD63
Stony Stratford: Bucks 11 SP74
Stormont: Perth. 15 NO05
Stornoway: Lewis 16 NB43
Storr, The: mt., Skye 16 NG45
Stort: r. 7 TL42
Stour: r., Dorset 9 ST80
Stour: r., Essex 7 TL83
Stour: r., Kent 7 TR15
Stour: r., War 11 SP23
Stour: r., Worcs 11 SO88
Stourbridge: Worcs 11 SO88
Stourhead: Wilts. 9 ST73
Stourport-on-Severn Worcs 11 SO87
Stowe School: Bucks 11 SP63
Stowmarket: Suff. 6 TM05
Stow on the Wold: Glos 11 SP12
Strabane: Tyr. 18 G8
Strait of Dover 7 TR32
Strangford: & L., Down 18 K7
Stranraer: Wig. 14 NX06
Strat: r. 8 SS20
Strata Florida: Card. 10 SN76
Stratford on Avon: War 11 SP15
Strathaven: Lan. 14 NS74
Strath Avon: Banff. 17 NJ12
Strathbogie: Aber. 17 NJ53
Strathcarron: Ross & Crom. 17 NH59
Strath Dearn: Inv. 17 NH82
Strathearn: Perth. 15 NN81
Strath Ettrick: Inv. 17 NH52
Strath Fleet: Suther. 17 NC70
Strath Halladale: Suther. 17 NC95
Strath Kanaird: Ross & Crom. 16 NC10
Strathmore: Scot. 15 NO45
Strathmore: r. 17 NC44
•Strathmore Water. 17 ND04
Strathnairn: Inv. 17 NH73
Strathnaver: Suther. 17 NC75
Strath of Kildonan: Suther. 17 NC82
Strath Oykell: Ross & Crom./Suther. 16 NC40
Strathpeffer: Ross & Crom. 17 NH45
Strathspey: Inv. 17 NH91
Strathy: r., Suther. 17 NC85
Strathy Pt.: Suther. 17 NC86
Stratton: Corn. 8 SS20
Stretford: Lancs 13 SJ89
Stroma: i., Caith. 17 ND37
Stromeferry: Ross & Crom. 16 NG83
Stromness: Ork. Is. 17 HY20
Stronsay: i., Ork. Is. 17 HY62
Stroud: Glos 11 SO80
Strule: r. 18 G8
Strumble Head: Pemb. 10 SM84
Sturminster Newton: Dorset 9 ST71
Suck: r. 19 E5
Sudbury: Suff. 7 TL84
SUFFOLK: Co., England 7TL/TM
Suie Hill: Kirkc. 15 NX75
Suilven: mt., Suther. 16 NC11
Suir: r. 19 G3
Sulby: r. 12 SC49
Sulgrave: Northants 11 SP54
Sumburgh Hd.: Shet. Is. 17 HU40
Summer Isles: Ross & Crom. 16 NB91
Sunart: Argyll 16 NM76
Sunderland: Dur. 13 NZ35
Surbiton: Surrey 7 TQ16
SURREY: Co., Eng. 7 TQ—
SUSSEX: Co., Eng. 7 TQ—
SUTHERLAND: Co., Scotland 17 NC—
Sutton: Surrey 7 TQ26
Sutton Coldfield: War. 11 SP19
Sutton in Ashfield: Notts 11 SK45
Sutton Scotney: Hants 9 SU43
Swadlincote: Derby 11 SK31
Swaffham: Norf. 6 TF80
Swale: r. 13 SE29
Swale, The: Kent 7 TR06
Swaledale: Yorks 13 NZ10
Swanage: Dorset 9 SZ07
Swansea: & bay, Glam. 10 SS69
Swift: r. 11 SP58
Swilly: L. & r., Don. 18 F9
Swindon: Wilts. 9 SU18
Swineford: Mayo 18 D6
Swords: Dublin 18 J5
Sybil Pt.: Kerry 19 Inset

Tadcaster: Yorks 13 SE44
Taf: r. 10 SN21
Taff: r. 10 ST18
Tain: Ross & Crom. 17 NH78
Talla: res., Peebles. 15 NT12
Tal-y-llyn: Mer. 10 SH70
Tamar: r. 8 SX46
Tame: r. 11 SP29
Tamworth: Staffs 11 SK20
Tanat: r. 10 SJ12
Tanera More: i., Ross & Crom. 16 NB90
Tantallon Castle: E. Loth. 15 NT58
Tara Hill: Meath 18 H6
Taransay: i., Inv. 16 NB00
Tarbat Ness: Ross & Crom. 17 NH98
Tarbert: Harris. 16 NB10
Tarf Water: r., Perth. 17 NN98
Tas: r. 6 TM19
Taunton: & vale, Som. 9 ST22
Tavistock: Devon. 8 SX47
Tavy: r. 8 SX58
Taw: r. 8 SS52
Tawe: r. 10 SN70
Tay: r. 15 NO13
Tayport: Fife 15 NO42
Tees: r. 13 NZ01
Teesdale: Yorks/Dur. 13 NY92
Teifi: r. 10 SN24
Teifiside: Card. 10 SN33
Teign: r. 8 SX88
Teignmouth: Devon. 8 SX97
Teise: r. 7 TQ63
Teith: r. 14 NN60
Teme: r. 11 SO85
Templemore: Tip. 19 F4
Tenbury Wells: Worcs 11 SO56
Tenby: Pemb. 10 SN10
Tenterden: Kent 7 TQ83
Ter: r. 7 TL71
Test: r. 7 SU33
Tetbury: Glos 9 ST89
Teviot: r. 15 NT40
Teviotdale: Rox. 15 NT41
Tewkesbury: Glos 11 SO83
Texa: i., Argyll 14 NR34
Thame: & r., Oxon. 11 SP70
Thames: r. 7SU/TQ
Thaw: r. 10 ST07
Thaxted: Essex 7 TL63
Thet: r. 6 TL88
Thetford: Norf. 6 TL88
Thetford Chase: Norf. 6 TL88
Thirsk: Yorks 13 SE48
Thomastown: Kilk. 19 G4
Thornaby on Tees: Yorks 13 NZ41
Thornbury: Glos 11 ST69
Thorne: Yorks 13 SE61
Thornhill: Dumf. 15 NX89
Thornton: Lancs 12 SD34
Thrapston: Northants 11 SP97
Threave Castle: Kirkc. 14 NX76
Thrushel: r. 8 SX48
Thurles: Tip. 19 F4
Thurso: & r., Caith. 17 ND16
Tickhill: Yorks 13 SK59
Tidworth: Hants 9 SU24
Tilbury: Essex 7 TQ67
Till: r., Lincs 11 SK88
Till: r., Northumb. 15 NT93
Tillicoultry: Clack. 15 NS99
Tilt: r. 17 NN86
Tintagel: Corn. 8 SX08
Tintern Abbey: Mon. 11 SO50
Tinto Hills: Lan. 15 NS93
TIPPERARY: Co., R. of Ireland 19 E4
Tiree: i., Argyll. 14 NL94
Tirga More: mt., Harris 16 NB01
Tirry: r. 17 NC51
Titterstone Clee: Salop 11 SO57
Tiumpan Head: Lewis 16 NB53
Tiverton: Devon. 8 SS91
Tobermory: Mull 14 NM55
Todmorden: Yorks 13 SD92
Toe Head: Cork 19 C1
Tolpuddle: Dorset 9 SY79
Tolsta Head: Lewis 16 NB54
Tonbridge: Kent 7 TQ54
Tone: r. 9 ST32
Tonypandy: Glam. 10 SS99
Topsham: Devon. 8 SX98
Tor Bay: Devon. 8 SX95
Torne: r. 13 SE70
Torpoint: Corn. 8 SX45
Torquay: Devon. 8 SX96
Torran Rocks: Argyll 14 NM21
Torridge: r. 8 SS41
Torridon: Ross & Crom. 16 NG95
Tory I.: Don. 18 E9
Totnes: Devon. 8 SX86
Tottenham: Middx. 7 TQ39
Tove: r. 11 SP74
Toward Point: Argyll 14 NS16
Towcester: Northants 11 SP64
Tower Point: Pemb. 10 SM71
Tow Law: Dur. 13 NZ13
Towyn: Mer. 10 SH50
Tralee: & B., Kerry 19 B3
Tramore: & B., Wat. 19 G3
Tranent: E. Loth. 15 NT47
Trecastle: Breck. 10 SN82
Tredegar: Mon. 10 SO10
Trefignath: Anglesey 10 SH28
Tregaron: Card. 10 SN65
Tregoney: Corn. 8 SW94
Treherbert: Glam. 10 SS99
Tremadoc B.: Caer. 10 SH53
Trent: r. 13 SK89
Tre'r Ceiri: Caer. 10 SH34
Tresco: Scilly Is. 8 SV81
Trevose Hd.: Corn. 8 SW87
Trim: Meath 18 H6
Tring: Herts 7 SP91
Troon: Ayr 14 NS33
Trossachs, The: Perth 14 NN50
Trostan: Antrim 18 J9
Trotternish: Skye 16 NG45
Troup Head: Banff. 17 NJ86
Troutbeck: Westmor. 12 NY40
Trowbridge: Wilts. 9 ST85
Truro: Corn. 8 SW84
Trwyn Cilan: Caer. 10 SH32
Trwyn-y-Tal: Caer. 10 SH34
Tryweryn: r. 10 SK84
Tuam: Gal. 18 D6
Tud: r. 6 TG01
Tullamore: Offaly 19 G5
Tullow: Carlow 19 H4
Tummel: r. 17 NN95
Tunbridge Wells: Kent 7 TQ54
Tunstall: Staffs 11 SJ85
Turnhouse: Midloth. 15 NT17
Turriff: Aber. 17 NJ74
Tusker Rock: Glam. 10 SS87
Tuxford: Notts 13 SK77
Tweed: r. 15 NT94
Tweedsmuir: Peeb. 15 NT12
Twelve Pins, The: Gal. 18 B6
Twickenham: Middx. 7 TQ17
Twomileborris: Tip. 19 F4
Twrch: r., Carm./Breck. 10 SN71
Twrch: r., Montg. 10 SH91
Twymyn: r. 10 SH80
Tyldesley: Lancs 12 SD60
Tyne: r., Dur. 13 NY96
Tyne: r., E. Loth. 15 NT57
Tyne Gap: Northumb. 12 NY66
Tynemouth: Northumb. 15 NZ36
TYRONE: Co., N. Ireland 18 G8
Tywi (Towy): r. 10 SN62

Uckfield: Sussex 7 TQ42
Uffculme: Devon. 9 ST01
Ugie: r. 14 NK14
Ullapool: Ross & Crom. 16 NH19
Ullswater: L., Cumb./Westmor. 12 NY42
Ulster: Prov., N. Ireland 18 —
Ulva: i., Argyll 14 NM43
Ulverston: Lancs 12 SD27
Unst: i., Shet. Is. 17 HP60
Upper Lough Erne: R. of Ireland 18 F7
Uppingham: Rut. 11 SP89
Upton upon Severn: Worcs 11 SO84
Ure: r. 13 SE46
Urie: r. 17 NJ72
Urmston: Lancs 13 SJ79
Urquhart Castle: Inv. 17 NH52
Urr Water: r. 15 NX77
Usk: Mon. 11 SO30
Usk: r. 11 ST39
Uttoxeter: Staffs 11 SK03
Uxbridge: Middx. 7 TQ08

Valentia I.: Kerry 19 Inset
Vale of Aylesbury: Bucks 7 SP70
Vale of Belvoir: Notts 11 SK74
Vale of Berkeley: Glos 11 SO70
Vale of Clwyd: Denb. 10 SJ06
Vale of Conway: Caer. 10 SH76
Vale of Evesham: Worcs 11 SP04
Vale of Glamorgan 10 ST82
Vale of Gloucester 11 SO81
Vale of Kent 7 TQ93
Vale of Llangollen: Denb. 10 SJ23
Vale of Pewsey: Wilts. 9 SU16
Vale of Pickering: Yorks 13 SE77
Vale of Powis: Montg. 10 SJ20
Vale of Sussex 7 TQ21
Vale of Taunton Deane: Som. 9 ST22
Vale of Wardour: Wilts. 9 SU03
Vale of White Horse: Berks 11 SU39
Vale of York 13 SE47
Valle Crucis Abbey: Denb. 10 SJ24
Valley: Anglesey 10 SH27
Vaternish: & point, Skye 16 NG25
Vatersay: i., Inv. 16 NL69
Ventnor: I. of Wight 7 SZ57
Ver: r. 7 TL10
Veryan Bay: Corn. 8 SW93
Vyrnwy: r. 10 SJ21
Vyrnwy, L.: Denb. 10 SH92

Wadebridge: Corn. 8 SW97
Wade's Causeway: Yorks 13 NZ80
Wainfleet All Saints: Lincs 6 TF49
Wakefield: Yorks 13 SE32
Waldon: r. 8 SS30
Walland Marsh: Kent 7 TQ92
Wallasey: Ches. 12 SJ39
Wallingford: Berks 11 SU58
Wallsend: Northumb. 15 NZ26
Walmer: Kent 7 TR35
Walsall: Staffs 11 SP09
Waltham Abbey: Essex 7 TL30
Walthamstow: Essex 7 TQ38
Walton: Surrey 7 TQ16
Walton le Dale: Lancs 12 SD52
Walton on the Naze: Essex 7 TM22
Wansbeck: r. 15 NZ08
Wantage: Berks 11 SU48
Ward Hill: Ork. Is. 17 HY20
Wardle: Lancs 13 SD91
Ward's Stone: Lancs 12 SD55
Ware: Herts 7 TL31
Wareham: Dorset 9 SY98
Warminster: Wilts 9 ST84
Warrenpoint: Down 18 J7
Warrington: Lancs. 12 SJ68
Warwick: War. 11 SP26
WARWICKSHIRE: England 11 SP—
Wasdale Head: Cumb. 12 NY10
Wash, The: England 6 TF53
Washburn: r. 13 SE15
Washington: Dur. 13 NZ35
Wast Water: L., Cumb. 12 NY10
Watchet: Som. 9 ST04
WATERFORD: Co., R. of Ireland 19 G3
Waterford Harbour 19 H3
Watergate Bay: Corn. 8 SW86
Water of Ae: r. 15 NX99
Water of Feugh: r. 17 NO59
Water of Fleet: r. 14 NX56
Water of Leith: r. 15 NT16
Water of Luce: r. 14 NX16
Water of Milk: r. 15 NY28
Watford: Herts 7 TQ19
Watlington: Oxon. 11 SU69
Watton: Norf. 6 TF90
Waun-oer: Mer. 10 SH71
Waveney: r. 6 TM39
Waver: r. 12 NY24
Weald, The: Kent 7 TQ—
Wear: r. 13 NZ35
Weardale: Dur. 13 NZ03
Weaver: r. 11 SJ64
Wednesbury: Staffs 11 SO99
Welland: r. 6 TF33
Wellingborough: Northants 11 SP86
Wellington: Here. 11 SO44
Wellington: Salop 11 SJ61
Wellington: Som. 9 ST12
Wellington College: Berks 7 SU86
Wells: Som. 9 ST54
Wells next The Sea: Norf. 6 TF94
Welshpool: Montg. 10 SJ20
Welwyn: Herts 7 TL21
Welwyn Garden City: Herts 7 TL21
Wem: Salop 11 SJ52
Wembley: Middx. 7 TQ18
Wemyss Castle: Fife 15 NT39
Wendover: Bucks 11 SP80
Wendron Moors: Corn. 8 SW63
Wenlock Edge: Salop 11 SO59
Wenning: r. 13 SD76
Wensley Dale: Yorks 13 SD89
Wensum: r. 6 TG01
Went: r. 13 SE51
Wenvoe: Glam. 10 ST17
West Allen: r. 13 NY75
West Bridgford: Notts 11 SK53
West Bromwich: Staffs 11 SP09
West Burra: i., Shet. Is. 17 HU33
Westbury: Wilts. 9 ST85
West Cleddau: r. 8 SM92
Westerham: Kent 7 TQ45
Wester Ross: Ross & Crom. 16 NH16
West Fen: Lincs 6 TF35
Westgate on Sea: Kent 7 TR37
West Ham: Essex 7 TQ48
West Hartlepool: Dur. 13 NZ53
West Kirby: Ches. 12 SJ28
West Loch Roag: Lewis 16 NB03
West Loch Tarbert: Argyll 14 NR86
West Loch Tarbert: Harris 16 NB00
West Looe: Corn. 8 SX25
WEST LOTHIAN: Co., Scotland 15 NT07
West Lulworth: Dorset 9 SY88
West Malling: Kent 7 TQ65
WESTMEATH: Co., R. of Irel. 18 F6
WESTMORLAND: Co., England 12 NY—
Westonbirt: Glos 11 ST88
Weston-super-Mare: Som. 9 ST36
Westport: Mayo 18 B6
Westray: i., Ork. Is. 17 HY44
West Riding: Admin. Co., Yorks 13 SE—
West Suffolk: Admin. Co., Suff. 6 TL86
West Sussex: Admin. Co., Sussex 7SU/TQ
Westward Ho!: Devon. 8 SS42
West Water: r. 17 NO57
West Wycombe: Bucks 7 SU89
Wetherby: Yorks 13 SE44
WEXFORD: Co., R. of Ireland 19 H3
Wexford: & bay, Wex. 19 J3
Wey: r. 7 SU94
Weybridge: Surrey 7 TQ06
Weymouth: Dorset 9 SY67
Whaley Bridge: Derby 13 SK08
Wharfe: r. 13 SE14
Wharfedale: Yorks 13 SE05
Whernside: mt., Yorks 13 SD78
Whickham: Dur. 13 NZ26
Whiddy I.: Cork 19 B2
Whipsnade: Beds 7 TL01
Whitburn: W. Loth 15 NS96
Whitby: Yorks 13 NZ81
Whitchurch: Bucks 11 SP82
Whitchurch: Hants 9 SU44
Whitchurch: Salop. 11 SJ54
White Castle: Mon. 11 SO31
White Coomb: mt., Dumf. 15 NT11
White Esk: r. 15 NY29
Whiteford Point: Glam. 10 SS49
Whitehaven: Cumb. 12 NX91
Whitehead: Antrim 18 K8
White Hill: Angus 17 NO47
Whitehorse Hill: Berks 11 SU38
Whitesand Bay: Corn. 8 SW32
Whitesand Bay: Corn. 8 SX35
Whitesand Bay: Pemb. 10 SM72
Whitfell: Cumb. 12 SD19
Whithorn: Wig. 14 NX44
Whitley Bay: Northumb. 15 NZ37
Whitstable: Kent 7 TR16
Whittlesey: Cambs. 6 TL29
Whitwick: Leics. 11 SK41
Whitworth: Lancs 13 SD81
Wiay: i. Skye 16 NG33
Wick: & r., Caith. 17 ND35
Wickham Market: Suff. 6 TM35
WICKLOW: Co., R. of Ireland 19 J4
Wicklow Hd.: Wick. 19 K4
Wicklow Mts.: Wick. 19 J4
Wickwar: Glos 11 ST78
Wid: r. 7 TL60
Widecombe in the Moor: Devon. 8 SX77
Wide Firth: Ork. Is. 17 HY41
Widnes: Lancs 12 SJ58
Wigan: Lancs 12 SD50
Wigston Magna: Leics. 11 SP69
Wigton: Cumb. 12 NY24
Wigtown: Wig. 14 NX45
WIGTOWNSHIRE: Scotland 14 NX—
Willenhall: Staffs 11 SO99
Willesden: Middx. 7 TQ28
Willington: Dur. 13 NZ13
Williton: Som. 9 ST04
Wilmslow: Ches. 11 SJ88
Wilton: Wilts. 9 SU03
WILTSHIRE: Eng. 9 ST/SU
Wimbledon: Surrey 7 TQ27
Wimborne Minster: Dorset 9 SZ09
Wincanton: Som. 9 ST72
Winchcombe: Glos. 11 SP02
Winchelsea: Sussex 7 TQ91
Winchester: Hants 7 SU42
Windermere: & L., Westmor./Lancs 12 SD39
Windrush: r. 11 SP21
Windsor: Berks 7 SU97
Winsford: Ches. 11 SJ66
Winsley: Wilts. 9 ST76
Winslow: Bucks 11 SP72
Winster: Westmor. 12 SD49
Wirksworth: Derby 11 SK25
Wirral: Ches. 10 SJ38
Wisbech: Cambs. 6 TF40
Wishaw: Lan. 15 NS75
Wisp Hill: Rox./Dumf. 15 NY39
Wissey: r. 6 TL69
Witham: Essex 7 TL81
Witham: r. 6 TF16
Witheridge: Devon 8 SS81
Withernsea: Yorks 13 TA32
Witney: Oxon. 11 SP31
Wiveliscombe: Som. 9 ST02
Wivenhoe: Essex 7 TM02
Wnion: r. 10 SH71
Woburn: Beds 7 SP93
Woden Law: Rox. 15 NT71
Woking: Surrey 7 TQ05
Wokingham: Berks 7 SU86
Wolf Rock: Corn. 8 SW21
Wolsingham: Dur. 13 NZ03
Wolverhampton: Staffs 11 SO99
Wolverton: Bucks 11 SP84
Wombwell: Yorks 13 SE30
Woodbridge: Suff. 7 TM24
Woodhall Spa: Lincs 6 TF16
Woodstock: Oxon. 11 SP41
Woolacombe: Devon. 8 SS44
Wooler: Northumb. 15 NT92
Woolsington: Northumb. 15 NZ17
Woolsthorpe Manor: Lincs 6 SK92
Woolwich: London 7 TQ47
Wootton Bassett: Wilts. 9 SU08
Worcester: Worcs 11 SO85
WORCESTERSHIRE: England 11 SO—
Workington: Cumb. 12 NX92
Worksop: Notts 13 SK57
Worms Head: Glam. 10 SS38
Worsborough: Yorks 13 SE30
Worsley: Lancs. 13 SD70
Worthing: Sussex 7 TQ10
Wotton under Edge: Glos 11 ST79
Wragby: Lincs 6 TF17
Wrath, Cape: Suther. 16 NC27
Wreake: r. 11 SK71
Wrekin, The: Salop 11 SJ60
Wrexham: Denb. 10 SJ35
Wrotham: Kent 7 TQ65
Wroxeter: Salop 11 SJ50
Wye: Kent 7 TR04
Wye: r., Derby. 13 SK26
Wye: r., Glos 11 SO50
Wylye: r. 9 ST94
Wymondham: Norf. 6 TG10
Wyre: r., Card. 10 SN67
Wyre: r., Lancs 12 SD33

Yar: r. 7 SZ58
Yare: r. 6 TG00
Yarm: Yorks 13 NZ41
Yarmouth: I. of Wight. 7 SZ38
Yarmouth: Norf. see Gt. Yarmouth
Yarnbury Castle: Wilts. 9 SU04
Yarrow Water: r. 15 NT22
Yarty: r. 9 ST20
Yeadon: Yorks 13 SE24
Yealm: r. 8 SX65
Yell: i., Shet. Is. 17 HU48
Yeo: r., Devon. 8 SS63
Yeo: r., Devon. 8 SS82
Yeo: r., Devon./Som. 8 SX89
Yeo: r., Som. 9 ST42
Yeo: r., Som. 9 ST36
Yeovil: Som. 9 ST51
Y Gaer: Breck. 10 SO02
Y Llethr: mt., Mer. 10 SH62
Ynysdeullyn: Pemb 10 SM83
Ynys Lochtyn: Card. 10 SN35
York: Yorks 13 SE65
YORKSHIRE: Eng. 13 —
Yorkshire Dales 13 SD99
Yorkshire Wolds: Yorks 13 SE/TA
Youghall: Cork. 19 F2
Yr Eifl: mt., Caer. 10 SH34
Ysbyty Ystwyth: Card. 10 SN77
Yscir: r. 10 SN93
Ystrad: r. 10 SJ06
Ystwyth: r. 10 SN77
Ythan: r. 17 NJ83

Zetland: i., Shet. Is. 17 HU35
Zone Point: Corn. 8 SW83

POPULATION

ENGLAND

County	1971
Bedfordshire	463 493
Berkshire	633 457
Buckinghamshire	586 211
Cambridgeshire	302 507
Cheshire	1 542 624
Cornwall	379 892
Cumberland	292 009
Derbyshire	884 339
Devonshire	896 245
Dorset	361 213
Durham	1 408 103
Essex	1 353 564
Gloucestershire	1 069 454
Greater London	7 379 014
Hampshire	1 561 605
Herefordshire	138 425
Hertfordshire	922 188
Huntingdonshire	202 337
Kent	1 396 030
Lancashire	5 106 123
Leicestershire	771 213
Lincolnshire	808 384
Norfolk	616 427
Northamptonshire	467 843
Northumberland	794 975
Nottinghamshire	974 640
Oxfordshire	380 814
Rutland	27 463
Shropshire	336 934
Somerset	681 974
Staffordshire	1 856 890
Suffolk	544 725
Surrey	999 588
Sussex	1 241 332
Warwickshire	2 079 799
Westmorland	72 724
Wight, Isle of	109 284
Wiltshire	486 048
Worcestershire	692 605
Yorkshire	5 047 567
Total population of England	45 870 062

WALES AND MONMOUTH

County	1971
Anglesey	59 705
Brecknockshire	53 234
Caernarvonshire	122 852
Cardiganshire	54 844
Carmarthenshire	162 313
Denbighshire	184 824
Flintshire	175 396
Glamorgan	1 255 374
Merionethshire	35 277
Montgomeryshire	42 761
Pembrokeshire	97 295
Radnorshire	18 262
Monmouth	461 459
Total population of Wales and Monmouth	2 723 596

NORTHERN IRELAND

County	1971
Antrim	352 549
Armagh	133 196
Belfast (Co. Bor.)	360 150
Down	310 617
Fermanagh	49 960
Londonderry	130 296
Londonderry (Co. Bor.)	51 850
Tyrone	138 975
Total population of Northern Ireland	1 527 593

TOTALS

	1971
Total population of Great Britain and Northern Ireland	59 049 070
Channel Is. Population	125 240
Isle of Man Population	49 743

REPUBLIC OF IRELAND

County	1971
Carlow	34 025
Cavan	52 674
Clare	74 844
Cork (incl. City)	351 735
Donegal	108 000
Dublin (incl. City)	849 542
Galway	148 220
Kerry	112 941
Kildare	71 522
Kilkenny	61 811
Laoighis	45 349
Leitrim	28 313
Limerick	140 370
Longford	28 227
Louth	74 899
Mayo	109 497
Meath	71 616
Monaghan	46 231
Offaly	51 834
Roscommon	53 497
Sligo	50 236
Tipperary	123 196
Waterford (incl. City)	76 932
Westmeath	53 557
Wexford	85 892
Wicklow	66 270
Total population of Republic of Ireland	2 971 230

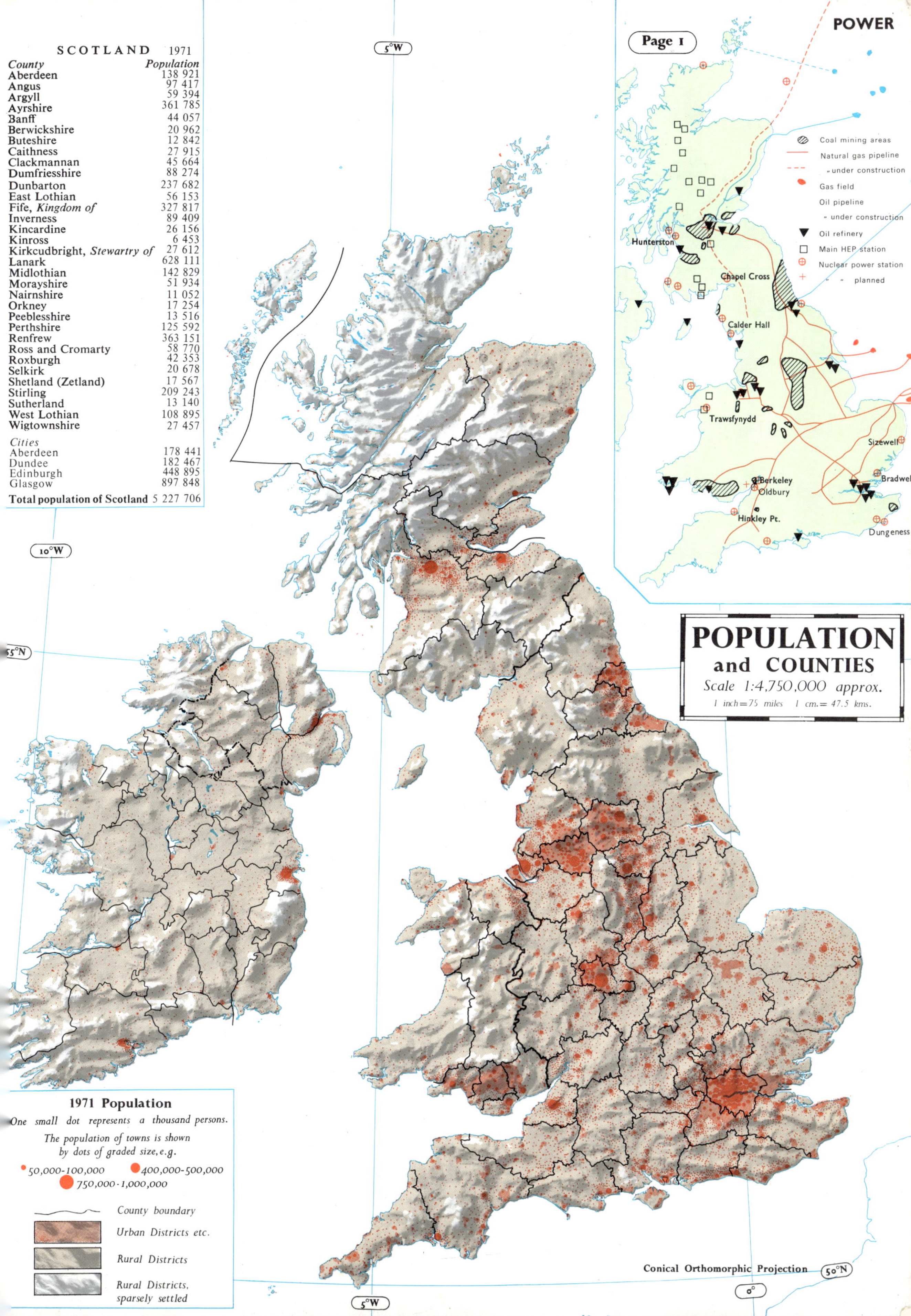

SCOTLAND 1971

County	Population
Aberdeen	138 921
Angus	97 417
Argyll	59 394
Ayrshire	361 785
Banff	44 057
Berwickshire	20 962
Buteshire	12 842
Caithness	27 915
Clackmannan	45 664
Dumfriesshire	88 274
Dunbarton	237 682
East Lothian	56 153
Fife, *Kingdom of*	327 817
Inverness	89 409
Kincardine	26 156
Kinross	6 453
Kirkcudbright, *Stewartry of*	27 612
Lanark	628 111
Midlothian	142 829
Morayshire	51 934
Nairnshire	11 052
Orkney	17 254
Peeblesshire	13 516
Perthshire	125 592
Renfrew	363 151
Ross and Cromarty	58 770
Roxburgh	42 353
Selkirk	20 678
Shetland (Zetland)	17 567
Stirling	209 243
Sutherland	13 140
West Lothian	108 895
Wigtownshire	27 457
Cities	
Aberdeen	178 441
Dundee	182 467
Edinburgh	448 895
Glasgow	897 848
Total population of Scotland	5 227 706

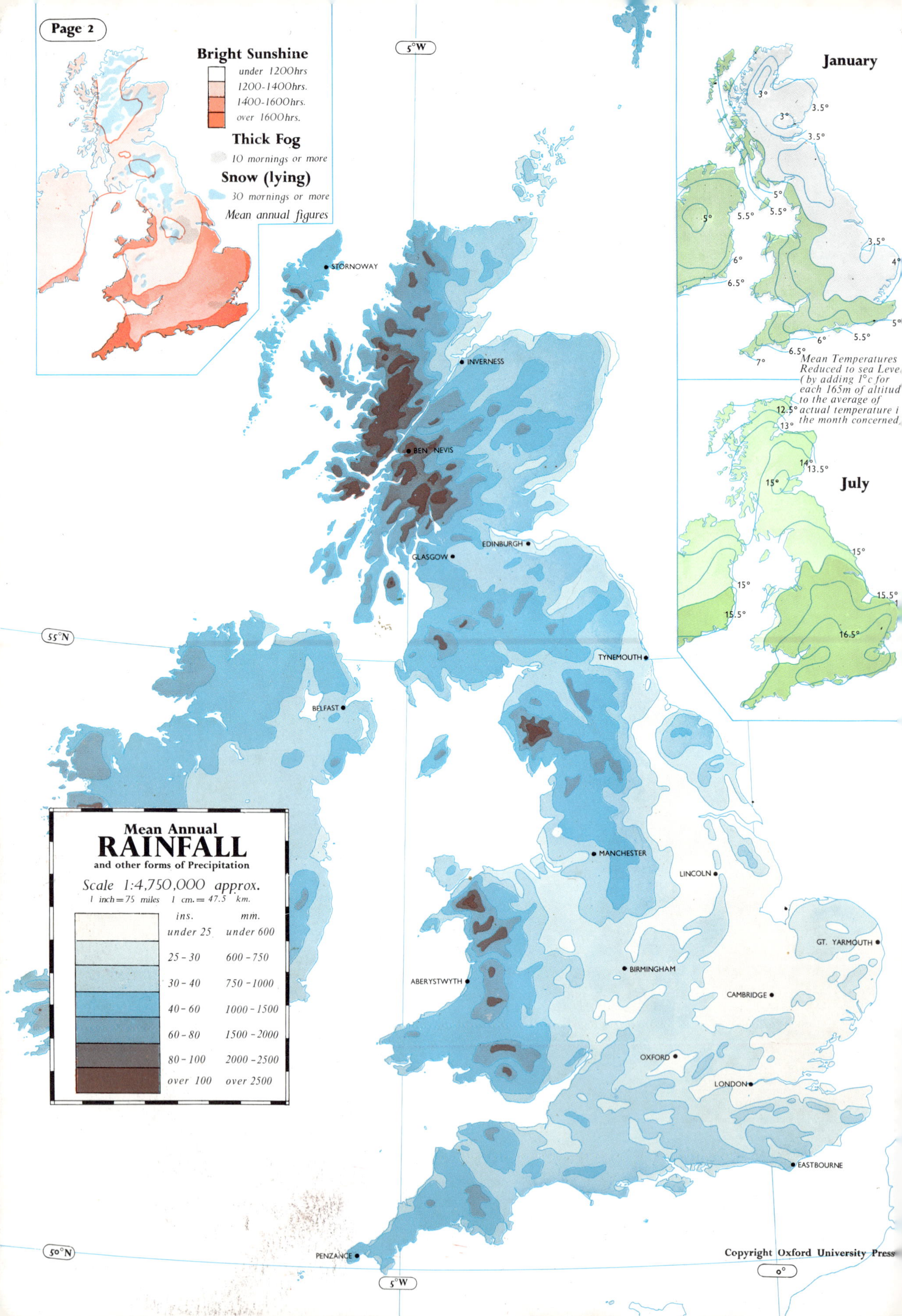

Bright Sunshine
under 1200hrs
1200-1400hrs.
1400-1600hrs.
over 1600hrs.
Thick Fog
10 mornings or more
Snow (lying)
30 mornings or more
Mean annual figures
5°W
January
3°
3.5°
5°
5.5°
6°
6.5°
7°
4°
Mean Temperatures Reduced to sea Leve
(by adding 1°c for each 165m of altitud
to the average of actual temperature i
the month concerned.
July
12.5°
13°
14°
13.5°
15°
15.5°
16.5°
STORNOWAY
INVERNESS
BEN NEVIS
EDINBURGH
GLASGOW
55°N
TYNEMOUTH
BELFAST
MANCHESTER
LINCOLN
GT. YARMOUTH
BIRMINGHAM
ABERYSTWYTH
CAMBRIDGE
OXFORD
LONDON
EASTBOURNE
PENZANCE
50°N
0°
Mean Annual
RAINFALL
and other forms of Precipitation
Scale 1:4,750,000 approx.
1 inch = 75 miles 1 cm. = 47.5 km.
ins. mm.
under 25 under 600
25 - 30 600 - 750
30 - 40 750 - 1000
40 - 60 1000 - 1500
60 - 80 1500 - 2000
80 - 100 2000 - 2500
over 100 over 2500

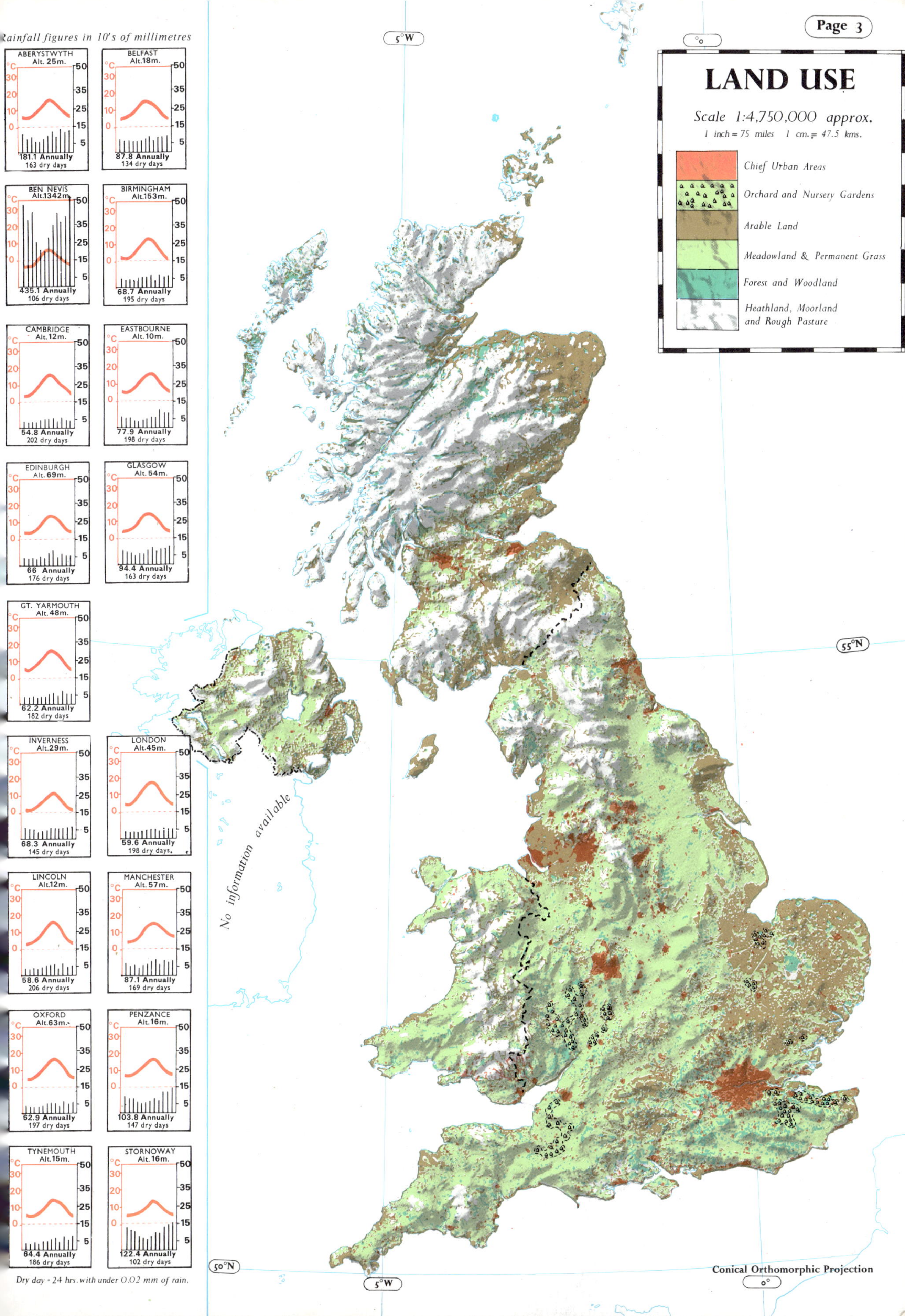

Rainfall figures in 10's of millimetres
ABERYSTWYTH Alt. 25m. 181.1 Annually 163 dry days
BELFAST Alt. 18m. 87.8 Annually 134 dry days
BEN NEVIS Alt. 1342m. 435.1 Annually 106 dry days
BIRMINGHAM Alt. 153m. 68.7 Annually 195 dry days
CAMBRIDGE Alt. 12m. 54.8 Annually 202 dry days
EASTBOURNE Alt. 10m. 77.9 Annually 198 dry days
EDINBURGH Alt. 69m. 66 Annually 176 dry days
GLASGOW Alt. 54m. 94.4 Annually 163 dry days
GT. YARMOUTH Alt. 48m. 62.2 Annually 182 dry days
INVERNESS Alt. 29m. 68.3 Annually 145 dry days
LONDON Alt. 45m. 59.6 Annually 198 dry days
LINCOLN Alt. 12m. 58.6 Annually 206 dry days
MANCHESTER Alt. 57m. 87.1 Annually 169 dry days
OXFORD Alt. 63m. 62.9 Annually 197 dry days
PENZANCE Alt. 16m. 103.8 Annually 147 dry days
TYNEMOUTH Alt. 15m. 64.4 Annually 186 dry days
STORNOWAY Alt. 16m. 122.4 Annually 102 dry days
Dry day = 24 hrs. with under 0.02 mm of rain.
LAND USE
Scale 1:4,750,000 approx.
1 inch = 75 miles 1 cm. = 47.5 kms.
Chief Urban Areas
Orchard and Nursery Gardens
Arable Land
Meadowland & Permanent Grass
Forest and Woodland
Heathland, Moorland and Rough Pasture
5°W
0°
55°N
50°N
No information available
Conical Orthomorphic Projection

Page 4
National Parks
1 Lake District
2 Snowdonia
3 N. Yorkshire Moors
4 Yorkshire Dales
5 Peak District
6 Pembrokeshire Coast
7 Exmoor
8 Dartmoor
9 Brecon Beacons
10 Northumberland
Pennine Way
Offa's Dyke Path
Existing Parks
Impressive scenery
Good coastal scenery
GEOLOG
River, estuary, marsh, coastal deposits.
Sands and clays forming subdued ridge-and-valley, plains.
Chalk scarps and undulating " downs "
Featureless claylands and sandy hills.
Clay lowlands and steep sandy ridges.
Successive scarps, dip-slopes and vales of limestones and clays.
Undulating clay lowlands and minor scarps of sands and ironst
Red marl lowlands, with salts, and sandy, pebbly ridges.
Limestone scarp E. of Pennines, elsewhere red sandstone hills, s
Grits, shales, and coal seams, with basalts in Scottish Lowlands, scarps, hills and undulating lowlands: concealed coalfields, esp and S. of Pennines, and in East Kent.
Massive limestone, forming rugged uplands and dissected pla shales and basalts in Scottish Lowlands.
Marls, and massive sandstones, with lavas in Scotland, formin rugged hills with deep valleys, plateaux.
Sandstones and slates; limestone and slates, forming moorland and valleys.
Slates, shales, forming rugged uplands; scarp-forming limestone etc. especially of Welsh Borderland.
Slates and volcanic rocks forming mountains; a few sandstone stone scarps.
Hard grits, shales and slates forming mountains and lowlands.
Rough sandstones, and volcanic rocks, forming rugged scarps a
Schists and other metamorphic rocks usually forming ver mountains and high or low moorlands.
Basalts of Tertiary age, forming plateaux and isolated hills a Note: pre-Tertiary volcanic rocks are included in their respecti
Granites and intrusive rocks of various ages forming bold isol
*These rocks are sometimes known by the collective
5°W
10°W
55°N
50°N
0°
Lerwick
Bergen & Oslo
Hambu
St. Malo
Dieppe
Boulogne
Calais
Helmsdale
Dykel
Findhorn
Spey
Don
Dee
Garry
Etive
Tay
Earn
Teith
Forth
Clyde
Esk
Tweed
Ayr
Nith
Teviot
Liddel
Annan
Aln
Coquet
Wansbeck
Blyth
Irthing
Cree
Tyne
Wear
Eden
Tees
Swale
Ure
Nidd
Derwent
Hull
Wharfe
Aire
Ribble
Calder
Don
Mersey
Weaver
Conwy
Clwyd
Dee
Idle
Witham
Trent
Slea
Wensum
Yare
Waveney
Welland
Ouse
Cam
Nene
Dyfi
Severn
Teme
Avon
Cherwell
Thame
Colne
Lea
Teifi
Wye
Towy
Neath
Ebbw
Usk
Taff
Avon
Thames
Kennet
Axe
Parrett
Exe
Torridge
Tamar
Dart
Fal
Test
Itchen
Wey
Arun
Medway
Rother
Stour
Foyle
Derg
Bann
Dee
Blackwater
Boyne
Liffey
Shannon
Avoca
Slaney
Barrow
Nore
Suir
Blackwater
Lee
Brandon
Ft.
M.
16,000
4,800
10,000
3,000
6,000
1,800
3,000
900
1,500
450
1,000
300
600
180
300
90
Sea Level
Land Depression
PHYSICAL
and
RAILWAYS
Scale 1:4,750,000 approx.
1 inch = 75 miles 1 cm. = 47.5 kms.
Conical Orthomorphic Projection
Copyright Oxford University Press

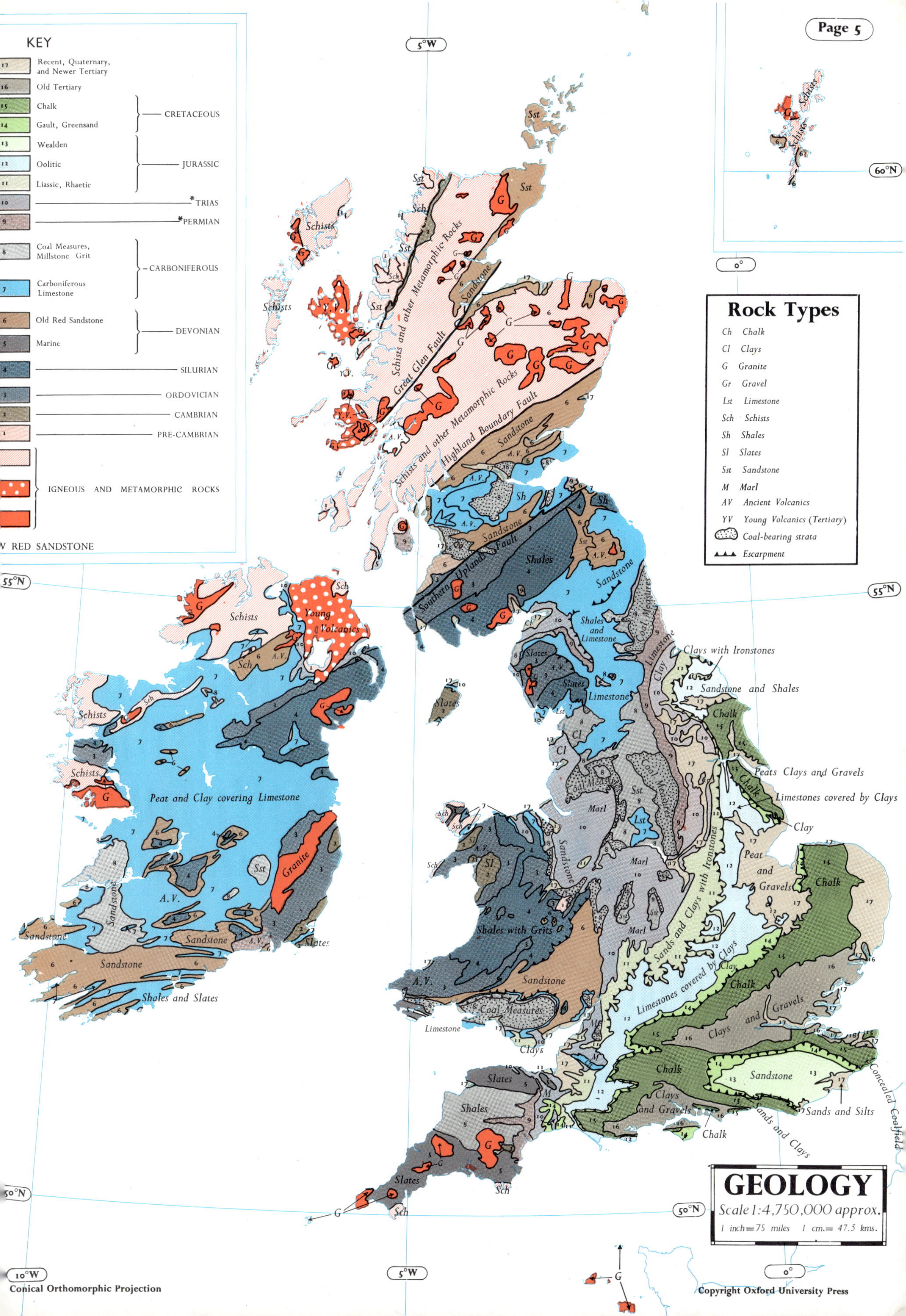

Page 5
KEY
17 Recent, Quaternary, and Newer Tertiary
16 Old Tertiary
15 Chalk
14 Gault, Greensand
CRETACEOUS
13 Wealden
12 Oolitic
11 Liassic, Rhaetic
JURASSIC
10 *TRIAS
9 *PERMIAN
8 Coal Measures, Millstone Grit
7 Carboniferous Limestone
CARBONIFEROUS
6 Old Red Sandstone
5 Marine
DEVONIAN
4 SILURIAN
3 ORDOVICIAN
2 CAMBRIAN
1 PRE-CAMBRIAN
IGNEOUS AND METAMORPHIC ROCKS
V RED SANDSTONE
Rock Types
Ch Chalk
Cl Clays
G Granite
Gr Gravel
Lst Limestone
Sch Schists
Sh Shales
Sl Slates
Sst Sandstone
M Marl
AV Ancient Volcanics
YV Young Volcanics (Tertiary)
Coal-bearing strata
Escarpment
GEOLOGY
Scale 1:4,750,000 approx.
1 inch=75 miles 1 cm.= 47.5 kms.
5°W
0°
55°N
60°N
50°N
10°W
Great Glen Fault
Highland Boundary Fault
Southern Uplands Fault
Schists and other Metamorphic Rocks
Young Volcanics
Peat and Clay covering Limestone
Shales and Slates
Shales with Grits
Coal Measures
Clays with Ironstones
Sandstone and Shales
Peats Clays and Gravels
Limestones covered by Clays
Peat and Gravels
Sands and Clays with Ironstones
Limestones covered by Clays
Clays and Gravels
Sands and Silts
Sands and Clays
Concealed Coalfield
Shales and Limestone
Conical Orthomorphic Projection
Copyright Oxford University Press

S.E. ENGLAND
Scale 1:1,000,000
0 Kilometres 10 15 20 25 30 35 40
0 Miles 5 10 15 20 25
One Inch to 16 Miles Approx.
Built up area
Motorway
Main road
Railway
County boundary
Airports
Canals
Sand
National Parks
new county boundaries
Ft. M.
16,000 4,800
10,000 3,000
6,000 1,800
3,000 900
1,500 450
1,000 300
600 180
300 90
Sea Level
Land Depression
SE
TA
SK
TF
TG
YORKS
HUMBERSIDE
SOUTH YORKS
DERBY
NOTTINGHAM
LINCOLN
LINCOLN.
KESTEVEN
HOLLAND
LEICESTER.
RUTLAND
NORTHANTS
HUNTS
CAMBRIDGE
NORFOLK
SUFFOLK
WEST SUFFOLK
EAST SUFFOLK
WARWICK
Lincoln Wolds
Lincoln Marsh
Lincoln Heath
The Fens
Norfolk Broads
Breckland
THE WASH
Burnham Flats
Mouth of the Humber
Spurn Head
Scolt Head
Blakeney Point
Leeds
Wakefield
Dewsbury
Castleford
Pontefract
Selby
Goole
Howden
Cottingham
Kingston upon Hull
Hedon
Withernsea
Patrington
Barton upon Humber
Scunthorpe
Grimsby
Cleethorpes
Barnsley
Doncaster
Rotherham
Sheffield
Worksop
Gainsborough
Market Rasen
Louth
Mablethorpe
Alford
Chesterfield
Mansfield
Lincoln
Horncastle
Spilsby
Skegness
Wainfleet All Saints
Newark upon Trent
Sleaford
Boston
Nottingham
Derby
Grantham
Matlock
Burton upon Trent
Loughborough
Melton Mowbray
Leicester
Oakham
Stamford
Spalding
Peterborough
Wisbech
King's Lynn
New Hunstanton
Hunstanton
Fakenham
Cromer
Sheringham
North Walsham
Norwich
Great Yarmouth
Lowestoft
Coventry
Nuneaton
Hinckley
Rugby
Kettering
Wellingborough
Northampton
Huntingdon
St. Ives
Ely
Thetford
Bury St. Edmunds
Newmarket
Diss
Southwold
Leamington Spa
Warwick
Kenilworth

FRANCE
Calais
Boulogne
Le Touquet
Cap Gris Nez
Strait of Dover
ENGLISH CHANNEL
SP
TL
TM
TQ
TR
SU
SZ
TV
LONDON
GREATER LONDON
Ipswich
Felixstowe
Harwich
Colchester
The Naze
Clacton on Sea
Chelmsford
Southend-on-Sea
Margate
Ramsgate
North Foreland
Canterbury
Dover
South Foreland
Folkestone
Maidstone
Ashford
Hastings
Eastbourne
Beachy Head
Brighton
Worthing
Portsmouth
Southampton
Winchester
Reading
Oxford
Luton
Watford
Guildford
Croydon
Isle of Wight
The Needles
St. Catherine's Pt.
Selsey Bill
Dungeness
ESSEX
KENT
SURREY
EAST SUSSEX
WEST SUSSEX
HAMPSHIRE
BERKS
OXFORD
HERTS
BEDS
BUCKS
North Downs
South Downs
The Weald

Bristol Channel
Pembrokeshire Coast Path
Somerset & N. Devon Coast Path
Cornish Coastal Footpath (North)
Cornish Coastal Footpath (South)
Devon S.Coast Path
Isles of Scilly
Sea Level
Land Depression
Transverse Mercator Projection

S.W. ENGLAND
Scale 1:1,000,000
Kilometres
Miles
One Inch to 16 Miles Approx.
Built up area
Motorway
Main road
Railway
National Parks
County boundary
Airports
Canals
Sand
new county boundaries
H E R E F O R D.
Black Mountains
Abergavenny
Monmouth
Ebbw Vale
M O N M O U T H
Pontypool
G W E N T
Newport
Caerphilly
Cardiff
Penarth
Barry
Chepstow
Severn Bridge
Mouth of the Severn
Bristol
A V O N
Weston-super-Mare
Bath
Mendip Hills
Wells
Bridgwater
S O M E R S E T
Taunton
Yeovil
Chard
Honiton
Tewkesbury
Cheltenham
Gloucester
Stroud
Cirencester
Forest of Dean
Swindon
Chippenham
Marlborough Downs
Devizes
Trowbridge
W I L T S.
Salisbury Plain
Salisbury
Oxford
O X F O R D
Vale of White Horse
Reading
Newbury
Basingstoke
Andover
Winchester
H A M P S H I R E
Southampton
Portsmouth
Isle of Wight
Newport
The Solent
The Needles
Bournemouth
Poole
Isle of Purbeck
Dorchester
Weymouth
Bill of Portland
D O R S E T
North Dorset Downs
Blandford Forum
Lyme Bay
Lyme Regis
Sidmouth
New Forest
Selsey Bill
Chiltern Hills
Aylesbury
Buckingham
Cowes
Ryde
Sandown
Shanklin
Ventnor
St. Alban's Head
St. Catherine's Pt.
Chesil Beach
Christchurch
Fareham
Gosport
Havant
Emsworth
SO
SP
ST
SU
SY
SZ
C H A N N E L
Channel Islands
Guernsey
St. Peter Port
Alderney
Sark
Herm
Jethou
Jersey
St. Helier
St. Aubin
Race of Alderney
C. de la Hague
FRANCE
Passage de la Deroute
Les Ecrehou
Casquets
Burhou
Casquet Banks
Schole Bank
Guernsey is 113 km. or 70 miles (11cm. or 4½" at this scale) due south of Bill of Portland
2° W
49° 30'

WALES and the MIDLANDS
Scale 1:1 ,000,000
One Inch to 16 Miles Approx.
Built up area
Motorway
Main road
Railway
National Parks
County boundary
Airports
Canals
Sand
new county boundaries
Sea Level
Land Depression
Pembrokeshire Coast Path
Cardigan Bay
Carmarthen Bay
Bristol Channel
Transverse Mercator Projection

LANCS.
GREATER MANCHESTER
YORKS.
Helens
Warrington
Widnes
Runcorn
Salford
Stretford
Manchester
Stockport
Altrincham
Hale
Cheadle
Stalybridge
Hyde
Glossop
Marple
New Mills
Bleaklow Hill
Kinder Scout
Peak
District
SOUTH YORKSHIRE
Stocksbridge
Rawmarsh
Rotherham
Conisbrough
Sheffield
Maltby
Tickhill
Bawtry
Gainsborough
Market Rasen
Lincoln
Wragby
LINCOLN
Ship Canal
Northwich
Knutsford
Wilmslow
Macclesfield
Buxton
Bollington
Whaley Bridge
Chesterfield
Dronfield
Eckington
Killamarsh
Worksop
East Retford
Staveley
Bolsover
Bakewell
Matlock
Alfreton
Mansfield
Mansfield Woodhouse
Sutton in Ashfield
Kirkby in Ashfield
Clay Cross
Ollerton
Tuxford
Newark upon Trent
Southwell
CHESHIRE
Winsford
Middlewich
Congleton
Sandbach
Crewe
Nantwich
Alsager
Biddulph
Leek
Kidsgrove
Tunstall
Burslem
Newcastle under Lyme
Hanley
Stoke on Trent
Longton
Cheadle
Ashbourne
Wirksworth
Ripley
Belper
Heanor
Ilkeston
Hucknall
Nottingham
Beeston
West Bridgford
Long Eaton
Derby
Bingham
Grantham
SJ
SK
TF
KESTEVEN
Cranwell
Sleaford
Holland Fen
Whitchurch
Market Drayton
Stone
Uttoxeter
Eccleshall
STAFFORD.
Stafford
Burton upon Trent
Repton
Melbourne
Swadlincote
Ashby de la Zouch
Coalville
Loughborough
Shepshed
Whitwick
Mountsorrel
Charnwood Forest
Melton Mowbray
Wreake
Bourne
Market Deeping
Stamford
Oakham
RUTLAND
Newport
Rugeley
Cannock Chase
Cannock
Lichfield
Tamworth
LEICESTER.
Leicester
Wigston Magna
Uppingham
Peterborough
Wellington
The Wrekin
Oakengates
Shifnal
Dawley
Coalbrookdale
Iron Bridge
Broseley
Much Wenlock
Brownhills
Walsall
Willenhall
Darlaston
Bilston
Wednesbury
W. Bromwich
Wolverhampton
Sutton Coldfield
Atherstone
Hinckley
Nuneaton
Bosworth Field
Market Harborough
Corby
Oundle
Bridgnorth
Church Stretton
Dudley
Brierley Hill
Smethwick
Birmingham
Edgbaston
Halesowen
Stourbridge
Coleshill
Solihull
Coventry
Kenilworth
Rugby
Lutterworth
Desborough
Rothwell
Kettering
Thrapston
Burton Latimer
Finedon
Raunds
Irthlingborough
Higham Ferrers
Kimbolton
Rushden
Wellingborough
TL
Kidderminster
Bewdley
Stourport-on-Severn
Cleobury Mortimer
Titterstone Clee
Ludlow
Tenbury Wells
Bromsgrove
Redditch
Droitwich
Alne
Henley in Arden
WARWICK.
Warwick
Leamington Spa
Southam
Daventry
Northampton Uplands
Northampton
St. Neots
HEREFORD
Leominster
Worcester
Bromyard
Alcester
Stratford on Avon
SO
SP
Malvern
Pershore
Evesham
Bredon Hill
Vale of Evesham
Chipping Campden
Shipston on Stour
Banbury
Towcester
Olney
Bedford
Sulgrave
Silverstone
Newport Pagnell
Wolverton
Stony Stratford
Fenny Stratford
Bletchley
Ampthill
Shefford
Hereford
Ledbury
Herefordshire Beacon
Upton upon Severn
Tewkesbury
Winchcombe
Moreton in Marsh
Bloxham
Deddington
Chipping Norton
Brackley
Buckingham
Woburn
Winslow
Leighton Buzzard
Dunstable
Luton
Hitchin
Ross on Wye
Newent
Cheltenham
Gloucester
Stow-on-the-Wold
Bourton on the Water
Charlbury
Woodstock
Blenheim Palace
Kidlington
Bicester
Aylesbury
Whitchurch
Harpenden
St. Albans
Mitcheldean
Forest of Dean
Cinderford
Coleford
Monmouth
Newnham
Painswick
Stroud
Cirencester
Fossebridge
Burford
Witney
Oxford
Cowley
Thame
Princes Risborough
Wendover
Tring
Berkhamsted
Hemel Hempstead
Chesham
Lydney
Blakeney
Berkeley
Dursley
Minchinhampton
Nailsworth
Tetbury
Fairford
Lechlade
Bampton
Abingdon
Radley
Watford
Bushey
Chepstow
Thornbury
Wotton under Edge
Wickwar
Malmesbury
Cricklade
Highworth
Faringdon
Shrivenham
Vale of White Horse
Wantage
Didcot
Wallingford
Chalgrove
Watlington
Chilterns
High Wycombe
Amersham
Rickmansworth
Beaconsfield
Ruislip
Harrow
Severn Tunnel
Chipping Sodbury
Wootton Bassett
Swindon
Whitehorse Hill
Lambourn Downs
Lambourn
Berkshire Downs
Henley on Thames
Marlow
Maidenhead
Slough
Eton
Uxbridge
Southall
Ealing
Windsor
Hounslow
Twickenham
Staines
Egham
Bristol
Clifton Gorge
Mangotsfield
Marshfield
Chippenham
Calne
Corsham
Marlborough Downs
Marlborough
Avebury
Milk Hill
Savernake Forest
Hungerford
Newbury
Pangbourne
Reading
Bracknell
Wokingham
Ascot
Chertsey
Weybridge
Walton-on-Thames
Esher
Keynsham
Bath
Melksham
Vale of Pewsey
Aldermaston
Silchester
ST
SU
TQ
WILTS.
BERKS.
HANTS
SOMERSET
AVON
OXFORD
BUCKS.
BEDS.
HERTS
NORTHANTS
HUNTS
GLOUCESTER
WORCESTER
SHROPSHIRE
Chew Res.
Copyright Oxford University Press

KIRKCUDBRIGHT
DUMFRIESSHIRE
Galloway
DUMFRIES AND GALLOWAY
WIGTOWNSHIRE
Stranraer
The Rhins
Luce Bay
Mull of Galloway
Whithorn
Wigtown
Newton Stewart
Kirkcudbright
Castle Douglas
Dalbeattie
Dumfries
Annan
Solway Firth
Carlisle
CUMBERLAND
CUMBRIA
WESTMORLAND
Lake District
Keswick
Cockermouth
Workington
Whitehaven
Maryport
Silloth
Wigton
Penrith
Ambleside
Windermere
Kendal
Coniston
Ulverston
Millom
Barrow-in-Furness
Morecambe Bay
Morecambe
Heysham
Lancaster
Carnforth
Isle of Man
Ramsey
Peel
Laxey
Douglas
Port Erin
Castletown
Calf of Man
Point of Ayre
IRISH SEA
Fleetwood
Blackpool
Lytham
St. Anne's on the Sea
Preston
Southport
Ormskirk
Crosby
Bootle
Wallasey
Birkenhead
Liverpool
Liverpool Bay
Hoylake
St. Helens
Warrington
Widnes
Chester
FLINT
Wrexham
Llangollen
Rhyl
Prestatyn
Llandudno
Colwyn Bay
Conwy
Abergele
Denbigh
Ruthin
DENBIGH
CLWYD
ANGLESEY
Holyhead
Amlwch
Llangefni
Menai Bridge
Beaumaris
Bangor
Caernarfon
Caernarfon Bay
Snowdon
CAERNARVON
GWYNEDD
Nevin
Ffestiniog
Blaenau-Ffestiniog
NX
NY
NW
SC
SD
SH
SJ
Transverse Mercator Projection
Ft.
M.
16,000
4,800
10,000
3,000
6,000
1,800
3,000
900
1,500
450
1,000
300
600
180
300
90
Sea Level
Land Depression

N. ENGLAND
Scale 1:1,000,000
0 Kilometres 10 15 20 25 30 35 40
0 Miles 5 10 15 20 25
One Inch to 16 Miles Approx.
Built up area
Motorway
Main road
Railway
County boundary
Airports
Canals
Sand
National Parks
new county boundaries
NORTH SEA
NZ
SE
SK
TA
TF
OV
NORTHUMBERLAND
TYNE AND WEAR
DURHAM
CLEVELAND
NORTH YORKSHIRE
HUMBERSIDE
SOUTH YORKSHIRE
WEST YORKSHIRE
NOTTINGHAM
LINCOLN
DERBY
STAFFORDSHIRE
MANCHESTER
Whitley Bay
Tynemouth
South Shields
Newcastle upon Tyne
Wallsend
Jarrow
Gosforth
Gateshead
Sunderland
Corbridge
Hexham
Blaydon
Whickham
Washington
Birtley
Stanley
Consett
Chester le Street
Houghton le Spring
Hetton le Hole
Seaham Harbour
Allendale Town
Blanchland
Durham
Peterlee
Stanhope
Wolsingham
Willington
Crook
Spennymoor
Bishop Auckland
Sedgefield
St.John's Chapel
Pawlaw Pike
Hartlepool
Middleton in Teesdale
Mickle Fell
Shildon
Newton Aycliffe
Billingham
Coatham
Redcar
Saltburn by the Sea
Brotton
Loftus
Grangetown
Stockton on Tees
Teesside
Middlesbrough
Thornaby on Tees
Skelton
Guisborough
Barnard Castle
Brough
Darlington
Yarm
Cleveland
Whitby
Kirkby Stephen
Stokesley
Cleveland Hills
Esk
Wade's Causeway
North Yorks. Moors
Richmond
Reeth
Swaledale
Catterick Camp
Northallerton
Hawes
Askrigg
Leyburn
Bedale
Middleham
Yorkshire Dales
Thirsk
Helmsley
Kirby Moorside
Pickering
Allerton Forest
Scarborough
Rievaulx Abbey
Ampleforth
Vale of Pickering
Masham
Ripon
Filey
Hunmanby
Malton
Easingwold
Howardian Hills
Flamborough Head
Bridlington
Boroughbridge
Pateley Bridge
Grassington
Settle
Ripley
Knaresborough
Harrogate
Spofforth
Bolton Abbey
Skipton
Ilkley
Otley
Wetherby
Stamford Bridge
Gt.Driffield
Pocklington
York
Marston Moor
Hornsea
Earby
Silsden
Keighley
Bingley
Guiseley
Yeadon
Tadcaster
Harewood
Market Weighton
Beverley
Colne
Nelson
Burnley
Shipley
Horsforth
Bradford
Leeds
Pudsey
Cawood
Selby
Sherburn in Elmet
Cottingham
Hessle
Kingston upon Hull
Hedon
Withernsea
Patrington
Accrington
Halifax
Brighouse
Batley
Dewsbury
Rothwell
Morley
Castleford
Normanton
Pontefract
Knottingley
Howden
Goole
Snaith
Wakefield
Barton upon Humber
New Holland
Winterton
Rawtenstall
Todmorden
Elland
Huddersfield
Mirfield
Horbury
Rochdale
Bury
Ramsbottom
Heywood
Slaithwaite
Meltham
Holmfirth
Kirkburton
Denby Dale
Barnsley
Royston
Cudworth
Darton
Adwick le Street
Thorne
Crowle
Scunthorpe
Immingham
Grimsby
Cleethorpes
Spurn Head
Radcliffe
Middleton
Oldham
Penistone
Wombwell
Dearne
Mexborough
Conisbrough
Doncaster
Isle of Axholme
Epworth
Brigg
Caistor
Ashton under Lyne
Stalybridge
Hyde
Glossop
Stocksbridge
Rawmarsh
Rotherham
Maltby
Tickhill
Bawtry
Kirton in Lindsey
Stretford
Manchester
Stockport
Marple
Peak District
Sheffield
Gainsborough
Market Rasen
Louth
Mablethorpe
Lincoln Wolds
Lincoln Marsh
Bramhall
Hazel Grove
New Mills
Whaley Bridge
Wilmslow
Alderley Edge
Bollington
Buxton
Macclesfield
Dronfield
Eckington
Worksop
East Retford
Wragby
Alford
Chesterfield
Staveley
Bolsover
Clowne
The Dukeries
Tuxford
Lincoln
Horncastle
Bakewell
Mansfield Woodhouse
Mansfield
Ollerton
Old Bolingbroke
Woodhall Spa
Spilsby
Burgh le Marsh
Skegness
Biddulph
Matlock
Matlock Bath
Clay Cross
Sutton in Ashfield
Kirkby in Ashfield
Southwell
Newark upon Trent
Wainfleet All Saints
Kidsgrove
Tunstall
Burslem
Leek
Wirksworth
Alfreton
Ripley
Belper
Heanor
Ilkeston
Hucknall Torkard
Nottingham
Stoke on Trent
Hanley
Longton
Cheadle
Ashbourne
Cranwell
Sleaford
Holland Fen
Boston
North Beck
East Fen
West Fen
Kesteven
Vale of Belvoir
Trent
Humber
Ouse
Aire
Tees
Wear
Tyne
Swale
Ure
Derwent
Dove
Idle
Witham
Ancholme
Hull
Holderness
Gypsey Race
Sand Hutton
Staffordshire

Ardnamurchan
Coll
Tiree
Inner Hebrides
Mull
Morvern
Ardgour
Appin
Benderloch
Rannoch Moor
Grampians
Ben Nevis
Mamore Forest
Glen Coe
Oban
Firth of Lorne
Ross of Mull
Iona
Colonsay
Jura
Islay
Sound of Jura
Lochgilphead
Knapdale
Kintyre
Campbeltown
Mull of Kintyre
Gigha
Arran
Buteshire
Cowal
Inveraray
Argyll
Loch Fyne
Dunbarton
Stirling
Renfrew
Glasgow
Paisley
Greenock
Helensburgh
Dumbarton
Clydebank
Firth of Clyde
Ayr
Kilmarnock
Irvine
Troon
Ardrossan
Kyle
Carrick
Girvan
Maybole
Ailsa Craig
Ayrshire
Galloway
Kirkcudbright
Stranraer
Wigtownshire
The Rhinns
Luce Bay
Whithorn
Wigtown
Newton Stewart
The Machars
The Moors
Mull of Galloway
North Channel
Rathlin I.
Giant's Causeway
Portrush
Coleraine
Ballymoney
Ballycastle
Ballymena
Larne
Antrim
Ballyclare
Lough Neagh
Belfast
Bangor
Belfast Lough
Northern Ireland
Londonderry
Antrim
Down
For detailed map of Ireland see Pages 18-19
Transverse Mercator Projection
55°N
6°W
NM
NN
NL
NR
NS
NQ
NW
NX
Ft.
M.
16,000
4,800
10,000
3,000
6,000
1,800
3,000
900
1,500
450
1,000
300
600
180
300
90
Sea Level
Land Depression

S. SCOTLAND
Scale 1:1 ,000,000
0 Kilometres 10 15 20 25 30 35 40
0 Miles 5 10 15 20 25
One Inch to 16 Miles Approx.
Built up area
Motorway
Main road
Railway
County boundary
Airports
Canals
Sand
National Parks
new county boundaries
NORTH SEA
NO
NP
NT
NU
NY
NZ
ANGUS
PERTH
KINROSS
CLACKMANNAN
FIFE
WEST LOTHIAN
MIDLOTHIAN
EAST LOTHIAN
BERWICKSHIRE
PEEBLESSHIRE
SELKIRK
ROXBURGH
BORDERS
DUMFRIESSHIRE
NORTHUMBERLAND
DURHAM
CUMBERLAND
CUMBRIA
TYNE AND WEAR
Blair Atholl
Ben Vrackie
Mt. Blair
Cat Law 669
Brechin
Montrose
Scurdie Ness
Lunan Bay
Pitlochry
Aberfeldy
Kirriemuir
Forfar
Alyth
Rattray
Blairgowrie
Dunkeld
Birnam
Coupar Angus
Glamis
Sidlaw Hills
Arbroath
Dighty W.
Carnoustie
Monifieth
Buddon Ness
Dundee
Tayport
Newport
Firth of Tay
Inchcape or Bell Rock
King's Seat 377
Meall nan Canraich 623
Perth
Crieff
Newburgh
St. Andrews Bay
St. Andrews
Abernethy
Cupar
Auchtermuchty
Gleneagles
Auchterarder
Ladybank
Eden
North Carr Beacon
Fife Ness
East Neuk of Fife
Crail
Falkland
Lomond Hills
Leslie
Kilrenny
Anstruther
Pittenweem
Kinross
Dunblane
Bridge of Allan
Alva
Dollar
Tillicoultry
Glenrothes
Markinch
Leven
Elie
Earlsferry
Isle of May
Buckhaven
Stirling
Alloa
Clackmannan
Cowdenbeath
Lochgelly
Dysart
Kirkcaldy
Kincardine
Dunfermline
Kinghorn
Firth of Forth
Bass Rock
North Berwick
Tantallon Cas.
Culross
Grangemouth
Burntisland
Inchkeith
Gullane
Falkirk
Bo'ness
Inverkeithing
Forth Bridge
Queensferry
Dunbar
Linlithgow
Leith
Portobello
Musselburgh
Prestonpans
Cockenzie
Tranent
Tyne
East Linton
Haddington
Edinburgh
Armadale
Bathgate
Livingston
Lasswade
Dalkeith
St. Abb's Head
Heart Law 391
Loanhead
Bonnyrigg
Eyemouth
Whitburn
The Hopes
Lammermuir Hills
Fala
Penicuik
Pentland Hills
Moorfoot Hills
Wishaw
Carluke
Berwick upon Tweed
Duns
Blackhope Scar 651
Lanark
Lauder
Greenlaw
Holy Island
Peebles
Coldstream
Galashiels
Farne Islands
Bamburgh
Biggar
Melrose
Kelso
Belford
Tinto Hills
Abbotsford
Dryburgh Abbey
St. Boswells
Roxburgh
Dun Rig 742
Selkirk
Beadnell Bay
Culter Fell 748
Dollar Law 817
Wooler
Tweedsmuir
Broad Law
St. Mary's L.
Yarrow W.
Ettrick Forest
Eckford
Crailing
Jedburgh
Hownam Law 449
The Cheviot 816
Breamish
Eglingham
Hart Fell 808
Ettrick
Teviotdale
Hawick
Woden Law 423
Cushat Law 616
Alnwick
Moffat
Ettrick Pen 692
Hott Hill
Chesters
Carter Bar
Cheviot Hills
Coquet
Long Crag 319
Amble
Queensberry 696
Davington
Cauldcleuch Head 608
Peel Fell 602
Catcleugh
Oh Me Edge
Ridlees Cairn
Rothbury
Rothbury Forest
Thornhill
Wisp Hill 594
Hermitage Cas.
Roan Fell 568
Redesdale
Rochester
Padon Hill 378
Otterburn
Font
Arkleton Hill 521
Larriston Fells
Ashington
Newbiggin by the Sea
Lochmaben
Lockerbie
Langholm
Elliott's Pike 478
North Tyne
Bellingham
Hart Burn
Wansbeck
Morpeth
Bedlington
Blyth
Holywood
Burnswark
Bewcastle Fells
Sighty Crag 519
Maxwelltown
Dumfries
Whitley Bay
Bell Crags 332
Chesters
Tynemouth
South Shields
Gosforth
Newcastle upon Tyne
Wallsend
Jarrow
Annan
Gretna Green
Longtown
Kirtlebridge
Corbridge
Hexham
Prudhoe
Blaydon
Whickham
Gateshead
Southwick
Sunderland
Criffell 569
Dalbeattie
Solway Firth
Hadrian's Wall
Naworth Cas.
Haltwhistle
Brampton
Washington
Birtley
Southerness Point
Silloth
Carlisle
Cold Fell
Pike Rigg 325
Allendale Town
Blanchland
Blackhill
Consett
Stanley
Annfield Plain
Chester le Street
Houghton le Spring
Hetton le Hole
Seaham
Balcary Point
Wigton
Alston
Cross Fell 893
Brownley
Durham
Peterlee
Inglewood Forest
Kirkoswald
Stanhope
Maryport
St. John's Chapel
Wolsingham
Tow Law
Weardale
Crook
Willington
Copyright Oxford University Press

N. SCOTLAND
Scale 1:1,000,000
One Inch to 16 Miles Approx.
Built up area
Main road
Railway
National Parks
County boundary
Airports
Canals
Sand
new county boundaries
Transverse Mercator Projection
Butt of Lewis
Stornoway
North Uist
South Uist
Benbecula
Barra
Castlebay
Trotternish
Portree
Minginish
Cuillin Hills
Sleat
Knoydart
Morar
Arisaig
Moidart
Ardnamurchan
Morvern
Ardgour
Coll
Tiree
Rhum
Eigg
Canna
Tobermory
Fort William
Ben Nevis
Kintail
Ullapool
Lochinver
Kinlochbervie
Cape Wrath
The Little Minch
Sound of Mull
STRATHCLYDE

NC
ND
Pentland Firth
Dunnet Head
Stroma
Castle of Mey
John o' Groats Ho.
Pentland Skerries
Duncansby Head
Brims Ness
Strathy Pt.
Lower Dounreay
Scrabster
Thurso
Dunnet Bay
Eilean nan Ròn
Kyle of Tongue
L. Calder
L. Watten
Sinclair's Bay
Noss Hd.
Wick
Beinn nam Bad Mor
Ben Loyal
Beinn Stumanadh
Loch Loyal
Strathnaver
Naver
Strathy
Halladale
CAITHNESS
Ben Griam More
Knockfin Heights
Loch Naver
Loch Rimsdale
Loch nan Clar
Ben Klibreck
Morven
Dunbeath W.
Berriedale W.
Strath of Kildonan
Helmsdale
Creag Riabhach na Creighe
Beinn Dhorain
Brora
Ben Horn
L. Brora
Lairg
Strath Fleet
Fleet
Dunrobin Cas.
Golspie
Loch Fleet
Inveran
Strathcarron
Carron
Evelix
Dornoch
Dornoch Firth
Tarbat Ness
Tain
Beinn Tharsuinn
Morie
Balnagown
Loch Glass
Wyvis
Alness
Invergordon
Cromarty Firth
Cromarty
Moray Firth
NH
Black Isle
Dingwall
Fortrose
Beauly Firth
Inverness
The Aird
Culloden Moor
Nairn
Ardersier
Dalcross
Cawdor
Culbin Wood
Forres
Burghead
Gordonstoun
Covesea Skerries
Lossiemouth
Spey Bay
Laich o' Moray
Elgin
Rafford
Dallas
Lossie
MORAY
Fochabers
Buckie
Cullen
Portsoy
Banff
Macduff
Troup Hd
Rosehearty
Kinnairds Head
Fraserburgh
Loch of Strathbeg
Rattray Head
NK
Peterhead
Buchan Ness
Buchan
Knock Hill
Aberchirder
Deveron
Turriff
Isla
Keith
Rothes
Ben Aigan
Charlestown of Aberlour
Dufftown
Huntly
Strathbogie
NJ
NAIRN
Lochindorb
Dorback Burn
Findhorn
Strathnairn
Drumnadrochit
Urquhart Cas.
L. Duntelchaig
Carn na Loine
Carn Glas-choire
Grantown-on-Spey
Ben Rinnes
Hills of Cromdale
Strath Avon
The Buck
Correen Hills
Callievar Hill
Ythan
Ellon
Formartine
Oldmeldrum
Port Erroll
Cruden Bay
Urie
Inverurie
Kintore
Don
Dyce
Aberdeen
Girdle Ness
Dee
Findon Ness
Carn Mor
Ladder Hills
Boat of Garten
Strathspey
Carn Coire na h-Easgainn
Geal-chàrn Mòr
Aviemore
Inverdruie
Alvie
Geal Chàrn
Avon
Monadhliath Mts.
Carn Ban
Kingussie
Spey
Cairn Gorm
Cairngorm Mts.
Glen Avon
Brown Cow Hill
Gairn
Morven
GRAMPIAN
Hill of Fare
Ben Macdhui
Beinn a'Bhuird
Braeriach
Cairn Toul
Crathie
Ballater
Aboyne
Deeside
Banchory
Water of Feugh
Mar Forest
Braemar
Balmoral Cas.
Badenoch
Highlands
Gaick Forest
Dalwhinnie
Càrn na Caim
Geldie Burn
Balmoral Forest
Lochnagar
Mount Keen
Peter Hill
Mount Battock
Kerloch
Cowie W.
Garron Pt.
Stonehaven
KINCARDINE
Tarf Water
Beinn Iutharn Mhor
Beinn Dearg
Forest of Atholl
Broad Cairn
Glas Maol
Mayar
Glen Clova
Glen Esk
North Esk
White Hill
Howe of the Mearns
Laurencekirk
Inverbervie
Ben Alder
Loch Ericht
Beinn Udlamain
Beinn A'Ghlo
Garry
Tilt
Blair Atholl
Ben Vrackie
Mt. Blair
West Water
South Esk
ANGUS
Brechin
Montrose
Scurdie Ness
Beinn A'Chuallaich
Kinloch Rannoch
Pass of Killiecrankie
Pitlochry
Tummel
L. Rannoch
Schiehallion
Carn Mairg
Aberfaldy
Tay
Cat Law
Braes of Angus
Kirriemuir
Strathmore
Forfar
Lunan W.
Lunan Bay
Glen Lyon
Bridge of Balgie
Drummond Hill
Blairgowrie
Rattray
Alyth
Ericht
Ruthven
Dean Water
Glamis
Isla
Black W.
Shee W.
NN
NO
NP
Orkney Islands
HY
Mull Hd.
Papa Westray
North Ronaldsay
Westray
The North Sound
North Ronaldsay Firth
Start Point
Sanday
Westray Firth
Eday
Rousay
Sanday Sound
ORKNEY
Brough Head
Mainland
Stronsay
Stronsay Firth
Shapinsay
Skara Brae
L. of Stenness
Wide Fth.
Grimsetter
Kirkwall
Stromness
Ward Hill
Hoy
Scapa Flow
St. Margaret's Hope
South Ronaldsay
Pentland Firth
Pentland Skerries
Duncansby Head
Scrabster
John o' Groats Ho.
Shetland Islands
HP
Herma Ness
Unst
Yell
Fetlar
Ronas Hill
Out Skerries
St. Magnus Bay
Muckle Roe
Whalsay
Papa Stour
Sandness
Aith
Zetland
SHETLAND
Bressay
Lerwick
The Deeps
Foula
West Burra
HU
Sumburgh
Jarlshof
Sumburgh Head
Sumburgh Roost
Scale 1:2,000,000
HZ
Stonybreck
Fair Isle

IRELAND
Scale 1:1,250,000
0 Kilometres 15 20 25 30 35 40 45 50
0 Miles 5 10 15 20 25 30
One Inch to 20 Miles Approx.
Built up area
Main road
Railway
County boundary
Airports
Canals
ATLANTIC OCEAN
North Channel
Irish
SCOTLAND
Kintyre
Campbeltown
Mull of Kintyre
Rathlin I.
Rathlin Sound
NORTHERN IRELAND
ULSTER
CONNAUGHT
LEINSTER
DONEGAL
LONDONDERRY
ANTRIM
TYRONE
FERMANAGH
ARMAGH
DOWN
MONAGHAN
CAVAN
LOUTH
MEATH
WESTMEATH
LONGFORD
LEITRIM
SLIGO
MAYO
ROSCOMMON
Belfast
Londonderry
Lough Neagh
Lower Lough Erne
Upper Lough Erne
Lough Foyle
Donegal Bay
Sligo Bay
Clew Bay
Dundalk Bay
Malin Head
Inishtrahull
Inishowen Peninsula
Giant's Causeway
Antrim Mts.
Sperrin Mts.
Mourne Mts.
Blue Stack Mts.
Derryveagh Mts.
Nephin Beg Range
Partry Mts.
Slieve Gamph or Ox Mts.
Achill I.
Mullet Peninsula
Tory I.
Aran I.
Gola I.
Portrush
Coleraine
Ballymena
Larne
Bangor
Newry
Dundalk
Drogheda
Enniskillen
Omagh
Strabane
Letterkenny
Donegal
Ballyshannon
Sligo
Ballina
Castlebar
Westport
Cavan
Monaghan
Armagh
Lisburn
Portadown
Lurgan
Dungannon
Cookstown
Downpatrick
Kilkeel
Newcastle
Carlingford Lough
Strangford Lough
Belfast Lough
Carrick on Shannon
Boyle
Roscommon
Longford
Mullingar
Navan
Kells
Trim
Balbriggan
Skerries
Rush
Swords
Shannon
10°W
9°W
8°W
7°W
6°W
55°N
54°N
A
B
C
D
E
F
G
H
J
K
L
9
8
7
6

Page 19
Copyright Oxford University Press
Conical Orthomorphic Projection
ATLANTIC OCEAN
St. George's Channel
MUNSTER
LEINSTER
REPUBLIC OF IRELAND
CLARE
LIMERICK
TIPPERARY
KERRY
CORK
WATERFORD
KILKENNY
WEXFORD
CARLOW
WICKLOW
KILDARE
LAOIGHIS
OFFALY
Galway Bay
Dingle Bay
Bantry Bay
Mouth of the Shannon
Galway
Limerick
Cork
Waterford
Wexford
Kilkenny
Killarney
Tralee
Dingle
Ennis
Clonmel
Tipperary
Wicklow
Arklow
Carlow
Athy
Kildare
Naas
Bray
Greystones
Tullamore
Birr
Nenagh
Thurles
Cashel
Mallow
Fermoy
Youghal
Dungarvan
Bantry
Skibbereen
Kinsale
Macroom
Listowel
Kilrush
Kilkee
Shannon
Wicklow Mts.
Blackstairs Mts.
Comeragh Mts.
Knockmealdown Mts.
Galtee Mts.
Silvermine Mts.
Slieve Bloom
Macgillycuddy's Reeks
Carrauntoohil 1041
Boggeragh Mts.
Nagles Mts.
Ballyhoura Hills
Caha Mts.
Shehy Mts.
Mizen Head
Carnsore Point
Hook Head
Loop Head
Kerry Head
Old Head of Kinsale
Fastnet Rock
Skellig Rocks
52°N
53°N
7°W
8°W
9°W
Ft.
M.
16,000
4,800
10,000
3,000
6,000
1,800
3,000
900
1,500
450
1,000
300
600
180
300
90
Sea Level
Land Depression
A
B
C
D
E
F
G
H
I
J
K
1
2
3
4
5

EUROPE
and the
MEDITERRANEAN
Scale 1:12,500,000 approx.
0 Kilometres 200 300 400
0 Miles 100 200 300
One Inch to 200 Miles
Towns over 1 million people
" over 100,000 people
Boundaries - international
- provincial etc.
Railways
Roads
Airports
Sand desert
Oil pipeline
Canal
Marsh
Ice cap
Ft. M.
16,000 4,800
10,000 3,000
6,000 1,800
3,000 900
1,500 450
1,000 300
600 180
300 90
Sea Level
Land Depression
Conical Orthomorphic Projection
20°W
15°W
10°W
5°W
0°
5°E
55°N
50°N
45°N
40°N
35°N
200 metres
ATLANTIC OCEAN
North Sea
Bay of Biscay
English Channel
Irish Sea
Shetland Is.
Orkney Is.
Hebrides
SCOTLAND
Inverness
Aberdeen
Dundee
Glasgow
Edinburgh
Londonderry
N. IRELAND
Belfast
REPUBLIC OF IRELAND
Shannon
Limerick
Dublin
Waterford
Cork
Newcastle
Middlesbrough
Liverpool
Leeds
Hull
Manchester
Sheffield
Stoke
Nottingham
Birmingham
Norwich
WALES
ENGLAND
Swansea
Cardiff
Bristol
London
Thames
Southampton
Dover
Land's End
Plymouth
Bergen
Haugesund
Stavanger
Kristiansand
Esbjerg
Emden
Bremen
Amsterdam
The Hague
Rotterdam
NETHERLANDS
Arnhem
Essen
Dortmund
Düsseldorf
Cologne
Bonn
Ostend
Calais
Lille
Ghent
Antwerp
Brussels
BELGIUM
Liège
LUX.
Luxembourg
Wiesbaden
Mannheim
Saarbrück
Cherbourg
Le Havre
Somme
Oise
Seine
Marne
Reims
Meuse
Moselle
Paris
Brest
Rennes
Mayenne
Le Mans
Loir
Loire
Nantes
Nancy
Strasbourg
Vosges
Rhine
Dijon
Belfort
Doubs
Basel
Bern
FRANCE
Cher
Vienne
Creuse
Saône
Geneva
SWITZERLAND
Rhône
Limoges
Clermont-Ferrand
Lyons
4810
Massif Central
Dordogne
Isère
Durance
Bordeaux
Garonne
Lot
Tarn
Milan
Turin
Tanaro
Bayonne
Toulouse
Nîmes
Nice
MONACO
Marseilles
Gulf of Lions
Ligurian Sea
Corsica (Fr.)
Ajaccio
Sassari
Sardinia (It.)
Cagliari
Corunna
C. Finisterre
Gijón
Cantabrian Mts.
Miño
Sil
León
Bilbao
San Sebastián
Pyrenees
ANDORRA
Vigo
Esla
Ebro
Oporto
Douro
Valladolid
Duero
Tormes
Saragossa
Segre
Coimbra
PORTUGAL
Tagus
Barcelona
Lisbon
Setúbal
Évora
Madrid
SPAIN
C. Tortosa
Guadiana
Badajoz
Ciudad Real
Jucar
Valencia
Sierra Morena
Balearic Islands (Sp.)
Minorca
Palma
Majorca
Iviza
C. de la Nao
C. St. Vincent
Faro
Guadalquivir
Córdoba
Segura
Murcia
Alicante
Seville
Gulf of Cádiz
Cádiz
Jerez
Sierra Nevada
3481
Cartagena
C. Trafalgar
Málaga
Almeria
Tangier
Gibraltar (Br.)
Ceuta (Sp.)
Tetuán
Mediterranean
Algiers
Bejaia
Annaba
Oran
El Asnam
Chéliff
Constantine
Medjerda
Melilla (Sp.)
3441
Er Rif
Sebou
Moulouya
Oudja
Tlemcen
Sidi-Bel-Abbès
Little Atlas
Tell Atlas
El Dar el Beida (Casablanca)
Rabat
Fès
Meknès
MOROCCO
ALGERIA
•2325
Djelfa
Oil Pipeline
Safi
Ksabi
Méchéria
Essaoira
Marrakech
Touggourt
Agadir
Béchar

Gävle
Turku
Åland Is.
Helsinki
Leningrad
Gulf of Finland
Tallinn
20°E
30°E
35°E
40°E
55°N
50°N
45°N
15°E
25°E
Kazan
Uppsala
L. Mälar
Stockholm
Örebro
Karlstad
Lake Väner
L. Vätter
Norrköping
Linköping
Borås
Göteborg
Visby
Gotland
Kalmar
Karlskrona
Hälsingborg
Malmö
S W E D E N
Baltic Sea
Gulf of Riga
Riga
West Dvina
Liepāja
Klaipeda
Kaunas
Vilnius
Daugavapils
Tartu
Lake Peipus
Volkhov
Novgorod
L. Ilmen'
Msta
Lovat
Velikiye Luki
Rzhev
Volga
Rybinsk
Yaroslavl'
Ivanovo
Gor'kiy
Dzerzhinsk
Vladimir
Kalinin
Moscow
Kolomna
Ryazan
Serpukhov
Tula
Novomoskovsk
Penza
Tambov
Lipetsk
Voronezh
Balashov
Borisoglebsk
Vitebsk
Smolensk
Dnieper
Mogilev
Minsk
Berezina
Bobruysk
Gomel'
Bryansk
Orel
Kursk
Seym
Don
Oka
U. S. S. R.
Bornholm
Rügen
Kaliningrad
Gdańsk
Grodno
Neman
Białystok
Rostock
Szczecin
Bydgoszcz
Vistula
Warsaw
Brest Litovskiy
Pinsk
Pripet
Chernigov
Kiev
Khar'kov
Poltava
Donets
Sula
Berlin
Poznań
Łódź
Lublin
Rovno
Zhitomir
Cherkassy
Dnepropetrovsk
Kramatorsk
Lugansk
Donetsk
Taganrog
Rostov-na-Donu
Manych
P O L A N D
Leipzig
Dresden
Wroclaw
Zabrze
Katowice
Kraków
L'vov
Kirovograd
Krivoy Rog
Zaporozh'ye
Zhdanov
Melitopol'
Sea of Azov
Kerch'
Krasnodar
Kuban
Armavir
Sudeten Mts.
Prague
Moravska Ostrava
Brno
Pilsen
CZECHOSLOVAKIA
Košice
Mukachevo
Carpathian Mountains
Chernovtsy
Dniester
Kishinev
Nikolayev
Kherson
Odessa
Bug
Crimea
Simferopol'
Sevastopol'
C. Tarkhankut
200 metres
Linz
Vienna
Bratislava
Győr
Miskolc
Satu Mare
Debrecen
Iaşi
Siret
Prut
Salzburg
AUSTRIA
Graz
Klagenfurt
Budapest
HUNGARY
Tisza
Cluj
ROMANIA
Braşov
Brăila
Szeged
Timişoara
Mureş
Olt
Pécs
Subotica
Ploeşti
Bucharest
Constanţa
Black Sea
Bolzano
Ljubljana
Zagreb
Trieste
Rijeka
Venice
Padua
Sava
Danube
Jiu
Craiova
Ruse
Pleven
Varna
Belgrade
YUGOSLAVIA
Morava
Drina
Niš
Balkan Mts.
Sofia
Burgas
Plovdiv
BULGARIA
Maritsa
Struma
Istanbul
Bosporus
Samsun
Zonguldak
Sivas
Ankara
Kizilirmak
Bologna
SAN MARINO
Florence
Adriatic Sea
Dinaric Alps
Sarajevo
Split
Dubrovnik
Skopje
Vardar
Assisi
ITALY
Tiber
Rome
C. Gargano
Tiranë
ALBANIA
Drin
Kavalla
Salonica
Bursa
Sakarya
Eskişehir
Kayseri
TURKEY
L. Tuz
Bari
Naples
Taranto
Vlonë
Pindus Mts.
Larisa
Yannina
Aegean Sea
Dardanelles
Balikesir
Mitilini
Afyonkarahisar
L. Eğridir
L. Beyşehir
Konya
Adana
Ceyhan
Tyrrhenian Sea
Ionian Sea
GREECE
İzmir
Gediz
Menderes
Muğla
Antalya
Antakya
Aksu
C. Gelidonya
Athens
Patras
MOREA
Palermo
Messina
Sicily
Catania
C. Passero
C. Matapan
Rhodes
Nicosia
CYPRUS
Latakia
SYRIA
Tripoli
LEBANON
Beirut
Tyre
Haifa
Jaffa-Tel Aviv
ISRAEL
Jerusalem
Canea
Candia
Crete
MALTA
Valletta
Mediterranean Sea
Bon
Port Said
Alexandria
Tanta
EGYPT
Cairo
Suez
Tarabulus (Tripoli)
LIBYA
Beida
Barce
Benghazi
Copyright Oxford University Press

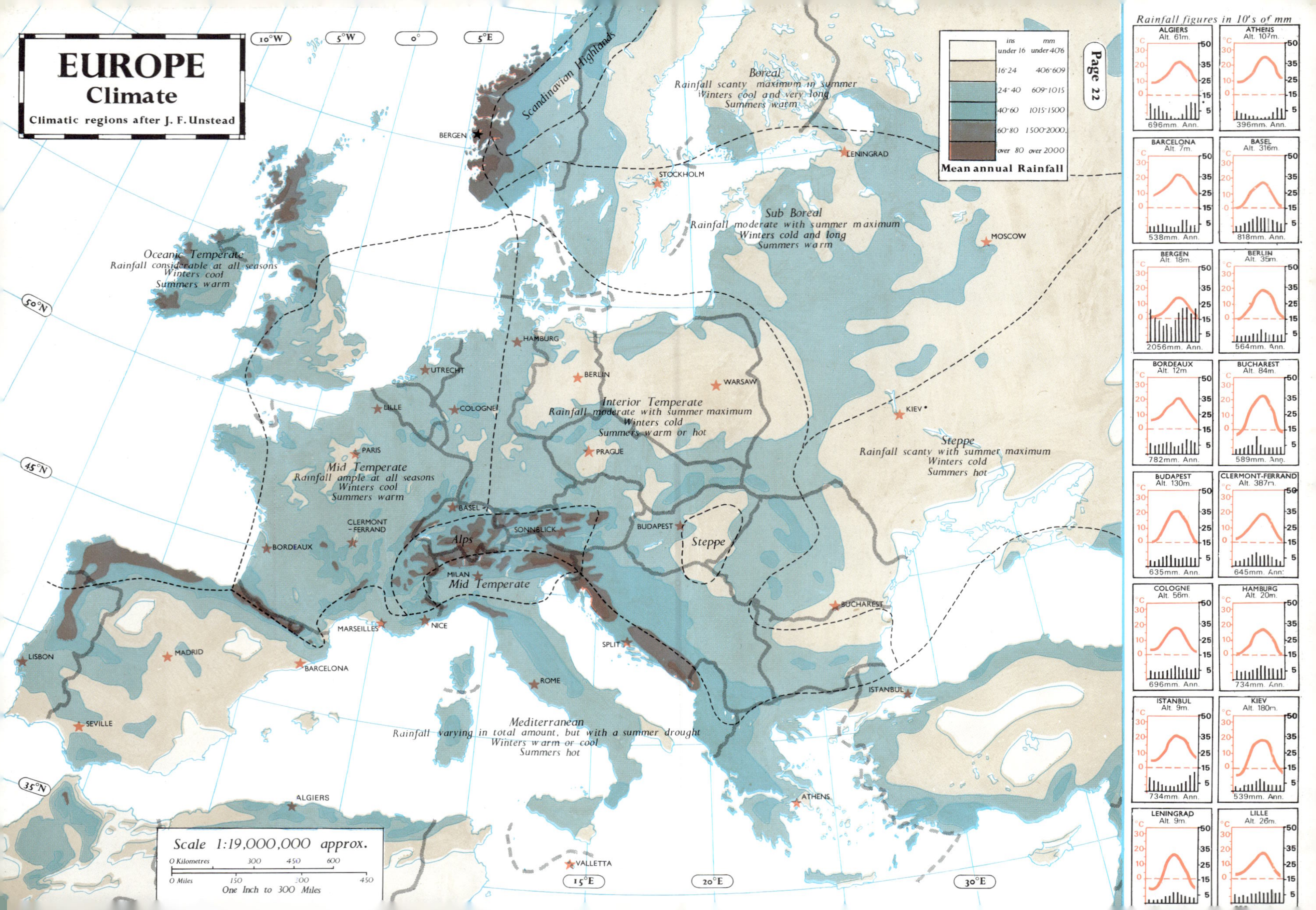
EUROPE
Climate
Climatic regions after J. F. Unstead
Page 22
Mean annual Rainfall
ins mm
under 16 under 406
16-24 406-609
24-40 609-1015
40-60 1015-1500
60-80 1500-2000
over 80 over 2000
Scale 1:19,000,000 approx.
0 Kilometres 300 450 600
0 Miles 150 200 450
One Inch to 300 Miles
10°W
5°W
0°
5°E
15°E
20°E
30°E
50°N
45°N
35°N
Scandinavian Highlands
Boreal
Rainfall scanty maximum in summer
Winters cool and very long
Summers warm
Sub Boreal
Rainfall moderate with summer maximum
Winters cold and long
Summers warm
Oceanic Temperate
Rainfall considerable at all seasons
Winters cool
Summers warm
Interior Temperate
Rainfall moderate with summer maximum
Winters cold
Summers warm or hot
Steppe
Rainfall scanty with summer maximum
Winters cold
Summers hot
Mid Temperate
Rainfall ample at all seasons
Winters cool
Summers warm
Alps
Mid Temperate
Steppe
Mediterranean
Rainfall varying in total amount, but with a summer drought
Winters warm or cool
Summers hot
BERGEN
STOCKHOLM
LENINGRAD
MOSCOW
HAMBURG
BERLIN
WARSAW
UTRECHT
LILLE
COLOGNE
KIEV
PARIS
PRAGUE
BASEL
CLERMONT-FERRAND
SONNBLICK
BUDAPEST
BORDEAUX
MILAN
BUCHAREST
MARSEILLES
NICE
SPLIT
LISBON
MADRID
BARCELONA
ROME
ISTANBUL
SEVILLE
ATHENS
ALGIERS
VALLETTA
Rainfall figures in 10's of mm
ALGIERS Alt. 61m. 696mm. Ann.
ATHENS Alt. 107m. 396mm. Ann.
BARCELONA Alt. 7m. 538mm. Ann.
BASEL Alt. 316m. 818mm. Ann.
BERGEN Alt. 18m. 2056mm. Ann.
BERLIN Alt. 35m. 564mm. Ann.
BORDEAUX Alt. 12m. 782mm. Ann.
BUCHAREST Alt. 84m. 589mm. Ann.
BUDAPEST Alt. 130m. 635mm. Ann.
CLERMONT-FERRAND Alt. 387m. 645mm. Ann.
COLOGNE Alt. 56m. 696mm. Ann.
HAMBURG Alt. 20m. 734mm. Ann.
ISTANBUL Alt. 9m. 734mm. Ann.
KIEV Alt. 180m. 539mm. Ann.
LENINGRAD Alt. 9m.
LILLE Alt. 26m.
°C 30 20 10 0
50 35 25 15 5

EUROPE
Physical

Page 23

EUROPE
Population

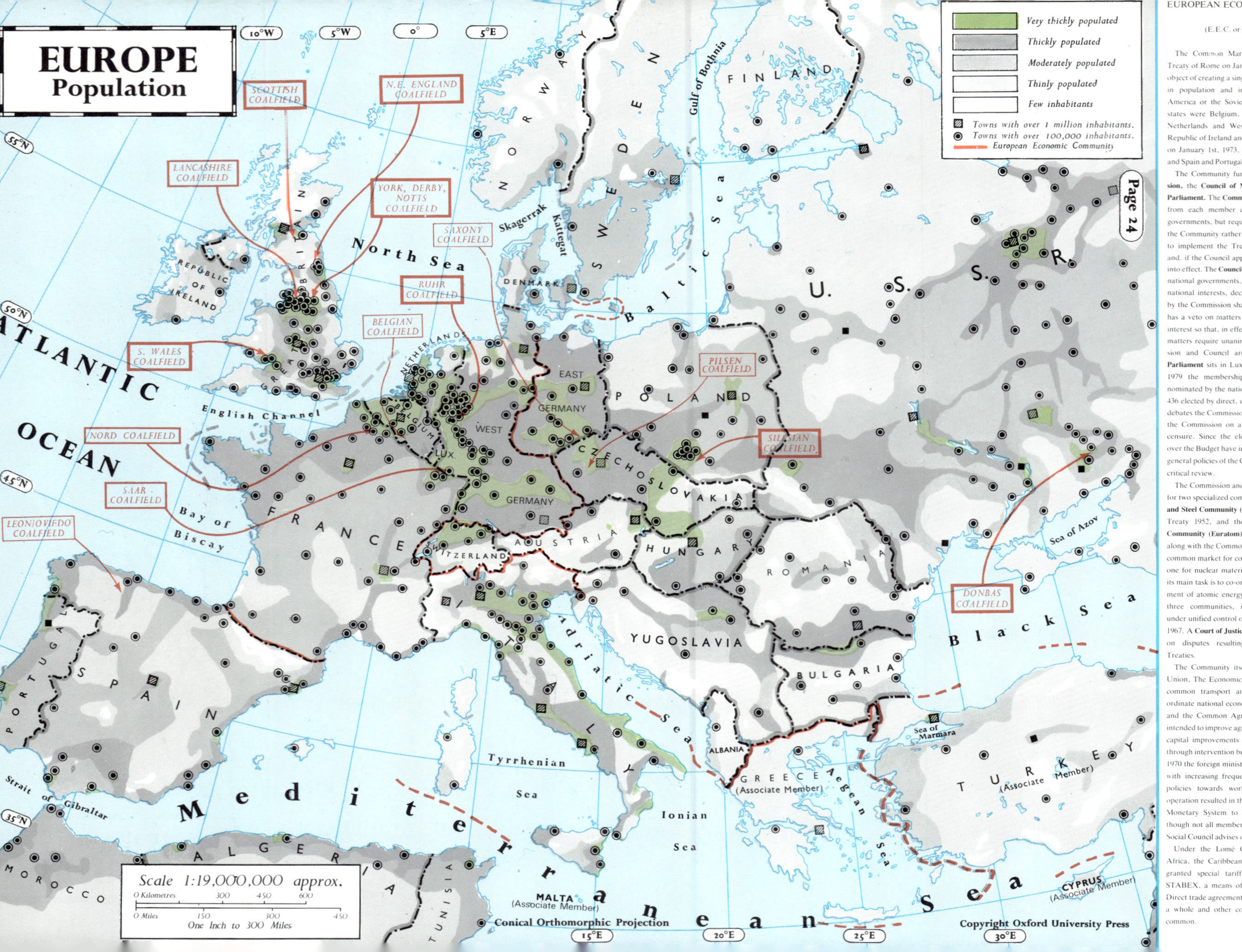

EUROPEAN ECONOMIC COMMUNITY

(E.E.C. or Common Market)

The Common Market was established by the Treaty of Rome on January 1st, 1958, with the main object of creating a single economic unit comparable in population and industrial capacity to North America or the Soviet Union. Founding member states were Belgium, France, Italy, Luxembourg, Netherlands and West Germany. Denmark, the Republic of Ireland and the United Kingdom joined on January 1st, 1973, Greece on January 1st, 1981 and Spain and Portugal have applied to join.

The Community functions through the **Commission**, the **Council of Ministers**, and the **European Parliament.** The **Commission** consists of 13 members from each member country, appointed by their governments, but required to act in the interests of the Community rather than nationally. Their task is to implement the Treaty, by formulating policies and, if the Council approves them, by putting them into effect. The **Council,** consisting of ministers of the national governments, and specifically representing national interests, decides which policies proposed by the Commission shall be adopted. Each member has a veto on matters regarded as vital to national interest so that, in effect, decisions on all important matters require unanimous support. Both Commission and Council are located in Brussels. The **Parliament** sits in Luxembourg and Strasbourg. In 1979 the membership was increased from 198, nominated by the national Parliamentary parties, to 436 elected by direct, universal suffrage. Parliament debates the Commission's proposals and can dismiss the Commission on a two-thirds majority vote of censure. Since the election Parliamentary powers over the Budget have increased and the financial and general policies of the Commission are coming under critical review.

The Commission and Council are also responsible for two specialized communities–the **European Coal and Steel Community (E.C.S.C.)** set up by the Paris Treaty 1952, and the **European Atomic Energy Community (Euratom)** set up by the Rome Treaty along with the Common Market itself. E.C.S.C. is a common market for coal, iron and steel; Euratom is one for nuclear materials and equipment, although its main task is to co-ordinate and promote development of atomic energy for peaceful purposes. The three communities, independent initially, came under unified control of Commission and Council in 1967. A **Court of Justice** in Luxembourg adjudicates on disputes resulting from implementing the Treaties.

The Community itself consists of The Customs Union, The Economic Union, designed to create a common transport and trade structure and co-ordinate national economic and social programmes, and the Common Agricultural Policy. This last is intended to improve agriculture by means of loans for capital improvements and by guaranteeing prices, through intervention buying and import levies. Since 1970 the foreign ministers of the members have met with increasing frequency to co-ordinate national policies towards world problems. Financial co-operation resulted in the formation of the European Monetary System to regulate exchange rates although not all members joined. The Economic and Social Council advises on employment and prices.

Under the Lomé Convention 57 countries in Africa, the Caribbean and the Pacific have been granted special tariff concessions and, through STABEX, a means of stabilizing export earnings. Direct trade agreements between the Community as a whole and other countries are becoming more common.

SPAIN AND PORTUGAL
Scale 1:6,300,000 approx.
One Inch to 100 Miles
Towns over 1 million people
,, over 100,000 people
Boundaries international
Railways
Canal
Airports
Bay of Biscay
Mediterranean Sea
Balearic Islands (Sp.)
FRANCE
SPAIN
PORTUGAL
MOROCCO
ALGERIA
CORSICA
SARDINIA
ITALY
Pyrenees
Cantabrian Mountains
Sierra Morena
OLD CASTILE
NEW CASTILE
ARAGON
CATALONIA
ANDALUSIA
Madrid
Lisbon (Lisboa)
Barcelona
Valencia
Seville (Sevilla)
Oporto
Saragossa (Zaragoza)
Bilbao
Málaga
Murcia
Granada
Córdoba
Valladolid
Palma
Majorca
Minorca
Ibiza (Iviza)
Formentera
Gibraltar (Br.)
Str. of Gibraltar
Algiers
Oran
Constantine
Marseilles
Toulouse
Gulf of Cádiz
200 metres
Conical Orthomorphic Projection
Copyright Oxford University Press

Page 26
EUROPE
France—Poland
Scale 1:6,300,000 approx.
0 Kilometres 100 150 200
0 Miles 50 100 150
One Inch to 100 Miles
For legend see page 25
Meridian of Greenwich
Conical Orthomorphic Projection
200 metres
5°W
45°N
0°
5°E
North Sea
Irish Sea
English Channel
Bay of Biscay
Gulf of Lions
Ligurian Sea
Bristol Channel
Cardigan Bay
St. George's Channel
Strait of Dover
Channel Islands
Frisian Islands
Heligoland Bight
IRELAND
REPUBLIC OF IRELAND
N. IRELAND
SCOT.
WALES
ENGLAND
FRANCE
BELGIUM
NETHERLANDS
WEST GERMANY
SWITZERLAND
SPAIN
ANDORRA
MONACO
LIECHTENSTEIN
CORSICA
BRITTANY
AQUITAINE
CHAMPAGNE
PIEDMONT
LIGURIA
CATALONIA
ARAGON
NAVARRE
BASQUE
OLD CASTILE
Massif Central
Pyrenees
Alps
Jura
Vosges
Ardennes
Eifel
Argonne
Black Forest
Cévennes
Maritime Alps
Cottian Alps
Graian Alps
Pennine Alps
Bernese Alps
Les Landes
Sauerland
Belfast
Dublin
Wexford
Newcastle
Carlisle
Middlesbrough
Isle of Man
Douglas
Blackpool
Leeds
York
Bradford
Preston
Hull
Liverpool
Birkenhead
Manchester
Sheffield
Grimsby
Anglesey
Holyhead
Caernarvon
Stoke
Derby
Nottingham
Wolverhampton
Birmingham
Leicester
Coventry
Northampton
King's Lynn
Norwich
Gt. Yarmouth
Lowestoft
Cambridge
Ipswich
Harwich
Fishguard
St. David's Head
Carmarthen
Swansea
Cardiff
Bristol
Gloucester
Oxford
Luton
London
Reading
Southend
Exeter
Southampton
Bournemouth
Portsmouth
Brighton
Folkestone
Dover
Plymouth
Falmouth
Penzance
Land's End
Lizard Point
Start Pt.
Portland Bill
I. of Wight
Newhaven
Dungeness
N. Foreland
Flamborough Hd.
The Wash
Severn
Thames
Esbjerg
Heligoland
Cuxhaven
Wilhelmshaven
Bremerhaven
Bremen
Emden
Oldenburg
Groningen
Terschelling
Texel
Wadden Zee
IJsselmeer
Ijmuiden
Haarlem
Amsterdam
The Hague
Hook of Holland
Europoort
Rotterdam
Utrecht
Deventer
Enschede
Arnhem
Nijmegen
Tilburg
Eindhoven
Schoonebeek
Emmen
Cloppenburg
Lingen
Osnabrück
Münster
Bielefeld
Bocholt
Gelsenkirchen
Essen
Dortmund
Bochum
Hagen
Duisburg
Düsseldorf
Mönchen-gladbach
Solingen
Cologne
Aachen
Bonn
Siegen
Koblenz
Limburg
Wiesbaden
Mainz
Frankfurt am Main
Darmstadt
Ludwigshafen
Mannheim
Heidelberg
Saarbrücken
Karlsruhe
Stuttgart
Freiburg
Flushing
Zeebrugge
Ostend
Bruges
Ghent
Antwerp
Brussels
Ypres
Tourcoing
Roubaix
Lille
Maastricht
Liege
Verviers
Waterloo
Namur
Charleroi
Dinant
Sedan
Luxembourg
Calais
Dunkirk
Boulogne
C. Gris Nez
Agincourt
Crécy
Arras
Douai
Valenciennes
Cambrai
Abbeville
Amiens
Somme
St. Quentin
Dieppe
Le Havre
Arromanches
Deauville
Caen
Cherbourg
C. de la Hague
C. d'Antifer
Alderney
Guernsey
Sark
Jersey
Rouen
Beauvais
Aisne
Oise
Soissons
Laon
Reims
Marne
Thionville
Verdun
Metz
Nancy
Châlons-sur-Marne
Bar-le-Duc
St. Dizier
Falaise
Seine
Versailles
Paris
Chartres
Fontainebleau
Troyes
Yonne
Chaumont
Strasbourg
Rhine
Île d'Ouessant (Ushant)
Brest
Lannion
St. Malo
Dinard
Lamballe
Pte. du Raz
Quimper
Lorient
Vannes
Rennes
Alençon
le Mans
Belle Île-en-Mer
St. Nazaire
Nantes
Loire
Angers
Tours
Orléans
Ile d'Yeu
Mulhouse
Belfort
Montbéliard
Basel (Bâle)
Olten
Zürich
Solothurn
Luzern
Schwyz
Bern
Neuchâtel
Besançon
Dijon
Saône
Bourges
Nevers
Châteauroux
Poitiers
le Creusot
Pontarlier
Lons-le-Saunier
Chalon-sur-Saône
Mâcon
Lausanne
Montreux
Geneva
Chamonix
Martigny
St. Gotthard P.
Simplon P.
L. Maggiore
Stresa
Varese
Bergamo
Monza
Milan
Biella
Novara
Pavia
Aosta
Annecy
M. Blanc
Chambéry
Île d'Oléron
la Rochelle
Rochefort
Pte. de Grave
Cognac
Limoges
Aubusson
Vichy
Clermont Ferrand
Lyons
St. Étienne
Grenoble
Modane
Turin
Mt. Cenis P.
Alessandria
Asti
Novi Ligure
Saluzzo
Cuneo
Genoa
Savona
Gulf of Genoa
Perigueux
Brive
Aurillac
Cap Ferret
Bordeaux
Garonne
Agen
Mont de Marsan
Albi
Montélimar
Durance
Barcelonnette
Rhône
Avignon
Nîmes
Arles
Montpellier
Béziers
Sète
C. d'Agde
Marseilles
Toulon
Iles d'Hyères
Draguignan
Cannes
Nice
Cap d'Antibes
San Remo
Imperia
Santander
C. Machichaco
San Sebastián
Biarritz
Bayonne
Irun
Hendaye
Bilbao
Tolosa
Vitoria
Roncesvalles
Pamplona
Pau
Tarbes
Lourdes
Toulouse
Mazamet
Carcassonne
Ariège
Narbonne
Perpignan
Port Bou
Burgos
Logroño
Jaca
Aneto
Huesca
Tudela
Ebro
Soria
Douro
Saragossa (Zaragoza)
Lérida
Ségre
Llanos de Urgel
Manresa
Tarrasa
Sabadell
Gerona
Barcelona
Reus
Tarragona
Sa. de Guadarrama
El Escorial
Guadalajara
Madrid
Calvi
Ajaccio

Page 27
Copenhagen
Zealand
Ringsted
Næstved
Malmö
Trelleborg
Bornholm
Rønne
15°E
Baltic
Sea
Lolland
Nykøbing
Gedser
C. Arkona
Sassnitz
Rügen
Fehmarn
Grossenbrode
Lübeck Bay
Stralsund
Rostock
Greifswald
Pomeranian Bay
Wismar
Świnoujście
Schwerin
Szczecin
(Stettin)
Neustrelitz
Wittenberge
Eberswalde
EAST
Rathenow
Stendal
Spandau
Berlin
Brandenburg
Potsdam
Frankfurt
Magdeburg
Dessau
Stassfurt
GERMANY
Cottbus
Halle
Torgau
Eilenburg
Elbe
Leipzig
Weimar
Jena
Gera
Dresden
Karl-Marx-Stadt
Zwickau
Saale
Erz gebirge
Hof
Bayreuth
Nuremberg
Regensburg
Ingolstadt
Passau
Danube (Donau)
BAVARIA
Inn
Munich
Oberammergau
Innsbruck
Salzburg
Linz
Steyr
Wiener-Neustadt
Vienna
(Wien)
AUSTRIA
Brenner Pass
Hohe Tauern
Niedere Tauern
Eisenerz
Leoben
Donawitz
Köflach
Graz
Lienz
Villach
Klagenfurt
Semmering P.
Merano
Bolzano
TRENTINO
Dolomites
Trento
Belluno
Venetian Alps
Carnic Alps
Julian Alps
Udine
Gorizia
Ljubljana
Trieste
VENETO
Verona
Padua
(Padova)
Venice
Chioggia
Gulf of Venice
Mantua
Adige
Ferrara
Mouths of the Po
Reggio
Emilia
Bologna
Ravenna
Forlì
Rimini
San Marino
Arno
Florence
(Firenze)
Arezzo
Siena
Rapolano
Perugia
L. Trasimeno
Assisi
Foligno
UMBRIA
Ancona
Macerata
Ascoli Piceno
THE MARCHES
Grosseto
L. Bolsena
Terni
Teramo
Pescara
Chieti
Lanciano
Aquila
ABRUZZI-MOLISE
LATIUM
Tiber
Civitavecchia
C. Linaro
Rome
(Roma)
Ostia
Frascati
Tivoli
Sulmona
Cassino
Lepini Mts.
Anzio
Campobasso
Termoli
San Severo
Foggia
Cerignola
Barletta
Molfetta
Bari
C. Gargano
ITALY
Adriatic Sea
200 metres
Istria
Pula
(Pola)
Cres
Rijeka
(Fiume)
Krk
Gdynia
Gdańsk
(Danzig)
Gulf of Danzig
Elbląg
Malbork
EAST PRUSSIA
Sovetsk
(Tilsit)
Kaliningrad
(Königsberg)
Chernyakhovsk
(Insterburg)
20°E
R. S. F. S. R.
Kaunas
LITH. S.S.R.
Vilnius
25°E
Minsk
Lida
Neman
Novogrudok
Grodno
BYELORUSSIAN S.S.R.
Volkovysk
Slonim
U.S.S.R.
Koszalin
Szczecinek
Chojnice
Vistula (Wisła)
Grudziądz
Olsztyn
Tannenberg
Białystok
Mława
Łomża
Ostrów Mazowiecki
Bydgoszcz
Toruń
Inowrocław
Włocławek
POLAND
Warsaw
(Warszawa)
Biała Podlaska
Kobrin
Brest Litovskiy
Gorzów Wielkopolski
(Landsberg)
Warta
Gniezno
Poznań
Kutno
Łódź
Skierniewice
Zielona Góra
(Grünberg)
Głogów
Jarocin
Kalisz
Krotoszyn
Ostrów Wielkopolski
Piotrków
Radom
Lublin
Chełm
Bug
Kovel
Vladimir-Volynskiy
Zamość
SILESIA
Wrocław
(Breslau)
Brzeg
Częstochowa
Kielce
Jędrzejów
Vistula
Kamienna Góra
(Landeshut)
Opole
Zawiercie
Bytom
Chorzów
Sosnowiec
Gliwice
Zabrze
Katowice
Kraków
Nowa Huta
Rzeszów
Jarosław
Przemyśl
L'vov
Dubno
Kremenets
50°N
Zolochev
Ternopol'
Berezhany
Sambor
UKRAINIAN S.S.R.
Borislav
Bolekhov
Ivano-Frankovsk
Kolomyya
Veretski Pass
Tatar Pass
Chernovtsy
Carpathian Mts.
Liberec
Sudeten Mts.
Kłodzko
Nysa
Sadowa
Nymburk
Prague
Nučice
Pardubice
Šumperk
Opava
Moravská Ostrava
Český Těšín
Cieszyn
Moravian Gate
Olomouc
Prostějov
Gottwaldov
BOHEMIA
CZECHOSLOVAKIA
Karlovy Vary
Cheb
Mariánské Lázně
Plzeň
(Plzen)
Bohemian Forest
Klatovy
Písek
Vltava
České Budějovice
Brno
Austerlitz
Znojmo
MORAVIA
Nowy Sącz
Jasło
Sanok
East Beskids
Ružomberok
Spiš
Košice
Uzhgorod
Chop
Mukachevo
Khust
SLOVAKIA
Lučenec
Levice
Ózd
Miskolc
Tokaj
Nyíregyháza
Matzen
Bratislava
Komárno
Danube
Esztergom
Budapest
Jászberény
Debrecen
Tisza
Sopron
Győr
Gánt
Csepel
Szolnok
Kisújszállás
Szombathely
Bakony Forest
Úrkút
Veszprém
Dunaújváros
HUNGARY
Kecskemét
Kiskunfélegyháza
Balaton L.
Alföld
Hódmezővásárhely
Lispeszentadorján
Nagykanizsa
Kaposvár
Komló
Pécs
Mohács
Szeged
Subotica
Sombor
Arad
Oradea
Satu-Mare
Baia-Mare
Bistrița
Câmpulung Moldovenesc
Zalău
Cluj
Turda
Dobrești
Salonta
Gheorgheni
Târgu Mureș
Odorhei
Sighișoara
Mediaș
TRANSYLVANIA
Alba Iulia
Sebeș
Sibiu
Deva
Timișoara
Lugoj
ROMANIA
Caransebeș
Petroșani
Transylvanian Alps
Câmpulung
Râmnicu Vâlcea
Reșița
Târgu Jiu
45°N
Pitești
25°E
BANAT
Iron Gates
Turnu Severin
Slatina
Craiova
WALLACHIA
Băilești
Calafat
Turnu Măgurele
Vidin
Oryakhovo
Danube (Dunare)
Pleven
Maribor
Dravograd
Drava
Varaždin
Celje
SLOVENIA
Zagreb
Virovitica
Osijek
Karlovac
Sisak
CROATIA
Brod
Temerin
Novi Sad
Danube (Dunav)
Ruma
Zrenjanin
(Petrovgrad)
Belgrade
(Beograd)
Sava
Požarevac
Bihać
Banja Luka
BOSNIA
Gospić
Dinaric Alps
Dalmatia
YUGOSLAVIA
HERCEGOVINA
Sarajevo
Kragujevac
Čačak
Rankovićevo
(Kraljevo)
Kruševac
Titovo Užice
Zlatibor
Bor
Niš
Zadar
Šibenik
Split
Šolta
Brač
Mostar
Ploče
Lastovo
Dubrovnik
Kotor (Cattaro)
Cetinje
MONTENEGRO
Titograd
Novi Pazar
Kopaonik Mts.
Trepča
Kosovska Mitrovica
Priština
Vranje
SERBIA
Dimitrovgrad
Bar
Shkodër
(Scutari)
ALBANIA
Tiranë
(Tirana)
Durrës
(Durazzo)
Elbasan
20°E
Đakovica
Prizren
Kukës
Skopje
Titov Veles
Štip
MACEDONIA
Prilep
Bitola
(Monastir)
Florina
Edhessa
Strumica
Vardar
Petrich
Drama
Serrai
Salonica
(Thessaloniki)
GREECE
BULGARIA
Vratsa
Botevgrad
Sofia
(Sofiya)
Dimitrovo
(Pernik)
Kyustendil
Pazardzhik
Struma
Pirin Mts.
Mesta Nestos
Ft.
M.
16,000
4,800
10,000
3,000
6,000
1,800
3,000
900
1,500
450
1,000
300
600
180
300
90
Sea Level
Land Depression
Copyright Oxford University Press

FRANCE
Scale 1:3,150,000 approx.
0 Kilometres 50 75 100 125
0 Miles 25 50 75
One Inch to 50 Miles
North Sea
English Channel
Strait of Dover (Pas de Calais)
GERMANY
BELGIUM
NETHERLANDS
LUXEMBOURG
WESTPHALIA
BRITTANY
NORMANDY
LORRAINE
ALSACE
PICARDY
CHAMPAGNE
MAINE
ARGONNE
ÎLE DE FRANCE
Paris
Amsterdam
The Hague ('s-Gravenhage)
Rotterdam
Antwerp (Anvers)
Brussels
Liège
Ghent (Gand)
Lille
Cologne (Köln)
Bonn
Düsseldorf
Luxembourg
Strasbourg
Nancy
Metz
Rheims (Reims)
Rouen
Le Havre
Cherbourg
Rennes
Brest
Calais
Dunkirk
Boulogne
Amiens
Dover
Folkestone
Margate
Channel Islands (Br.)
St. Peter Port
St. Helier
Meridian of Greenwich
50°N
5°W
5°E

F R A N C E
SWITZERLAND
S P A I N
Bay of Biscay
Gulf of Lions
Côte d'Azur
Ft. M.
16,000 4,800
10,000 3,000
6,000 1,800
3,000 900
1,500 450
1,000 300
600 180
300 90
Sea Level
Land Depression
45°N
5°E
0°
Meridian of Greenwich
Conical Orthomorphic Projection
Copyright Oxford University Press
Nantes
Paimboeuf
Loire
Saumur
Tours
Amboise
Cher
TOURAINE
Chinon
Montreuil Bellay
Cholet
Sèvre Nantaise
Hauteurs de Gâtine
Thouars
Bressuire
Parthenay
la Roche-sur-Yon
Les Sables-d'Olonne
POITOU
Poitiers
Châtellerault
Vienne
Châteauroux
Indre
le Blanc
Lussac-les-Châteaux
Vierzon-Ville
Bourges
BERRY
Issoudun
St. Amand Mont-Rond
la Châtre
Sancerre
Cosne
Clamecy
NIVERNAIS
Nevers
Loire
Allier
Moulins
BOURBONNAIS
Montluçon
Boussac
Creuse
MARCHE
Guéret
Bessines
Aubusson
Niort
Sèvre Niortaise
La Rochelle
AUNIS
Île de Ré
Île d'Oléron
Rochefort-sur-Mer
Saintes
SAINTONGE
ANGOUMOIS
Cognac
Charente
Angoulême
Ruffec
Bellac
St. Junien
Limoges
Rochechouart
LIMOUSIN
Pte. de la Coubre
Pte. de Grave
Royan
le Verdon
Gironde
Médoc
Pauillac
Étg. d'Hourti
Blaye
Périgueux
Périgord
Brive
Tulle
Dordogne
Libourne
Bordeaux
Pessac
la Bastide
Bergerac
Issigeac
Garonne
Cap Ferret
Arcachon
Leyre
Langon
Sauternes
Marmande
AQUITAINE
Lot
Cahors
Lacapelle-Marival
Figeac
Decazeville
Villeneuve-sur-Lot
Agenais
Agen
Molières
Parentis
Mimizan
Les Landes
Pays d'Albret
Roquefort
Mont de Marsan
Adour
Eauze
Lectoure
Montauban
Aveyron
Gers
Auch
Mirande
GASCONY
Dax
Bayonne
Biarritz
St. Jean-de-Luz
Orthez
Lacq
BÉARN
Pau
Oloron-Ste-Marie
Lourdes
Tarbes
St. Jean-Pied-de-Port
Roncesvalles
Aoiz
Urdos
Jaca
Mont Perdu 3333
Maladetta
Massif Aneto 3404
Viella
Pic de Montvalier 2840
Pic d'Estats 3141
ANDORRA
Andorra
l'Hospitalet
Bourg Madame
Prades
Fenouillèdes
ROUSSILLON
Perpignan
Port Vendres
Corbières
Montagnes du Plantaurel
FOIX
Foix
Pamiers
Ariège
Aurignac
Muret
Toulouse
Carcassonne
Aude
Olonzac
Narbonne
Béziers
Hérault
C. d'Agde
Sète
Thore
Castres
Mazamet
Mts. de Lacaune
Monts de l'Espinouse
St. Pons
Carmaux
Tarn
Albi
Roquefort
St. Affrique
Causse du Larzac
Millau
Rodez
Monts d'Aubrac
Aurillac
Plomb du Cantal 6095
Murat
St. Flour
Massif Central
Puy de Sancy 1886
les Bains-du-Mont-Dore
Massif du Livradois
Auvergne
Clermont-Ferrand
Riom
Limagne
Vichy
Thiers
Monts du Forez
Dore
Lapalisse
Roanne
LYONNAIS
Tarare
Monts du Beaujolais
Charolles
Monts du Charollais
Montceau-les-Mines
Luzy
le Creusot
Autun
Morvan
Chalon-sur-Saône
Beaune
Côte d'Or
Nuits-St. Georges
Dijon
BURGUNDY
Mâcon
Saône
Villefranche-sur-Saône
Bourg
Revermont
Lons-le-Saunier
Dôle
Loue
Besançon
Doubs
FRANCHE COMTÉ
Pontarlier
la Chaux-de-Fonds
Neuchâtel
L. Neuchâtel
Biel
Aare
Solothurn
Olten
Burgdorf
Bern
Fribourg
Thun
L. Thun
L. Brienz
Interlaken
Yverdon
Gruyères
Lausanne
Vevey
Montreux
Bernese Alps
L. of Geneva (Lac Léman)
Nyon
Thonon
Evian
Rhône
Brig
Sion
St. Maurice
Weisshorn 4453
Martigny
Zermatt
Pennine Alps
Matterhorn
Gt. St. Bernard P.
Aosta
Geneva
St. Julien
Champéry
Chamonix
M. Blanc 4810
Génissiat Dam
Bellegarde
St. Claude
Oyonnax
la Chaux
Jura
Annecy
Culoz
L. du Bourget
Aix les Bains
Lt. St. Bernard P.
Tignes Res.
Chambéry
SAVOY
Graian Alps
Villeurbanne
Lyons (Lyon)
Givors
Vienne
Rive-de-Gier
St. Chamond
St. Étienne
le Chambon Feugerolles
Annonay
le Puy
le Monastier
Monts du Velay
Monts de la Margeride
Loire
Allier
la Tour-du-Pin
Voiron
Isère
Grenoble
Dauphiné
St. Jean de Maurienne
Modane
M. Cenis P.
Susa
Cottian Alps
M. Pelvoux
Alps
Briançon
M. de Lans
Romans
Valence
Drôme
Dévoluy
Gap
Embrun
Larche
Maddalena P.
Barcelonnette
Maritime Alps
Tende
Tenda P.
Privas
Montélimar
Donzère
Ardèche
Rhône
Cévennes
Bessèges
Alès
Garrigues
Lasalle
le Vigan
Ganges
Sommières
Montpellier
Aigues-Mortes
Étang de Vaccarès
Camargue
les Stes. Maries
G. d'Aigues Mortes
Nîmes
Gard
Remoulins
Tarascon
Arles
les Baux
Avignon
Orange
Carpentras
Cavaillon
Montagne du Lubéron
Durance
Forcalquier
Oraison
Verdon
Salon de Provence
PROVENCE
Aix-en-Provence
Étg. de Berre
Martigues
Chaîne de l'Étoile
Marseilles
Aubagne
la Ciotat
Toulon
la Seyne-sur-mer
Hyères
Îles d'Hyères
St. Tropez
Fréjus
St. Raphaël
Draguignan
Grasse
Cannes
Cap d'Antibes
Nice
Menton
Monte Carlo MONACO
Ventimiglia
San Remo
Sisteron
Digne

ITALY and THE BALKANS
Scale 1:6,300,000 approx.
0 Kilometres 100 150 200
0 Miles 50 100 150
One Inch to 100 Miles
Towns over 1 million people
" over 100,000 people
Boundaries international
- provincial etc
Railway
Airports
Marsh
Autobahn
Canal
Ice cap
Ft. M.
16,000 4,800
10,000 3,000
6,000 1,800
3,000 900
1,500 450
1,000 300
600 180
300 90
Sea Level
Land Depression
200 metres
Conical Orthomorphic Projection
5°E
10°E
15°E
45°N
35°N
GERMANY
AUSTRIA
SWITZERLAND
FRANCE
ALPS
ITALY
YU
HER
SLOVENIA
CROATIA
BOSNIA and
H
ALGERIA
TUNISIA
CORSICA
SARDINIA
SICILY
MALTA
Strasbourg
Stuttgart
Tübingen
Ulm
Blenheim
Ingolstadt
Augsburg
Munich
Passau
České Budějovice
Znojmo
Vltava
Danube (Donau)
Linz
Vienna (Wien)
Matzen
Bratis
Steyr
Wiener-Neustadt
Salzburg
Memmingen
Tuttlingen
Danube
Freiburg
Black Forest
Rhine
Vosges
Seine
Chaumont
Mulhouse
Belfort
Dijon
Saône
Doubs
Besançon
Nevers
Bourges
le Creusot
Loire
Chalon-sur-Saône
Pontarlier
Lons-le-Saunier
Basel (Bâle)
Olten
Zürich
Solothurn
Luzern
Schwyz
L. Constance
Bregenz
Oberammergau
LIECHTENSTEIN
Innsbruck
Brenner Pass
Bern
L. Neuchâtel
Vichy
Lausanne
Montreux
Bernese Alps
Geneva
L. Geneva
Clermont Ferrand
Lyons
Annecy
Chamonix
M. Blanc 4810
Martigny
Rhône
Brig
St. Gotthard P.
Andermatt
Davos
Rhaetian Alps
Simplon P.
Pennine Alps
Maggiore
Bellinzona
Lugano
L. Como
Bergamo Alps
Lecco
Merano
Bolzano
TRENTINO
Dolomites
Trento
Belluno
Hohe Tauern 3739
3523
Niedere Tauern
Eisenerz
Leoben
Donawitz
Semmering P.
Sopron
Szombathely
Köflach
Graz
Lienz
Carnic Alps
Villach
Klagenfurt
Dravograd
Maribor
Drava
Varaždin
Celje
Lisspeszenta
Nagyka
Balaton
St. Étienne
Chambéry
Aosta
Graian Alps
4061
Varese
Como
Monza
Bergamo
Brescia
L. of Garda
Verona
Venetian Alps
Udine
Gorizia
Julian Alps
Ljubljana
Zagreb
Virovitica
Karlovac
Sisak
Sava
Grenoble
Modane
M. Cenis P.
Turin
Biella
Novara
Milan
Pavia
Po
Plain of Lombardy
Adda
Cremona
Mantua
Padua (Padova)
Adige
Venice
Chioggia
Gulf of Venice
Trieste
Istria
Rijeka (Fiume)
Krk
Cres
Pula (Pola)
Mouths of the Po
Ferrara
Montélimar
Durance
Cottian Alps
Alessandria
PIEDMONT
Piacenza
Parma
Reggio nell'Emilia
Acqui
Novi Ligure
Saluzzo
Barcelonnette
Maritime Alps
Cuneo
Ligurian Apennines
LIGURIA
Genoa
Savona
Gulf of Genoa
Rapallo
3297
Nîmes
Avignon
Arles
Montpellier
Sète
Marseilles
Toulon
Îles d'Hyères
Draguignan
Cannes
Nice
MONACO
San Remo
Imperia
C. d'Antibes
Ligurian Sea
La Spezia
EMILIA ROMAGNA
Bologna
Ravenna
Forlì
Etruscan Apennines
Rimini
San Marino
Pisa
Arno
Florence (Firenze)
TUSCANY
Leghorn (Livorno)
Arezzo
Siena
Rapolano
L. Trasimeno
Perugia
Assisi
Foligno
THE MARCHES
Ancona
Macerata
Ascoli Piceno
Teramo
Bihać
Banja Luka
Gospić
Dinaric Alps
Dalmatia
Zadar
Šibenik
Split
Šolta
Brač
Hvar
Korčula
Lastovo
Ploce
Most
Adriatic Sea
Bastia
Calvi
Casamozza
Elba
Grosseto
Bolsena
L.
UMBRIA
Tiber
Terni
Monte Cristo
Civitavecchia
C. Linaro
LATIUM
Aquila
2951
ABRUZZI
Pescara
Chieti
Lanciano
Ajaccio
Rome (Roma)
Ostia
Tivoli
Frascati
Sulmona
MOLISE
Termoli
San Severo
C. Gargano
Bonifacio
Str. of Bonifacio
Lepini Mts.
Cassino
Campobasso
Foggia
Anzio
C. Circeo
Gaeta
Olbia
Sassari
Chilivani
Nuoro
C. Comino
Capua
Caserta
Benevento
Cerignola
Barletta
Molfetta
Bari
Naples (Napoli)
Vesuvius 1176
Ischia
Pompeii
Capri
Salerno
Potenza
Matera
BASILICATA
Taranto
CAMPANIA
APULIA
Oristano
Tyrrhenian Sea
Iglesias
Cagliari
Gulf of Ta
Cosenza
CALABRIA
Crotone
Catanzaro
Stromboli
Lipari Is.
Vulcano
Str. of Messina
Messina
Reggio di Calabria
C. Spartivento
Trapani
Palermo
Bagheria
Marsala
Etna 3274
Caltanissetta
Agrigento
Catania
Licata
Ragusa
Syracuse (Siracusa)
C. Passero
Sicilian Channel
Pantelleria
Malta Channel
Gozo
Rabat
Valletta
Lampedusa
Mediterranean Sea
Bejaia
Djidjelli
Skikda
Annaba
Tabarka
Menzel Bourguiba
Binzert
Mateur
G. of Tunis
Tunis
Carthage
Halq el Oued
C. Bon
Medjerda
Medjez-el-Bab
Constantine
Sétif
Tell Atlas
Souk Ahras
El Kef
Gulf of Hammamet
Enfida
Sousse
Kairouan
Tébessa
2325
Biskra
5065
Kasserine
Sfax
Kerkenna Is.

Veretski Pass
Kolomyya
Mogilev Podol'skiy
Tul'chin
Krivoy Rog
Pervomaysk
E C H.
Košice
Uzhgorod
Carpathian Mountains
U.
25°E
Tatar Pass
Chernovtsy
S.
30°E
Balta
S.
Lučenec
Chop
Mukachevo
Khust
Floreshty
Dniester
Bel'tsy
Rybnitsa
Anan'yev
Voznesensk
Ozd
Miskolc
Tokaj
Nyíregyháza
Satu-Mare
Botoşani
Suceava
Prut
MOLDAVIAN
S.S.R.
Orgeyev
Bug
Berezovka
R.
Esztergom
Budapest
Jászberény
Tisza
Debrecen
Baia-Mare
Câmpulung Moldovenesc
Iaşi
Kishinev
Bessarabia
Razdel'naya
Nikolayev
Dnieper
Berislav
Kherson
Tsyurupinsk
Csepel
Szolnok
Kisújszállás
Oradea
Zălău
Bistriţa
Piatra-Neamţ
Roman
Bendery
Tiraspol'
Ochakov
Odessa
Skadovsk
GARY
Kecskemét
Dobreşti
Salonta
Cluj
Turda
Târgu Mureş
Gheorgheni
Bacău
Siret
Vaslui
Belgorod-Dnestrovskiy
Karkinitsky Bay
skunfélegyháza
Hodmezővásárhely
TRANSYLVANIA
Odorhei
Bârlad
MOLDAVIA
UKRAINIAN S.S.R.
Artsiz
Pack-ice average max. Jan.-Feb.
Szeged
Arad
Mediaş
Sighişoara
Sfântu Gheorghe
Tecuci
Kagul
Bolgrad
Kiliya
C. Tarkhankut
CRIMEA
Yevpatoriya
Subotica
Alba Iulia
Sebeş
Sibiu
Braşov
Izmail
45°N
Sombor
Timişoara
Lugoj
Deva
ROMANIA
Galaţi
Brăila
Mouths of the Danube
Sevastopol
Temerin
Novi Sad
Caransebeş
Petroşani
2529
Transylvanian Alps
Râmnicu Sărat
Buzău
Danube (Dunav)
Ruma
Zrenjanin (Petrovgrad)
Reşiţa
BANAT
Râmnicu Vâlcea
Târgu Jiu
Câmpulung
Piteşti
Ploeşti
Dobruja
Black Sea
Belgrade (Beograd)
Iron Gates
Turnu Severin
Bucharest (Bucureşti)
Feteşti
Călăraşi
Constanţa
Morava
Požarevac
Slatina
Craiova
WALLACHIA
Silistra
YUGOSLAVIA
Bor
Bäileşti
Calafat
Vidin
Giurgiu
Ruse (Ruschuk)
Turnu Măgurele
Tolbukhin
200 metres
Kragujevac
Čačak
Titovo Užice
Rankovićevo (Kraljevo)
Oryakhovo
Danube (Dunarea)
Svishtov
Sarajevo
Zlatibor
Kruševac
Pleven
Shumen
Varna
SERBIA
Niš
Vratsa
Veliko Turnovo
Gabrovo
Novi Pazar
Kopaonik Mts.
Dimitrovgrad
Botevgrad
Shipka P.
Balkan Mts.
Kazanlŭk
Sliven
Yambol
Burgas
G. of Burgas
MONTENEGRO
Trepča
Kosovska Mitrovica
Priština
Vranje
Sofia (Sofiya)
BULGARIA
Dimitrovo (Pernik)
Kyustendil
Stara Zagora
Plovdiv (Philippopolis)
Pazardzhik
Dimitrovgrad
Zonguldak
Titograd
Cetinje
Dakovica
Prizren
2921
Asenovgrad
Maritsa
Strandzha
Kirklareli
Edirne (Adrianople)
Bar
Shkodër (Scutari)
Kukës
2760
Skopje
Titov Veles
Struma
Pirin Mts.
Rhodope Mts.
Mesta
Khaskovo
Ivailovgrad
Zlatograd
Lüleburgaz
Bosporus
ALBANIA
MACEDONIA
Štip
Strumica
Petrich
Nestos
THRACE
Çatalca
İstanbul (Constantinople)
Üsküdar (Scutari)
Adapazarı
Durrës (Durazzo)
Tiranë (Tirana)
Elbasan
Prilep
Bitola (Monastir)
Vardar
Serrai
Drama
Xanthi
Kavalla
Alexandroúpolis (Dedeagach)
Çorlu
Tekirdağ
Sea of Marmara
Dardanelles
Edhessa
Florina
Ptolemais
Salonica (Thessaloniki)
Thasos
Samothrace (Samothraki)
Imroz
Gallipoli
Bandırma
Bursa
Sakarya
40°N
Korçë (Koritsa)
Vlonë (Valona)
Kozani
Polyiros
Athos
Çanakkale
Mustafa Kemalpaşa
Eskişehir
Strait of Otranto
Gjinokastër (Argyrokastro)
Pindus Mts.
Olympus 2916
G. of Thermai
C. Helles
Lemnos
Mudros
Balıkesir
Edremit
Kütahya
Yannina
Trikkala
Larisa
Northern Sporades
Lesbos
Savaştepe
Ayvalık
Afyonkarahisar
Corfu (Kerkira)
Corfu
EPIRUS
GREECE
Volos
THESSALY
Iliodhromia
Skopelos
Skiros
Mitilini
Bergama
Akhisar
Uşak
TURKEY
Akşehir
Sultan Mts.
Arta
Preveza
Lamia
Aegean Islands
Menemen
Manisa
Turgutlu
L. Eğridir
Thermopylae
G. of Euboea
Euboea
Chios (Khios)
Chios
İzmir (Smyrna)
Ödemiş
Ionian Is.
Parnassus 2459
Mesolongion
Chalcis (Khalkis)
Tire
Aydın
L. Acı
Burdur
L. Beyşehir
Ithaca (Ithaki)
G. of Patras
Patras
G. of Corinth
Megara
Marathon
Menderes
Denizli
Argostolion
Cephalonia (Kefallinia)
PELOPONNESE (MOREA)
Corinth
Athens (Athinai)
Andros
Samos
Ikaria
Zante (Zakinthos)
Zante
Katakolon
Pirgos
Olympia
Mycenae
Argos
Nauplia
Kea
Ermoupolis
Patmos
Muğla
L. Söğüt
Antalya
Tripolis
Thermia (Kithnos)
Cyclades
Leros
Kalimnos
Dodecanese (Sporades)
Spetsai
Paros
Naxos
Cos (Kos)
G. of Kerme
Fethiye
3056
Kalamata
Sparta
Mirtoon Sea
Nisiros
Bay of Navarino
Rhodes
Kaş
C. Gelidonya
Ios
Tilos
C. Akritas
Milos
Thira
Astipalaia
Rhodes
Kastellorizo
C. Matapan
Cerigo (Kithira)
Sea of Crete
Karpathos
C. Spatha
Crete (Kriti)
Kasos
Kasos Str.
35°N
Canea (Khania)
Rethimnon
Candia (Iraklion)
2148
Ionian Sea
20°E
25°E

BERLIN
Built-up area
Administrative districts of Western Berlin.
Administrative districts of Soviet Sector.
Ft.
M.
16,000
4,800
10,000
3,000
6,000
1,800
3,000
900
1,500
450
1,000
300
600
180
300
90
Sea Level
Land Depression
North Sea
Heligoland
Heligoland Bight
East Frisian Islands
West Frisian Islands
Waddenzee
Ijsselmeer (Zuider Zee)
Pomeranian Bay
Lübeck Bay
5°E
50°N
WEST GERMANY
EAST GERMANY
NETHERLANDS
BELGIUM
LUXEMBOURG
POLAND
CZECH.
F
MECKLENBURG
HOLSTEIN
FRIESLAND
WESTPHALIA
THURINGIA
HAINAULT
LIMBURG
SAAR
Hamburg
Bremen
Hanover
Berlin
Amsterdam
The Hague ('s-Gravenhage)
Rotterdam
Brussels
Antwerp (Anvers)
Ghent (Gand)
Liège
Cologne (Köln)
Bonn
Düsseldorf
Essen
Dortmund
Frankfurt am Main
Mainz
Wiesbaden
Kassel
Magdeburg
Leipzig
Dresden
Halle
Erfurt
Karl-Marx-Stadt (Chemnitz)
Prague (Praha)
Pilsen (Plzeň)
Nuremberg (Nürnberg)
Würzburg
Mannheim
Heidelberg
Saarbrücken
Luxembourg
Szczecin (Stettin)
Frankfurt an der Oder
Rostock
Lübeck
Kiel Canal
Mittelland Canal
Dortmund-Ems Canal
Elbe
Weser
Rhine
Main
Mosel
Lüneburg Heath
Teutoburger Wald
Sauerland
Westerwald
Taunus
Eifel
Hunsrück
Odenwald
Harz
Thüringer Wald
Erzgebirge
Franconian Jura
Bavarian Forest
Brocken 3746

GERMANY and THE ALPS
Scale 1:3,150,000 approx.
0 Kilometres 25 50 75 100 125
0 Miles 25 50 75
One Inch to 50 Miles
Conical Orthomorphic Projection
Copyright Oxford University Press
AUSTRIA
SWITZERLAND
ITALY
FRANCE
YUGOSLAVIA
Adriatic Sea
Gulf of Venice
Gulf of Genoa
Munich (München)
Augsburg
Ulm
Salzburg
Innsbruck
Zürich
Bern
Basel (Bâle)
Luzern (Lucerne)
Lausanne
Geneva
Milan (Milano)
Turin (Torino)
Genoa (Genova)
Venice (Venezia)
Verona
Trieste
Bologna
Florence (Firenze)
Lyons (Lyon)
Grenoble
Marseilles
Nice
Dijon
Mulhouse
Trento
Bolzano
Padua (Padova)
Ferrara
Ravenna
Rimini
Leghorn
Pisa
Lucca
Ljubljana
Klagenfurt
Linz
Passau

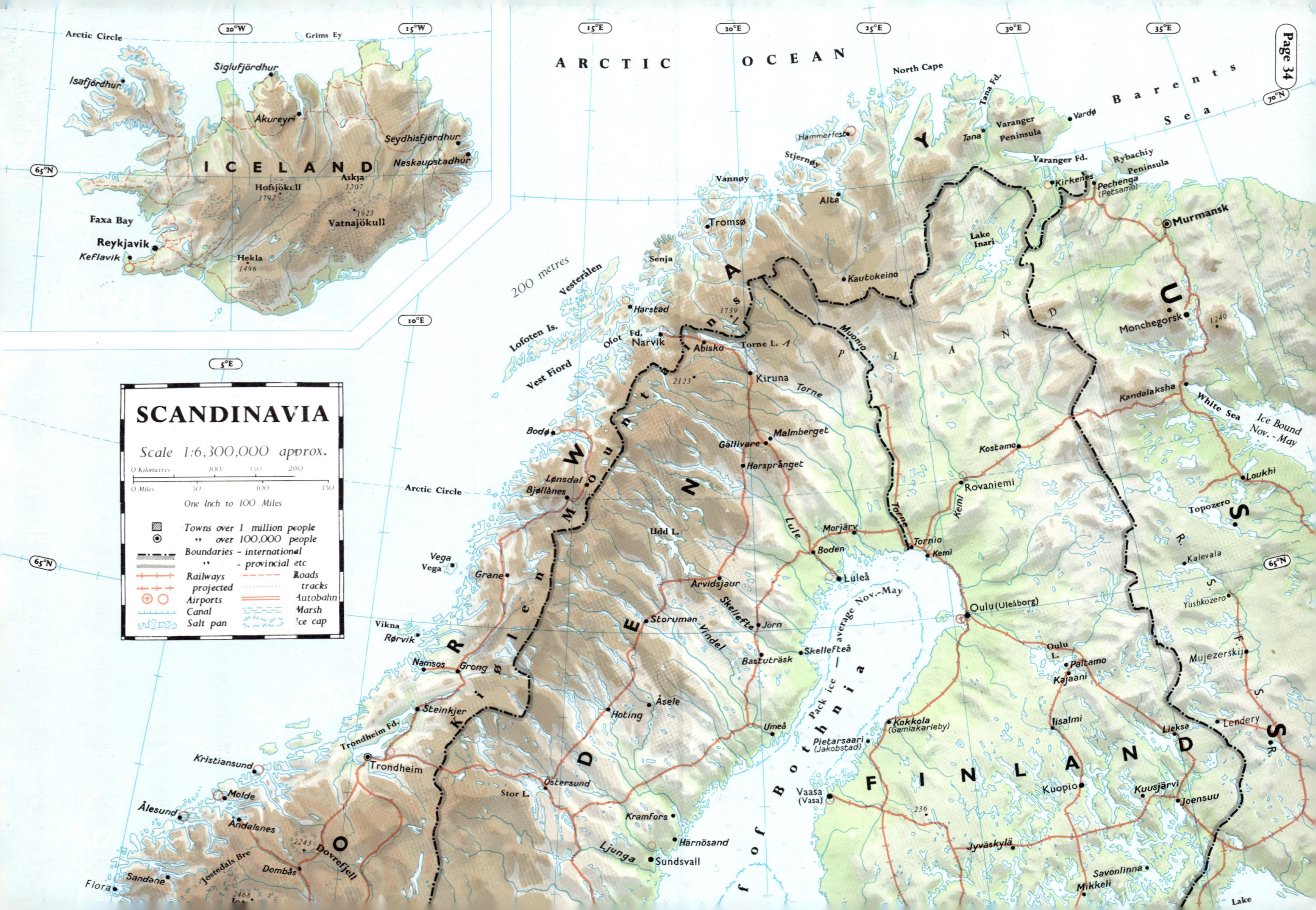
SCANDINAVIA
Scale 1:6,300,000 approx.
0 Kilometres 100 150 200
0 Miles 50 100 150
One Inch to 100 Miles
Towns over 1 million people
" over 100,000 people
Boundaries - international
" - provincial etc
Railways
projected
Airports
Canal
Salt pan
Roads
tracks
Autobahn
Marsh
Ice cap
ARCTIC OCEAN
Barents Sea
White Sea
Ice Bound Nov. - May
Gulf of Bothnia
Pack ice — average Nov.-May
200 metres
ICELAND
Arctic Circle
Grims Ey
Isafjördhur
Siglufjördhur
Akureyri
Seydhisfjördhur
Neskaupstadhur
Askja
1207
Hofsjökull
1792
1923
Vatnajökull
Faxa Bay
Reykjavik
Keflavik
Hekla
1496
20°W
15°W
10°E
5°E
15°E
20°E
25°E
30°E
35°E
65°N
70°N
North Cape
Tana Fd.
Varanger Peninsula
Vardø
Tana
Hammerfest
Stjernøy
Varanger Fd.
Rybachiy Peninsula
Kirkenes
Pechenga (Petsamo)
Murmansk
Vannøy
Alta
Tromsø
Lake Inari
Kautokeino
Senja
Vesterålen
Harstad
Lofoten Is.
Ofot Fd.
Narvik
Abisko
Torne L.
1739
Vest Fiord
Kiruna
Torne
2123
Muonio
Monchegorsk
1240
Kandalaksha
LAPLAND
Bodø
Malmberget
Gällivare
Harsprånget
Kostamo
Loukhi
Rovaniemi
Kemi
Topozero
Lønsdal
Bjøllånes
Arctic Circle
Udd L.
Lule
Morjärv
Tornio
Kemi
Boden
Luleå
Vega
Vega
Grane
Arvidsjaur
Kalevala
Oulu (Uleåborg)
Skellefte
Jörn
Yushkozero
Storuman
Vindel
Vikna
Rørvik
Namsos
Grong
Bastuträsk
Skellefteå
Oulu L.
Paltamo
Kajaani
Mujezerskij
Steinkjer
Åsele
Hoting
Iisalmi
Umeå
Kokkola (Gamlakarleby)
Lieksa
Lendery
Trondheim Fd.
Trondheim
Pietarsaari (Jakobstad)
Kristiansund
Östersund
Stor L.
Vaasa (Vasa)
Kuopio
Kuusjärvi
Joensuu
236
Molde
Ålesund
Åndalsnes
2243
Dovrefjell
Kramfors
Härnösand
Jyväskylä
Sandane
Jostedals Bre
Dombås
Ljunga
Sundsvall
Savonlinna
Mikkeli
Flora
2468
Lake
NORWAY
SWEDEN
FINLAND
U.S.S.R.
Kjölen Mountains

Baltic Sea
Gulf of Finland
Gulf of Riga
Gulf of Danzig
Skagerrak
Kattegat
The Sound
Great Belt
Little Belt
Kiel Bay
Lübeck Bay
Heligoland Bight
Pomeranian Bay
Hanö Bay
North Frisian Islands
West Frisian Islands
East
Heligoland
200 metres
Feb.-March
Pack ice — average max.
Helsinki
(Helsingfors)
Turku
(Åbo)
Tallinn
Riga
Leningrad
Pushkin
Kronshtadt
Narva
Pskov
Tartu
Lake Peipus
Daugavpils
Vilnius
Kaunas
Minsk
Grodno
Kaliningrad
(Königsberg)
Sovetsk
(Tilsit)
Klaipeda
(Memel)
Liepāja
Ventspils
Hiiumaa
Saaremaa
ESTONIAN S.S.R.
LATVIAN S.S.R.
LITHUANIAN S.S.R.
BYELORUSSIAN S.S.R.
UKRAINIAN S.S.R.
R.S.F.S.R.
Stockholm
Uppsala
Gävle
Västerås
Örebro
Norrköping
Linköping
Jönköping
Göteborg
Malmö
Hälsingborg
Karlskrona
Kalmar
Växjö
Gotland
Öland
Bornholm
Lake Väner
L. Vätter
L. Mälar
Oslo
Drammen
Bergen
Stavanger
Kristiansand
Hardangervidda
Lake Mjøsa
Copenhagen
(København)
Odense
Aarhus
Aalborg
Esbjerg
Funen
Zealand
Lolland
DENMARK
Hamburg
Berlin
Bremen
Hanover
Kiel
Lübeck
Rostock
Leipzig
Dresden
Magdeburg
Cologne
Düsseldorf
Essen
Dortmund
Bonn
Warsaw
(Warszawa)
Gdańsk
(Danzig)
Gdynia
Szczecin
(Stettin)
Poznań
Wrocław
(Breslau)
Łódź
Bydgoszcz
Toruń
Lublin
POLAND
EAST PRUSSIA
Oder (Odra)
Neisse (Nysa)
Vistula (Wisła)
Elbe
Weser
Ems
Bug
West Dvina
Ft. M.
16,000 4,800
10,000 3,000
6,000 1,800
3,000 900
1,500 450
1,000 300
600 180
300 90
Sea Level
Land Depression
60°N
55°N
15°E
20°E
Modified Conical Orthomorphic Projection
Copyright Oxford University Press

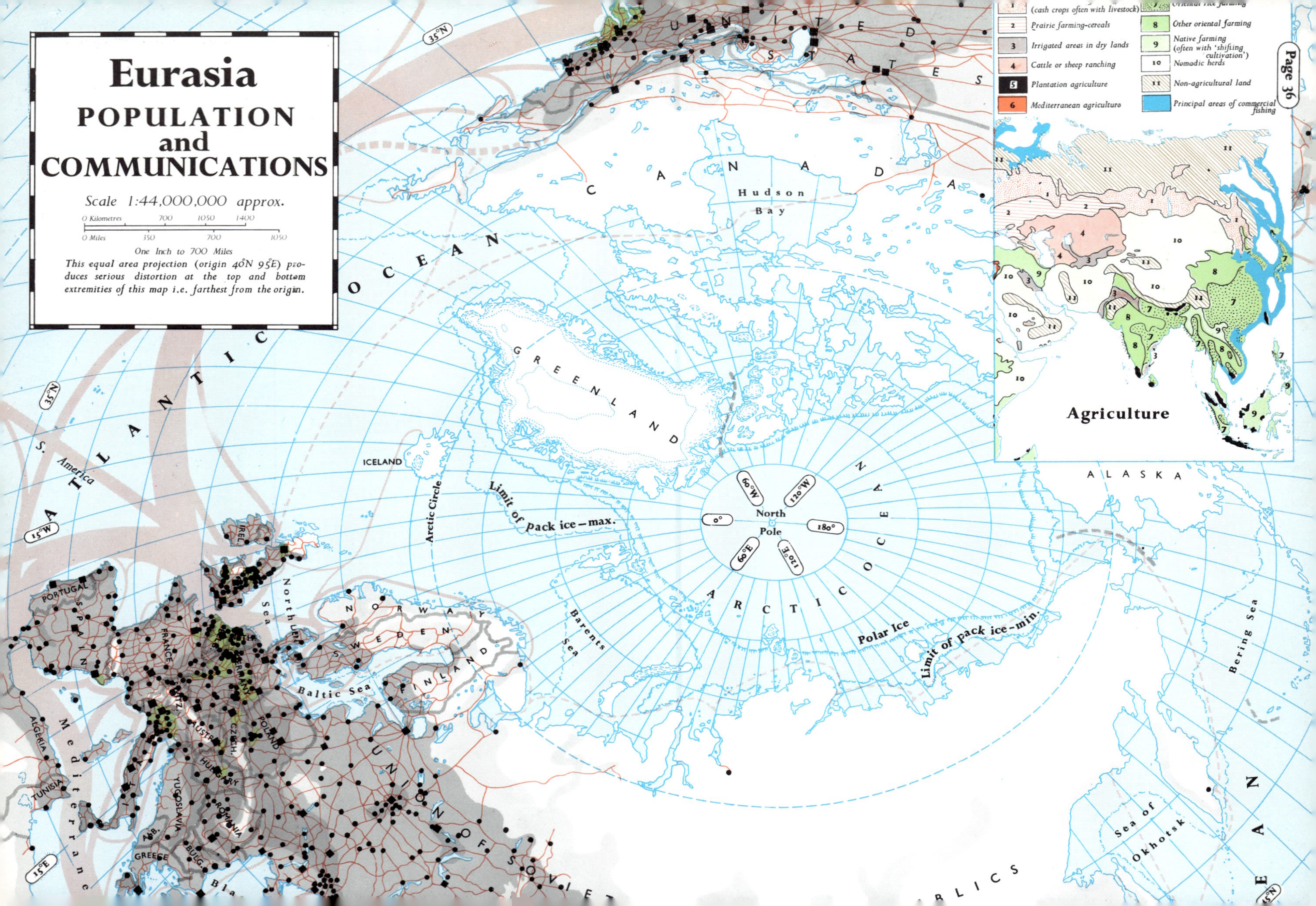
Eurasia
POPULATION
and
COMMUNICATIONS
Scale 1:44,000,000 approx.
0 Kilometres 700 1050 1400
0 Miles 350 700 1050
One Inch to 700 Miles
This equal area projection (origin 40°N 95°E) produces serious distortion at the top and bottom extremities of this map i.e. farthest from the origin.
1 (cash crops often with livestock)
2 Prairie farming-cereals
3 Irrigated areas in dry lands
4 Cattle or sheep ranching
5 Plantation agriculture
6 Mediterranean agriculture
7 Oriental rice farming
8 Other oriental farming
9 Native farming (often with 'shifting cultivation')
10 Nomadic herds
11 Non-agricultural land
Principal areas of commercial fishing
Agriculture
UNITED STATES
CANADA
Hudson Bay
GREENLAND
ICELAND
ALASKA
ATLANTIC OCEAN
ARCTIC OCEAN
North Pole
0°
60°W
120°W
180°
120°E
60°E
35°N
15°W
15°E
S. America
Arctic Circle
Limit of pack ice – max.
Limit of pack ice – min.
Polar Ice
Barents Sea
Bering Sea
Sea of Okhotsk
NORWAY
SWEDEN
FINLAND
North Sea
Baltic Sea
IREL.
PORTUGAL
SPAIN
FRANCE
SWITZ.
GERMANY
AUSTRIA
CZECH.
POLAND
HUNGARY
ROMANIA
YUGOSLAVIA
BULG.
ALB.
GREECE
ALGERIA
TUNISIA
Mediterrane
Bla
UNION OF SOVIET
REPUBLICS

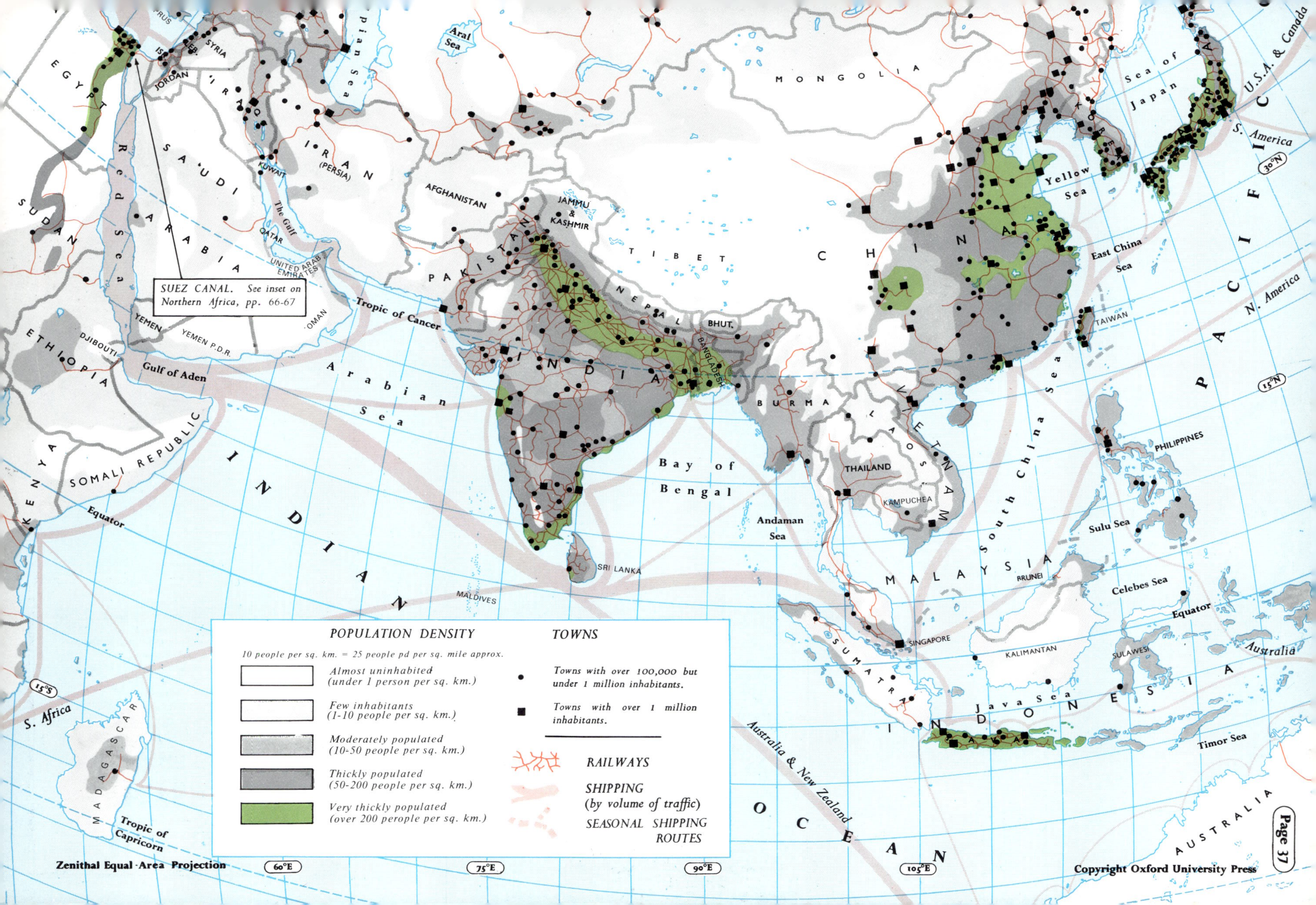

SUEZ CANAL. See inset on Northern Africa, pp. 66-67
POPULATION DENSITY
10 people per sq. km. = 25 people pd per sq. mile approx.
Almost uninhabited (under 1 person per sq. km.)
Few inhabitants (1-10 people per sq. km.)
Moderately populated (10-50 people per sq. km.)
Thickly populated (50-200 people per sq. km.)
Very thickly populated (over 200 perople per sq. km.)
TOWNS
Towns with over 100,000 but under 1 million inhabitants.
Towns with over 1 million inhabitants.
RAILWAYS
SHIPPING (by volume of traffic)
SEASONAL SHIPPING ROUTES
EGYPT
SUDAN
ETHIOPIA
DJIBOUTI
KENYA
SOMALI REPUBLIC
YEMEN
YEMEN P.D.R.
OMAN
SAUDI ARABIA
JORDAN
SYRIA
'IRAQ
KUWAIT
QATAR
UNITED ARAB EMIRATES
IRAN (PERSIA)
AFGHANISTAN
PAKISTAN
JAMMU & KASHMIR
INDIA
NEPAL
BHUT.
BANGLADESH
SRI LANKA
MALDIVES
TIBET
CHINA
MONGOLIA
KOREA
JAPAN
TAIWAN
BURMA
THAILAND
LAOS
VIETNAM
KAMPUCHEA
MALAYSIA
SINGAPORE
BRUNEI
PHILIPPINES
KALIMANTAN
SULAWESI
SUMATRA
INDONESIA
MADAGASCAR
AUSTRALIA
Red Sea
Gulf of Aden
The Gulf
Aral Sea
Arabian Sea
Bay of Bengal
Andaman Sea
South China Sea
East China Sea
Yellow Sea
Sea of Japan
Sulu Sea
Celebes Sea
Java Sea
Timor Sea
INDIAN OCEAN
PACIFIC
Tropic of Cancer
Tropic of Capricorn
Equator
S. Africa
Australia & New Zealand
Australia
S. America
N. America
U.S.A. & Canada
15°S
60°E
75°E
90°E
105°E
15°N
30°N
Zenithal Equal-Area Projection

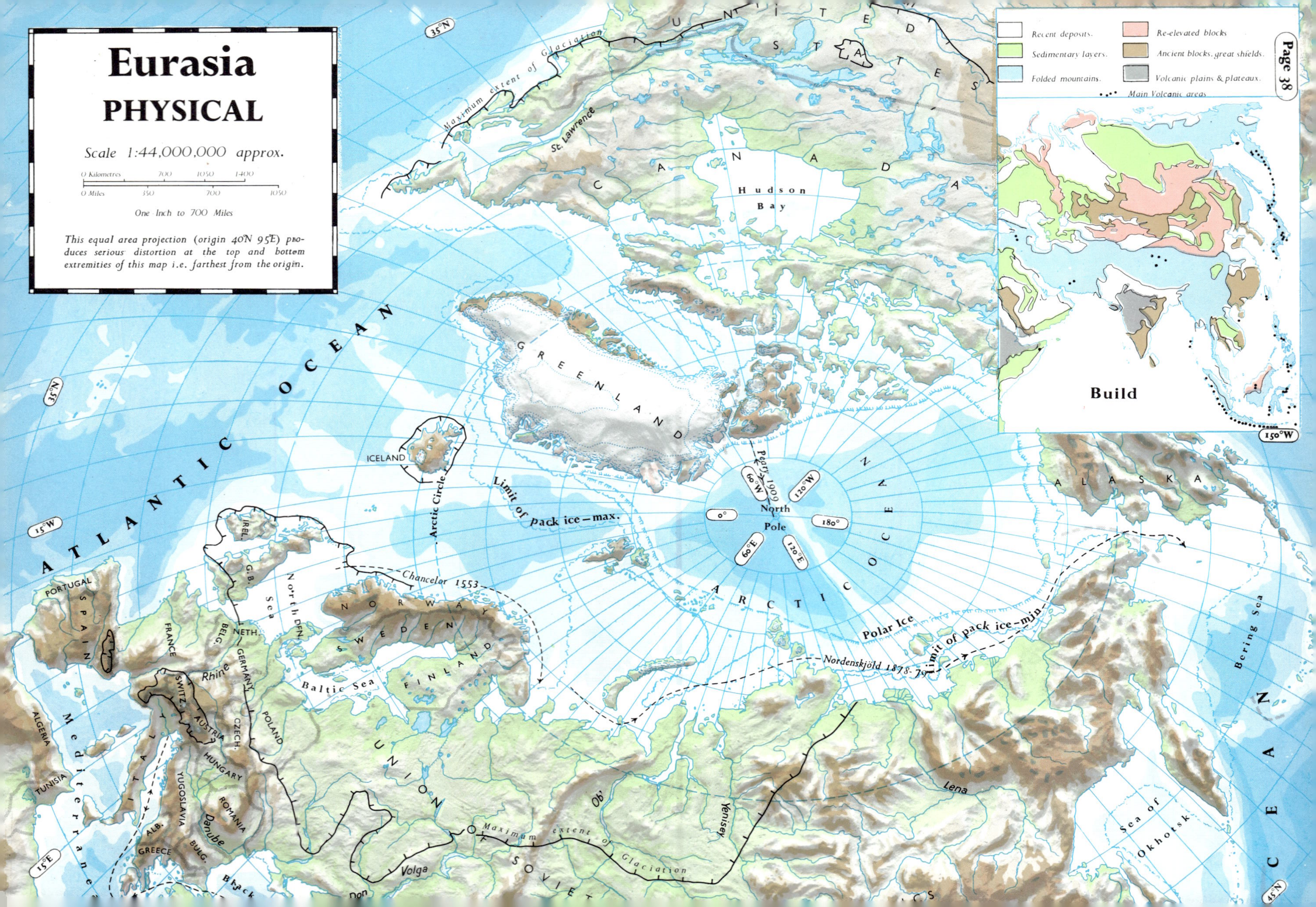

Eurasia
PHYSICAL
Scale 1:44,000,000 approx.
0 Kilometres 700 1050 1400
0 Miles 350 700 1050
One Inch to 700 Miles
This equal area projection (origin 40°N 95°E) produces serious distortion at the top and bottom extremities of this map i.e. farthest from the origin.
Page 38
Recent deposits.
Sedimentary layers.
Folded mountains.
Re-elevated blocks
Ancient blocks, great shields.
Volcanic plains & plateaux.
Main Volcanic areas
Build
150°W
ATLANTIC OCEAN
ARCTIC OCEAN
UNITED STATES
CANADA
Hudson Bay
St. Lawrence
Maximum extent of Glaciation
GREENLAND
ICELAND
Arctic Circle
Limit of pack ice–max.
Limit of pack ice–min.
Polar Ice
Peary 1909
North Pole
0°
60°W
120°W
180°
60°E
120°E
Chancelor 1553
Nordenskjöld 1878-79
NORWAY
SWEDEN
FINLAND
North Sea
DEN.
Baltic Sea
IREL.
G.B.
NETH.
BELG.
GERMANY
POLAND
CZECH.
FRANCE
SWITZ.
AUSTRIA
HUNGARY
ROMANIA
YUGOSLAVIA
BULG.
ALB.
GREECE
ITALY
PORTUGAL
SPAIN
ALGERIA
TUNISIA
Mediterranean
Black
Rhine
Danube
Volga
Don
Ob'
Yenisey
Lena
UNION OF SOVIET
ALASKA
Bering Sea
Sea of Okhotsk
35°N
15°W
15°E
45°N

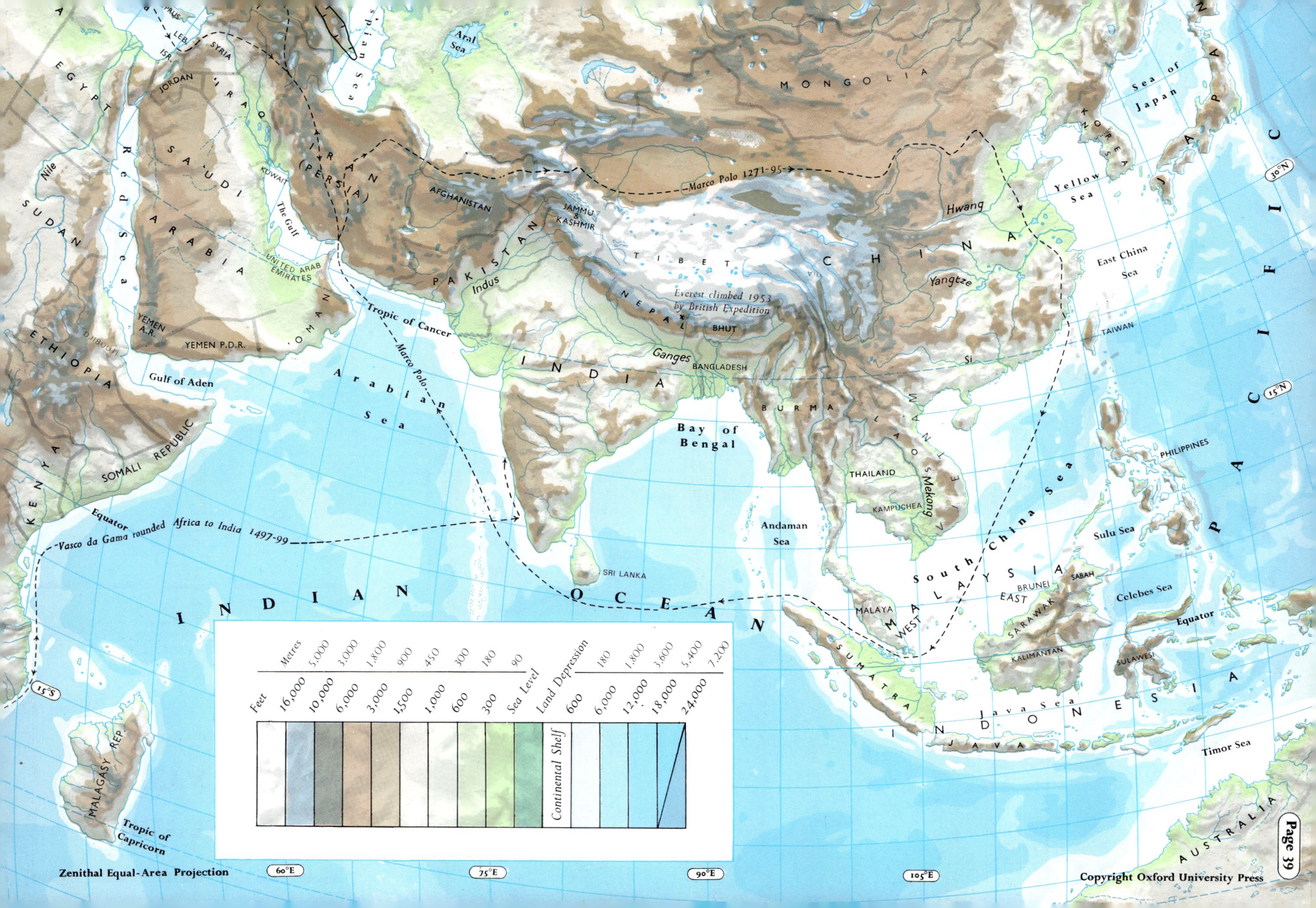

MONGOLIA
CHINA
TIBET
INDIA
PAKISTAN
AFGHANISTAN
IRAN (PERSIA)
SAUDI ARABIA
IRAQ
SYRIA
JORDAN
LEB.
ISR.
EGYPT
SUDAN
ETHIOPIA
DJIBOUTI
SOMALI REPUBLIC
KENYA
YEMEN A.R.
YEMEN P.D.R.
OMAN
KUWAIT
UNITED ARAB EMIRATES
JAMMU & KASHMIR
NEPAL
BHUT
BANGLADESH
BURMA
THAILAND
LAOS
KAMPUCHEA
VIETNAM
MALAYA
WEST MALAYSIA
EAST MALAYSIA
BRUNEI
SABAH
SARAWAK
KALIMANTAN
SULAWESI
SUMATRA
JAVA
INDONESIA
PHILIPPINES
TAIWAN
KOREA
JAPAN
SRI LANKA
MALAGASY REP.
AUSTRALIA
Aral Sea
Caspian Sea
Red Sea
The Gulf
Gulf of Aden
Arabian Sea
Bay of Bengal
Andaman Sea
South China Sea
Sulu Sea
Celebes Sea
Java Sea
Timor Sea
East China Sea
Yellow Sea
Sea of Japan
INDIAN OCEAN
PACIFIC
Nile
Indus
Ganges
Mekong
Yangtze
Hwang
Si
Everest climbed 1953 by British Expedition
Marco Polo 1271-95
Marco Polo
Vasco da Gama rounded Africa to India 1497-99
Tropic of Cancer
Equator
Tropic of Capricorn
30°N
15°N
15°S
60°E
75°E
90°E
105°E
Feet
Metres
16,000
5,000
10,000
3,000
6,000
1,800
3,000
900
1,500
450
1,000
300
600
180
300
90
Sea Level
Land Depression
600
180
6,000
1,800
12,000
3,600
18,000
5,400
24,000
7,200
Continental Shelf
Zenithal Equal-Area Projection

Eurasia

VEGETATION

Scale 1:44,000,000 approx.

0 Kilometres 700 1050 1400
0 Miles 350 700 1050

One Inch to 700 Miles

This equal area projection (origin 40°N 95°E) produces serious distortion at the top and bottom extremities of this map i.e. farthest from the origin.

Rainfall figures in 10's of millimetres

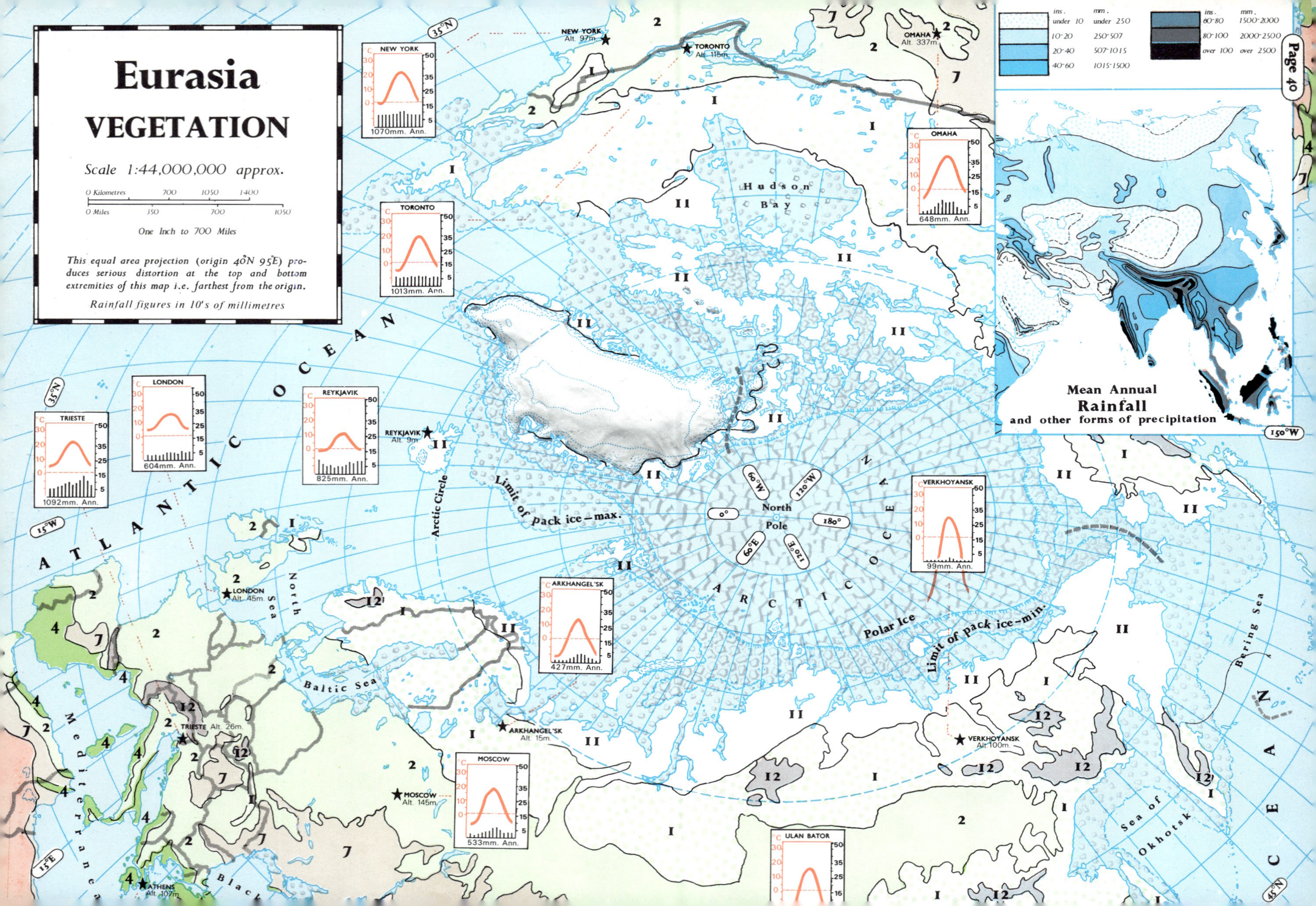

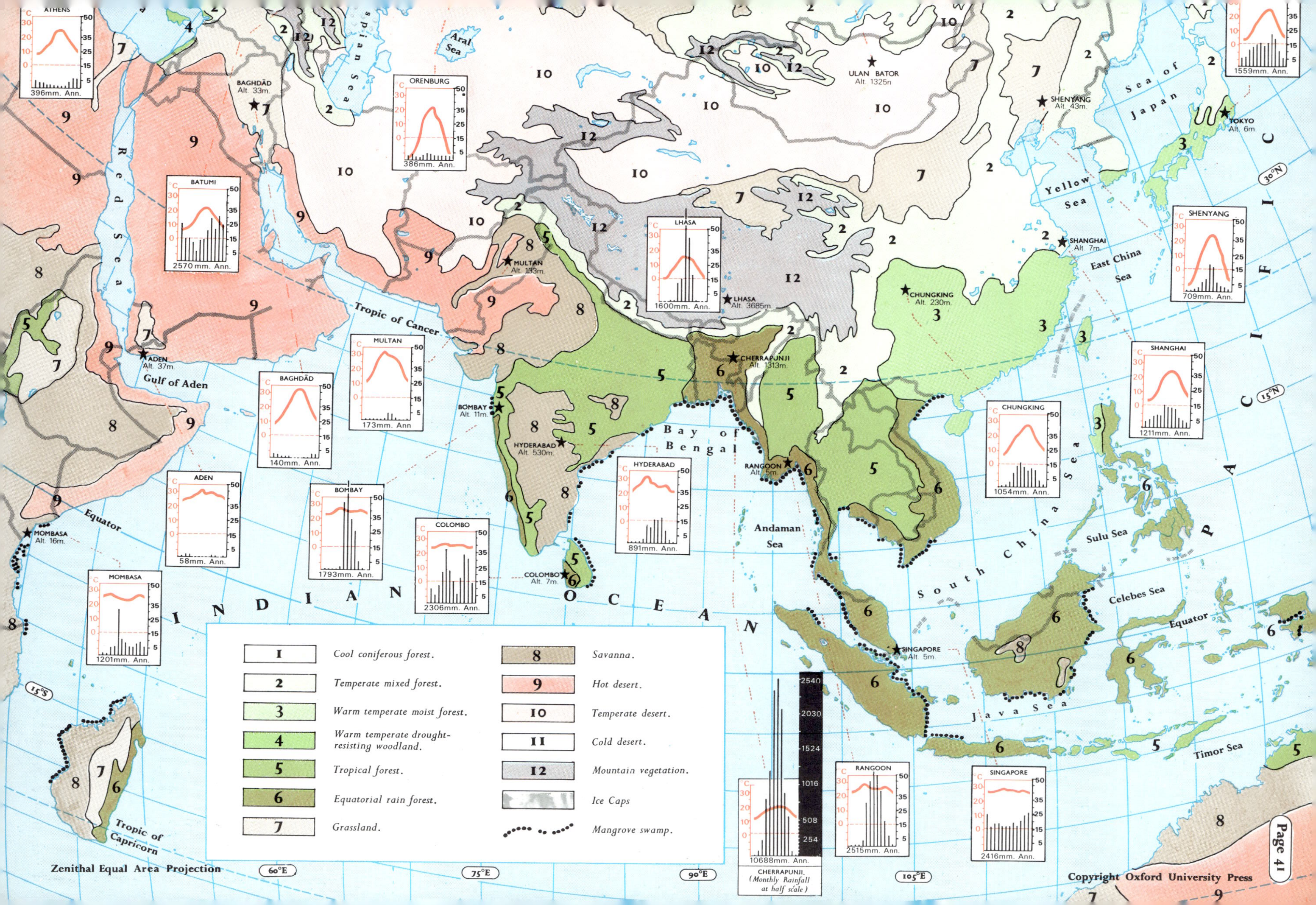

Cool coniferous forest.
Temperate mixed forest.
Warm temperate moist forest.
Warm temperate drought-resisting woodland.
Tropical forest.
Equatorial rain forest.
Grassland.
Savanna.
Hot desert.
Temperate desert.
Cold desert.
Mountain vegetation.
Ice Caps
Mangrove swamp.
ATHENS 396mm. Ann.
BAGHDĀD Alt. 33m.
ORENBURG 386mm. Ann.
ULAN BATOR Alt. 1325m
SHENYANG Alt. 43m.
TOKYO Alt. 6m.
1559mm. Ann.
BATUMI 2570 mm. Ann.
LHASA 1600mm. Ann.
LHASA Alt. 3685m.
SHANGHAI Alt. 7m.
SHENYANG 709mm. Ann.
CHUNGKING Alt. 230m.
MULTAN Alt. 133m.
ADEN Alt. 37m.
MULTAN 173mm. Ann
BAGHDĀD 140mm. Ann.
BOMBAY Alt. 11m.
HYDERABAD Alt. 530m.
CHERRAPUNJI Alt. 1313m.
SHANGHAI 1211mm. Ann.
CHUNGKING 1054mm. Ann.
ADEN 58mm. Ann.
BOMBAY 1793mm. Ann.
COLOMBO 2306mm. Ann.
HYDERABAD 891mm. Ann.
RANGOON Alt. 5m.
MOMBASA Alt. 16m.
MOMBASA 1201mm. Ann.
COLOMBO Alt. 7m.
SINGAPORE Alt. 5m.
CHERRAPUNJI 10688mm. Ann. (Monthly Rainfall at half scale)
RANGOON 2515mm. Ann.
SINGAPORE 2416mm. Ann.
Aral Sea
Caspian Sea
Red Sea
Gulf of Aden
Tropic of Cancer
Equator
Tropic of Capricorn
Bay of Bengal
Andaman Sea
South China Sea
Sulu Sea
Celebes Sea
Java Sea
Timor Sea
Yellow Sea
East China Sea
Sea of Japan
INDIAN OCEAN
PACIFIC
30°N
15°N
15°S
60°E
75°E
90°E
105°E
Zenithal Equal Area Projection

U.S.S.R.
Scale 1:25,000,000 approx.
0 Kilometres 400 600 800
0 Miles 200 300 400 500
One Inch to 400 Miles
Conical Orthomorphic Projection
ATLANTIC OCEAN
ICELAND
GREENLAND (DENMARK)
Arctic Circle
Limit of pack ice-average maximum (Spring)
Unnavigable Polar Ice
Spitsbergen (Svalbard) (Norway)
Bear I.
North Cape
Barents Sea
Novaya Zemlya
Kara Sea
Vaygach I.
C. Kanin
Kola Peninsula
Murmansk
White Sea
NORWAY
SWEDEN
FINLAND
Narvik
Trondheim
Bergen
Oslo
Göteborg
Stockholm
Helsinki
Gulf of Bothnia
Gulf of Finland
Baltic Sea
Gotland
Faeroe Is. (Den.)
Shetland Is.
Orkney Is.
North Sea
GREAT BRITAIN
REPUBLIC OF IRELAND
Glasgow
Edinburgh
Dublin
Liverpool
Birmingham
London
Scilly Is.
English Channel
B. of Biscay
200 metres
FRANCE
Paris
Loire
Rhône
Rhine
Marseilles
Gulf of Lions
Corsica
Brussels
Amsterdam
NETH.
LUX.
Bonn
Hamburg
Elbe
Berlin
GERMANY
DENMARK
Copenhagen
Bern
Turin
Milan
AUSTRIA
Vienna
Prague
CZECHOSLOVAKIA
POLAND
Warsaw
Szczecin
Wroclaw
Krakow
Gdansk
Kaliningrad
Vistula
Oder
HUNGARY
Budapest
ITALY
Rome
Naples
Adriatic Sea
YUGOSLAVIA
Belgrade
Sava
ALBANIA
GREECE
Athens
Aegean Sea
Crete
BULGARIA
Sofia
ROMANIA
Bucharest
Danube
Galati
Prut
Mediterranean Sea
Riga
Tallinn
ESTONIAN S.S.R.
LATVIAN S.S.R.
LITHUANIAN S.S.R.
Vilnius
Minsk
BYELORUSSIAN S.S.R.
Pripet Marshes
Pinsk
L'vov
Dniester
UKRAINIAN
Kiev
Bug
Kishinev
Odessa
Nikolayev
Nikopol'
Dnepropetrovsk
Dnieper
Kharkov
DONBASS
Donets
Zhdanov
Simferopol'
Sevastopol
Kerch
Sea of Azov
Black Sea
Novorossiysk
Krasnodar
Armavir
Rostov
Tsimlyansk Res.
Volgograd
Don
Leningrad
L. Ladoga
Lake Onega
Petrozavodsk
Novgorod
Vitebsk
Smolensk
Gomel'
Moscow
Kalinin
Yaroslavl'
Vologda
Ivanovo
Gor'kiy
Ryazan'
Tula
Orel'
Kursk
Voronezh
Tambov
Saratov
Penza
Volga
Kazan'
Kirov
Izhevsk
Kama
Perm
Arkhangel'sk
N. Dvina
Pechora
Naryan-Mar
Vorkuta
Kara
Usa
Salekhard
Izhma
Kotlas
Vychegda
RUSSIAN SOVIET
N.Sos'va
Ural Mts.
Serov
Nizhniy-Tagil
Sverdlovsk
Tobol'sk
Tyumen'
Irtysh
Chelyabinsk
Kurgan
Magnitogorsk
Tobol
Ishim
Petukhovo
Petropavlovsk
Omsk
Ufa
Belaya
Kuybyshev
Orenburg
Ural'sk
Ural
Orsk
Astrakhan'
Gur'yev
Emba
KAZAKH
Steppe
Turgay
Tselinograd
Karaganda
Kazakh Upland
Baykonur
Sarisu
Kounrad
Balkhash
Lake Balkhash
Chu
Mu'yun-Kum
Aral Sea
Aral'sk
Ust'-Urt Plateau
Kungrad
Mangyshlak Pen.
Shevchenko
Kara-Bogaz-Gol
Caspian Sea
Krasnovodsk
Baku
Kura
Makhachkala
Groznyy
Caucasus Mts.
GEORGIAN S.S.R.
Tbilisi
ARMENIAN S.S.R.
Yerevan
Batumi
Turan
Kara-Kum
TURKMEN S.S.R.
UZBEK
Kyzyl-Kum
Khiva
Sy Darya
Chimkent
Tashkent
Frunze
Alma-Ata
KIRGIZ S.S.R.
Fergana
Samarkand
Bukhara
Dyushambe
TADZHIK S.S.R.
Amu Dar'ya
Mary
Ashkhabad
Kashgar
Yarkand
KASHMIR
Gilgit
PAKISTAN
Kabul
AFGHANISTAN
Herat
Mashhad
IRAN (PERSIA)
Tehran
Shahrud
Bandar-e Shah
Hamadan
Esfahan (Isfahan)
Dasht-e Kavir
Shiraz
Kerman
Bushehr
Abadan
Basra
KUWAIT
Kuwait
The Gulf
Tabriz
Lake Urmia
Lake Van
Erzurum
Mosul
Baghdad
IRAQ
SYRIA
Aleppo
Damascus
Beirut
LEBANON
ISRAEL
Jerusalem
Amman
JORDAN
Aqaba
EGYPT
Cairo
Suez
Port Said
Alexandria
CYPRUS
TURKEY
Istanbul
Ankara
Zonguldak
Izmir
Adana
SAUDI ARABIA
Nafud
Medina
Riyadh
Dhahran
10°W
10°E
20°E
35°E
50°E
55°E
60°E
65°E
70°E
75°E
80°E
25°N
35°N
40°N
45°N
50°N
55°N
60°N
65°N
70°N
75°N
80°N

Towns over 1 million people
" over 100,000 people
Boundaries - international
- provincial etc.
Railways
projected
Roads
track
Airports
Canal
Sand desert
Salt pan
Marsh
Ice cap
Ft.
M
Sea Level
Land Depression
North Pole
180°
160°E
140°E
120°E
100°E
80°E
60°E
40°E
85°N
80°N
75°N
70°N
60°N
55°N
50°N
45°N
40°N
30°N
85°E
90°E
95°E
100°E
105°E
110°E
115°E
O C E A N
Severnaya
Zemlya
Bol'shevik I.
C. Chelyuskin
Wiese I. (Vize)
Unnavigable Polar Ice
Novosibirskiye Ostrova
Laptev Sea
Lyakhov Islands
Laptev Str.
East Siberian Sea
Wrangel I.
Chukchi Sea
Bering Strait
St. Lawrence (U.S.)
International Date Line
Bering Sea
Gulf of Anadyr'
Anadyr'
C. Navarin
Nome
Kivak
Komandor Is.
Kamchatka
Kamchatka Bay
Petropavlovsk-Kamchatskiy
Sea of Okhotsk
Magadan
Okhotsk
Taymyr Penin.
L. Taymyr
Nordvik
Khatanga
Tiksi
Kazach'ye
Indigirka
Kolyma Plain
Kolyma
Yukagir Plateau
Gydan (Kolyma) Range
Shelekhov Bay
Ambarchik
Ostrovnoye
Markovo
Kamenskoye
Kavacha
Cherskiy Range
Susuman
Verkhoyansk
Verkhoyansk Range
Lena
Sangar
Vilyuy
Yakutsk
Amga
Aldan
Buyaga
El'gyay
Olekminsk
Dzherba
Vitim
Korshunova
Central Siberian Plateau
Putoran Mts.
Dudinka
Noril'sk
Karaul
Igarka
Lower Tunguska
Stony Tunguska
Yenisey
Tarko-Sale
FEDERATED SOCIALIST REPUBLIC
R
S
Yeniseysk
Angara
Chuna
Ust'-Kut
Tayshet
Bratsk
Krasnoyarsk
Tomsk
Kemerovo
Novokuznetsk
Abakan
Minusinsk
Shelym
Biysk
Kyzyl
Zhigalovo
Lake Baykal
Cheremkhovo
Usol'ye
Irkutsk
Ulan-Ude
Chita
Darasun
Nerchinsk
Sretensk
Bukachacha
Mogoche
Never
Zeya
Tygda
Amur
Blagoveshchensk
Bureya
Birobidzhan
Khabarovsk
Soviet Harbour
Komsomol'sk
Amgun
Nikolayevsk
Aleksandrovsk
Sakhalin (USSR)
Kholmsk
Yuzhno Sakhalinsk
Wakkanai
Hokkaido
Sapporo
Muroran
Hakodate
Aomori
Sea of Japan
Vladivostok
Suchan
Ussuriysk
Sikhote Alin Range
Shihchan
Nunkiang
Tsitsihar
Harbin (Pinkiang)
Kirin
Mutankiang
Changchun
Shenyang
Anshan
Yingkow
Lü-ta
Chefoo
NORTH KOREA
Pyongyang
Chinnampo
Seoul
SOUTH KOREA
Pusan
Hiroshima
Shimonoseki
Kitakyushu
Nagasaki
Kyushu
Shikoku
Kobe
Kyoto
JAPAN
Yellow Sea
East China Sea
Ryukyu Is.
Hulun
Erentsab
Choibalsan
Tamtsak Bulak
Ulanhoto
Great Khingan Mts.
Ulan Bator (Urga)
MONGOLIA
Selenga
Bulagan
Jibhalanta
Jirgalantu
Ulangom
Altai Range
Sain Shanda
Gobi Desert
Changkiakow (Kalgan)
Peking (Peiping)
Chengteh
Tientsin
Huhehot
Paotow
Shihkiachwang
Tsinan
Tsingtao
Taiyüan
Yinchwan (Ningshia)
Anyang
Süchow
Loyang
Sian
Tungkwan
Lanchow (Kaolan)
Sining
Nanking
Shanghai
Hwang
Urumchi
Turfan
Qomul (Hami)
Ansi
UIGHUR
REGION
Tsaidam Swamps
C H I N A
Kan
Leninogorsk
Aksha
Uldza

Page 44
20°E
25°E
30°E
35°E
40°E
45°E
50°E
55°E
50°N
45°N
40°N
Henko
Helsinki
Gulf of Finland
Vyborg
Lake Ladoga
Petrozavodsk
Lake Onega
Ukh
Gotland
Khiumaa
Saaremaa
Tallinn
Baltic Sea
Ventspils
Liepāja
Gulf of Riga
ESTONIAN S.S.R.
Narva
Leningrad
Pushkin
L. Peipus
Tartu
LATVIAN S.S.R.
Riga
Klaipeda
Svir'
Konosha
North Dvina
Kotlas
Vychegda
Syktyvkar
Sukhona
Novgorod
L. Ilmen'
Pskov
Kaliningrad
Gdańsk
R.S.F.S.R.
Sovetsk
Siauliai
LITHUANIAN S.S.R.
Kaunas
Vilnius
W. Dvina
Vitebsk
Velikiye Luki
Valdai Hills
Vyshniy Volochek
Cherepovets
Vologda
Rybinsk
Rybinsk Reservoir
RUSSIAN SOVIET FEDE
Kama
Rudnichnyy
Kirov
Glazov
Kostroma
Yaroslavl'
Ivanovo
Kineshma
Kalinin
Volga
Rzhev
POLAND
Grodno
Białystok
Warsaw
Minsk
BYELORUSSIAN S.S.R.
Baranovichi
Smolensk
Yel'nya
Vyaz'ma
Moscow
Vladimir
Kovrov
Orekhovo-Zuyevo
Dzerzhinsk
Gor'kiy
Yoshkar-Ola
Izhevsk
Kazan'
Mogilev
Pripet Marshes
Pinsk
Brest Litovskiy
Kovel'
Kaluga
Kolomna
Oka
Murom
Arzamas
Tula
Novomoskovsk
Ryazan'
Bryansk
Bezhitsa
Sarny
Gomel'
L'vov
Rovno
Ivano-Frankovsk
Chernigov
Orel'
U
Saransk
Ul'yanovsk
S
Korosten'
Zhitomir
Berdichev
Kiev
Konotop
Kursk
Lipetsk
Tambov
Penza
Syzran'
Kuybyshev
Sterlitar
UKRAINIAN S.S.R.
Chernovtsy
Dniester
Vinnitsa
Dnieper
Sumy
Voronezh
Volga Hills
Chapayevsk
Samara
Buzuluk
Ishim
Botoşani
Bistriţa
Prut
MOLD. S.S.R.
Kirovograd
Poltava
Belgorod
Khar'kov
Borisoglebsk
Balashov
Saratov
Vol'sk
Kremenchug
Don
Krasnyy Kut
Ural'sk
Ural
Sol'-Ilet
Bacău
ROMANIA
Iaşi
Bug
Dneprodzerzhinsk
Krivoy Rog
Dnepropetrovsk
Donets
Novouzensk
Aleksandrov Gay
Kishinev
Odessa
Nikopol'
Nikolayev
Zaporozh'ye
DONBAS
Voroshilovgrad
Donetsk
Makeyevka
Yenakiyevo
Krasnyy Luch
Tsimlyansk Reservoir
Volgograd
Galaţi
Bucharest
Danube
Kherson
Zhdanov
Taganrog
Shakhty
Rostov
Novocherkassk
Baskunchak
Caspian Lowlands
K
Sulina
Nogaysk
Yeysk
Sal'sk
Makat
BULGARIA
CRIMEA
Sea of Azov
Simferopol'
Sevastopol'
Kerch'
Varna
200 metres
Balaklava
Inkerman
Yalta
Astrakhan'
Gur'yev
Burgas
Kuban
Krasnodar
Novorossiysk
Armavir
Stavropol'
Black Sea
Tuapse
Maykop
Sochi
Caucasus
Pyatigorsk
İstanbul
Zonguldak
Sukhumi
Mangyshlak Peninsula
Fort Shevchenko
Pontic
Sinop
Elbrus
Adapazari
Karabük
Shevchenko
Samsun
Poti
GEORGIAN S.S.R.
Ordzhonikidze
Groznyy
Eskişehir
Kutahya
Ankara
Batumi
Kutaisi
Makhachkala
Afyonkarahisar
TURKEY
Mountains
Trabzon
Tbilisi
Derbent
Lake Tuz
Sivas
Divriği
Erzurum
Alaverdi
Leninakan
L. Sevan
Kirovabad
Kara-Bogaz-Gol
Konya
Kayseri
Yerevan
ARMENIAN S.S.R.
AZERBAYDZHAN S.S.R.
Sumgait
Baku
Caspian Sea
Surface Height 28 m. below m.s.l.
Malatya
Elâzığ
Mt. Ararat
Taurus Mts
Cilician Gates
Adana
Maraş
Lake Van
Muş
Nakhichevan
Krasnovodsk
Diyarbakır
Araks (Araxes)
Cheleken
Nebit-Da
Mersin
Gaziantep
Urfa
Siirt
İskenderun
Tigris
CYPRUS
Nicosia
Latakia
Baniyās
Antakya (Antioch)
Aleppo
Mardin
Tabrīz
Astara
Euphrates
Mianeh
L. Urmia
Rasht
Tripoli
Beirut
LEBANON
Homs
SYRIA
Mosul
Irbil
Alborz Mts.
Bandar-e
Gorgān
Qazvin
Damāvand
Conical Orthomorphic Projection
Palmyra
Kirkuk
Damascus
ISRAEL
'IRAQ
IRAN
Tehrān
Semnān
PER
Ft.
M.
16,000
4,800
10,000
3,000
6,000
1,800
3,000
900
1,500
450
1,000
300
600
180
300
90
Sea Level
Land Depression

Western
U.S.S.R.
Scale 1:12,500,000 approx.
0 Kilometres 200 300 400
0 Miles 100 200 300
One Inch to 200 Miles
Towns over 1 million people
" over 100,000 people
Boundaries international
- provincial etc
Railways
projected
Roads
tracks
Airports
Canal
Sand desert
Marsh
Salt pan
Ice cap
Copyright Oxford University Press
West
Siberian
Plain
SOCIALIST REPUBLIC
R
S
KUZBAS
Steppes
Kazakh Uplands
KAZAKH S.S.R.
Hunger Steppe
UZBEK S.S.R.
TURKMEN S.S.R.
KIRGIZ S.S.R.
TADZHIK S.S.R.
Turan Plain
Kyzyl-Kum
Kara-Kum
Muyun-Kum
Kara-Tau
CHINA
SINKIANG
MONGOLIA
AFGHANISTAN
PAKISTAN
KASHMIR
TIBET
Tien Shan
Dzungaria
Takla Makan
Alai Range
Pamirs
Hindu Kush
Western Sayan Mts
Altai Ra.
Kopet Dagh
Dzungarian Gate
Lenin Pk. 7134
Mt. Communism 7495
Khan Tengri 7190
Aral Sea
Surface Height 48m above m.s.l.
Lake Balkhash
Issyk-Kul'
Lake Chany
Lake Tengiz
Lake Selety-Tengiz
L. Kulundinskoye
L. Chelkar-Tengiz
L. Zaysan
Ulyungur Nor
Ebi Nor
Ob
Ob'
Irtysh
Black Irtysh
Yenisey
Angara
Tobol'
Ishim
Tavda
Tura
Chulym
Vakh
Vasyugan
Turgay
Chu
Ili
Syr Darya (Jaxartes)
Amu Darya (Oxus)
Tarim
Yarkand
Khotan
Indus
Kulunda Steppe
Berezovo
Faktoriye
Surgut
Khanty-Mansiysk
Yeniseysk
Kansk
Tayshet
Krasnoyarsk
Achinsk
Mariinsk
Belyy Yar
Asino
Tomsk
Anzhero-Sudzhensk
Kemerovo
Leninsk-Kuznetskiy
Prokop'yevsk
Novokuznetsk
Kolyvan'
Akademgorodok
Novosibirsk
Kuybyshev
Tatarsk
Barnaul
Biysk
Gorno-Altaysk
Chernogorsk
Minusinsk
Abakan
Shalym
Polunochnoye
Ivdel'
Severoural'sk
Serov
Sos'va
Tobol'sk
Tavda
Kushva
Alapayevsk
Nizhniy-Tagil
Artemovskiy
Kamyshlov
Tyumen'
Sverdlovsk
Kamensk-Ural'skiy
Omutinskoye
Novonazyvayevka
Tara
Omsk
Kalachinsk
Kasli
Zlatoust
Chelyabinsk
Kurgan
Makushino
Petukhovo
Petropavlovsk
Troitsk
Ust'Uyskoye
Kokchetav
Magnitogorsk
Kartaly
Kustanay
Semiozernoye
Bredy
Dzhetygara
Orsk
Khrom-Tau
Pavlodar
Danilovka
Spasskoye
Atbasar
Tselinograd
Rubtsovsk
Kolyvan'
Leninogorsk
Zyryanovsk
Belousovka
Semipalatinsk
Ust'-Kamenogorsk
Cherdoyak
Zharma
Temir-Tau
Karaganda
Ayaguz
Chuguchak
Yamatu
Turgay
Ulu-Tau
Marganets
Atasuskiy
Uspenskiy
Mointy
Kounradskiy
Balkhash
Ala Kul'
Andreyevka
Dzhezkazgan
Baykonur
Aral'sk
Kazalinsk
Tekely
Kzyl-Orda
Suzak
Chu
Alma-Ata
Frunze
Rybach'ye
Turkestan
Chulak-Tau
Dzhambul
Arys'
Chimkent
Tashkent
Namangan
Angren
Andizhan
Osh
Kokand
Fergana
Leninabad
Kashgar (Shufu)
Khodzheyli
Khiva
Begovat
Bukhara
Samarkand
Dyushambe
Khorog
Chardzhou
Falzabad
Kerki
Termez
Mary (Merv)
Ashkhabad
Kirovsk
Kishm
Gilgit
Chitral
Mazar-i-Sharif
Maimana
Mashhad
Kushka
Kabul
Jalalabad
Peshawar
Abbottabad
60°E
65°E
70°E
75°E
80°E
85°E
90°E
95°E
60°N
55°N
50°N
45°N
40°N
35°N
7315

Page 46
MIDDLE EAST
PAKISTAN
and INDIA
Scale 1:19,000,000 approx.
0 Kilometres 300 450 600
0 Miles 150 300
One Inch to 300 Miles
Towns over 1 million people
" over 100,000 people
Boundaries - international
- provincial etc.
Railways
projected
Airports
Sand desert
Marsh
Roads
track
Canal
Salt pan
Ice cap
Conical Orthomorphic Projection
30°E
35°E
45°E
50°E
55°E
60°E
65°E
40°N
35°N
25°N
20°N
15°N
5°N
200 metres
Tropic of Cancer
Black Sea
Mediterranean Sea
Caspian Sea
Aral Sea
Red Sea
The Gulf
Gulf of Oman
Gulf of Aden
Arabian Sea
Sea of Azov
TURKEY
SYRIA
LEBANON
ISRAEL
JORDAN
IRAQ
IRAN
(PERSIA)
KUWAIT
SAUDI ARABIA
BAHRAIN
QATAR
UNITED ARAB EMIRATES
OMAN
YEMEN
San'a
A.R.
YEMEN P.D.R.
EGYPT
SUDAN
ETHIOPIA
(ABYSSINIA)
DJIBOUTI
SOMALI REPUBLIC
KENYA
AFGHANISTAN
CYPRUS
U.S.S.R.
R.S.F.S.R.
UKRAINIAN S.S.R.
GEORGIAN S.S.R.
ARMENIAN S.S.R.
AZERBAYDZHAN S.S.R.
TURKMEN S.S.R.
UZBEK
KAZAKH
ROMANIA
BULGARIA
GREECE
Istanbul
Ankara
Izmir
Konya
Adana
Aleppo
Damascus
Beirut
Jerusalem
Amman
Baghdad
Basra
Kuwait
Tehrān
Eşfahān
(Isfahan)
Mashhad
Tabriz
Shīrāz
Kermān
Riyadh
Jidda
Mecca
Medina
Manama
Dauha
Muscat
Aden
Hodeida
Djibouti
Addis Ababa
Cairo
Alexandria
Port Said
Suez
Port Sudan
Baku
Tbilisi
Yerevan
Volgograd
Astrakhan
Rostov
Krasnodar
Ashkhabad
Krasnovodsk
Bukhara
Herat
Zāhedān
Bandar 'Abbās
Caucasus Mountains
Pontic Mountains
Taurus Mts.
Zagros Mts.
Alborz Mts.
Kopeh Dagh
Dasht-e Kavīr
Dasht-e Lūt
Nafud
Rub' al Khali
Hijaz
Asir
Hadramaut
Dhufar
Ogaden
Kara-Kum
Turanian Plain
Ust-Urt Plateau
Syrian Desert
Nubian Desert
Ethiopian Plateau
Socotra
(Yemen P.D.R.)
Kuria Muria Is.
Masira
Ras al Hadd
Str of Hormuz
Bab el Mandeb

S. S. R.
Kazakh Uplands
80°E
Ayaguz
85°E
90°E
Altai
MONGOLIA
Range
100°E
105°E
Gobi Desert
Mointy
Kounradskiy
Balkhash
Lake Balkhash
Andreyevka
Ebi Nor
Dzungaria
Urumchi (Tihwa)
Turfan
Qomul (Hami)
Paotow
(Yellow)
40°N
Ordos Plateau
Yin Shan
Hwang
Chu
Alma-Ata
Frunze
Rybach'ye
Issyk-Kul'
Tien Shan
Bagrach Kol
Ansi
Kiuchuan
Ala Shan
Yinchwan (Ningsia)
KIRGIZ S.S.R.
Osh
Fergana
Tarim
SINKIANG – UIGHUR
Takla Makan
AUTONOMOUS REGION
Nan Shan
Great Wall
Sining
Lanchow (Kaolan)
Tsing Hai (Koko Nor)
35°N
Fengsiang
Tsinling Shan
Tsaidam Swamps
Kashgar
Yarkand
Khotan
TADZHIK S.S.R.
Altyn Tagh
Amne Machen Shan
Bayan Kara Shan
Nancheng
Faizabad
Khorog
Pamirs
Kunlun Mountains
Jyekundo
Yangtze
Mekong
Nangchen Japo
Chengtu
Yaan
Red
30°N
Gilgit
Chitral
KASHMIR
Karakoram
Leh
Indus
Jalalabad
Khyber Pass
Peshawar
Srinagar
Rawalpindi
Islamabad
Jammu
Sialkot
Jhelum
Lahore
Amritsar
Faisalabad
Ravi
Multan
Sutlej
Simla
Patiala
Saharanpur
TIBET
Salween
Chamdo
Kangting
Batang (Paan)
Ipin
Basin
Hsichang
Nyenchen Tangtha Range
Lhasa
Tsangpo
Shigatse
Gyangtse
Everest 8847
Great Himalayan Range
NEPAL
Katmandu
SIKKIM
BHUTAN
Darjeeling
Dibrugarh
ASSAM
Naga Hills
Irrawaddy
Kunming (Yunnanfu)
25°N
Chengkiang
Huitse
Meerut
Moradabad
Bareilly
Shahjahanpur
Delhi
Ganges
Bikaner
Thar Desert
Agra
Jaipur
Jamuna
Lucknow
Kanpur
Ajmer
Gwalior
Jhansi
Jodhpur
Allahabad
Varanasi
Patna
Bhagalpur
Rangpur
Shillong
Brahmaputra
Sylhet
BANGLADESH
Dacca
Kohima
Imphal
Myitkyina
Tengchung
Bhamo
Indaw
Mawlaik
Bawdwin
Lashio
SHAN STATES
Shwebo
Mandalay
Chindwin
Chin Hills
Pakokku
Yenangyaung
Magwe
BURMA
LAOS
Houeisai
Luangprabang
Chiang Rai
Chiang Mai
Mekong
INDIA
Vindhya Range
Jabalpur
Jamshedpur
Howrah
Calcutta
Plassey
Sundarbans
Chittagong
Mouths of the Ganges
Hooghly
Ahmadabad
Vadodara
Indore
Rajkot
Narbada
Satpura Range
Nagpur
Mahanadi
Cuttack
Akyab
Arakan Yoma
Thayetmyo
Prome
Toungoo
Sittang
Salween
Uttaradit
Tak (Rahaeng)
G. of Cambay
Surat
Tapti
(BHARAT)
Cheduba
Pegu
Rangoon
Moulmein
Bassein
Gulf of Martaban
Pagoda Pt.
15°N
Ayutthaya
THAILAND
Bombay
Pune
Godavari
Eastern Ghats
Vishakhapatnam
Sholapur
Hyderabad
Kakinada
Krishna
Vijayawada
Western Ghats
Bay of Bengal
Tavoy
Krung Thep (Bangkok)
Mergui
Andaman Islands (India)
Andaman Sea
200 metres
Mergui Arch.
Chumphon
Isthmus of Kra
Deccan
Coromandel Coast
Madras
Bangalore
Arcot
Mysore
Mangalore
Malabar Coast
Lakshadweep (Laccadive Islands) (India)
Laccadive Sea
Nilgiri Hills
Pondicherry
Cauvery
Calicut
Palghat Gap
Tiruchirapalli
Palk Strait
Cochin
Phuket I.
Nicobar Islands (India)
OCEAN
Trincomalee
SRI LANKA
Kandy
2524
Colombo
Galle
Trivandrum
70°E
75°E
85°E
90°E
5°N
Kutaradja
Sumatra
MALDIVE ISLANDS
M.
4,800
3,000
1,800
900
450
300
180
90
Level
Depression

Page 48.
MIDDLE EAST
Scale 1:12,500,000 approx.
0 Kilometres 200 300 400
0 Miles 100 200 300
One Inch to 200 Miles
Towns over 1 million people
" over 100,000 people
Boundaries - international
" - provincial etc.
Railways
projected
Roads
track
Airports
Canal
Sand desert
Salt pan
Marsh
Ice cap
Mediterranean Sea
LIBYA
EGYPT
SUDAN
NORTHERN
KORDOFAN
DARFUR
CHAD REPUBLIC
ISRAEL
LEBANON
CYPRUS
GREECE
TURKEY
ITALY
YUGO
ALB.
Aegean Sea
Libyan Desert
Western Desert
Eastern Desert
Nubian Desert
Libyan Plateau
Qattara Depression
Serir of Kalanshu
Gilf Kebir Plateau
Tropic of Cancer
Lake Nasser
Sinai
Tripoli
Benghazi
Jebel el Akhdar
Gulf of Sidra
Tobruk
Alexandria
Cairo
Port Said
Suez
Aswân
Luxor
Wadi Halfa
Khartoum
Omdurman
Atbara
El Obeid
El Fasher
Istanbul
Ankara
Izmir
Athens
Crete
Rhodes
Nicosia
Beirut
Damascus
Haifa
Jaffa - Tel Aviv
Conical Orthomorphic Projection
Holy Land
Scale 1:2,500,000
0 Kilometres 30
0 Miles 20
One Inch to 40 Miles
Old Testament names thus, Gath
New Testament names thus, Cana
PHOENICIA
GALILEE
SAMARIA
EPHRAIM
JUDAEA
JUDAH
IDUMAEA
PHILISTIA
DECAPOLIS
GILEAD
AMMON
MOAB
EDOM
Sea of Galilee
Dead Sea
R. Jordan
Plain of Sharon
Tyre
Acre
Haifa
Nazareth
Caesarea
Joppa
Jerusalem
Bethlehem
Jericho
Hebron
Gaza
Beersheba
The Negeb

Caspian Sea
U. S. S. R.
TURKMEN S.S.R.
I R A N (PERSIA)
I R A Q
SAUDI ARABIA
The Gulf
Gulf of 'Oman
UNITED ARAB EMIRATES
OMAN
QATAR
BAHRAIN
KUWAIT
YEMEN A. R.
YEMEN P. D. R.
Arabian Sea
Gulf of Aden
AFGHANISTAN
Baghdād
Tehrān
Riyadh
Kuwait
Baku
Aden
Rub' al Khali
Nafud
Zagros Mountains
Alborz Mts.
Dasht-e Kavīr
Dasht-e Lūt
Ft.
M.
16,000
4,800
10,000
3,000
6,000
1,800
3,000
900
1,500
450
1,000
300
600
180
300
90
Sea Level
Land Depression

Page 50
FAR EAST
Scale 1:19,000,000 approx.
0 Kilometres 300 450 600
0 Miles 150 300 450
One Inch to 300 Miles
Towns over 1 million people
" over 100,000 people
Boundaries - international
provincial etc.
Railways
projected
Roads
track
Airports
Canal
Marsh
Ice cap
MONGOLIA
CHINA
JAPAN
U.S.S.R.
NORTH KOREA
SOUTH KOREA
INDIA
BURMA
TAIWAN (Formosa)
Gobi Desert
Altai Range
Sea of Japan
Yellow Sea
East China Sea
Po Hai (G. of Chihli)
Ryukyu (Nansei) Islands
200 metres
Tropic of Cancer
Formosa Strait
Limit of pack ice average maximum Jan.-Mar.
Gulf of Tartary
Ulan Bator
Peking (Peiping)
Tientsin
Tangshan
Shanghai
Nanking
Wuhan
Chungking
Chengtu
Canton
Hong Kong (Br.)
Victoria
Macao (Port.)
Harbin (Pinkiang)
Shenyang
Fushun
Anshan
Changchun
Kirin
Sian (Changan)
Lanchow (Kaolan)
Taiyüan (Yangku)
Tsinan
Tsingtao
Kaifeng
Chengchow
Suchow (Tungshan)
Hangchow
Foochow
Amoy
Swatow
Kunming (Yunnanfu)
Kweiyang (Kweichu)
Changsha
Nanchang
Lhasa
Vladivostok
Khabarovsk
Blagoveshchensk
Sapporo
Hakodate
Tokyo
Yokohama
Nagoya
Osaka
Kobe
Kyoto
Hiroshima
Shimonoseki
Kitakyushu
Nagasaki
Kagoshima
Seoul (Kyongsong)
Pyongyang
Pusan
Taegu
Taejon
Inchon
Taipeh
Kao-hsiung
Mandalay
Hanoi
Hokkaido
Honshu
Shikoku
Kyushu
Okinawa
Naha
Sakhalin (USSR)
Yellow
Hwang (Yellow)
Yangtze
Amur
Sungari
Mekong
Salween (Lu)
90°E
95°E
100°E
105°E
110°E
115°E
120°E
125°E
130°E
135°E
140°E
20°N
25°N
30°N
35°N
40°N
45°N

Philippine Sea
South China Sea
THAILAND
(Siam)
Rangoon
Moulmein
Uttaradit
Tak (Rahaeng)
Udon Thani
Gulf of Martaban
Ye
Tavoy
Krung Thep
(Bangkok)
Ayutthaya
Nakhon Ratchasima
Phanom Dongrak
Dawna Range
Mergui
Andaman Sea
Mergui Arch
Chanthaburi
Chumphon
Isthmus of Kra
Phuket I.
Gulf of Siam
Kompong Som
KAMPUCHEA
Tonle Lake
Angkor
Phnom Penh
Kratie
Vinh Loi
Ho Chi Minh City
(Saigon)
Phanrang
Da Nang
Hué
Savannakhet
Ubon
Mekong
VIETNAM
Range
Samah
Paracel Is. (China)
Songkhla
(Singora)
Alor Star
George Town
Penang
Taiping
Kota Bharu
2102
Ipoh
PENINSULAR MALAYA
Kuantan
Kuala Lumpur
Seremban
Strait of Malacca
Malacca
Johore Bahru
SINGAPORE
Bintan
Riau Archipelago
Lingga
Equator
Singkep
MALAYSIA
Medan
Nias
Batu Is.
Padang
Mentawai Is.
Sumatra
(Sumatera)
3800
Pakanbaru
Djambi
Bangka
Palembang
Enggano
Telukbetung
Krakatau
Sunda Strait
Djakarta
Bandung
Semarang
Surakarta
Jogjakarta
Surabaja
Madiun
Madura
Malang
Java
(Djawa)
Java Sea
Christmas I.
(Austl.)
Anambas Is.
(Indon.)
Bunguran Is. (Indon.)
(Natuna)
200 metres
Belitung
(Billiton)
Kuching
Serian
Simanggang
Sibu
SARAWAK
Seria
BRUNEI
Bandar Seri Begawan
Labuan
Weston
Kota Kinabalu
Kudat
Mt. Kinabalu
4101
SABAH
Sandakan
Tarakan
Borneo
(Kalimantan)
Müller Mts.
1999
Pontianak
Samarinda
Balikpapan
Strait of Makassar
Bandjarmasin
Laut
INDONESIA
Kangean Is.
Bali Sea
Singaradja
Bali
3142
Lombok Str.
Lombok
3726
Sumbawa
Flores Sea
Flores
Maumere
Lomblen
Pantar
Alor
Sumba
Waingapu
Sawu Sea
Sawu
Roti
Kupang
Timor
Dili
Wetar
Timor Sea
Luzon
Aparri
San Fernando
2930
Quezon City
Manila
Bataan Peninsula
Legaspi
Mindoro
Calamian Group
Palawan
THE PHILIPPINES
Samar
Leyte
Panay
Iloilo
Bacolod
Cebu
Negros
Bohol
Sulu Sea
2627
Mindanao
Davao
Zamboanga
Basilan
Jolo
Tawitawi
Celebes Sea
Talaud Is.
Manado
Gulf of Tomini
Celebes
(Sulawesi)
7458
Gulf of Tolo
3107
Gulf of Bone
Ujung Pandang
Muna
Butung
Kabaena
Molucca Sea
Sula Is.
Obi Is.
Morotai
Halmahera
Ternate
Moluccas
(Maluku)
Waigeo
Misoöl
Seram Sea
Seram
Buru
Amboina
Ambon
Banda Sea
Kai Is.
Aru Is.
Tanimbar Is.
Babar Is.
Arafura Sea
Doberai Peninsula
Manokwari
Biak
Japen
DJAYA PURA
New Guinea
Palau Is.
Caroline Islands
(U.S. Trust.)
Bathurst I.
Melville I.
AUSTRALIA
Ft. M.
16,000 4,800
10,000 3,000
6,000 1,800
3,000 900
1,500 450
1,000 300
600 180
300 90
Sea Level
Land Depression
15°N
10°N
5°N
5°S
10°S
110°E
115°E
120°E
125°E
Conical Orthomorphic Projection

Conical Orthomorphic Projection

CHINA
Scale 1:12,500,000 approx.
One Inch to 200 Miles
Railway gauges are not distinguished on the map of China
Conical Orthomorphic Projection

Page 54
130°E
135°E
140°E
45°N
40°N
35°N
JAPAN
Scale 1:6,300,000 approx.
0 Kilometres 100 150 200
0 Miles 50 100 150
One Inch to 100 Miles
POPULATION
of Japan
116 million approx.
(1979)
Zenithal Equidistant Projection
Copyright Oxford University Press
Sea of Japan
JAPAN
PACIFIC
HOKKAIDO
HONSHU
SHIKOKU
KYUSHU
CHINA
U. S. S. R.
NORTH KOREA
SOUTH KOREA
Lishuchen
Lake Khanka
Mutankiang
Mulingchen
Ningan
Grodekovo
Spassk Dal'niy
Sikhote Alin Range
Tetyukhe
Tetyukhe-Pristan'
Tungning
Ussuriisk
Ol'ga
Wangching
Artem
Margaritovo
1853
Suchan
Vladivostok
Hunchun
Yenki
Posyet
Nakhoda
Limit of pack ice average maximum (Feb.-Mar.)
200 metres
Hoeryong
Unggi
Chongjin
Kilchu
Songjin
Ullung Do.
Take Rks.
Ulchin
Yongdok
Pohang
Kyongju
Pusan
Korea Strait
Tsu Islands
Oki Is.
Rishiri
Embetsu
Asahikawa
Otaru
Ishikari
Sapporo
Suttsu
Tomakomai
Uchiura Bay
Muroran
Okushiri I.
Esashi
Hakodate
1072
Fukuyama
Tsugaru Channel
Ohata
Misawa
Aomori
Hachin
Hirosaki
Kosaka
Noshiro
2040
Morioka
Akita
Kitakami Mountains
Yokote
Ou Mts.
Sakata
Tsuruoka
Shinjo
Ishinom
Yamagata
Sendai
Sado
Yonezawa
Niigata
Shibata
Fukushima
2024
Sanjo
Nagaoka
Wakamatsu
Koriyama
Kashiwazaki
Shirakawa
Abukuma Mts.
Iwaki
Takada
Mikuni Mts.
Shinano
Wajima
Noto Peninsula
Nanao
2933
Nikko
Hitachi
Takaoka
Toyama
Nagano
Utsunomiya
Kanazawa
Maebashi
Kiryu
Mito
Takasaki
Hida Mts.
Matsumoto
Chichibu
Kawagoe
Urawa
Tone
Choshi
Fukui
2702
Tokyo
Chiba
Kofu
Hachioji
Kawasaki
3172
Yokohama
Akaishi Mts.
Fuji
1776
Boso Peninsula
Yokosuka
Omiya
Sagami Gulf
Tateyama
Numazu
Shizuoka
Kyoga Point
Wakasa Bay
Tsuruga
Matsue
Tottori
Gifu
Ogaki
Ichinomiya
Chugoku Mountains
L. Biwa
Nagoya
Tsuyama
Yokkaichi
Kyoto
Otsu
Okazaki
Anjo
Hamada
Okayama
Himeji
Osaka
Ueno
Ise Bay
Toyohashi
Kobe
Nara
Tsu
Hamamatsu
Kurashiki
Ise
Totomi Gulf
Harima Gulf
Osaka Bay
Hiroshima
Kure
Inland Sea
Sumoto
Takamatsu
Yamaguchi
Iwakuni
Tokushima
Wakayama
Izu Islands
Shimonoseki
Kitakyushu
Ube
Imabari
Kii Mts.
Kii Channel
1957
Suo Gulf
Nogata
Fukuoka
Takawa
Matsuyama
Iyo Gulf
Shikoku Mts.
Kochi
Tanabe
Shingu
Sakawa
Yawatahama
Hoyo Str.
Tosa Bay
Sasebo
Kurume
Oita
Usuki
Uwajima
C. Muroto
Shimabara G.
Omuta
1788
Nagasaki
Kumamoto
Shimabara
C. Ashizuri
Nobeoka
Kyushu Mts.
Yatsushiro B.
Minamata
Miyazaki
Kagoshima
Kanoya
Makurazaki

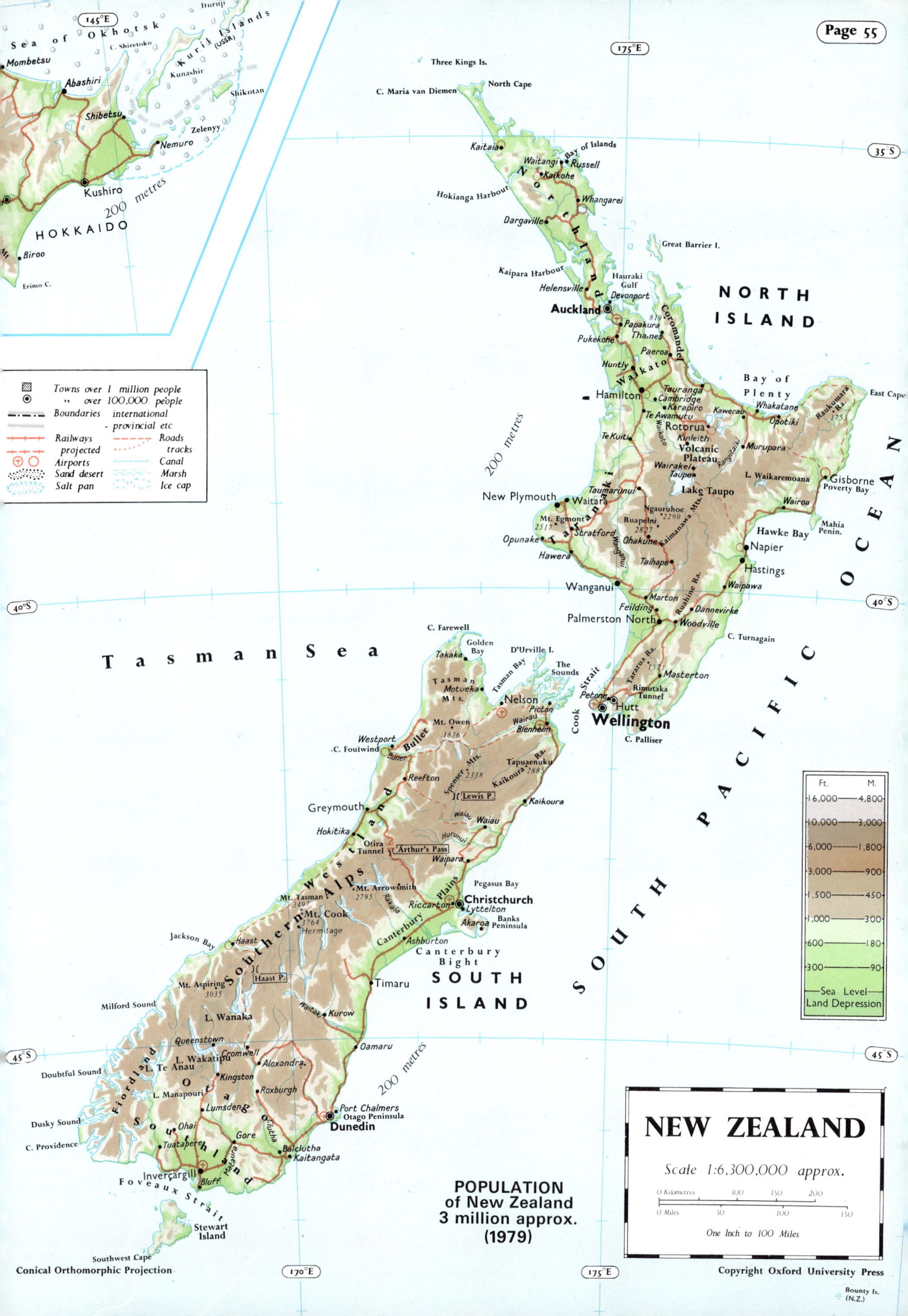
NEW ZEALAND
Scale 1:6,300,000 approx.
One Inch to 100 Miles
POPULATION of New Zealand 3 million approx. (1979)
Towns over 1 million people
,, over 100,000 people
Boundaries international
- provincial etc
Railways
projected
Roads
tracks
Airports
Canal
Sand desert
Marsh
Salt pan
Ice cap
NORTH ISLAND
SOUTH ISLAND
Tasman Sea
SOUTH PACIFIC OCEAN
Sea of Okhotsk
HOKKAIDO
Kuril Islands (USSR)
Auckland
Wellington
Christchurch
Dunedin
Hamilton
Conical Orthomorphic Projection

Australia and the Far East
POPULATION and COMMUNICATIONS
Scale 1:44,000,000 approx.
One Inch to 700 Miles
POPULATION DENSITY
10 people per sq. km. = 25 people per sq. mile approx.
Almost uninhabited (under 1 person per sq.km.)
Few inhabitants (1-10 people per sq. km.)
Moderately populated (10-50 people per sq. km.)
Thickly populated (50-200 people per sq. km.)
Very thickly populated (over 200 people per sq.km.)
TOWNS
Towns with over 100,000 but under 1 million inhabitants.
Towns with over 1 million inhabitants.
RAILWAYS
SHIPPING (by volume of traffic)
SEASONAL SHIPPING
Agriculture
1 "Western" mixed farming
2 Prairie farming-cereals
3 Irrigated areas in dry lands
4 Cattle or sheep ranching
5 Plantation agriculture
11 Non-agricultural land
MONGOLIA
MANCHURIA
U.S.S.R.
CHINA
KOREA
Sea of Japan
JAPAN
East China Sea
HONG KONG
TAIWAN
Tropic of Cancer
Philippine Sea
PACIFIC OCEAN
South China Sea
LAOS
VIETNAM
THAILAND
KAMPUCHEA
PHILIPPINE IS.
Sulu Sea
MALAYSIA
BRUNEI
SABAH
SARAWAK
Celebes Sea
PENINSULAR
SINGAPORE
KALIMANTAN
SULAWESI
Equator
INDONESIA
DJAYA PURA
PAPUA-NEW GUINEA
SOLOMON ISLANDS
Banda Sea
Java Sea
SUMATRA
JAVA
Arafura Sea
Timor Sea
Gulf of Carpentaria
Coral Sea
INDIAN OCEAN
NORTHERN TERRITORY
QUEENSLAND
WESTERN AUSTRALIA
SOUTH AUSTRALIA
AUSTRALIA
NEW SOUTH WALES
VICTORIA
TASMANIA
Great Australian Bight
Tasman Sea
NEW ZEALAND
VANUATU
NEW CALEDONIA
Tropic of Capricorn
Canada
U.S.A.
S. America
U.S.A. & Canada via Hawaii
America & Europe via Panama
India & Europe
Suez
closed 1967
Europe via the Cape
150°E
160°E
170°E
180°
40°N
30°N
20°N
10°N
10°S
20°S
30°S
40°S
100°E
110°E
120°E
Modified Zenithal Equidistant Projection

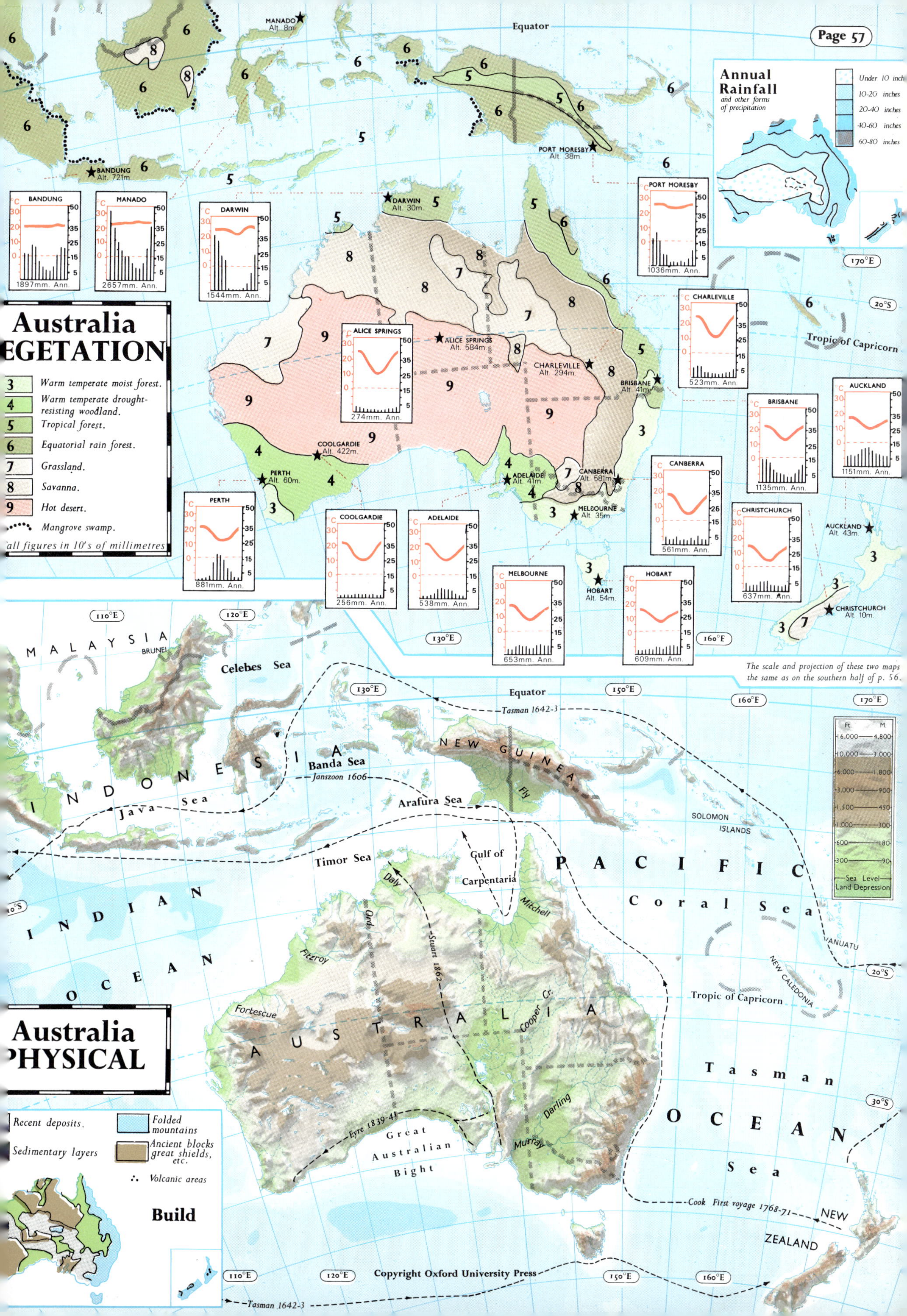
Australia
VEGETATION
3 Warm temperate moist forest.
4 Warm temperate drought-resisting woodland.
5 Tropical forest.
6 Equatorial rain forest.
7 Grassland.
8 Savanna.
9 Hot desert.
Mangrove swamp.
All figures in 10's of millimetres
Annual Rainfall
and other forms of precipitation
Under 10 inches
10-20 inches
20-40 inches
40-60 inches
60-80 inches
BANDUNG 1897mm. Ann.
MANADO 2657mm. Ann.
DARWIN 1544mm. Ann.
PORT MORESBY 1036mm. Ann.
CHARLEVILLE 523mm. Ann.
ALICE SPRINGS 274mm. Ann.
BRISBANE 1135mm. Ann.
AUCKLAND 1151mm. Ann.
CANBERRA 561mm. Ann.
PERTH 881mm. Ann.
COOLGARDIE 256mm. Ann.
ADELAIDE 538mm. Ann.
MELBOURNE 653mm. Ann.
HOBART 609mm. Ann.
CHRISTCHURCH 637mm. Ann.
MANADO Alt. 8m.
BANDUNG Alt. 721m.
PORT MORESBY Alt. 38m.
DARWIN Alt. 30m.
ALICE SPRINGS Alt. 584m.
CHARLEVILLE Alt. 294m.
BRISBANE Alt. 41m.
COOLGARDIE Alt. 422m.
PERTH Alt. 60m.
ADELAIDE Alt. 41m.
CANBERRA Alt. 581m.
MELBOURNE Alt. 35m.
HOBART Alt. 54m.
AUCKLAND Alt. 43m.
CHRISTCHURCH Alt. 10m.
Equator
Tropic of Capricorn
The scale and projection of these two maps the same as on the southern half of p. 56.
Australia
PHYSICAL
MALAYSIA
BRUNEI
Celebes Sea
Banda Sea
Janszoon 1606
INDONESIA
Java Sea
Arafura Sea
NEW GUINEA
Fly
Tasman 1642-3
SOLOMON ISLANDS
Timor Sea
Gulf of Carpentaria
PACIFIC
Coral Sea
VANUATU
NEW CALEDONIA
INDIAN OCEAN
Daly
Ord
Stuart 1862
Mitchell
Fitzroy
Fortescue
Cooper Cr.
AUSTRALIA
Tasman
OCEAN
Sea
Darling
Murray
Eyre 1839-41
Great Australian Bight
Cook First voyage 1768-71
NEW ZEALAND
Recent deposits.
Sedimentary layers
Folded mountains
Ancient blocks great shields, etc.
Volcanic areas
Build
Ft. M.
6,000 4,800
10,000 3,000
6,000 1,800
3,000 900
1,500 450
1,000 300
600 180
300 90
Sea Level
Land Depression
110°E
120°E
130°E
150°E
160°E
170°E
20°S
30°S

Page 58
AUSTRALASIA
Scale 1:22,000,000 approx.
0 Kilometres 350 525 700 850
0 Miles 200 350 525
One Inch to 350 Miles
Towns over 1 million people
,, over 100,000 people
Boundaries - international
- provincial etc.
Railways
projected
Roads
track
Sand desert
Marsh
Airports
Salt pan
Ft. M.
16,000 4,800
10,000 3,000
6,000 1,800
3,000 900
1,500 450
1,000 300
600 180
300 90
Sea Level
Land Depression
Zenithal Equidistant Projection
110°E
120°E
125°E
130°E
135°E
100°E
115°E
5°N
0°
5°S
10°S
15°S
20°S
25°S
30°S
40°S
45°S
Kota Bharu
PENINSULAR MALAYSIA
Kuantan
MALAYA
Malacca
Johore Bahru
SINGAPORE
Bintan
Lingga
Anambas Is. (Indon.)
Bunguran Is. (Natuna) (Indon.)
BRUNEI
Seria
SABAH
Sandakan
SARAWAK
Sibu
Kuching
Serian
Müller Mts.
Borneo (Kalimantan)
Pontianak
Samarinda
Balikpapan
Bandjarmasin
Laut
Belitung (Billiton)
Bangka
Djambi
Sumatra
3800
Palembang
Telukbetung
Enggano
Sunda Str.
Djakarta
Bandung
Semarang
Jogjakarta
Madiun
Surabaja
Malang
3676
Madura
Java (Djawa)
Java Sea
INDONESIA
Bali
Bali Sea
Lombok Str.
Lombok
3726
Kangean Is.
Sumbawa
Flores Sea
Flores
Sumba
Waingapu
Sawu Sea
Sawu
Kupang
Roti
Timor
Timor Sea
Dili
Pantar
Alor
Lomblen
Wetar
Banda Sea
Tanimbar Is.
Kai Is.
Aru Is.
Frederik Hendrik I.
C. Valsch
Arafura Sea
PHILIPPINE IS.
Tawitawi
Celebes Sea
200 metres
Strait of Makassar
Manado
Gulf of Tomini
Celebes (Sulawesi)
3106
Gulf of Tolo
Gulf of Bone
Ujung Pandang
Muna
Butung
Kabaena
Molucca Sea
Moluccas (Maluku)
Sula Is.
Obi Is.
Buru
Seram
Ambon
Misool
Talaud Is.
Morotai
Halmahera
Ternate
Caroline Is. (U.S. Trust.)
Manokwari
Biak
Japen
Doberai Peninsula
DJAYA
PURA
New
Nassau Mts.
Christmas I. (Austl.)
INDIAN OCEAN
Melville I.
Bathurst I.
Darwin
Rum Jungle
Arnhem Land
Daly
Katherine
Groote Eyland
C. Talbot
Joseph Bonaparte Gulf
Victoria
Wyndham
Ord
Birdum
Daly Waters
NORTHERN TERRITORY
Stuart
Barkly Tableland
Tennant Creek
Yampi Sound
C. Leveque
Dampier Land
Derby
Fitzroy
Halls Creek
Broome
80 Mile Beach
Great Sandy Desert
L. Mackay
Highway
Alice Springs
Macdonnell Ranges
Port Hedland
Monte Bello Is.
Dampier
Marble Bar
Fortescue
Exmouth Gulf
Hamersley Ra.
1226
Ashburton
Lake Disappointment
Gibson Desert
WESTERN AUSTRALIA
AUSTRALIA
1515
Oodnadatta
SOUTH AUSTRALIA
Carnarvon
Dirk Hartogs I.
Murchison
Wiluna
Great Victoria Desert
Mt. Magnet
Laverton
Mt. Eba
Nullarbor Plain
Forrest
Ooldea
L. Gairdner
Geraldton
Kalgoorlie
Zanthus
Eucla
Ceduna
Port Augusta
Coolgardie
Southern Cross
Northam
Perth
Fremantle
Esperance
Recherche Arch.
Great Australian Bight
Port Lincoln
C. Catastrophe
C. Naturaliste
Bunbury
1109
Albany
C. Leeuwin

Page 59
145°E
150°E
155°E
160°E
165°E
170°E
175°E
Equator
0°
5°S
10°S
15°S
20°S
25°S
30°S
35°S
40°S
45°S
140°E
P A C I F I C
O C E A N
Tarawa
KIRIBATI
Nauru
NAURU
Ocean I.
Pura
Manus
Admiralty Is.
Kavieng
Aitape
Wewak
New Ireland
Bismarck Archipelago
Rabaul
P A P U A - N E W G U I N E A
Madang
Central Ra.
New Britain
3106
Bougainville
Shortland Is.
Choiseul
SOLOMON ISLANDS
Finschhafen
Lae
Owen Stanley Ra.
3993
Fly
Gulf of Papua
Vella Lavella
New Georgia
Santa Ysabel
Vanguna
Malaita
Stewart Is.
TUVALU
Honiara
Guadalcanal
2440
Port Moresby
D'Entrecasteaux Is.
Ulawa
San Cristobal
Funafuti
Str.
C. York
Louisiade Arch.
Rennell I.
Santa Cruz Is.
Cherry I.
Mitre I.
Cape York Peninsula
Great Barrier Reef
C o r a l
S e a
Cooktown
Mitchell
Cairns
Gilbert
Herberton
Forsayth
Norman
Townsville
Espiritu Santo
Malekula
VANUATU
Vila
Efate
Erromanga
Loyalty Is. (Fr.)
Vanua Levu
FIJI
Viti Levu
Suva
Lau Group
Chesterfield Is. (Fr.)
Charters Towers
Hughenden
Mackay
Winton
New Caledonia (Fr.)
Nouméa
Rockhampton
Mt. Morgan
Gladstone
Longreach
Barcoo
Tropic of Capricorn
Yaraka
Bundaberg
Maryborough
Charleville
Great Dividing Range
Quilpie
Creek
Darling Downs
Toowoomba
Brisbane
Ipswich
Cunnamulla
Lismore
Grafton
Bourke
Norfolk I. (Austl.)
Darling
NEW SOUTH WALES
Broken Hill
Tamworth
1494
Dubbo
520
Maitland
1274
Newcastle
Lachlan
Orange
Lithgow
Katoomba
Sydney
Wollongong
Mildura
Murray
Murrumbidgee
Goulburn
Swan Hill
Riverina
Echuca
Canberra
Albury
Australian Alps
Mt. Kosciusko 2233
VICTORIA
Bendigo
1167
Ballarat
Geelong
Gippsland
Orbost
Cape Howe
Melbourne
T a s m a n
S e a
North Cape
Kaikohe
Auckland
Hamilton
NORTH ISLAND
New Plymouth
Gisborne
2827
Napier
Palmerston N.
King I.
Bass Strait
Furneaux Group
Burnie
1573
Mt. Lyell
St. Marys
Launceston
TASMANIA
Hobart
Cook Strait
Nelson
Westport
Greymouth
SOUTH ISLAND
Wellington
NEW ZEALAND
Mt. Cook 3764
Southern Alps
Christchurch
Invercargill
Stewart I.
Dunedin
Copyright Oxford University Press

South-West
AUSTRALIA
SAME SCALE
WESTERN AUSTRALIA
INDIAN OCEAN
SOUTH
QUEENSLAND
Coral Sea
Great Barrier Reef
Great Dividing Range
Darling Downs
Tropic of Capricorn
200 metres
115°E
120°E
150°E
20°S
25°S
30°S
35°S
Cue
Mt. Magnet
Greenough
Ajana
Northampton
Mullewa
Geraldton
Houtman Abrolhos
Dongara
Three Springs
Lake Barlee
Laverton
Leonora
Menzies
Kalgoorlie
Boulder
Coolgardie
Koolyanobbing
Southern Cross
Goomalling
Cunderdin
Merredin
Swan
Northam
Perth
Midland
Rottnest I.
Fremantle
Kwinana
Darling Ra.
Narrogin
Bunbury
Collie
Wagin
Newdegate
Lake Cowan
Norseman
Cap Naturaliste
Busselton
Boyup Brook
Katanning
Blackwood
Bridgetown
Augusta
Cape Leeuwin
Northcliffe
Stirling Ra.
Hood Point
Esperance
Recherche Archipelago
Point D'Entrecasteaux
Nornalup
Albany
Flinders Reef
Abington Reef
Palm Is.
Flinders Passage
Magnetic I.
Townsville
C. Bowling Green
Ayr
Home Hill
Marion Reef
Merinda
Hook I.
Whitsunday I.
Ravenswood
Burdekin
Proserpine
Shaw I.
Repulse B.
Cumberland Is.
Leichhardt Ra.
Owens Creek
Clarke Ra.
Mackay
Northumberland Islands
Percy Is.
Swain Reefs
Suttor
Belyando
Denham Ra.
Broad Sd.
Long I.
Shoalwater B.
Townshend I.
Capricorn Channel
Port Clinton
C. Manifold
Clermont
Marlborough
Fitzroy
Mackenzie
Emerald
Rockhampton
Gt. Keppel I.
Keppel B.
Capricorn Group
Curtis Channel
Mount Morgan
Gladstone
Lady Elliot I.
Springsure
Expedition Ra.
Dawson
Jambin
Nagoorin
Lawgi
Moura
Buckland Tableland
Tambo
Carnarvon Ra.
Burnett Heads
Sandy Cape
Bundaberg
Hervey Bay
Childers
Burnett
Maryborough
Fraser or Great Sandy I.
Taroom
Augathella
Lake Yamma Yamma
Simpson Desert
Bulloo
Quilpie
Charleville
Mitchell
Roma
Boyne
Gympie
Murgon
Kingaroy
Nanango
Nambour
Eromanga
Chinchilla
Condamine
Surat
Glenmorgan
Cabawin
Dalby
Redcliffe
Crow's Nest
Moreton Bay
Brisbane
Sandgate
Toowoomba
Ipswich
N. Stradbroke I.
Leyburn
Cooper Creek
Innamincka
Wilson
Noccundra
Warrego
Cunnamulla

Eastern
AUSTRALIA
Scale 1:6,300,000 approx.
0 Kilometres 100 150 200
0 Miles 50 100 150
One Inch to 100 Miles
Towns over 1 million people
" over 100,000 people
Boundaries - international
- provincial etc
3' 6" 4' 8½" 5' 3" Railways
projected
Airports
Sand desert
Roads
tracks
Canal
Marsh
Salt pan
Ft. M.
6,000 4,800
10,000 3,000
6,000 1,800
3,000 900
1,500 450
1,000 300
600 180
300 90
Sea Level
Land Depression
NEW SOUTH WALES
SOUTH AUSTRALIA
VICTORIA
Great Dividing Range
Great Valley
Gippsland
Riverina
Flinders Range
Main Barrier Range
New England Ra.
Hastings Ra.
Hunter Ra.
Blue Mts.
Gourock Ra.
Australian Alps
Snowy Mts.
Mt. Kosciusko 2233
Mt. Hotham 1860
Barry Mts.
The Grampians 1167
Mt. Lofty Ra.
Liverpool Plains
Lake Eyre South
Lake Torrens
L. Frome
L. Bancannia
L. Menindee
L. Tandou
Traveller's L.
L. Cowal
L. George
L. Alexandrina
L. Hume
L. Eildon
Wyangala Res.
Burrinjuck Res.
Caryapundy Swamp
Darling
Murray
Murrumbidgee
Lachlan
Macquarie
Barwon
Namoi
Bland
Hunter
Macleay
Clarence
Severn
Ovens
Mitchell
Snowy
Tumut
Hopkins
Yarra
Marree
Leigh Creek
Brachina
Hawker
Bookaloo
Quorn
Port Augusta
Iron Knob
Whyalla
Port Pirie
Peterborough
Gladstone
Burra
Clare
Wallaroo
Kadina
Balaklava
Eudunda
Waikerie
Renmark
Berri
Gawler
Elizabeth
Salisbury
Port Adelaide
Adelaide
Murray Bridge
Meribah
Peebinga
Pinnaroo
Kingston
Naracoorte
Bordertown
Beachport
Millicent
Mt. Gambier
Callabonna
Milparinka
Urisino
Wanaaring
Yantabulla
Angledool
Bourke
Cobar
Barnato
Nyngan
Wilcannia
Purnamoota
Silverton
Broken Hill
Menindee
Pooncarie
Ivanhoe
Mossgiel
Roto
Hillston
Wentworth
Mildura
Red Cliffs
Morkalla
Balranald
Hay
Griffith
Leeton
Narrandera
Temora
Wyalong
Condobolin
Parkes
Forbes
Cowra
Young
Cootamundra
Junee
Wagga Wagga
Yass
Goulburn
Canberra
A.C.T.
Queanbeyan
Holbrook
Albury
Adaminaby
Cooma
Nimmitabel
Bega
Deniliquin
Tocumwal
Moree
Walgett
Narrabri
Barraba
Inverell
Glen Innes
Tenterfield
Grafton
Coff's Harbour
Armidale
Macksville
Kempsey
Gunnedah
Tamworth
Nundle
Port Macquarie
Taree
Coonamble
Gilgandra
Dubbo
Wellington
Mudgee
Kandos
Muswellbrook
Singleton
Maitland
Cessnock
Newcastle
Belmont
Gosford
Orange
Bathurst
Lithgow
Katoomba
Penrith
Jenolan Caves
Parramatta
Liverpool
Sydney
Port Jackson
Botany Bay
Cronulla
Bulli
Wollongong
Port Kembla
Shoalhaven
Jervis Bay
Sugarloaf Pt.
Cape Howe
C. Everard
Orbost
Bairnsdale
Sale
Yallourn
Warragul
Korumburra
Wonthaggi
90 Mile Beach
Wangaratta
Benalla
Shepparton
Whitfield
Mansfield
Kilmore
Echuca
Picola
Kerang
Swan Hill
Nyahwest
Yungera
Ouyen
Warracknabeal
Charlton
Bendigo
Castlemaine
Maryborough
Ballarat
Ararat
Horsham
Dimboola
Nhill
Morea
Edenhope
Glenelg
Hamilton
Melbourne
Port Philip Bay
Geelong
Colac
Warrnambool
Portland
C. Otway
South East Point
Bass Strait
Tasmania 150 miles
200 metres
Spencer Gulf
Gulf St. Vincent
Yorke Peninsula
C. Spencer
Investigator Str.
Kangaroo I.
Encounter Bay
C. Willoughby
The Coorong
C. Jaffa
30°S
35°S
140°E
145°E
150°E
Transverse Mercator Projection
Copyright Oxford University Press

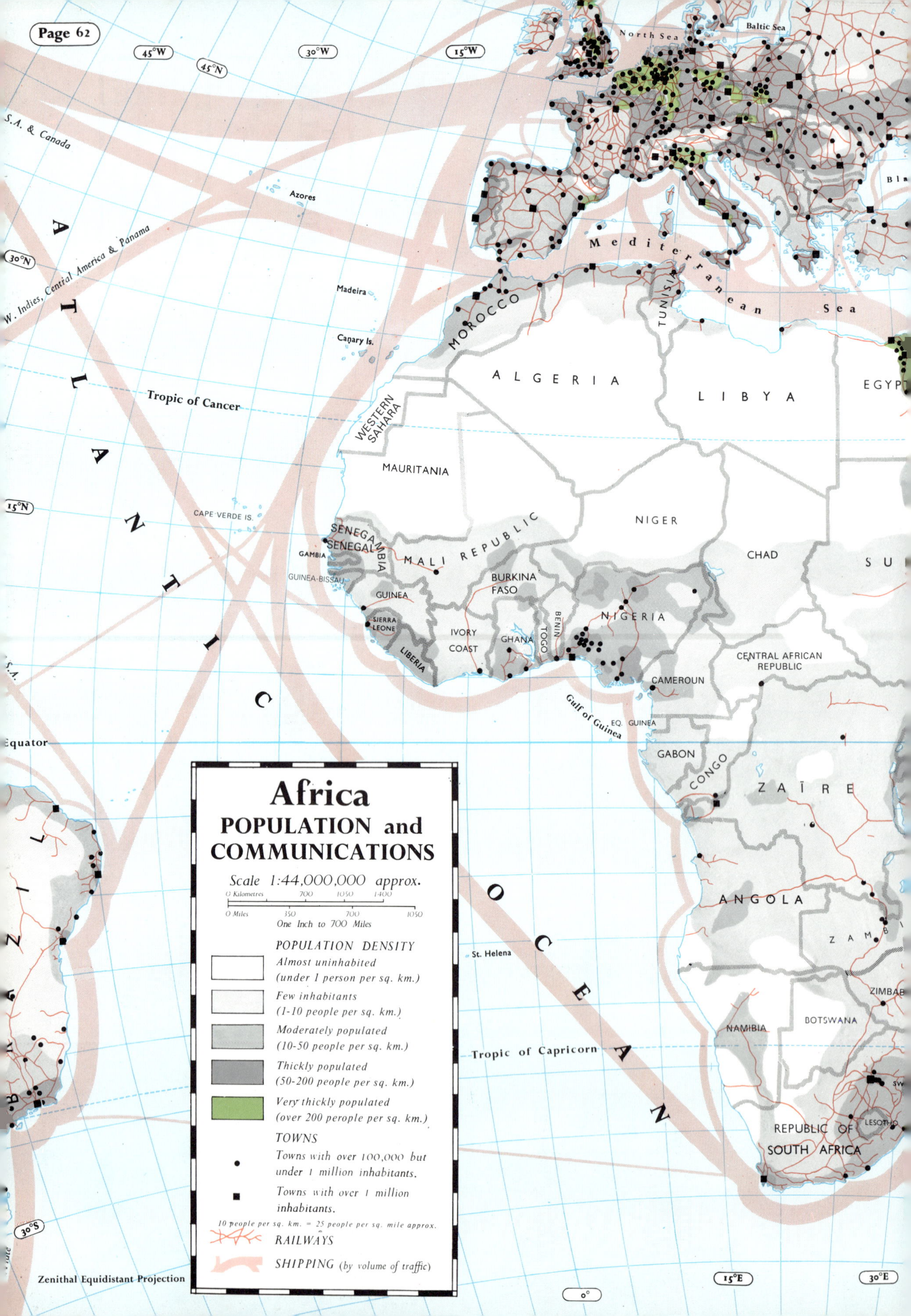

Africa
POPULATION and COMMUNICATIONS
Scale 1:44,000,000 approx.
0 Kilometres 700 1050 1400
0 Miles 350 700 1050
One Inch to 700 Miles
POPULATION DENSITY
Almost uninhabited (under 1 person per sq. km.)
Few inhabitants (1-10 people per sq. km.)
Moderately populated (10-50 people per sq. km.)
Thickly populated (50-200 people per sq. km.)
Very thickly populated (over 200 perople per sq. km.)
TOWNS
Towns with over 100,000 but under 1 million inhabitants.
Towns with over 1 million inhabitants.
10 people per sq. km. = 25 people per sq. mile approx.
RAILWAYS
SHIPPING (by volume of traffic)
Zenithal Equidistant Projection
45°W
30°W
15°W
0°
15°E
30°E
45°N
30°N
15°N
30°S
Equator
Tropic of Cancer
Tropic of Capricorn
ATLANTIC OCEAN
North Sea
Baltic Sea
Mediterranean Sea
Gulf of Guinea
Azores
Madeira
Canary Is.
Cape Verde Is.
St. Helena
U.S.A. & Canada
W. Indies, Central America & Panama
MOROCCO
ALGERIA
TUNISIA
LIBYA
EGYPT
WESTERN SAHARA
MAURITANIA
MALI REPUBLIC
NIGER
CHAD
SENEGAMBIA
SENEGAL
GAMBIA
GUINEA-BISSAU
GUINEA
SIERRA LEONE
LIBERIA
IVORY COAST
BURKINA FASO
GHANA
TOGO
BENIN
NIGERIA
CAMEROUN
CENTRAL AFRICAN REPUBLIC
EQ. GUINEA
GABON
CONGO
ZAÏRE
ANGOLA
NAMIBIA
BOTSWANA
REPUBLIC OF SOUTH AFRICA
LESOTHO

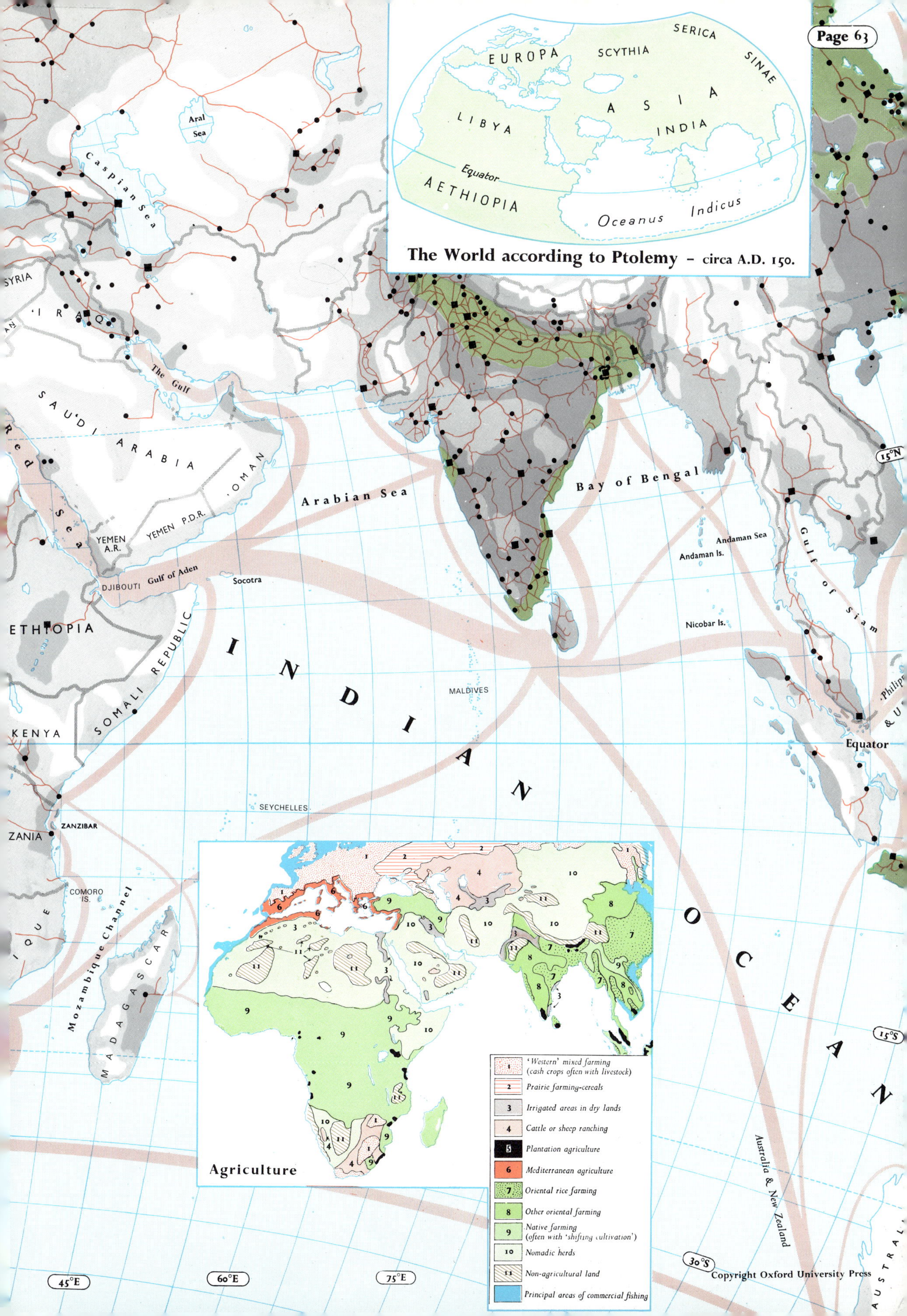

EUROPA
SCYTHIA
SERICA
SINAE
ASIA
LIBYA
INDIA
Equator
AETHIOPIA
Oceanus Indicus
The World according to Ptolemy – circa A.D. 150.
Aral Sea
Caspian Sea
SYRIA
'IRAQ
The Gulf
SAUDI ARABIA
Red Sea
OMAN
YEMEN P.D.R.
YEMEN A.R.
DJIBOUTI
Gulf of Aden
Socotra
Arabian Sea
Bay of Bengal
Andaman Sea
Andaman Is.
Nicobar Is.
Gulf of Siam
15°N
ETHIOPIA
SOMALI REPUBLIC
KENYA
INDIAN OCEAN
MALDIVES
Equator
SEYCHELLES
ZANZIBAR
COMORO IS.
Mozambique Channel
MADAGASCAR
15°S
30°S
45°E
60°E
75°E
Australia & New Zealand
Agriculture
'Western' mixed farming (cash crops often with livestock)
Prairie farming-cereals
Irrigated areas in dry lands
Cattle or sheep ranching
Plantation agriculture
Mediterranean agriculture
Oriental rice farming
Other oriental farming
Native farming (often with 'shifting cultivation')
Nomadic herds
Non-agricultural land
Principal areas of commercial fishing

Africa
PHYSICAL
Scale 1:44,000,000 approx.
0 Kilometres 700 1050 1400
0 Miles 350 700 1050
One Inch to 700 Miles
Ft M
16,000 5,000
10,000 3,000
6,000 1,800
3,000 900
1,500 450
1,000 300
600 180
300 90
Sea Level
Land Depression
Continental Shelf
600 180
6,000 1,800
12,000 3,600
18,000 5,400
24,000 7,200
Zenithal Equal-Area Projection
Build
Recent deposits
Sedimentary layers
Folded mountains
Re-elevated blocks
Ancient blocks, great shields, etc.
Volcanic plains & plateaux
Main volcanic areas
Mean Annual Rainfall
ins mm
under 10 under 250
10-20 250-507
20-40 507-1015
40-60 1015-1500
60-80 1500-2000
80-100 2000-2500
over 100 over 2500
PORTUGAL
SPAIN
Ebro
ITALY
GREECE
Danube
Black Sea
U. S. S. R.
Caspian Sea
TURKEY
Mediterranean Sea
TUNISIA
MOROCCO
ALGERIA
LIBYA
EGYPT
SYRIA
LEB
ISR
JORDAN
Tigris
Euphrates
IRAQ
IRAN (PERSIA)
KUWAIT
The Gulf
SA'UDI ARABIA
Red Sea
Nile
Dra
WESTERN SAHARA
MAURITANIA
Tropic of Cancer
Senegal
SENEGAL
SENEGAMBIA
GAMBIA
GUINEA-BISSAU
GUINEA
Niger
Mungo Park 1805
MALI REPUBLIC
NIGER
CHAD
SUDAN
Atbara
Bruce 1768
YEMEN A.R.
YEMEN P.D.R.
Gulf of Aden
DJIBOUTI
BURKINA FASO
SIERRA LEONE
LIBERIA
IVORY COAST
GHANA
Volta
TOGO
BENIN
NIGERIA
Mungo Park drowned
Benue
Lake Chad Basin
Chari
White Nile
Blue Nile
ETHIOPIA
SOMALI REPUBLIC
Shibeli
Juba
CENTRAL AFRICAN REPUBLIC
Marchand 1898
CAMEROUN
EQ GUINEA
GABON
CONGO
Oubangui
Congo
Uele
Equator
ZAÏRE
Kasai
UGANDA
KENYA
Speke & Grant 1861
RWANDA
BURUNDI
TANZANIA
Stanley & Livingstone met, 1871
Livingstone 1866
Lualaba
Livingstone died 1873
MALAWI
Ruvuma
ANGOLA
ZAMBIA
Zambezi
Livingstone 1853-56
MOZAMBIQUE
MADAGASCAR
Cubango
NAMIBIA
BOTSWANA
ZIMBABWE
Tropic of Capricorn
Limpopo
Livingstone 1849-51
Vaal
SWAZILAND
Orange
REPUBLIC OF SOUTH AFRICA
LESOTHO
ATLANTIC OCEAN
Gulf of Guinea
Vasco da Gama Round Africa to India & back, 1497-99
INDIAN OCEAN
To & from
35°N
30°N
25°N
20°N
15°N
10°N
5°N
5°S
10°S
15°S
20°S
25°S
30°S
15°W
10°W
5°W
0°
5°E
10°E
15°E
30°E
35°E
40°E
45°E
50°E

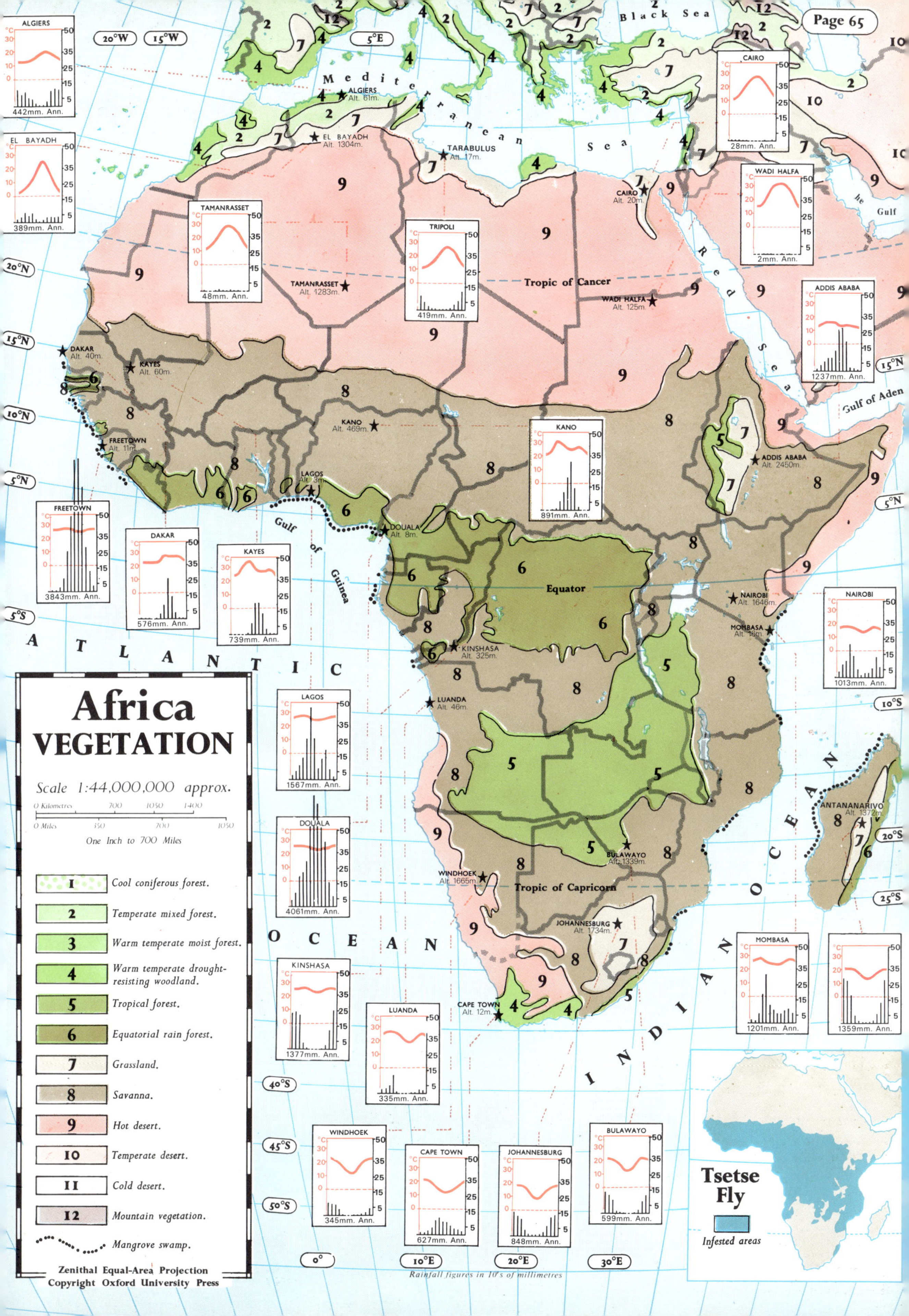

Africa
VEGETATION
Scale 1:44,000,000 approx.
One Inch to 700 Miles
1 Cool coniferous forest.
2 Temperate mixed forest.
3 Warm temperate moist forest.
4 Warm temperate drought-resisting woodland.
5 Tropical forest.
6 Equatorial rain forest.
7 Grassland.
8 Savanna.
9 Hot desert.
10 Temperate desert.
11 Cold desert.
12 Mountain vegetation.
Mangrove swamp.
Zenithal Equal-Area Projection
Mediterranean Sea
Black Sea
Red Sea
Gulf of Aden
Gulf of Guinea
ATLANTIC OCEAN
INDIAN OCEAN
Tropic of Cancer
Equator
Tropic of Capricorn
ALGIERS Alt. 61m.
EL BAYADH Alt. 1304m.
TARABULUS Alt. 17m.
CAIRO Alt. 20m.
TAMANRASSET Alt. 1283m.
WADI HALFA Alt. 125m.
DAKAR Alt. 40m.
KAYES Alt. 60m.
FREETOWN Alt. 11m.
KANO Alt. 469m.
LAGOS Alt. 3m.
ADDIS ABABA Alt. 2450m.
DOUALA Alt. 8m.
NAIROBI Alt. 1646m.
MOMBASA Alt. 16m.
KINSHASA Alt. 325m.
LUANDA Alt. 46m.
ANTANANARIVO Alt. 1372m.
BULAWAYO Alt. 1339m.
WINDHOEK Alt. 1665m.
JOHANNESBURG Alt. 1734m.
CAPE TOWN Alt. 12m.
ALGIERS 442mm. Ann.
EL BAYADH 389mm. Ann.
TAMANRASSET 48mm. Ann.
TRIPOLI 419mm. Ann.
CAIRO 28mm. Ann.
WADI HALFA 2mm. Ann.
ADDIS ABABA 1237mm. Ann.
KANO 891mm. Ann.
FREETOWN 3843mm. Ann.
DAKAR 576mm. Ann.
KAYES 739mm. Ann.
NAIROBI 1013mm. Ann.
LAGOS 1567mm. Ann.
DOUALA 4061mm. Ann.
KINSHASA 1377mm. Ann.
LUANDA 335mm. Ann.
MOMBASA 1201mm. Ann.
1359mm. Ann.
WINDHOEK 345mm. Ann.
CAPE TOWN 627mm. Ann.
JOHANNESBURG 848mm. Ann.
BULAWAYO 599mm. Ann.
Tsetse Fly
Infested areas
Rainfall figures in 10's of millimetres

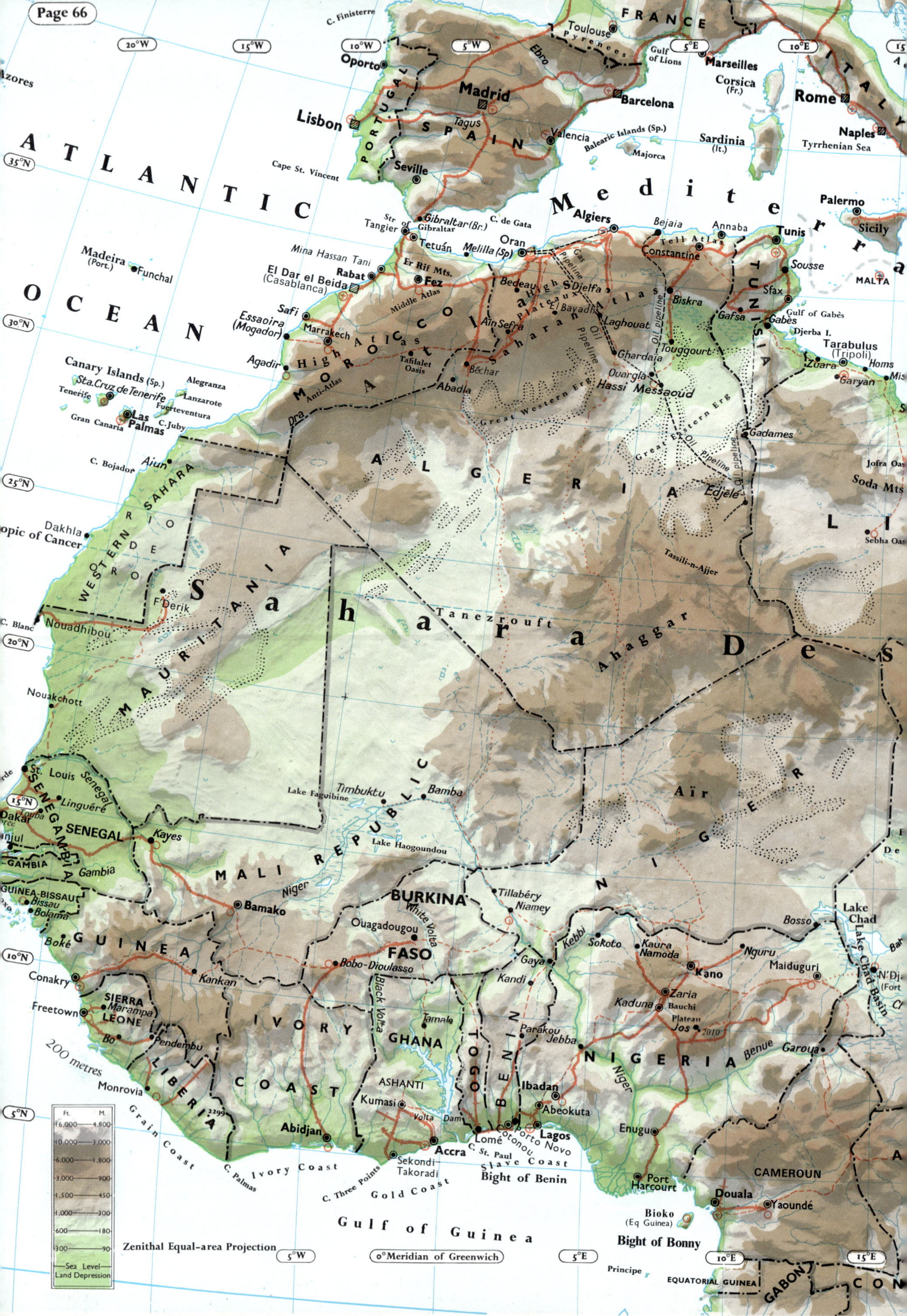

ATLANTIC OCEAN
Mediterra
Sahara Des
20°W
15°W
10°W
5°W
5°E
10°E
35°N
30°N
25°N
20°N
15°N
10°N
5°N
C. Finisterre
FRANCE
Toulouse
Pyrenees
Gulf of Lions
Marseilles
ITALY
Azores
Oporto
PORTUGAL
Madrid
Ebro
Barcelona
Corsica (Fr.)
Rome
Lisbon
Tagus
SPAIN
Valencia
Balearic Islands (Sp.)
Majorca
Sardinia (It.)
Naples
Tyrrhenian Sea
Cape St. Vincent
Seville
Str. of Gibraltar
Gibraltar (Br.)
C. de Gata
Tangier
Tetuán
Melilla (Sp.)
Oran
Algiers
Bejaia
Annaba
Tell Atlas
Constantine
Tunis
Palermo
Sicily
Sousse
MALTA
Madeira (Port.)
Funchal
Mina Hassan Tani
Rabat
El Dar el Beida (Casablanca)
Er Rif Mts.
Fez
Middle Atlas
Bedeau
High Plateaux
Djelfa
El Bayadh
Biskra
Gas Pipeline
TUNISIA
Sfax
Gafsa
Gulf of Gabès
Gabès
Djerba I.
Safi
Essaoira (Mogador)
Marrakech
MOROCCO
High Atlas
Tafilalet Oasis
Aïn Sefra
Saharan Atlas
Laghouat
Oil Pipeline
Touggourt
Ghardaia
Tarabulus (Tripoli)
Zuara
Homs
Garyan
Agadir
Anti-Atlas
Béchar
Abadla
Ouargla
Hassi Messaoud
Canary Islands (Sp.)
Sta. Cruz de Tenerife
Tenerife
Alegranza
Lanzarote
Fuerteventura
Las Palmas
Gran Canaria
C. Juby
Dra
Great Western Erg
Great Eastern Erg
Oil pipeline
Gadames
C. Bojador
Aiun
ALGERIA
Jofra Oas
Soda Mts
Edjelé
LI
Dakhla
Tropic of Cancer
WESTERN SAHARA
RIO DE ORO
Sebha Oas
Tassili-n-Ajjer
MAURITANIA
F'Derik
C. Blanc
Nouadhibou
Tanezrouft
Ahaggar
Nouakchott
St. Louis
Senegal
Linguéré
SENEGAMBIA
Dakar
SENEGAL
Kayes
GAMBIA
Gambia
Lake Faguibine
Timbuktu
Bamba
REPUBLIC
Lake Haogoundou
MALI
Niger
Aïr
NIGER
Lake Chad
GUINEA-BISSAU
Bissau
Bolama
Bamako
BURKINA
Tillabéry
Niamey
White Volta
Ouagadougou
FASO
Bosso
Boké
GUINEA
Kebbi
Sokoto
Kaura Namoda
Nguru
Maiduguri
Conakry
Kankan
Bobo-Dioulasso
Gaya
Kandi
Kano
SIERRA LEONE
Freetown
Marampa
Bo
Pendembu
IVORY COAST
Black Volta
Tamale
GHANA
TOGO
BENIN
Parakou
Jebba
Zaria
Kaduna
Bauchi Plateau
Jos
NIGERIA
Benue
Garoua
200 metres
Monrovia
LIBERIA
ASHANTI
Kumasi
Volta
Dam
Ibadan
Abeokuta
Lagos
Porto Novo
Cotonou
Lomé
Enugu
Grain Coast
Abidjan
Accra
C. St. Paul
Slave Coast
Bight of Benin
C. Palmas
Ivory Coast
C. Three Points
Sekondi-Takoradi
Gold Coast
Port Harcourt
CAMEROUN
Douala
Yaoundé
Bioko (Eq Guinea)
Bight of Bonny
Gulf of Guinea
Zenithal Equal-area Projection
0° Meridian of Greenwich
Principe
EQUATORIAL GUINEA
GABON
Ft.
M.
16,000
4,800
10,000
3,000
6,000
1,800
3,000
900
1,500
450
1,000
300
600
180
300
90
Sea Level
Land Depression

N. AFRICA
Aden to Dakar
Scale 1:19,000,000 approx.
0 Kilometres 300 450 600
0 Miles 150 300 450
One Inch to 300 Miles
Towns over 1 million people
,, over 100,000 people
Boundaries - international
- provincial etc
Railways
projected
Roads
tracks
Airports
Canal
Sand desert
Marsh
Salt pan
Ice cap
Suez Canal
174km. long including approaches (actual canal 163km). Minimum depth 10m., minimum width 60m. Time of passage 13 hrs. It is level throughout and therefore has no locks.
The canal was opened in 1869, taken over by Egypt in 1956 It was closed by war in 1967 and reopened in 1975 In 1978 21 999 Vessels passed through the canal
SCALE
1cm to 15km. approx.
1" to 24 miles approx
This map has been made at the same scale as that of the Panama Canal, on page 83
Damietta
To Gibraltar 1915 n. miles
Lake Manzala
Port Said
Port Fuad
Bay of Pelusium
El Matariya
El Qantara
El Ballâh
El Firdân
(Swing Br.)
To Cairo 129km.
Ismailia
Moascar
Tell el Kebir
Sweetwater canal
Lake Timsah
Great Bitter Lake
Fayid
Little Bitter Lake
Gineifa
Suez
El Shatt
Port Taufîq
To Aden 1305 n. mls.
ROMANIA
Bucharest
Belgrade
Sevastopol
U.S.S.R.
Black Sea
Danube
Varna
Sofia
BULGARIA
YUGOSLAVIA
Skopje
Tirane
ALBANIA
Salonica
GREECE
Aegean Sea
Istanbul
Zonguldak
Sinop
Samsun
Batumi
Erzurum
Ankara
TURKEY
Afyonkarahisar
Kayseri
Malatya
Izmir
Athens
Adana
Aleppo
Euphrates
Rhodes
Nicosia
CYPRUS
Famagusta
SYRIA
Iraklion
Crete
LEBANON
Beirut
Damascus
IRAQ
ISRAEL
Amman
JORDAN
Dead Sea
Jerusalem
Gaza
Mediterranean Sea
200 metres
Beida
Benghazi
Tobruk
Rosetta
Damietta
Alexandria
Port Said
Suez Canal
Ismailia
Suez
El 'Alamein
Libyan Plateau
Cairo
Pyramids
Memphis
Qattara Depression
-134
Siwa
El Faiyûm
Sinai
2641
Eilat
'Aqaba
Oil Pipeline
Ras Lanuf
Gulf of Suez
Red Sea Hills
Barrage
Asyut
Qasr Farafra
EGYPT
Girga
Thebes
Luxor
Isna
Dakhla Oasis
El Khârga
Libyan Desert
Kufra Oases
Aswân
1st. Cataract
Aswân Dam
Foul Bay
Lake Nasser
Wadi Halfa
2nd. Cataract
Nile
Nubian Desert
SA'UDI ARABIA
Yanbu'
Jidda
Mecca
Red Sea
Port Sudan
Suakin
3rd. Cataract
4th. Cataract
5th. Cataract
Berber
Atbara
Ed Damer
Koussi
3415
6th. Cataract
Omdurman
Khartoum
Jebel Aulia Dam
Kassala
Agordat
Tessenei
Asmara
Massawa
Kamaran Is. (S.Yemen)
YEMEN
Sa'na
P.D.R. YEMEN
Mukalla
SUDAN
Gezira
Wad Medani
Aduwa
Aden
As Shaab
Assab
Bab el Mandeb
G. of Aden
C. Guardafui
El Fasher
El Obeid
Sennar Dam
Gondar
Marra Mts.
KORDOFAN
DARFUR
Nyala
BLUE NILE
White Nile
Roseires
Lake Tana
DJIBOUTI
Djibouti
Zeila
Berbera
Erigavo
Blue Nile
Diredawa
Harar
Hargeisa
Fashoda
Malakal
Ethiopian Plateau
Addis Ababa
Awash
ETHIOPIA
(ABYSSINIA)
Haud
Gore
Ginir
Ogaden
BAHR EL GHAZAL
Jur
Sudd
Bahr el Jebel (White Nile)
Wau
CENTRAL AFRICAN REPUBLIC
Jonglei
Shibeli
SOMALI REPUBLIC
Obbia
Juba
Nimule
Lake Turkana
East Rift Valley
Mega
Moyale
Mobaye
Zongo
Oubangui
Bondo
ZAÏRE
Komba
Isiro
Mungbere
UGANDA
Lake Albert
KENYA
Juba
Mogadiscio
Equator
20°E
25°E
30°E
35°E
40°E
40°N
35°N
30°N
25°N
20°N
15°N
10°N
5°N

Nigeria & Ghana
Scale 1:12,500,000 approx.
0 Kilometres 200 300 400
0 Miles 100 200 300
One Inch to 200 Miles
South Africa &
Page 68
NIGER
NIGERIA
BURKINA FASO
GHANA
TOGO
BENIN
CAMEROUN
EQUATORIAL GUINEA
RIO MUNI
GABON
SUDAN
ETHIOPIA
(ABYSSINIA)
UGANDA
KENYA
TANZANIA
RWANDA
BURUNDI
ZAÏRE
Gulf of Guinea
Bight of Bonny
Slave Coast
Gold Coast
Lake Chad
Lake Victoria
L. Tanganyika
L. Rukwa
L. Mweru
Lake Albert
Lake Turkana
L. Kyoga
L. Natron
L. Edward
L. Kivu
East Rift Valley
Ethiopian Plateau
Meridian of Greenwich
Equator
200 metres
Niamey
Ouagadougou
Kano
Zaria
Kaduna
Jos
Bauchi
Maiduguri
Ibadan
Lagos
Abeokuta
Oyo
Oshogbo
Ede
Benin City
Enugu
Onitsha
Aba
Port Harcourt
Warri
Calabar
Douala
Yaoundé
Libreville
Port Gentil
Accra
Kumasi
Tamale
Sekondi-Takoradi
Lomé
Cotonou
Porto Novo
Addis Ababa
Nairobi
Mombasa
Kampala
Entebbe
Dar es Salaam
Zanzibar
Dodoma
Tabora
Mwanza
Kigoma
Ujiji
Juba
Bujumbura
Kigali
Principe
São Tomé
Annobón
Bioko (Eq. Guinea)
Mt. Kenya
Uhuru (Kilimanjaro) 5895
Mt. Ruwenzori 5128
Mafia I.
Pemba

Page 69
ANGOLA
ZAMBIA
MOZAMBIQUE
MALAWI
ZIMBABWE
BOTSWANA
NAMIBIA
REPUBLIC OF SOUTH AFRICA
CAPE PROVINCE
TRANSVAAL
ORANGE FREE STATE
NATAL
LESOTHO
SWAZI-LAND
TRANSKEI
ATLANTIC OCEAN
INDIAN OCEAN
Mozambique Channel
Tropic of Capricorn
Bassas da. India (Fr.)
Europa (Fr.)
200 metres
Lubango
Menongue
Moçâmedes
Chibia
Pôrto Alexandre
Mutano
Kunene
Cubango
Cuito
Balovale
Kasempa
Luanshya
Ndola
Mankoya
Mongu
Senanga
Zambezi
Mulobezi
Kalomo
Pemba
Kabwe
Lusaka
Kafue
Kariba Dam
Kariba Gorge
Kariba Lake
Maramba
Mosjao-Joenga (Victoria Falls)
Hwange
Shangani
Gwaai
Sanyati
Kildonan
Shamva
Mazoe
Harare
Kadoma
Sebakwe
Kwekwe
Gweru
Shurugwi
Bulawayo
Matopo Hills
Plumtree
West Nicholson
Zimbabwe
Mutare
Chipata
Malawi
Salima
Lilongwe
Mangache
Vila Cabral
Zomba
Blantyre
Shire
Tete
Entre Rios
Nacala
Mozambique
Nampula
Mocuba
Xai Xai
Inhaminga
Macequece
Sofala
Nova Sofala
Spungabera
Okovango
Caprivi Strip
Etosha Pan
Tsumeb
Grootfontein
Outjo
Omaruru
Karibib
Usakos
Windhoek
Gobabis
Swakopmund
Pelican Pt.
Walvis Bay
Namib Desert
Mariental
Keetmanshoop
Seeheim
Elizabeth Pt.
Lüderitz
Pomona
Karasburg
Warmbad
Orange
Okovango Basin
Maun
Lake Ngami
Makarikari Salt Pan
Francistown
Serowe
Palapye Road
Kalahari Desert
Gaberone
Nossob
Molopo
Witdraai
Beit Bridge
Messina
Louis Trichardt
Pafuri
Limpopo
Leydsdorp
Thabazimbi
Potgietersrus
Lydenburg
Komatipoort
Magude
Vila de João Beia
Delagoa Bay
Maputo
Inhambane
Zeerust
Pretoria
Middelburg
Witbank
Johannesburg
Heidelberg
Mafikeng
Lichtenburg
Vaal
Vereeniging
Klerksdorp
Vryburg
Sishen
Kroonstad
Welkom
Piet Retief
Newcastle
Harrismith
Bethlehem
Ladysmith
Ulundi
Eshowe
Greytown
Pietermaritzburg
Durban
Griqualand
Barkly West
Kimberley
Postmasburg
Griquatown
Modder River
Bloemfontein
Maseru
Belmont
High Veld
Drakensberg
Matatiele
Port Shepstone
Margate
Port Nolloth
O'okiep
Springbok
Prieska
Carnarvon
De Aar
Burgersdorp
Umtata
Butterworth
King William's Town
East London
Bitterfontein
Calvinia
Victoria West
Nieuwveld Ra.
Beaufort West
Great Karroo
Fraserburg
Graaff-Reinet
Klipplaat
Grahamstown
Port Alfred
Uitenhage
Algoa Bay
Port Elizabeth
St. Helena Bay
Moorreesburg
Malmesbury
Paarl
Cape Town
Simonstown
Cape of Good Hope
False B.
Stellenbosch
Worcester
Ladismith
Little Karroo
Swellendam
Oudtshoorn
Uniondale
Knysna
George
Mossel Bay
C. Seal
C. St. Francis
15°S
20°S
25°S
30°S
35°S
15°E
20°E
30°E
35°E
40°E
Ft.
M.
16,000
4,800
10,000
3,000
6,000
1,800
3,000
900
1,500
450
1,000
300
600
180
300
90
Sea Level
Land Depression
Towns over 1 million people
" over 100,000 people
Boundaries international
- provincial etc
Railways
projected
Roads
tracks
Airports
Canal
Sand desert
Marsh
Salt pan
Ice cap
Zenithal Equal Area Projection
Copyright Oxford University Press

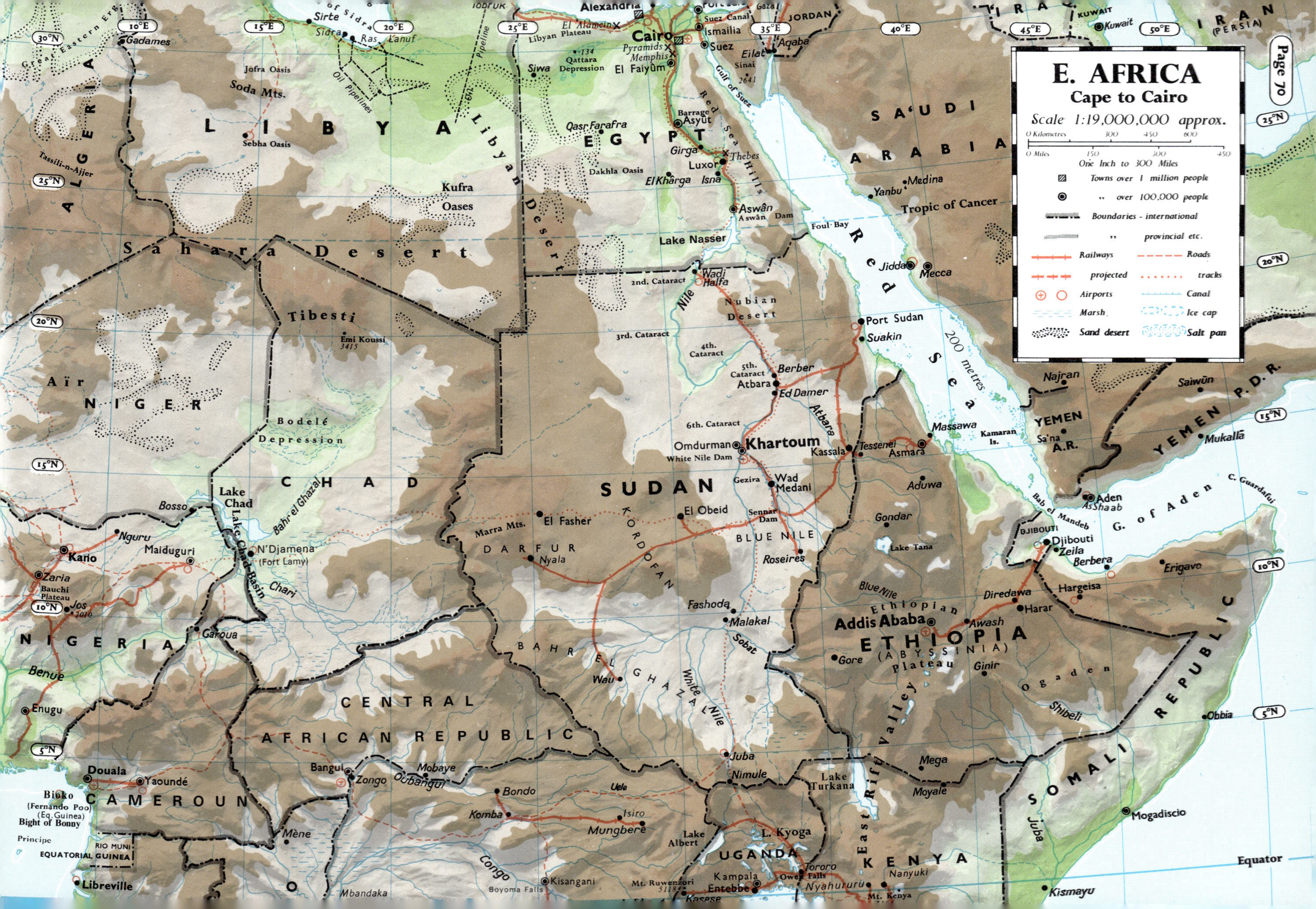

E. AFRICA
Cape to Cairo
Scale 1:19,000,000 approx.
0 Kilometres 150 300 450 600
0 Miles 150 300 450
One Inch to 300 Miles
Towns over 1 million people
,, over 100,000 people
Boundaries - international
,, provincial etc.
Railways
projected
Airports
Marsh
Sand desert
Roads
tracks
Canal
Ice cap
Salt pan
LIBYA
EGYPT
SAUDI ARABIA
SUDAN
CHAD
NIGER
NIGERIA
CAMEROUN
CENTRAL AFRICAN REPUBLIC
ETHIOPIA
(ABYSSINIA)
SOMALI REPUBLIC
KENYA
UGANDA
YEMEN A.R.
YEMEN P.D.R.
DJIBOUTI
EQUATORIAL GUINEA
RIO MUNI
ALGERIA
IRAN (PERSIA)
KUWAIT
JORDAN
Red Sea
200 metres
G. of Aden
Gulf of Suez
Bab el Mandeb
Foul Bay
Sahara Desert
Libyan Desert
Nubian Desert
Tibesti
Emi Koussi 3415
Bodelé Depression
Kufra Oases
Lake Nasser
Lake Chad
Lake Chad Basin
Lake Turkana
L. Kyoga
Lake Albert
Lake Tana
East Rift Valley
Ethiopian Plateau
KORDOFAN
DARFUR
BAHR EL GHAZAL
BLUE NILE
White Nile
Blue Nile
Nile
Atbara
Sobat
Chari
Benue
Congo
Ubangi
Uele
Juba
Shibeli
Ogaden
Tropic of Cancer
Equator
Cairo
Alexandria
Suez
Ismailia
Aswân
Luxor
Asyût
Khartoum
Omdurman
Port Sudan
Suakin
Kassala
Atbara
Berber
Ed Damer
El Obeid
El Fasher
Nyala
Wad Medani
Juba
Malakal
Fashoda
Wau
Addis Ababa
Asmara
Massawa
Djibouti
Aden
Mecca
Jidda
Medina
Mogadiscio
Kismayu
Kampala
Entebbe
N'Djamena (Fort Lamy)
Bangui
Douala
Yaoundé
Libreville
Kano
Maiduguri
Zaria
Jos
Kisangani
Gadames
Sebha Oasis
Siwa
Qattara Depression
El Faiyûm
Pyramids
Memphis
Thebes
Wadi Halfa
2nd. Cataract
3rd. Cataract
4th. Cataract
5th. Cataract
6th. Cataract
White Nile Dam
Sennar Dam
Aswân Dam
Marra Mts.
Soda Mts.
Red Sea Hills
Hargeisa
Harar
Diredawa
Berbera
Zeila
Sa'na
Mukalla
Najran
Kamaran Is.
Kuwait
Bight of Bonny
Bioko (Fernando Poo) (Eq. Guinea)
Principe

ATLANTIC OCEAN
INDIAN OCEAN
ZAÏRE
ANGOLA
NAMIBIA
BOTSWANA
ZAMBIA
ZIMBABWE
MOZAMBIQUE
MALAWI
TANZANIA
MADAGASCAR
REPUBLIC OF SOUTH AFRICA
CAPE PROVINCE
ORANGE FREE STATE
TRANSVAAL
NATAL
LESOTHO
SWAZILAND
TRANSKEI
BURUNDI
CABINDA
ZANZIBAR
COMORO ISLANDS
Mozambique Channel
Kalahari Desert
Namib Desert
Okovango Basin
Makarikari Salt Pan
Etosha Pan
Lake Ngami
Lake Tanganyika
L. Rukwa
L. Mweru
L. Bangweulu
Lake Nyasa
Kariba Dam
Zambezi
Limpopo
Orange
Vaal
Molopo
Nossob
Lualaba
Kasai
Congo
Ruvuma
Muchinga Mts.
Ankaratra Mts.
High Veld
Drakensberg
Kilimanjaro 5895
Pool Malebo
Mateka Falls
Gumbe Falls
Mosi-oa-Tunya (Victoria Falls)
Kinshasa
Brazzaville
Matadi
Boma
Mayoumba
Pointe Noire
Ilebo
Lusambo
Kananga
Kindu
Kongola
Kamina
Bukama
Likasi
Lubumbashi
Kalemi
Kigoma
Mpanda
Tabora
Mwanza
Dodoma
Moshi
Mombasa
Tanga
Pemba
Zanzibar
Dar es Salaam
Mtwara
Nachingwea
Songea
Mbala
Chipata
Kitwe
Ndola
Kabwe
Lusaka
Kafue
Maramba
Mongu
Malonga
Luanda
Malange
Lobito
Benguela
Huambo
Serpa Pinto
Lubango
Moçâmedes
Tsumeb
Windhoek
Walvis Bay
Pelican Pt.
Lüderitz
Elizabeth Point
Port Nolloth
Hwange
Bulawayo
Kwekwe
Harare
Mutare
Tete
Blantyre
Zomba
Salima
Vila Cabral
Entre Rios
Nampula
Mozambique
Mocuba
Xai Xai
Sofala
Maputo
Francistown
Serowe
Gaberone
Messina
Leydsdorp
Lydenburg
Middelburg
Pretoria
Johannesburg
Mafikeng
Vryburg
Kimberley
Bloemfontein
Ladysmith
Pietermaritzburg
Durban
East London
Port Elizabeth
C. St. Francis
De Aar
Victoria West
Beaufort West
Oudtshoorn
Great Karroo
Worcester
Swellendam
Malmesbury
Cape Town
Cape of Good Hope
St. Helena Bay
C. Agulhas
Antsirane (Diego Suarez)
Nossi Bé
Toamasina
Antananarivo
Fianarantsoa
Faradofay
C. Sainte Marie
Toliary
Mahajanga
Bassas da India (Fr.)
Europa (Fr.)
Aldabra Is. (Seychelles)
200 metres
Tropic of Capricorn
5°S
10°S
15°S
20°S
25°S
30°S
15°E
30°E
35°E
40°E
45°E
Ft.
M.
16,000
4,800
10,000
3,000
6,000
1,800
3,000
900
1,500
450
1,000
300
600
180
300
90
Sea Level
Land Depression
Zenithal Equal-area Projection

North & South America
POPULATION and COMMUNICATIONS
Scale 1:44,000,000 approx.
0 Kilometres 350 700 1050 1400
0 Miles 350 700 1050
One Inch to 700 Miles
This projection produces great exaggeration of scale
ALASKA
CANADA
UNITED STATES OF AMERICA
MEXICO
GREENLAND
ICELAND
IRELAND
GREAT BRITIAN
ARCTIC OCEAN
Polar Ice
Hudson Bay
NORTH ATLANTIC OCEAN
NORTH PACIFIC OCEAN
Gulf of Mexico
WEST INDIES
CUBA
JAMAICA
HAITI
DOM. REP.
BERMUDA
GUAT.
HOND.
Limit of pack ice—min.
Limit of pack ice—max.
Arctic Circle
Tropic of Cancer
Axis of Projection
45°N
60°N
75°N
120°W
90°W
60°W
30°N
15°N

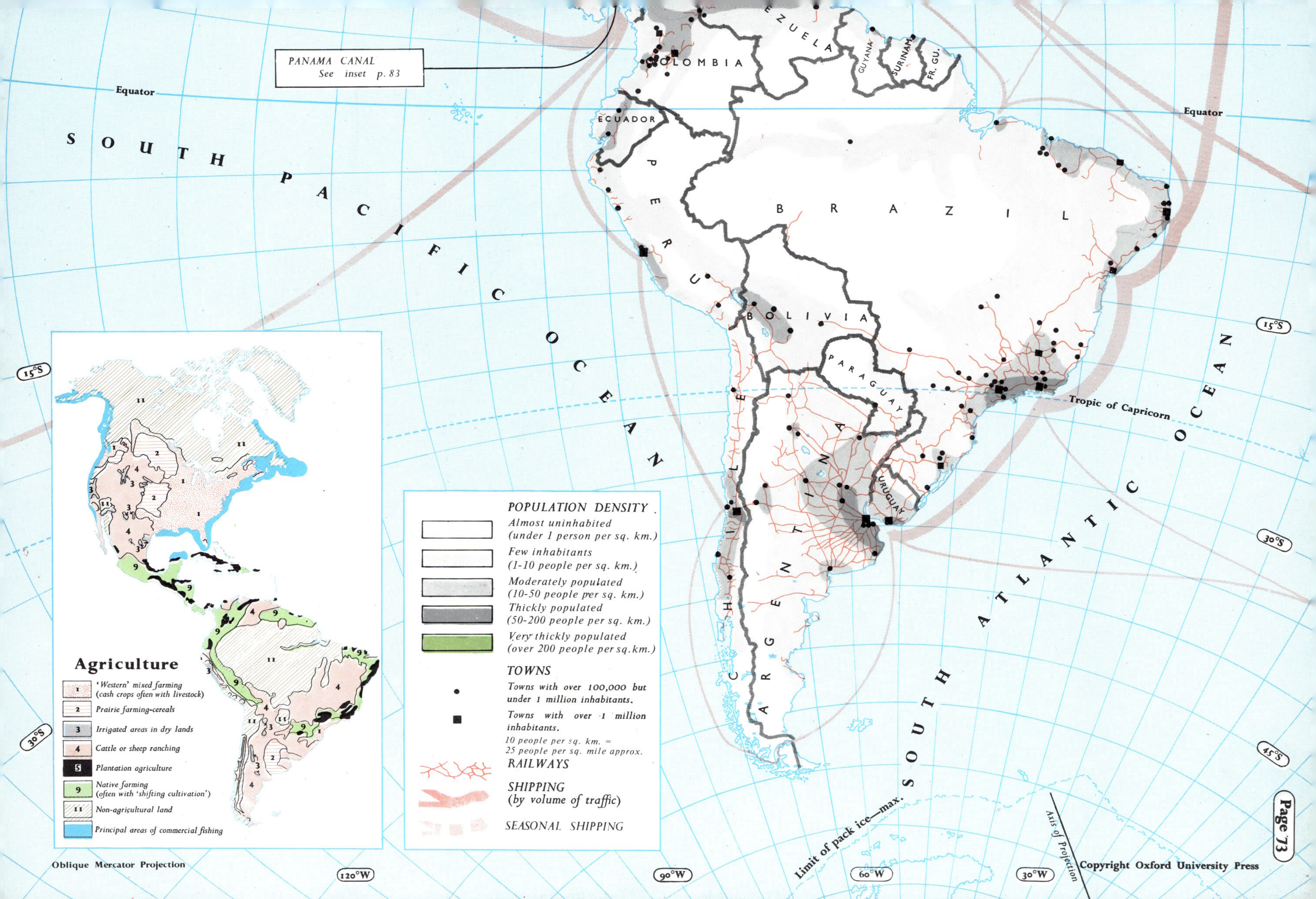

PANAMA CANAL
See inset p. 83
Equator
SOUTH PACIFIC OCEAN
SOUTH ATLANTIC OCEAN
COLOMBIA
VENEZUELA
GUYANA
SURINAM
FR. GU.
ECUADOR
PERU
BRAZIL
BOLIVIA
PARAGUAY
URUGUAY
CHILE
ARGENTINA
Tropic of Capricorn
15°S
30°S
45°S
120°W
90°W
60°W
30°W
Limit of pack ice—max.
Axis of Projection
POPULATION DENSITY
Almost uninhabited
(under 1 person per sq. km.)
Few inhabitants
(1-10 people per sq. km.)
Moderately populated
(10-50 people per sq. km.)
Thickly populated
(50-200 people per sq. km.)
Very thickly populated
(over 200 people per sq. km.)
TOWNS
Towns with over 100,000 but under 1 million inhabitants.
Towns with over 1 million inhabitants.
10 people per sq. km. = 25 people per sq. mile approx.
RAILWAYS
SHIPPING
(by volume of traffic)
SEASONAL SHIPPING
Agriculture
'Western' mixed farming (cash crops often with livestock)
Prairie farming-cereals
Irrigated areas in dry lands
Cattle or sheep ranching
Plantation agriculture
Native farming (often with 'shifting cultivation')
Non-agricultural land
Principal areas of commercial fishing
Oblique Mercator Projection

Page 74
North & South America
PHYSICAL
Scale 1:44,000,000 approx.
0 Kilometres 700 1050 1400
0 Miles 350 700 1050
One Inch to 700 Miles
This projection produces great exaggeration of scale
NORTH ATLANTIC OCEAN
NORTH PACIFIC OCE
ARCTIC OCEAN
Polar Ice
GREENLAND
ICELAND
IRELAND
GREAT BRITAIN
Maximum extent of Glaciation
Arctic Circle
Limit of pack ice—min.
Limit of pack ice—max.
Vikings Leif & Karlsefni c 1000 A.D.
Henry Hudson 1610-11
J. Cabot 1497
Cartier 1535
Columbus 1st. Voyage 1492-3
Sir J. Franklin died 1847
Amundsen 1903-5
Axis of Projection
Cook
Vancouver
Cook 1778
Vancouver 1792-5
Tropic of Cancer
ALASKA
Yukon
Mackenzie
Mackenzie 1789
Peace
1793
Fraser
CANADA
Hudson Bay
UNITED STATES
Oregon Trail
Snake
California Trail
Spanish Trail
Colorado
Santa Fe Trail
Platte
Missouri
Red
Arkansas
La Salle 1681
Mississippi
Ohio
Maximum extent of Glaciation
Hudson
St. Lawrence
Rio Grande
MEXICO
Gulf of Mexico
BERMUDA
CUBA
JAMAICA
HAITI
DOM. REP.
WEST INDIES
GUAT.
HOND.
15°N
30°N
45°N
60°N
75°N
60°W
90°W
120°W

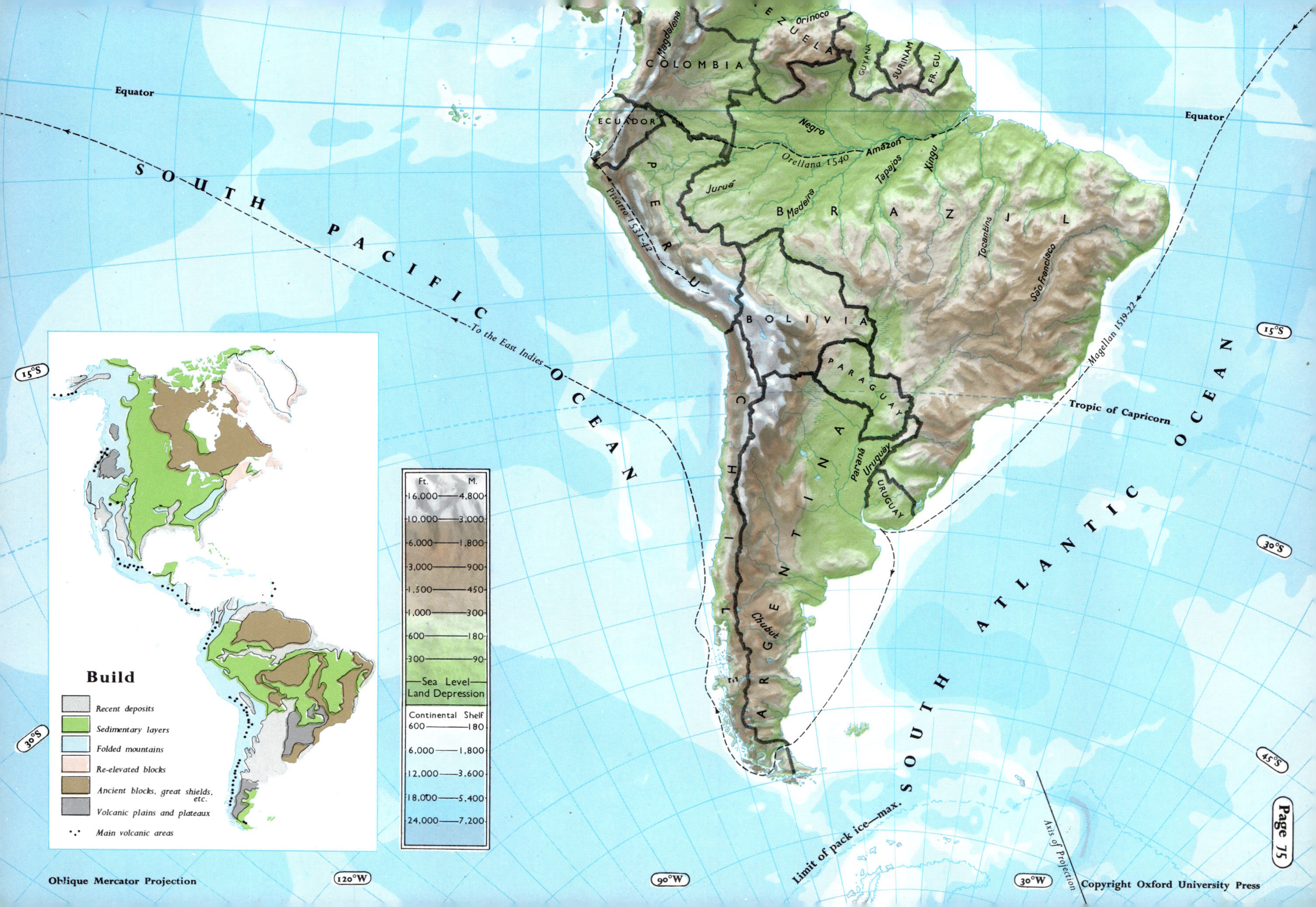

SOUTH PACIFIC OCEAN
SOUTH ATLANTIC OCEAN
Equator
Tropic of Capricorn
COLOMBIA
VENEZUELA
GUYANA
SURINAM
FR. GU.
ECUADOR
PERU
BRAZIL
BOLIVIA
PARAGUAY
URUGUAY
CHILE
ARGENTINA
Magdalena
Orinoco
Negro
Amazon
Orellana 1540
Tapajos
Xingu
Juruá
Madeira
Tocantins
São Francisco
Paraná
Uruguay
Chubut
Pizarro 1531-42
Magellan 1519-22
To the East Indies
Limit of pack ice—max.
Axis of Projection
15°S
30°S
45°S
30°W
90°W
120°W
Ft. M.
16,000—4,800
10,000—3,000
6,000—1,800
3,000—900
1,500—450
1,000—300
600—180
300—90
Sea Level
Land Depression
Continental Shelf
600—180
6,000—1,800
12,000—3,600
18,000—5,400
24,000—7,200
Build
Recent deposits
Sedimentary layers
Folded mountains
Re-elevated blocks
Ancient blocks, great shields, etc.
Volcanic plains and plateaux
Main volcanic areas
Oblique Mercator Projection

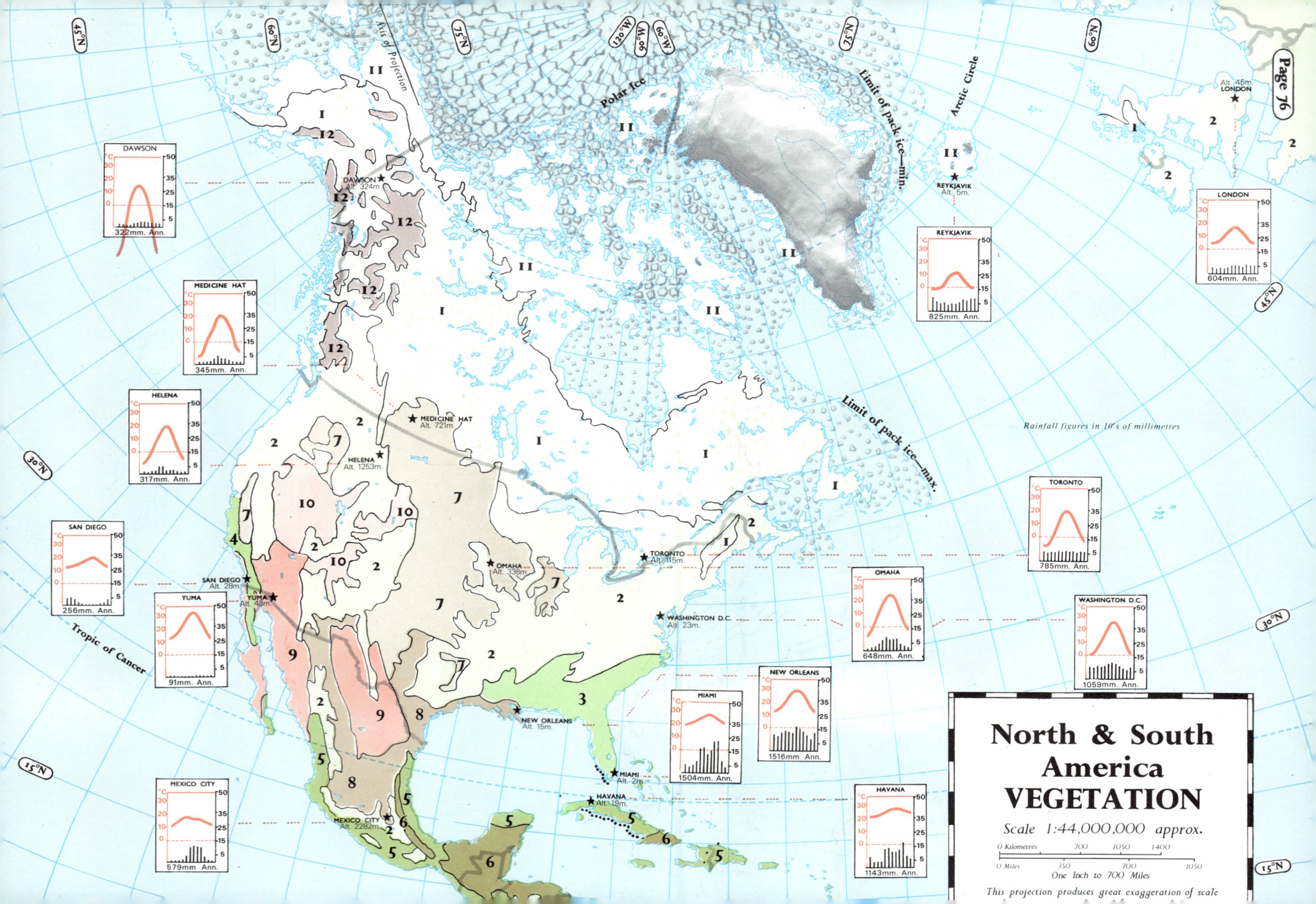

Page 76
North & South America
VEGETATION
Scale 1:44,000,000 approx.
0 Kilometres 700 1050 1400
0 Miles 350 700 1050
One Inch to 700 Miles
This projection produces great exaggeration of scale
Rainfall figures in 10's of millimetres
Polar Ice
Limit of pack ice—min.
Limit of pack ice—max.
Arctic Circle
Tropic of Cancer
Axis of Projection
45°N
60°N
75°N
120°W
90°W
60°W
30°N
15°N
DAWSON Alt. 324m.
MEDICINE HAT Alt. 721m.
HELENA Alt. 1253m.
SAN DIEGO Alt. 28m.
YUMA Alt. 43m.
MEXICO CITY Alt. 2282m.
OMAHA Alt. 336m.
TORONTO Alt. 115m.
WASHINGTON D.C. Alt. 23m.
NEW ORLEANS Alt. 15m.
MIAMI Alt. 2m.
HAVANA Alt. 19m.
REYKJAVIK Alt. 5m.
LONDON Alt. 45m.
DAWSON 322mm. Ann.
MEDICINE HAT 345mm. Ann.
HELENA 317mm. Ann.
SAN DIEGO 256mm. Ann.
YUMA 91mm. Ann.
MEXICO CITY 579mm. Ann.
OMAHA 648mm. Ann.
TORONTO 785mm. Ann.
WASHINGTON D.C. 1059mm. Ann.
NEW ORLEANS 1516mm. Ann.
MIAMI 1504mm. Ann.
HAVANA 1143mm. Ann.
REYKJAVIK 825mm. Ann.
LONDON 604mm. Ann.
°C 30 20 10 0
50 35 25 15 5

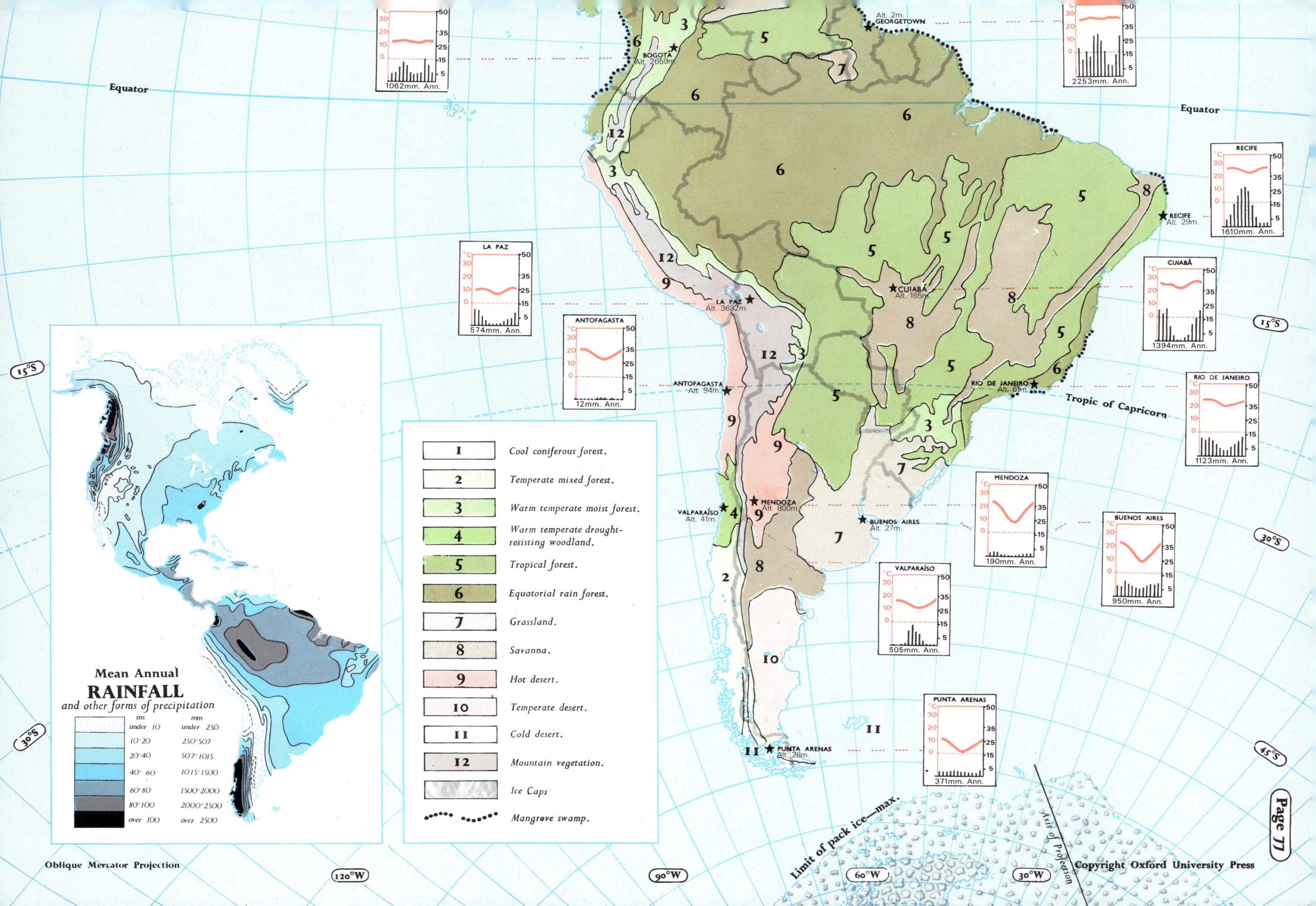
Equator
Tropic of Capricorn
GEORGETOWN Alt. 2m.
BOGOTÁ Alt. 2659m.
RECIFE Alt. 29m.
CUIABÁ Alt. 165m.
LA PAZ Alt. 3632m.
ANTOFAGASTA Alt. 94m.
RIO DE JANEIRO Alt. 61m.
VALPARAÍSO Alt. 41m.
MENDOZA Alt. 800m.
BUENOS AIRES Alt. 27m.
PUNTA ARENAS Alt. 28m.
1062mm. Ann.
2253mm. Ann.
LA PAZ 574mm. Ann.
ANTOFAGASTA 12mm. Ann.
RECIFE 1610mm. Ann.
CUIABÁ 1394mm. Ann.
RIO DE JANEIRO 1123mm. Ann.
MENDOZA 190mm. Ann.
BUENOS AIRES 950mm. Ann.
VALPARAÍSO 505mm. Ann.
PUNTA ARENAS 371mm. Ann.
1 Cool coniferous forest.
2 Temperate mixed forest.
3 Warm temperate moist forest.
4 Warm temperate drought-resisting woodland.
5 Tropical forest.
6 Equatorial rain forest.
7 Grassland.
8 Savanna.
9 Hot desert.
10 Temperate desert.
11 Cold desert.
12 Mountain vegetation.
Ice Caps
Mangrove swamp.
Mean Annual
RAINFALL
and other forms of precipitation
ins mm
under 10 under 250
10-20 250-507
20-40 507-1015
40-60 1015-1500
60-80 1500-2000
80-100 2000-2500
over 100 over 2500
Limit of pack ice—max.
Axis of Projection
15°S
30°S
45°S
120°W
90°W
60°W
30°W
Oblique Mercator Projection

NORTH MAGNETIC POLE
The North Magnetic Pole moves about, slowly (and unpredictably) in central arctic Canada In 1946 it was at 74°N 96°W approx.; and see map for 1966 position. This movement affects "Magnetic Variation from True North"—i.e. the angle between true north and "compass" north. For example in London in 1820 a compass would have pointed approximately 24° west of true north; in 1962, 8° west.
ARCTIC OCEAN
Beaufort Sea
Bering Sea
Bering Strait
International Date Line
U.S.S.R.
ALASKA
Brooks Range
Alaska Range
Aleutian Range
Alaska Peninsula
Gulf of Alaska
PACIFIC OCEAN
YUKON
Mackenzie Mountains
NORTHWEST
Victoria Island
Banks Island
Queen Eliza
ROCKY MOUNTAINS
BRITISH COLUMBIA
ALBERTA
SASKATCHEWAN
PRAIRIES
CANADA
UNITED STATES
Coast Mountains
Columbia Mountains
Cascade
Coast Ranges
Bitterroot Range
Salmon River Mts.
Blue Mts.
Point Barrow
Prudhoe Bay
Fairbanks
Anchorage
Nome
Kotzebue
Bethel
Fort Yukon
Seward
Valdez
Cordova
Kodiak I.
Juneau
Skagway
Ketchikan
Prince Rupert
Whitehorse
Dawson
Inuvik
Aklavik
Norman Wells
Great Bear Lake
Great Slave Lake
Yellowknife
Fort Simpson
Watson Lake
Ft. Nelson
Dawson Creek
Ft. Smith
Uranium City
Goldfields
Edmonton
Calgary
Saskatoon
Regina
Lethbridge
Medicine Hat
Prince George
Kamloops
Vancouver
Vancouver I.
New Westminster
Victoria
Bellingham
Seattle
Tacoma
Spokane
Portland
Oregon City
Great Falls
Helena
Butte
Boise
Idaho Falls
Pocatello
Ogden
Salt Lake City
Great Salt Lake
Cheyenne
Bismarck
Eureka
Cape Mendocino
Klamath Falls
Sacramento
Carson City
Queen Charlotte Is.
Queen Charlotte Sound
Chichagof I.
Prince of Wales I.
200 metres
180°
175°W
150°W
140°W
120°W
130°W
125°W
120°W
115°W
110°W
105°W
60°N
55°N
50°N
45°N
40°N
35°N
Ft. / M.
16,000 — 4,800
10,000 — 3,000
6,000 — 1,800
3,000 — 900
1,500 — 450
1,000 — 300
600 — 180
300 — 90
Sea Level
Land Depression
Zenithal Equidistant Projection

CANADA
Scale 1:19,000,000 approx.
Kilometres
Miles
One Inch to 300 Miles
Towns over 1 million people
,, over 100,000 people
Boundaries international
- provincial etc
Railways
projected
Roads
tracks
Airports
Canal
Sand desert
Marsh
Salt pan
Ice cap
GREENLAND
(Denmark)
ICELAND
Baffin Bay
Davis Strait
Baffin Island
Foxe Basin
Hudson Strait
Hudson Bay
Ungava Peninsula
Ungava Bay
James Bay
LABRADOR
NEWFOUNDLAND
QUEBEC
ONTARIO
MANITOBA
TERRITORIES
ATLANTIC OCEAN
Gulf of St. Lawrence
Arctic Circle
Limit of pack ice - average min. (autumn)
Limit of pack ice - average max. (spring)
Montreal
Ottawa
Quebec
Toronto
Detroit
Chicago
New York
Philadelphia
Boston
Washington
Halifax
St. John's
Lake Superior
Lake Huron
Lake Michigan
Lake Ontario
Lake Erie
200 metres
Grand Banks
95°W
90°W
85°W
80°W
75°W
70°W
35°N
40°N
45°N
50°N
55°N

Page 80
50°N
125°W
120°W
115°W
110°W
105°W
100°W
BRITISH COLUMBIA
ALBERTA
SASKATCHEWAN
MANIT
CANADA
Edmonton
Vermilion
Prince Albert
N. Battleford
Saskatchewan
Cedar Lake
L. Winnipeg
Hudson Bay
L. Winnipegosis
Winnipegosis
Saskatoon
Biggar
Yorkton
Assiniboine
L. Manitoba
Regina
Moose Jaw
Medicine Hat
Brandon
Winnip
St. Boni
Souris
Estevan
Assiniboia
Fraser
Lillooet
Lytton
Kamloops
Selkirk Mountains
Kicking Horse Pass
Banff
Golden
Revelstoke
Calgary
Turner Valley
Columbia
Kootenay
Fort Macleod
Crowsnest Pass
Cranbrook
Lethbridge
Trail
Princeton
Nootka Sound
Vancouver I.
Vancouver
Squamish
Nanaimo
Strait of Juan de Fuca
Victoria
New Westminster
Bellingham
Everett
Seattle
Okanogan
Chief Joseph Dam
Grand Coulee Dam
Olympia
Mt. Rainier 4392
Tacoma
WASHINGTON
Spokane
Coeur d'Alene
Yakima
Astoria
Mt. St. Helens 2950
Vancouver
Bonneville Dam
Portland
Columbia
McNary Dam
Snake
Mt. Hood 3428
Oregon City
Salem
La Grande
Eugene
Willamette
Blue Mts.
OREGON
Bend
Cascade Range
Ashland
Klamath Falls
Shelby
Havre
Chinook
Milk
Fort Peck Dam
Fort Peck Reservoir
Great Falls
Missouri
Missoula
MONTANA
Helena
Butte
Billings
Yellowstone
Salmon
Warren
Salmon River Mts.
Bitterroot Range
IDAHO
Boise
Snake
Idaho Falls
Pocatello
Yellowstone National Park
Bighorn Mts.
Powder
ROCKY MOUNTAINS
Williston
Minot
Grand Fork
NORTH DAKOTA
Bismarck
Fa
Aberd
SOUTH DAKOTA
Pierre
Rapid City
Sioux
Missouri
WYOMING
Casper
Seminoe Dam
Pathfinder Dam
Laramie Peak 3132
Rock Springs
Green River
Laramie
Cheyenne
Scottsbluff
NEBRASKA
North Platte
Platte
Linc
PACIFIC OCEAN
Eureka
Mt. Shasta 4317
Shasta Dam
Lassen Peak 3187
40°N
Red Bluff
Sacramento
Sierra Nevada
Coast Ranges
Reno
Carson City
Austin
Elko
Great Salt Lake
Ogden
Salt Lake City
Provo
Tintic
UNITED
Berkeley
Sacramento
Oakland
Stockton
San Francisco
Mt. Grant 4445
NEVADA
UTAH
Green
Longs Peak 4345
Denver
COLORADO
Grand Junction
Colorado Springs
Pueblo
La Junta
KANSAS
Hutchinson
Wichita
Dodge City
Monterey
S. Joaquin
Fresno
Mt. Whitney 4418
Tulare
CALIFORNIA
Iron Mtn. 2386
St. George
Colorado
Las Vegas
L. Mead
Hoover Dam
35°N
Bakersfield
Sta. Barbara
Colorado Plateaux
Grand Canyon
Raton
Hollywood
Los Angeles
Pasadena
Long Beach
San Bernardino
Los Alamos
Santa Fe
Canadian
OKLA
Oklahoma City
Amarillo
Albuquerque
Salton Sea
Aqueduct
Blythe
ARIZONA
San Diego
Tijuana
Calexico
Imperial Dam
Yuma
Mexicali
Phoenix
Miami
Globe
NEW MEXICO
Ensenada
Gila
Ajo
Tucson
Roswell
Llano Estacado
Lubbock
Wichita Falls
BAJA CALIFORNIA
Las Cruces
Carlsbad
Dal
Fort Worth
Abilene
30°N
Nogales
Bisbee
Ciudad Juárez
El Paso
Midland
TEXAS
Cananea
San Angelo
Wace
Pecos
Guadalupe (Mex.)
Angel de la Guarda
Nacozari
Edwards Plateau
Austin
SONORA
Moctezuma
Hermosillo
San Benito Islands
Rio Grande
San Antonio
Madera
CHIHUAHUA
Chihuahua
Yaqui
Guaymas
MEXICO
Aquiles Serdán
COAHUILA
Eagle Pass
Nueva Rosita
Corpus Chris
Gulf of California
Lower California
Ciudad Obregon
Conchos
Jiménez
Laredo
Nuevo Laredo
Hidalgo del Parral
TERRITORY OF BAJA CALIFORNIA SUR
Topolobampo
Brownsville
Ft.
M.
16,000
4,800
10,000
3,000
6,000
1,800
3,000
900
1,500
450
1,000
300
600
180
300
90
Sea Level
Land Depression
Conical Orthomorphic Projection

James Bay
90°W
85°W
80°W
75°W
70°W
50°N
Fort Albany
Moosonee
L. Mistassini
Sept Iles
Port Cartier
Gaspé
Gaspé Penin.
C A N A D A
O N T A R I O
Q U E B E C
Chibougamau
Nakina
Kapuskasing
Dolbeau
Chicoutimi
St. Lawrence
Tadoussac
L. St. John
Rivière du Loup
Edmundston
NEW BRUNSWICK
MARITIME
Saint John
Lake Nipigon
Kenora
Lake of the Woods
Atikokan
Nipigon
Thunder Bay
Cochrane
L. Abitibi
Timmins
Noranda
Rouyn
Kirkland Lake
Gouin Reservoir
Quebec
Michipicoten Harbour
Cobalt
Lake Timiskaming
Timiskaming
Shawinigan
Trois Rivières
Thetford Mines
Lake Superior
Mesabi Range
Vermilion Lake
Keweenaw Peninsula
Grand Rapids
Duluth
Superior
Ironwood
Iron Mountain
Sault Ste. Marie
Sudbury
North Bay
Ottawa
Hull
Montreal
Beauharnois
Parry Sound
Georgian Bay
Midland
Lake Huron
Owen Sound
Kingston
Burlington
Montpelier
Watertown
Adirondacks
MAINE
Bangor
Augusta
Mt. Washington 1917
Portland
NEW HAMPSHIRE
VERMONT
NEW ENGLAND
Concord
Manchester
MINNESOTA
St. Cloud
Minneapolis
St. Paul
Eau Claire
Green Bay
WISCONSIN
Oshkosh
Mississippi
MIDDLE
Lake Michigan
MICHIGAN
Toronto
Lake Ontario
Niagara Falls
Rochester
Syracuse
Utica
Albany
Boston
Cape Cod
MASS.
Worcester
Springfield
Providence
New Bedford
Nantucket
Hartford
CONN.
R.I.
Kitchener
Hamilton
Buffalo
Bay City
Grand Rapids
Flint
Lansing
London
Lake Erie
NEW YORK
New Haven
Long Island
Bridgeport
New York
Jersey City
Hudson R.
40°N
Milwaukee
Madison
Detroit
Windsor
Scranton
Sioux City
Ft. Dodge
Dubuque
Cedar Rapids
IOWA
Des Moines
Chicago
Gary
Clinton
Toledo
Cleveland
Akron
Canton
PENNSYLVANIA
Trenton
Philadelphia
South Bend
Fort Wayne
Rock Island
Council Bluffs
Omaha
Pittsburgh
Harrisburg
Wilmington
N.J.
Atlantic City
Dover
Wheeling
Columbus
UNITED STATES
Peoria
Springfield
Illinois
Quincy
Indianapolis
Dayton
OHIO
Baltimore
Washington
D.C.
Annapolis
DEL.
MARYLAND
Delaware Bay
St. Joseph
ILLINOIS
INDIANA
Cincinnati
Ohio
WEST VIRGINIA
Charleston
Huntington
VIRGINIA
Richmond
James
Kansas City
Missouri
Jefferson City
St. Louis
Louisville
Frankfort
Lexington
Chesapeake Bay
Newport News
Norfolk
Appalachian
Evansville
Owensboro
Lynchburg
Roanoke
MISSOURI
KENTUCKY
Bristol
Winston-Salem
NORTH CAROLINA
Raleigh
Springfield
Spruce Pine
Cape Hatteras
35°N
Joplin
Plateau
Ozark
Norris Dam
Knoxville
Asheville
Gastonia
Charlotte
New Bern
Nashville
TENNESSEE
Tennessee Valley
Jackson
Chattanooga
Spartanburg
Wilmington
ARKANSAS
Fort Smith
Memphis
Wilson Dam
Greenville
SOUTH CAROLINA
Columbia
Corinth
Florence
Tennessee
Rome
Athens
Little Rock
Arkansas
Gadsden
Atlanta
Augusta
Red
Camden
Birmingham
GEORGIA
Macon
Charleston
Texarkana
MISSISSIPPI
ALABAMA
Columbus
Savannah
Monroe
Vicksburg
Meridian
Montgomery
Shreveport
Jackson
Alabama
LOUISIANA
Natchez
Jacksonville
Alexandria
Mobile
Tallahassee
Baton Rouge
Gulfport
Pensacola
Gainesville
Beaumont
Lake Charles
Daytona Beach
Houston
Port Arthur
New Orleans
Port Sulphur
C. Canaveral
Texas City
Galveston
200 metres
Orlando
FLORIDA
Melbourne
Tampa
St. Petersburg
Lakeland
Lake Okeechobee
Palm Beach
Gulf of Mexico
Everglades
Miami
THE BAHAMAS
Nassau
Florida Keys
25°N
95°W
90°W
85°W
ATLANTIC OCEAN
UNITED STATES
Scale 1:12,500,000 approx.
0 Kilometres 200 300 400
0 Miles 100 200 300
One Inch to 200 Miles
Towns over 1 million people
" over 100,000 people
Boundaries - international
state, etc.
Roads
- motorway
- projected
- main
Airports
Canal
Marsh

U.S.A. and CENTRAL AMERICA
Scale 1:19,000,000 approx.
Kilometres 0 150 300 450 600
Miles 0 150 300 450
One Inch to 300 Miles
Towns over 1 million people
,, over 100,000 people
Boundaries - international
- state
Railways
projected
Roads
proposed
Airports
Canal
Sand desert
Marsh
Salt pan
Ice cap
THE UNITED STATES
Alabama 23; Arizona 44; Arkansas 30; California 48; Colorado 40; Connecticut 6; Delaware 10; Florida 17; Georgia 16; Idaho 42; Illinois 28; Indiana 20; Iowa 27; Kansas 35; Kentucky 21; Louisiana 31; Maine 1; Maryland 11; Massachusetts 4; Michigan 18; Minnesota 26; Mississippi 24; Missouri 29; Montana 38; Nebraska 34; Nevada 47; New Hampshire 2; New Jersey 8; New Mexico 41; New York 7; North Carolina 14; North Dakota 32; Ohio 19; Oklahoma 36; Oregon 46; Pennsylvania 9; Rhode Island 5; South Carolina 15; South Dakota 33; Tennessee 22; Texas 37; Utah 43; Vermont 3; Virginia 13; Washington 45; West Virginia 12; Wisconsin 25; Wyoming 39. Alaska became a state on January 3rd. 1959 Hawaii became a state on August 21st. 1959
Zenithal Equidistant Projection
UNITED STATES
CANADA
MEXICO
PACIFIC OCEAN
Gulf of Mexico
Bay of Campeche
GUATEMALA
EL SALVADOR
Rocky Mountains
Colorado Plateau
Llano Estacado
Mexican Plateau
Western Sierra Madre
Eastern Sierra Madre
Southern Sierra Madre
Lower California
Gulf of California
Isthmus of Tehuantepec
Gulf of Tehuantepec
Tropic of Cancer
San Francisco
Los Angeles
San Diego
Portland
Spokane
Denver
El Paso
Houston
San Antonio
Dallas
Fort Worth
New Orleans
Minneapolis
St. Paul
Omaha
Des Moines
Kansas City
Oklahoma City
Memphis
Monterrey
Guadalajara
Mexico City
Puebla
Veracruz
Mérida
Guatemala
San Salvador

Page 83
Ft.
M.
16,000
4,800
10,000
3,000
6,000
1,800
3,000
900
1,500
450
1,000
300
600
180
300
90
Sea Level
Land Depression
85°W
80°W
75°W
70°W
55°W
50°W
45°W
40°N
35°N
15°N
10°N
65°W
Moosonee
Lake Mistassini
Sept Îles
Gaspé
Gaspé Peninsula
Gulf of St. Lawrence
Magdalen Is.
Cabot Strait
Port-aux-Basques
Miquelon (Fr.)
Placentia Bay
C. Race
Kapuskasing
L. Abitibi
Gouin Res.
L. St. John
Tadoussac
Edmundston
PRINCE EDWARD I.
Charlottetown
Pictou
Cape Breton I.
Sydney Mines
Sydney
Canso
S. Porcupine
Timmins
Kirkland Lake
Cobalt
Quebec
Trois Rivières
St. Lawrence
Fredericton
Moncton
NOVA SCOTIA
Halifax
Saint John
Bay of Fundy
Cape Sable
200 metres
Sault Ste. Marie
Sudbury
Ottawa
Montreal
Thetford Mines
Bangor
Georgian Bay
Midland
L. Champlain
Mt. Washington
Portland
Lake Huron
Kingston
Burlington
Manchester
Toronto
Hamilton
L. Ontario
Rochester
Utica
Albany
Boston
Grand Rapids
Flint
Niagara Falls
Syracuse
Hartford
Providence
Cape Cod
Detroit
Windsor
Lake Erie
Buffalo
Hudson
Fall River
New Haven
Long Island
Toledo
Cleveland
Scranton
New York
Fort Wayne
Pittsburgh
Jersey City
Trenton
Philadelphia
Indianapolis
Columbus
Wilmington
Baltimore
Washington
Delaware Bay
Cincinnati
Ohio
Louisville
Lexington
Charleston
James
Richmond
Newport News
Chesapeake Bay
Bristol
Norfolk
Knoxville
Mt. Mitchell 2038
Winston-Salem
Raleigh
Cape Hatteras
Chattanooga
Charlotte
Columbia
Wilmington
Gadsden
Atlanta
Augusta
Birmingham
Macon
Charleston
Columbus
Montgomery
Savannah
Jacksonville
Daytona Beach
C. Canaveral
Melbourne
Tampa
Lake Okeechobee
Palm Beach
Everglades
Miami
Key West
Florida Keys
Straits of Florida
Nassau
THE BAHAMAS
San Salvador (Watling)
Tropic of Cancer
BERMUDA
ATLANTIC OCEAN
Havana
Yucatan Channel
Cienfuegos
Camagüey
CUBA
Caicos Islands (Br.)
Turks Is.
WEST INDIES
Windward Passage
DOMINICAN REPUBLIC
Santiago
Santiago de Cuba
HAITI
Hispaniola
Port-au-Prince
Santo Domingo
Mona Passage
San Juan
PUERTO RICO (U.S.)
St. Thomas (U.S.)
Anegada (Br.)
Virgin Is.
St. Croix (U.S.)
Sombrero Passage
Sombrero
Anguilla (Br.)
St. Martin (Fr. & Neth.)
St. Christophers (St. Kitts)
Nevis
Barbuda
ANTIGUA
Montserrat (Br.)
Guadeloupe (Fr.)
Basse-Terre
Marie-Galante (Fr.)
Les Saintes
Leeward Islands
DOMINICA
Fort de France
Martinique (Fr.)
ST. LUCIA
ST. VINCENT
BARBADOS
Grenadines
GRENADA
Windward Islands
Lesser Antilles
Cayman Is.
Montego Bay
Greater Antilles
JAMAICA
Kingston
Spanish Town
Caribbean Sea
Trujillo
C. Gracias a Dios
Segovia
Tobago
Port of Spain
TRINIDAD & TOBAGO
Aruba (Neth.)
Curaçao (Neth.)
Bonaire (Neth)
Puerto Cabello
Margarita I.
Gulf of Venezuela
Pt. de Gallinas
Sta. Marta
Maracay
La Guaira
Cumaná
Barcelona
Maturín
Tucupita
Managua
Lake Nicaragua
Barranquilla
Maracaibo
Valencia
Caracas
Barquisimeto
Calabozo
Cartagena
Magdalena
Lake of Maracaibo
Cord. de Mérida
VENEZUELA
Orinoco
Ciudad Bolívar
GUYANA
Georgetown
Mackenzie
COSTA RICA
San José
Puerto Limón
Panama Canal
Portobello
Colón
Panamá
PANAMA
G. of Darien
COLOMBIA
Turbo
Copyright Oxford University Press
Gaillard Cut (Culebra)
Maximum elevation 95m
Minimum depth 12m
ATLANTIC
PACIFIC
Sea Level
0km 10 20 30 40 50 60 70 80
Gatun Locks 3 pairs
Length 304m
Width 33m
Lift 26m
Pedro Miguel Locks 1 pair
Length 304m
Width 33m
Lift 9m
Miraflores Locks 2 pairs
Length 304m
Width 33m
Lift 16m
Panama Canal
1 cm. = 15 km. approx.
1'' to 24 miles approx.
ATLANTIC OCEAN
80°W
Colón
Gatun Locks
Gatun Lake
CANAL ZONE
PANAMÁ
Pedro Miguel Locks
Miraflores Locks
9°N
Balboa
Panamá
PACIFIC OCEAN
PANAMA The canal, opened in 1914, is 80km long incl. approaches (actual canal 58km). Min. depth 13m, min. width 91m. (Galliard Cut). Time of passage 8hrs. In 1978 the Canal Zone became Panamanian territory but the U.S.A. will operate the Canal until 1999. In 1978 12 677 vessels passed through carrying 142 518 288 t of cargo.

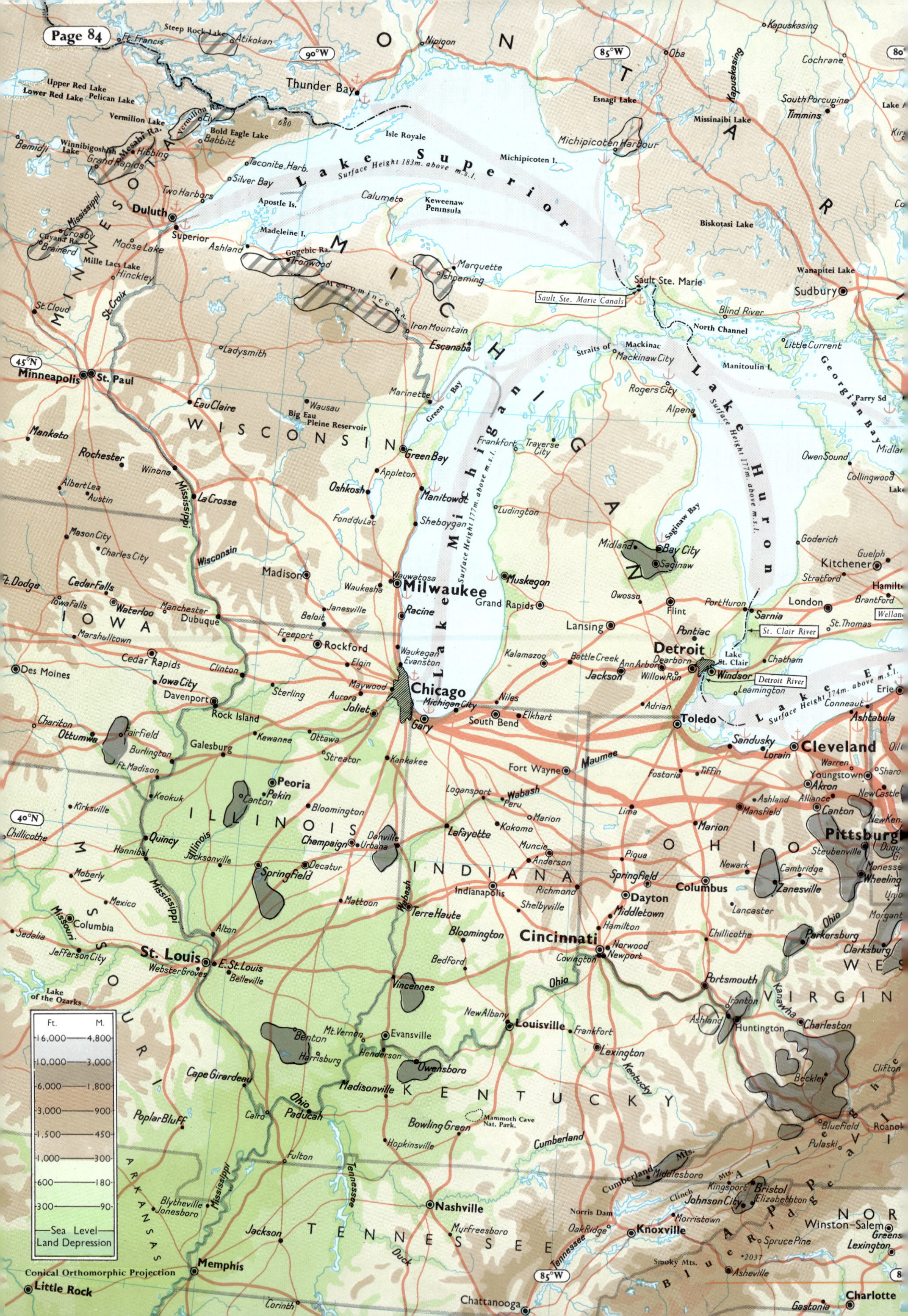

Page 84
Steep Rock Lake
Atikokan
Ft. Francis
90°W
85°W
Nipigon
Thunder Bay
Kapuskasing
Cochrane
Oba
Esnagi Lake
South Porcupine
Timmins
Missinaibi Lake
Upper Red Lake
Lower Red Lake
Pelican Lake
Vermilion Lake
Vermilion Ra.
Ely
Bold Eagle Lake
Babbitt
Isle Royale
Michipicoten I.
Michipicoten Harbour
Bemidji
Winnibigoshish Lake
Mesabi Ra.
Hibbing
Grand Rapids
Taconite Harb.
Silver Bay
Lake Superior
Surface Height 183m. above m.s.l.
Two Harbors
Calumet
Keweenaw Peninsula
Apostle Is.
Duluth
Superior
Ashland
Madeleine I.
Gogebic Ra.
Ironwood
Marquette
Ishpeming
Biskotasi Lake
Wanapitei Lake
Sudbury
Crosby
Cuyuna Ra.
Brainerd
Moose Lake
Mille Lacs Lake
Hinckley
Menominee Ra.
Sault Ste. Marie
Sault Ste. Marie Canals
Blind River
North Channel
Little Current
St. Cloud
St. Croix
Iron Mountain
Escanaba
Mississippi
MINNESOTA
MICHIGAN
ONTARIO
Ladysmith
Straits of Mackinac
Mackinaw City
Manitoulin I.
Georgian Bay
45°N
Minneapolis
St. Paul
Marinette
Green Bay
Rogers City
Alpena
Parry Sd
Eau Claire
Wausau
Big Eau Pleine Reservoir
WISCONSIN
Lake Michigan
Surface Height 177m. above m.s.l.
Lake Huron
Surface Height 177m. above m.s.l.
Mankato
Rochester
Winona
Green Bay
Appleton
Frankfort
Traverse City
Owen Sound
Midland
Collingwood
Albert Lea
Austin
Oshkosh
La Crosse
Manitowoc
Fond du Lac
Sheboygan
Ludington
Saginaw Bay
Mason City
Charles City
Wisconsin
Goderich
Guelph
Kitchener
Midland
Bay City
Saginaw
Madison
Ft. Dodge
Cedar Falls
Wauwatosa
Milwaukee
Muskegon
Stratford
Hamilton
Iowa Falls
Waterloo
Waukesha
Janesville
Racine
Grand Rapids
Owosso
Flint
Port Huron
Sarnia
London
Brantford
IOWA
Manchester
Dubuque
Beloit
Lansing
Pontiac
St. Clair River
St. Thomas
Marshalltown
Freeport
Rockford
Waukegan
Evanston
Kalamazoo
Battle Creek
Detroit
Lake St. Clair
Chatham
Des Moines
Cedar Rapids
Clinton
Elgin
Jackson
Ann Arbor
Dearborn
Willow Run
Windsor
Detroit River
Iowa City
Sterling
Maywood
Chicago
Niles
Leamington
Lake Erie
Surface Height 174m. above m.s.l.
Erie
Davenport
Aurora
Joliet
Michigan City
Elkhart
Adrian
Conneaut
Chariton
Rock Island
South Bend
Toledo
Ashtabula
Ottumwa
Fairfield
Kewanee
Ottawa
Gary
Burlington
Galesburg
Streator
Kankakee
Sandusky
Lorain
Cleveland
Ft. Madison
Fort Wayne
Maumee
Fostoria
Tiffin
Warren
Youngstown
Akron
Peoria
Canton
Pekin
Logansport
Wabash
Peru
Ashland
Mansfield
Alliance
Canton
New Castle
Keokuk
Kirksville
ILLINOIS
Bloomington
Marion
Lima
Marion
40°N
Chillicothe
Quincy
Hannibal
Illinois
Champaign
Urbana
Danville
Lafayette
Kokomo
Pittsburgh
Steubenville
OHIO
Jacksonville
Decatur
Muncie
Anderson
Piqua
Newark
Cambridge
Wheeling
Moberly
Springfield
INDIANA
Springfield
Columbus
Zanesville
Mexico
Mississippi
Mattoon
Indianapolis
Richmond
Dayton
Lancaster
Missouri
Columbia
Wabash
Terre Haute
Shelbyville
Middletown
Hamilton
Chillicothe
Sedalia
Alton
Bloomington
Cincinnati
Norwood
Newport
Covington
Ohio
Parkersburg
Jefferson City
St. Louis
E. St. Louis
Belleville
Webster Groves
Bedford
Clarksburg
Portsmouth
Lake of the Ozarks
MISSOURI
Vincennes
Ohio
New Albany
Ironton
Kanawha
WEST VIRGINIA
Ft.
M.
16,000
4,800
10,000
3,000
6,000
1,800
3,000
900
1,500
450
1,000
300
600
180
300
90
Sea Level
Land Depression
Benton
Mt. Vernon
Evansville
Louisville
Frankfort
Ashland
Huntington
Charleston
Harrisburg
Henderson
Owensboro
Lexington
Cape Girardeau
Madisonville
KENTUCKY
Kentucky
Beckley
Clifton
Ohio
Paducah
Cairo
Poplar Bluff
Bowling Green
Mammoth Cave Nat. Park
Bluefield
Roanoke
Pulaski
Cumberland
Hopkinsville
Fulton
Tennessee
ARKANSAS
Mississippi
Cumberland Mts.
Middlesboro
Kingsport
Bristol
Elizabethton
Johnson City
Clinch
Blytheville
Jonesboro
Nashville
Norris Dam
Morristown
Winston-Salem
Jackson
TENNESSEE
Murfreesboro
Oak Ridge
Knoxville
Spruce Pine
Lexington
Duck
Tennessee
Blue Ridge
Appalachian
Smoky Mts.
2037
Asheville
Memphis
Conical Orthomorphic Projection
Little Rock
Corinth
Chattanooga
Gastonia
Charlotte

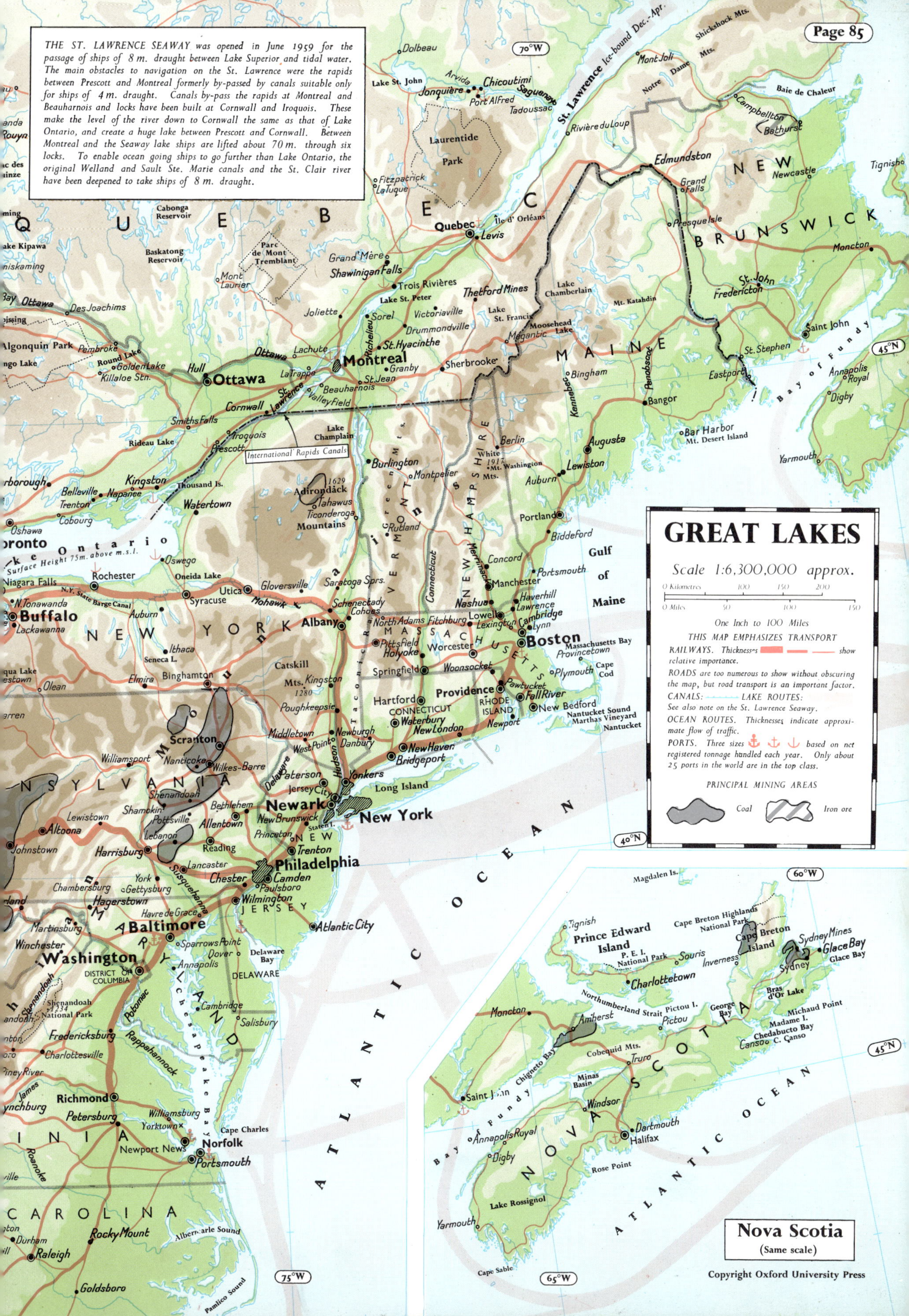

Page 85
THE ST. LAWRENCE SEAWAY was opened in June 1959 for the passage of ships of 8 m. draught between Lake Superior and tidal water. The main obstacles to navigation on the St. Lawrence were the rapids between Prescott and Montreal formerly by-passed by canals suitable only for ships of 4 m. draught. Canals by-pass the rapids at Montreal and Beauharnois and locks have been built at Cornwall and Iroquois. These make the level of the river down to Cornwall the same as that of Lake Ontario, and create a huge lake between Prescott and Cornwall. Between Montreal and the Seaway lake ships are lifted about 70 m. through six locks. To enable ocean going ships to go further than Lake Ontario, the original Welland and Sault Ste. Marie canals and the St. Clair river have been deepened to take ships of 8 m. draught.
GREAT LAKES
Scale 1:6,300,000 approx.
0 Kilometres 100 150 200
0 Miles 50 100 150
One Inch to 100 Miles
THIS MAP EMPHASIZES TRANSPORT
RAILWAYS. Thicknesses show relative importance.
ROADS are too numerous to show without obscuring the map, but road transport is an important factor.
CANALS: LAKE ROUTES:
See also note on the St. Lawrence Seaway.
OCEAN ROUTES. Thicknesses indicate approximate flow of traffic.
PORTS. Three sizes based on net registered tonnage handled each year. Only about 25 ports in the world are in the top class.
PRINCIPAL MINING AREAS
Coal
Iron ore
QUEBEC
NEW BRUNSWICK
MAINE
VERMONT
NEW HAMPSHIRE
MASSACHUSETTS
CONNECTICUT
RHODE ISLAND
NEW YORK
NEW JERSEY
PENNSYLVANIA
MARYLAND
DELAWARE
DISTRICT OF COLUMBIA
CAROLINA
NOVA SCOTIA
ATLANTIC OCEAN
Lake Ontario
Surface Height 75m. above m.s.l.
International Rapids Canals
Gulf of Maine
Bay of Fundy
St. Lawrence Ice-bound Dec.-Apr.
Montreal
Ottawa
Quebec
Boston
New York
Philadelphia
Baltimore
Washington
Buffalo
Newark
Providence
Albany
Halifax
Prince Edward Island
Cape Breton Island
Nova Scotia
(Same scale)
70°W
75°W
65°W
60°W
45°N
40°N
Copyright Oxford University Press

Page 86
JAMAICA
HAITI
DOMINICAN REPUBLIC
PUERTO RICO (U.S.A.)
Virgin Is. (Br. & U.S.)
St. Christophers (St. Kitts)
Montserrat (Br.)
Guadeloupe (Fr.)
Leeward Islands
DOMINICA
Martinique (Fr.)
ST. LUCIA
ST. VINCENT
Windward Islands
GRENADA
C A R I B B E A N S E A
Guatemala
HONDURAS
2310
Tegucigalpa
Segovia
C. Gracias a Dios
EL SAL.
San Salvador
NICARAGUA
Managua
Lake of Nicaragua
COSTA RICA
San José
Puerto Limón
Panama Canal
Colón
Portobello
PANAMA
Panama
Gulf of Panama
Gulf of Darien
Turbo
Pt. de Gallinas
Gulf of Venezuela
Aruba (Neth.)
Curaçao (Neth.)
Sta. Marta
Barranquilla
Cartagena
Maracaibo
Lake of Maracaibo
Cabimas
Magdalena Basin
Pto. Cabello
La Guaira
Valencia
Caracas
Barquisimeto
Calabozo
Barcelona
Cumaná
Margarita I.
Maturín
Tucupita
TRINID.
TOBA
Cordillera de Mérida
Cúcuta
San Cristóbal
Arauca
VENEZUELA
Orinoco
Ciudad Bolív
Cerro Bolivar
Caroni
Angel Fal
Pto. Ayacucho
Bucaramanga
5750
Magdalena
Cauca
Medellín
Tunja
Manizales
Central
Oriental
Ibagué
Bogotá
COLOMBIA
Cordillera Occidental
Cordillera Central
Cordillera Oriental
Buenaventura
Cali
Neiva
Florencia
Orinoco
Casiquiare
Boa Vist
Branco
Cocos Is. (C.R.)
Malpelo I. (Col.)
Tumaco
San Lorenzo
Pasto
Vaupés
Mitú
Chaves I. (Indefatigable I.)
Equator
S. Cristobal (Chatham I.)
Galápagos Islands (Ecuador)
Isabela (Albemarle I.)
Quito
Cotopaxi 5895
Manta
ECUADOR
Chimborazo 6272
Riobamba
Guayaquil
Gulf of Guayaquil
Negro
Putumayo
Morona
Amazon
Iquitos
(Solimoes)
Leticia
Manaus
Loja
Talara
Marañon
Piura
Sechura Desert
Chiclayo
Cajamarca
Ucayali
Juruá
Purús
Cruzeiro do Sul
Trujillo
Huallaga
Chimbote
Huaras
Cordillera
Pôrto Velho
Santo Antônio
Rio Branco
Huánuco
Goyllarisquizga
Cerro de Pasco
Minaragra
La Montaña
Riberalta
Guajará-mirim
Beni
La Oroya
Callao
Lima
Huancayo
Ayacucho
6246
Macchu Picchu
Huancavelica
Abancay
Cusco (Cuzco)
Pisco
Ica
Occidental
5816
Las Yungas
L. Titicaca
Llanos de Guarayos
Chiquit
200 metres
Puno
La Paz
Illimani 6462
Arequipa
Mollendo
Corocoro
Cochabamba
Mizque
Santa Cru
Tacna
Oruro
6670
L. Poopó
Arica
Sucre
Potosí
Pisagua
Uyuni
Iquique
Tarija
Pilcomayo
Chuquicamata
Atacama Desert
Tropic of Capricorn
Antofagasta
Jujuy
Salta
Taltal
CHILE
ARGENTINA
BOLIVIA
PERU
BRAZIL
P A C I F I C O C E A N
Ft. M.
16,000 4,800
10,000 3,000
6,000 1,800
3,000 900
1,500 450
1,000 300
600 180
300 90
Sea Level
Land Depression
Transverse Mercator Projection
15°N
10°N
5°N
5°S
10°S
15°S
20°S
90°W
85°W
80°W
75°W
70°W
65°W

S. AMERICA (North)

Scale 1:19,000,000 approx.

75°W
70°W
65°W
60°W
55°W
50°W
45°W
40°W
10°S
15°S
20°S
25°S
30°S
35°S
Tropic of Capricorn
200 metres
PERU
BOLIVIA
BRAZIL
PARAGUAY
URUGUAY
ARGENTINA
CHILE
PACIFIC
OCEAN
La Montaña
Cordillera Occidental
Cordillera Real
Plateau of Mato Grosso
Serra dos Parecis
Brazilian Plateau
Highlands of Brazil
Goiás Massif
Plateau of Minas Gerais
Llanos de Guarayos
Chiquitos Plateau
Las Yungas
Gran Chaco
Pampas
Atacama Desert
Costa
Paraná Plateau
RIO GRANDE DO SUL
Serra Geral
Serra Geral de Goiás
Serra dos Aimorés
ESPÍRITO SANTO
Huaras
Huánuco
Cerro de Pasco
Minaragra
La Oroya
Callao
Lima
Huancayo
Ayacucho
Macchu Picchu
Huancavelica
Abancay
Cusco (Cuzco)
Apurimac
Ica
Puno
Arequipa
Mollendo
Corocoro
Tacna
Arica
Rio Branco
Riberalta
Guajará-mirim
Pôrto Velho
Santo Antônio
Madeira
Beni
Juruena
Xingu
Araguaia
Tocantins
São Francisco
Jequitinhonha
5816
L. Titicaca
La Paz
Illimani 6462
Cochabamba
Mizque
Santa Cruz
Oruro
3670
L. Poopó
Sucre
Potosí
Uyuni
Tarija
1995
Pisagua
Iquique
Chuquicamata
Antofagasta
Jujuy
Salta
Taltal
Chañaral
Caldera
Potrerillos
Ojos del Salado 7100
Copiapó
Tucumán
Santiago del Estero
Catamarca
La Rioja
Dulce
Salado
La Serena
Coquimbo
San Juan
Aconcagua 7013
Uspallata Pass
Mendoza
Viña del Mar
Valparaíso
Los Andes
Santiago
Rancagua
San Fernando
Curicó
San Rafael
San Luis
Córdoba
Venado Tuerto
Pergamino
Juan Fernández Is. (Chile)
Chillán
Concepción
Coronel
Lebu
Temuco
Zapala
Neuquén
Colorado
Santa Rosa
Bahía Blanca
Tandil
Mar del Plata
Buenos Aires
Avellaneda
La Plata
River Plate
Montevideo
Rosario
Santa Fé
Paraná
Pilcomayo
Paraguay
Uruguay
Resistencia
Corrientes
Asunción
Concepción
Posadas
Corumbá
Campo Grande
Ponta Porã
Cuiabá
Goiás
Goiânia
Anápolis
Brasília
Pirapora
Montes Claros
Diamantina
Dôres do Indaiá
Uberaba
Itabira
Colatina
Belo Horizonte
2904
Vitória
Caravelas
Ribeirão Prêto
Juiz de Fóra
Petrópolis
Niterói
Rio de Janeiro
2821
Volta Redonda
Campinas
Socarbo
São Paulo
Santos
Curitiba
Florianópolis
Uruguaiana
Sta. Maria
São Leopoldo
Pôrto Alegre
Salto
Rivera
Paysandú
Fray Bentos
Pelotas
Rio Grande
Angical
Poções
Itabuna
Ilhéus
Nazaré
Salvador (Bahia)
Feira de Santana
Aracajú
Maceió
Paulo Afonso Falls
Paulista
Recife (Pernambuco)

S. AMERICA
(South)
Scale 1:19,000,000 approx.
0 Kilometres 300 450 600
0 Miles 150 300 450
One Inch to 300 Miles
Towns over 1 million people
" over 100,000 people
Boundaries international
- provincial etc
Railways
projected
Airports
Sand desert
Salt pan
Roads
tracks
Canal
Marsh
Ice cap
Ft. M.
16,000 4,800
10,000 3,000
6,000 1,800
3,000 900
1,500 450
1,000 300
600 180
300 90
Sea Level
Land Depression
ATLANTIC
OCEAN
SCOTIA SEA
WEDDELL SEA
Chiloé I.
Chonos Archipelago
Taitao Peninsula
Rawson
Chubut
Las Plumas
Chico
Comodoro Rivadavia
Balmaceda
L. Cochrane
Puerto Deseado
Río Gallegos
Gallegos
Strait of Magellan
Queen Adelaide Archipelago
Punta Arenas (Magallanes)
Tierra del Fuego
Ushuaia
Ile de los Estados (Staten I.)
Cape Horn
FALKLAND IS. (Br.)
Port Stanley
SOUTH GEORGIA (Br.)
Grytviken
2934
South Sandwich Islands (Br.)
Drake Passage
Limit of pack ice—average max (spring)
South Shetland Islands
Elephant I.
Coronation I.
South Orkney Islands
Deception I.
Hope Bay
Antarctic Pen.
Graham Land
Larsen Ice Shelf
200 metres
Adelaide I.
Antarctic Circle
Limit of pack ice – average min. (autumn)
Charcot I.
Alexander I.
Palmer Land
Peter I Island (Nor.)
3581
4066
3375
2350
40°S
45°S
50°S
55°S
60°S
65°S
90°W
80°W
70°W
60°W
50°W
40°W
30°W
20°W
Transverse Mercator Projection

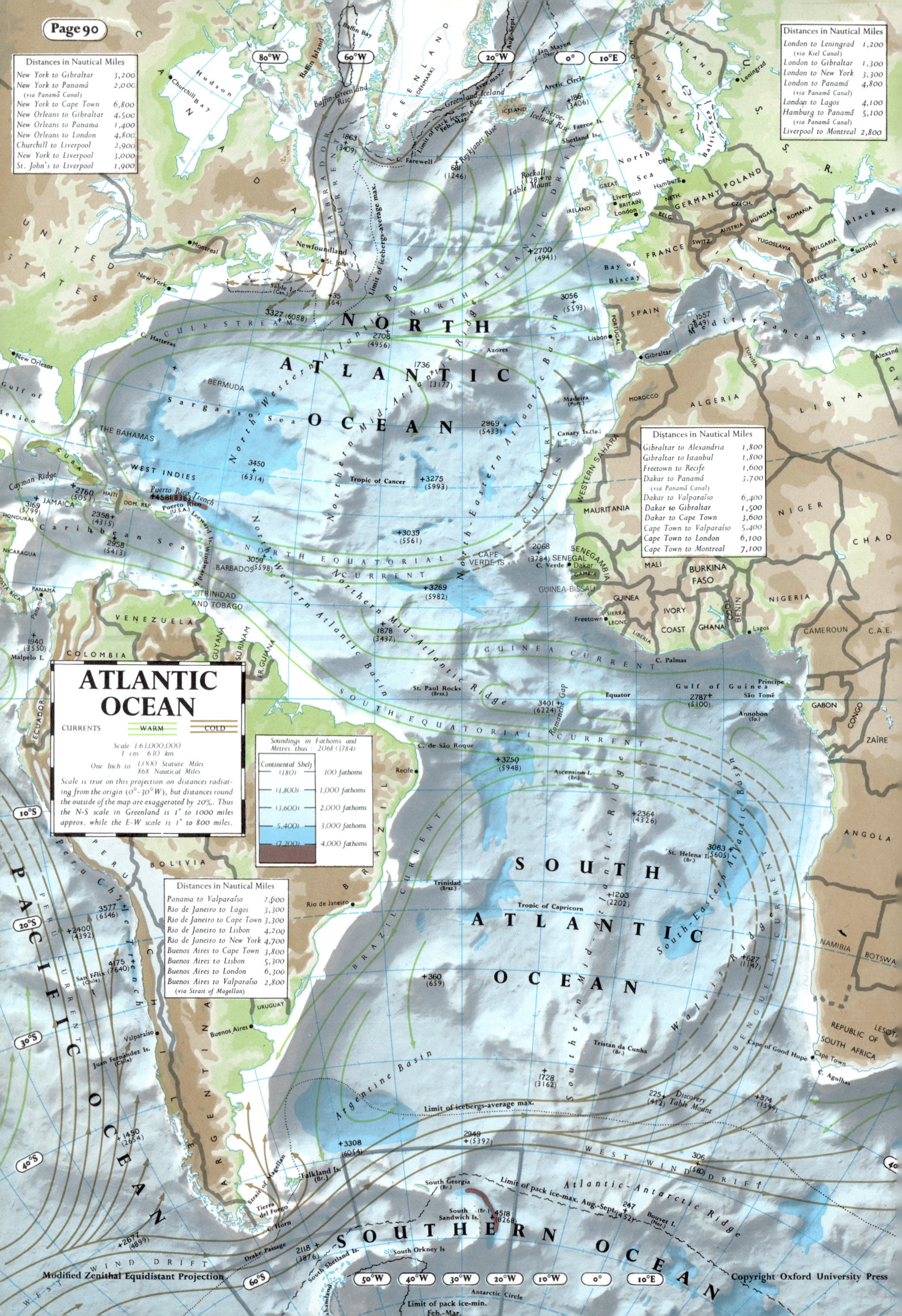
ATLANTIC OCEAN
CURRENTS WARM COLD
Scale 1:63,000,000
1 cm 630 km
One Inch to 1,000 Statute Miles 868 Nautical Miles
Scale is true on this projection on distances radiating from the origin (0°–30°W), but distances round the outside of the map are exaggerated by 20%. Thus the N-S scale in Greenland is 1" to 1000 miles approx. while the E-W scale is 1" to 800 miles.
Soundings in Fathoms and Metres thus: 2068 (3784)
Continental Shelf (180) 100 fathoms
(1,800) 1,000 fathoms
(3,600) 2,000 fathoms
(5,400) 3,000 fathoms
(7,200) 4,000 fathoms
Distances in Nautical Miles
New York to Gibraltar 3,200
New York to Panamá 2,000
(via Panamá Canal)
New York to Cape Town 6,800
New Orleans to Gibraltar 4,500
New Orleans to Panama 1,400
New Orleans to London 4,800
Churchill to Liverpool 2,900
New York to Liverpool 3,000
St. John's to Liverpool 1,900
Distances in Nautical Miles
London to Leningrad 1,200
(via Kiel Canal)
London to Gibraltar 1,300
London to New York 3,300
London to Panamá 4,800
(via Panamá Canal)
London to Lagos 4,100
Hamburg to Panamá 5,100
(via Panamá Canal)
Liverpool to Montreal 2,800
Distances in Nautical Miles
Gibraltar to Alexandria 1,800
Gibraltar to Istanbul 1,800
Freetown to Recife 1,600
Dakar to Panamá 3,700
(via Panamá Canal)
Dakar to Valparaíso 6,400
Dakar to Gibraltar 1,500
Dakar to Cape Town 3,600
Cape Town to Valparaíso 5,400
Cape Town to London 6,100
Cape Town to Montreal 7,100
Distances in Nautical Miles
Panama to Valparaíso 2,600
Rio de Janeiro to Lagos 3,300
Rio de Janeiro to Cape Town 3,300
Rio de Janeiro to Lisbon 4,200
Rio de Janeiro to New York 4,700
Buenos Aires to Cape Town 3,800
Buenos Aires to Lisbon 5,300
Buenos Aires to London 6,300
Buenos Aires to Valparaíso 2,800
(via Strait of Magellan)
NORTH ATLANTIC OCEAN
SOUTH ATLANTIC OCEAN
SOUTHERN OCEAN
PACIFIC OCEAN
GULF STREAM
NORTH EQUATORIAL CURRENT
GUINEA CURRENT
SOUTH EQUATORIAL CURRENT
BRAZIL CURRENT
BENGUELA CURRENT
CANARY CURRENT
LABRADOR CURRENT
WEST WIND DRIFT
Sargasso Sea
North-Western Atlantic Basin
North-Eastern Atlantic Basin
Northern Mid-Atlantic Ridge
Southern Mid-Atlantic Ridge
South-Eastern Atlantic Basin
Walvis Ridge
Argentine Basin
Atlantic-Antarctic Ridge
Romanche Gap
Limit of icebergs-average max.
Limit of pack ice-max. Aug.-Sept.
Limit of pack ice-min. Feb.-Mar.
Tropic of Cancer
Tropic of Capricorn
Equator
Arctic Circle
Antarctic Circle
Modified Zenithal Equidistant Projection
80°W 60°W 20°W 0° 10°E
50°W 40°W 30°W 20°W 10°W 0° 10°E
10°S 20°S 30°S 40°S 60°S

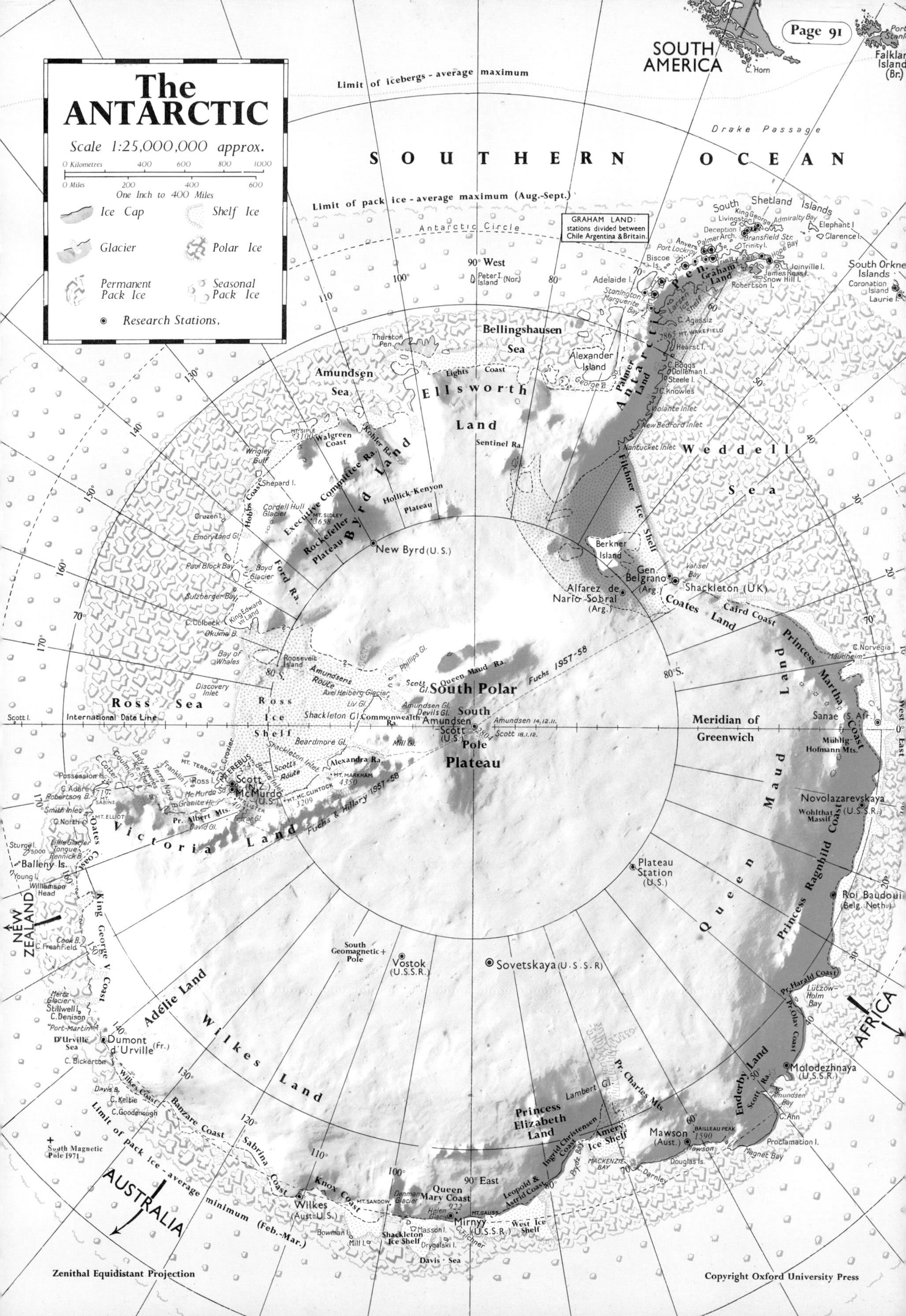
The ANTARCTIC
Scale 1:25,000,000 approx.
0 Kilometres 400 600 800 1000
0 Miles 200 400 600
One Inch to 400 Miles
Ice Cap
Shelf Ice
Glacier
Polar Ice
Permanent Pack Ice
Seasonal Pack Ice
Research Stations,
SOUTH AMERICA
C. Horn
Falkland Islands (Br.)
Limit of icebergs - average maximum
Drake Passage
SOUTHERN OCEAN
Limit of pack ice - average maximum (Aug.-Sept.)
Antarctic Circle
GRAHAM LAND: stations divided between Chile Argentina & Britain.
South Shetland Islands
King George I.
Livingston I.
Admiralty Bay
Deception I.
Elephant I.
Clarence I.
Anvers I.
Palmer Arch.
Bransfield Str.
Trinity I.
Hope Bay
Port Lockroy
Biscoe Is.
Joinville I.
James Ross I.
Snow Hill I.
Robertson I.
South Orkney Islands
Coronation Island
Laurie I.
90° West
Peter I. Island (Nor.)
Adelaide I.
Stonington I.
Marguerite Bay
Graham Land
Antarctic Pen.
Larsen Ice Shelf
C. Agassiz
MT. WAKEFIELD 2865
Hearst I.
C. Boggs
Dolleman I.
Steele I.
C. Knowles
Bellingshausen Sea
Alexander Island
George VI Sound
Palmer Land
Thurston Pen.
Eights Coast
Amundsen Sea
Ellsworth Land
Sentinel Ra.
Bolante Inlet
New Bedford Inlet
Nantucket Inlet
Weddell Sea
MT. SIPLE 3100
Walgreen Coast
Kohler Ra.
Wrigley Gulf
Shepard I.
Hobbs Coast
Executive Committee Ra.
Byrd Land
Hollick-Kenyon Plateau
Cordell Hull Glacier
MT. SIDLEY 3658
Rockefeller Plateau
Cruzen I.
Emory Land Gl.
New Byrd (U.S.)
Filchner Ice Shelf
Berkner Island
Vahsel Bay
Gen. Belgrano (Arg.)
Shackleton (UK)
Alfarez de Nario Sobral (Arg.)
Coates Land
Caird Coast
Paul Block Bay
Boyd Glacier
Ford Ra.
Sulzberger Bay
King Edward VII Land
C. Colbeck
Okuma B.
Bay of Whales
Roosevelt Island
Phillips Gl.
Queen Maud Ra.
Fuchs 1957-58
Princess Martha Coast
C. Norvegia
Maudheim
80° S.
Amundsens Route
Axel Heiberg Glacier
Liv Gl.
Scott Gl.
South Polar
Discovery Inlet
Ross Sea
Ross Ice Shelf
Amundsen Gl.
Devils Gl.
South
Amundsen Scott (U.S.)
2804
Pole
Plateau
Amundsen 14.12.11.
Scott 18.1.12.
Scott I.
International Date Line
Shackleton Gl.
Commonwealth Ra.
Meridian of Greenwich
Sanae (S. Afr.)
West
East
Beardmore Gl.
Mill Gl.
Shackleton Inlet
Scott's Route
Alexandra Ra.
MT. MARKHAM 4350
MT. TERROR
MT. EREBUS
Ross I.
Scott (N.Z.)
McMurdo (U.S.)
Mc Murdo Sd.
Granite Hr.
Franklin I.
Terra Nova B.
Lady Newnes Ice Shelf
Coulman I.
C. Cotter
Possession Is.
C. Adare
Robertson B.
Smith Inlet
MT. SABINE
MT. MC CLINTOCK 3209
Fuchs & Hillary 1957-58
Mühlig-Hofmann Mts.
Queen Maud Land
MT. ELLIOT
C. North
Pr. Albert Mts.
David Gl.
Victoria Land
Oates Coast
Novolazarevskaya (U.S.S.R.)
Wohlthat Massif
Princess Ragnhild Coast
Sturge I.
5000
Lillie Glacier Tongue
Rennick B.
Balleny Is.
Young I.
Williamson Head
Plateau Station (U.S.)
Roi Baudouin (Belg. Neth.)
NEW ZEALAND
Cook B.
C. Freshfield
King George V Coast
South Geomagnetic Pole
Vostok (U.S.S.R.)
Sovetskaya (U.S.S.R.)
Princess Ragnhild Coast
Pr. Harald Coast
Lützow-Holm Bay
AFRICA
Adélie Land
Mertz Glacier
Stillwell I.
C. Denison
"Port-Martin"
D'Urville Sea
Dumont d'Urville (Fr.)
C. Bickerton
Wilkes Land
Pr. Olav Coast
Pr. Charles Mts.
Enderby Land
Molodezhnaya (U.S.S.R.)
Scott Ra.
Amundsen Bay
C. Ann
Wilkes Coast
Davis B.
C. Keltie
C. Goodenough
Banzare Coast
Lambert Gl.
Princess Elizabeth Land
Ingrid Christensen Coast
Amery Ice Shelf
Mawson (Aust.)
BAILLEAU PEAK 1590
Proclamation I.
Magnet Bay
Douglas Is.
Mackenzie Bay
C. Darnley
Sabrina Coast
Limit of pack ice - average minimum (Feb.-Mar.)
South Magnetic Pole 1971
AUSTRALIA
Knox Coast
MT. SANDOW
Denman Glacier
Queen Mary Coast
922
Helen Glacier
90° East
Leopold & Astrid Coast
MT. GAUSS
Mirnyy (U.S.S.R.)
West Ice Shelf
Wilkes (Aust.-U.S.)
Bowman I.
Masson I.
Mill I.
Shackleton Ice Shelf
C. Filchner
Drygalski I.
Davis Sea
Zenithal Equidistant Projection

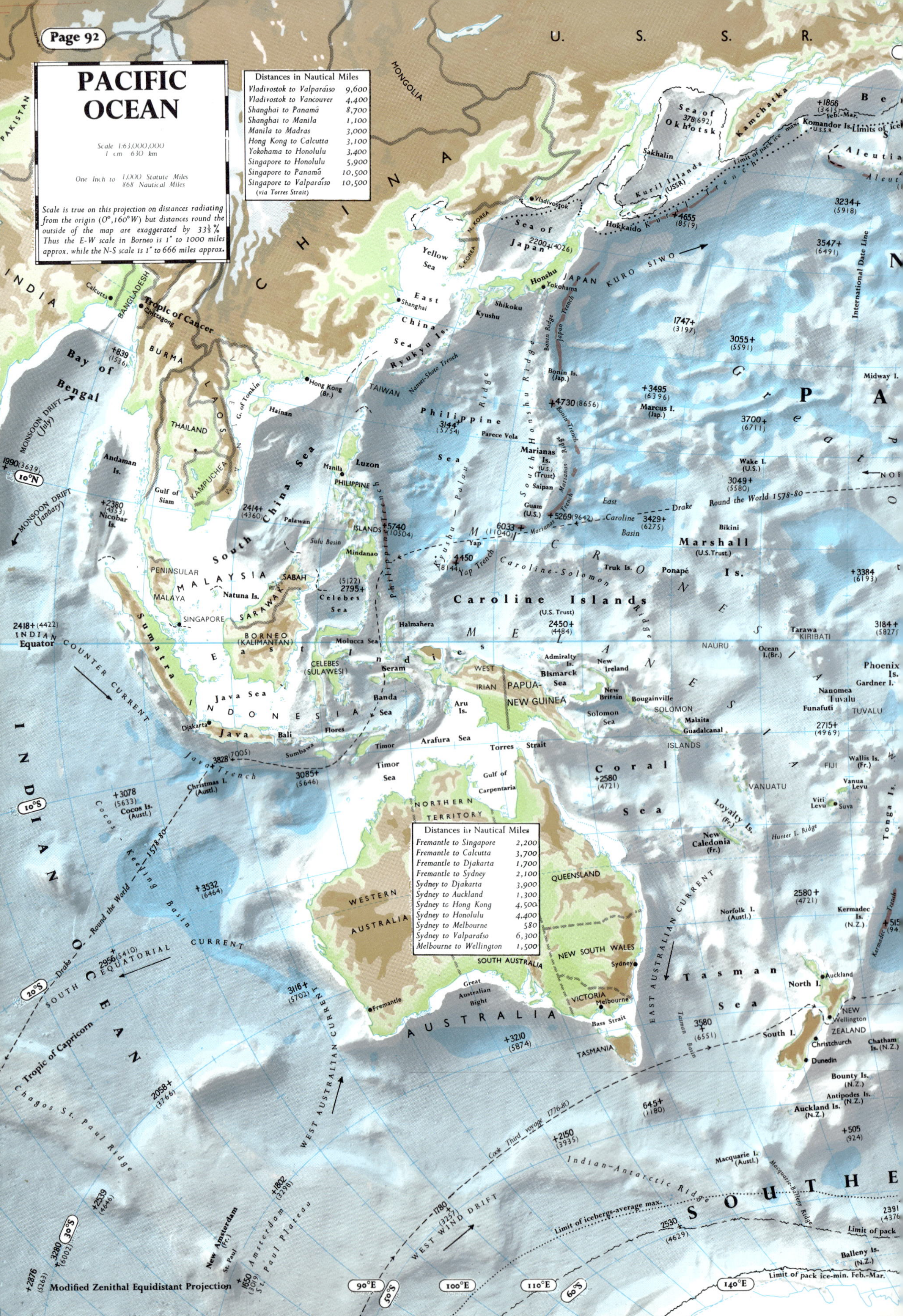
PACIFIC OCEAN
Scale 1:63,000,000
1 cm 630 km
One Inch to 1,000 Statute Miles 868 Nautical Miles
Scale is true on this projection on distances radiating from the origin (0°, 160°W) but distances round the outside of the map are exaggerated by 33⅓%. Thus the E-W scale in Borneo is 1" to 1000 miles approx. while the N-S scale is 1" to 666 miles approx.
Distances in Nautical Miles
Vladivostok to Valparaiso 9,600
Vladivostok to Vancouver 4,400
Shanghai to Panamá 8,700
Shanghai to Manila 1,100
Manila to Madras 3,000
Hong Kong to Calcutta 3,100
Yokohama to Honolulu 3,400
Singapore to Honolulu 5,900
Singapore to Panamá 10,500
Singapore to Valparaiso (via Torres Strait) 10,500
Distances in Nautical Miles
Fremantle to Singapore 2,200
Fremantle to Calcutta 3,700
Fremantle to Djakarta 1,700
Fremantle to Sydney 2,100
Sydney to Djakarta 3,900
Sydney to Auckland 1,300
Sydney to Hong Kong 4,500
Sydney to Honolulu 4,400
Sydney to Melbourne 580
Sydney to Valparaiso 6,300
Melbourne to Wellington 1,500
U. S. S. R.
MONGOLIA
CHINA
PAKISTAN
INDIA
BANGLADESH
BURMA
LAOS
VIETNAM
THAILAND
KAMPUCHEA
Tropic of Cancer
Bay of Bengal
Sea of Okhotsk
Kamchatka
Sakhalin
Kuril Islands (USSR)
Hokkaido
Sea of Japan
Yellow Sea
East China Sea
Honshu
Shikoku
Kyushu
Ryukyu Is.
TAIWAN
Hong Kong (Br.)
Hainan
Philippine Sea
Luzon
Manila
PHILIPPINE ISLANDS
Mindanao
South China Sea
Gulf of Siam
Andaman Is.
Nicobar Is.
MALAYSIA
SINGAPORE
Sumatra
BORNEO (KALIMANTAN)
SARAWAK
SABAH
Celebes Sea
CELEBES (SULAWESI)
Molucca Sea
Halmahera
Seram
Banda Sea
Java Sea
Java
Bali
INDONESIA
Timor Sea
Arafura Sea
Torres Strait
WEST IRIAN
PAPUA-NEW GUINEA
Bismarck Sea
Solomon Sea
Coral Sea
Caroline Islands
Marianas Is. (U.S.) (Trust)
Marshall Is. (U.S.Trust.)
MICRONESIA
MELANESIA
POLYNESIA
NAURU
KIRIBATI
TUVALU
SOLOMON ISLANDS
VANUATU
FIJI
New Caledonia (Fr.)
AUSTRALIA
NORTHERN TERRITORY
WESTERN AUSTRALIA
SOUTH AUSTRALIA
QUEENSLAND
NEW SOUTH WALES
VICTORIA
TASMANIA
Tasman Sea
NEW ZEALAND
North I.
South I.
INDIAN OCEAN
SOUTHERN OCEAN
Equator
Tropic of Capricorn
Drake Round the World 1578-80
Cook Third voyage 1776-80
WEST WIND DRIFT
SOUTH EQUATORIAL CURRENT
WEST AUSTRALIAN CURRENT
EAST AUSTRALIAN CURRENT
KURO SIWO
INDIAN COUNTER CURRENT
MONSOON DRIFT (July)
MONSOON DRIFT (January)
Limit of icebergs-average max.
Limit of pack ice-min. Feb.-Mar.
International Date Line
Modified Zenithal Equidistant Projection
10°N
Equator
10°S
20°S
30°S
50°S
60°S
90°E
100°E
110°E
140°E

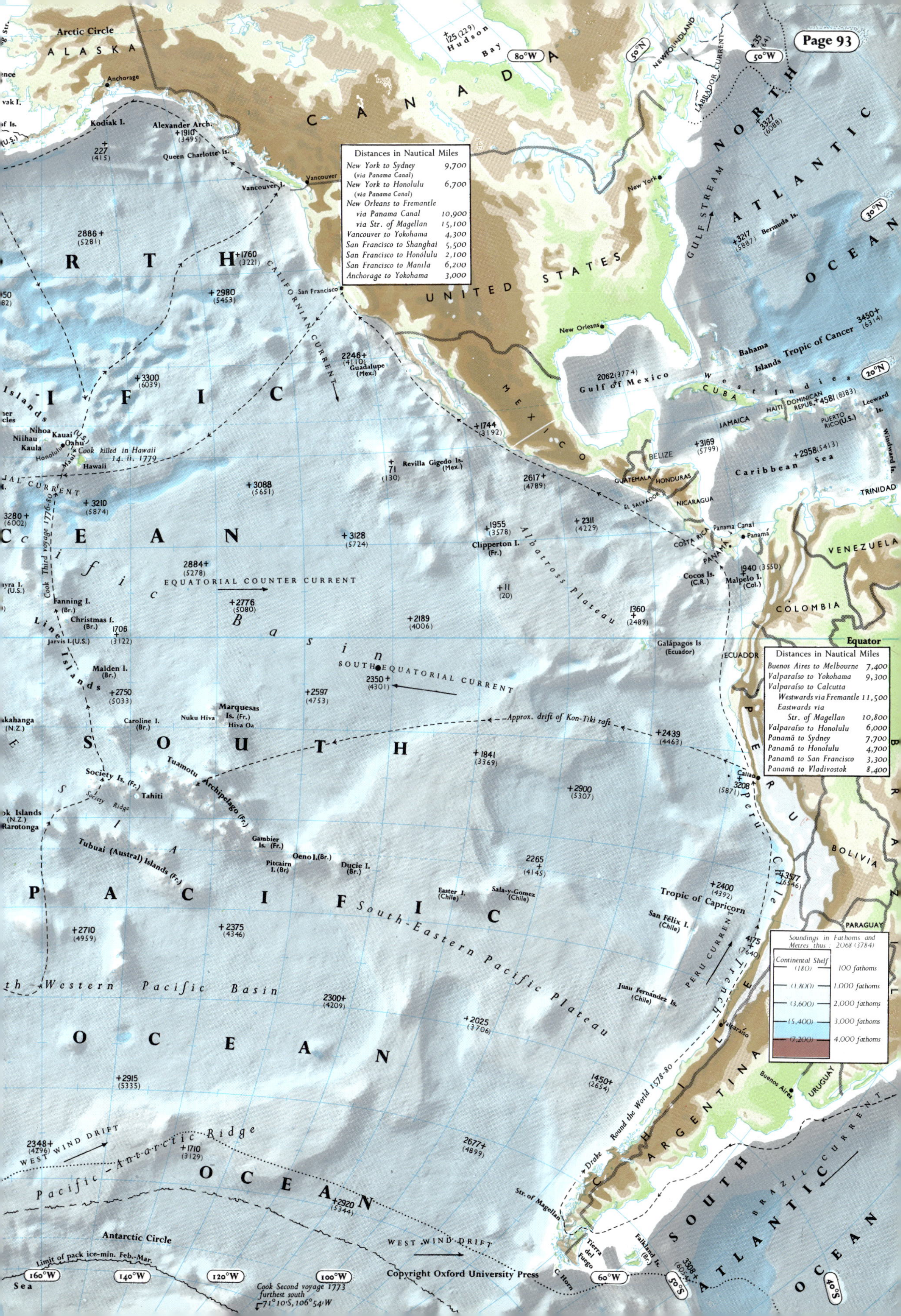
Distances in Nautical Miles
New York to Sydney (via Panama Canal) 9,700
New York to Honolulu (via Panama Canal) 6,700
New Orleans to Fremantle via Panama Canal 10,900
via Str. of Magellan 15,100
Vancouver to Yokohama 4,300
San Francisco to Shanghai 5,500
San Francisco to Honolulu 2,100
San Francisco to Manila 6,200
Anchorage to Yokohama 3,000
Distances in Nautical Miles
Buenos Aires to Melbourne 7,400
Valparaíso to Yokohama 9,300
Valparaíso to Calcutta
Westwards via Fremantle 11,500
Eastwards via Str. of Magellan 10,800
Valparaíso to Honolulu 6,000
Panamá to Sydney 7,700
Panamá to Honolulu 4,700
Panamá to San Francisco 3,300
Panamá to Vladivostok 8,400
Soundings in Fathoms and Metres thus 2068 (3784)
Continental Shelf (180) 100 fathoms
(1,800) 1,000 fathoms
(3,600) 2,000 fathoms
(5,400) 3,000 fathoms
(7,200) 4,000 fathoms
Arctic Circle
ALASKA
Anchorage
Kodiak I.
Alexander Arch.
Queen Charlotte Is.
Vancouver I.
Vancouver
CANADA
Hudson Bay
80°W
50°N
NEWFOUNDLAND
LABRADOR CURRENT
50°W
New York
UNITED STATES
NORTH ATLANTIC OCEAN
GULF STREAM
Bermuda Is.
30°N
San Francisco
CALIFORNIAN CURRENT
New Orleans
Guadalupe (Mex.)
Gulf of Mexico
MEXICO
Bahama Islands
Tropic of Cancer
20°N
West Indies
CUBA
HAITI
DOMINICAN REPUB.
JAMAICA
PUERTO RICO (U.S.)
Leeward Is.
Windward Is.
BELIZE
GUATEMALA
HONDURAS
EL SALVADOR
NICARAGUA
COSTA RICA
PANAMA
Panama Canal
Panamá
Caribbean Sea
TRINIDAD
VENEZUELA
COLOMBIA
Revilla Gigedo Is. (Mex.)
Clipperton I. (Fr.)
Albatross Plateau
Cocos Is. (C.R.)
Malpelo I. (Col.)
Galápagos Is (Ecuador)
ECUADOR
Equator
PERU
Callao
Peru-Chile Trench
BOLIVIA
BRAZIL
PARAGUAY
Tropic of Capricorn
San Félix I. (Chile)
Juan Fernández Is. (Chile)
Valparaíso
PERU CURRENT
CHILE
ARGENTINA
URUGUAY
Buenos Aires
Islands
Nihoa
Kauai
Oahu
Niihau
Kaula
Honolulu
Maui
Hawaii
Cook killed in Hawaii 14. ii. 1779
Cook Third voyage 1776-80
PACIFIC OCEAN
EQUATORIAL COUNTER CURRENT
Pacific Basin
Fanning I. (Br.)
Christmas I. (Br.)
Jarvis I. (U.S.)
Line Islands
Malden I. (Br.)
SOUTH EQUATORIAL CURRENT
Approx. drift of Kon-Tiki raft
Caroline I. (Br.)
Marquesas Is. (Fr.)
Nuku Hiva
Hiva Oa
SOUTH PACIFIC OCEAN
Society Is. (Fr.)
Tahiti
Society Ridge
Tuamotu Archipelago (Fr.)
Rarotonga
Tubuai (Austral) Islands (Fr.)
Gambier Is. (Fr.)
Oeno I. (Br.)
Pitcairn I. (Br.)
Ducie I. (Br.)
Easter I. (Chile)
Sala-y-Gomez (Chile)
South-Eastern Pacific Plateau
Western Pacific Basin
Pacific-Antarctic Ridge
WEST WIND DRIFT
Antarctic Circle
Limit of pack ice-min. Feb.-Mar.
Drake Round the World 1578-80
Str. of Magellan
Tierra del Fuego
C. Horn
Falkland Is. (Br.)
SOUTH ATLANTIC OCEAN
BRAZIL CURRENT
160°W
140°W
120°W
100°W
60°W
50°S
40°S
Cook Second voyage 1773 furthest south 71°10'S, 106°54'W

PHYSICAL

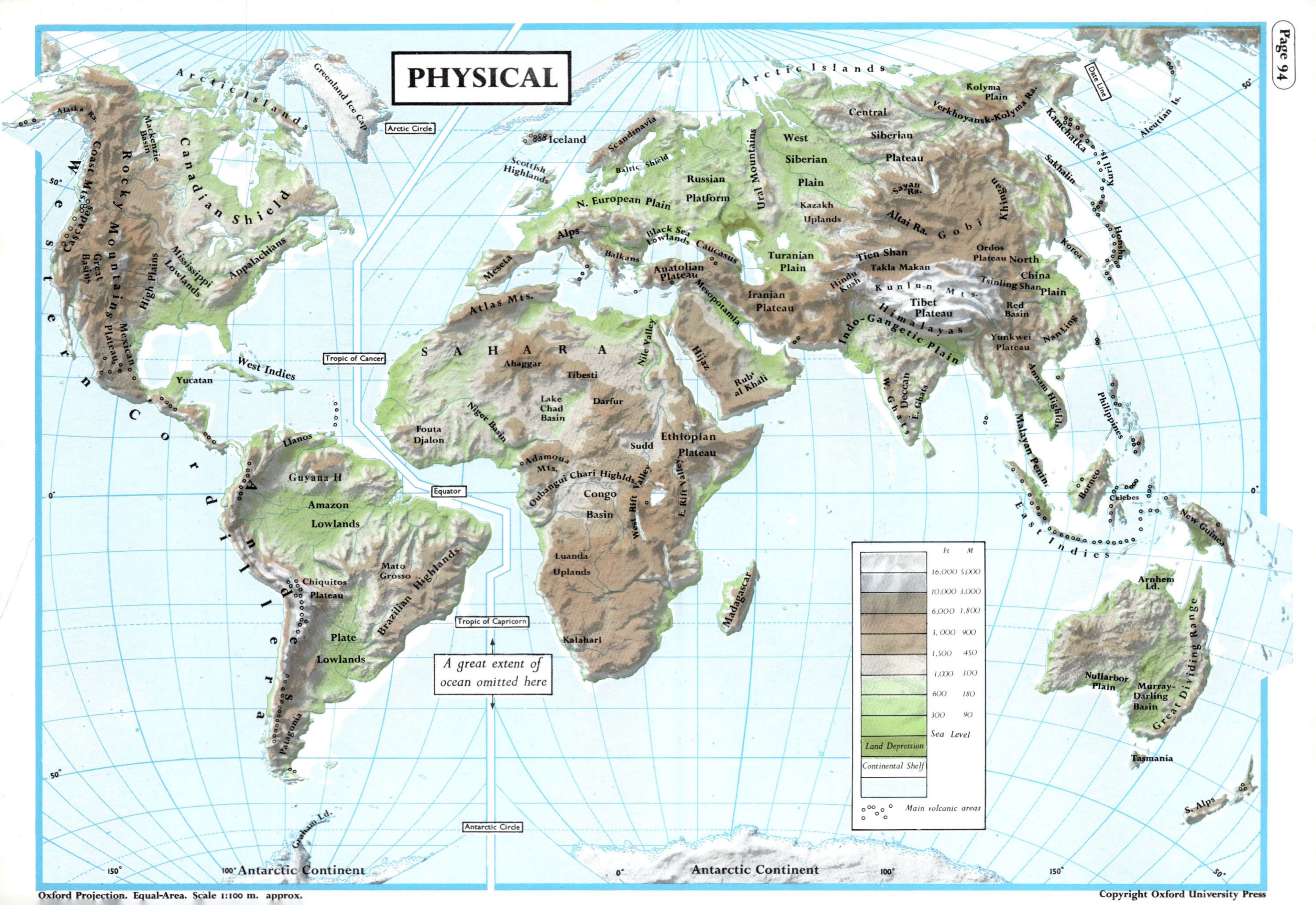

Oxford Projection. Equal-Area. Scale 1:100 m. approx.

BUILD

Oxford Projection. Equal-Area. Scale 1 : 100 m. approx.

VEGETATION

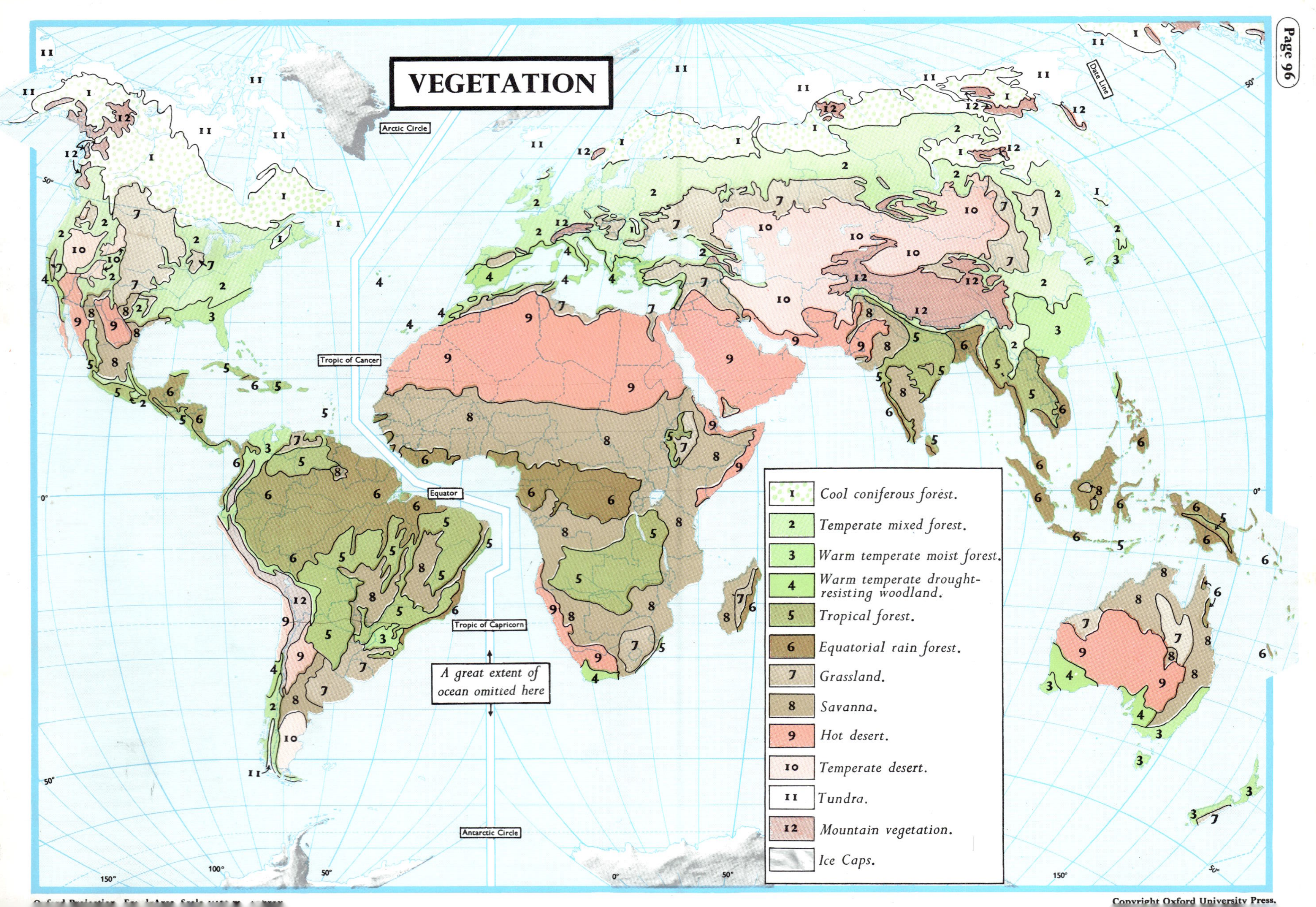
VEGETATION
Arctic Circle
Tropic of Cancer
Equator
Tropic of Capricorn
Antarctic Circle
Date Line
A great extent of ocean omitted here
1 Cool coniferous forest.
2 Temperate mixed forest.
3 Warm temperate moist forest.
4 Warm temperate drought-resisting woodland.
5 Tropical forest.
6 Equatorial rain forest.
7 Grassland.
8 Savanna.
9 Hot desert.
10 Temperate desert.
11 Tundra.
12 Mountain vegetation.
Ice Caps.

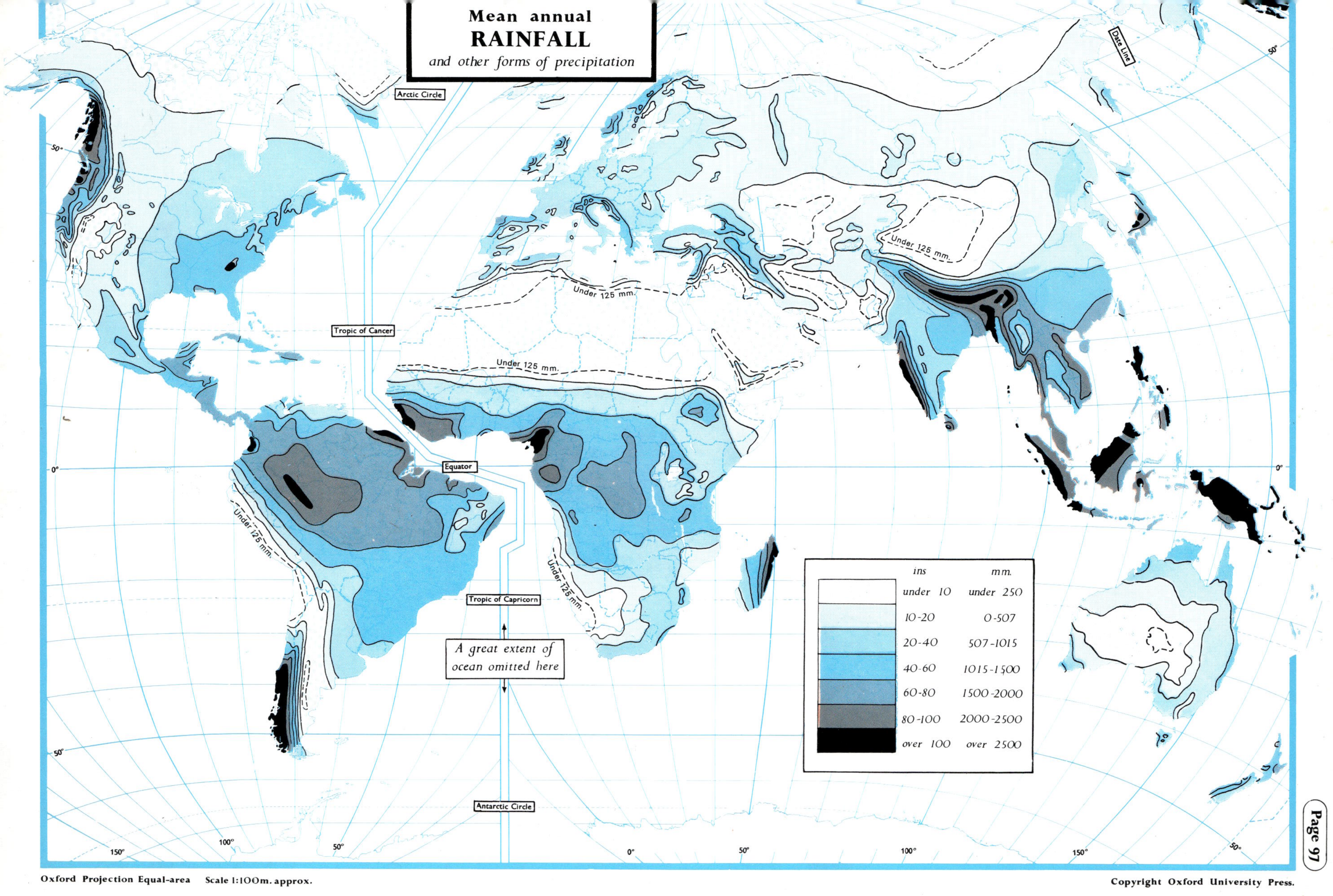

Oxford Projection Equal-area Scale 1:100m. approx.

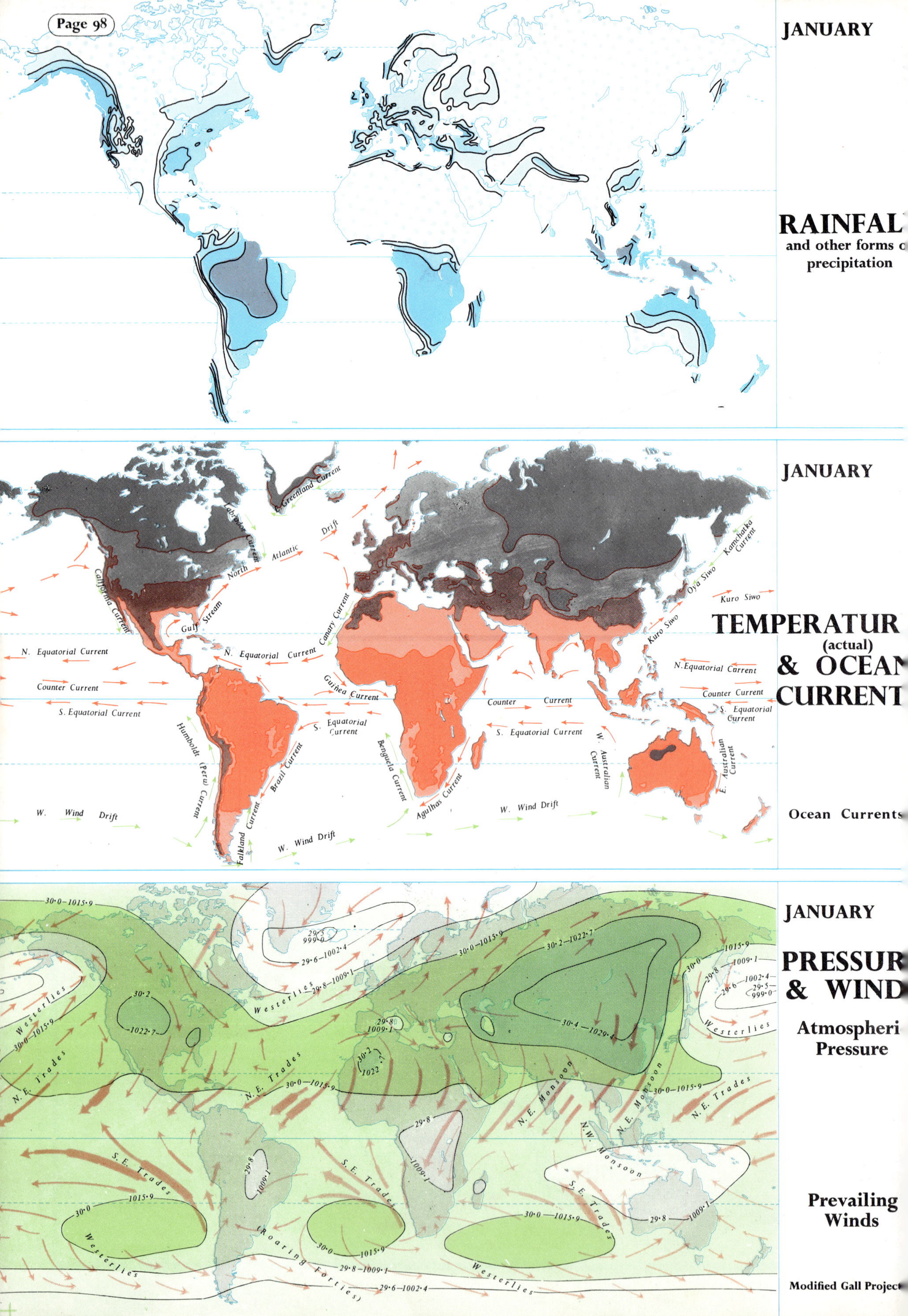

Page 98
JANUARY
RAINFAL
and other forms o
precipitation
JANUARY
TEMPERATUR
(actual)
& OCEA
CURRENT
Ocean Currents
E. Greenland Current
Labrador Current
North Atlantic Drift
California Current
Gulf Stream
Canary Current
N. Equatorial Current
N. Equatorial Current
Counter Current
S. Equatorial Current
Guinea Current
S. Equatorial Current
Humboldt (Peru) Current
Brazil Current
Benguela Current
Agulhas Current
Falkland Current
W. Wind Drift
W. Wind Drift
W. Wind Drift
Counter Current
S. Equatorial Current
W. Australian Current
Kamchatka Current
Oya Siwo
Kuro Siwo
Kuro Siwo
N.Equatorial Current
Counter Current
S. Equatorial Current
E. Australian Current
JANUARY
PRESSUR
& WIND
Atmospheri
Pressure
Prevailing
Winds
Modified Gall Project
30·0–1015·9
29·5
999·0
29·6–1002·4
30·0–1015·9
30·2–1022·7
1015·9
29·8–1009·1
29·6
1002·4
29·5
999·0
Westerlies
30·0–1015·9
30·2
1022·7
Westerlies
29·8–1009·1
29·8
1009·1
30·2
1022
30·4–1029·4
N.E. Trades
N.E. Trades
30·0–1015·9
N.E. Monsoon
N.E. Monsoon
30·0–1015·9
N.E. Trades
Westerlies
29·8
1009·1
29·8
1009·1
N.W. Monsoon
S.E. Trades
S.E. Trades
S.E. Trades
1015·9
30·0
30·0–1015·9
29·8
1009·1
Westerlies
30·0
1015·9
(Roaring Forties)
29·8–1009·1
Westerlies
29·6–1002·4

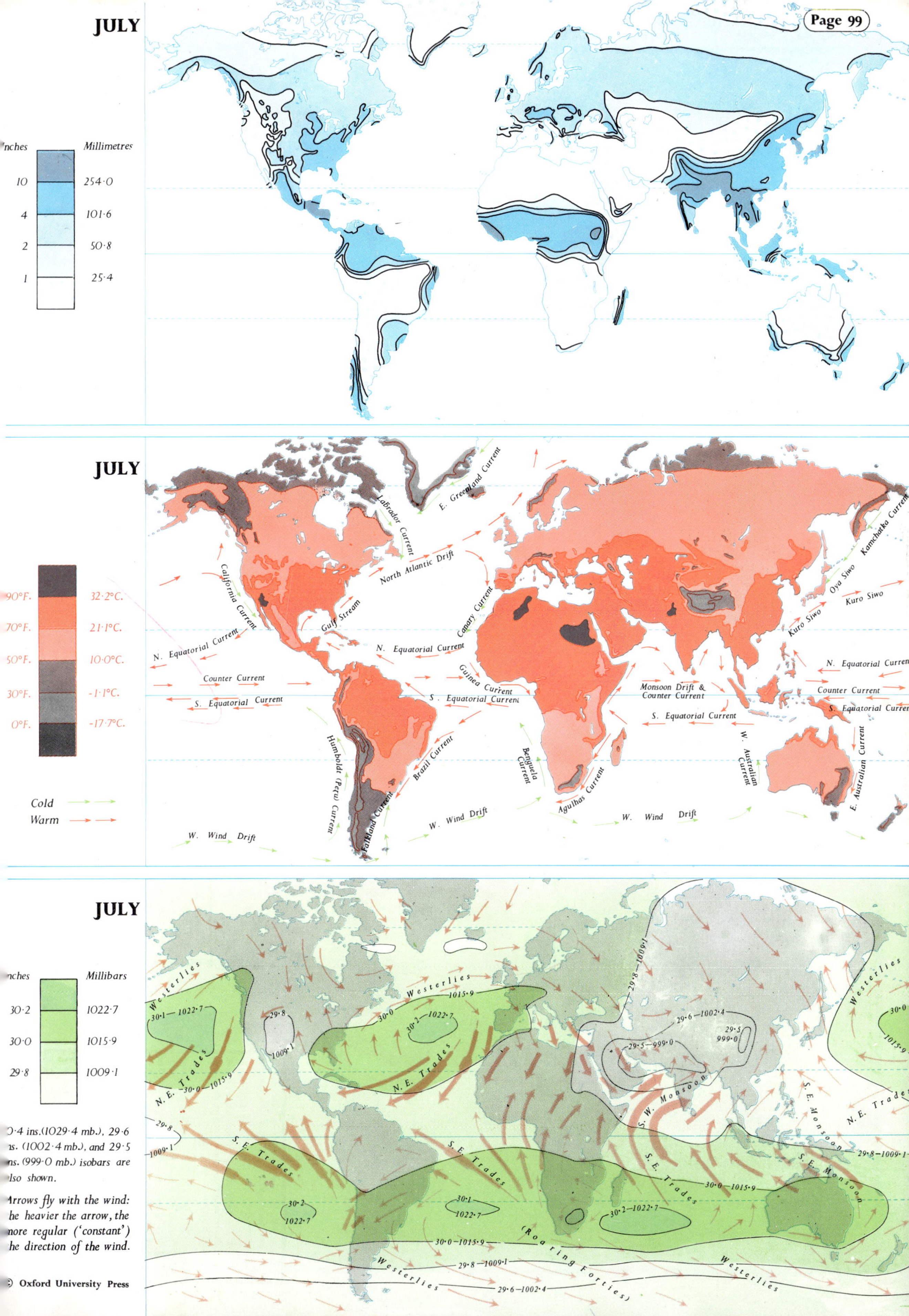
JULY
nches
Millimetres
10
254·0
4
101·6
2
50·8
1
25·4
JULY
90°F.
32·2°C.
70°F.
21·1°C.
50°F.
10·0°C.
30°F.
-1·1°C.
0°F.
-17·7°C.
Cold
Warm
E. Greenland Current
Labrador Current
North Atlantic Drift
California Current
Gulf Stream
Canary Current
N. Equatorial Current
Counter Current
S. Equatorial Current
Guinea Current
Monsoon Drift & Counter Current
Kamchatka Current
Oya Siwo
Kuro Siwo
Humboldt (Peru) Current
Brazil Current
Benguela Current
Agulhas Current
W. Australian Current
E. Australian Current
Falkland Current
W. Wind Drift
JULY
nches
Millibars
30·2
1022·7
30·0
1015·9
29·8
1009·1
0·4 ins.(1029·4 mb.), 29·6 ns. (1002·4 mb.), and 29·5 ns. (999·0 mb.) isobars are lso shown.
Arrows fly with the wind: he heavier the arrow, the nore regular ('constant') he direction of the wind.
Westerlies
N. E. Trades
S. E. Trades
S. W. Monsoon
S. E. Monsoon
(Roaring Forties)
29·6—1002·4
29·5—999·0
29·8—1009·1
30·0—1015·9
30·2—1022·7
30·1—1022·7
© Oxford University Press

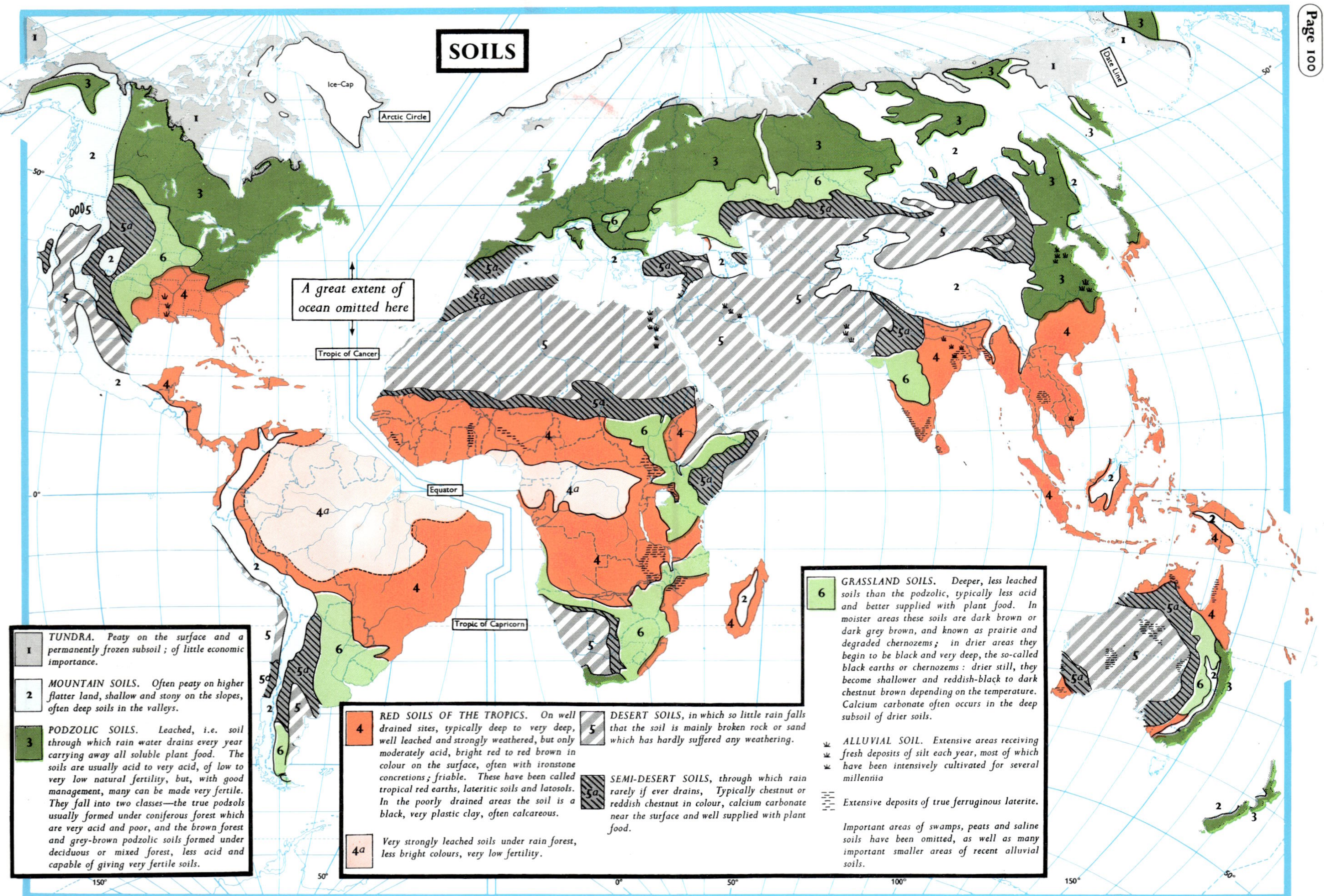
SOILS
Ice-Cap
Arctic Circle
Date Line
A great extent of ocean omitted here
Tropic of Cancer
Equator
Tropic of Capricorn
1 TUNDRA. Peaty on the surface and a permanently frozen subsoil; of little economic importance.
2 MOUNTAIN SOILS. Often peaty on higher flatter land, shallow and stony on the slopes, often deep soils in the valleys.
3 PODZOLIC SOILS. Leached, i.e. soil through which rain water drains every year carrying away all soluble plant food. The soils are usually acid to very acid, of low to very low natural fertility, but, with good management, many can be made very fertile. They fall into two classes—the true podsols usually formed under coniferous forest which are very acid and poor, and the brown forest and grey-brown podzolic soils formed under deciduous or mixed forest, less acid and capable of giving very fertile soils.
4 RED SOILS OF THE TROPICS. On well drained sites, typically deep to very deep, well leached and strongly weathered, but only moderately acid, bright red to red brown in colour on the surface, often with ironstone concretions; friable. These have been called tropical red earths, lateritic soils and latosols. In the poorly drained areas the soil is a black, very plastic clay, often calcareous.
4a Very strongly leached soils under rain forest, less bright colours, very low fertility.
5 DESERT SOILS, in which so little rain falls that the soil is mainly broken rock or sand which has hardly suffered any weathering.
5a SEMI-DESERT SOILS, through which rain rarely if ever drains, Typically chestnut or reddish chestnut in colour, calcium carbonate near the surface and well supplied with plant food.
6 GRASSLAND SOILS. Deeper, less leached soils than the podzolic, typically less acid and better supplied with plant food. In moister areas these soils are dark brown or dark grey brown, and known as prairie and degraded chernozems; in drier areas they begin to be black and very deep, the so-called black earths or chernozems: drier still, they become shallower and reddish-black to dark chestnut brown depending on the temperature. Calcium carbonate often occurs in the deep subsoil of drier soils.
ALLUVIAL SOIL. Extensive areas receiving fresh deposits of silt each year, most of which have been intensively cultivated for several millennia
Extensive deposits of true ferruginous laterite.
Important areas of swamps, peats and saline soils have been omitted, as well as many important smaller areas of recent alluvial soils.
150°
50°
0°
100°
Oxford Projection Equal-area Scale 1:100m. approx.

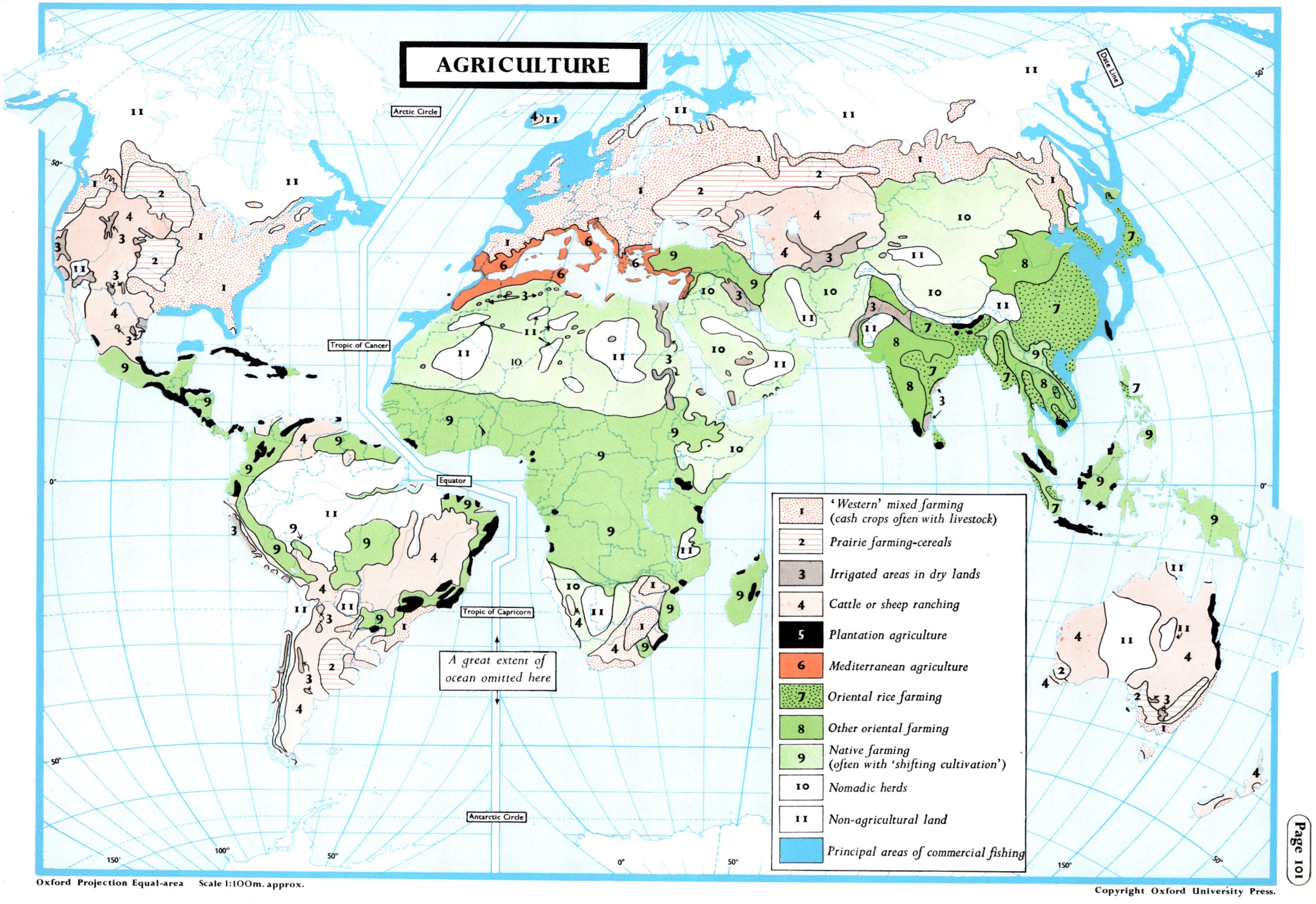
AGRICULTURE
Arctic Circle
Tropic of Cancer
Equator
Tropic of Capricorn
Antarctic Circle
Date Line
A great extent of ocean omitted here
1 'Western' mixed farming (cash crops often with livestock)
2 Prairie farming-cereals
3 Irrigated areas in dry lands
4 Cattle or sheep ranching
5 Plantation agriculture
6 Mediterranean agriculture
7 Oriental rice farming
8 Other oriental farming
9 Native farming (often with 'shifting cultivation')
10 Nomadic herds
11 Non-agricultural land
Principal areas of commercial fishing
Oxford Projection Equal-area Scale 1:100m. approx.

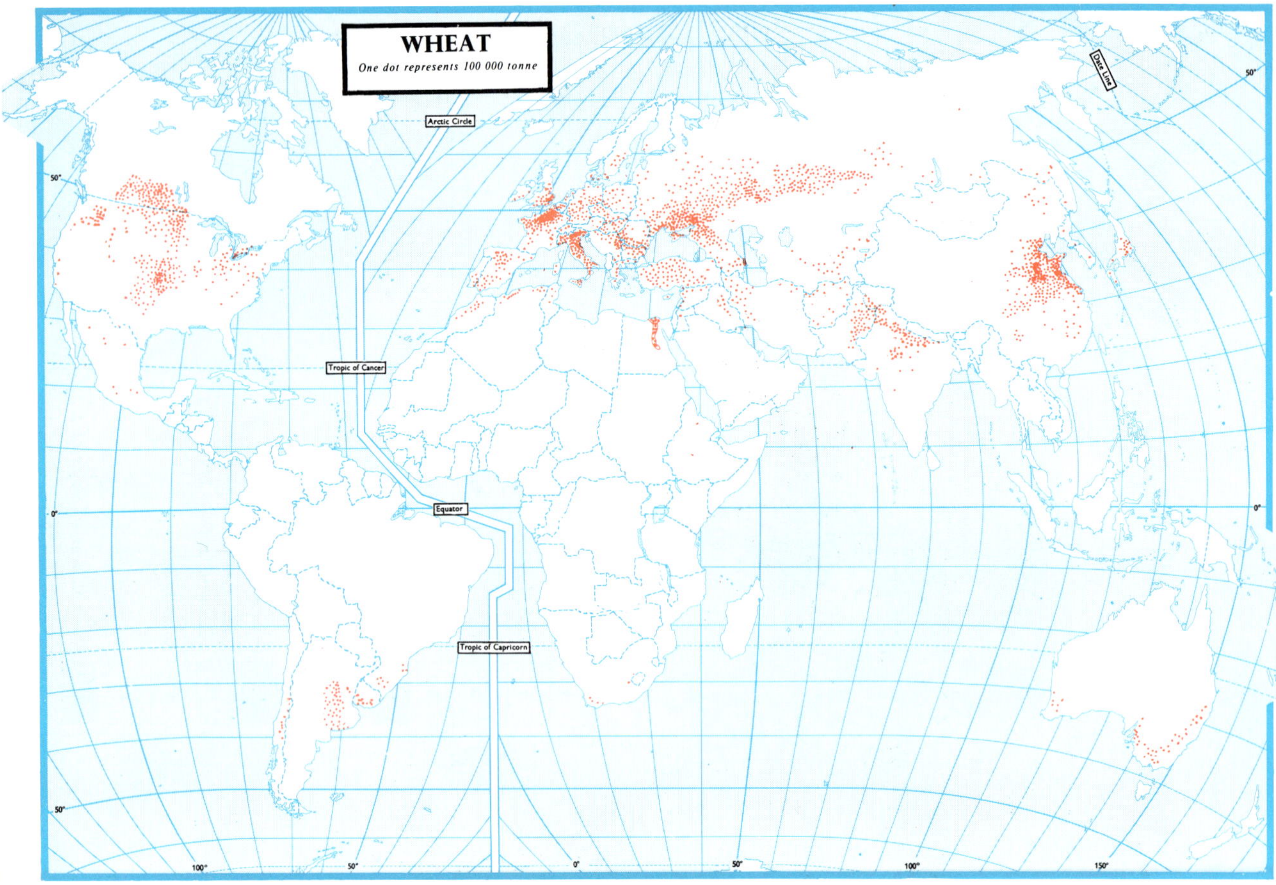

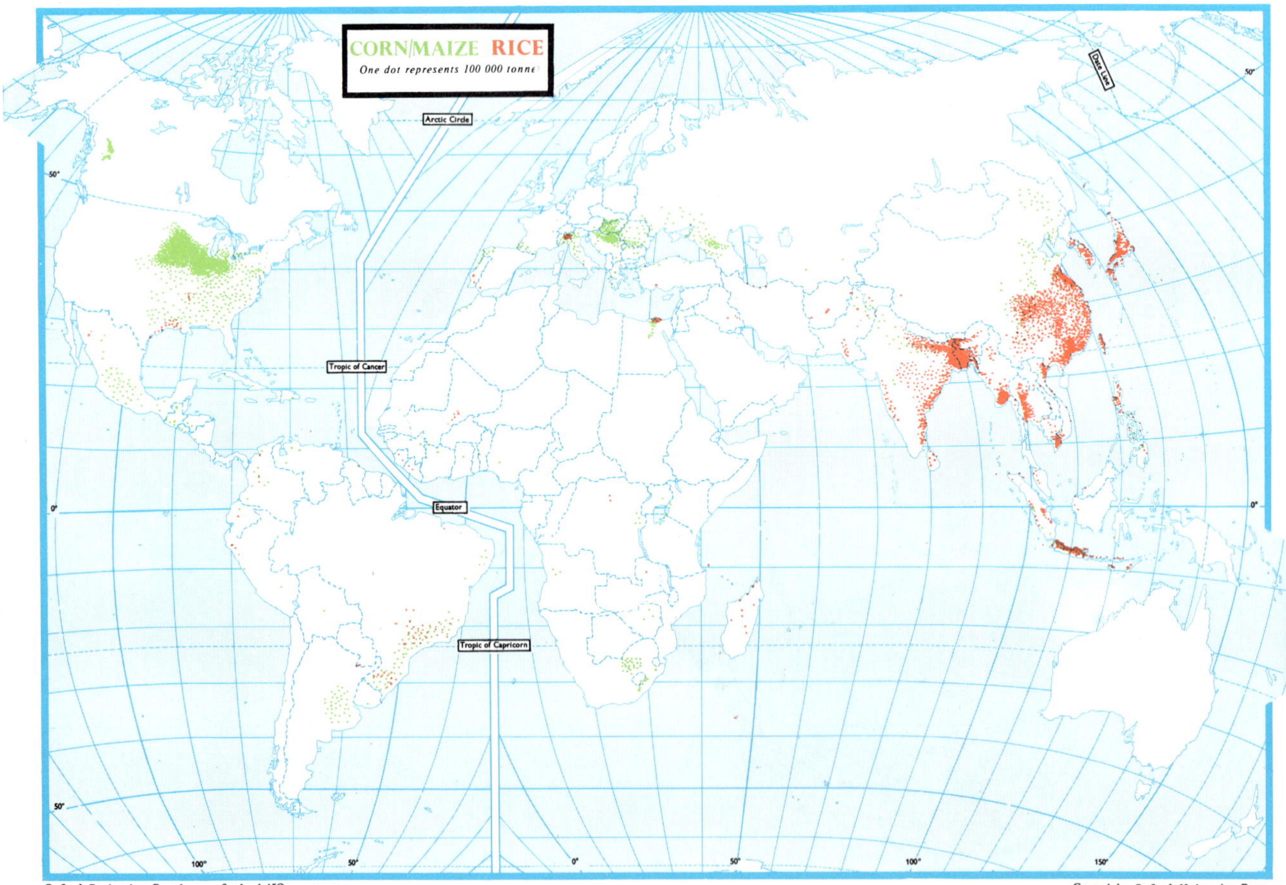

WHEAT

One dot represents 100 000 tonne

Arctic Circle

Tropic of Cancer

Equator

Tropic of Capricorn

Date Line

CORN/MAIZE RICE

One dot represents 100 000 tonne

Arctic Circle

Tropic of Cancer

Equator

Tropic of Capricorn

Date Line

Oxford Projection Equal-area Scale 1:150m. approx.

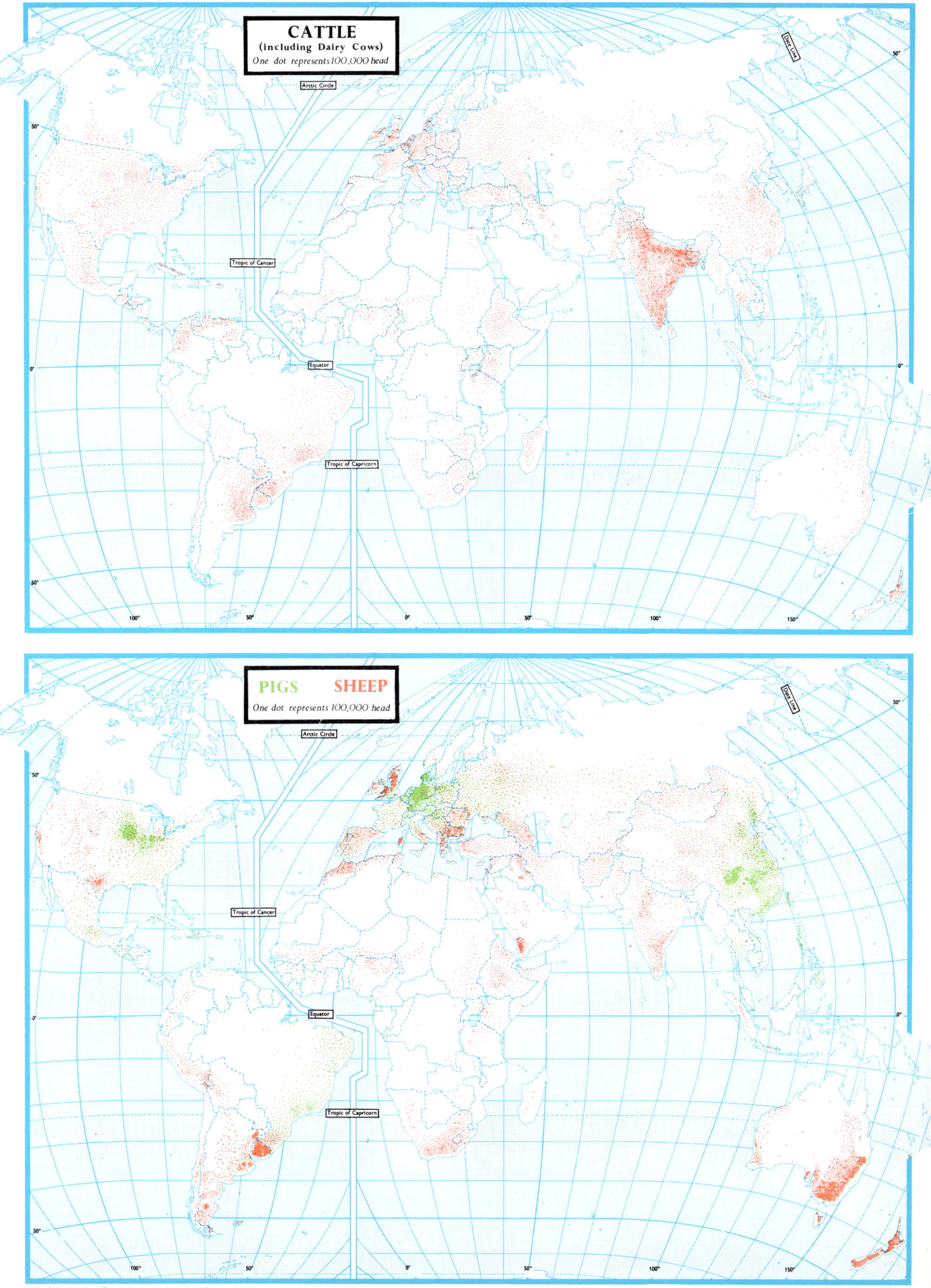

Oxford Projection Equal-area Scale 1:150m. approx.

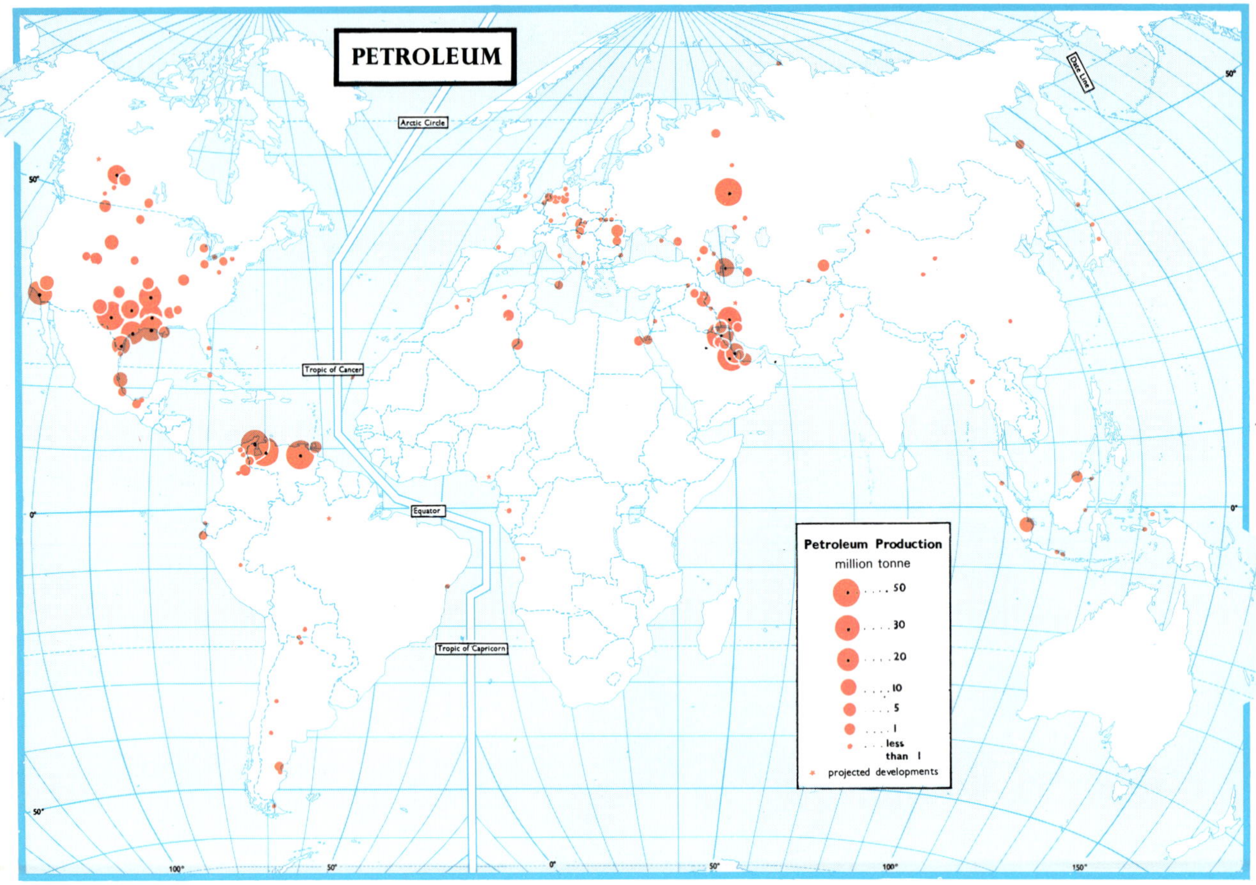

PETROLEUM

Arctic Circle
Tropic of Cancer
Equator
Tropic of Capricorn
Date Line

Petroleum Production
million tonne

- 50
- 30
- 20
- 10
- 5
- 1
- . . . . less than 1
- projected developments

COAL

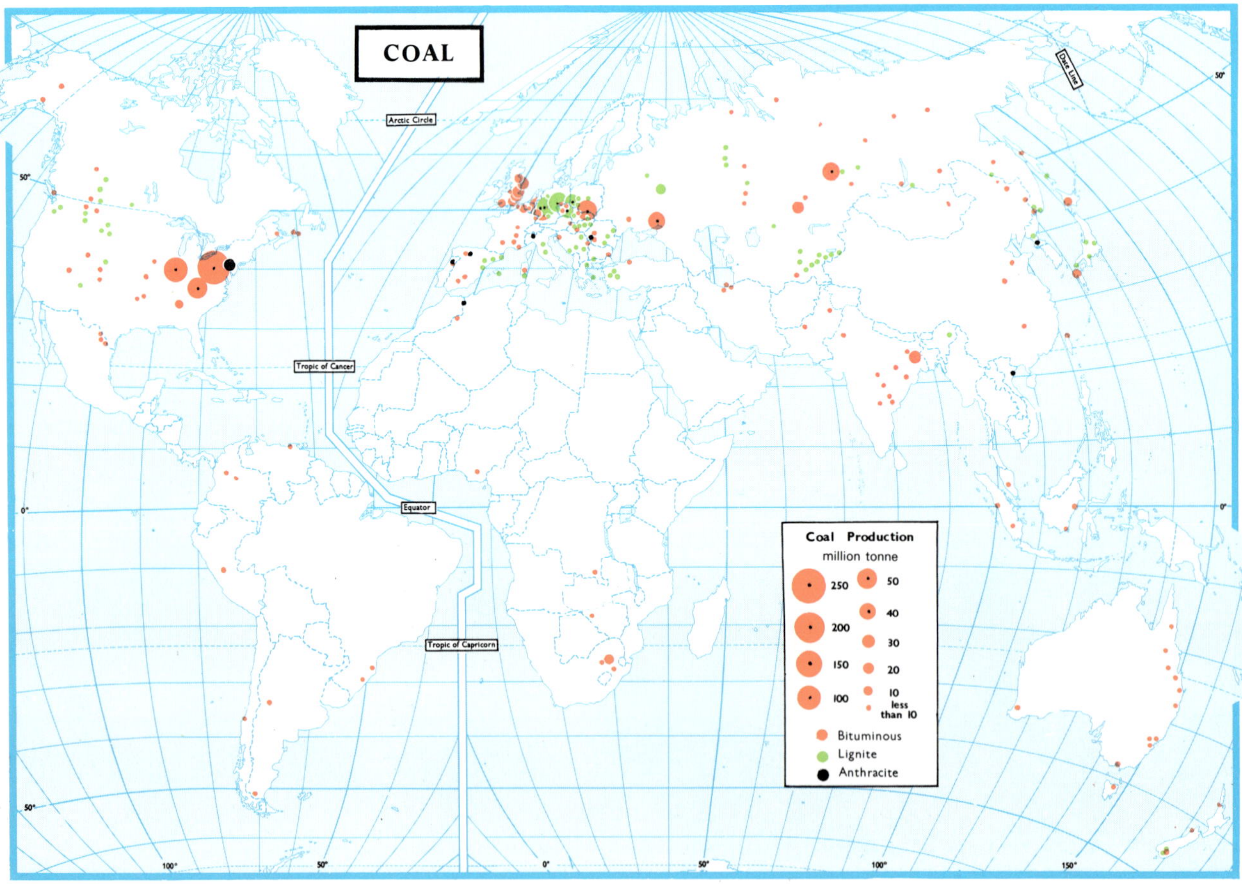

Arctic Circle
Tropic of Cancer
Equator
Tropic of Capricorn
Date Line

Coal Production
million tonne

- 250
- 200
- 150
- 100
- 50
- 40
- 30
- 20
- 10
- less than 10

- Bituminous
- Lignite
- Anthracite

Oxford Projection Equal-area Scale 1:150m. approx.

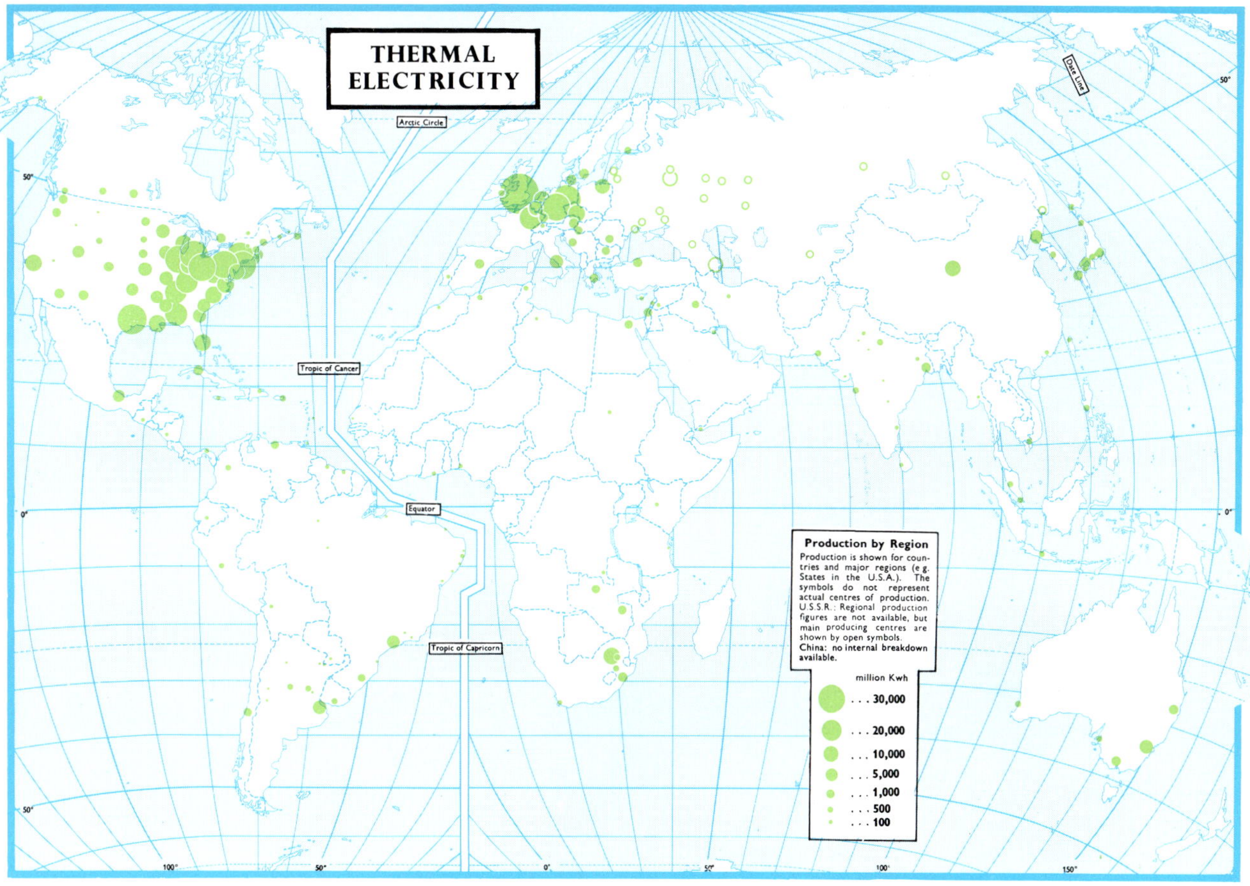

THERMAL ELECTRICITY

Production by Region

Production is shown for countries and major regions (e.g. States in the U.S.A.). The symbols do not represent actual centres of production. U.S.S.R.: Regional production figures are not available, but main producing centres are shown by open symbols. **China: no internal breakdown available.**

million Kwh

- . . . 30,000
- . . . 20,000
- . . . 10,000
- . . . 5,000
- . . . 1,000
- . . . 500
- . . . 100

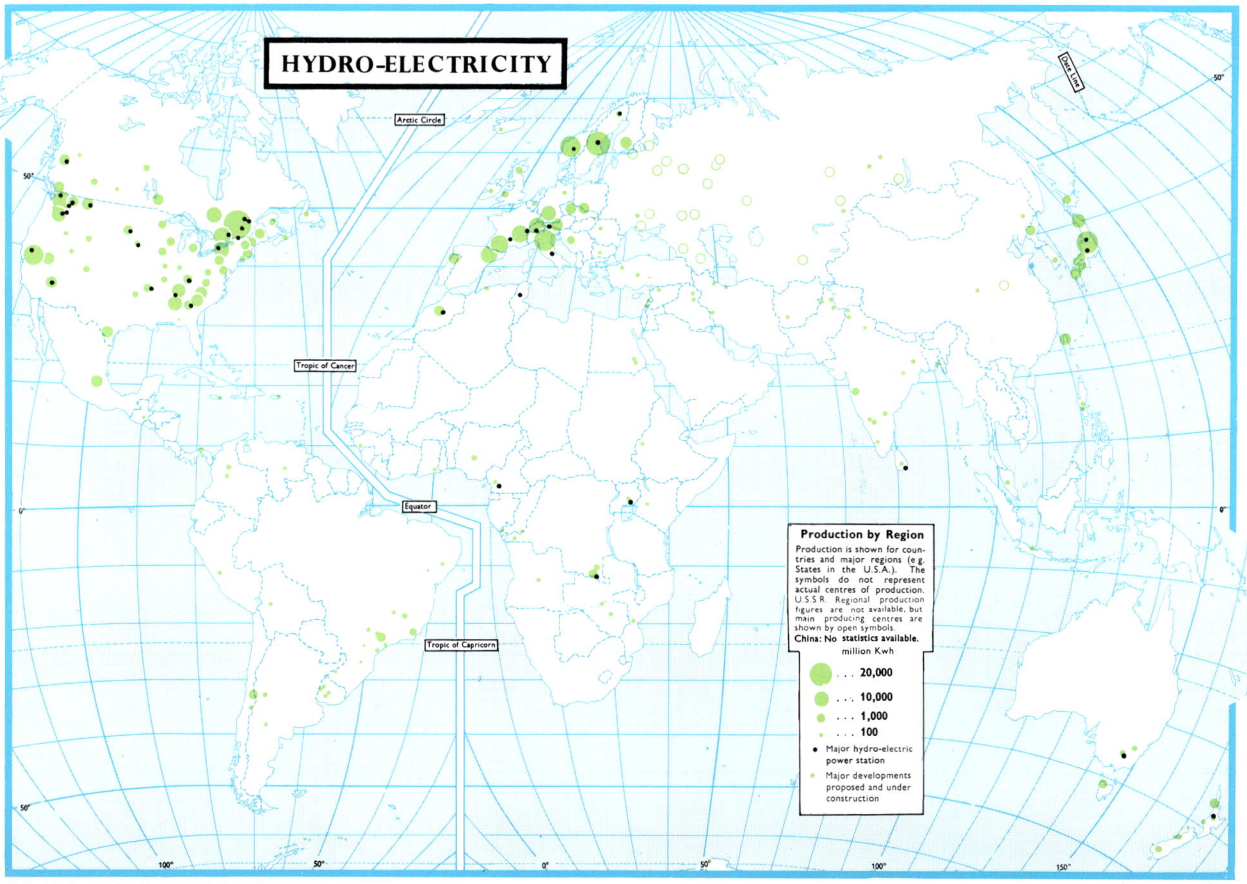

HYDRO-ELECTRICITY

Production by Region

Production is shown for countries and major regions (e.g. States in the U.S.A.). The symbols do not represent actual centres of production. U.S.S.R. Regional production figures are not available, but main producing centres are shown by open symbols. **China: No statistics available.**

million Kwh

- . . . 20,000
- . . . 10,000
- . . . 1,000
- . . . 100
- Major hydro-electric power station
- Major developments proposed and under construction

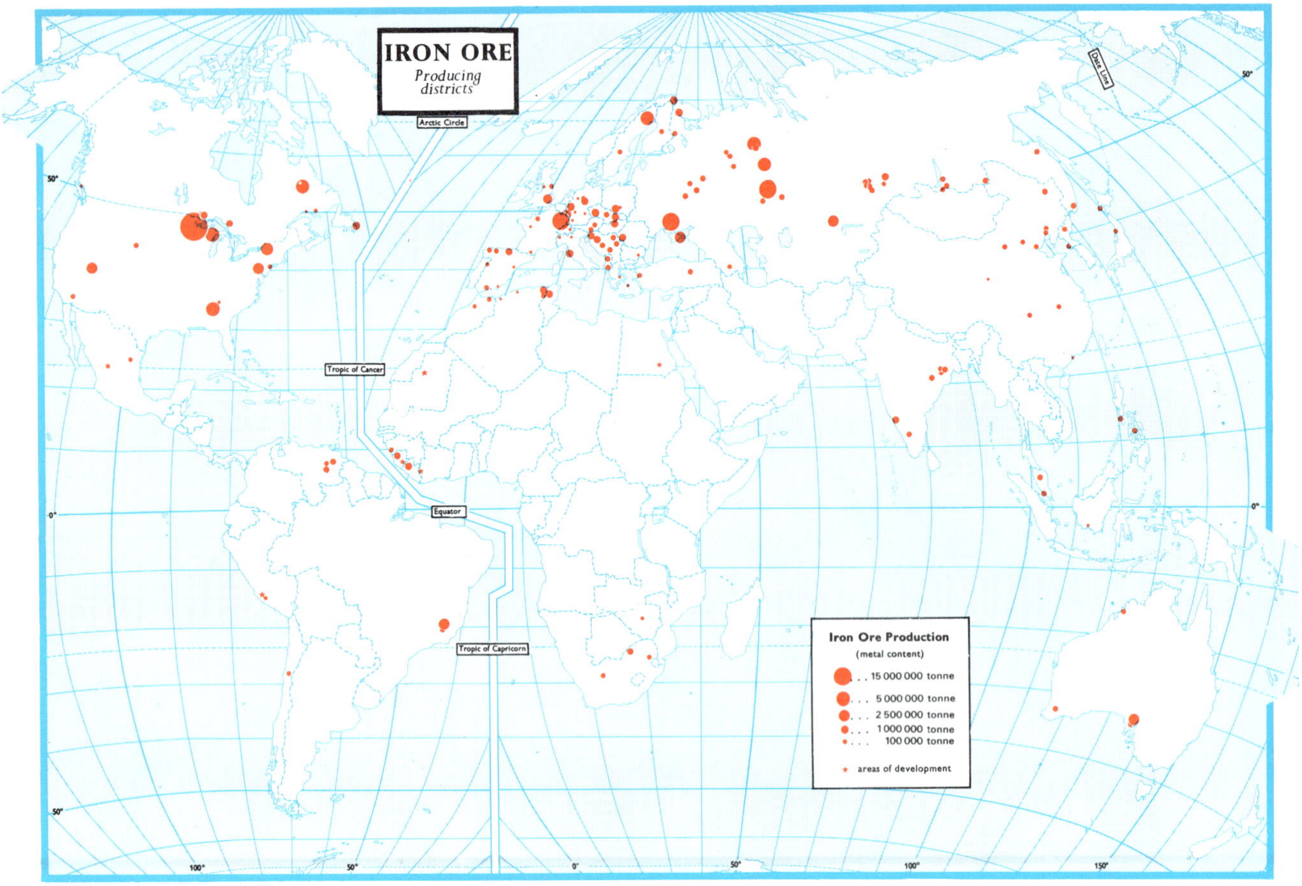

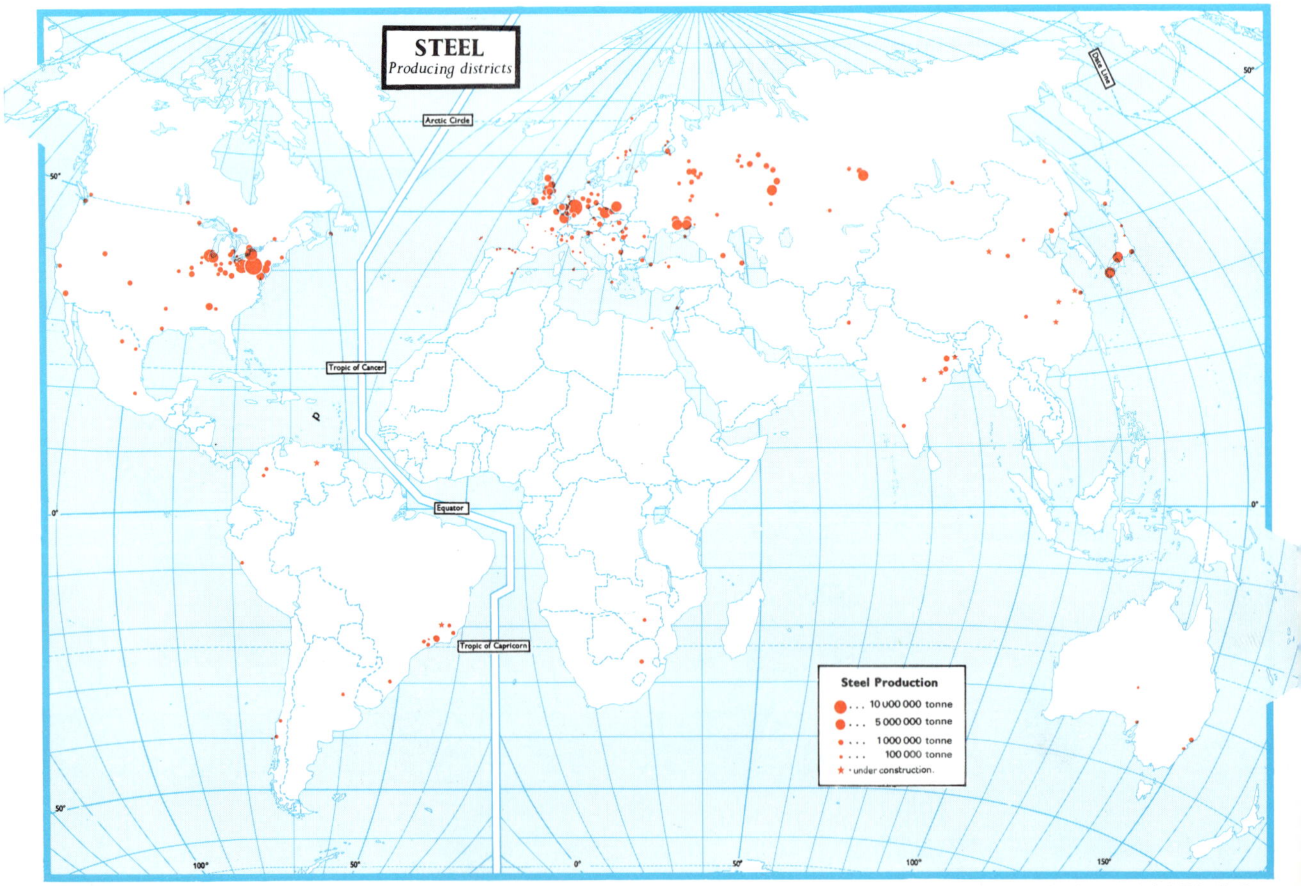

IRON ORE

Producing districts

Arctic Circle

Tropic of Cancer

Equator

Tropic of Capricorn

Date Line

Iron Ore Production

(metal content)

- . . . 15 000 000 tonne
- . . . 5 000 000 tonne
- . . . 2 500 000 tonne
- . . . 1 000 000 tonne
- . . . 100 000 tonne
- ★ areas of development

STEEL

Producing districts

Arctic Circle

Tropic of Cancer

Equator

Tropic of Capricorn

Date Line

Steel Production

- . . . 10 000 000 tonne
- . . . 5 000 000 tonne
- . . . 1 000 000 tonne
- . . . 100 000 tonne
- ★ under construction.

Oxford Projection Equal-area Scale 1:150m. approx.

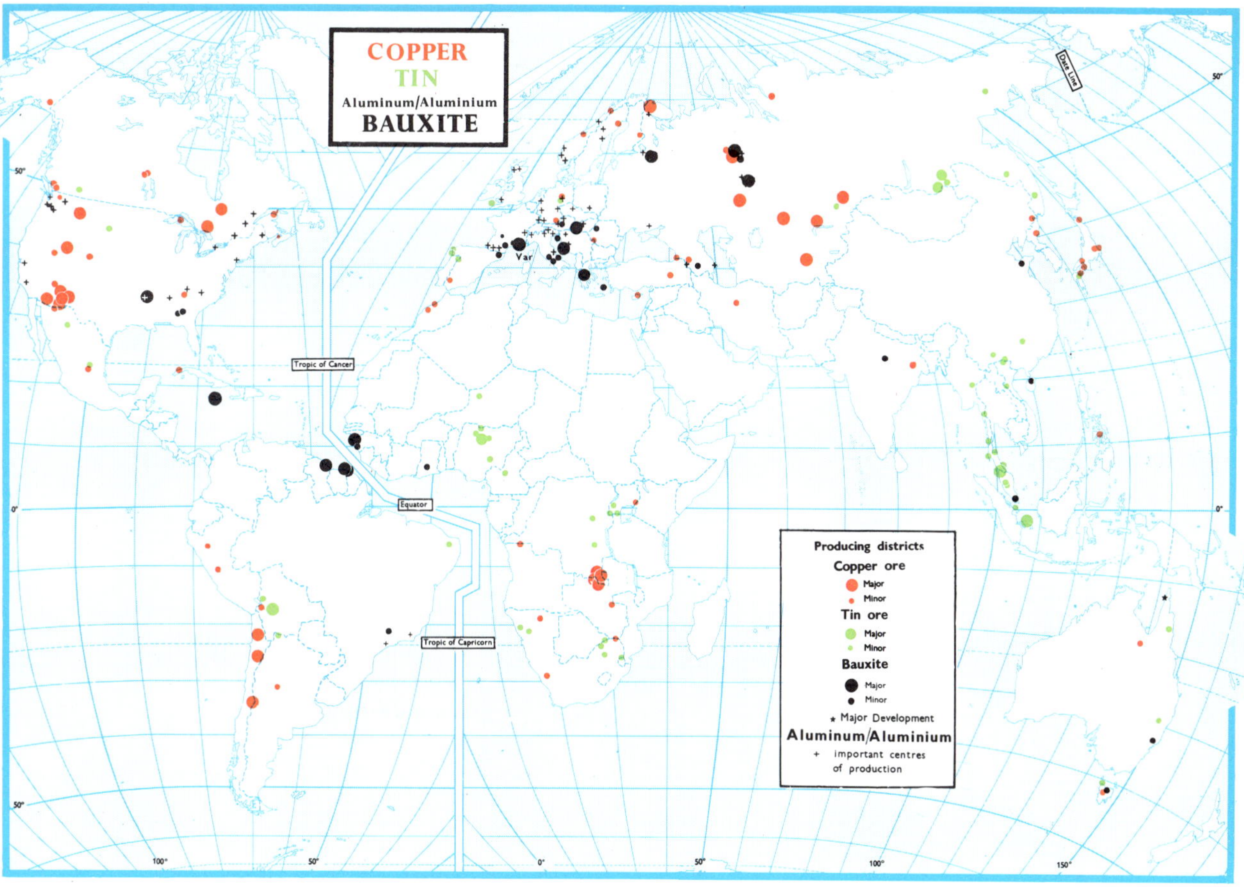

COPPER TIN Aluminum/Aluminium BAUXITE

Producing districts

Copper ore
- Major
- Minor

Tin ore
- Major
- Minor

Bauxite
- Major
- Minor

* Major Development

Aluminum/Aluminium
+ important centres of production

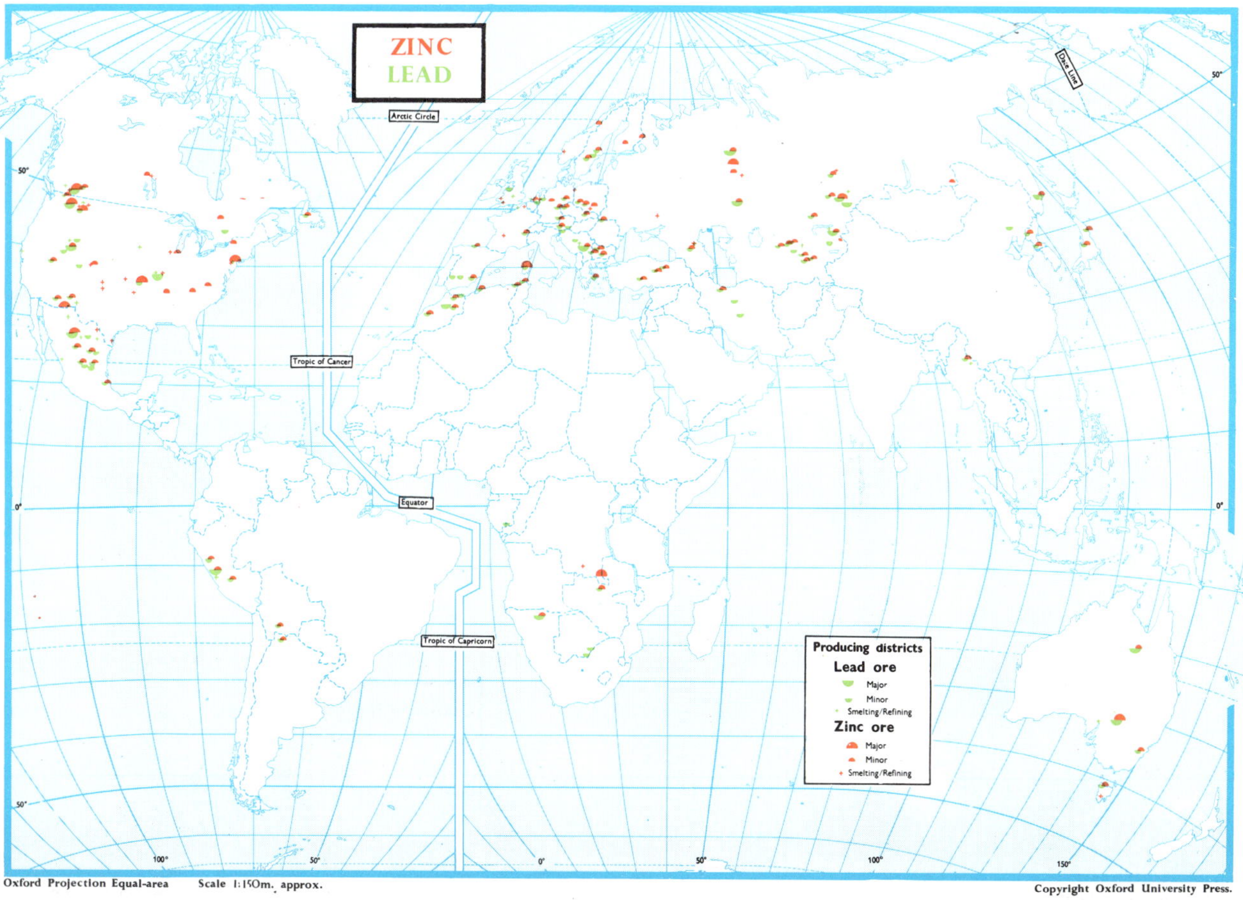

Tropic of Cancer
Equator
Tropic of Capricorn
Date Line
Var

ZINC LEAD

Producing districts

Lead ore
- Major
- Minor
- Smelting/Refining

Zinc ore
- Major
- Minor
- Smelting/Refining

Arctic Circle
Tropic of Cancer
Equator
Tropic of Capricorn
Date Line

Oxford Projection Equal-area Scale 1:150m. approx.

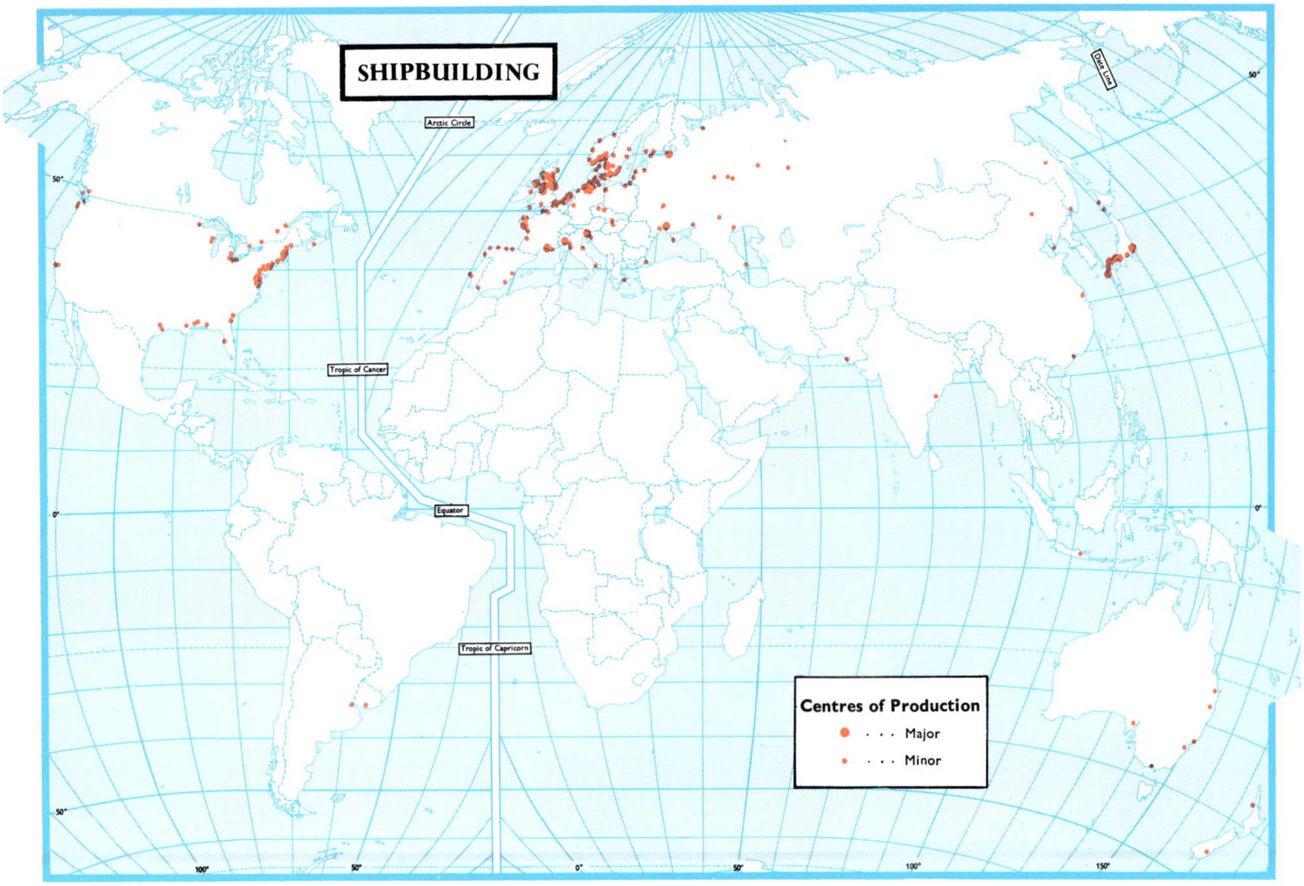

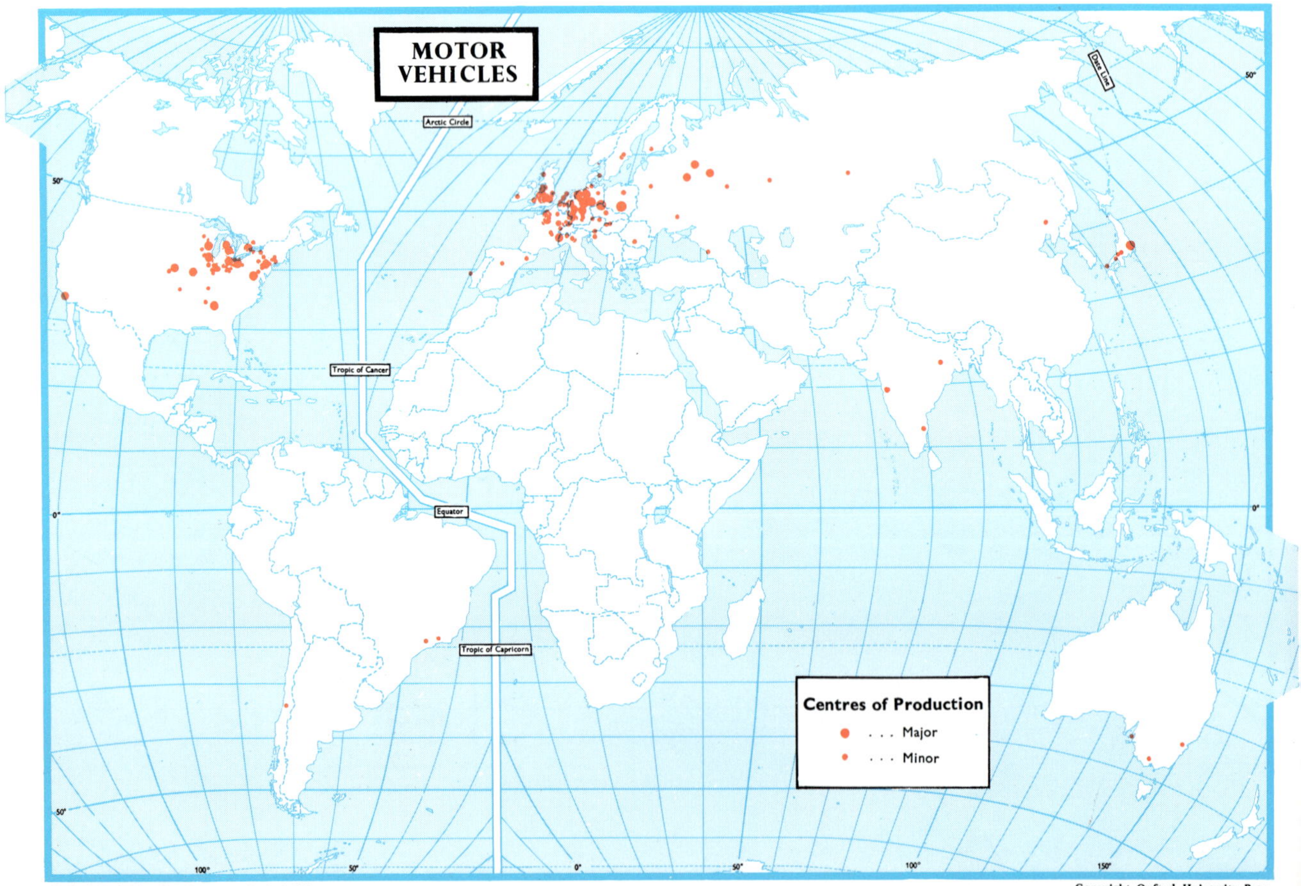

SHIPBUILDING

MOTOR VEHICLES

Oxford Projection Equal-area Scale 1:150m. approx.

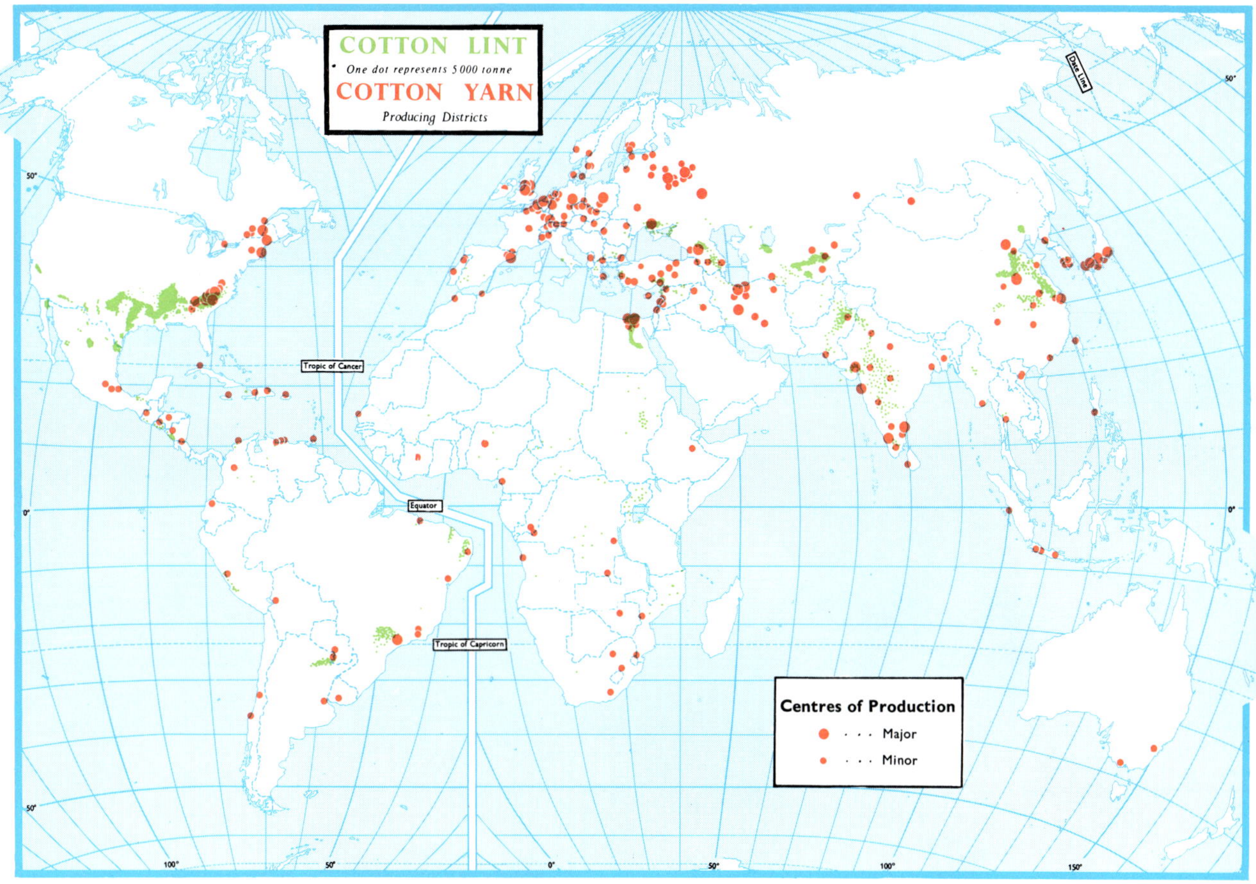

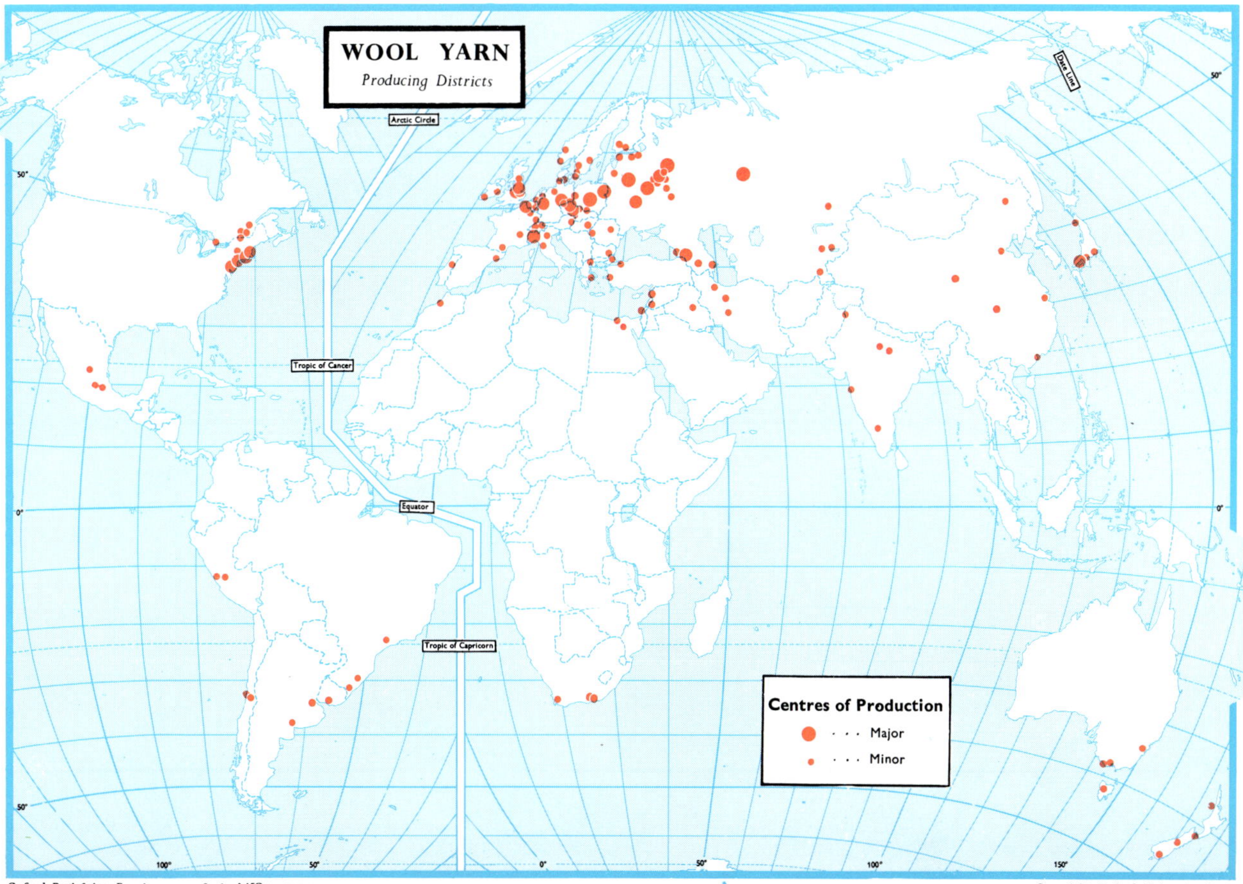

COTTON LINT
One dot represents 5 000 tonne
COTTON YARN
Producing Districts
Date Line
50°
Tropic of Cancer
Equator
Tropic of Capricorn
0°
Centres of Production
. . . Major
. . . Minor
100°
50°
0°
50°
100°
150°

WOOL YARN
Producing Districts
Date Line
Arctic Circle
50°
Tropic of Cancer
Equator
Tropic of Capricorn
0°
Centres of Production
. . . Major
. . . Minor
100°
50°
0°
50°
100°
150°

POPULATION

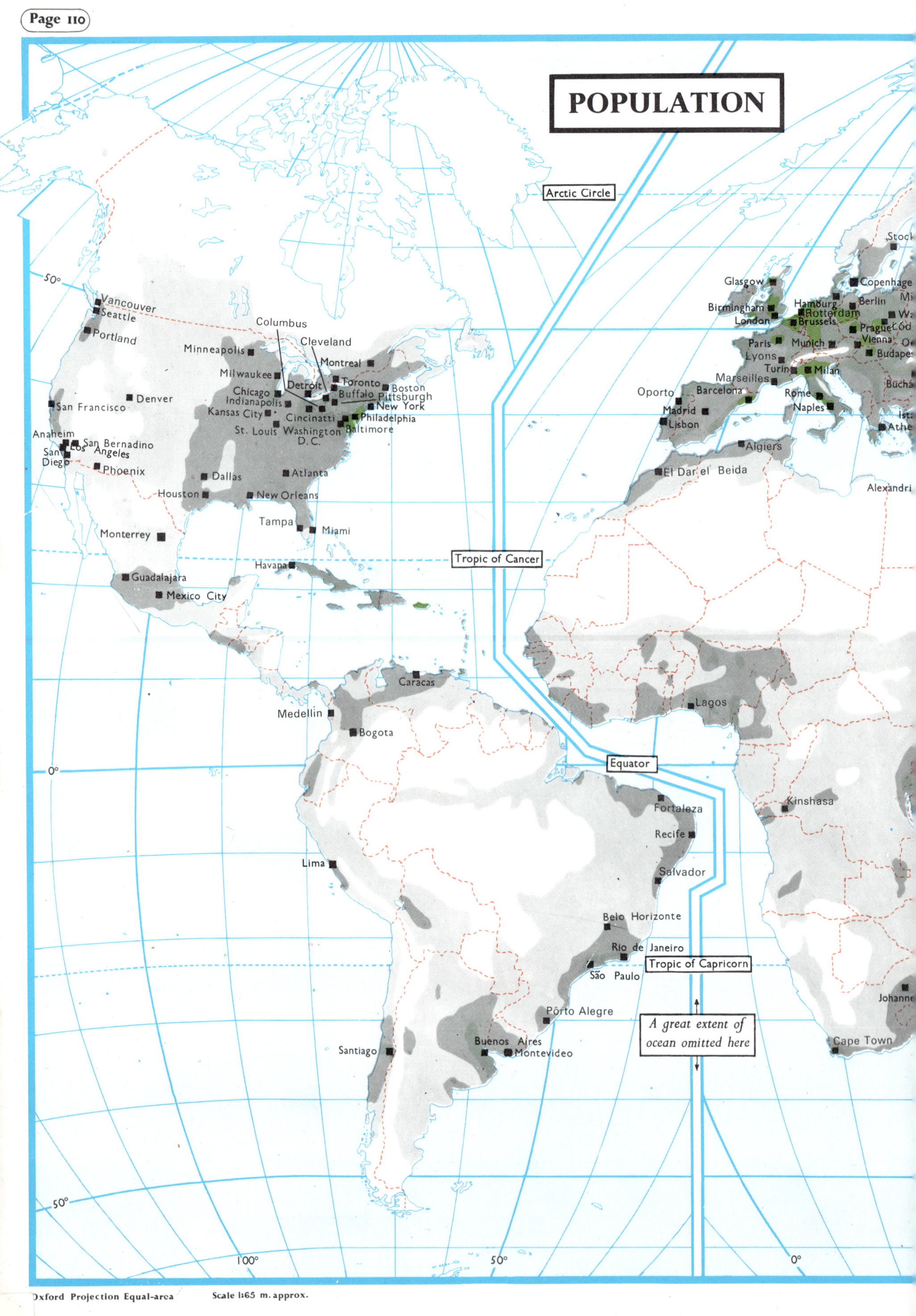

Oxford Projection Equal-area   Scale 1:65 m. approx.

POPULATION DENSITY

Key	Description
(white)	*Almost uninhabited (under 1 person per sq. km.)*
(light grey)	*Few inhabitants (1-10 people per sq. km.)*
(grey)	*Moderately populated (10-50 people per sq. km.)*
(dark grey)	*Thickly populated (50-200 people per sq. km.)*
(green)	*Very thickly populated (over 200 people per sq. km.)*
■	*Towns with over 1 million inhabitants.*

10 people per sq. km. = 25 people per sq. mile approx.

COUNTRIES OF THE WORLD

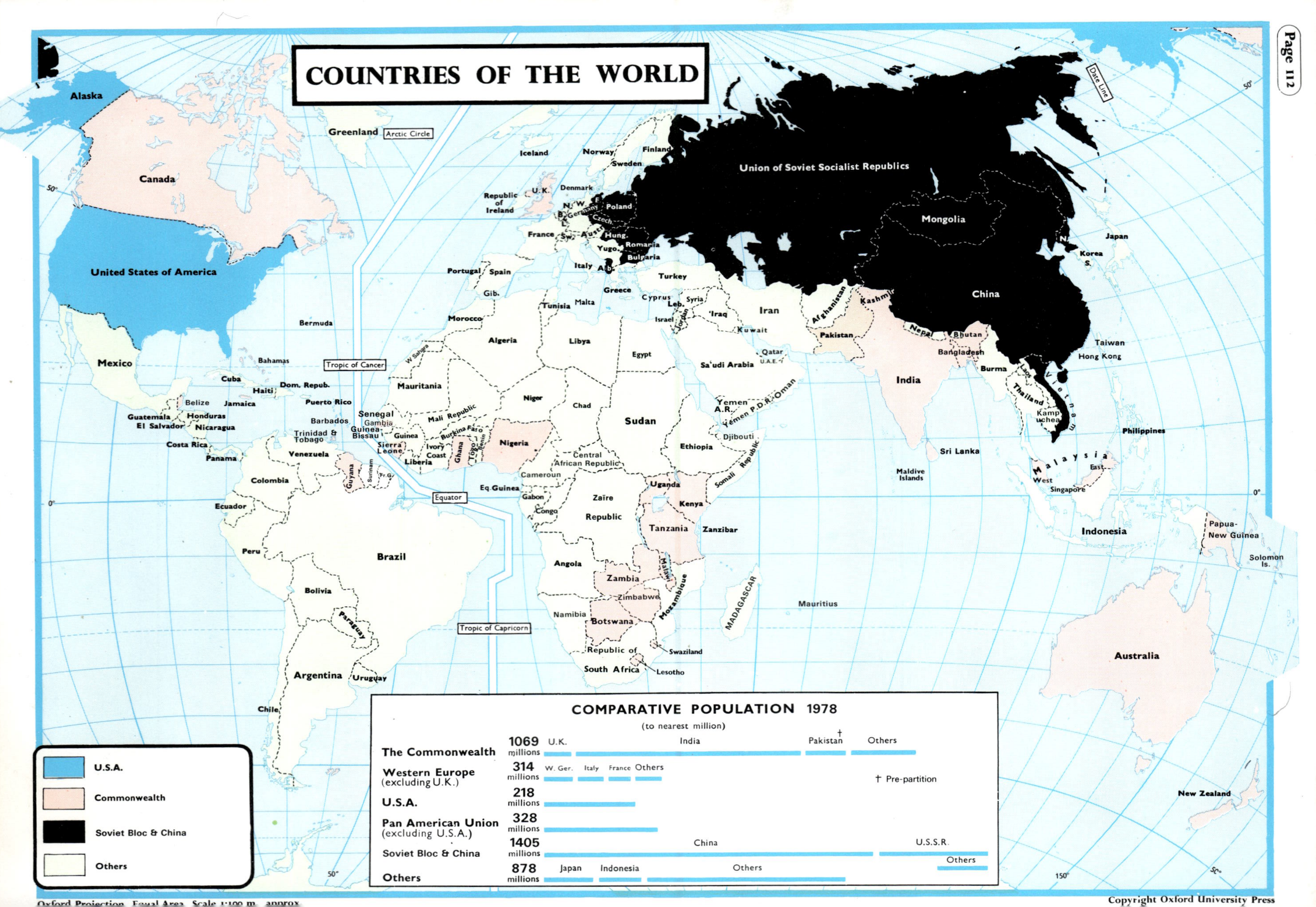

Oxford Projection Equal Area Scale 1:100 m approx.

Countries of the World — Population, Area and Land Use

* See Page 131

COUNTRIES	POPULATION (to nearest thousand) *a*	DENSITY (per sq. mile) *a ÷ b*	AREA (in sq. miles) *b*	APPROX. LAND USE PERCENTAGES† Arable & orchard	Permanent meadow & pasture	Forest & woodland	Waste, city areas etc.
*Afars and Issas (Fr.)	125,000	14	8,900	—	11.1	0.4	88.5
Afghanistan	17,480,000	70	250,000	13.7	4.9	2.3	79.1
Albania	2,075,000	189	·11,000	17.4	25.4	43.7	13.5
Algeria	14,770,000	15.5	952,000	3.0	16.1	1.3	79.6
Andorra	19,000	100	190	n.a.	n.a.	n.a.	n.a.
Angola	5,430,000	11	481,000	0.7	23.3	34·6	41.4
Antilles (Neth.)	218,000	574	380	5.2	—	—	94.8
Argentina	23,983,000	22	1,080,000	7.0	42.6	25.2	25.2
Australia	12,296,000	4·4	2,975,000	4.6	58.1	4.6	32.7
Austria	7,371,000	230	32,000	20.6	26.9	37.9	14·6
Bahamas, The	195,000	44	4,404	1.1	0.1	28.4	70.4
Bahrain	207,000	900	230	n.a.	n.a.	n.a.	n.a.
Bangladesh	75,000,000	1,360	55,000	64.0		—	17.1
Barbados	254,000	1,530	166	60.5	9.3	—	30.2
Belgium	9,646,000	804	12,000	30.7	23.6	19.7	26.0
Benin	2,640,000	58	45,000	13.7	3.9	19.2	63.2
Bermuda	67,000	3,190	21	4.0	4.0	60.0	32.0
Bolivia	5,060,000	12.2	415,000	2.8	10.3	42.8	44.1
Botswana	629,000	2.0	275,000	0.3	72.2	1.7	25.8
Brazil	92,238,000	28	3,286,000	3.5	12.6	60.8	23.1
Bulgaria	8,436,000	196	43,000	41.1	11.1	32.6	15.2
Burma	27,584,000	105	262,000	23.4	0.5	66.8	9.3
Burundi	3,475,000	315	11,000	37.3	22.6	2.5	37.6
Cambodia (Kampuchea)	6,701,000	96	70,000	16.2	n.a.	73.9	n.a.
Cameroun	5,680,000	31	183,000	30.2	6.9	27.7	35.2
Canada	21,854,000	5.7	3,851,809	4.2	2.1	44.4	49.3
Cape Verde Is.	272,000	174	1,560	7.4	n.a.	0.2	n.a.
*Central African Republic	1,518,000	6.4	238,000	9.4	0.2	11.8	78.5
Ceylon (Sri Lanka)	12,240,000	490	25,000	28.6	0.2	50.7	20.5
Chad	3,510,000	7.7	496,000	5.5	35.0	12.0	47.5
Chile	9,566,000	33	286,000	6.1	13.6	27.9	52.4
China	787,000,000	209	3,759,000	11.2	18.2	7.9	62.7
Colombia	21,720,000	50	439,000	4.4	12.8	61.0	21.0
Comoro Islands	270,000	320	838	36.9	13.8	16.1	33.2
Congo	960,000	6.6	132,000	1.8	n.a.	47.5	n.a.
Costa Rica	1,695,000	85	20,000	12.3	18.2	58.8	10.7
Cuba	8,250,000	188	44,000	17.2	34.0	26.1	22.7
Cyprus	630,000	175	3,600	46.7	10.0	18.5	24.8
Czechoslovakia	14,418,000	292	49,000	42.5	13.9	34.8	9.2
Denmark	4,910,000	288	17,000	62.9	7.5	9.3	20.3
Dominican Rep.	4,174,000	222	19,000	21.9	17.8	45.7	14.6
Ecuador	6,300,000	59	106,000	10.7	8.1	54.9	26.3
Egypt	34,130,000	88	386,000	2.7	—	—	97.3
El Salvador	3,390,000	414	8,200	30.3	28.2	23.7	17.8
Equatorial Guinea	286,000	26	11,000	7.9	3.7	81.6	6.8
Ethiopia	24,769,000	65	395,000	10.3	56.4	7.3	26.0
Fiji	519,000	74	7,000	16.4	44.0	38.5	1.1
Finland	4,703,000	36	130,000	8.1	0.4	64.6	26.9
France	51,280,000	241	213,000	38.1	24.3	21.8	15.8
Gabon	485,000	4.7	·103,000	0.5	n.a.	74.7	n.a.
Gambia, The	375,000	93	4,000	17.7	35.4	3.0	43.9
Germany, East	17,097,000	407	42,000	46.2	13.3	27.2	13.3
Germany, West	61,682,000	643	96,000	33.4	23.5	29.0	14.1
Ghana	8,600,000	93	92,000	10.7	—	10.3	n.a.
Greece	8,835,000	173	51,000	29.2	30.0	19.7	12.1
Greenland (Dan.)	47,000	—	840,000	—	—	—	100.0
Guadeloupe (Fr.)	323,000	468	690	29.2	9.0	32.6	29.2
Guatemala	5,350,000	127	42,000	13.5	5.3	44.4	36.8
Guiana, French	44,000	1.3	35,000	—	0.6	95.0	4.4
Guinea	4,010,000	42	95,000	n.a.	n.a.	4.3	n.a.
Guinea Bissau	530,000	37	14,000	7.3	n.a.	6.3	n.a.
Guyana	742,000	8.9	83,000	0.9	11.8	84.3	3.0
Haiti	4,768,000	476	11,000	13.4	18.0	25.2	43.4
Honduras	2,495,000	58	43,000	7.3	30.5	26.9	35.3
Honduras, (Belize)	120,000	13	8,900	1.4	0.7	45.8	52.1
Hong Kong (Br.)	4,050,000	10,125	400	12.6	—	9.7	77.7
Hungary	10,295,000	286	36,000	60.7	14.0	15.3	10.0
Iceland	203,000	5.0	40,000	—	22.1	—	77.9
India	550,370,000	436	1,263,000	49.6	4.3	17.1	29.0
Indonesia	124,890,000	170	736,000	9.3	*	63.8	26.9
Iran	29,780,000	47	628,000	7.0	4.1	7.3	81.6
Iraq	9,750,000	57	172,000	16.7	9.5	4.3	69.5
Ireland	2,921,000	108	27,000	18.0	49.0	2.8	30.2
Israel	3,010,000	376	8,000	19.9	33.9	4.6	41.6
Italy	54,080,000	466	116,000	50.8	17.1	20.2	11.9
Ivory Coast	4,195,000	33	124,000	6.4	n.a.	74.4	n.a.
Jamaica	1,959,000	445	4,400	21.1	23.4	19.2	36.3
Japan	104,660,000	732	143,000	16.2	2.6	68.7	12.5
Jordan	2,160,000	58	37,000	11.6	2.2	0.7	85.5
Kenya	11,690,000	53	220,000	2.9	6.7	2.9	85.5
Korea, North	14,280,000	304	47,000	15.7	n.a.	74.4	n.a.
Korea, South	32,430,000	853	38,000	22.9	0.2	67.1	9.8
Kuwait	830,000	143	5,800	—	—	n.a.	n.a.
Laos	3,030,000	34	90,000	3.4	3.4	59.3	33.9
Lebanon	2,645,000	780	3,400	28.5	1.0	9.1	61.4
Leeward Is.	141,000	385	418	43.0	12.0	13.0	32.0
Lesotho	1,040,000	87	12,000	11.7	82.2	—	6.1
Liberia	1,150,000	27	43,000	34.5	2.2	32.5	30.8
Libya	2,010,000	3	679,000	1.9	8.0	0.2	89.9
Liechtenstein	21,000	334	62	12.5	43.7	25.0	18.8
Luxembourg	337,000	337	1,000	26.7	24.7	33.2	15.4
Madagascar	6,643,000	29	230,000	4.9	52.0	21.7	21.4
Malawi	4,398,000	119	37,000	10.7	3.4	8.8	77.1
Malaysia	10,583,000	82	128,000	18.9	n.a.	65.7	n.a.
Maldive Islands	115,000	1,000	115	n.a.	n.a.	n.a.	n.a.
Mali	5,140,000	11	465,000	1	n.a.	3.8	n.a.
Malta	323,000	2,608	121	50.0	—	—	50.0
Martinique (Fr.)	332,000	795	420	29.1	18.2	24.5	28.2
Mauritania	1,140,000	2.7	419,000	0.2	36.2	13.9	79.7
Mauritius	823,000	1,160	720	50.6	16.1	21.5	11.8
Mexico	50,830,000	67	760,000	12.1	40.1	22.1	25.7
Mongolia	1,240,000	2.0	604,000	2.3	n.a.	16.3	n.a.
Morocco	15,050,000	88	171,000	17.7	17.2	12.0	53.1
Mozambique	8,233,000	28	298,000	3.4	56.2	24.8	15.6
Nepal	10,845,000	200	54,000	13.0	14.2	32.2	40.6
Netherlands	13,190,000	1,015	13,000	28.8	38.3	8.6	24.3
New Caledonia (Fr.)	100,600	13.7	7,330	4.3	21.4	14.5	59.8
New Zealand	2,850,000	27	104,000	3.0	47.8	23.2	26.0
Nicaragua	1,915,000	34	57,000	6.2	6.6	46.2	41.1
Niger	4,130,000	9	459,000	11.8	2.3	12.3	73.6
Nigeria	63,870,000	179	357,000	23.6	n.a.	34.2	n.a.
Norway	3,851,000	32	125,000	2.6	0.5	21.7	75.2
'Oman	680,000	8.3	82,000	n.a.	n.a.	n.a.	n.a.
Pakistan	58,500,000	160	366,000	27.5	n.a.	3.8	n.a.
Panama	1,417,000	49	29,000	7.5	11.0	80.5	1.0
Papua New Guinea	2,315,000	12.5	184,000	0.6	—	n.a.	n.a.
Paraguay	2,303,000	14.6	157,000	2.2	24.3	51.0	22.5
Peru	14,010,000	28	496,000	2.0	21.7	67.7	8.6
Philippines	38,493,000	332	116,000	26.4	11.0	41.2	21.4
Poland	32,555,000	274	120,000	50.3	13.7	25.8	10.2
Portugal	9,560,000	273	35,000	49.2	6.0	28.1	16.7
Puerto Rico (U.S.)	2,754,000	800	3,400	30.4	35.3	13.3	21.0
Qatar	100,000	250	4,000	n.a.	n.a.	—	n.a.
Réunion (Fr.)	445,500	459	970	24.7	8.0	38.2	29.1
*Rhodesia (Zimbabwe)	5,090,000	33	150,000	4.7	12.5	60.0	22.8
Romania	20,101,000	218	92,000	44.1	18.2	26.8	10.9
Rwanda	3,500,000	350	10,000	37.8	33.0	5.9	23.3
São Tomé and Principe	66,000	186	372	31.3	n.a.	—	n.a.
Sa'udi Arabia	7,200,000	7.8	927,000	0.2	37.7	0.8	61.3
Senegal	3,780,000	49	76,000	28.0	n.a.	27.1	n.a.
Seychelles	51,000	318	160	42.1	1.0	12.4	44.5
Sierre Leone	2,512,000	87	28,000	51.1	30.7	4.2	14.0
Singapore	2,017,000	9,000	244	22.4	—	20.7	56.9
Somali Rep.	2,730,000	11	246,000	1.5	32.3	22.6	43.6
South Africa	21,282,000	45	472,000	9.9	74.0	1.3	14.8
*S.W. Africa (Namibia)	615,000	1.9	318,000	0.8	64.2	6.4	28.6
Spain	34,130,000	175	195,000	40.8	28.1	23.0	8.1
Spanish North Africa	164,000	13,666	12	n.a.	n.a.	n.a.	n.a.
Sudan	15,186,000	15	967,000	2.8	9.6	36.5	51.1
Surinam (Neth.)	389,000	7.1	55,000	0.3	—	45.0	19.9
Swaziland	410,000	61	6,700	14.5	73.4	7.4	4.7
Sweden	8,110,000	47	173,260	7.1	1.2	50.0	41.7
Switzerland	6,230,000	389	16,000	16.2	42.2	23.8	23.8
Syria	6,450,000	90	72,000	35.9	33.0	2.4	28.7
Taiwan	14,350,000	1,025	14,000	24.7	n.a.	70.9	n.a.
Tanzania	13,630,000	37	364,000	12.7	36.9	37.6	12.8
Thailand	34,738,000	175	198,000	21.9	—	52.8	25.3
Togo	1,815,000	86	21,000	38.2	3.5	9.4	48.9
Trinidad and Tobago	1,040,000	515	1,980	34.1	1.0	45.0	19.9
Tunisia	5,027,000	79	63,362	34.6	45.2	6.7	13.5
Turkey	36,160,000	122	296,000	33.5	36.2	13.5	16.8
Uganda	10,130,000	111	91,000	16.0	n.a.	7.0	n.a.
Union of Soviet Socialist Republics	242,000,000	28	8,648,000	10.3	16.6	40.6	32.5
United Arab Emirates	135,000	4.2	32,000	n.a.	n.a.	n.a.	n.a.
United Kingdom	55,534,000	588	94,500	30.7	49.7	7.4	12.2
United States of America	207,010,000	58	3,554,000	19.8	27.4	32.2	20.6
Upper Volta (Burkina Faso)	5,278,000	49	106,000	17.9	n.a.	7.3	n.a.
Uruguay	2,852,000	37	72,000	12.0	74.1	3.2	10.7
Venezuela	10,035,000	28	352,000	5.7	18.3	52.6	23.4
Viet-Nam	39,672,000	308	129,000	29.9	n.a.	82 6	n.a.
Western Sahara	63,000	0.6	105,000	n.a.	7.5	n.a.	n.a.
Windward Is.	384,000	464	826	33.9	3.0	36.2	26.9
Yemen A. R.	5,900,000	79	75,000	n.a.	n.a.	0.8	n.a.
Yemen, P. D. R.	1,220,000	10.9	112,000	6.9	31.3	8.9	58.9
Yugoslavia	20,500,000	207	99,000	32.5	25.2	34.4	7.9
Zaïre	22.480.000	25	906,000	20.9	1.0	42.7	35.4
Zambia	4,208,000	14	290,000	2.6	43.8	50.0	3.6

* Included in other groups. — None. n.a. Not Available. For further information *see* The Oxford Economic Atlas of the World. † Percentages are calculated from figures given in FAO Year-Book. They do not necessarily total 100 per cent. Water is included as waste land.

WORLD AIR ROUTES

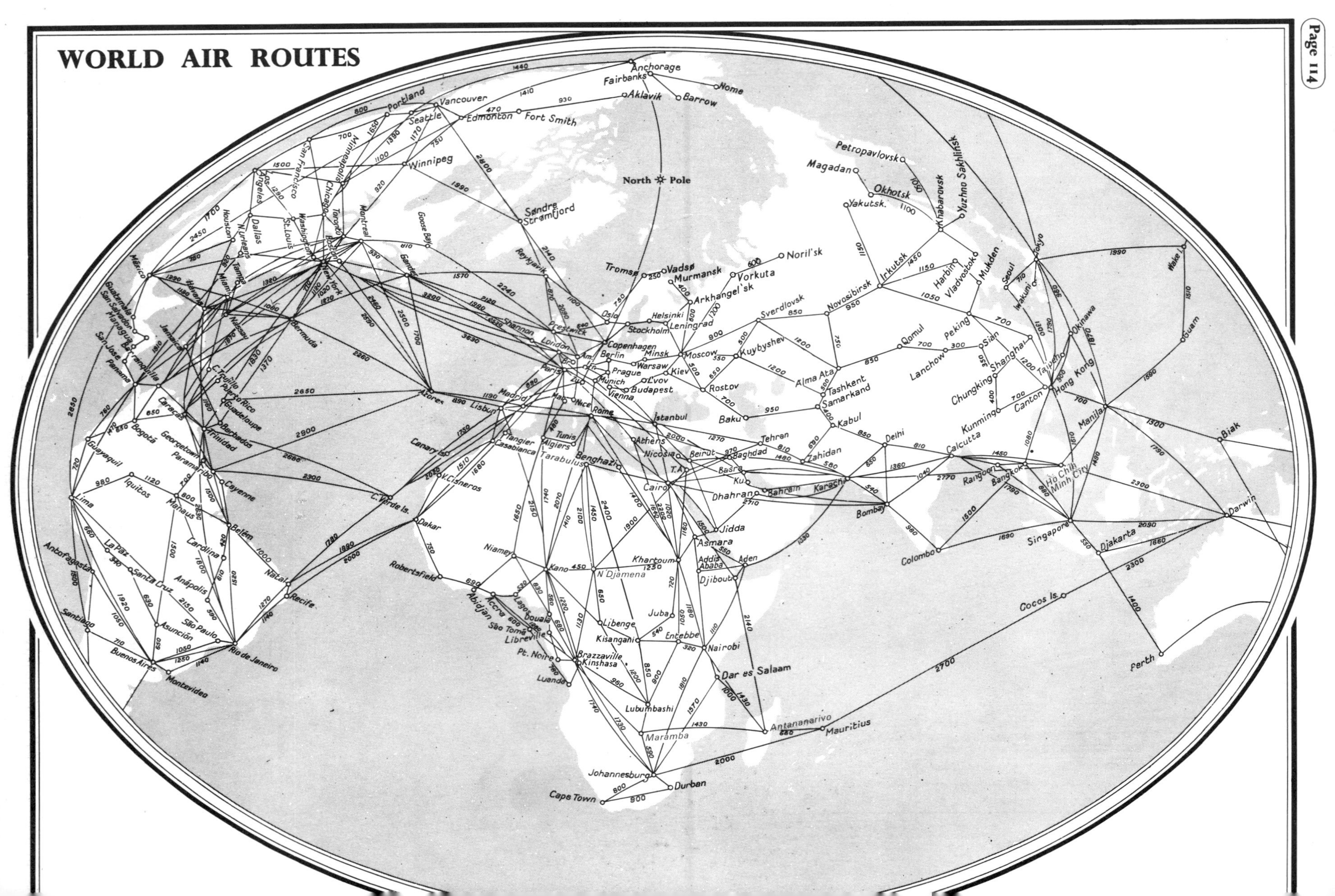

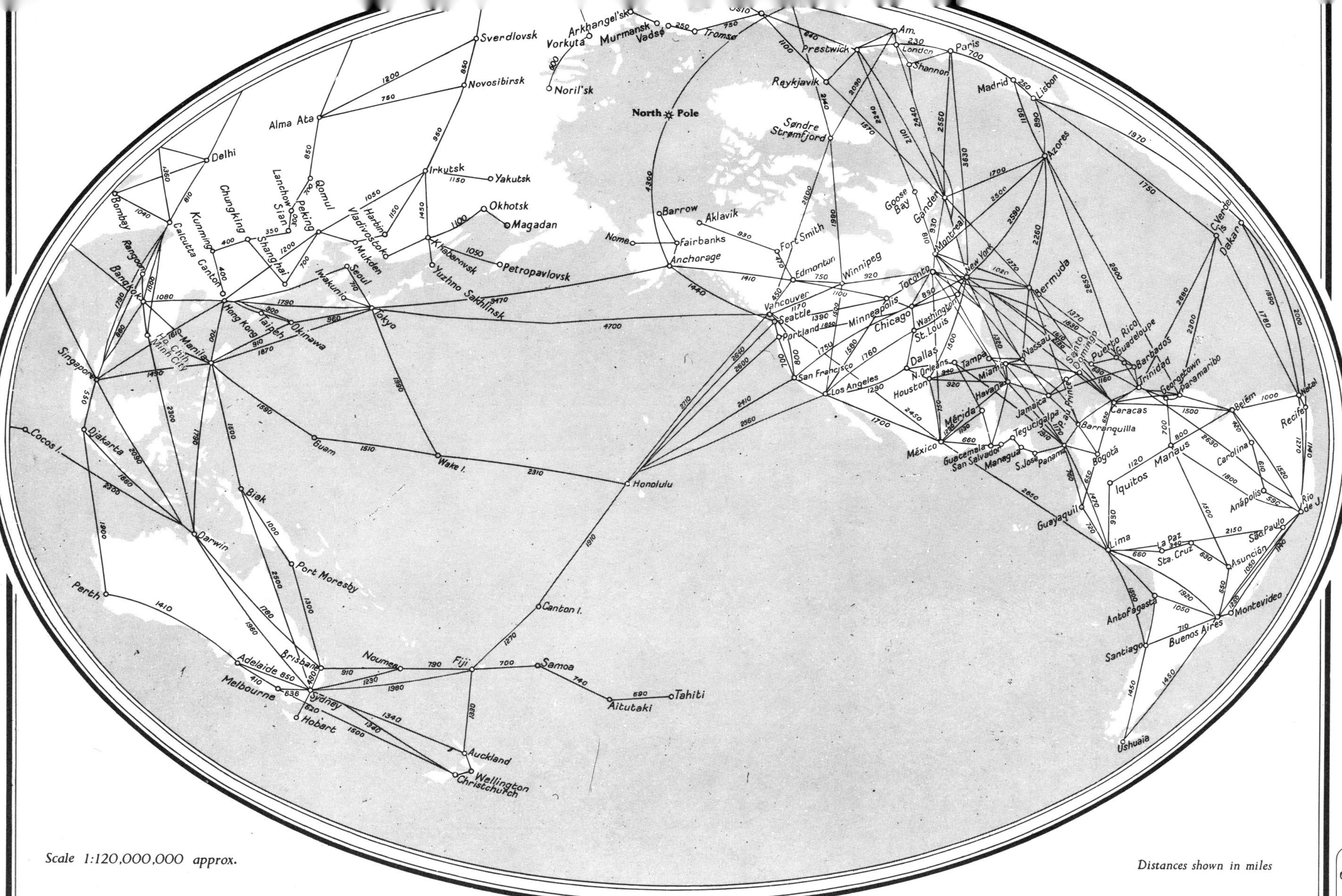

Scale 1:120,000,000 approx.

Distances shown in miles

Oblique Aitoff Projection

Selected World Geographic

Listed below are Countries and Cities which have changed their names since the end of World War II. Wh names have changed more than once, the intermediate name is annoted 'q.v.' in the new column. By cross reference the latest name can be found. For example the old name Belgian Congo became Congo (Kinshas

COUNTRY NAME CHANGES

Arranged chronologically

YEAR	OLD NAME	NEW NAME(S)
1945	Netherlands East Indies	Indonesia
1946	French Indochina (part)	Vietnam
1946	Trans-Jordan	Jordan
1947	India	India & Pakistan
1949	Eire	Irish Republic
1949	French Indochina (part)	Cambodia & Laos
1956	Anglo-Egyptian Sudan	Sudan
1957	The Gold Coast	Ghana
1959–62	Aden Protectorate	Fed. of S. Arabia q.v.
1960	Belgian Congo	Congo (Kinshasa) q.v.
1960	British and Italian Somaliland	Somali Democratic Republic
1960	French Equatorial Africa	Cameroon, Central African Republic, Chad, Gabon
1960	French West Africa	Dahomey, Mali, Mauritania, Niger, Senegal, Upper Volta
1961	Ruanda-Urundi	Rwanda & Burundi
1961	Union of South Africa	Republic of S. Africa
1963	Malaya, Sabah, Sarawak	Malaysia
1964	Northern Rhodesia	Zambia
1964	Nyasaland	Malawi
1964	Tanganyika/Zanzibar	Tanzania
1966	Basutoland	Lesotho
1966	Bechuanaland	Botswana
1966	British Guiana	Guyana
1967	Fed. of South Arabia	Southern Yemen q.v.
1967	French Somaliland	French Territory of the Afars & Issas q.v.
1968	Spanish Territories of the Gulf of Guinea	Equatorial Guinea
1970	Cambodia	Khmer Republic q.v.
1970	Southern Yemen	Yemen Peoples' Democratic Republic
1971	East Pakistan	Bangladesh
1971	Trucial States	United Arab Emirates
1971	Congo (Kinshasa)	Zaïre
1972	Ceylon	Sri Lanka
1973	British Honduras	Belize
1973	Papua & Terr. of New Guinea	Papua-New Guinea
1974	Portuguese Guinea	Guinea-Bissau
1975	Dahomey	Benin
1975	Malagasy Republic	Madagascar
1975	Ellice Islands	Tuvalu
1976	Spanish Sahara	Western Sahara
1976	N. & S. Vietnam	Vietnam
1977	French Territories of Afars & Issas	Djibouti
1979	Khmer Republic	Kampuchea
1979	Gilbert Islands	Kiribati
1980	Southern Rhodesia	Zimbabwe
1980	New Hebrides	Vanuatu
1984	Upper Volta	Burkina Faso

CITY NAME CHANGES

Arranged alphabetically. Cities which have

OLD NAME	NEW NAME	COUN
Abercorn	Mbala	Zambia
Akmolinsk	Celinograd	U.S.S.R
Akyab	Sittwe	Burma
Alexandretta	İskenderun	Turkey
Albertville	Kalemi	Zaïre
Alger (Algiers)	El Djezair	Algeria
Al Ittihad	Madīnat Ash Sha'b	Yemen D
Bakwanga	Mbuji-Mayi	Zaïre
Bancroft	Chililabombwe	Zambia
Bangkok	Krung Thep	Thailand
Banningville	Bandundu	Zaïre
Baroda	Vadodara	India
Batavia	Djakarta	Indonesi
Bathurst	Banjul	The Gam
Beaverlodge	Goldfields	Canada
Bedeau	Ras el Ma	Algeria
Benares	Varanasi	India
Bizerta	Binzert	Tunisia
Bône	'Annaba	Algeria
Bougie	Bejaïa	Algeria
Breslau	Wrocław	German Poland
Broken Hill	Kabwe	Zambia
Brunei town	Bandar Seri Begawan	Brunei
Calicut	Kozhikode q.v.	India
Canton	Guangzhou	China
Casablanca	El-Dar-el-Beida	Morocco
Cawnpore	Kānpur	India
Chefoo	Yantai	China
Chemnitz	Karl-Marx-Stadt	E. Germ
Chkalov	Orenburg	U.S.S.R
Ciudad Trujillo	Santo Domingo	Dominic Repub
Coquilhatville	Mbandaka	Zaïre
Cuamba	Nova Freixo	Mozamb
Dairen	Lüda	China
Djambi	Telanaipura	Indonesi
Elisabethville	Lubumbashi	Zaïre
Fort Jameson	Chipata	Zambia
Fort Lamy	N'djamena	Chad
Fort William & * Port Arthur	Thunder Bay	Canada
Fort Rosebery	Mansa	Zambia
Georgetown	Pinang	Malaysi
Gzhatsk	Gagarin	U.S.S.R

ame Changes from 1945

960 but Congo (Kinshasa) is itself listed as the old name for Zaïre for 1971. Variations in spelling through erent methods of transliteration, or differences between the vernacular and anglicized forms, are not included e.

*rporated into a larger conurbation are marked *. In general, only cities of over 100,000 are included.*

OLD NAME	NEW NAME	COUNTRY
ankow*	Wuhan	China
anyang*	Wuhan	China
ollandia	Kotabaru q.v.	Indonesia
ønefoss*	Ringerike	Norway
ot Springs	Truth or Consequences	U.S.A.
sinking	Changchun	China
dotville	Likasi	Zaïre
sselton	Kota Kinabalu	Malaysia
algan	Zhangjiakou	China
enitra	Mina Hassan Tani	Morocco
irin	Jilin	China
okura*	Kitakyūshū	Japan
ongmoon	Jiangmen	China
önigsberg	Kaliningrad	Germany→ U.S.S.R.
otabaru	Sukarnapura q.v.	Indonesia
ozhikode	Calicut	India
uldja	Yining	China
weihwa	Huhehaote	China
opoldville	Kinshasa	Zaïre
vingstone	Maramba	Zambia
ourenço Marques	Can Phumo	Mozambique
ugansk	Voroshilovgrad	U.S.S.R.
luabourg	Kananga	Zaïre
ngkiang	Qiqihaer	China
achilīpatnam	Bandar	India
ariupol	Ždanov	U.S.S.R.
asulipatam	Machilīpatnam q.v.	India
emel	Klaipėda	Germany→ U.S.S.R.
iddlesbrough*	Teesside	England
oji*	Kitakyūshū	Japan
olotov	Perm'	U.S.S.R.
olotovsk	Nolinsk	U.S.S.R.
ukden	Shenyang	China
cosia	Levkosia	Cyprus
ulis	Isiro	Zaïre
tsamo	Pečenga	Finland→ U.S.S.R.
ilippeville	Skikda	Algeria
nthierville	Ubundi	Zaïre
ona	Pune	India
rt Arthur	Lüshun	China

OLD NAME	NEW NAME	COUNTRY
Port Arthur & Fort William *	Thunder Bay	Canada
Port Étienne	Nouadhibou	Mauritania
Port Francqui	Ilebo	Zaïre
Port Herald	Nsanje	Malawi
Port Lyautey	Kenitra q.v.	Morocco
Prome	Pyè	Burma
Saigon-Cholon	Ho Chih Minh City	Vietnam
Sihanoukville	Kompong Som	Khmer Republic
Stalinabad	Dušanbe	U.S.S.R.
Stalingrad	Volgograd	U.S.S.R.
Stalino	Doneck	U.S.S.R.
Stalinogorsk	Novomoskovsk	U.S.S.R.
Stalinogrod	Katowice	Poland
Stalinsk	Novokuzneck	U.S.S.R.
Stanislav	Ivano-Frankovsk	U.S.S.R.
Stanisławów	Stanislav q.v.	Poland→ U.S.S.R.
Stanleyville	Kisangani	Zaïre
Stavropol'	Toljatti	U.S.S.R. (on R. Volga)
Stockton-on-Tees*	Teesside	England
Sukarnapura	Djajapura	Indonesia
Taihoku	T'aipei	Japanese Formosa → Taiwan
Takao	Kaohsiung	Japanese Formosa → Taiwan
Tananarive	Antananarivo	Madagascar
Tourane	Da Nang	Vietnam
Thysville	Songolo	Zaïre
Tiflis	Tbilisi	U.S.S.R.
Tihua	Urumchi q.v.	China
Tobata*	Kitakyūshū	Japan
Tripoli	Ţarābulus	Lebanon
Tripoli	Ţarābulus	Libya
Urumchi	Wulumuqi	China
Usumbura	Bujumbura	Burundi
Voroshilov	Ussurijsk	U.S.S.R.
Voroshilovgrad	Lugansk q.v.	U.S.S.R.
Wakamatsu*	Kitakyūshū	Japan
Waldenburg	Wałbrzych	Germany→ Poland
Wuchang*	Wuhan	China
Yarkand	Suoche	China
Yawata*	Kitakyūshū	Japan

GAZETTEER OF THE WORLD

Place	Page	Lat.	Long.
Aabenraa: Denmark	35	55n	9e
Aachen: Germany	32	51n	6e
Aalborg: Denmark	35	57n	10e
Aalst: Belgium	28	51n	4e
Aare: r., Switzerland	33	47n	7e
Aarhus: Denmark	35	56n	10e
Aba: Nigeria	68	5n	7e
Ābādān: Iran	49	30n	48e
Abadla: Algeria	66	31n	3w
Abakan: USSR	45	54n	91e
Abancay: Peru	86	13s	73w
Abashiri: Japan	55	44n	144e
Abbeville: France	28	50n	2e
Abbottabad: W. Pak.	52	34n	73e
Abd al Kuri: i., Arabian Sea	49	12n	52e
Abeokuta: Nigeria	68	7n	3e
*Abercorn: N. Rhod.	68	9s	31e
Aberdeen: USA	80	46n	99w
Abha: Sau. Arab.	49	18n	43e
Abidjan: Ivory Coast	66	5n	4w
Abilene: USA	80	32n	100w
Abington Reef: Coral Sea	60	18s	150e
Abisko: Sweden	34	68n	19e
Abitibi L.: Canada	84	49n	80w
Åbo: Finland	35	61n	22e
Abqaiq: Sau. Arab.	49	26n	49e
Abruzzi-Molise: Italy	30	42n	14e
Abu: India	52	25n	73e
Abukuma Mts.: Japan	54	37n	141e
ABYSSINIA	67	10n	40e
Acapulco: Mexico	82	17n	100w
Accra: Ghana	68	5n	0
Achinsk: USSR	45	56n	90e
Acı, L.: Turkey	31	38n	30e
Aconcagua: mt., Arg.	88	33s	70w
Acqui: Italy	33	45n	8e
Acre: Holy Land	48	Inset	
Ada: Ghana	68	6n	0
Adaminaby: Aust.	61	36s	149e
Adam's Bridge: India/Ceylon	52	9n	79e
Adana: Turkey	48	37n	35e
Adapazarı: Turkey	31	41n	30e
Adare, C.: Antarc.	91	71s	170e
Adda: r., Italy	33	46n	10e
Addis Ababa: Ethiopia	67	9n	39e
Adelaide: Australia	61	35s	139e
Adelaide I.: Antarc.	91	68s	69w
Adélie Land: Antarc.	91	70s	140e
*Aden: & G., Aden	49	13n	45e
*ADEN PROTECTORATE	49	15n	50e
Adige: r., Italy	33	47n	11e
Adirondack Mts.: USA	85	44n	74w
Admiralty B.: Antarc.	91	62s	59w
*Admiralty Is.: Pac. O.	92	2s	147e
Adour: r., France	29	44n	1w
Adrian: USA	84	42n	84w
Adrianople: Turkey	31	42n	26e
Adriatic Sea	30	43n	15e
Aduwa: Ethiopia	67	14n	39e
Aegean Is.: & sea, Grc.	31	38n	25e
AFGHANISTAN	46	35n	65e
Afyonkarahisar: Turkey	31	39n	30e
Agadir: Morocco	66	30n	10w
Agartala: India	53	24n	91e
Agassiz, C.: Antarc.	91	69s	63w
Agde, C.d': France	29	43n	4e
Agen: France	29	44n	1e
Agenais: France	29	44n	1e
Agincourt: France	28	50n	2e
Agordat: Ethiopia	67	15n	37e
Agra: India	52	27n	78e
Agrigento: Sicily	30	37n	14e
Agulhas, C.: S. Africa	71	35s	20e
Ahaggar: Algeria	66	23n	6e
Ahmadabad: India	52	23n	73e
Ahvāz: Iran	49	31n	49e
Ahvenanmaa: is., Fin.	35	60n	20e
Aigues-Mortes: France	29	44n	4e
Aïn Sefra: Algeria	66	33n	1w
Aïr: Niger	66	18n	8e
Aisne: r., France	28	49n	3e
*Aitape: New Guinea	59	3s	143e
Aiun: Sp. Sahara	66	27n	14w
Aix-en-Provence: Fr.	29	44n	5e
Aix-les-Bains: France	29	46n	6e
Ajaccio: Corsica	30	42n	9e
Ajana: Australia	60	28s	115e
Ajedabya: Libya	48	31n	20e
*Ajena: Ghana	68	6n	0
Ajmer: India	52	27n	75e
Ajo: USA	80	32n	113w
Akaishi Mts.: Japan	54	35n	138e
Akaroa: NZ	55	44s	173e
Akhisar: Turkey	31	39n	28e
Akita: Japan	54	40n	140e
Aklavik: Canada	78	68n	134w
Akmolinsk: see Tselinograd			
Akola: India	52	21n	77e
Akritas, C.: Greece	31	37n	22e
Akron: USA	84	41n	81w
Akşehir: Turkey	31	38n	31e
Aksha: USSR	43	50n	113e
Aktyubinsk: USSR	45	50n	57e
Akureyri: Iceland	34	66n	18w
Akyab: Burma	47	20n	93e
Alabama: r., USA	81	32n	87w
Albama: State, USA	81	33n	87w
Alai Range: USSR	45	40n	72e
Ala Kul': L., USSR	45	46n	82e
Al 'Amārah: 'Iraq	49	32n	47e
Åland Is.: Finland	35	60n	20e
Alapayevsk: USSR	45	58n	62e
Ala Shan: China	50	40n	103e
Alaska: USA	78	—	—
Alaskan Highway: Alaska/Canada	78	60n	132w
Alaska Range: USA	78	63n	150w
Alassio: Italy	33	44n	8e
Alaverdi: USSR	44	41n	45e
Alba: Italy	33	45n	8e
Albacete: Spain	25	39n	2w
Alba Iulia: Romania	31	46n	24e
ALBANIA	31	41n	20e
Albany: Australia	60	35s	118e
Albany: USA	85	43n	74w
Albermarle I.: Pac. O.	86	1s	91w
Albermarle Sd.: USA	85	36n	76w
Albert: France	28	50n	3e
Albert, L.: Africa	70	2n	31e
Alberta: Canada	78	57n	115w
Albert Lea: USA	84	44n	93w
*Albertville: Congo Rep.	71	6s	29e
Albi: France	29	44n	2e
Alborz Mts.: Iran	49	36n	52e
Albret, Pays d': France	29	44n	0
Albula Pass: Switz.	33	47n	10e
Albuquerque: USA	80	35n	107w
Albury: Australia	61	36s	147e
Alcazar: Spain	25	39n	3w
Alcazarquivir: Morocco	25	35n	6w
Alcoy: Spain	25	39n	1w
Aldabra Is.: Ind. O.	71	9s	47e
Aldan: USSR	43	58n	125e
Aldan: r., USSR	43	59n	132e
Alegranza: i., Can. Is.	66	29n	13w
Aleksandrov Gay: USSR	44	50n	49e
Aleksandrovsk: USSR	43	51n	142e
Alençon: France	28	48n	0
Aleppo: Syria	48	36n	37e
Alès: France	29	44n	4e
Alessandria: Italy	33	45n	9e
Ålesund: Norway	34	62n	6e
Aletschhorn: mt., Switz.	33	46n	8e
Aleutian Is.: USA	92	52n	175w
Aleutian Range: USA	78	58n	155w
Alexandra: NZ	55	45s	169e
Alexandra Ra.: Antarc.	91	84s	165e
Alexandria: Egypt	67	31n	30e
Alexandria: USA	81	31n	93w
Alexandrina, L.: Aust.	61	35s	139e
Alexandroúpolis: Grc.	31	41n	26e
Alföld: Hungary	27	47n	21e
Algarve: Portugal	25	37n	8w
Algeciras: & B., Spain	25	36n	5w
ALGERIA	66	—	—
Algiers: Algeria	66	37n	3e
Algonquin Park: Can.	85	46n	78w
Al Hajara: Sau. Arab.	49	31n	42e
Alicante: Spain	25	38n	0
Alice Springs: Aust.	58	24s	134e
Aligarh: India	52	28n	78e
Aling Kangri: Kashmir/China	52	33n	79e
Alingsås: Sweden	35	58n	13e
Alkmaar: Neth.	32	53n	5e
Al Kūt: 'Iraq	49	33n	46e
Allahabad: India	52	25n	82e
Allard L.: Canada	79	51n	64w
Alleghenies: USA	84	38n	80w
Allegheny: r., USA	85	42n	79w
Allentown: USA	85	41n	75w
Allepey: India	52	9n	77e
Allgäuer Alps: Germany/Austria	33	47n	10e
Alliance: USA	84	41n	81w
Allier: r., France	29	47n	4e
Alma-Ata: USSR	45	43n	77e
Almaden: Spain	25	39n	5w
Al-Masilah, Wadi: Aden Prot.	49	16n	51e
Almeida: Portugal	25	41n	7w
Almeria: Spain	25	37n	2w
Alor: i., Indonesia	51	8s	125e
Alor Star: Malaya	51	6n	100e
Alps, The: Europe	30	46n	10e
Alsace: France	28	48n	7e
Alta: Norway	34	70n	23e
Altai Range: Mongolia	50	46n	93e
Altenburg: Germany	32	51n	12e
Altiplano: Peru/Bolivia	86	15s	70w
Alton: USA	84	39n	90w
Altona: Germany	32	54n	10e
Altoona: USA	85	40n	78w
Altyn Tagh: China	47	37n	86e
Alvesta: Sweden	35	57n	14e
Alwar: India	52	27n	77e
Al Wudyan: Sau. Arab.	49	32n	40e
Amarillo: USA	80	35n	102w
Amazon: r., Brazil	86	3s	61w
Ambala: India	52	30n	77e
Ambarchik: USSR	43	70n	162e
Amberg: Germany	32	50n	12e
Amboina: Indonesia	51	4s	128e
Amboise: France	29	47n	1e
Ambon: i., Indonesia	51	4s	128e
Amersfoort: Neth.	32	52n	5e
Amga: r., USSR	43	61n	132e
Amgun: r., USSR	43	53n	138e
Amherst: Canada	85	46n	64w
Amiens: France	28	50n	2e
Amlekganj: Nepal	52	27n	85e
'Amman: Jordan	48	32n	36e
Ammon: Holy Land	48	Inset	
Amne Machen Shan: China	50	35n	100e
Amoy: China	53	24n	118e
Amritsar: India	52	32n	75e
Amsterdam: Neth.	32	52n	5e
Amu Dar'ya: r., USSR	45	38n	64e
Amundsen B.: Antarc.	91	67s	50e
Amundsen Glacier: Antarctica	91	86s	160w
Amundsen Sea: Antarc.	91	72s	110w
Amur: r., USSR/China	43	52n	127e
Anabar: r., USSR	43	72n	113e
Anadyr': & r., USSR	43	65n	177e
Anaimudi: India	52	10n	77e
Anaiza: Sau. Arab.	49	26n	44e
Anambas Is.: Indonesia	51	3n	107e
Anan'yev: USSR	31	48n	30e
Anapolis: Brazil	87	16s	49w
Ancenis: France	29	47n	1w
Anchorage: USA	78	61n	150w
Ancona: Italy	33	44n	14e
Åndalsnes: Norway	34	63n	7e
Andalusia: Spain	25	37n	5w
Andaman Is.: & sea, B. of Bengal	47	12n	92e
Andermatt: Switz.	33	47n	9e
Andernach: Germany	32	50n	7e
Anderson: USA	84	40n	86w
Andes: range, S. Amer.	86	—	—
Andhra Pradesh: India	52	17n	79e
Andizhan: USSR	45	41n	73e
ANDORRA	29	42n	2e
Andreyevka: USSR	45	46n	81e
Andros: i., Greece	31	38n	25e
Anegada: i., W. Indies	83	19n	64w
Aneto: mt., Spain	25	43n	1e
Angara: r., USSR	45	58n	94e
Angel Falls: Venezuela	86	6n	63w
Angers: France	29	47n	1w
Angical: Brazil	87	12s	45w
Angkor: Cambodia	51	13n	103e
Angledool: Aust.	61	29s	148e
ANGOLA	71	—	—
Angoulême: France	29	46N	0
Angoumois: France	29	46N	0
Angren: USSR	45	41n	70e
Anguilla: i.,W. Indies	83	18n	63w
Anhwei: China	53	32N	117e
Aniak: USA	78	62n	160w
Aniva Bay: USSR	43	46n	143e
Anjo: Japan	54	35n	137e
Anjou: France	29	48n	0
Ankara: Turkey	48	40n	33e
Ankarata Mts.: Madag.	71	19s	47e
Anking: China	53	31n	117e
Ann, C.: Antarc.	91	66s	51e
Annaberg: Germany	32	51n	13e
Annam Range: Laos	51	18n	105e
Annapolis: USA	85	39n	77w
Annapolis Royal: Can.	85	45n	66w
Ann Arbor: USA	84	42n	84w
Annecy: & L., France	29	46n	6e
Annobón: i., G. of Guin.	68	2s	6e
Annonay: France	29	45n	5e
Ansbach: Germany	32	49n	11e
Anshan: China	53	41n	123e
Anshun: China	53	26n	106e
Ansi: China	50	41n	96e
Antakya: Turkey	48	36n	36e
Antalya: Turkey	31	37n	31e
Antarctica	91	—	—
Antequera: Spain	25	37n	5w
Anti-Atlas: Morocco	66	30n	8w
Antibes, C. d': France	29	44n	7e
Anticosti I.: Canada	79	49n	63w
Antifer, C. d': France	28	50n	0
Antigua: Guatemala	82	15n	91w
Antigua: i., W. Indies	83	17n	62w
Antilles, see Greater & Lesser			
Antioch: Turkey	48	36n	36e
Antipodes Is.: NZ	92	50s	179e
Antofagasta: Chile	88	24s	70w
*Antsirane: Madag.	71	13s	49e
Antung: China	53	40n	124e
Antwerp (Anvers): Belg.	28	51n	4e
Anvers: i., Antarc.	91	64s	64w
Anyang: China	53	36n	114e
Anzhero-Sudzhensk: USSR	45	56n	86e
Anzio: Italy	30	41n	13e
Aoiz: Spain	29	43n	1w
Aomori: Japan	54	41n	141e
Aosta: Italy	33	46n	7e
Aparri: Philippines	51	18n	122e
Apeldoorn: Neth.	32	52n	6e
Apennines: Italy	30	43n	12e
Apostle Is.: USA	84	47n	90w
Appalachians: USA	83	—	—
Apulia: Italy	30	41n	16e
'Aqaba: Jordan	48	29n	35e
Aquila: Italy	30	43n	13e
Aquiles Serdán: Mex.	80	28n	106w
Aquitaine: France	29	45n	1e
Arabian Sea	47	—	—
Aracajú: Brazil	87	11s	37w
Arad: Romania	31	46n	21e
Arafura Sea	58	10s	132e
Aragon: Apain	25	42n	0
Araguaia: r., Brazil	87	12s	51w
Arakan Yoma: Burma	50	20n	94e
Araks: r., Asia	44	39n	48e
Aral Sea: USSR	45	45n	60e
Aral'sk: USSR	45	47n	62e
Ararat: Australia	61	37s	143e
Ararat, Mt.: Turkey	49	40n	44e
Arauca: Venez.	86	7n	71w
Aravalli Hills: India	52	27n	74e
Araxes: r., Asia	44	39n	48e
Arcot: India	52	13n	79e
Arctic Ocean	78	—	—
Ardabīl: Iran	49	38n	48e
Ardèche: France	29	44n	4e
Ardennes: mts., Belg.	28	50n	5e
Arendal: Norway	35	59n	9e
Arequipa: Peru	86	17s	72w
Arezzo: Italy	30	43n	12e
Argaum: India	52	21n	77e
Argentan: France	28	49n	0
Argenteuil: France	28	49n	2e
ARGENTINA	88/89	—	—
Argonne: & for., France	28	49n	5e
Argos: Greece	31	38n	23e
Argostolion: Greece	31	38n	20e
Argyrokastro: Albania	31	40n	20e
Arica: Chile	86	18s	70w
Ariège: r., France	29	43n	2e
Arimathaea: Holy Land	48	Inset	
Arizona: State, USA	80	35n	112w
Arkansas: r., USA	81	34n	92w
Arkansas: State, USA	81	35n	92w
Arkhangel'sk: USSR	42	65n	40e
Arkona, C.: Germany	35	55n	14e
Arlberg P.: Austria	33	47n	10e
Arles: France	29	44n	5e
Arlon: Belgium	28	50n	6e
Armavir: USSR	44	45n	41e
Armenian SSR: USSR	44	40n	45e
Armentières: France	28	51n	3e
Armidale: Aust.	61	30s	152e
Arnhem: Netherlands	32	52n	6e
Arnhem Land: Aust.	58	14s	132e
Arno: r., Italy	33	44n	11e
Arnsberger Wald: Ger.	32	51n	9e
Arras: France	28	50n	3e
Arvée, M. d': France	28	48n	4w
Arromanches: France	28	49n	1w
Arrowsmith, Mt.: NZ	55	43s	171e
Arta: Greece	31	39n	21e
Artachon: France	29	45n	1w
Artem: USSR	54	43n	132e
Artemovskiy: USSR	45	57n	62e
Arthur's Pass: NZ	55	43s	172e
Artois: France	28	50n	2e
Artsiz: USSR	31	46n	29e
Aruba: i., S. America	86	12n	70w
Aru Is.: Indon.	51	6s	134e
*Arusha: Tangan.	68	3s	36e
Arvida: Canada	85	48n	71w
Arvidsjaur: Sweden	34	66n	19e
Arvika: Sweden	35	60n	12e
Arys': USSR	45	43n	69e
Arzamas: USSR	44	55n	44e
Asahikawa: Japan	54	44n	142e
Asansol: India	52	24n	87e
Ascension I.: Atl. O.	90	9s	15w
Aschaffenburg: Ger.	32	50n	9e
Ascoli Piceno: Italy	30	44n	14e
Åsele: Sweden	34	64n	17e
Asenovgrad: Bulgaria	31	42n	25e
Ashanti: Ghana	68	7n	2w
Ashburton: NZ	55	44s	172e
Ashburton: r., Aust.	58	23s	117e
Asheville: USA	84	36n	83w
Ashizuri, C.: Japan	54	33n	133e
Ashkelon: Holy Land	48	Inset	
Ashkhabad: USSR	45	38n	58e
Ashland: Ky., USA	84	38n	83w
Ashland: Ohio, USA	84	41n	82w
Ashland: Oreg., USA	80	42n	123w
Ashland: Wis., USA	84	47n	91w
Ashtabula: USA	84	42n	81w
Ashuanipi L.: Canada	79	53n	66w
Asino: USSR	45	57n	86e
Asir: Sau. Arab.	49	19n	42e
Askja: volc., Iceland	34	65n	17w
Asl: Egypt	48	29n	33e
Asmara: Ethiopia	67	15n	39e
Aspiring, Mt.: NZ	55	44s	169e
Assab: Ethiopia	67	13n	42e
Assam: India	53	27n	93e
Assaye: India	52	20n	76e
'Assen: Netherlands	32	53n	7e
Assiniboia: Canada	80	49n	106w
Assiniboine: r., Canada	80	51n	102w
Assisi: Italy	30	44n	13e
Astara: USSR/Iran	44	38n	49e
Asti: Italy	33	45n	8e
Astipalaia: i., Greece	31	36n	26e
Astoria: USA	80	46n	124w
Astrakhan': USSR	44	46n	48e
Asturias: Spain	25	43n	6w
Asunción: Paraguay	88	25s	57w
Aswân: & dam, Egypt	67	24n	33e
Asyût: Egypt	67	27n	31e
Atacama Desert: Chile	88	22s	69w
Atasuskiy: USSR	45	49n	72e
Atbara: & r., Sudan	67	18n	34e
Atbasar: USSR	45	52n	68e
Athabasca: r., Canada	78	54n	117w
Athabasca, L.: Canada	78	59n	110w
Athens: Greece	31	38n	24e
Athens: USA	81	34n	83w
Athinai: Greece	31	38n	24e
Athos: mt., Greece	31	40n	24e
Atikokan: Canada	84	49n	91w
Atlanta: USA	81	34n	85w
Atlantic City: USA	85	39n	74w
Atlantic Ocean, N. & S.	90	—	—
Atlas: mts., Mor./Algeria	66	32n	3w
Atrak: r., Iran	49	38n	57e
*Atshan: Libya	66	27n	11e
Aubagne: France	29	43n	6e
Aube: r., France	28	48n	4e
Aubrac, M. d': France	29	45n	3e
Auburn: Maine, USA	85	44n	70w
Auburn: N.Y., USA	85	43n	77w
Aubusson: France	29	46n	2e
Auch: France	29	44n	1e
Auckland: NZ	55	37s	175e
Auckland Is.: NZ	92	50s	166e
Aude: r., France	29	43n	2e
Audierne: & B., France	28	48n	5w
Augathella: Aust.	60	26s	147e
Augsburg: Germany	33	48n	11e
Augusta: Australia	60	34s	115e
Augusta: Ga., USA	81	33n	82w
Augusta: Maine, USA	85	44n	70w
Aujila: Libya	48	29n	22e
Aunis: France	29	46n	1w
Aurangabad: India	52	20n	75e
Aurich: Germany	32	54n	7e
Aurignac: France	29	43n	1e
Aurillac: France	29	45n	2e
Aurora: USA	84	42n	88w
Aussig: Czech.	32	51n	14e
Austerlitz: Czech.	27	49n	17e
Austin: Minn., USA	84	44n	93w
Austin: Nevada, USA	80	39n	117w
Austin: Texas, USA	80	30n	98w
Austral: is., Pac. O.	93	22s	150w
AUSTRALIA	58/59	—	—
Australian Alps	61	36s	149e
*Australian Antarctic Territory	91	—	—
Australian Capital Territory	61	36s	149e
AUSTRIA	27	47n	14e
Autun: France	29	47n	4e
Auvergne: & mts., Fr.	29	45n	3e
Auxerre: France	28	48n	3e
Avallon: France	29	47n	4e
Aveiro: Portugal	25	41n	9w
Avellanada: Arg.	88	35s	58w
Aveyron: r., France	29	44n	2e
Avignon: France	29	44n	5e
Ávila: Spain	25	41n	5w
Avranches: France	28	49n	1w
Awash: Ethiopia	67	9n	40e
Awaso: Ghana	68	6n	2w
Axel Heiberg Glacier: Antarctica	91	86s	165w
Axel-Heiberg I.: Canada	79	80n	90w
Ayacucho: Peru	86	13s	74w
Ayaguz: USSR	45	48n	80e
Aydın: Turkey	31	38n	28e
Aylmer, L.: Canada	78	64n	108w
Ayon I.: USSR	43	70n	168e
Ayr: Australia	60	19s	148e
Ayutthaya: Thailand	51	14n	100e
Ayvalık: Turkey	31	39n	27e
Azerbaydzhan SSR: USSR	45	40n	47e
Azores: is., Atl. O.	66	39n	29w
Azotus: Holy Land	48	Inset	
Azov, Sea of: USSR	44	46n	37e
Babar Is.: Indon.	51	8s	129e
Babbitt: USA	84	48n	92w
Bab el Mandeb: str., Red Sea	67	12n	43e
Babylon: 'Iraq	49	33n	44e
Bacău: Romania	31	47n	27e
Bacolod: Philippines	51	11n	123e
Badajoz: Spain	25	39n	7w
Baden: Switzerland	33	47n	8e
Baden-Baden: Germany	33	49n	8e
Bad Ischl: Austria	33	48n	14e
Bad Kissingen: Ger.	32	50n	10e
Bad Kreuznach: Ger.	32	50n	8e
Bad Reichenhall: Ger.	33	48n	13e
*Badulla: Ceylon	52	7n	81e
Baffin Bay: Canada	79	73n	65w
Baffin I.: Canada	79	70n	75w
Baghdād: 'Iraq	49	33n	44e
Bagheria: Sicily	30	38n	14e
Bagrach Kol: China	47	42n	87e
Bahama Is.: W. Indies	83	25n	75w
*Baharîya Oasis: Egypt	48	28n	29e
Bahawalpur: W. Pak.	52	29n	72e
Bahia: Brazil	87	13s	38w
Bahía Blanca: Arg.	88	39s	62w
Bahraich: India	52	27n	82e
BAHRAIN	49	26n	51e
Bahr el Ghazal: Sudan	67	8n	27e
Bahr el Ghazal: r., Chad	66	13n	16e
Bahr el Jebel: r., Sudan	67	7n	31e
Baia-Mare: Romania	31	48n	24e
Bailen: Spain	25	38n	4w
Băileşti: Romania	31	44n	23e
Bailleau Pk.: Antarc.	91	68s	60e
Bailleul: France	28	51n	3e
Bairnsdale: Australia	61	38s	148e
Bakersfield: USA	80	35n	119w
Bakony Forest: Hung.	27	47n	18e
Baku: USSR	44	40n	50e
Balaghat: India	52	22n	80e
Balaklava: Australia	61	34s	138e
Balaklava: USSR	44	45n	34e
Balashov: USSR	44	52n	43e
Balasore: India	52	22n	87e
Balaton, L.: Hungary	27	47n	17e
Balboa: Panamá	83	Inset	
Balclutha: NZ	55	46s	170e
Bâle: Switzerland	33	48n	8e
Balearic Is.: Spain	25	—	—
Balen: Belgium	28	51n	5e
Bali: i., Indonesia	51	8s	115e
Balıkesir: Turkey	31	40n	28e
Balikpapan: Borneo	51	1s	117e
Balkan Mts.: Bulgaria	31	43n	25e
Balkhash: & L., USSR	45	47n	75e
Ballarat: Australia	61	38s	144e

* See Page 131

Page; Lat. Long.
Balleny Is.: Antarc. 91; 67s 163e
Ballina: Australia 61; 29s 153e
Balmaceda: Chile 89; 46s 72w
*Balovale: N. Rhod. 69; 13s 23e
Balranald: Australia 61; 35s 144e
Balsas: r., Mexico 82; 18n 99w
Balta: USSR 31; 48n 30e
Baltic Sea 35; — —
Baltimore: USA 85; 39n 77w
Baltrum: i., Germany 32; 54n 7e
Baluchistan: Iran 49; 28n 60e
Baluchistan: W. Pak. 52; Inset
Bamako: Mali 66; 13n 8w
Bamba: Mali 66; 17n 2w
Bamberg: Germany 32; 50n 11e
Bamenda: Cameroon 68; 6n 10e
Banat: Romania 31; 45n 22e
Bancannia, L.: Aust. 61; 31s 142e
Bandar 'Abbas: Iran 49; 27n 56e
Bandar-e Shāh: Iran 49; 37n 54e
Bandar-e Shāhpūr: Iran 49; 30n 49e
Banda Sea 51; 6s 128e
Banderas Bay: Mexico 82; 21n 106w
Bandırma: Turkey 31; 40n 28e
Bandjarmasin: Borneo 51; 4s 115e
Bandra: India 52; 19n 73e
Bandung: Java 51; 7s 108e
Banff: Canada 80; 51n 115w
Bangka: i., Indon. 51; 2s 106e
*Bangkok: Thailand 51; 13n 100e
Bangor: USA 85; 45n 69w
Bangui: Cen. Afr. Repub. 67; 4n 18e
*Bangweulu, L.: N. Rhod. 68; 11s 30e
Ban Houeisai: Laos 50; 20n 100e
Baniyâs: Syria 44; 35n 36e
Banja Luka: Yugo. 27; 45n 17e
Banks I.: Canada 78; 73n 120w
Banks Penin.: NZ 55; 44s 173e
Bannu: W. Pak. 52; 33n 71e
Banzare Coast: Antarc. 91; 67s 125e
Bapaume: France 28; 50n 3e
Baranovichi: USSR 44; 53n 26e
Barbados: i., W. Indies 83; 13n 60w
Barbuda: i., W. Indies 83; 18n 62w
Barce: Libya 48; 33n 21e
Barcelona: Spain 25; 41n 2e
Barcelona: Venez. 86; 10n 65w
Barcelonnette: France 29; 44n 7e
Barcoo: r., Aust. 59; 24s 144e
Bardia: Libya 48; 32n 25e
Bareilly: India 52; 28n 79e
Barents Sea 42; 73n 40e
Bar Harbor: USA 85; 44n 68w
Bari: Italy 30; 41n 17e
Barkly Tableland: Aust. 58; 18s 136e
Barkly West: S. Africa 69; 28s 25e
Bârlad: Romania 31; 46n 28e
Bar-le-Duc: France 28; 49n 5e
Barlee, L.: Australia 60; 29s 119e
Barletta: Italy 30; 41n 16e
Barlin: France 28; 50n 3e
Barnato: Australia 61; 32s 145e
Barnaul: USSR 45; 53n 84e
Barne Inlet: Antarc. 91; 80s 160e
*Baroda: India 52; 22n 73e
Barquisimeto: Venez. 86; 10n 69w
Barraba: Australia 61; 30s 151e
Barrackpore: India 52; 23n 88e
Barranquilla: Col. 86; 11n 75w
Barrow, Pt.: Canada 78; 71n 155w
Barrow Str.: Canada 79; 74n 93w
Barry Mts.: Australia 61; 37s 147e
Bar-sur-Seine: France 28; 48n 4e
Barwon: r., Australia 61; 30s 148e
Basel: Switzerland 33; 48n 8e
Basilan: i., Phil. 51; 7n 122e
Basilicata: Italy 30; 40n 16e
Baskatong Res.: Can. 85; 47n 76w
Baskunchak: USSR 44; 48n 47e
Basque: Spain 25; 43n 2w
Basra: 'Iraq 49; 30n 48e
Bassas da India: i., Ind. O. 69; 22s 40e
Bassein: Burma 51; 17n 95e
Basse-Terre:
Guadeloupe 83; 16n 62w
Bastia: Corsica 30; 43n 9e
Bastogne: Belgium 28; 50n 6e
Bastuträsk: Sweden 34; 65n 20e
*BASUTOLAND 69; 30s 28e
*Bata: Sp. Guinea 68; 2n 10e
Bataan Penin.: Phil. 51; 15n 120e
Batang: China 50; 30n 99e
Batan Is.: Philippines 53; 21n 122e
Bathurst: Australia 61; 33s 150e
Bathurst: Canada 85; 47n 66w
*Bathurst: Gambia 66; 13n 17w
Bathurst, C.: Canada 78; 70n 128w
Bathurst I.: Australia 58; 11s 131e
Bathurst I.: Canada 79; 75n 100w
Baton Rouge: USA 81; 31n 91w
*Batticaloa: Ceylon 52; 8n 82e
Battle Creek: USA 84; 42n 85w
Battle Harbour: Canada 79; 52n 56w
Batu Is.: Indonesia 51; 0 99e
Batumi: USSR 44; 42n 42e
Batz, Î. de: France 28; 49n 4w
Bauchi: Nigeria 68; 10n 10e
Bautzen: Germany 32; 51n 14e
Bavaria: Germany 32; 49n 11e
Bawdwin: Burma 50; 23n 97e
Bayan Kara Shan: China 50; 34n 98e
Bay City: USA 84; 44n 84w
Bayeux: France 28; 49n 1w
Baykal, L.: USSR 43; 53n 108e
Baykonur: USSR 45; 48n 66e
Baymak: USSR 45; 52n 58e
Bayonne: France 29; 43n 1w
Bayreuth: Germany 32; 50n 12e
Baza: Spain 25; 37n 3w
Bazdar: W. Pakistan 52; Inset
Beachport: Australia 61; 37s 140e
Beardmore Glacier:
Antarctica 91; 85s 170e
Béarn: France 29; 43n 1w
Beas: r., India 52; 32n 77e
Beauce: France 28; 48n 2e
Beaufort Sea 78; 72n 140w
Beaufort West: S. Africa 69; 32s 23e
Beauharnois: Canada 85; 45n 74w
Beaujolais, M. du: Fr. 29; 46n 4e
Beaumont: USA 81; 30n 94w
Beaune: France 29; 74n 5e
Beauvais: France 28; 49n 2e
*Beaverlodge: Canada 78; 60n 109w
*BECHUANALAND 69; 22s 25e
Beckley: USA 84; 38n 81w
*Bedeau: Algeria 66; 34n 1w
Bedford: USA 84; 39n 87w
Beersheba: Holy Land 48; Inset
Bega: Australia 61; 37s 150e
Begovat: USSR 45; 40n 69e
*Beira: Mozambique 69; 20s 35e
Beirut: Lebanon 48; 34n 36e
*Beit Bridge: S. Rhod. 69; 22s 30e
Beja: Portugal 25; 38n 8w
Bela: W. Pakistan 52; Inset
Belaya: r., USSR 44; 54n 56e
Belém: Brazil 87; 2s 48w
Belfort: France 29; 48n 7e
Belgaum: India 52; 16n 75e
BELGIUM 28; 51n 4e
Belgorod: USSR 44; 51n 37e
Belgorod-Dnestrovskiy:
USSR 31; 46n 30e
Belgrade: Yugoslavia 27; 45n 20e
Belitung: i., Indonesia 51; 3s 108e
*Belize: Br. Honduras 82; 18n 88w
Bellac: France 29; 46n 1e
Bellano: Italy 33; 46n 9e
Bellary: India 52; 15n 77e
Bellegarde: France 29; 46n 6e
Belle I., Str. of: Canada 79; 52n 56w
Belle Île-en-Mer: France 28; 47n 3w
Belleville: Canada 85; 44n 77w
Belleville: USA 84; 39n 90w
Bellingham: USA 80; 49n 123w
Bellingshausen Sea:
Antarctica 91; 72s 85w
Bellinzona: Switzerland 33; 46n 9e
Belluno: Italy 33; 46n 12e
Belmont: Australia 61; 33s 152e
Belmont: S. Africa 69; 29s 24e
Belo Horizonte: Brazil 87; 20s 44w
Beloit: USA 84; 43n 89w
Belousovka: USSR 45; 50n 83e
Bel'tsy: USSR 31; 48n 28e
Belyando: r., Australia 60; 22s 147e
Belyy I.: USSR 43; 74n 71e
Bemidji: USA 84; 47n 95w
Benalla: Australia 61; 37s 146e
Bend: USA 80; 44n 121w
Bender Cassim: Som. 46; 11n 49e
Bendery: USSR 31; 47n 29e
Bendigo: Australia 61; 37s 144e
Benevento: Italy 30; 41n 15e
Bengal, B. of 47; — —
Benghazi: Libya 67; 32n 20e
Benguela: Angola 69; 13s 13e
Beni: r., Bolivia 86; 13s 67w
Beni Mansour: Algeria 25; 36n 4e
Benin, Bight of:
G. of Guinea 66; 5n 3e
Benin City: Nigeria 68; 6n 6e
Beni Saf: Algeria 25; 35n 1w
Bensersiel: Germany 32; 54n 8e
Benton: USA 84; 38n 89w
Benue: r., Nigeria 68; 9n 11e
Beograd: Yugoslavia 27; 45n 20e
Berar: India 52; 21n 77e
Berber: Sudan 67; 18n 34e
*Berbera: Som. Prot. 67; 10n 45e
Berdichev: USSR 44; 50n 29e
Berezovka: USSR 31; 47n 31e
Berezovo: USSR 45; 64n 65e
Bergama: Turkey 31; 39n 27e
Bergamo: Italy 33; 46n 10e
Bergen: Norway 35; 60n 5e
Bergen op Zoom: Neth. 32; 52n 4e
Bergerac: France 29; 45n 0
Bergisch Gladbach: Ger. 32; 51n 7e
Berhampore: India 52; 24n 88e
Bering Str.: USSR/USA 78; 66n 170w
Berislav: USSR 31; 47n 33e
Berkeley: USA 80; 38n 122w
Berlin: Germany 32; 53n 14e
Berlin: USA 85; 44n 71w
Bermuda: i., Atl. O. 83; 32n 65w
Bern: Switzerland 33; 47n 7e
Bernay: France 28; 49n 1e
Bernese Alps: Switz. 33; 47n 8e
Bernina P.: Switz. 33; 46n 10e
Berre, Étg. de: France 29; 44n 5e
Berri: Australia 61; 34s 141e
Berry: France 29; 47n 2e
Besançon: France 29; 47n 6e
Bessarabia: USSR 31; 47n 28e
Bessèges: France 29; 44n 4e
Bessines: France 29; 46n 1e
Bethany: Holy Land 48; Inset
Bethel: Holy Land 48; Inset
Bethlehem: Holy Land 48; Inset
Bethlehem: S. Africa 69; 28s 28e
Bethlehem: USA 85; 41n 75w
Bethsaida: Holy Land 48; Inset
Béthune: France 28; 51n 3e
Betwa: r., India 52; 26n 79e
Beuvron: r., France 29; 47n 3e
Beyşehir, L.: Turkey 31; 38n 32e
Bezhitsa: USSR 44; 53n 34e
Béziers: France 29; 43n 3e
Bhagalpur: India 52; 25n 87e
Bhamo: Burma 50; 24n 97e
BHARAT (INDIA) 52; — —
Bhaunagar: India 52; 22n 72e
Bhima: r., India 52; 17n 77e
Bhopal: India 52; 23n 77e
Bhubaneswar: India 52; 20n 86e
Bhuj: India 52; 23n 70e
BHUTAN 52; 28n 90e
Biafra, Bight of 68; 3n 8e
*Biak: Neth. New Guin. 58; 1s 136e
Biała Podlaska: Poland 35; 52n 23e
Białystok: Poland 35; 53n 23e
Biarritz: France 29; 43n 2w
Bickerton, C.: Antarc. 91; 66s 137e
Biddeford: USA 85; 43n 70w
Biel: Switzerland 33; 47n 7e
Bielefeld: Germany 32; 52n 9e
Biella: Italy 33; 46n 8e
Big Eau Pleine Res.: USA 84; 45n 90w
Biggar: Canada 80; 52n 108w
Bighorn Mts.: USA 80; 44n 107w
Bihać: Yugoslavia 27; 45n 16e
Bihar: India 52; 25n 85e
*Biharamulo: Tanganyika 68; 3s 31e
Bikaner: India 52; 28n 73e
Bikini: i., Pac. O. 92; 12n 165e
Bilaspur: India 52; 22n 82e
Bilbao: Spain 25; 43n 3w
Billings: USA 80; 46n 109w
Billiton: i., Indonesia 51; 3s 108e
Bingen: Germany 32; 50n 8e
Bingham: USA 85; 45n 70w
Binghampton: USA 85; 42n 76w
Bintan: i., Indonesia 51; 1n 104e
Birdum: Australia 58; 16s 133e
Bir el Harash: Libya 48; 26n 22e
Bīrjand: Iran 49; 33n 59e
Birmingham: USA 81; 33n 87w
Birni N'Konni: Niger 68; 14n 5e
Birobidzhan: USSR 43; 49n 133e
Biroo: Japan 55; 42n 143e
Bisbee: USA 80; 31n 110w
Biscay, B. of 26; 45n 3w
Biscoe Is.: Antarc. 91; 66s 67w
Biskotasi L.: Canada 84; 47n 82w
Biskra: Algeria 66; 35n 6e
Bismarck: USA 80; 47n 100w
*Bismarck Arch.:
New Guinea 59; 4s 149e
*Bissau: Port. Guinea 66; 12n 16w
Bistriţa: Romania 31; 47n 25e
Bitola: Yugoslavia 27; 41n 21e
Bitterfeld: Germany 32; 52n 12e
Bitterfontein: S. Africa 69; 31s 18e
Bitterroot Ra.: USA 80; 46n 114w
Biwa, L.: Japan 54; 35n 136e
Biysk: USSR 45; 53n 85e
*Bizerta: Tunisia 30; 37n 10e
Bjøllånes: Norway 34; 67n 15e
Björneborg: Finland 34; 62n 22e
Black Forest: Germany 33; 48n 8e
Black Irtysh: r.,
China/USSR 45; 48n 85e
Black Sea 44; — —
Black Volta: r., Africa 68; 10n 3w
Blackwood: r., Aust. 60; 34s 116e
Blagoveshchensk: USSR 43; 51n 127e
Blanc, C.: Sp. Sahara 66; 21n 17w
Blanc, Mt.: Fr./It. 29; 46n 7e
Bland: r., Australia 61; 34s 148e
Blankenberghe: Belg. 28; 51n 3e
*Blantyre: Nyasaland 69; 16s 35e
Blavet: r., France 28; 48n 3w
Blaye: France 29; 45n 1w
Blenheim: Germany 33; 49n 10e
Blenheim: NZ 55; 42s 174e
Blida: Algeria 25; 36n 3e
Blind River: Canada 84; 46n 83w
Blitta: Togo 68; 8n 1e
Bloemfontein: S. Africa 69; 29s 26e
Blois: France 29; 48n 1e
Bloomington: Ill., USA 84; 41n 89w
Bloomington: Ind., USA 84; 39n 87w
Bluefield: USA 84; 37n 81w
Blue Mts.: Australia 61; 33s 150e
Blue Mts.: USA 80; 45n 119w
Blue Nile Prov., Sudan 67; 12n 33e
Blue Nile: r.,
Sudan/Ethiopia 67; 10n 37e
Blue Ridge: USA 84; 36n 82w
Bluff: NZ 55; 47s 168e
Blumenthal: Germany 32; 53n 9e
Blythe: USA 80; 34n 115w
Blytheville: USA 84; 36n 90w
Bo: Sierra Leone 66; 8n 12w
Boa Vista: Brazil 86; 3n 61w
*Bobo-Dioulasso: Volta 66; 11n 4w
Bocholt: Germany 32; 52n 7e
Bochum: Germany 32; 51n 7e
Bodelé Depr.: Chad 66; 17n 17e
Boden: Sweden 34; 66n 22e
Bodø: Norway 34; 67n 14e
Boggs, C.: Antarc. 91; 71s 60w
Bogotá: Colombia 86; 5n 74w
Bohemian Forest:
Germany/Czech. 27; 49n 14e
Bohol: i., Philippines 51; 10n 124e
Boise: USA 80; 44n 116w
Bojador, C.: Sp. Sahara 66; 26n 15w
Boké: Guinea 66; 11n 14w
Bokn Fiord: Norway 35; 59n 6e
*Bolama: Port. Guinea 66; 12n 16w
Bolan Pass: W. Pak. 52; 30n 67e
Bold Eagle L.: USA 84; 48n 92w
Bole: Ghana 68; 9n 2w
Bolgrad: USSR 31; 46n 29e
Boling: USA 81; 29n 96w
BOLIVIA 86; 15s 65w
Bollwiller: France 28; 48n 7e
Bologna: Italy 33; 44n 11e
Bolsena, L.: Italy 30; 43n 12e
Bol'shevik I.: USSR 43; 78n 103e
Bolzano: Italy 33; 47n 11e
*Boma: Congo Rep. 71; 6s 13e
Bombay: India 52; 19n 73e
Bon, C.: Tunisia 30; 37n 11e
*Bondo: Congo Rep. 70; 4n 24e
*Bône: Algeria 66; 37n 8e
Bone, G. of: Indon. 51; 4s 121e
Bonifacio: Corsica 30; 41n 9e
Bonin Is.: Pac. O. 92; 27n 142e
Bonn: Germany 32; 51n 7e
Bonneville Dam: USA 80; 46n 122w
Bonny: Nigeria 68; 4n 7e
Bookaloo: Australia 61; 32s 137e
Boothia Penin.: Can. 79; 70n 95w
Bor: Sudan 68; 6n 32e
Bor.: Yugoslavia 27; 44n 22e
Borås: Sweden 35; 58n 13e
Bordeaux: France 29; 45n 1w
Borden I.: Canada 78; 78n 112w
Bordertown: Aust. 61; 36s 141e
Borgholm: Sweden 35; 57n 17e
Borgo Val di Taro: Italy 33; 45n 10e
Borisoglebsk: USSR 44; 52n 42e
Borkum: i., Germany 32; 54n 7e
Borlänge: Sweden 35; 61n 15e
Borneo: i., Indon. 51; 0 115e
Bornholm: i., Den. 35; 55n 15e
*Boromo: Volta 68; 12n 3w
Bosnia & Hercegovina:
Yugoslavia 27; 44n 17e
Boso Penin.: Japan 54; 35n 140e
Bosporus: Turkey 31; 41n 29e
Bosso: Niger 66; 14n 13e
Boston: USA 85; 42n 71w
Botany Bay: Australia 61; 34s 151e
Botevgrad: Bulgaria 31; 43n 24e
Bothnia, G. of 34; 63n 20e
Botoşani: Romania 31; 48n 27e
Bottrop: Germany 32; 52n 7e
*Bougainville: i., Pac. O. 92; 8s 155e
*Bougie: Algeria 66; 37n 5e
Boulder: Australia 60; 31s 122e
Boulogne: France 28; 51n 2e
Bounty Is., NZ 92; 48s 179e
Bourbonnais: France 29; 46n 3e
Bourg: France 29; 46n 5e
Bourges: France 29; 47n 2e
Bourget, L. du: France 29; 46n 6e
Bourg Madame: France 29; 42n 2e
Bourke: Australia 61; 30s 146e
Bourtanger Moor:
Neth./Germany 32; 53n 7e
Bou Saâda: Algeria 25; 35n 4e
Boussac: France 29; 46n 2e
Bouvet I.: S. Ocean 90; 54s 4e
Bowling Green: USA 84; 37n 86w
Bowling Green, C.:
Australia 60; 19s 148e
Bowman I.: Antarc. 91; 66s 103e
Boyd Glac.: Antarc. 91; 78s 146w
Boyne: r., Australia 60; 26s 151e
Boyup Brook: Aust. 60; 34s 117e
Brabant: Belgium 28; 51n 4e
Brač: i., Yugo. 27; 43n 17e
Brachina: Australia 61; 31s 138e
Braga: Portugal 25; 41n 8w
Brahmani: r., India 52; 22n 85e
Brahmaputra: r., India 53; 27n 93e
Brăila: Romania 31; 45n 28e
Brainerd: USA 84; 46n 94w
Branco: r., Brazil 86; 2n 62w
Brandenburg: Ger. 32; 52n 13e
Brandon: Canada 80; 50n 100w
Brantford: Canada 84; 43n 80w
Bras d'Or Lake: Can. 85; 46n 61w
Brasília: Brazil 87; 16s 48w
Braşov: Romania 31; 46n 26e
Bratislava: Czech. 27; 48n 17e
Bratsk: USSR 43; 56n 102e
Braunau: Austria 33; 48n 13e
Braunschweig: Ger. 32; 52n 11e
BRAZIL 86 87; — —
Brazilian Highlands 87; — —
Brazoria: USA 81; 29n 96w
Brazos: r., USA 81; 31n 96w
Brazzaville: Congo 71; 4s 15e
Breda: Netherlands 32; 52n 5e
Bredy: USSR 45; 52n 60e
Bregenz: Austria 33; 48n 10e
Bréhat: i., France 28; 49n 3w
Breisach: Germany 33; 48n 8e
Bremen: Germany 32; 53n 9e
*Bremerhaven Wesermünde:
Germany 32; 53n 9e
Brenner Pass: It./Aus. 33; 47n 12e
Brescia: Italy 33; 46n 10e
Breslau: Poland 35; 51n 17e
Bressuire: France 29; 47n 0
Brest: France 28; 48n 4w
Brest Litovskiy: USSR 35; 52n 24e
Briançon: France 29; 45n 7e
Bridgeport: USA 85; 41n 73w
Bridgetown: Australia 60; 34s 116e
Brie: France 28; 49n 3e
Brienz, L.: Switz. 33; 47n 8e
Briey: France 28; 49n 6e
Brindisi: Italy 30; 41n 18e
Brisbane: Australia 60; 27s 153e
*BRITISH ANTARCTIC
TERRITORY 91; 65s 50w
*BRITISH BORNEO 51; 3n 113e
British Columbia: Can. 78; 55n 125w
*BRITISH GUIANA 87; 5n 60w
*BRITISH HONDURAS 82; 17n 88w
Brittany: France 28; 48n 3w
Brive: France 29; 45n 1e
Brno: Czechoslovakia 27; 49n 17e
Broad Sd.: Australia 60; 22s 150e
Brocken: mt., Ger. 32; 52n 11e
Brod: Yugoslavia 27; 45n 18e
Broken Hill: Australia 61; 32s 142e
*Broken Hill: N. Rhod. 68; 14s 28e
Brooks Range: USA 78; 68n 155w
Broome: Australia 58; 18s 122e
Brothers, The: is.,
Arabian Sea 46; 12n 53e
Brownsville: USA 82; 26n 97w
Bruchsal: Germany 32; 49n 9e
Bruges (Brugge): Belg. 28; 51n 3e
Brühl: Germany 32; 51n 7e
BRUNEI 51; 5n 115e
Brunswick: Germany 32; 52n 11e
Brussels: Belgium 28; 51n 4e
Bryansk: USSR 44; 53n 34e
Brzeg: Poland 27; 51n 18e
Bucaramanga: Col. 86; 7n 73w
Bucharest (Bucureşti):
Romania 31; 44n 26e
Buckland Tableland:
Australia 60; 25s 148e
Budapest: Hungary 27; 47n 19e
Buea: Nigeria 68; 4n 9e
Buenaventura: Col. 86; 4n 77w
Buenos Aires: Arg. 88; 35s 58w
Buffalo: USA 85; 43n 79w
Bug: r., USSR 44; 48n 30e
Buganda: Uganda 68; 0 31e
Bukachacha: USSR 43; 53n 117e
*Bukama: Congo Rep. 71; 9s 26e
Bukavu: Congo Rep. 71; 2s 29e
Bukhara: USSR 45; 40n 65e
*Bukoba: Tanganyika 68; 2s 32e
Bulagan: Mongolia 50; 48n 103e
*Bulawayo: S. Rhodesia 69; 20s 29e
BULGARIA 31; 42n 25e
Buller: & r., NZ 55; 42s 172e
Bulli: Australia 61; 34s 151e
Bulloo Downs: Aust. 61; 29s 143e
Bumtang: Bhutan 52; 28n 91e
Bunbury: Australia 60; 33s 116e
Bundaberg: Aust. 60; 25s 152e
Bunguran Is.: Indonesia 51; 4n 108e
Buraida: Sau. Arab. 49; 26n 44e
Buraimi:
Muscat & 'Oman 49; 24n 56e
Burdekin: r., Aust. 60; 20s 147e
Bureya: USSR 43; 50n 130e
Burgas: & G., Bulgaria 31; 42n 28e
Burgdorf: Switz. 33; 47n 8e
Burgersdorp: S. Africa 69; 31s 26e
Burgos: Spain 25; 42n 4w
Burgundy: France 29; 47n 5e
Burlington: Iowa, USA 84; 41n 91w
Burlington: N.C., USA 85; 36n 79w
Burlington: Vt., USA 85; 44n 73w
BURMA 50; 20n 95e
Burnett Heads: Aust. 60; 25s 152e
Burra: Australia 61; 34s 139e
Burrinjuck Res.: Aust. 61; 35s 149e
Bursa: Turkey 31; 40n 29e
Buru: i., Indonesia 51; 3s 127e
BURUNDI 68; 3s 30e
Būshehr: Iran 49; 29n 51e
Bussa: Nigeria 68; 10n 5e
Busselton: Aust. 60; 34s 115e
Butere: Kenya 68; 0 35e
Butte: USA 80; 46n 113w
Butterworth: S. Africa 69; 32s 28e
Butung: i., Indonesia 51; 5s 123e
Buxar: India 52; 26n 84e
Buyaga: USSR 43; 60n 127e
Buzău: Romania 31; 45n 27e
Buzuluk: USSR 44; 53n 52e
Byam Martin I. 78; 75n 105w
Bydgoszcz: Poland 35; 53n 17e
Byelorussian SSR: USSR 44; 53n 28e
Bylot I.: Canada 79; 73n 78w
Bytom: Poland 27; 50n 19e

Cabinda: (Port.) Congo 71; 5s 12e
Cabonga Res.: Canada 85; 47n 77w
Cabot Strait: Canada 79; 47n 60w
Čačak: Yugoslavia 27; 44n 20e
Cáceres: Spain 25; 39n 6w
Cádiz: & G., Spain 25; 36n 6w
Caen: France 28; 49n 0
Caesarea: Holy Land 48; Inset
Caesarea Philippi:
Holy Land 48; Inset
Cagliari: Sardinia 30; 39n 9e
Cahors: France 29; 44n 1e
Caicos Is.: W. Indies 83; 22n 71w
Caird Coast: Antarc. 91; 76s 26w
Cairns: Australia 59; 16s 146e
Cairo: Egypt 67; 30n 31e
Cairo: USA 84; 37n 89w
Cajamarca: Peru 86; 7s 78w
Calabar: Nigeria 68; 5n 8e
Calabozo: Venezuela 86; 9n 67w
Calabria: Italy 30; 39n 16e
Calafat: Romania 31; 44n 23e
Calais: France 28; 51n 2e
Calamian Gp.: Phil. 51; 12n 120e
Călăraşi: Romania 31; 44n 27e
Calcutta: India 52; 22n 88e
Caldera: Chile 88; 27s 71w
Calexico: USA 80; 33n 115w
Calgary: Canada 80; 51n 114w
Cali: Colombia 86; 3n 77w
California: USA 80; 35n 120w
California, G. of 82; 28n 113w
Callabonna: Australia 61; 30s 140e
Callao: Peru 86; 12s 77w
Caltanissetta: Sicily 30; 37n 14e
Calumet: USA 84; 47n 88w
Calvi: Corsica 30; 43n 9e
Calvinia: S. Africa 69; 32s 20e
Camagüey: Cuba 83; 21n 78w
Camargue: France 29; 43n 4e
Cambay: & G., India 52; 22n 72e
CAMBODIA 51; 12n 105e
Cambrai: France 28; 50n 3e
Cambridge: Mass., USA 85; 42n 71w
Cambridge: Md., USA 85; 38n 76w
Cambridge: Ohio, USA 84; 40n 82w
Cambridge: NZ 55; 38s 175e
Camden: Ark., USA 81; 33n 93w
Camden: N.J., USA 85; 40n 75w
CAMEROON 70; 5n 12e
Camooweal: Aust. 58; 20s 138e
Campania: Italy 30; 41n 15e
Campbellton: Canada 85; 48n 67w
Campeche, B. of: Mex. 82; 20n 93w
Campinas: Brazil 88; 23s 47w
Campine: Belgium 28; 51n 5e
Campobasso: Italy 30; 41n 15e
Campo Grande: Brazil 88; 20s 55w
Câmpulung: Romania 31; 45n 25e
Câmpulung-Moldovenesc:
Romania 31; 48n 26e
CANADA 78/79; — —
Canadian: r., USA 80; 36n 107w
Çanakkale: Turkey 31; 40n 26e
Canal Zone: Panamá 83; Inset
Cananea: Mexico 80; 31n 110w
Canary Is.: Atl. O. 66; 28n 15w
Canaveral, C.: USA 81; 28n 81w
Canberra: Australia 61; 35s 149e
Candia: Crete 31; 35n 25e
Canea: Crete 31; 35n 24e
Cannes: France 29; 44n 7e
Canso: Canada 85; 45n 61w
Cantabrian Mts.: Spain 25; 43n 5w
Canterbury Bight: NZ 55; 44s 172e
Canton: China 53; 23n 113e
Canton: Ill., USA 84; 41n 90w
Canton: Ohio, USA 84; 41n 81w
Canton I.: Pac. O. 92; 3s 171w
Canudos: Brazil 87; 7s 58w
Cape Breton I.: Canada 85; 46n 61w
Cape Girardeau: USA 84; 37n 90w
Cape Province: S. Afr. 69; 33s 25e
Capernaum: Holy Land 48; Inset
Cape Town: S. Africa 69; 34s 18e
Cape Verde Is.: Atl. O. 90; 18n 24w
Cape Yorke Penin.:
Australia 59; 10s 143e

*See Page 131

Place	Page	Lat.	Long.
Capri: i., Italy	30	41n	14e
Capricorn Chan.: & is., Australia	60	22s	152e
Caprivi Strip: SW. Afr.	69	18s	23e
Capua: Italy	30	41n	14e
Caracas: Venezuela	86	10n	67w
Caransebeş: Romania	31	45n	22e
Caravelas: Brazil	87	18s	39w
Carcassonne: France	29	43n	2e
Cardamon Hills: India	52	10n	77e
Caribbean Sea	83	—	—
Carinthia: Austria	33	47n	14e
Carlsbad: USA	80	32n	104w
Carmaux: France	29	44n	2e
Carmel, Mt.: Holy Land	48	Inset	
Carnac: France	28	47n	3w
Carnarvon: Australia	58	25s	114e
Carnarvon: S. Africa	69	31s	22e
Carnarvon Ra.: Aust.	60	25s	149e
Carnic Alps: Aus. It.	33	47n	13e
Carolina: Brazil	87	7s	48w
Caroline I.: Pac. O.	93	10s	150w
Caroline Is.: Pac. O.	92	2n	145e
Caroni: r., Venezuela	86	6n	63w
Carpathian Mts.: USSR Romania	31	48n	25e
Carpentaria, G. of	58	15s	138e
Carpentras: France	29	44n	5e
Carrara: Italy	33	44n	10e
Carson City: USA	80	39n	120w
Cartagena: Colombia	86	10n	75w
Cartagena: Spain	25	38n	1w
Carthage: Tunisia	30	37n	10e
Carvin: France	28	50n	3e
Caryapundy Swamp: Australia	61	29s	143e
Casablanca: Morocco	66	34n	8w
Casale Monferrato: Italy	33	45n	8e
Casamozza: Corsica	30	43n	10e
Cascade Ra.: Can. USA	80	49n	121w
Cascavel: Brazil	87	4s	38w
Caserta: Italy	30	41n	14e
Casino: Australia	61	29s	153e
Casiquiare: r., Venez.	86	2n	67w
Caspian Lowlands: USSR	44	52n	50e
Caspian Sea	44	—	—
Casquets: Chan. Is.	28	50n	2w
Cassel: France	28	51n	2e
Cassino: Italy	30	41n	14e
Castellón de la Plana: Spain	25	40n	0
Castelo Branco: Port.	25	40n	7w
Castlemaine: Aust.	61	37s	144e
Castres: France	29	44n	2e
Çatalca: Turkey	31	41n	28e
Catalonia: Spain	25	41n	1e
Catamarca: Argentina	88	28s	66w
Catania: Sicily	30	37n	15e
Catanzaro: Italy	30	39n	16e
Catastrophe, C.: Aust.	58	35s	136e
Catoche, C.: Mexico	83	21n	87w
Catskill Mts.: USA	85	42n	74w
Cauca: r., Colombia	86	7n	76w
Caucasus Mts.: USSR	44	43n	45e
Causse du Larzac: Fr.	29	44n	3e
Cauvery: India	52	12n	77e
Cavado: r., Portugal	25	42n	8w
Cavaillon: France	29	44n	5e
Cáxias: Brazil	87	5s	44w
Cayenne: Fr. Guiana	87	5n	52w
Cayman Is.: W. Indies	83	20n	81w
Ceará: Brazil	87	4s	38w
Cebu: Philippines	51	10n	123e
Cedar Falls: USA	84	43n	92w
Cedar Rapids: USA	82	42n	92w
Ceduna: Australia	58	32s	134e
Celebes: i., Indonesia	51	2s	120e
Celebes Sea	51	3n	122e
Celje: Yugoslavia	27	46n	15e
Celle: Germany	32	53n	10e
CENTRAL AFRICAN REPUBLIC	67	5n	20e
*Central Range: New Guinea	59	6s	144e
Central Siberian Plateau: USSR	43	—	—
Cephalonia: i., Greece	31	38n	21e
Cerignola: Italy	30	41n	16e
Cerigo: i., Greece	31	36n	23e
Cerro Bolivar: mt., Venezuela	86	7n	63w
Cerro de Pasco: Peru	86	11s	76w
Cesena: Italy	33	44n	12e
České Budějovice: Czechoslovakia	27	49n	15e
Český Těšín: Czech.	27	50n	19e
Cessnock: Australia	61	33s	151e
Cetinje: Yugoslavia	27	42n	19e
Ceuta: (Sp.), Morocco	25	36n	5w
Cévennes: France	29	44n	4e
CEYLON	52	8n	81e
Chablis: France	28	48n	4e
CHAD	66	15n	20e
Chad, L.: & basin, Chad	66	13n	15e
Chalcis: Greece	31	38n	24e
Chaleur, B. de: Canada	85	48n	65w
Châlons-sur-Marne: Fr.	28	49n	4e
Chalon-sur-Saône: Fr.	29	47n	5e
Chaman: W. Pakistan	52	31n	67e
Chamba: India	52	32n	76e
Chambal: r., India	52	27n	77e
Chamberlain, L.: USA	85	46n	69w
Chambersburg: USA	85	40n	78w
Chambéry: France	29	46n	6e
Chamdo: China	50	31n	97e
Chamonix: France	29	46n	7e
Champagne: France	28	49n	4e
Champagne Pouilleuse: France	28	49n	4e
Champaign: USA	84	40n	88w
Champéry: Switz.	33	46n	7e
Champlain, L.: USA	85	44n	73w
Chañaral: Chile	88	26s	71w
Chanchiang: China	53	21n	110e
Changan: China	53	34n	109e
Changchew: China	53	32n	120e
Changchih: China	53	36n	113e
Changchun: China	53	44n	125e
Changkiakow: China	53	41n	115e
Changsha: China	53	28n	113e
Changshu: China	53	32n	121e
Chanthaburi: Thai.	51	13n	102e
Chany, L.: USSR	45	55n	78e
Chaoan: China	53	24n	117e
Chaoyangchen: China	50	43n	127e
Chapala, L.: Mexico	82	20n	103w
Chapayevsk: USSR	44	53n	50e
Chapel Hill: USA	85	36n	79w
Chapra: India	52	26n	85e
Charcot I.: Antarc.	91	70s	76w
Chardzhou: USSR	45	39n	64e
Charente: France	29	46n	0
Chari: r., Chad	66	11n	16e
Chariton: USA	84	41n	93w
Charleroi: Belgium	28	50n	5e
Charles, C.: USA	85	37n	76w
Charles City: USA	84	43n	93w
Charleston: S. C., USA	81	33n	80w
Charleston: W. Va., USA	84	38n	82w
Charleville: Aust.	60	26s	146e
Charleville: France	28	50n	5e
Charlotte: USA	81	35n	81w
Charlottesville: USA	85	38n	78w
Charlottetown: Can.	85	46n	63w
Charlton: Australia	61	36s	143e
Charolles: France	29	46n	4e
Charters Towers: Aust.	59	20s	146e
Chartres: France	28	48n	1e
Château, Pte. de: Fr.	28	49n	3w
Châteaubriant: Fr.	28	48n	1w
Châteaudun: France	28	48n	1e
Châteaulin: France	28	48n	4w
Château Renault: Fr.	29	48n	1e
Châteauroux: France	29	47n	2e
Château-Thierry: Fr.	28	49n	3e
Châtellerault: France	29	47n	1e
Chatham: Canada	84	42n	82w
Chatham I.: Pac. O.	86	1s	81w
Chatham Is.: NZ	92	44s	177w
Châtillon-sur-Seine: Fr.	28	48n	5e
*Chatrapur: India	52	19n	85e
Chattanooga: USA	81	35n	85w
Chaumont: France	28	48n	5e
Chausey, Î. de: France	28	49n	2w
Chautauqua L.: USA	85	42n	79w
Chaves I.: Pacific O.	86	1s	90w
Cheb: Czech.	32	50n	12e
Chedabucto B.: Can.	85	45n	61w
Cheduba: i., Burma	47	18n	93e
Chefoo: China	53	37n	121e
Cheju I.: S. Korea	50	33n	127e
Chekiang: China	53	29n	120e
Chekunda: USSR	43	51n	132e
Cheleken: USSR	44	39n	53e
Chéliff: r., Algeria	25	36n	2e
Chelkar-Tengiz, L.: USSR	45	48n	63e
Chełm: Poland	35	51n	23e
Chelyabinsk: USSR	45	55n	62e
Chelyuskin, C.: USSR	43	78n	105e
Chemnitz: see Karl-Marx-Stadt			
Chenab: r., Kashmir/W. Pak.	52	33n	75e
Chengchow: China	53	35n	113e
Chengkiang: China	50	25n	103e
Chengteh: China	53	29n	112e
Chengteh (Jehol): China	53	41n	118e
Chengtu: China	53	31n	104e
Cher: r., France	29	47n	1e
Cherbourg: France	28	50n	2w
Cherdoyak: USSR	45	49n	84e
Cheremkhovo: USSR	43	53n	103e
Cherepovets: USSR	44	59n	38e
Chernigov: USSR	44	51n	31e
Chernogorsk: USSR	45	54n	91e
Chernovtsy: USSR	44	48n	26e
Chernyakhovsk: USSR	35	55n	23e
Cherrapunji: India	53	25n	92e
Cherry I.: Pac. O.	59	11s	170e
Cherskiy Ra.: USSR	43	65n	145e
Chesapeake B.: USA	85	38n	76w
Chester: USA	85	40n	75w
Chesterfield: Canada	79	63n	90w
Chesterfield Is.: Pac. O.	59	20s	160e
Cheyenne: USA	80	41n	105w
Chhindwara: India	52	22n	79e
Chiang Mai: Thailand	50	19n	99e
Chiang Rai: Thailand	50	20n	100e
Chiari: Italy	33	46n	10e
Chiba: Japan	54	36n	140e
Chibia: Angola	69	15s	14e
Chibougamau: Canada	81	50n	75w
Chicago: USA	84	42n	88w
Chichagof I.: USA	78	58n	136w
Chichén Itzá: Mexico	83	21n	89w
Chichibu: Japan	54	36n	139e
Chiclayo: Peru	86	7s	80w
Chico: r., Argentina	89	45s	67w
Chicoutimi: Canada	85	48n	71w
Chief Joseph Dam: USA	80	48n	119w
Chiemsee: Germany	33	48n	12e
*Chiengi: N. Rhod.	68	9s	29e
Chieti: Italy	30	42n	14e
Chigneto B.: Canada	85	45n	65w
Chihfeng: China	53	42n	119e
Chihli Gulf: China	53	38n	118e
Chihuahua: Mexico	80	29n	106w
Childers: Australia	60	25s	152e
CHILE	88/89	—	—
Chilivani: Sardinia	30	41n	9e
Chillán: Chile	88	37s	72w
Chillicothe: Mo., USA	84	40n	93w
Chillicothe: Ohio, USA	84	39n	83w
Chiloé I.: Chile	89	43s	74w
Chimborazo: mt., Ec.	86	2s	79w
Chimbote: Peru	86	9s	79w
Chimkent: USSR	45	42n	70e
CHINA	50	—	—
Chinchilla: Aust.	60	27s	151e
Chinchow: China	53	41n	121e
Chindwin: r., Burma	50	25n	94e
Chingwangtao: China	53	40n	119e
Chin Hills: Burma	50	22n	93e
Chinkiang: China	53	32n	120e
Chinnampo: N. Korea	50	39n	125e
Chinon: France	29	47n	0
Chinook: USA	80	49n	109w
Chioggia: Italy	33	45n	12e
Chios: i., Greece	31	38n	26e
Chiquitos Plat.: Bolivia	86	17s	62w
Chita: USSR	43	52n	113e
Chitral: W. Pakistan	47	36n	72e
*Chittagong: E. Pakistan	53	23n	92e
Choibalsan: Mongolia	50	48n	114e
Choiseul: i., Pac. O.	59	7s	157e
Chojnice: Poland	35	54n	18e
Cholet: France	29	47n	1w
*Cholon: S. Viet Nam	51	10n	107e
Chongjin: N. Korea	50	42n	130e
Chonos Arch.: Chile	89	45s	74w
Chop: USSR	31	49n	22e
Chorzów: Poland	27	50n	19e
Choshi: Japan	54	36n	141e
Chott Djerid: Tun.	66	34n	8e
Christchurch: NZ	55	43s	173e
Christmas I.: Ind. O.	92	11s	106e
Christmas I.: Pac. O.	93	2n	157w
Chu: & r., USSR	45	44n	74e
Chuanchow: China	53	25n	118e
Chubut: r., Argentina	89	43s	66w
Chuckchi Sea	43	70n	170w
Chugoku Mts.: Japan	54	35n	134e
Chuguchak: China	45	47n	83e
Chuho: China	43	45n	128e
Chulak-Tau: USSR	45	43n	71e
Chulym: r., USSR	45	57n	88e
Chumphon: Thailand	51	10n	99e
Chungking: China	53	30n	107e
*Chunya: Tanganyika	68	8s	34e
Chuquicamata: Chile	88	23s	69w
Chur (Coire): Switz.	33	47n	10e
Churchill: & r., Canada	79	59n	94w
Cienfuegos: Cuba	83	22n	80w
Cieszyn: Poland	27	50n	19e
Cilician Gates: Turkey	48	37n	35e
Cincinnati: USA	84	39n	84w
Circeo, C.: Italy	30	41n	13e
Ciudad Bolívar: Venez.	86	8n	63w
Ciudad Juárez: Mexico	80	32n	106w
Ciudad Real: Spain	25	39n	4w
Ciudad Rodrigo: Spain	25	41n	6w
Civitavecchia: Italy	30	42n	12e
Clamecy: France	29	47n	4e
Clare: Australia	61	34s	138e
Clarence: r., Australia	61	30s	153e
Clarence I.: Antarctica	91	61s	54w
Clarke Ra.: Australia	60	21s	149e
Clarksburg: USA	84	39n	80w
Clausthal-Zellerfeld: Germany	32	52n	10e
Clermont: Australia	60	23s	148e
Clermont: France	28	49n	2e
Clermont-Ferrand: Fr.	29	46n	3e
Cles: Italy	33	46n	11e
Cleveland: USA	84	41n	82w
Clifton Forge: USA	84	38n	80w
Clinch Mts.: USA	84	36n	83w
Clinton: USA	84	42n	90w
Clipperton I.: Pac. O.	93	10n	110w
Cloppenburg: Germany	32	53n	8e
Clovis: USA	80	34n	103w
Cluj: Romania	31	47n	24e
Clutha: r., NZ	55	46s	169e
Coahuila: Mexico	80	29n	102w
Coast Mts.: Canada	78	55n	130w
Coast Ranges: USA	80	—	—
Coats Land: Antarc.	91	78s	30w
Cobalt: Canada	84	47n	80w
Cobar: Australia	61	31s	146e
Cobequid Mts.: Canada	85	46n	64w
Cobourg: Canada	85	44n	78w
Coburg: Germany	32	50n	11e
Cochabamba: Bolivia	86	17s	66w
Cochin: India	52	10n	77e
Cochin China: S. Viet Nam	51	10n	106e
Cochrane: Canada	84	49n	81w
Cochrane, L.: Chile Arg.	89	47s	72w
Cocos Is.: Australia	92	11s	97e
Cocos Is.: Pacific O.	86	6n	87w
Cod, C.: USA	85	42n	70w
Coeur d'Alene: USA	80	48n	117w
Coff's Harbour: Aust.	61	30s	153e
Cognac: France	29	46n	0
Cohoes: USA	85	43n	74w
Coimbatore: India	52	11n	77e
Coimbra: Portugal	25	40n	8w
Coire (Chur): Switz.	33	47n	10e
Colac: Australia	61	38s	144e
Colatina: Brazil	87	20s	40w
Colbeck, C.: Antarc.	91	77s	158w
Collie: Australia	60	33s	116e
Colmar: France	28	48n	7e
Cologne: Germany	32	51n	7e
*Colomb Béchar: Alg.	66	32n	2w
COLOMBIA	86	5n	73w
*Colombo: Ceylon	52	7n	80e
Colón: Panamá	83	9n	80w
Colorado: r., Argentina	88	39s	65w
Colorado: r., Texas, USA	80	30n	97w
Colorado: r., USA	80	37n	111w
Colorado: State, USA	80	39n	105w
Colorado Plateaux: USA	80	35n	110w
Colorado Springs: USA	80	39n	105w
Columbia, District of: USA	81	39s	77w
Columbia: Mo., USA	84	39n	92w
Columbia: S.C., USA	81	34n	81w
Columbia: r., Can. USA	80	46n	120w
Columbia Mts.: Canada	78	52n	118w
Columbus: Ga., USA	81	32n	85w
Columbus: Ohio, USA	84	40n	83w
Colville L.: Canada	78	67n	125w
Comacchio, L.: It.	33	45n	12e
*Comilla: E. Pakistan	53	23n	91e
Commonwealth Range: Antarctica	91	86s	179w
Communism, Mt.: USSR	45	38n	73e
Como: & L., Italy	33	46n	9e
Comodoro Rivadavia: Argentina	89	46s	67w
Comorin, C.: India	52	8n	77e
*Comoro Arch.: Ind. O.	71	12s	43e
Compiègne: France	28	49n	3e
Conakry: Guinea	66	10n	14w
Concarneau: France	28	48n	4w
Concepción: Chile	88	37s	73w
Conchos: r., Mexico	80	28n	106w
Concord: USA	85	43n	71w
Condamine: r., Aust.	60	27s	150e
Condobolin: Aust.	61	33s	147e
CONGO (ex-French)	71	0	15e
CONGO REPUBLIC	71	2s	22e
*Congo: r., Africa	71	3s	16e
Conneaut: USA	84	42n	81w
Connecticut: r., USA	85	43n	72w
Connecticut: State, USA	85	42n	73w
Constance, L.: Ger. Switz.	33	48n	9e
Constanța: Romania	31	44n	29e
Constantine: Alg.	66	37n	7e
Constantinople: Tur.	31	41n	29e
Cooch Behar: India	52	27n	90e
Cook, Mt.: NZ	55	43s	170e
Cook Bay: Antarc.	91	68s	152e
Cook Is.: Pac. O.	93	20s	160w
Cook Strait: NZ	55	41s	175e
Cooktown: Australia	59	16s	145e
Coolangatta: Aust.	60	28s	153e
Coolgardie: Aust.	60	31s	121e
Coonamble: Aust.	61	31s	149e
Cooper's Ck.: Aust.	60	27s	141e
Coorong, The: Aust.	61	34s	139e
Cootamundra: Aust.	61	35s	148e
Copenhagen: Den.	35	56n	12e
Copiapó: Chile	88	27s	70w
Coppermine: Canada	78	68n	115w
*Coquilhatville: Congo Republic	70	0	18e
Coquimbo: Chile	88	30s	72w
Coral Sea	92	15s	155e
Corbières: France	29	43n	3e
Cordell Hull Glacier: Antarctica	91	75s	136w
Córdoba: Argentina	88	31s	64w
Córdoba: Spain	25	38n	5w
Cordova: Alaska	78	61n	145w
Corfu: & i., Greece	31	39n	20e
Corinth: & G., Greece	31	38n	23e
Corinth: USA	81	35n	89w
Çorlu: Turkey	31	41n	28e
Corner Brook: Canada	79	49n	58w
Cornwall: Canada	85	45n	75w
Cornwall I.: Canada	79	77n	95w
Cornwallis I.: Canada	79	75n	95w
Corocoro: Bolivia	86	17s	68w
Coromandel: NZ	55	37s	175e
Coromandel Coast: Ind.	52	15n	81e
Coronation G.: Can.	78	68n	112w
Coronation I.: Antarc.	91	61s	46w
Coronel: Chile	88	37s	73w
Corpus Christi: USA	80	28n	97w
Corrientes: Arg.	87	27s	59w
CORSICA	30	42n	9e
Corsicana: USA	81	32n	96w
Çoruh: r., Turkey	49	41n	41e
Corumbá: Brazil	87	19s	57w
Corunna: Spain	25	43n	8w
Cos: i., Greece	31	37n	27e
Cosenza: Italy	30	39n	16e
Cosne: France	29	47n	4e
COSTA RICA	83	10n	85w
Costermansville: Congo Republic	71	2s	29e
Côte d'Azur: France	29	43n	7e
Côte d'Or: France	29	47n	5e
Cotentin: France	28	49n	2w
Cotonou: Dahomey	68	6n	2e
Cotopaxi: Ecuador	86	1s	78w
Cottbus: Germany	32	52n	14e
Cotter, C.: Antarc.	91	72s	170e
Cottian Alps: Fr. It.	29	45n	7e
Coubre, Pte de la: Fr.	29	46n	1w
Coulman I.: Antarc.	91	73s	170e
Council Bluffs: USA	81	41n	96w
Coutances: France	28	49n	2w
Covilhã: Portugal	25	40n	7w
Covington: USA	84	39n	84w
Cowal, L.: Australia	61	34s	147e
Cowan, L.: Australia	60	32s	122e
Cowra: Australia	61	34s	149e
*Cox's Bazar: E. Pak.	53	22n	92e
Craiova: Romania	31	44n	24e
Cranbrook: Canada	80	49n	115w
Crécy: France	28	50n	2e
Creil: France	28	49n	2e
Cremona: Italy	33	45n	10e
Cres: i., Yugoslavia	27	45n	14e
Crete: i., Greece	31	35n	25e
Creuse: r., France	29	46n	2e
Crimea: USSR	44	46n	34e
Croatia: Yugo.	27	45n	16e
Cromwell: NZ	55	45s	169e
Cronulla: Australia	61	34s	151e
Crosby: USA	84	46n	94w
Crotone: Italy	30	39n	17e
Crow's Nest: Aust.	60	27s	152e
Crowsnest P.: Canada	80	49n	115w
Crozier, C.: Antarc.	91	78s	170e
Cruzeiro do Sul: Braz.	86	8s	73w
Cruzen I.: Antarc.	91	74s	141w
Csepel: Hungary	27	47n	19e
CUBA	83	23n	80w
Cubango: r., Africa	69	16s	18e
Cúcuta: Colombia	86	8n	73w
Cuddalore: India	52	12n	80e
Cuddapah: India	52	14n	79e
Cue: Australia	60	27s	118e
Cuenca: Spain	25	40n	2w
Cuiabá: Brazil	87	16s	56w
Cuito: r., Angola	69	17s	20e
Culebra: Panamá	83	Inset	
Culoz: France	29	46n	6e
Cumaná: Venezuela	86	10n	64w
Cumberland: USA	85	40n	79w
Cumberland: r., USA	84	37n	85w
Cumberland Is.: Aust.	60	21s	150e
Cumberland Mts.: USA	84	36n	84w
Cumberland Sd.: Can.	79	65n	65w
Cunderdin: Australia	60	31s	117e
Cuneo: Italy	33	44n	8e
Cunnamulla: Australia	60	28s	146e
Curaçao: i., S. Amer.	86	12n	69w
Curicó: Chile	88	35s	72w
Curitiba: Brazil	88	25s	49w
Curtis Chan.: Aust.	60	24s	152e
Cusco (Cuzco): Peru	86	13s	72w
Cuttack: India	52	21n	86e
Cuxhaven: Germany	32	54n	9e
Cuyana Ra.: USA	84	46n	94w
Cyclades: is., Greece	31	37n	25e
CYPRUS	48	35n	33e
*Cyrenaica: Libya	48	30n	22e
CZECHOSLOVAKIA	27	—	—
Częstochowa: Poland	35	51n	19e
*Dacca: E. Pakistan	52	24n	90e
Dahlak Arch.: Red Sea	49	16n	40e
Dahna: Sau. Arab.	49	26n	47e
*DAHOMEY	68	10n	2e
*Dairen: China	53	38n	122e
Dajarra: Australia	59	22s	139e
Dakar: Senegal	66	15n	17w
Dakhla Oasis: Egypt	67	25n	29e
Dakovica: Yugoslavia	27	42n	20e
Dalabandin: W. Pak.	52	Inset	
Dalby: Australia	60	27s	151e
Dalhousie, C.: Canada	78	70n	130w
Dalhousie: India	52	33n	76e
Dallas: USA	80	33n	97w
Dalmatia: Yugoslavia	27	44n	16e
Dalmenhorst: Germany	32	53n	9e
Dal'niy: China	53	38n	122e
Daltonganj: India	52	24n	84e
Daly: r., Australia	58	14s	131e
Daly Waters: Australia	58	16s	133e
Dam: Surinam	87	5n	55w
Damão: India	52	20n	73e
Damascus: Syria	48	34n	36e
Damatura: Nigeria	68	12n	12e
Damāvand: mt., Iran	49	36n	52e
Damietta: Egypt	67	31n	32e
Damodar: r., India	52	24n	87e
Dampier Land: Aust.	58	17s	122e
Dan: Holy Land	48	Inset	
Danbury: USA	85	41n	73w
Danilovka: USSR	45	53n	70e
Dannemora: Sweden	35	60n	18e
Dannevirke: NZ	55	40s	176e
Danube: r., Europe	31	44n	24e
Danushkodi: India	52	9n	79e
Danville: Ill., USA	84	40n	88w
Danville: Va., USA	85	37n	79w
Danzig: Poland	35	54n	19e
Darasun: USSR	43	53n	116e
Dardanelles: Turkey	31	40n	27e
*Dar es Salaam: Tangan.	68	7s	39e
Darfur: Sudan	67	12n	25e
Dargaville: NZ	55	36s	174e
Darien, G. of: S. Amer.	86	9n	77w
Darjeeling: India	52	27n	88e
Darling: r., Australia	61	31s	145e
Darling Downs: Aust.	60	27s	152e
Darling Ra.: Australia	60	32s	116e
Darmstadt: Germany	32	50n	9e
Darnley, C.: Antarc.	91	68s	69e
Dartmouth: Canada	85	45n	64w
Darwin: Australia	58	12s	131e
Dasht: r., W. Pakistan	52	Inset	
Dasht-e Kavīr: Iran	49	34n	54e
Dasht-e Lūt: Iran	49	32n	57e
Daugavpils: USSR	35	56n	27e
Dauha: Qatar	49	25n	51e
Dauphiné: France	33	45n	6e
Davao: Philippines	51	7n	125e
Davenport: USA	84	42n	91w
David Glacier: Antarc.	91	75s	162e
Davis Bay: Antarctica	91	66s	135e
Davis Sea: Antarctica	91	65s	94e
Davis Strait: Canada	79	67n	58w
Davos: Switzerland	33	47n	10e
Dawna Ra.: Burma/Thai.	51	13n	99e
Dawson: Canada	78	64n	139w
Dawson: r., Australia	60	24s	150e
Dawson Creek: Canada	78	56n	120w
Dax: France	29	44n	1w
Dayton: USA	84	40n	84w
Daytona Beach: USA	81	29n	81w
De Aar: S. Africa	69	31s	24e
Dead Sea: Isr. Jordan	48	32n	35e
Dearborn: USA	84	42n	83w
Deauville: France	28	49n	0
Debrecen: Hungary	27	47n	21e
Decapolis: Holy Land	48	Inset	
Decatur: USA	84	40n	89w
Decazeville: France	29	45n	2e
Deccan: India	52	17n	77e
Deception I.: Antarc.	91	63s	60w
Děčín: Czechoslovakia	32	51n	14e
Dedeagach: Greece	31	41n	26e
Dehra Dun: India	52	30n	78e
Deir ez Zor: Syria	49	36n	40e
Delagoa B.: S. Africa	69	26s	33e
Delaware: r., USA	85	41n	75w
Delaware: State, USA	85	39n	75w
Delft: Netherlands	32	52n	4e
Delhi: India	52	28n	77e
Demarcation Pt.: Canada/USA	78	70n	141w
Demmin: Germany	32	54n	13e
Dendermonde: Belgium	28	51n	4e
Denham Ra.: Australia	60	22s	148e
Den Helder: Neth.	32	53n	5e
Deniliquin: Australia	61	35s	145e
Denison, C.: Antarc.	91	67s	143e
Denizli: Turkey	31	38n	29e
Denman Glac.: Antarc.	91	67s	99e
DENMARK	35	55n	10e
*D'Entrecasteaux Is.: New Guinea	59	10s	151e
D'Entrecasteaux, Pt.: Australia	60	35s	116e
Denver: USA	80	40n	105w
Dera Ghazi Khan: W. Pakistan	52	30n	70e
Dera Ismail Khan: W. Pakistan	52	32n	71e
Derbent: USSR	44	42n	48e
Derby: Australia	58	17s	124e
Derna: Libya	48	33n	23e
Des Joachims: Canada	85	46n	78w
Des Moines: USA	84	42n	94w
Dessau: Germany	32	52n	12e
Detroit: USA	84	42n	83w
Dettingen: Germany	32	50n	9e
Deva: Romania	31	46n	23e

* See Page 131

	Page;	Lat.	Long.
Deventer: Netherlands	32;	52n	6e
Devils Glacier: Antarc.	91;	87s	170w
Dévoluy: France	29;	45n	6e
Devon I.: Canada	79;	75n	85w
Devonport: NZ	55;	37s	175e
Dhahran: Sau. Arab.	49;	26n	50e
Dharwar: India	52;	15n	75e
Dhufar: Muscat & 'Oman	46;	17n	55e
Dhulia: India	52;	21n	75e
Diamantina: Brazil	87;	18s	43w
Dibrugarh: India	53;	27n	95e
*Diego Suarez: Madag.	71;	13s	49e
Dieppe: France	28;	50n	1e
Dikwa: Nigeria	68;	12n	14e
Digby: Canada	85;	45n	66w
Digne: France	29;	44n	6e
Dijon: France	29;	47n	5e
Dili: Timor	51;	9s	126e
Dillingen: Germany	33;	49n	10e
Dimboola: Australia	61;	36s	142e
Dimitrovgrad: Bulg.	31;	42n	26e
Dimitrovgrad: Yugo.	27;	43n	23e
Dimitrovo: Bulgaria	31;	43n	23e
*Dinajpur: E. Pak.	52;	25n	89e
Dinan: France	28;	48n	2w
Dinant: Belgium	28;	50n	5e
Dinard: France	28;	49n	2w
Dinaric Alps: Yugo.	27;	44n	16e
Dinkelsbühl: Ger.	32;	49n	10e
Diomede Is.: USSR USA	78;	66n	169w
Diredawa: Ethiopia	67;	10n	42e
Dirk Hartogs I.: Aust.	58;	26s	113e
Dirranbandi: Aust.	60;	28s	148e
Disappointment, L.: Australia	58;	23s	123e
Discovery Inlet: Antarc.	91;	78s	171w
Disko: i., Greenland	79;	70n	53w
Diu I.: Arabian Sea	52;	21n	71e
Divriği: Turkey	49;	39n	38e
Dixmude: Belgium	28;	51n	3e
Diyarbakır: Turkey	49;	38n	40e
Djakarta: Java	51;	6s	107e
Djawa: i., Indon.	51;	7s	110e
Djelfa: Algeria	66;	35n	3e
Djerba I.: Tunisia	66;	34n	11e
*Djibouti: Fr. Som.	67;	12n	43e
Djidjelli: Algeria	25;	37n	6e
Dneprodzerzhinsk: USSR	44;	49n	34e
Dnepropetrovsk: USSR	44;	48n	35e
Dnieper: r., USSR	44;	50n	31e
Dniester: r., USSR	44;	48n	28e
Dobreşti: Romania	31;	47n	22e
Dobruja: Bulg. Rom.	31;	44n	28e
Dodecanese: is., Grc.	31;	37n	26e
Dodge City: USA	80;	38n	100w
*Dodoma: Tanganyika	68;	6s	36e
Dolbeau: Canada	79;	49n	72w
Dôle: France	29;	47n	5e
Dolleman I.: Antarc.	91;	70s	60w
Dolomites: mts., Italy	33;	46n	12e
Dom: mt., Switz.	33;	46n	8e
Domažlice: Czech.	32;	50n	13e
Dombås: Norway	34;	62n	9e
Dominica: i., W. Indies	83;	16n	62w
DOMINICAN REPUBLIC	83;	19n	70w
Don: r., USSR	44;	50n	40e
Donau: r., Ger. Aus.	33;	49n	13e
Donauwörth: Ger.	33;	49n	11e
Donawitz: Austria	27;	47n	15e
Donbass: USSR	44;	48n	40e
*Dondra Hd.: Ceylon	52;	6n	81e
Donets: r., USSR	44;	49n	37e
Donetsk: USSR	44;	48n	38e
Dongola: Sudan	48;	19n	31e
Donzère: France	29;	45n	5e
Doonerak, Mt.: USA	78;	68n	152w
Dordogne: r., France	29;	45n	0
Dordrecht: Neth.	32;	52n	5e
Dore: r., France	29;	46n	4e
Dôres do Indaiá: Braz.	87;	19s	46w
Dornbirn: Austria	33;	47n	10e
Dortmund: Germany	32;	52n	7e
Dortmund Ems Canal: Germany	32;	52n	8e
Dothan: Holy Land	48;	Inset	
Douai: France	28;	50n	3e
Douala: Cameroon	66;	4n	10e
Douarnenez: & B., Fr.	28;	48n	4w
Doubs: r., France	29;	47n	6e
Doubtful Sound: NZ	55;	45s	167e
Douglas Is.: Antarc.	91;	67s	64e
Douro: r., Spain Port.	25;	41n	8w
Dover: USA	85;	39n	76w
Dover, Str. of: Eng. Fr.	28;	51n	1e
Dovrefjell: mts., Nor.	34;	62n	10e
Dra: r., Mor. Alg.	66;	29n	9w
Draguignan: France	29;	44n	6e
Drake Passage: S. Amer.	89;	58s	65w
Drakensberg: S. Africa	69;	30s	29e
Drama: Greece	31;	41n	24e
Drammen: Norway	35;	60n	10e
Drau: r., Austria	33;	47n	13e
Drava: r., Europe	27;	46n	18e
Drave: r., Austria	33;	47n	13e
Dravograd: Yugo.	27;	47n	15e
Dresden: Germany	32;	51n	14e
Dreux: France	28;	49n	1e
Drôme: r., France	29;	45n	5e
Drummondville: Can.	85;	46n	72w
Drygalski I.: Antarc.	91;	66s	93e
Dubai: Trucial 'Oman	49;	25n	55e
Dubawnt L.: Canada	78;	63n	102w
Dubbo: Australia	61;	32s	149e
Dubrovnik: Yugo.	27;	43n	18e
Dubuque: USA	84;	42n	91w
Ducie I.: Pac. O.	93;	25s	124w
Duck: r., USA	84;	36n	87w
Ducktown: USA	81;	35n	84w
Dudelange: Lux.	32;	50n	6e
Dudinka: USSR	43;	70n	86e
Duisburg: Germany	32;	51n	7e
Dulce: r., Argentina	88;	29s	64w
Duluth: USA	84;	47n	92w
Dunarea: r., Europe	31;	44n	25e
Dunedin: NZ	55;	46s	170e
Dunkirk: France	28;	51n	2e
Duquesne: USA	84;	40n	80e
Durance: r., France	29;	44n	6e
Durango: Mexico	82;	24n	105w
Durazzo: Albania	31;	41n	19e
Durban: S. Africa	69;	30s	31e
Düren: Germany	32;	51n	7e
Durge Nor: Mongolia	50;	48n	93e
Durham: USA	85;	36n	79w
Durrës: Albania	31;	41n	19e
D'Urville I.: NZ	55;	41s	174e
D'Urville Sea: Antarc.	91;	65s	142e
Dusky Sound: NZ	55;	46s	167e
Düsseldorf: Germany	32;	51n	7e
Dyushambe: USSR	45;	38n	69e
Dzerzhinsk: USSR	44;	56n	43e
Dzhambul: USSR	45;	43n	72e
Dzherba: USSR	43;	60n	117e
Dzhetygara: USSR	45;	52n	61e
Dzhezkazgan: USSR	45;	48n	68e
Dzungaria: China	47;	45n	88e
Dzungarian Gate USSR China	45;	45n	82e
Eagle Pass: USA	80;	29n	100w
East Beskids: Poland	27;	49n	22e
East China Sea	53;	—	—
Easter I.: Pac. O.	93;	27s	110w
Eastern Desert: Egypt	48;	27n	32e
Eastern Ghats: India	52;	—	—
Eastern Reg.: Ghana	68;	6n	1w
Eastern Reg.: Nigeria	68;	6n	8e
Eastern Sierra Madre: Mexico	82;	23n	100w
East London: S. Africa	69;	33s	28e
EAST PAKISTAN	52;	23n	90e
Eastport: USA	85;	45n	67w
East Prussia: Poland	35;	54n	20e
East Rift Valley: Africa	68;	5n	37e
East St. Louis: USA	84;	39n	90w
East Siberian Sea	43;	73n	160e
Eau Claire: USA	84;	45n	91w
Eauze: France	29;	44n	0
Eberswalde: Germany	35;	53n	14e
Ebi Nor: China	47;	45n	83e
Ebro: r., Spain	25;	42n	1w
Echuca: Australia	61;	36s	145e
ECUADOR	86;	2s	78w
Edam: Netherlands	32;	53n	5e
Ed Dacar: Libya	48;	26n	23e
Ed Damer: Sudan	67;	17n	34e
Ede: Netherlands	32;	52n	6e
Ede: Nigeria	68;	8n	4e
Edenhope: Australia	61;	37s	141e
Edhessa: Greece	31;	41n	22e
Edirne: Turkey	31;	42n	26e
Edjelé: Algeria	66;	28n	10e
Edmonton: Canada	80;	53n	113w
Edmunston: Canada	85;	47n	68w
Edremit: Turkey	31;	40n	27e
*Edsel Ford Ra.: Antarc.	91;	78s	141w
Edward, L.: Africa	68;	0	30e
Edwards Plat.: USA	80;	31n	100w
Eekloo: Belgium	28;	51n	4e
Efate: i., Pacific Ocean	59;	17s	168e
Eger: r., Czech.	32;	50n	14e
Egersund: Norway	35;	58n	6e
Egmont, Mt.: NZ	55;	39s	174e
Egridir, L.: Turkey	31;	38n	31e
Eifel: mts., Germany	32;	50n	7e
Eighty Mile Beach: Aust.	58;	19s	121e
Eilat: Israel	48;	29n	35e
Eildon Res.: Australia	61;	37s	146e
Eilenburg: Germany	32;	51n	13e
Eindhoven: Neth.	32;	51n	6e
Eisenach: Germany	32;	51n	10e
Eisenerz: Austria	27;	47n	15e
Eisenhüttenstadt: E. Ger.	32;	52n	15e
El Agheila: Libya	48;	30n	19e
El 'Alamein: Egypt	67;	31n	29e
El Atrun Oasis: Sudan	48;	18n	27e
Elâziğ: Turkey	49;	38n	39e
Elba: i., Italy	30;	43n	10e
El Ballâh: Egypt	67;	Inset	
Elbasan: Albania	31;	41n	20e
Elbe: r., Germany	32;	53n	11e
Elbeuf: France	28;	49n	1e
Elbląg: Poland	35;	54n	20e
E'lbrus: mt., USSR	44;	43n	42e
Elche: Spain	25;	38n	1w
Eldoret: Kenya	68;	1n	35e
Elephant I.: Antarc.	91;	61s	55w
El Escorial: Spain	25;	41n	4w
El Faiyûm: Egypt	67;	29n	31e
El Fasher: Sudan	67;	13n	25e
El Ferrol: Spain	25;	43n	8w
El Firdân: Egypt	67;	Inset	
El Gatrun: Libya	48;	25n	15e
Elgin: USA	84;	42n	89w
*El Giza: Egypt	48;	30n	30e
El'gyay: USSR	43;	62n	117e
*Elisabethville: Congo	68;	12s	27e
Elizabeth Pt.: SW. Afr.	69;	27s	15e
Elizabethton: USA	84;	36n	82w
El Jauf: Libya	48;	24n	23e
El Khârga: Egypt	67;	25n	30e
Elkhart: USA	84;	42n	86w
Elko: USA	80;	41n	116w
Ellesmere I.: Canada	79;	80n	80w
*Ellice Is.: Pacific Ocean	92;	8s	180
Elliot, Mt.: Antarc.	91;	71s	166e
Ellsworth Highland: Antarctica	91;	78s	90w
El Matarîya: Egypt	67;	Inset	
El Milk, Wadi: Sudan	48;	17n	30e
El Minya: Egypt	48;	28n	31e
Elmira: USA	85;	42n	77w
Elmshorn: Germany	32;	54n	10e
El Obeid: Sudan	67;	13n	30e
El Paso: USA	80;	32n	106w
El Qantara: Egypt	67;	Inset	
EL SALVADOR	82;	14n	89w
El Shatt: Egypt	67;	Inset	
Elvas: Portugal	25;	39n	7w
Ely: USA	84;	48n	92w
Emba: USSR	45;	49n	58e
Embetsu: Japan	54;	45n	142e
Embrun: France	29;	45n	6e
Emden: Germany	32;	53n	7e
Emerald: Australia	60;	23s	148e
Emi Koussi: Chad	67;	20n	18e
Emilia Romagna: Italy	33;	45n	11e
Emmaboda: Sweden	35;	57n	16e
Emmaus: Holy Land	48;	Inset	
Emmen: Netherlands	32;	53n	7e
Emmerich: Germany	32;	52n	6e
Emory Land Glacier: Antarctica	91;	76s	141w
Ems: r., Germany	32;	52n	8e
Encounter B.: Aust.	61;	36s	139e
Enderby Land: Antarc.	91;	68s	50e
*Enfidaville: Tunisia	30;	36n	10e
Engadine: Switzerland	33;	47n	10e
En-gedi: Holy Land	48;	Inset	
Enggano: i., Indon.	51;	5s	102e
English Channel	26;	50n	3w
Enns: r., Austria	33;	48n	14e
Enschede: Neth.	32;	42n	7e
Ensenada: Mexico	80;	32n	117w
Entebbe: Uganda	68;	0	32e
Entre Rios: Moz.	69;	15s	37e
Entreves: Italy	33;	46n	7e
Enugu: Nigeria	68;	7n	7e
Épernay: France	28;	49n	4e
Ephraim: Holy Land	48;	Inset	
Épinal: France	28;	48n	6e
Epirus: Greece	31;	39n	21e
Erebus, Mt.: Antarc.	91;	78s	167e
Erentsab: Mongolia	50;	50n	115e
Erfurt: Germany	32;	51n	11e
Erie: & L., USA	84;	42n	80w
*Erigavo: Som. Prot.	67;	10n	47e
Erimo, C.: Japan	55;	42n	143e
Eritrea: Ethiopia	67;	15n	40e
Erlangen: Germany	32;	50n	11e
Ermoupolis: Greece	31;	37n	25e
Eromanga: Australia	60;	27s	143e
Er Rif Mts.: Morocco	66;	35n	5w
Erromanga: i., Pac. O.	59;	19s	169e
Erzgebirge: Ger. Czech.	32;	50n	13e
Erzincan: Turkey	49;	40n	40e
Erzurum: Turkey	49;	40n	41e
Esashi: Japan	54;	42n	140e
Esbjaerg: Denmark	35;	55n	8e
Escanaba: USA	84;	46n	87w
Esch: Luxembourg	32;	50n	6e
Eschwege: Germany	32;	51n	10e
Eşfahān: Iran	49;	33n	52e
Eshowe: S. Africa	69;	29s	32e
Eskilstuna: Sweden	35;	59n	16e
Eskişehir: Turkey	31;	40n	30e
Esnagi, L.: Canada	84;	49n	84w
Esperance: Australia	60;	34s	122e
Espinouse, M. de l': Fr.	29;	43n	3e
Espírito Santo: Braz.	87;	20s	41w
Espiritu Santo: i., Pacific Ocean	59;	15s	167e
Essaoira: Morocco	66;	31n	10w
Essen: Germany	32;	51n	7e
*Essequibo: r., Br. Guiana	87;	5n	59w
Esslingen: Germany	33;	49n	9e
Estados, I. de los: Arg.	89;	55s	64w
Estats, Pic d'.: Fr. Sp.	29;	43n	1e
Estevan: Canada	80;	49n	103w
Estonian SSR: USSR	35;	59n	26e
Estremadura: Port.	25;	39n	5w
Esztergom: Hungary	27;	48n	19e
Étampes: France	28;	48n	2e
Étaples: France	28;	51n	2e
Etawah: India	52;	27n	79e
ETHIOPIA	67;	10n	40e
Etna: volc., Sicily	30;	38n	15e
Etosha Pan: SW. Africa	69;	19s	16e
Etruscan Apennines: It.	33;	44n	10e
Euboea: i., Greece	31;	38n	24e
Eucla: Australia	58;	32s	129e
Eudunda: Australia	61;	34s	139e
Eugene: USA	80;	44n	123w
Eupen: Belgium	28;	51n	6e
Euphrates: r., Asia	49;	35n	40e
Eure: r., France	28;	49n	1e
Eureka: USA	80;	41n	124w
Europa: i., Indian O.	69;	23s	40e
Evanston: USA	84;	42n	88w
Evansville: USA	84;	38n	88w
Everard, C.: Aust.	61;	38s	149e
Everest: Nepal China	52;	28n	88e
Everett: USA	80;	48n	122w
Everglades: USA	81;	26n	81w
Evian: France	29;	46n	7e
Évora: Portugal	25;	39n	8w
Évreux: France	28;	49n	1e
Executive Committee Range: Antarctica	91;	77s	125w
Exmouth G.: Aust.	58;	22s	114e
Expedition Ra.: Aust.	60;	24s	149e
Eyre, L.: Australia	58;	28s	137e
Faenza: Italy	33;	44n	12e
Faeroe Is.: N. Atl. O.	90;	62n	8w
Fagersta: Sweden	35;	60n	16e
Faguibine, L.: Mali	66;	17n	4w
Fairbanks: USA	78;	65n	148w
Fairfield: USA	84;	41n	92w
Faizabad: Afghan.	47;	37n	71e
Faktoriye: USSR	45;	62n	75e
Falaise: France	28;	49n	0
Falkland Is.: Atl. O.	89;	52s	60w
*Falkland Is. Dependencies see Br. Antarctic Territory			
Falköping: Sweden	35;	58n	14e
Fall River: USA	85;	42n	71w
False B.: S. Africa	69;	34s	18e
Falun: Sweden	35;	61n	16e
Famagusta: Cyprus	48;	35n	38e
Fanning I.: Pac. O.	93;	4n	159w
Fano: Italy	33;	44n	13e
Farafra Oasis: Egypt	48;	27n	28e
Farah: Afghanistan	46;	32n	62e
Farasan Is.: Red Sea	47;	17n	42e
Farewell: USA	78;	63n	154w
Farewell, C.: Grnld.	79;	60n	44w
Farewell, C.: NZ	55;	40s	173e
Fargo: USA	80;	47n	97w
Faro: Portugal	25;	37n	8w
Fārs: Iran	49;	29n	52e
Fashoda: Sudan	67;	10n	32e
Faxa B.: Iceland	34;	64n	23w
Fayîd: Egypt	67;	Inset	
Fécamp: France	28;	50n	0
Fehmarn: i., Germany	35;	54n	11e
Feilding: NZ	55;	40s	175e
Feira de Santana: Braz.	87;	13s	39w
Feldkirch: Austria	33;	47n	10e
Fen: r., China	53;	36n	111e
Fengsiang: China	53;	34n	107e
Fenouillèdes: France	29;	43n	3e
Fengyang: China	50;	33n	118e
Fenyang: China	53;	37n	112e
Fergana: USSR	45;	41n	72e
Fernando de Noronha: i., Brazil	87;	4s	32w
*Fernando Poo: i., G. of Guinea	68;	4n	8e
Ferrara: Italy	33;	45n	12e
Ferrar Glac.: Antarc.	91;	78s	163e
Ferret, C.: France	29;	45n	1w
*Ferryville: Tunisia	30;	37n	10e
Feteşti: Romania	31;	44n	28e
Fethiye: Turkey	31;	37n	29e
Fez: Morocco	66;	34n	5w
*Fezzan: Libya	48;	25n	15e
Fianarantsoa: Madag.	71;	22s	47e
Fichtelgebirge: Ger.	32;	50n	12e
Fidenza: Italy	33;	45n	10e
Figeac: France	29;	45n	2e
Fiji Is.: Pacific Ocean	92;	18s	178e
Filchner, C.: Antarc.	91;	66s	92e
Filchner Ice Shelf: Antarctica	91;	78s	50w
Finistère: France	28;	48n	4w
Finisterre, C.: Spain	25;	43n	9w
FINLAND	34 35;	—	—
Finland, G. of	35;	60n	25e
*Finschhafen: New Guinea	59;	7s	147e
Finsteraarhorn: mt., Switzerland	33;	47n	8e
Fiordland: NZ	55;	45s	167e
Firenze: Italy	33;	44n	10e
Fitchburg: USA	85;	43n	72w
Fitzpatrick: Canada	85;	47n	73w
Fitzroy: r., Australia	58;	18s	124e
Fitzroy: r., Australia	60;	23s	150e
Fiume: Yugoslavia	27;	45n	14e
Flanders: Belgium	28;	51n	4e
Flensburg: Germany	35;	55n	9e
Flers: France	28;	49n	1w
Flinders: r., Australia	59;	20s	142e
Flinders Ra.: Australia	61;	31s	139e
Flinders Reef: Coral Sea	60;	18s	149e
Flin Flon: Canada	80;	55n	102w
Flint: USA	84;	43n	84w
Florence: Italy	33;	44n	11e
Florence: USA	81;	35n	88w
Florencia: Colombia	86;	2n	76w
Flores: i., Indonesia	51;	8s	121e
Floreshty: USSR	31;	48n	28e
Floriano: Brazil	87;	7s	43w
Florianópolis: Brazil	88;	28s	49w
Florida: State, USA	81;	30n	83w
Florida Keys: USA	83;	25n	81w
Florina: Greece	31;	41n	21e
*Florø: Norway	34;	62n	5e
Flushing: Netherlands	32;	52n	4e
*Fly: r., Papua	59;	7s	142e
Foggia: Italy	30;	41n	15e
Foix: France	29;	43n	2e
Foligno: Italy	30;	44n	13e
Fond du Lac: USA	84;	44n	88w
Fontainebleau: France	28;	48n	3e
Fontenoy: Belgium	28;	51n	3e
Foochow: China	53;	26n	119e
Forbes: Australia	61;	33s	148e
Forcalquier: France	29;	44n	6e
Fordlândia: Brazil	87;	4s	55w
Forel, Mt.: Greenland	79;	67n	37w
Forez, M. du: France	29;	46n	4e
Forli: Italy	33;	44n	12e
Formentera: i., Spain	25;	39n	1e
FORMOSA (TAIWAN)	53;	24n	122e
Forrest: Australia	58;	31s	128e
Forsayth: Australia	59;	19s	144e
Fort Albany: Canada	81;	52n	82w
Fortaleza: Brazil	87;	4s	38w
Fort Chimo: Canada	79;	58n	68w
*Fort Dauphin: Madag.	71;	25s	47e
Fort de France: Martinique	83;	15n	61w
Fort Dodge: USA	84;	42n	94w
Fortescue: r., Australia	58;	22s	118e
Fort Francis: Canada	84;	49n	93w
*Fort Gouraud: Mauritania	66;	23n	12w
Fort Hall: Kenya	68;	1s	37e
*Fort Jameson: N. Rhod.	69;	13s	33e
*Fort Johnston: Nyasa.	69;	14s	35e
*Fort Lamy: Chad	66;	12n	15e
Fort Macleod: Canada	80;	50n	113w
Fort Madison: USA	84;	41n	91w
Fort Nelson: Canada	78;	59n	123w
Fort Peck Res.: USA	80;	48n	107w
*Fort Rosebery: N. Rhod.	68;	11s	29e
Fort Sandeman: W. Pak.	52;	32n	69e
Fort Shevchenko: USSR	44;	45n	50e
Fort Simpson: Canada	78;	62n	122w
Fort Smith: Canada	78;	60n	112w
Fort Smith: USA	81;	35n	94w
Fort Wayne: USA	84;	41n	85w
Fort William: Canada	84;	48n	89w
Forth Worth: USA	80;	33n	97w
Fort Yukon: USA	78;	67n	145w
Fostoria: USA	84;	41n	83w
Fougères: France	28;	48n	1w
Foul Bay: Egypt Sudan	67;	23n	36e
Foulwind, C.: NZ	55;	42s	171e
Fourmies: France	28;	50n	4e
Foveaux Str.: NZ	55;	47s	168e
Foxe Basin: Canada	79;	67n	77w
FRANCE	28 29;	—	—
Franche Comté: France	29;	47n	6e
*Francistown: Bech.	69;	21s	27e
Franconian Jura: Ger.	32;	50n	12e
Frankfort: Ky., USA	84;	38n	85w
Frankfort: Mich., USA	84;	45n	86w
Frankfurt am Main: Ger.	32;	50n	9e
Frankfurt an der Oder: Germany	32;	52n	15e
Franklin I.: Antarctica	91;	76s	168e
Franz Josef Land: USSR	42;	80n	55e
Frascati: Italy	30;	42n	13e
Fraser: r., Canada	80;	51n	122w
Fraserburg: S. Africa	69;	33s	22e
Fraser I.: Australia	60;	25s	153e
Fray Bentos: Uruguay	88;	33s	58w
Fredericia: Denmark	35;	56n	10e
Fredericksburg: USA	85;	38n	77w
Fredericton: Canada	85;	46n	67w
*Frederik Hendrik I.: Neth. New Guinea	58;	8s	138e
Frederikshavn: Den.	35;	57n	10e
Fredrikstad: Norway	35;	59n	11e
Freeport: USA	84;	42n	90w
Freetown: Sierra Leone	66;	8n	13w
Freiburg im Breisgau: Germany	33;	48n	8e
Freising: Germany	33;	48n	12e
Fréjus: France	29;	43n	7e
Fremantle: Australia	60;	32s	116e
FRENCH GUIANA	87;	4n	53w
*FRENCH SOMALILAND	67;	12n	43e
Freshfield, C.: Antarc.	91;	68s	151e
Fresnillo: Mexico	82;	23n	103w
Fresno: USA	80;	37n	120w
Freudenstadt: Germany	33;	48n	8e
Fribourg: Switzerland	33;	47n	7e
Friedrichshafen: Ger.	33;	48n	9e
Friesland: Netherlands	32;	53n	6e
Frisian Is.: Neth. Ger.	32;	54n	7e
Frobisher Bay: Canada	79;	63n	69w
Frome, L.: Australia	61;	31s	140e
Frunze: USSR	45;	43n	75e
Fuentes de Oñoro: Sp.	25;	40n	7w
Fuerteventura: i., Canary Is.	66;	28n	14w
Fuji: mt. & r., Japan	54;	35n	139e
Fukien: China	53;	26n	118e
Fukui: Japan	54;	36n	136e
Fukuoka: Japan	54;	34n	130e
Fukushima: Japan	54;	38n	140e
Fukuyama: Japan	54;	41n	140e
Fulda: & r., Germany	32;	51n	10e
Fulton: USA	84;	37n	89w
Funafuti: i., Pac. O.	92;	8s	178e
Funchal: Madeira	66;	33n	17w
Fundy, B. of: Canada	85;	45n	66w
Funen: i., Denmark	35;	55n	10e
Furka Pass: Switzerland	33;	47n	8e
Fürth: Germany	32;	50n	11e
Fushun: China	53;	42n	123e
Fusin: China	53;	42n	122e
*Gaberones: Bech.	69;	24s	26e
Gabès: & G., Tunisia	66;	34n	10e
GABON	70;	1s	12e
Gabrovo: Bulgaria	31;	43n	25e
Gadames: Libya	66;	30n	9e
Gadsden: USA	81;	34n	86w
Gaeta: Italy	30;	41n	14e
Gafsa: Tunisia	66;	34n	9e
Gail: r., Austria	33;	47n	13e
Gaillard Cut: Panamá	83;	Inset	
Gairdner, L.: Australia	58;	27s	136e
Galana: r., Kenya	68;	3s	39e
Galápagos Is.: Pac. O.	86;	2s	90w
Galaţi: Romania	31;	45n	28e
Galena: USA	78;	65n	157w
Galesburg: USA	84;	41n	90w
Galicia: Spain	25;	42n	8w
Galilee: & sea, Holy Land	48;	Inset	
Gallarate: Italy	33;	46n	9e
*Galle: Ceylon	52;	6n	80e
Gallegos: r., Argentina	89;	52s	71w
Gallinas, Pt. de: Col.	86;	12n	72w
Gallipoli: Turkey	31;	40n	27e
Gällivare: Sweden	34;	67n	20e
Galveston: USA	81;	29n	95w
Gambeila: Ethiopia	68;	8n	35e
GAMBIA: & r.	66;	13n	15w
Gambier Is.: Pac. O.	93;	22s	135w
Gamlakarleby: Finland	34;	64n	23e
Gand: Belgium	28;	51n	4e
Gandak: r., India	52;	27n	85e
Gander: Canada	79;	49n	55w
Ganga: r., India	52;	25n	86e
Ganges: France	29;	44n	4e
Ganges: r., India	52;	25n	86e
Ganongga: i., Pac. O.	59;	7s	157e
Gánt: Hungary	27;	47n	18e
Gap: France	29;	45n	6e
Gard: r., France	29;	44n	4e
Garda, L. of: Italy	33;	46n	11e
Gardez: Afghanistan	52;	34n	69e
Gardner I.: Pac. O.	92;	5s	175w
Gardner Pinnacles: Pacific Ocean	93;	25n	168w
Gardula: Ethiopia	68;	6n	37e
Gargano, C.: Italy	30;	42n	16e
Garissa: Kenya	68;	0	40e
Garonne: r., France	29;	45n	0
Garoua: Cameroon	66;	10n	13e
Garrigues, Mts.: France	29;	44n	4e
Garry, L.: Canada	78;	66n	100w
Gartok: China	52;	32n	80e
Gary: USA	84;	42n	87w
Garyan: Libya	66;	32n	13e
Gasan-Kuli: USSR	49;	38n	54e
Gascony: France	29;	44n	0
Gaspé: & penin., Can.	79;	49n	65w
Gastonia: USA	81;	36n	82w
Gata, C. de: Spain	25;	37n	2w
Gath: Holy Land	48;	Inset	
Gâtine, Hauteurs de: Fr.	29;	47n	1w
*Gatooma: S. Rhodesia	69;	18s	30e
Gatun, L.: Panamá	83;	Inset	
Gauhati: India	53;	26n	92e
Gävle: Sweden	35;	61n	17e
Gawler: Australia	61;	35s	138e
Gaya: India	52;	25n	85e
Gaya: Niger	66;	12n	3e
*Gaza: Egypt	67;	32n	34e
Gaziantep: Turkey	49;	37n	37e
Gdańsk: Poland	35;	54n	19e
Gdov: USSR	35;	59n	28e
Gdynia: Poland	35;	55n	18e
Gedser: Denmark	35;	55n	12e
Geelong: Australia	61;	38s	144e
Geeradsbergen: Belg.	28;	51n	4e
Gelidonya, C.: Turkey	31;	36n	30e
Gelsenkirchen: Ger.	32;	51n	7e
Geneva: Switzerland	33;	46n	6e

* See Page 131

Page; Lat. Long.

Geneva, L. of: Switz. 33; 46n 6e
Genghis Khan, Wall of:
China 53; 42n 112e
Genil: r., Spain 25; 37n 4w
Génissiat Dam: France 29; 46n 6e
Gennesaret: Holy Land 48; Inset
Genoa: & G., Italy 33; 44n 9e
Genova: Italy 33; 44n 9e
George: S. Africa 69; 34s 22e
George B.: Canada 85; 46n 62w
George, L.: Australia 61; 35s 150e
*Georgetown: Br. Guiana 87; 7n 58w
George Town: Malaya 51; 5n 100e
Georgia: State, USA 81; 33n 83w
Georgian B.: Canada 84; 46n 81w
Georgian SSR: USSR 44; 42n 45e
Gera: Germany 32; 51n 12e
Geraldton: Australia 60; 29s 115e
Gerizim, Mt.:
Holy Land 48 Inset
GERMANY 32/33; — —
Gerona: Spain 25; 42n 3e
Gers: r., France 29; 44n 1e
Geryville: Algeria 66; 34n 1e
Gettysburg: USA 85; 40n 77w
Gezer: Holy Land 48; Inset
Gezira: Sudan 67; 14n 32e
Ghaghra: r., India 52; 27n 82e
GHANA 68; 8n 2w
Ghardaïa: Algeria 66; 32n 4e
Ghazipur: India 52; 26n 83e
Ghent: Belgium 28; 51n 4e
Gheorgheni: Romania 31; 47n 26e
Giarabub: Libya 48; 30n 24e
Gibeah: Holy Land 48; Inset
Gibeon: Holy Land 48; Inset
Gibraltar: (Br.), Spain 25; 36n 5w
Gibson Desert: Aust. 58; 24s 123e
Gidole: Ethiopia 68; 6n 37e
Gien: France 29; 48n 3e
Giessen: Germany 32; 51n 9e
Gifu: Japan 54; 35n 137e
Gijón: Spain 25; 43n 6w
Gila: r., USA 80; 33n 111w
Gilbert: r., Australia 59; 17s 142e
Gilbert Is.: Pac. O. 92; 0 175e
Gilboa, Mt.: Holy Land 48; Inset
Gilead: Holy Land 48; Inset
Gilf Kebir Plat.: Egypt 48; 24n 26e
Gilgal: Holy Land 48; Inset
Gilgandra: Australia 61; 32s 149e
Gilgit: Kashmir 47; 36n 74e
Gilgunnia: Australia 61; 32s 146e
Gineifa: Egypt 67; Inset
Ginir: Ethiopia 67; 7n 41e
Gippsland: Australia 61; 38s 147e
Girga: Egypt 48; 26n 32e
Gironde: r., France 29; 45n 1w
Gisborne: NZ 55; 39s 178e
Giurgiu: Romania 31; 44n 26e
Givors: France 29; 46n 5e
Gjinokastër: Albania 31; 40n 20e
Glace Bay: Canada 85; 46n 60w
Gladbeck: Germany 32; 52n 7e
Gladstone: Australia 60; 24s 151e
Gladstone: Australia 61; 33s 138e
Glarus: Switzerland 33; 47n 9e
Glauchau: Germany 32; 51n 12e
Glazov: USSR 44; 58n 52e
Glenelg: r., Australia 61; 37s 142e
Glen Innes: Australia 61; 30s 152e
Glenmorgan: Australia 60; 27s 150e
Gliwice: Poland 27; 50n 18e
Globe: USA 80; 33n 111w
Głogów: Poland 35; 52n 16e
Glomma: r., Norway 35; 61n 11e
Gloversville: USA 85; 43n 74w
Gniezno: Poland 35; 52n 18e
Goa: (Port.) India 52; 15n 74e
Gobabis: SW. Africa 69; 22s 19e
Gobi Desert: Mongolia 50; 43n 105e
Godavari: r., India 52; 18n 81e
Goderich: Canada 84; 44n 82w
Godthaab: Greenland 79; 64n 52w
Gogebic Range: USA 84; 47n 90w
Goiânia: Brazil 87; 17s 49w
Goiás: Brazil 87; 16s 50w
Goiás Massif: Brazil 87; 15s 48w
Gol: Norway 35; 61n 9e
Gold Coast: G. of Guin. 68; 4n 1w
Golden: Canada 80; 51n 117w
Golden B.: NZ 55; 41s 173e
Golden Lake: Canada 85; 46n 77w
Goldsboro: USA 85; 35n 78w
Gomati: r., India 52; 27n 82e
Gomel': USSR 44; 52n 31e
Gomorrah: Holy Land 48; Inset
Gondar: Ethiopia 67; 13n 37e
Good Hope, C. of:
South Africa 69; 34s 18e
Goomalling: Australia 60; 31s 117e
Goondiwindi: Australia 60; 29s 150e
Goose Bay: Canada 79; 53n 60w
Göppingen: Germany 33; 49n 10e
Gorakhpur: India 52; 27n 83e
Gore: Ethiopia 67; 8n 36e
Gore: NZ 55; 46s 169e
Goree: Senegal 66; 15n 17w
Gorgān: Iran 49; 37n 55e
Gorizia: Italy 33; 46n 14e
Gor'kiy: USSR 44; 56n 44e
Gorno-Altaysk: USSR 45; 52n 86e
Gorzów Wielkopolski:
Poland 35; 53n 15e
Gosford: Australia 61; 33s 151e
Goslar: Germany 32; 52n 10e
Gospić: Yugoslavia 27; 44n 15e
Göta: r., Sweden 35; 58n 12e
Göteborg: Sweden 35; 58n 12e
Gotha: Germany 32; 51n 11e
Gotland: i., Sweden 35; 57n 19e
Göttingen: Germany 32; 51n 10e
Gottwaldov: Czech. 27; 49n 18e
Goude: Netherlands 32; 52n 5e
Gouin Res.: Canada 81; 49n 75w
Goulburn: Australia 61; 35s 150e
Gourock Range: Aust. 61; 36s 149e
Goyllarisquizga: Peru 86; 11s 76w
Gozo: I., Medit. Sea 30; 36n 14e
Graaff-Reinet: S. Afr. 69; 32s 25e

Page; Lat. Long.

Gracias a Dios, C.: Nic. 83; 15n 83w
Grafton: Australia 61; 30s 153e
Grahamland: Antarc. 91; 66s 65w
Grahamstown: S. Afr. 69; 33s 27e
Graian Alps: Fr./It. 33; 45n 7e
Grain Coast: Africa 66; 5n 10w
Grampians: & mts.
Australia 61; 37s 143e
Granada: Spain 25; 37n 4w
Granby: Canada 85; 45n 73w
Gran Canaria: i.,
Canary Is. 66; 28n 16w
Gran Chaco: S. Amer. 88; 24s 60w
Grand Banks: Canada 79; 46n 53w
Grand Canyon: USA 80; 36n 112w
Grand Coulee Dam:
USA 80; 48n 119w
Grand Falls: N.B., Can. 85; 47n 68w
Grand Falls: Newf.,
Canada 79; 49n 56w
Grand Forks: USA 80; 48n 97w
Grand Junction: USA 80; 39n 108w
Grand' Mère: Canada 85; 47n 73w
Grand Popo: Dahomey 68; 6n 2e
Grand Rapids: Mich.,
USA 84; 43n 86w
Grand Rapids: Minn.,
USA 84; 47n 93w
Grane: Norway 34; 66n 13e
Grant, Mt.: USA 80; 38n 118w
Granville: France 28; 49n 2w
Grasse: France 29; 44n 7e
Grave, Pte de: France 29; 46n 1w
Gravelines: France 28; 51n 2e
Graz: Austria 27; 47n 16e
Great Australian Bight 58; 33s 130e
Great Barrier I.: NZ 55; 36s 175e
Great Barrier Reef 60; 19s 149e
Great Bear L.: Canada 78; 66n 120w
Great Belt: str., Den. 35; 55n 11e
Great Bitter Lake: Egypt 67; Inset
Great Dividing Range:
Australia 59; — —
Great Eastern Erg: Alg. 66; 30n 7e
Greater Antilles 83; — —
Great Falls: USA 80; 47n 111w
Great Himalayan Range 52; — —
Great Karroo: S. Afr. 69; 33s 22e
Great Keppel I.: Aust. 60; 23s 151e
Great Khingan Mts.:
China 50; 48n 121e
Great Plain: Holy Land 48; Inset
Great Rann of Kutch:
India/Pakistan 52; 24n 70e
Great St. Bernard Pass:
Switzerland/Italy 33; 46n 7e
Great Salt Lake: USA 80; 41n 113w
Great Sandy Desert:
Australia 58; 21s 125e
Great Sandy I.: Aust. 60; 25s 153e
Great Slave L.: Canada 78; 62n 115w
Great Valley: Aust. 61; 38s 145e
Great Victoria Desert:
Australia 58; 28s 130e
Great Wall: China 53; — —
Great Western Erg: Alg. 66; 31n 1e
GREECE 31; 39n 22e
Green: r., USA 80; 40n 110w
Green B.: USA 84; 45n 88w
GREENLAND 79; — —
Green Mts.: USA 85; 44n 73w
Greenough: r., Aust. 60; 28s 116e
Green River: USA 80; 42n 109w
Greensboro: USA 84; 36n 80w
Greensburg: USA 84; 40n 80w
Greenville: USA 81; 35n 82w
Greifswald: Germany 32; 54n 13e
Grenada: i., W. Indies 83; 12n 62w
Grenadines: is., W. Ind. 83; 13n 62w
Grenay: France 28; 50n 3e
Grenoble: France 29; 45n 6e
Greymouth: NZ 55; 42s 171e
Grey Range: Australia 61; 29s 142e
Greytown: S. Africa 69; 29s 31e
Griffith: Australia 61; 34s 146e
Grimsel Pass: Switz. 33; 47n 8e
Grims Ey: i., Iceland 34; 66n 18w
Grindelwald: Switz. 33; 47n 8e
Griqualand: S. Africa 69; 28s 22e
Griquatown: S. Africa 69; 29s 23e
Gris Nez, C.: France 28; 51n 2e
Grodekovo: USSR 54; 44n 131e
Grodno: USSR 44; 54n 24e
Groix, Î. de: France 28; 48n 3w
Gronau: Germany 32; 52n 7e
Grong: Norway 34; 65n 12e
Groningen: Neth. 32; 53n 7e
Groote Eylandt: Aust. 58; 14s 137e
Grootfontein: SW. Afr. 69; 20s 18e
Grossenbrode: Ger. 35; 54n 11e
Grosseto: Italy 30; 43n 11e
Gross Glockner: Aus. 33; 47n 13e
Groznyy: USSR 44; 43n 46e
Grudziądz: Poland 35; 53n 19e
Grünberg: Poland 35; 52n 16e
Gruyères: Switzerland 33; 47n 7e
Grytviken: S. Georgia 89; 54s 37w
Guadalajara: Mexico 82; 21n 103w
Guadalajara: Spain 25; 41n 3w
Guadalcanal: i., Pac. O. 92; 10s 160e
Guadalcanal: Spain 25; 38n 6w
Guadalquivir: r., Spain 25; 38n 5w
Guadeloupe: i., W. Ind. 83; 17n 62w
Guadiana: r., Sp./Port. 25; 38n 7w
Guadix: Spain 25; 37n 3w
Guajará-mirim: Brazil 86; 11s 65w
Guam: i., Pacific Ocean 92; 14n 145e
Guarda: Portugal 25; 41n 7w
Guardafui, C.: Somalia 67; 12n 51e
GUATEMALA 82; 15n 90w
Guatemala: Guatemala 82; 15n 91w
Guayaquil: Ecuador 86; 2s 80w
Guaymas: Mexico 80; 28n 111w
Gubakha: USSR 45; 59n 58e
Gubin: Poland 32; 52n 15e
Guebwiller: France 28; 48n 7e
Guelph: Canada 84; 43n 80w
Guéret: France 29; 46n 2e
Guiana Highlands:
S. America 86/87; — —

Page; Lat. Long.

GUINEA 66; 10n 10w
Guinea, G. of 68; 2n 0
Guingamp: France 28; 48n 3w
Gujerat: India 52; 23n 72e
Gujranwala: W. Pak. 52; 32n 74e
Gulfport: USA 81; 30n 89w
Gulf Stream: N. Atl. O. 90; — —
Gunnedah: Australia 61; 31s 150e
Guntur: India 52; 16n 81e
Gur'yev: USSR 44; 47n 52e
*Gwaai: S. Rhodesia 69; 19s 28e
Gwadar: W. Pakistan 52; Inset
Gwalior: India 52; 27n 78e
*Gwelo: S. Rhodesia 69; 19s 30e
Gyangtse: China 47; 29n 90e
Gydan Range: USSR 43; 63n 160e
Gyda Penin.: USSR 43; 71n 80e
Gympie: Australia 60; 26s 153e
Győr: Hungary 27; 48n 18e

Haarlem: Netherlands 32; 52n 5e
Haast: & pass, NZ 55; 44s 169e
Hab: r., W. Pakistan 52; Inset
Habbānīyah: 'Iraq 49; 33n 43e
Hachinohe: Japan 54; 41n 141e
Hachioji: Japan 54; 36n 139e
Hadibu: Socotra 49; 13n 54e
Hadithah: 'Iraq 49; 34n 42e
*Hadramaut: Aden. Prot. 49; 16n 50e
Haft-Gel: Iran 49; 31n 50e
Hageland: Belgium 28; 51n 5e
Hagen: Germany 32; 51n 8e
Hagerstown: USA 85; 40n 78w
Hague, C. de la: France 28; 50n 2w
Hague, The: Neth. 32; 52n 4e
Haguenau: France 28; 49n 8e
Haifa: Israel 48; 33n 35e
Hail: Sa'udi Arabia 49; 27n 42e
Hailar: China 50; 49n 120e
Hainan: China 51; 19n 110e
Hainault: Belgium 28; 51n 4e
Haiphong: N. Viet Nam 53; 21n 107e
HAITI 83; 19n 73w
Hakodate: Japan 54; 42n 141e
Halaib: Sudan 48; 22n 36e
Halberstadt: Germany 32; 52n 11e
Haldensleben: Germany 32; 52n 11e
Halifax: Canada 85; 45n 64w
Halle: Germany 32; 51n 12e
Halls Creek: Aust. 58; 18s 128e
Halmahera: i., Indon. 51; 1n 128e
Halmstad: Sweden 35; 57n 13e
Hälsingborg: Sweden 35; 56n 13e
Halunarshan: China 53; 47n 120e
Hama: Syria 48; 35n 36e
Hamada: Japan 54; 35n 132e
Hamadān: Iran 49; 35n 48e
Hamamatsu: Japan 54; 35n 138e
Hamar: Norway 35; 61n 11e
*Hambantota: Ceylon 52; 6n 82e
Hamburg: Germany 32; 54n 10e
Hämeenlinna: Finland 35; 61n 25e
Hameln: Germany 32; 52n 9e
Hamersley Ra.: Aust. 58; 22s 117e
Hami: China 47; 43n 93e
Hamilton: Australia 61; 38s 142e
Hamilton: Canada 84; 43n 80w
Hamilton: NZ 55; 38s 175e
Hamilton: USA 84; 39n 84w
Hamm: Germany 32; 52n 8e
Hammamet, G. of: Tun. 30; 36n 11e
Hammerfest: Norway 34; 71n 24e
Hāmūn-i Helmand: Iran 46; 32n 61e
Han: r., China 53; 32n 112e
Hangchow: China 53; 30n 120e
Hangö (Hanko): Fin. 35; 60n 23e
*Hankow: China 53; 31n 114e
Hannibal: USA 84; 40n 91w
Hanö Bay: Sweden 35; 56n 15e
Hanoi: N. Viet Nam 53; 21n 106e
Hanover: Germany 32; 52n 10e
Hanyang: see Wuhan
Haogoundou, L.: Mali 66; 16n 3w
Haradh: Sa'udi Arabia 49; 24n 49e
Harar: Ethiopia 67; 9n 42e
Harbin: China 53; 46n 126e
Harburg-Wilhelmsburg:
Germany 32; 53n 10e
Hardanger Fd.: Norway 35; 60n 6e
Hardangervidda: Nor. 35; 60n 7e
Hardenberg: Neth. 32; 53n 7e
*Hargeisa: Som. Prot. 67; 10n 44e
Hari: r., Afghanistan 49; 35n 61e
Harima Gulf: Japan 54; 34n 135e
Harlingen: Neth. 32; 53n 5e
Härnösand: Sweden 34; 63n 18e
Harrisburg: Ill., USA 84; 38n 89w
Harrisburg: Pa., USA 85; 40n 77w
Harrismith: S. Africa 69; 28s 29e
Harsprånget: Sweden 34; 67n 20e
Harstad: Norway 34; 69n 17e
Hartford: USA 85; 42n 73w
Harz: mts., Germany 32; 52n 11e
Hasa: Sa'udi Arabia 49; 27n 48e
Hassan: India 52; 13n 76e
Hasselt: Belgium 28; 51n 5e
Hassi Messaoud: Alg. 66; 32n 6e
Hässleholm: Sweden 35; 56n 14e
Hastings: NZ 55; 40s 177e
Hastings Range: Aust. 61; 31s 152e
Hatinh: N. Viet Nam 51; 18n 106e
Hatteras, C.: USA 81; 35n 75w
Haud: Ethiopia 67; 8n 45e
Haugesund: Norway 35; 59n 5e
Hauraki Gulf: NZ 55; 37s 175e
Havana: Cuba 83; 23n 83w
Haverhill: USA 85; 43n 71w
Havre: USA 80; 49n 110w
Havre de Grace: USA 85; 39n 76w
Hawaii: i., Pac. O. 93; 20n 155w
Hawaiian Is.: Pac. O. 92/93; — —
Hawera: NZ 55; 40s 174e
Hawke Bay: NZ 55; 39s 177e
Hawker: Australia 61; 32s 138e
Hay: Australia 61; 34s 145e
Hazaribagh: India 52; 24n 85e
Hazebrouck: France 28; 51n 2e
Hazelton: Canada 78; 55n 128w
Hazor: Holy Land 48; Inset
Hearst I.: Antarctica 91; 70s 62w

Page; Lat. Long.

Hebron: Holy Land 48; Inset
Heerenveen: Neth. 32; 53n 6e
Heidelberg: Germany 32; 49n 9e
Heidelberg: S. Africa 69; 26s 28e
Heilbronn: Germany 32; 49n 9e
Heilungkiang: China 53; 46n 124e
Hekla: mt., Iceland 34; 64n 20w
Helena: USA 80; 47n 112w
Helen Glacier: Antarc. 91; 67s 94e
Helensville: NZ 55; 37s 174e
Heligoland: i. & B., Ger. 35; 54n 8e
Helles, C.: Turkey 31; 40n 26e
Helmand: r., Afghan. 46; 30n 63e
Helsingfors: Finland 35; 60n 25e
Helsingør: Denmark 35; 56n 13e
Helsinki: Finland 35; 60n 25e
Henderson: USA 84; 38n 88w
Hengelo: Netherlands 32; 52n 7e
Henyang: China 53; 27n 112e
Herat: Afghanistan 46; 34n 62e
Hérault: France 29; 43n 3e
Herberton: Australia 59; 17s 145e
Herford: Germany 32; 52n 9e
Herisau: Switzerland 33; 47n 9e
Hermitage: NZ 55; 44s 170e
Hermosillo: Mexico 80; 29n 111w
Herne: Germany 32; 52n 7e
Herning: Denmark 35; 56n 9e
Herschel I.: Canada 78; 70n 139w
Herstal: Belgium 28; 51n 6e
Hervey B.: Australia 60; 25s 153e
Hibbing: USA 84; 47n 93w
Hidaka Mts.: Japan 55; 42n 143e
Hidalgo del Parral:
Mexico 82; 27n 106w
Hida Mts.: Japan 54; 36n 138e
High Atlas: Morocco 66; 32n 7w
High Plateaux: Alg. 66; 34n 1e
High Veld: S. Africa 69; 28s 27e
Hiiumaa: i., USSR 35; 59n 23e
Hijaz: Sa'udi Arabia 49; 25n 39e
Hildesheim: Germany 32; 52n 10e
Hillah: 'Iraq 49; 32n 44e
Hillegom: Netherlands 32; 52n 5e
Hillston: Australia 61; 34s 146e
Hilversum: Neth. 32; 52n 5e
Himachal Pradesh: India 52; 32n 77e
Himeji: Japan 54; 35n 135e
Hinckley: USA 84; 46n 93w
Hindu Kush: Afghan. 47; 36n 70e
*Hingshan: China 50; 47n 130e
Hirfanlı: Turkey 48; 39n 34e
Hirosaki: Japan 54; 41n 140e
Hiroshima: Japan 54; 34n 133e
Hirson: France 28; 50n 4e
Hispaniola: W. Indies 83; 19n 72w
Hitachi: Japan 54; 37n 141e
Hiva Oa: i., Pac. O. 93; 10s 140w
Hjørring: Denmark 35; 58n 10e
Hobart: Tasmania 59; 43s 147e
Hoboken: Belgium 28; 51n 4e
Hoch Moor: Germany 32; 53n 8e
Hodeida: Yemen 49; 15n 43e
Hodmezövásárhely:
Hungary 27; 46n 20e
Hoeryong: N. Korea 54; 42n 130e
Hof: Germany 32; 50n 12e
Hofei: China 53; 32n 117e
Hofsjökull: mt., Iceland 34; 65n 19w
Hohe Rhön: mts., Ger. 32; 50n 10e
Hohe Tauern: Austria 33; 47n 13e
Hohsien: China 53; 24n 112e
Hoihow: China 50; 20n 110e
Hokianga Harb.: NZ 55; 35s 173e
Hokitika: NZ 55; 43s 171e
Hokkaido: i., Japan 54/55; — —
Holbaek: Denmark 35; 56n 12e
Holbrook: Australia 61; 36s 147e
*Hollandia:
Neth. New Guinea 59; 2s 141e
Hollick-Kenyon Plat.:
Antarctica 91; 79s 100w
Hollywood: USA 80; 34n 118w
Holstebro: Denmark 35; 56n 9e
Holstein: Germany 32; 54n 10e
Holyoke: USA 85; 42n 73w
Home Hill: Australia 60; 20s 148e
Homs: Libya 66; 32n 14e
Homs: Syria 48; 35n 37e
Hon: Libya 48; 29n 16e
Honan: China 53; 34n 113e
HONDURAS 83; 15n 88w
*Hønefoss: Norway 35; 60n 10e
Honfleur: France 28; 49n 0
HONG KONG 53; 22n 114e
Honiara: Guadalcanal 59; 9s 160e
Honolulu: Pac. O. 93; 21n 158w
Honshu: i., Japan 54; — —
Hood, Mt.: USA 80; 45n 122w
Hood Pt.: Australia 60; 34s 120e
Hoogezand: Neth. 32; 53n 7e
Hooghly: r., India 52; 22n 88e
Hook I.: Australia 60; 20s 149e
Hook of Holland: Neth. 32; 52n 4e
Hoover Dam: USA 80; 36n 115w
Hope Bay: Antarctica 91; 63s 57w
Hopeh: China 53; 38n 116e
Hopkins: r., Australia 61; 38s 143e
Hopkinsville: USA 84; 37n 87w
Hormuz, Str. of 49; 27n 57e
Horn, C.: Chile 89; 56s 67w
Horsham: Australia 61; 37s 142e
Hoshangabad: India 52; 23n 78e
Hotham, Mt.: Aust. 61; 36s 147e
Hoting: Sweden 34; 64n 16e
Hourtin, Etg. d': France 29; 45n 1w
Houston: USA 81; 30n 95w
Houtman Abrolhos:
rocks, Australia 60; 29s 114e
Howe, C.: Australia 61; 37s 150e
Howrah: India 52; 23n 88e
Hoyo Str.: Japan 54; 33n 132e
Hsichang: China 50; 28n 102e
Hsin-chu: Formosa 50; 25n 121e
Hsinhai: China 53; 35n 119e
Hsinhsiang: China 53; 35n 114e
Hsintai: China 53; 36n 118e
Hsinyang: China 53; 32n 114e
Hualiel: Formosa 53; 24n 122e
Huallaga: r., Peru 86; 8s 77w

Page; Lat. Long.

Huancavelica: Peru 86; 13s 75w
Huancayo: Peru 86; 12s 75w
Huánuco: Peru 86; 10s 76w
Huaras: Peru 86; 10s 77w
Hubli: India 52; 15n 75e
Hudson: r., USA 85; 41n 74w
Hudson Bay: Canada 79; 60n 85w
Hudson Bay: town, Can. 80; 53n 102w
Hudson Strait: Canada 79; 62n 72w
Hué: S. Viet Nam 51; 16n 107e
Huelva: Spain 25; 37n 7w
Huesca: Spain 25; 42n 0
Hufhuf: Sa'udi Arabia 49; 25n 50e
Hughenden: Australia 59; 21s 144e
Huhehot: China 53; 41n 112e
Huitse: China 53; 26n 103e
Hull: Canada 85; 45n 76w
Hüls: Germany 32; 52n 7e
Hulun: China 50; 49n 120e
Hulun Nor: China 50; 49n 117e
Humboldt Glac.: Grnld. 79; 80n 60w
Hume: r., Australia 61; 36s 144e
Hume Res.: Australia 61; 36s 147e
Hunan: China 53; 28n 111e
Hunchun: China 54; 43n 130e
Hunger Steppe: USSR 45; 47n 70e
Hunsrück: mts., Ger. 32; 50n 7e
Hunter: r., Australia 61; 32s 151e
Hunter Range: Aust. 61; 33s 150e
Huntington: USA 84; 38n 83w
Huntly: NZ 55; 37s 175e
Hupeh: China 53; 31n 112e
Hurghada: Egypt 48; 27n 33e
Huron, L.: Can./USA 84; 45n 83w
Hurunui: r., NZ 55; 43s 173e
Huskvarna: Sweden 35; 58n 14e
Hutchinson: USA 80; 38n 98w
Hutt: NZ 55; 41s 175e
Hvar: i., Yugoslavia 27; 43n 17e
Hwaining: China 53; 31n 117e
Hwang: r., China 53; 37n 117e
Hyderabad: India 52; 17n 78e
Hyderabad: W. Pakistan 52; 25n 68e
Hyères: France 29; 43n 6e

Iaşi: Romania 31; 47n 28e
Ibadan: Nigeria 68; 7n 4e
Ibagué: Colombia 86; 4n 75w
Ibi: Nigeria 68; 8n 10e
Ibiza: i., Spain 25; 39n 1e
Ica: Peru 86; 14s 76w
ICELAND 34; — —
Ichang: China 53; 31n 112e
Ichinomiya: Japan 54; 35n 137e
Idaho: State, USA 80; 44n 115w
Idaho Falls: USA 80; 43n 112w
Idumaea: Holy Land 48 Inset
Ifni: (Sp.) Morocco 66; 29n 10w
Igarka: USSR 43; 67n 86e
Iglesias: Sardinia 30; 39n 9e
Iisalmi: Finland 34; 64n 27e
Ijebu Ode: Nigeria 68; 7n 4e
Ijmuiden: Netherlands 32; 52n 5e
Ijssel: r., Neth. 32; 52n 6e
Ijsselmeer: Neth. 32; 53n 5e
Ikaria: i., Greece 31; 38n 26e
Île de France: France 28; 49n 2e
Île d'Orléans: Canada 85; 47n 71w
Ilhéus: Brazil 87; 15s 40w
Ili: r., USSR 45; 44n 78e
Iliamna L.: Alaska 78; 60n 155w
Illimani: mt., Bolivia 86; 17s 68w
Illinois: r., USA 84; 40n 90w
Illinois: State, USA 84; 40n 90w
Il'men', L.: USSR 44; 58n 31e
Ilmenau: Germany 32; 51n 11e
Iliodhromia: i., Greece 31; 39n 24e
Iloilo: Philippines 51; 11n 122e
Imabari: Japan 54; 34n 133e
Imatra: Finland 34; 61n 29e
Imperia: Italy 33; 44n 8e
Imperial Dam: USA 80; 33n 114w
Imphal: India 53; 25n 94e
Imroz: i., Turkey 31; 40n 26e
Inari, L.: Finland 34; 69n 28e
Inchon: S. Korea 50; 38n 127e
Indaw: Burma 50; 24n 96e
Indefatigable I.: Pac. O. 86; 1s 90w
INDIA (BHARAT) 52; — —
Indiana: State, USA 84; 40n 86w
Indianapolis: USA 84; 40n 86w
Indian Ocean 47; — —
Indigirka: r., USSR 43; 68n 147e
INDONESIA 51; — —
Indore: India 52; 23n 76e
Indre: r., France 29; 47n 1e
Indus: r., W. Pak. 52; 26n 68e
Ingolstadt: Germany 33; 49n 11e
Ingrid Christensen Coast:
Antarctica 91; 70s 79e
Inhambane: Moz. 69; 24s 35e
Inhaminga: Moz. 69; 18s 35e
Inkerman: USSR 44; 45n 34e
Inland Sea: Japan 54; 34n 133e
Inn: r., Austria 33; 47n 12e
Innamincka: Australia 60; 28s 141e
Inner Mongolian Auton.
Reg.: China 53; — —
Innsbruck: Austria 33; 47n 11e
Inntal: Austria 33; 47n 11e
Inowrocław: Poland 35; 53n 18e
Insterburg: USSR 35; 55n 23e
Interlaken: Switz. 33; 47n 8e
Inverall: Australia 61; 30s 151e
Invercargill: NZ 55; 46s 168e
Inverness: Canada 85; 46n 61w
Investigator Str.: Aust. 61; 35s 137e
Ionian Is.: & sea, Greece 31; 38n 20e
Ios: i., Greece 31; 37n 25e
Iowa: State, USA 81; 42n 94w
Iowa City: USA 84; 42n 92w
Iowa Falls: USA 84; 42n 93w
Ipin: China 53; 28n 104e
Ipoh: Malaya 51; 5n 101e
Ipswich: Australia 60; 28s 153e
Iquique: Chile 88; 20s 70w
Iquitos: Peru 86; 4s 73w
Iraklion: Crete 31; 35n 25e
IRAN (PERSIA) 49; 32n 55e
'IRAQ 49; 33n 45e

*See Page 131

Page; Lat. Long.
Irbil: 'Iraq 49; 36n 44e
*Iringa: Tanganyika 68; 8s 36e
Irkutsk: USSR 43; 53n 104e
Irtysh: r., USSR 45; 52n 77e
Irun: Spain 25; 43n 2w
Iron Gates: Romania 31; 45n 23e
Iron Knob: Australia 61; 33s 137e
Iron Mt.: USA 80; 38n 114w
Iron Mountain: USA 84; 46n 88w
Ironton: USA 84; 39n 83w
Ironwood: USA 84; 46n 90w
Iroquois: Canada 85; 45n 75w
Irrawaddy: r., Burma 50; 25n 97e
Isabela I.: Pac. O. 86; 1s 91w
Isafjördhur: Iceland 34; 66n 23w
Isar: r., Germany 33; 49n 12e
Isarco: r., Italy 33; 47n 12e
Ischia: i., Italy 30; 41n 14e
Ise Bay: Japan 54; 35n 137e
Iseo, L.: Italy 33; 46n 10e
Isère: r., France 29; 45n 5e
Iserlohn: Germany 32; 51n 8e
Iseyin: Nigeria 68; 8n 3e
Isfahan: Iran 49; 33n 52e
Ishikari: r., Japan 54; 43n 142e
Ishim: r., USSR 45; 53n 67e
Ishimbay: USSR 44; 53n 56e
Ishinomaki: Japan 54; 38n 141e
Ishpeming: USA 84; 47n 88w
İskenderun: Turkey 48; 37n 36e
Islands, B. of: NZ 55; 35s 174e
Isle Royale: USA 84; 48n 89w
Ismailia: Egypt 67; 30n 32e
Isna: Egypt 67; 25n 32e
Isonzo: r., Yugo./Italy 33; 46n 14e
ISRAEL 48; 32n 35e
Issigeac: France 29; 45n 1e
Issoudun: France 29; 47n 2e
Issyk-Kul: L., USSR 45; 42n 77e
İstanbul: Turkey 31; 41n 29e
Istria: Yugoslavia 27; 45n 14e
Itabira: Brazil 87; 19s 43w
Itabuna: Brazil 87; 15s 40w
Ithaca: USA 85; 42n 77w
Ithaca (Ithaki): i., Grc. 31; 38n 21e
*Ittihad: Aden 67; 13n 45e
Iturup: i., USSR 55; 45n 147e
Ivailovgrad: Bulgaria 31; 41n 26e
Ivanhoe: Australia 61; 33s 144e
Ivanovo: USSR 44; 57n 41e
Ivdel': USSR 45; 61n 60e
Iviza: i., Spain 25; 39n 1e
IVORY COAST 66; 8n 5w
Ivory Coast: G. of Guin. 66; 4n 5w
Iwakuni: Japan 54; 34n 132e
Iyo Gulf: Japan 54; 34n 132e
Izhevsk: USSR 44; 57n 53e
Izhma: r., USSR 42; 64n 54e
Izmail: USSR 31; 45n 29e
İzmir: Turkey 31; 38n 27e
İzmit: Turkey 48; 41n 30e
Izu Is.: Japan 54; 34n 140e

Jabal Akhdhar:
Muscat & 'Oman 49; 23n 57e
Jabalpur: India 52; 23n 80e
Jabal Shammar:
Sa'udi Arabia 49; 27n 41e
Jabal Shifa: Sau. Arab. 48; 27n 36e
Jabal Tuwaiq:
Sa'udi Arabia 49; 25n 46e
Jabesh-gilead:
Holy Land 48; Inset
Jaca: Spain 25; 43n 1w
Jáchymov: Czech. 32; 50n 13e
Jackson: Mich., USA 84; 42n 84w
Jackson: Miss., USA 81; 32n 90w
Jackson: Tenn., USA 84; 36n 89w
Jackson Bay: NZ 55; 44s 169e
Jacksonville: Fla., USA 81; 30n 82w
Jacksonville: Ill., USA 84; 40n 90w
Jacobabad: W. Pakistan 52; 28n 68e
Jadotville: Congo Rep. 71; 11s 27e
Jaén: Spain 25; 38n 4w
Jaffa, C.: Australia 61; 37s 140e
Jaffa-Tel Aviv: Israel 48; 32n 35e
Jaffna: Ceylon 52; 9n 80e
Jaipur: India 52; 27n 76e
Jaisalmer: India 52; 27n 71e
Jakobstad: Finland 34; 64n 23e
Jalalabad: Afghanistan 47; 35n 70e
Jalo Oasis: Libya 48; 28n 22e
JAMAICA 83; 18n 77w
Jambin: Australia 60; 24s 150e
James: r., USA 85; 38n 79w
James B.: Canada 79; 53n 80w
James Ross I.: Antarc. 91; 64s 58w
Jamestown: USA 85; 42n 79w
Jammu: Kashmir 52; 33n 75e
JAMMU & KASHMIR 52; 34n 76e
Jamnagar: India 52; 22n 70e
Jamshedpur: India 52; 23n 86e
Janesville: USA 84; 43n 89w
Jan Mayen I.: N. Atl. O. 90; 70n 5w
JAPAN 54/55; — —
*Japen: i., Neth. N. Guin. 58; 2s 137e
Jarocin: Poland 35; 52n 18e
Jarosław: Poland 27; 50n 23e
Jarvis I.: Pacific Ocean 93; 0 160w
Jask: Iran 49; 26n 58e
Jasło: Poland 27; 50n 21e
Jaszberény: Hungary 27; 47n 20e
Jauf: Sa'udi Arabia 49; 30n 40e
Java: i., Indonesia 51; 7s 110e
Jaxartes: r., USSR 45; 44n 66e
Jebba: Nigeria 68; 9n 5e
Jebel Akhdar: Libya 48; 32n 22e
Jebel Aulia Dam: Sudan 48; 15n 32e
Jedrzejów: Poland 27; 51n 20e
Jefferson City: USA 84; 39n 92w
Jehol: China 53; 41n 118e
Jena: Germany 32; 51n 12e
Jenolan Caves: Aust. 61; 34s 150e
Jequitinhonha: r., Brazil 87; 16s 40w
Jerez de la Frontera: Sp. 25; 37n 6w
Jericho: Holy Land 48; Inset
Jersey City: USA 85; 41n 74w
Jerusalem: Isr./Jordan 48; 32n 35e
Jervis B.: Australia 61; 35s 151e
*Jesselton: N. Borneo 51; 6n 116e

Page; Lat. Long.
*Jessore: E. Pakistan 52; 23n 89e
Jezreel, V. of: Holy Land 48; Inset
Jhansi: India 52; 25n 78e
Jhelum: r., W. Pakistan 52; 31n 72e
Jibhalanta: Mongolia 50; 48n 97e
Jidda: Sa'udi Arabia 49; 21n 39e
Jiménez: Mexico 82; 27n 105w
Jimma: Ethiopia 68; 7n 37e
João Pessoa: Brazil 87; 7s 35w
Jodhpur: India 52; 27n 73e
Joensuu: Finland 34; 63n 30e
Jofra Oasis: Libya 66; 29n 15e
Jogjakarta: Java 51; 8s 110e
Johannesburg: S. Africa 69; 26s 28e
Johnson City: USA 84; 36n 82w
Johnston I.: Pac. O. 93; 18n 170w
Johnstown: USA 85; 40n 79w
Johore Bahru: Malaya 51; 2n 104e
Joinville I.: Antarc. 91; 63s 56w
Joliet: USA 84; 42n 88w
Joliette: Canada 85; 46n 73w
Jolo: i., Philippines 51; 6n 121e
Jonesboro: USA 84; 36n 91w
Jones Sd.: Canada 79; 76n 85w
Jonglei: Sudan 67; 7n 32e
Jönköping: Sweden 35; 58n 14e
Jonquière: Canada 85; 48n 71w
Joplin: USA 81; 37n 95w
Joppa: Holy Land 48; Inset
JORDAN 48; 32n 37e
Jordan: r., Holy Land 48; Inset
Jorhat: India 53; 27n 94e
Jörn: Sweden 34; 65n 20e
Jos: Nigeria 68; 10n 9e
Joseph Bonaparte G.:
Australia 58; 14s 128e
Josselin: France 28; 48n 3w
Jostedals Bre: Norway 34; 62n 7e
Jotunheimen: Norway 34; 62n 8e
Juan de Fuca, Str.:
Canada/USA 80; 48n 125w
Juan Fernández Is.: Chile 88; 34s 79w
Juba: Sudan 67; 5n 32e
Juba: r., Eth./Somalia 70; 2n 42e
Juby, C.: Morocco 66; 28n 13w
Jucar: r., Spain 25; 39n 2w
Judaea: Holy Land 48; Inset
Judah: Holy Land 48; Inset
Juist: i., Germany 32; 54n 7e
Juiz de Fóra: Brazil 88; 22s 43w
Jujuy: Argentina 88; 24s 65w
Jukao: China 53; 32n 121e
Julian Alps: It./Yugo. 27; 46n 14e
Julier Pass: Switzerland 33; 46n 10e
Jülich: Germany 32; 51n 6e
Jullundur: India 52; 32n 76e
Juneau: USA 78; 58n 134w
Junee: Australia 61; 35s 148e
Jungfrau: mt., Switz. 33; 47n 8e
Jur: r., Sudan 67; 8n 28e
Jura, The: Fr./Switz. 29; 47n 6e
Juruá: r., Brazil 86; 6s 68w
Juruena: r., Brazil 87; 11s 58w
Jussey: France 28; 48n 6e
Jutland: Denmark 35; 56n 9e
Jyekundo: China 50; 33n 97e
Jyväskylä: Finland 34; 62n 26e

Kakaena: i., Indonesia 51; 5s 122e
Kabalo: Congo Rep. 71; 6s 27e
Kabul: Afghanistan 47; 35n 69e
Kade: Ghana 68; 6n 1w
Kadina: Australia 61; 34s 138e
Kaduna: Nigeria 68; 11n 7e
*Kafue: & r., N. Rhod. 69; 16s 28e
Kagoshima: Japan 54; 32n 130e
Kagul: USSR 31; 46n 28e
*Kaieteur Falls: Br. Gu. 87; 5n 59w
Kaifeng: China 53; 35n 115e
Kai Is.: Indon. 51; 6s 133e
Kaikohe: NZ 55; 35s 174e
Kaikoura: & mts., NZ 55; 42s 174e
Kailas Ra.: China 52; 32n 81e
Kaimanawa Mts.: NZ 55; 39s 176e
Kaipara Harb.: NZ 55; 36s 174e
Kairouan: Tunisia 30; 36n 10e
Kaiserslautern: Ger. 32; 49n 8e
Kaiser Wilhelm II Ld.:
Antarctica 91; 70s 89e
Kaitaia: NZ 55; 35s 173e
Kaitangata: NZ 55; 46s 170e
Kajaani: Finland 34; 64n 28e
Kakinada: India 52; 17n 82e
Kalabagh: W. Pakistan 52; 33n 72e
Kalachinsk: USSR 45; 55n 75e
Kaladan: r., India 53; 24n 93e
*Kalahari Desert: Bech. 69; 24s 23e
Kalamata: Greece 31; 37n 22e
Kalamazoo: USA 84; 42n 85w
Kalat: W. Pakistan 52; 29n 67e
Kalgan: China 53; 41n 115e
Kalgoorlie: Australia 60; 31s 122e
Kalimantan: i., Indon. 51; 0 115e
Kalimnos: i., Greece 31; 37n 27e
Kalinin: USSR 44; 57n 36e
Kaliningrad: USSR 35; 55n 20e
Kalisz: Poland 35; 52n 18e
Kalmar: Sweden 35; 57n 16e
*Kalomo: N. Rhodesia 69; 17s 26e
Kaluga: USSR 44; 55n 36e
Kama: r., USSR 44; 55n 51e
Kamaishi: Japan 54; 39n 142e
Kamaran Is.: Red Sea 49; 15n 43e
Kamchatka: & B., USSR 43; 55n 160e
Kamenskoye: USSR 43; 63n 165e
Kamensk-Uralskiy:
USSR 45; 56n 62e
Kamet: China/India 52; 31n 79e
Kamienna Góra: Poland 27; 51n 16e
*Kamina: Congo Rep. 71; 9s 25e
Kamloops: Canada 80; 51n 120w
Kampala: Uganda 68; 0 32e
Kampen: Netherlands 32; 53n 6e
Kamyshlov: USSR 45; 57n 63e
Kanawha: r., USA 84; 39n 82w
Kanazawa: Japan 54; 36n 137e
Kandagach: USSR 45; 49n 58e
Kandahar: Afghanistan 47; 32n 66e
Kandalaksha: USSR 34; 67n 33e
Kandi: Dahomey 68; 11n 3e

Page; Lat. Long.
Kandla: India 52; 23n 70e
Kandos: Australia 61; 33s 150e
*Kandy: Ceylon 52; 7n 81e
Kane Basin: Grnld. 79; 79n 70w
Kangaroo I.: Aust. 61; 36s 137e
Kangchenjunga:
Nepal/Sikkim 52; 28n 88e
Kangean Is.: Indon. 51; 7s 115e
Kangting: China 50; 30n 102e
Kanin, C.: USSR 42; 69n 43e
Kankan: Guinea 66; 10n 9w
Kankanee: USA 84; 41n 88w
Kano: Nigeria 68; 12n 8e
Kanoya: Japan 54; 31n 131e
Kanpur: India 52; 27n 80e
Kansas: State, USA 80; 38n 98w
Kansas City: Kansas,
USA 81; 39n 95w
Kansas City: Mo., USA 81; 39n 95w
Kansk: USSR 45; 56n 95e
Kansu: China 53; 35n 105e
Kao-hsiung: Formosa 50; 23n 120e
Kaolan: China 53; 36n 104e
Kapuskasing: & r., Can. 84; 49n 83w
Kaposvár: Hungary 27; 46n 18e
Kapurthala: India 52; 32n 75e
Kara: USSR 42; 69n 65e
Kara-Bogaz-Gol: USSR 44; 42n 53e
Karabük: Turkey 48; 41n 33e
Karachi: W. Pakistan 52; 25n 67e
Karaganda: USSR 45; 50n 73e
Karakoram: mts., Kash. 47; 35n 77e
Kara-Kum: USSR 45; 40n 60e
Karapiro: NZ 55; 38s 176e
Karasburg: SW. Africa 69; 28s 18e
Kara Sea: USSR 42; 73n 60e
Kara-Tau: USSR 45; 44n 68e
Karaul: USSR 43; 70n 83e
Karbalā: 'Iraq 49; 33n 44e
Kargil: Kashmir 52; 34n 76e
Kariba L.: & dam, Afr. 69; 17s 28e
Karibib: SW. Africa 69; 22s 16e
Karima: Sudan 48; 18n 32e
Karl-Marx-Stadt: E. Ger. 32; 51n 13e
Karlovac: Yugoslavia 27; 45n 15e
Karlovy Vary (Karlsbad):
Czechoslovakia 32; 50n 13e
Karlshamn: Sweden 35; 56n 15e
Karlskoga: Sweden 35; 59n 14e
Karlskrona: Sweden 35; 56n 16e
Karlsruhe: Germany 32; 49n 9e
Karlstad: Sweden 35; 59n 13e
*Karonga: Nyasaland 68; 10s 34e
Karpathos: i., Greece 31; 35n 27e
Kartaly: USSR 45; 53n 61e
Karwar: India 52; 15n 74e
Kaş: Turkey 31; 36n 30e
*Kasai: r., Congo Rep. 71; 4s 19e
Kasba L.: Canada 78; 60n 102w
*Kasempa: N. Rhodesia 69; 13s 26e
*Kasenga: Congo Rep. 68; 11s 29e
Kasese: Uganda 68; 0 30e
Kāshān: Iran 49; 34n 52e
Kashgar: China 45; 40n 76e
Kashmir see Jammu and
Kashmir
Kasos: i., Greece 31; 35n 27e
Kassala: Sudan 67; 15n 36e
Kassel: Germany 32; 51n 10e
Kasserine: Tunisia 30; 35n 9e
Kastellorizo: i., Grc. 31; 36n 30e
Katahdin, Mt.: USA 85; 46n 69w
Katakolon: Greece 31; 38n 21e
*Katanga: Congo Rep. 68; 10s 28e
Katanning: Australia 60; 34s 118e
Katcha: Nigeria 68; 9n 6e
Katherine: Australia 58; 14s 132e
Kathiawar: India 52; 22n 71e
Katmandu: Nepal 52; 28n 85e
Katoomba: Australia 61; 34s 150e
Katowice: Poland 27; 50n 19e
Katrineholm: Sweden 35; 59n 16e
Katsina: Nigeria 68; 8n 8e
Kattaro: Yugoslavia 27; 42n 19e
Kattegat: Swed./Den. 35; 57n 11e
Kauai: i., Pacific Ocean 93; 22n 160w
Kaula: i., Pacific Ocean 93; 22n 160w
Kaunas: USSR 35; 55n 24e
Kaura Namoda: Nigeria 68; 13n 7e
Kautokeino: Norway 34; 69n 23e
Kavalla: Greece 31; 41n 24e
*Kavieng: New Guinea 59; 3s 151e
Kawagoe: Japan 54; 36n 139e
Kawasaki: Japan 54; 35n 140e
Kawerau: NZ 55; 38s 177e
*Kaya: Volta 68; 13n 1w
Kayes: Mali 66; 14n 11w
Kayseri: Turkey 48; 38n 35e
Kazach'ye: USSR 43; 71n 136e
Kazakh SSR: USSR 44/45; — —
Kazakh Uplands: USSR 45; 49n 75e
Kazalinsk: USSR 45; 46n 62e
Kazan': USSR 44; 56n 49e
Kazanlik: Bulgaria 31; 43n 25e
Kea: i., Greece 31; 38n 24e
Kebbi: r., Nigeria 68; 13n 4e
Kecskemét: Hungary 27; 47n 20e
Kedesh: Holy Land 48; Inset
Keetmanshoop:
SW. Africa 69; 27s 18e
Kefallinia: i., Greece 31; 38n 21e
Keflavik: Iceland 34; 64n 23w
Keltie, C.: Antarctica 91; 66s 132e
Kemerovo: USSR 45; 55n 86e
Kemi: & r., Finland 34; 66n 25e
Kemp Land: Antarc. 91; 71s 58e
Kempsey: Australia 61; 31s 153e
*Kenitra: Morocco 66; 34n 7w
Kennebec: r., USA 85; 45n 70w
Kennicott: USA 78; 62n 143w
Kentucky: r., USA 84; 38n 84w
Kentucky: State, USA 84; 37n 85w
KENYA 68; 0 37e
Kenya, Mt.: Kenya 68; 0 37e
Keokuk: USA 84; 41n 91w
Keppel B.: Australia 60; 23s 151e
Kerang: Australia 61; 36s 144e
Kerch': USSR 44; 45n 36e
Kerkenna Is.: Tunisia 30; 35n 11e
Kerki: USSR 45; 38n 65e

Page; Lat. Long.
Kerkira: i., Greece 31; 39n 20e
Kermadec Is.: Pac. O. 92; 30s 179w
Kermān: Iran 49; 30n 57e
Kermānshāh: Iran 49; 34n 47e
Kerme, G. of: Turkey 31; 37n 28e
Kerulen: r., Mongolia 50; 47n 111e
Kewanee: USA 84; 41n 90w
Keweenaw Pen.: USA 84; 47n 88w
Key West: USA 83; 25n 82w
Khabarovsk: USSR 43; 49n 135e
Khaipur: W. Pakistan 52; 27n 68e
Khalkis: Greece 31; 38n 24e
Khānaqin: 'Iraq 49; 34n 45e
Khandwa: India 52; 22n 77e
Khania: Crete 31; 35n 24e
Khanka, L.: USSR/China 54; 45n 132e
Khan Tengri: China 45; 42n 80e
Khanty-Mansiysk: USSR 45; 61n 70e
Kharaghoda: India 52; 23n 72e
Kharagpur: India 52; 22n 87e
Kharan: W. Pakistan 52; Inset
Khara Usu Nor: Mong. 50; 48n 92e
Kharga Oasis: Egypt 48; 24n 31e
Khārk: i., Persian G. 49; 29n 50e
Khar'kov: USSR 44; 50n 36e
Khartoum: Sudan 67; 16n 32e
Khasi Hills: India 53; 26n 92e
Khaskovo: Bulgaria 31; 42n 26e
Khasm el Girba: Sudan 48; 15n 36e
Khatanga: USSR 43; 72n 103e
Kherson: USSR 44; 47n 33e
Khios: i., Greece 31; 38n 26e
Khiumaa: i., USSR 44; 59n 23e
Khiva: USSR 45; 41n 60e
Khobso Gol: Mongolia 50; 51n 100e
Khodzheyli: USSR 45; 42n 59e
Kholmsk: USSR 43; 47n 142e
Khorāsān: Iran 49; 35n 58e
Khorog: USSR 45; 38n 72e
Khorramshahr: Iran 49; 31n 48e
Khotan: r., China 47; 37n 80e
Khrom-Tau: USSR 45; 50n 58e
Khust: USSR 31; 48n 23e
Khuzdar: W. Pakistan 52; Inset
Khuzestān: Iran 49; 31n 50e
Khyber P.: Afghan./Pak. 52; 34n 71e
Kiamusze: China 50; 47n 130e
Kian: China 53; 27n 115e
Kiangsi: Prov., China 53; 28n 116e
Kiangsu: Prov., China 53; 33n 119e
Kiangtu: China 53; 32n 119e
Kicking Horse P.: Can. 80; 51n 116w
Kiel: Germany 35; 54n 10e
Kiel Canal: Germany 32; 54n 9e
Kielce: Poland 35; 51n 21e
Kiev: USSR 44; 50n 30e
*Kigoma: Tanganyika 68; 5s 30e
Kii Chan.: Japan 54; 34n 135e
Kii Mts.: Japan 54; 34n 136e
Kilchu: N. Korea 54; 41n 130e
*Kildonan: S. Rhod. 69; 17s 31e
*Kilimanjaro, Mt.:
Tanganyika 68; 3s 37e
Kiliya: USSR 31; 45n 29e
Killaloe Stn.: Canada 85; 46n 77w
Kilmore: Australia 61; 37s 145e
*Kilwa Kivinje: Tangan. 68; 9s 39e
Kimberley: S. Africa 69; 29s 25e
*Kinabalu, Mt.:
N. Borneo 51; 7n 117e
*Kindu: Congo Rep. 71; 3s 26e
Kineshma: USSR 44; 57n 42e
Kingaroy: Australia 60; 27s 152e
King Edward VII Land:
Antarctica 91; 78s 155w
King George I.: Antarc. 91; 62s 58w
King George V Coast:
Antarctica 91; 68s 145e
*King George VI Sd.:
Antarctica 91; 73s 70w
King Leopold & Queen Astrid
Coast: Antarctica 91; 67s 84e
Kingsport: USA 84; 37n 83w
Kingston: Australia 61; 37s 140e
Kingston: Canada 85; 44n 76w
Kingston: Jamaica 83; 18n 77w
Kingston: NZ 55; 45s 169e
Kingston: USA 85; 42n 74w
King William I.: Can. 79; 69n 97w
King William's Town:
South Africa 69; 33s 27e
Kinhwa: China 53; 29n 120e
Kinleith: NZ 55; 38s 176e
Kinsha: r., China 50; 32n 98e
*Kinyangiri: Tangan. 68; 4s 35e
Kiølen Mts.:
Norway/Sweden 34; 67n 16e
Kipawa, L.: Canada 85; 47n 79w
Kipini: Kenya 68; 2s 40e
*Kipushi: Congo Rep. 68; 12s 27e
Kirchheim: Germany 33; 49n 10e
Kirgiz Nor.: Mong. 50; 49n 94e
Kirgiz SSR: USSR 45; 42n 75e
Kirin: China 53; 44n 126e
Kirkenes: Norway 34; 70n 30e
Kirkūk: 'Iraq 49; 35n 45e
Kirkland Lake: Can. 84; 48n 80w
Kırklareli: Turkey 31; 42n 27e
Kirksville: USA 84; 40n 93w
Kirov: USSR 44; 59n 50e
Kirovabad: USSR 44; 41n 47e
Kirovograd: USSR 44; 49n 32e
Kirovsk: USSR 45; 38n 61e
Kiruna: Sweden 34; 68n 20e
Kiryu: Japan 54; 36n 139e
Kishi: Nigeria 68; 9n 4e
Kishinev: USSR 44; 47n 29e
Kishm: Afghanistan 45; 37n 70e
Kiskunfelegyháza:
Hungary 27; 47n 20e
Kismayu: Somalia 70; 0 42e
Kisújszállás: Hungary 27; 47n 21e
Kisumu: Kenya 68; 0 35e
Kitaka Mts.: Japan 54; 39n 141e
Kitchener: Canada 84; 43n 80w
Kitgum: Uganda 68; 3n 33e
Kithira: i., Greece 31; 36n 23e
Kithirai Str.: Greece 31; 36n 23e
Kithnos: i., Greece 31; 37n 24e
Kitimat: Canada 78; 54n 129w

Page; Lat. Long.
Kitzbühel Alps: Aus. 33; 47n 12e
Kiuchuan: China 50; 40n 98e
Kivak: USSR 43; 64n 173w
Kivu, L.: Congo Rep. 71; 2s 29e
Kızılırmak: r., Turkey 48; 41n 34e
Klagenfurt: Austria 33; 47n 14e
Klaipeda: USSR 35; 56n 21e
Klamath Falls: USA 80; 42n 122w
Klatovy: Czech. 27; 49n 13e
Klepp: Norway 35; 59n 6e
Klerksdorp: S. Africa 69; 27s 26e
Klipplaat: S. Africa 69; 33s 24e
Kłodzko: Poland 27; 50n 17e
Knob Lake: Canada 79; 55n 67w
Knokke: Belgium 28; 51n 3e
Knowles, C.: Antarc. 91; 72s 60w
Knox Coast: Antarc. 91; 67s 108e
Knoxville: USA 84; 36n 84w
Knysna: S. Africa 69; 34s 23e
Kobe: Japan 54; 35n 135e
København: Denmark 35; 56n 12e
Koblenz: Germany 32; 50n 8e
Kobrin: USSR 35; 52n 24e
Kochel: Germany 33; 48n 11e
Kochi: Japan 54; 33n 134e
Kodiak I.: USA 78; 57n 153w
Köflach: Austria 27; 47n 15e
Kofu: Japan 54; 36n 138e
Kohat: W. Pakistan 52; 33n 71e
Kohima: India 53; 26n 94e
Kohler Ra.: Antarctica 91; 76s 110w
Kokand: USSR 45; 41n 71e
Kokchetav: USSR 45; 53n 70e
Kokiu: China 53; 23n 103e
Kokkola: Finland 34; 64n 23e
Kokomo: USA 84; 41n 86w
Koko Nor: China 50; 37n 100e
*Kokura: Japan 54; 34n 131e
Kola Penin.: USSR 42; 68n 37e
*Kolarovgrad: Bulgaria 31; 43n 27e
Kolhapur: India 52; 17n 74e
Köln: Germany 32; 51n 7e
Kolomna: USSR 44; 55n 39e
Kolomyya: USSR 31; 49n 25e
Kolyma: r., USSR 43; 67n 155e
Kolymna Range: USSR 43; 63n 160e
Kolyuchin, G. of: USSR 43; 67n 175w
Kolyvan': USSR 45; 55n 83e
Kolyvan': USSR 45; 51n 82e
Komandor Is.: USSR 43; 55n 166e
Komárno: Czech. 27; 48n 18e
Komatipoort: S. Africa 69; 25s 32e
*Komba: Congo Rep. 70; 3n 24e
Komsomol'sk: USSR 43; 51n 137e
*Kongola: Congo Rep. 71; 5s 27e
Kongsvinger: Norway 35; 60n 12e
Königsberg: USSR 35; 55n 20e
Konosha: USSR 44; 61n 40e
Konotop: USSR 44; 51n 33e
Konstanz: Germany 33; 48n 9e
Konya: Turkey 48; 38n 33e
Kootenay L.: Canada 80; 50n 117w
Kopaonik Mts.: Yugo. 27; 43n 21e
Kopar: Yugoslavia 33; 46n 14e
Koppeh Dāgh: Iran 49; 37n 59e
Korcë: Albania 31; 41n 21e
Korčula: i., Yugo. 27; 43n 17e
Kordofan: Sudan 67; 12n 29e
Korea Strait 54; 34n 129e
Koritsa: Albania 31; 41n 21e
Koriyama: Japan 54; 37n 140e
Korosten': USSR 44; 51n 29e
*Korsakov: USSR 43; 46n 143e
Kortrijk: Belgium 28; 51n 3e
Korumburra: Aust. 61; 38s 146e
Kos: i., Greece 31; 37n 27e
Kosaka: Japan 54; 40n 141e
Kosciusko, Mt.: Aust. 61; 36s 148e
Kosh-Agach: USSR 45; 50n 88e
Kosi: r., India 52; 26n 87e
Košice: Czechoslovakia 27; 49n 21e
Kosovska Mitrovica:
Yugoslavia 27; 43n 21e
Kostamo: Finland 34; 67n 28e
Kosti: Sudan 48; 13n 33e
Kostroma: USSR 44; 58n 41e
Kostrzyn Odrz: Poland 32; 53n 14e
Koszalin: Poland 35; 54n 16e
Kota: India 52; 25n 76e
Kota Bharu: Malaya 51; 6n 102e
Köthen: Germany 32; 52n 12e
Kotka: Finland 35; 60n 27e
Kotlas: USSR 44; 61n 47e
Kotor: Yugoslavia 27; 42n 19e
Kotri: W. Pakistan 52; 25n 68e
Kounradskiy: USSR 45; 47n 75e
Kovel': USSR 35; 51n 25e
Kowloon: China 53; 22n 114e
Kozani: Greece 31; 40n 22e
*Kozhikode: India 52; 11n 76e
Kra, Isthmus of: Thai 51; 10n 99e
Kragujevac: Yugoslavia 27; 44n 21e
Krakatau: Indonesia 51; 6s 105e
Kraków: Poland 27; 50n 20e
Kraljevo: Yugoslavia 27; 44n 21e
Kramfors: Sweden 34; 63n 18e
Krasnodar: USSR 44; 45n 39e
Krasnovodsk: USSR 44; 40n 53e
Krasnoyarsk: USSR 45; 56n 93e
Krasnyy Kut: USSR 44; 51n 47e
Krasnyy Luch: USSR 44; 48n 39e
Kratié: Cambodia 51; 12n 106e
Krefeld: Germany 32; 51n 6e
Kremenchug: USSR 44; 49n 33e
Krishna: r., India 52; 16n 78e
Krishnanagar: India 52; 24n 88e
Kristiansand: Norway 35; 58n 8e
Kristianstad: Sweden 35; 56n 14e
Kristiansund: Norway 34; 63n 8e
Kristinehamn: Sweden 35; 59n 14e
Kriti: i., Greece 31; 35n 25e
Krivoy Rog: USSR 44; 48n 34e
Krk: i., Yugoslavia 30; 45n 15e
Kronotskiy B.: USSR 43; 54n 161e
Kronshtadt: USSR 35; 60n 30e
Kroonstad: S. Africa 69; 28s 27e
Krotoszyn: Poland 35; 52n 17e
Kruševac: Yugoslavia 27; 44n 21e
Kuala Lumpur: Malaya 51; 3n 102e
Kuantan: Malaya 51; 4n 103e

*See Page 131

Page; Lat. Long.
Kuban': r., USSR 44; 45n 38e
*Kuching: Sarawak 51; 2n 110e
*Kudat: N. Borneo 51; 7n 117e
Kufra Oases: Libya 67; 25n 22e
Kufstein: Austria 33; 48n 12e
Kukës: Albania 31; 42n 20e
Kukiang: China 53; 30n 116e
Kukong: China 50; 25n 113e
Kulmbach: Germany 32; 50n 12e
Kulunda Steppe: USSR 45; 52n 78e
Kulundinskoye, L.: USSR 45; 53n 80e
Kumamoto: Japan 54; 33n 131e
Kumasi: Ghana 68; 7n 2w
Kunashir: i., USSR 55; 44n 146e
Kunene: r., Africa 69; 17s 13e
Kungrad: USSR 45; 43n 59e
Kunlun Mts.: China 47; 36n 80e
Kunming: China 50; 25n 103e
Kuopio: Finland 34; 63n 28e
Kupang: Timor 51; 10s 124e
Kurashiki: Japan 54; 35n 134e
Kurdistan: Tur. Iran 49; 37n 45e
Kure: Japan 54; 34n 133e
Kurgan: USSR 45; 56n 65e
Kuria Muria Is.: Arabian Sea 49; 17n 56e
Kuril Is.: USSR 92; 45n 150e
Kurnool: India 52; 16n 78e
Kurow: NZ 55; 45s 170e
Kursk: USSR 44; 52n 36e
Kurume: Japan 54; 33n 131e
Kushiro: Japan 55; 43n 144e
Kushka: Afghanistan 45; 36n 62e
Kushva: USSR 45; 58n 60e
Kustanay: USSR 45; 53n 64e
Kütahya: Turkey 31; 39n 30e
Kutaisi: USSR 44; 42n 42e
Kutaradja: Sumatra 47; 5n 95e
Kutno: Poland 35; 52n 19e
Kutum: Sudan 48; 14n 24e
Kuusjärvi: Finland 34; 63n 29e
KUWAIT 49; 29n 47e
Kuybyshev: USSR 44; 53n 50e
Kuybyshev: USSR 45; 56n 79e
Kuyeh: China 53; 35n 116e
Kuzbass: USSR 45; 55n 85e
Kwanghwa: China 53; 32n 112e
Kwangsi Chuan Auton. Region: China 53; 24n 108e
Kwantung: Prov., China 53; 23n 113e
Kweichow: Prov., China 53; 27n 107e
Kweichu: China 50; 27n 107e
Kweilin: China 53; 25n 110e
Kweisu: China 53; 41n 112e
Kweiyang: China 50; 27n 107e
Kyoga, L.: Uganda 70; 2n 33e
Kyoga Pt.: Japan 54; 36n 135e
Kyongju: S. Korea 54; 36n 129e
Kyongsong: S. Korea 50; 38n 127e
Kyoto: Japan 54; 35n 136e
Kyushu: i., Japan 54; 32n 131e
Kyustendil: Bulgaria 31; 42n 23e
Kyzyl: USSR 43; 52n 95e
Kyzyl-Kum: USSR 45; 43n 65e
Kzyl-Orda: USSR 45; 45n 65e

La Albuera: Spain 25; 39n 7w
La Baule: France 28; 47n 2w
Labe: r., Czech. 32; 50n 14e
Labrador: Canada 79; 54n 60w
La Bastide: France 29; 45n 1w
*Labuan: i., N. Borneo 51; 5n 115e
Lacapelle-Marival: Fr. 29; 45n 2e
Lacaune, M. de: France 29; 44n 3e
*Laccadive Is.: Arabian Sea 47; 13n 72e
La Châtre: France 29; 47n 2e
La Chaux: France 29; 47n 6e
La Chaux de Fonds: Switzerland 33; 47n 7e
Lachlan: r., Australia 61; 34s 145e
Lachute: Canada 85; 46n 74w
La Ciotat: France 29; 43n 6e
Lackawanna: USA 85; 43n 79w
Lac Léman: Switz. 33; 46n 6e
La Coruña: Spain 25; 43n 8w
Lacq: France 29; 43n 1w
La Crosse: USA 84; 44n 91w
Ladakh Range: Kashmir 52; 33n 78e
Ladismith: S. Africa 69; 34s 21e
Ladoga, L.: USSR 44; 61n 31e
Lady Elliot I.: Aust. 60; 24s 153e
Lady Newnes Ice Shelf: Antarctica 91; 74s 168e
Ladysmith: S. Africa 69; 29s 30e
Ladysmith: USA 84; 45n 91w
*Lae: New Guinea 59; 7s 147e
Lafayette: USA 84; 41n 87w
La Flèche: France 28; 48n 0
Lågen: r., Norway 34; 62n 10e
Laghouat: Algeria 66; 34n 3e
Lagos: Nigeria 68; 6n 3e
Lagos: Portugal 25; 37n 9w
*La Goulette: Tunisia 30; 37n 10e
La Grande: USA 80; 46n 118w
La Guaira: Venez. 86; 10n 67w
*Lahej: Aden 49; 13n 45e
Lahn: r., Germany 32; 50n 8e
Lahore: W. Pakistan 52; 32n 74e
Lahr: Germany 33; 48n 8e
Lahti: Finland 35; 61n 26e
La Junta: USA 80; 38n 104w
Lake Charles: USA 81; 30n 93w
Lake Eyre South: Aust. 61; 29s 138e
Lake of the Ozarks: USA 84; 38n 93w
Lake of the Woods: Canada 81; 49n 94w
Lakhimpur: India 52; 28n 81e
La Linea: Spain 25; 36n 5w
La Louvière: Belgium 28; 50n 4e
Lamballe: France 28; 48n 3w
Lamia: Greece 31; 39n 22e
La Montana: Peru 86; 12s 72w
Lampedusa: i., Italy 30; 35n 13e
Lanak P.: Kash./China 52; 34n 80e
Lancaster: Ohio, USA 84; 40n 83w
Lancaster: Pa., USA 85; 40n 76w
Lancaster Sd.: Canada 79; 74n 83w

Page; Lat. Long
Lanchow: China 53; 36n 104e
Lanciano: Italy 30; 42n 14e
Landau: Germany 33; 49n 13e
Landerneau: France 28; 48n 4w
Landeshut: Poland 27; 51n 16e
Landsberg: Poland 35; 53n 15e
Landshut: Germany 33; 49n 12e
Langensalza: Germany 32; 51n 11e
Langeoog: i., Germany 32; 54n 7e
Langon: France 29; 45n 0
Langreo: Spain 25; 43n 6w
Langres: & plat., Fr. 28; 48n 5w
Languedoc: France 29; 44n 4e
Lannion: France 28; 49n 4w
Lans, M. de: France 29; 45n 5e
Lansing: USA 84; 43n 85w
Lanzarote: i., Canary Is. 66; 29n 14w
Lao Kay: N. Viet Nam 53; 22n 104e
Laon: France 28; 50n 4e
La Oroya: Peru 86; 12s 76w
LAOS 51; 18n 105e
Lapalisse: France 29; 46n 4e
La Paz: Bolivia 86; 17s 68w
Lapland: Scandinavia 34; 68n 25e
La Plata: Argentina 88; 35s 58w
Lappeenranta: Finland 35; 61n 28e
Laptev Sea 43; 75n 125e
Laptev Str.: USSR 43; 73n 142e
Larache: Morocco 25; 35n 6w
Laramie: Pk., USA 80; 41n 106w
Larche: France 29; 44n 7e
Laredo: USA 80; 28n 100w
Lārestan: Iran 49; 28n 54e
La Rioja: Argentina 88; 29s 67w
Larisa: Greece 31; 39n 22e
La Rochelle: France 29; 46n 1w
La Roche-sur-Yon: Fr. 29; 47n 1w
Larsen Ice Shelf: Antarc. 91; 67s 64w
La Serena: Chile 88; 30s 72w
La Seyne-sur-mer: Fr. 29; 43n 6e
Lashio: Burma 50; 23n 97e
Las Marismas: Spain 25; 37n 6w
Las Palmas: Canary Is. 66; 28n 16w
La Spezia: Italy 33; 44n 10e
Lassalle: France 29; 44n 4e
Lassen Peak: USA 80; 41n 122w
Lastoursville: Gabon 71; 1s 13e
Lastovo: i., Yugo. 27; 43n 17e
Las Vegas: USA 80; 36n 115w
Las Yungas: Bolivia 86; 16s 67w
Latakia: Syria 48; 35n 36e
Latium: Italy 30; 42n 13e
La Tour-du-Pin: Fr. 29; 45n 5e
La Trappe: Canada 85; 45n 74w
La Tuque: Canada 85; 47n 73w
Latvian SSR: USSR 44; 57n 25e
Launceston: Tasmania 59; 42s 147e
Laurentide Park: Can. 85; 48n 71w
Laurie I.: Antarc. 91; 61s 44w
Lausanne: Switzerland 33; 47n 7e
Laut: i., Borneo 51; 4s 116e
Lawgi: Australia 60; 25s 151e
Lawra: Ghana 68; 11n 3w
Lawrence: USA 85; 43n 71w
Laval: France 28; 48n 1w
Laverton: Australia 60; 29s 122e
Leamington: Canada 84; 42n 83w
LEBANON 48; 34n 36e
Lebanon: USA 85; 40n 76w
Le Blanc: France 29; 47n 1e
Lebu: Chile 88; 38s 74w
Le Cateau: France 28; 50n 4e
Lecce: Italy 31; 40n 18e
Lecco: Italy 33; 46n 9e
Lech: r., Ger. Aus. 33; 48n 11e
Le Chambon-Feugerolles: France 29; 45n 4e
Lechtal: Austria 33; 47n 10e
Le Conquet: France 28; 48n 5w
Le Creusot: France 29; 47n 4e
Le Croisic: France 28; 47n 3w
Lectoure: France 29; 44n 1e
Leer: Germany 32; 53n 7e
Leeton: Australia 61; 35s 147e
Leeuwarden: Neth. 32; 53n 6e
Leeuwin, C.: Australia 60; 34s 115e
Leeward Is.: W. Indies 83; 17n 62w
Legaspi: Philippines 51; 13n 124e
Leghorn: Italy 33; 44n 10e
Legnano: Italy 33; 46n 9e
Leh: Kashmir 52; 34n 78e
Le Havre: France 28; 49n 0
Lehrte: Germany 32; 52n 10e
Leichhardt Ra.: Aust. 60; 21s 148e
Leiden: Netherlands 32; 52n 5e
Leigh Creek: Aust. 61; 30s 138e
Leikanger: Norway 34; 61n 7e
Leipzig: Germany 32; 51n 12e
Lek: r., Netherlands 32; 52n 5e
*Le Kef: Tunisia 30; 36n 9e
Les Landes: France 29; 44n 1w
Le Mans: France 28; 48n 0
Lemnos: i., Greece 31; 40n 25e
Le Monastier: France 29; 45n 4e
Lena: r., USSR 43; 65n 125e
Leninabad: USSR 45; 40n 70e
Leninakan: USSR 44; 41n 44e
Leningrad: USSR 44; 60n 30e
Leninogorsk: USSR 45; 50n 84e
Lenin Pk.: USSR 45; 39n 73e
Leninskiy: USSR 43; 58n 115e
Leninsk-Kuznetskiy: USSR 45; 55n 86e
Lens: France 28; 50n 3e
Leoben: Austria 27; 47n 15e
León: Mexico 82; 22n 102w
León: Spain 25; 42n 6w
Leonora: Australia 60; 29s 121e
Léopold II, L.: Congo Rep. 71; 2s 18e
*Léopoldville: Congo Rep. 71; 4s 15e
Lepini Mts.: Italy 30; 41n 13e
Lepontine Alps: Switzerland Italy 33; 46n 8e
Le Puy: France 29; 45n 4e
Lérida: Spain 25; 42n 1e
Leros: i., Greece 31; 37n 27e
Les Bains-du-Mont-Dore: France 29; 46n 3e

Page; Lat. Long.
Les Baux: France 29; 44n 5e
Lesbos: i., Greece 31; 39n 26e
Les Mts. Faucilles: Fr. 28; 48n 6e
Les Sables d'Olonne: Fr. 29; 47n 2w
Les Saintes: is., W. Ind. 83; 16n 62w
Les Saintes Maries: Fr. 29; 43n 4e
Les Sept Îles: France 28; 49n 4w
Lesser Antilles 83; 15n 61w
Lethbridge: Canada 80; 50n 113w
Leticia: Colombia 86; 4s 70w
L'Étoile, Chaîne de: Fr. 29; 43n 6e
Le Touquet: France 28; 51n 2e
Le Tréport: France 28; 50n 1e
Leuven: Belgium 28; 51n 5e
Leveque, C.: Australia 58; 16s 123e
Le Verdon: France 29; 46n 1w
Leverkusen: Germany 32; 51n 7e
Levice: Czechoslovakia 27; 48n 19e
Le Vigan: France 29; 44n 4e
Levis: Canada 85; 47n 71w
Lewis Pass: NZ 55; 42s 173e
Lewiston: USA 85; 44n 70w
Lewistown: USA 85; 41n 78w
Lexington: Ky., USA 84; 38n 84w
Lexington: Mass., USA 85; 42n 71w
Lexington: N.C., USA 84; 36n 80w
Leyburn: Australia 60; 28s 152e
Leydsdorp: S. Africa 69; 24s 31e
Leyre: r., France 29; 44n 1w
Leyte: i., Philippines 51; 11n 125e
Lhasa: China 47; 30n 91e
L'Hospitalet: France 29; 42n 2e
Liao: r., China 53; 41n 122e
Liaoning: China 53; 42n 122e
Liaotung Penin.: China 53; 40n 122e
Liaoyang: China 53; 42n 123e
Liard: r., Canada 78; 61n 122w
Liberec: Czech. 27; 51n 15e
LIBERIA 66; 7n 9w
Libourne: France 29; 45n 0
Libreville: Gabon 70; 0 9e
LIBYA 66 67; — —
Libyan Desert 67; 25n 25e
Libyan Plat.: Egypt 67; 30n 26e
Licata: Sicily 30; 37n 14e
Lichtenburg: S. Africa 69; 26s 26e
Lida: USSR 35; 54n 25e
Lidköping: Sweden 35; 59n 13e
LIECHTENSTEIN 33; 47n 10e
Liège: Belgium 28; 51n 6e
Lieksa: Finland 34; 63n 30e
Lienz: Austria 33; 47n 13e
Liepāja: USSR 35; 57n 21e
Lier: Belgium 28; 51n 5e
Liestal: Switzerland 33; 47n 8e
Liévin: France 28; 50n 3e
Ligny: Belgium 28; 51n 5e
Liguria: Italy 33; 44n 9e
Ligurian Alps: Italy 33; 44n 8e
Ligurian Sea 26; 43n 9e
Lille: France 28; 51n 3e
Lillehammer: Norway 35; 61n 10e
Lillie Glacier Tongue: Antarctica 91; 70s 163e
Lillooet: Canada 80; 51n 122w
*Lilongwe: Nyasaland 69; 14s 34e
Lima: Peru 86; 12s 77w
Lima: USA 84; 41n 84w
Limagne: France 29; 46n 3e
Limassol: Cyprus 48; 35n 38e
Limburg: Germany 32; 50n 8e
Limburg: Netherlands 32; 51n 6e
Limoges: France 29; 46n 1e
Limousin: France 29; 46n 1e
Limpopo: r., Africa 69; 23s 32e
Linaro, C.: Italy 30; 42n 12e
Linares: Spain 25; 38n 4w
Lincoln: USA 80; 41n 97w
*Lindi: Tanganyika 68; 10s 40e
Line Is.: Pacific Ocean 93; 0 159w
Lingen: Germany 32; 52n 7e
Lingga: i., Indonesia 51; 0 105e
Linggi: N. Korea 54; 42n 130e
Linguéré: Senegal 66; 15n 15w
Lini: China 53; 35n 118e
Linköping: Sweden 35; 58n 16e
Linz: Austria 33; 48n 14e
Lions, G. of: France 29; 43n 4e
Lipari Is.: Sicily 30; 38n 15e
Lipetsk: USSR 44; 53n 39e
Lippstadt: Germany 32; 52n 8e
Lisbon (Lisboa): Port. 25; 39n 9w
Lisburne, C.: USA 78; 69n 166w
Lishuchen: China 54; 45n 131e
Lisianski: i., Pac. O. 92; 27n 175w
Lisieux: France 28; 49n 0
Lismore: Australia 61; 29s 153e
Lispeszentadorján: Hungary 27; 46n 17e
Lister, Mt.: Antarc. 91; 78s 163e
Litang: China 53; 23n 109e
Lithgow: Australia 61; 33s 150e
Lithuanian SSR: USSR 44; 56n 24e
Little Atlas: mts., Alg. 25; 36n 2e
Little Belt: str., Den. 35; 55n 10e
Little Bitter Lake: Egypt 67; Inset
Little Current: Can. 84; 46n 82w
Little Karroo: S. Africa 69; 34s 22e
Little Rock: USA 81; 35n 93w
Little St. Bernard P.: France Italy 33; 46n 7e
Liuchow: China 53; 24n 109e
Liverpool: Australia 61; 34s 151e
Liverpool Plains: Aust. 61; 31s 150e
Liv Glacier: Antarc. 91; 85s 167w
*Livingstone: N. Rhod. 69; 18s 26e
*Livingstone Falls: Congo Rep. 71; 5s 14e
Livingston I.: Antarc. 91; 63s 60w
*Livingstonia: Nyasa. 68; 10s 34e
Livorno: Italy 33; 44n 10e
Livradois, Massif du: France 29; 45n 3e
Ljubliana: Yugoslavia 27; 46n 15e
Ljunga: r., Sweden 34; 63n 16e
Llano Estacado: USA 80; 33n 102w
Llanos de Guarayos: Bolivia 86; 15s 63w
Llanos de Urgel: Spain 25; 41n 1e
Lo: r., China 53; 37n 109e

Page; Lat. Long.
Lobito: Angola 69; 12s 13e
Locarno: Switzerland 33; 46n 9e
Lodi: Italy 33; 45n 9e
Lodwar: Kenya 68; 3n 35e
Łódź: Poland 35; 52n 20e
Lofoten Is.: Norway 34; 68n 14e
Lofty, Mt.: Australia 61; 35n 139e
Logan: Mt.: Canada 78; 60n 140w
Logansport: USA 84; 41n 86w
Logroño: Spain 25; 42n 2w
Loir: r., France 28; 48n 1e
Loire: r., France 29; 47n 1w
Loja: Ecuador 86; 4s 79w
Lokchong: China 53; 25n 113e
Lokoja: Nigeria 68; 8n 7e
Lolland: i., Denmark 35; 55n 11e
Lombardy: Italy 33; 46n 9e
Lomblen: i., Indon. 51; 8s 123e
Lombok: i., Indon. 51; 8s 116e
Lomé: Togo 68; 6n 1e
Lommel: Belgium 28; 51n 5e
Łomża: Poland 35; 53n 22e
London: Canada 84; 43n 81w
Long Beach: USA 80; 34n 118w
Long I.: Australia 60; 22s 150e
Long I.: USA 85; 41n 73w
Longreach: Australia 59; 23s 144e
Longs Peak: USA 80; 40n 106w
Longuyon: France 28; 49n 6e
Longwy: France 28; 49n 6e
Lønsdal: Norway 34; 67n 15e
Lons-le-Saunier: Fr. 29; 47n 6e
Lopei: China 50; 48n 131e
Lopez, C.: Gabon 70; 1s 8e
Lorain: USA 84; 41n 82w
Lorca: Spain 25; 38n 2w
Lorestān: Iran 49; 33n 48e
Lorient: France 28; 48n 3w
Lörrach: Germany 33; 48n 8e
Lorraine: France 28; 49n 6e
Los Alamos: USA 80; 36n 106w
Los Andes: Chile 88; 33s 71w
Los Angeles: USA 80; 34n 118w
Lot: r., France 29; 44n 1e
Loue: r., France 29; 47n 6e
*Louisiade Arch.: New Guinea 59; 11s 152e
Louisiana: USA 81; 32n 93w
Louis Trichardt: South Africa 69; 23s 30e
Louisville: USA 84; 38n 86w
Loukhi: USSR 34; 66n 34e
Lourdes: France 29; 43n 0
*Lourenço Marques: Mozambique 69; 26s 32e
Lowell: USA 85; 43n 71w
Lower California: Mex. 82; 30n 115w
Lower Red Lake: USA 84; 48n 95w
Lower Tunguska: r., USSR 43; 64n 95e
Loyalty Is.: Pac. O. 92; 20s 165e
Loyang: China 53; 35n 112e
Lu: r., China 50; 31n 96e
Lualaba: r., Congo 71; 7s 27e
Luanda: Angola 71; 9s 13e
Luangprabang: Laos 50; 20n 102e
*Luanshya: N. Rhod. 69; 13s 28e
Lubbock: USA 80; 34n 102w
Lübeck: & B., Ger. 32; 54n 11e
Lubéron, M. du: Fr. 29; 44n 6e
Lublin: Poland 35; 51n 22e
Lucca: Italy 33; 44n 11e
Lučenec: Czech. 27; 48n 20e
Lucerne: & L., Switz. 33; 47n 8e
Luckenwalde: Ger. 32; 52n 13e
Lucknow: India 52; 27n 81e
Lüdenscheid: Ger. 32; 51n 8e
Lüderitz: SW. Africa 69; 27s 15e
Ludhiana: India 52; 31n 76e
Ludington: USA 84; 44n 86w
Ludwigsburg: Ger. 32; 49n 9e
Ludwigshafen: Ger. 32; 50n 8e
Ludwigslust: Germany 32; 53n 12e
Ludvika: Sweden 35; 60n 15e
Luga: USSR 35; 59n 30e
Lugano: Switzerland 33; 46n 9e
*Lugansk: USSR 44; 48n 39e
Lugo: Spain 25; 43n 7w
Lugoj: Romania 31; 46n 22e
Luhsien: China 53; 29n 106e
Luichow Penin.: China 53; 21n 110e
Luitpold Coast: Antarc. 91; 78s 30w
Lukuga: r., Congo Rep. 68; 6s 28e
Luleå: Sweden 34; 66n 22e
Lüleburgaz: Turkey 31; 41n 27e
*Luluabourg: Congo 71; 6s 22e
Lund: Sweden 35; 56n 13e
Lunéville: France 28; 49n 7e
Lüneburg: & Heath, Ger. 32; 53n 10e
Lungkiang: China 50; 47n 124e
Lungsi: China 53; 35n 105e
Lure: France 28; 48n 6e
*Lusaka: N. Rhodesia 69; 15s 28e
*Lusambo: Congo Rep. 71; 5s 23e
Lushai Hills: India 53; 23n 93e
Lussac-les-Châteaux: France 29; 46n 1e
Lutsk: USSR 35; 51n 25e
Lützow-Holm Bay: Antarctica 91; 69s 38e
LUXEMBOURG 32; 50n 6e
Luxor: Egypt 67; 26n 33e
Luzern: Switzerland 33; 47n 8e
Luzon: i., Philippines 51; 15n 121e
Luzy: France 29; 47n 4e
L'vov: USSR 44; 50n 24e
Lyakhov Is.: USSR 43; 74n 142e
*Lyallpur: W. Pakistan 52; 32n 73e
Lydda: Holy Land 48; Inset
Lydenburg: S. Africa 69; 25s 30e
Lynchburg: USA 85; 37n 79w
Lynn: USA 85; 42n 71w
Lynn Lake: Canada 78; 57n 101w
Lyonnais: France 29; 46n 4e
Lyons (Lyon): France 29; 46n 5e
Lys: r., France 28; 51n 3e
Lys'va: USSR 45; 58n 58e
Lyttelton: NZ 55; 43s 173e
Lytton: Canada 80; 50n 121w

Page; Lat. Long.
Ma'ān: Jordan 48; 30n 36e
Maarianhamina: Åland Is. 35; 60n 20e
Maas: r., Netherlands 32; 52n 6e
Maastricht: Belgium 28; 51n 6e
Macao: (Port.) China 53; 22n 113e
Macchu Picchu: Peru 86; 13s 73w
McClintock, Mt.: Antarctica 91; 80s 160e
Macdonnell Ranges: Australia 58; 24s 132e
Macedonia: Yugo. Grc. 31; 41n 23e
Maceió: Brazil 87; 10s 36w
Macequece: Moz. 69; 19s 33e
Macerata: Italy 30; 44n 14e
Machichaco, C.: Spain 25; 43n 3w
Macintyre: r., Australia 61; 29s 150e
Mackay: Australia 60; 21s 149e
Mackay, L.: Australia 58; 22s 129e
*Mackenzie: Br. Guiana 87; 6n 58w
Mackenzie: r., Aust. 60; 23s 149e
Mackenzie: r., Canada 78; 67n 130w
Mackenzie B.: Antarc. 91; 69s 72e
Mackenzie B.: Canada 78; 70n 136w
Mackenzie Highway: Canada 78; 58n 118w
Mackenzie Mts.: Canada 78; 63n 130w
Mackinac, Str. of: USA 84; 46n 85w
Mackinaw City: USA 84; 46n 85w
McKinley, Mt.: USA 78; 63n 151w
Macksville: Australia 61; 31s 153e
Macleay: r., Australia 61; 31s 152e
McMurdo Sd.: Antarc. 91; 78s 165e
McMurray: Canada 78; 57n 111w
McNary Dam: USA 80; 46n 119w
Macquarie: r., Aust. 61; 31s 148e
Macquarie I.: Australia 92; 55s 159e
Mâcon: France 29; 46n 5e
Macon: USA 81; 33n 84w
Mac-Robertson Land: Antarctica 91; 70s 68e
MADAGASCAR 71; 20s 47e
Madame I.: Canada 85; 45n 61w
*Madang: New Guinea 59; 5s 146e
Madaoua: Niger 68; 9n 6e
Maddalena P.: Fr. It. 29; 44n 7e
Madeira: i., Atl. O. 66; 33n 17w
Madeira: r., Brazil 86; 5s 61w
Madeleine I.: USA 84; 47n 91w
Madera: Mexico 80; 29n 108w
Madhya Pradesh: India 52; 23n 78e
Madison: USA 84; 43n 89w
Madisonville: USA 84; 37n 87w
Madiun: Java 51; 7s 112e
*Madras: India 52; 13n 80e
Madrid: Spain 25; 40n 4w
Madura: i., Indonesia 51; 7s 113e
Madurai: India 52; 10n 78e
Maebashi: Japan 54; 36n 139e
*Mafeking: S. Africa 69; 26s 26e
*Mafia I.: Tanganyika 68; 8s 40e
Magadan: USSR 43; 60n 150e
Magadi: Kenya 68; 2s 36e
Magallanes: Chile 89; 53s 71w
Magdalena: r., Col. 86; 7n 74w
Magdalena Basin: Col. 86; 9n 74w
Magdalen Is.: Canada 79; 47n 62w
Magdeburg: Germany 32; 52n 12e
Magellan, Str. of: Chile 89; 53s —
Magenta: Italy 33; 45n 9e
Maggiore, L.: Switzerland Italy 33; 46n 9e
Magnet Bay: Antarc. 91; 66s 56e
Magnetic I.: Australia 60; 19s 147e
Magnitogorsk: USSR 45; 53n 59e
Magude: Moz. 69; 25s 33e
Magwe: Burma 50; 20n 95e
Mahanadi: r., India 52; 22n 83e
*Mahenge: Tanganyika 68; 9s 37e
Mahia Penin.: NZ 55; 39s 178e
Mahón: Minorca 25; 40n 4e
Maiduguri: Nigeria 68; 12n 13e
Maimana: Afghanistan 46; 36n 65e
Main: r., Germany 32; 50n 11e
Main Barrier Ra.: Aust. 61; 31s 142e
Maine: France 28; 48n 0
Maine: State, USA 85; 45n 70w
Maine, G. of: USA 85; 43n 70w
Mainz: Germany 32; 50n 8e
Maitland: Australia 61; 33s 152e
Maji: Ethiopia 68; 6n 35e
Majorca: i., Spain 25; 40n 3e
*Majunga: Madagascar 71; 16s 46e
*Makarikari Salt Pan: Bechuanaland 69; 21s 26e
Makassar: & str., Indon. 51; 5s 119e
Makat: USSR 44; 48n 53e
Makeyevka: USSR 44; 48n 38e
Makhachkala: USSR 44; 43n 48e
Makran: Iran 49; 27n 60e
Makran: W. Pakistan 52; Inset
Makurazaki: Japan 54; 31n 130e
Makurdi: Nigeria 68; 8n 9e
Makushino: USSR 45; 55n 67e
Malabar Coast: India 52; 11n 75e
*Malacca: & str., Malaya 51; 2n 102e
Maladetta Massif: Spain France 29; 43n 1e
Málaga: Spain 25; 37n 4w
Malaita: i., Pac. O. 92; 9s 161e
Malakal: Sudan 67; 10n 32e
Malang: Java 51; 8s 113e
Malange: Angola 71; 10s 16e
Mälar, L.: Sweden 35; 59n 17e
Malatya: Turkey 49; 38n 38e
*MALAYA 51; 5n 102e
Malbork: Poland 35; 54n 19e
Malden I: Pac. O. 93; 5s 155w
Maldive Is.: Indian O. 47; 7n 73e
Malekula: i., Pac. O. 59; 16s 167e
Malesherbes: France 28; 48n 2e
MALI, REPUBLIC OF 66; 15n 5w
Malindi: Kenya 68; 3s 40e
Malmberget: Sweden 34; 67n 21e
Malmédy: Belgium 28; 50n 6e
Malmesbury: S. Africa 69; 34s 18e
Malmö: Sweden 35; 56n 13e
Maloja Pass: Switz. 33; 46n 10e
*Malonga: Congo Rep. 71; 10s 23e
Malpelo I.: Colombia 86; 4n 82w
Malplaquet: France 28; 50n 4e

* See Page 131

Page; Lat. Long.

Malta: i., Medit. Sea . 30; 36n 14e
Maluku: i., Indon. . 51; 1n 128e
Malvan: India . 52; 16n 73e
Mammoth Cave Nat. Park: USA . 84; 37n 86w
*Manaar: & G., Ceylon . 52; 8n 80e
Manado: Celebes . 51; 1n 125e
Managua: Nicaragua . 83; 12n 86w
Manama: Bahrain . 49; 26n 51e
Mana Pass: China . 52; 32n 79e
Manapouri, L.: NZ . 55; 45s 168e
Manaus (Manaós): Braz. 86; 3s 60w
Manchester: Iowa, USA 84; 42n 91w
Manchester: N.H., USA 85; 43n 71w
Manchuria: China . 50; 43n 125e
Mandalay: Burma . 50; 22n 96e
Mandasor: India . 52; 24n 75e
Mangalore: India . 52; 13n 75e
Mangyshlak Penin.: USSR . 44; 45n 50e
Manifold, C.: Aust. . 60; 23s 151e
Manila: Philippines . 51; 15n 121e
Manipur: India . 53; 25n 94e
Manisa: Turkey . 31; 39n 28e
Manitoba: Prov., Can. 79; 55n 95w
Manitoba, L.: Canada 80; 51n 99w
Manitoulin I.: Canada 84; 46n 82w
Manitowoc: USA . 84; 44n 88w
Manizales: Colombia 86; 5n 75w
Manjra: r., India . 52; 18n 77e
Mankato: USA . 84; 44n 94w
*Mankoya: N. Rhod. . 69; 15s 25e
Mannheim: Germany 32; 50n 9e
*Manokwari: Neth. New Guinea . 58; 1s 134e
Manresa: Spain . 25; 42n 2e
Mansfeld: Germany . 32; 52n 12e
Mansfield: Australia . 61; 37s 146e
Mansfield: USA . 84; 41n 82w
Manta: Ecuador . 86; 1s 81w
Mantes-Gassicourt: Fr. 28; 49n 2e
Mantua (Mantova): It. 33; 45n 11e
Manus: i., New Guinea 59; 2s 147e
Manzala, L.: Egypt . 67; Inset
Manzanillo: Mexico 82; 19n 104w
Maracaibo: & L., Venez. 86; 11n 72w
Marada: Libya . 48; 29n 19e
Marajó, I. of: Brazil . 87; 1s 50w
Marampa: Sierra Leone 66; 8n 12w
Maranhão: Brazil . 87; 3s 44w
Marañon: r., Peru . 86; 5s 77w
Maraş: Turkey . 44; 38n 37e
Marathon: Greece . 31; 38n 24e
Marble Bar: Australia 58; 21s 120e
Marburg: Germany 32; 51n 9e
Marche: France . 29; 46n 2e
Marches, The: Italy . 33; 44n 13e
Marchienne: Belgium 28; 50n 5e
Marcus I.: Pac. O. . 92; 25n 154e
Mar del Plata: Arg. . 88; 38s 58w
Mardin: Turkey . 49; 37n 41e
Marganets: USSR . 45; 48n 67e
Margarita I.: S. Amer. 86; 11n 64w
Margaritovo: USSR . 54; 43n 135e
Margate: S. Africa . 69; 31s 30e
Margeride, M. de la: Fr. 29; 45n 3e
Marguerite B.: Antarc. 91; 69s 69w
Marianas Is.: Pac. O. 92; 18n 145e
Mariánské Lázně: Czechoslovakia . 32; 50n 13e
Maria van Diemen, C.: New Zealand . 55; 34s 173e
Maribor: Yugoslavia . 27; 47n 16e
*Marie Byrd Land: Antarctica . 91; 80s 140w
Marie-Galante: i., West Indies . 83; 16n 61w
Marienbad: Czech. . 32; 50n 13e
Mariental: SW. Africa 69; 25s 18e
Mariinsk: USSR . 45; 56n 88e
Marinette: USA . 84; 45n 88w
Marion: Ind., USA . 84; 41n 86w
Marion: Ohio, USA . 84; 41n 83w
Marion Reef: Coral Sea 60; 19s 152e
Maritime Alps: Fr./It. 29; 44n 7e
Maritimes, The: Can. 79; 46n 65w
Maritsa: r., Europe . 31; 42n 26e
Markham, Mt.: Antarc. 91; 83s 160e
Markovo: USSR . 43; 65n 170e
Marlborough: Aust. 60; 23s 150e
Marles: France . 28; 51n 2e
Marmande: France . 29; 44n 0
Marmara, S. of: Turkey 31; 41n 28e
Marne: r., France . 28; 49n 4e
Marquesas Is.: Pac. O. 93; 9s 140w
Marquette: USA . 84; 47n 87w
Marrakech: Morocco 66; 32n 8w
Marra Mts.: Sudan . 67; 13n 24e
Marree: Australia . 61; 30s 138e
Marsabit: Kenya . 68; 2n 38e
Marsala: Sicily . 30; 38n 12e
Marseilles: France . 29; 43n 5e
Marshall Is.: Pac. O. 92; 10n 166e
Marshalltown: USA . 84; 42n 93w
Martaban, G. of: Burma 51; 16n 97e
Martha's Vineyard: USA 85; 41n 71w
Martigny: Switzerland 33; 46n 7e
Martiques: France . 29; 43n 5e
Martinique: i., W. Ind. 83; 15n 61w
Martinsburg: USA . 85; 39n 78w
Marton: NZ . 55; 40s 175e
Martos: Spain . 25; 38n 4w
Mary (Merv): USSR . 45; 38n 62e
Maryborough: Queens. Australia . 60; 25s 153e
Maryborough: Victoria, Australia . 61; 37s 144e
Maryland: State, USA 85; 39n 77w
Mascara: Algeria . 25; 35n 0
*Maseru: Basutoland 69; 29s 28e
Mashhad: Iran . 49; 36n 60e
Mashkel: W. Pakistan . 52; Inset
Masira: i., Muscat & 'Oman . 49; 21n 59e
Mason City: USA . 84; 43n 93w
Massachusetts: State, USA . 85; 42n 72w
Massawa: Ethiopia . 67; 15n 39e
Massif Centrale: France 29; 45n 3e
Masterton: NZ . 55; 41s 176e

Page; Lat. Long.

Mastung: W. Pakistan . 52; 29n 67e
*Masulipatnam: India . 52; 16n 81e
*Matadi: Congo Rep. . 71; 6s 13e
Matapan, C.: Greece . 31; 36n 22e
Matatiele: S. Africa . 69; 31s 29e
Mataura: r., NZ . 55; 46s 169e
*Mateka Falls: Congo Rep. . 71; 5s 15e
Matera: Italy . 30; 41n 17e
Mateur: Tunisia . 30; 37n 10e
Mathura: India . 52; 27n 78e
Mato Grosso, Plat. of: Brazil . 87; 15s 53w
*Matopo Hills: S. Rhod. 69; 21s 28e
Matrah: Muscat & 'Oman . 49; 24n 58e
Matruh: Egypt . 48; 31n 27e
Matsang: r., China . 47; 29n 86e
Matsue: Japan . 54; 35n 133e
Matsumoto: Japan . 54; 36n 138e
Matsuyama: Japan . 54; 34n 133e
Matterhorn: mt., Italy/Switzerland . 33; 46n 8e
Mattoon: USA . 84; 39n 88w
Maturín: Venezuela . 86; 10n 63w
Matzen: Austria . 27; 48n 17e
Matzu: i., Formosa . 50; 26n 120e
Maubeuge: France . 28; 50n 4e
Maudheim: Antarctica 91; 71s 11w
Maui: i., Pacific Ocean 93; 20n 155w
Maumee: r., USA . 84; 41n 85w
Maumere: Flores . 51; 8s 122e
*Maun: Bechuanaland 69; 20s 29e
MAURITANIA . 66; 20n 10w
Mawlaik: Burma . 50; 24n 94e
Mawson: Antarctica 91; 68s 62e
Mayenne: & r., France 28; 48n 1w
Maykop: USSR . 44; 45n 40e
Mayoumba: Gabon . 71; 4s 11e
Maywood: USA . 84; 42n 88w
Mazamet: France . 29; 43n 2e
Mazar-i-Sharif: Afghan. 49; 37n 67e
Mazarrón: Spain . 25; 38n 1w
Mazatlán: Mexico . 82; 23n 107w
*Mazoe: S. Rhodesia . 69; 17s 31e
Mbarara: Uganda . 68; 1s 31e
*Mbeya: Tanganyika . 68; 9s 33e
*Mbunga: Tanganyika . 68; 10s 36e
M'Clintock Chan.: Can. 78; 72n 103w
Mead, L.: USA . 80; 36n 114w
Meaux: France . 28; 49n 3e
Mecca: Sa'udi Arabia 49; 21n 40e
Mechelen: Belgium . 28; 51n 5e
Mecklenburg: Germany 32; 54n 12e
Medan: Sumatra . 51; 3n 98e
Medéa: Algeria . 25; 36n 3e
Medellín: Colombia . 86; 6n 76w
Mediaş: Romania . 31; 46n 24e
Medicine Hat: Canada 80; 50n 111w
Medina: Sa'udi Arabia 49; 24n 39e
Mediterranean Sea . 30 31; — —
Medjerda: r., Tunisia 30; 36n 9e
Medjez-el-Bab: Tunisia 30; 36n 10e
Mednogorsk: USSR . 45; 52n 58e
Médoc: France . 29; 45n 1w
Meerut: India . 52; 29n 78e
Mega: Ethiopia . 67; 4n 38e
Megantic: Canada . 85; 46n 71w
Megara: Greece . 31; 38n 23e
Megiddo: Holy Land . 48; Inset
Meiningen: Germany 32; 51n 10e
Meissen: Germany . 32; 51n 14e
Mekong: r., SE. Asia 51; 15n 106e
Melanesia: Pac. O. . 92; — —
Melbourne: Australia 61; 38s 145e
Melbourne: USA . 81; 28n 81w
Melilla: (Sp.), Mor. . 66; 35n 3w
Melun: France . 28; 48n 3e
Melville Bay: Grnld. 79; 70n 63w
Melville I.: Australia 58; 12s 131e
Melville I.: Canada . 78; 75n 110w
Memel: USSR . 35; 56n 21e
Memmingen: Germany 33; 48n 10e
Memphis: Egypt . 67; 30n 31e
Memphis: USA . 84; 35n 90w
Menderes: r., Turkey 31; 38n 29e
Mendoza: Argentina 88; 33s 69w
Mène: Congo . 70; 2n 17e
Menemen: Turkey . 31; 39n 27e
Mengtsz: China . 53; 23n 103e
Menindee: & L., Aust. 61; 32s 142e
Menominee Range: USA 84; 46n 89w
Mentawai Is.: Indon. 51; 2s 99e
Menton: France . 29; 44n 7e
Menzies: Australia . 60; 30s 121e
Meppel: Netherlands 32; 53n 6e
Merano: Italy . 33; 47n 11e
*Merauke: Neth. New Guinea 58; 8s 140e
Mercara: India . 52; 12n 76e
Mergui: & arch., Burma 51; 12n 97e
Meribah: Australia . 61; 35s 141e
Mérida: Mexico . 82; 21n 90w
Mérida: Spain . 25; 39n 6w
Meridian: USA . 81; 32n 89w
Merinda: Australia . 60; 20s 148e
Merowe: Sudan . 48; 18n 32e
Merredin: Australia 60; 31s 118e
Merrimack: r., USA 85; 43n 72w
Merseburg: Germany 32; 51n 12e
Mersin: Turkey . 48; 37n 35e
Mertz Glacier: Antarc. 91; 67s 146e
Meru: Kenya . 68; 0 38e
Merv (Mary): USSR . 45; 38n 62e
Mesabi Range: USA . 84; 47n 93w
Mesolongion: Greece 31; 38n 21e
Messina: Sicily . 30; 38n 16e
Messina: S. Africa . 69; 22s 30e
Mesta: r., Bulg. Grc. 31; 42n 24e
Mestre: Italy . 33; 46n 12e
Mettur: India . 52; 12n 78e
Metz: France . 28; 49n 6e
Meuse: r., Belgium . 28; 50n 5e
Mexicali: Mexico . 80; 33n 115w
Mexican Plateau . 82; 23n 103w
MEXICO . 82; — —
Mexico: USA . 84; 39n 92w
Mexico, G. of . 82 83; — —
Mexico City: Mexico 82; 19n 99w
Mézières: France . 28; 50n 5e

Page; Lat. Long.

Miami: Ariz., USA . 80; 33n 111w
Miami: Fla., USA . 81; 26n 80w
Mīāneh: Iran . 49; 37n 48e
Michaud Pt.: Canada 85; 46n 61w
Michigan: State, USA 84; — —
Michigan, L.: USA . 84; 45n 87w
Michigan City: USA 84; 42n 87w
Michipicoten Harb.: USA . 84; 48n 85w
Michipicoten I.: USA 84; 48n 86w
Micronesia: Pac. O. 92; — —
Middelburg: Neth. . 32; 52n 4e
Middelburg: S. Africa 69; 26s 30e
Middle Atlas: Mor. . 66; 33n 5w
Middlesboro: USA . 84; 37n 84w
Middletown: N.Y., USA 85; 41n 74w
Middletown: Ohio, USA 84; 39n 84w
Middle West: USA . 80 81; —
Midland: Australia . 60; 32s 116e
Midland: Canada . 84; 45n 80w
Midland: USA . 84; 44n 84w
Midnapore: India . 52; 22n 87e
Midway I.: Pac. O. . 92; 29n 179w
Mijares: r., Spain . 25; 40n 1w
Mikkeli: Finland . 34; 62n 27e
Mikuni Mts.: Japan . 54; 37n 139e
Milan (Milano): Italy 33; 45n 9e
Mildura: Australia . 61; 34s 142e
Milford Sound: NZ . 55; 44s 168e
Milk: r., USA . 80; 48n 109w
Millau: France . 29; 44n 3e
Mille Lacs L.: USA . 84; 46n 94w
Mill Glacier: Antarc. 91; 85s 168e
Millicent: Australia 61; 38s 140e
Mill I.: Antarc. . 91; 65s 101e
Milos: i., Greece . 31; 37n 24e
Milparinka: Australia 61; 30s 142e
Milwaukee: USA . 84; 43n 88w
Mimizan: France . 29; 44n 1w
Min: r., China . 53; 27n 117e
Minamata: Japan . 54; 32n 130e
Minaragra: Peru . 86; 11s 77w
Minas Basin: Canada 85; 45n 64w
Minas de Riotinto: Spain 25; 38n 7w
Minas Gerais: Brazil 87; 19s 45w
Mindanao: i., Phil. . 51; 7n 125e
Minden: Germany . 32; 52n 9e
Mindoro: i., Phil. . 51; 13n 121e
Minna: Nigeria . 68; 10n 7e
Minneapolis: USA . 84; 45n 93w
Minnesota: State, USA 81; 47n 95w
Miño: r., Sp. Portugal 25; 42n 8w
Minorca: i., Spain . 25; 40n 4e
Minot: USA . 80; 48n 101w
Minquiers, Plat. des: France . 28; 49n 2w
Minsk: USSR . 44; 54n 28e
Minusinsk: USSR . 45; 54n 91e
Miquelon: i., N. Amer. 79; 47n 56w
Miraflores Locks: Pan. 83; Inset
Miram Shah: W. Pak. 52; 33n 70e
Mirande: France . 29; 43n 0
Mirecourt: France . 28; 48n 6e
Mirtoon Sea: Greece 31; 37n 23e
Mirzapur: India . 52; 25n 83e
Misawa: Japan . 54; 41n 141e
Miskolc: Hungary . 27; 48n 21e
*Misoöl: i., Neth. New Guinea 58; 2s 130e
Missinaibi L.: Canada 84; 48n 84w
Mississippi: r., USA 81; — —
Mississippi: State, USA 81; 33n 90w
Missoula: USA . 80; 47n 114w
Missouri: r., USA 80 81; — —
Missouri: State, USA 81; 38n 92w
Mistassini, L.: Canada 81; 51n 74w
Misurata: Libya . 66; 32n 15e
Mitchell: Australia . 60; 26s 148e
Mitchell: r., Australia 59; 16s 143e
Mitchell: r., Australia 61; 37s 147e
Mitilini: Lesbos . 31; 39n 26e
Mito: Japan . 54; 36n 140e
Mitre I.: Pacific Ocean 59; 12s 170e
Mittelland Canal: Ger. 32; 52n 9e
Mitú: Colombia . 86; 1n 70w
*Mitumba Mts.: Congo Rep. . 68; 8s 28e
Miyako: Japan . 54; 40n 142e
Miyazaki: Japan . 54; 32n 131e
Mizque: Bolivia . 86; 18s 65w
Mjøsa, L.: Norway . 35; 61n 11e
Mława: Poland . 35; 53n 20e
Moab: Holy Land . 48; Inset
Moascar: Egypt . 67; Inset
Mobaye: Cen. Afr. Repub. 67; 4n 21e
Moberly: USA . 84; 39n 92w
Mobile: USA . 81; 31n 88w
Moçâmedes: Angola 69; 15s 12e
Mocimboa da Praia: Mozambique . 68; 11s 10e
Moctezuma: Mexico 80; 30n 110w
Mocuba: Mozambique 69; 17s 37e
Modane: France . 29; 45n 7e
Modder River: S Afr. 69; 29s 25e
Modena: Italy . 33; 45n 11e
Moengo: Surinam . 87; 6n 54w
*Mogadiscio: Somalia 70; 2n 45e
Mogador: Morocco . 66; 31n 10w
Mogilev Podol'skiy: USSR . 31; 49n 28e
Mogocha: USSR . 43; 54n 120e
Mohács: Hungary . 27; 46n 19e
Mohawk: r., USA . 85; 43n 75w
Mointy: USSR . 45; 48n 73e
*Moji: Japan . 54; 34n 131e
*Mokambo: Congo Rep. 69; 12s 28e
Moldau: r., Czech. . 32; 50n 14e
Moldavia: Romania . 31; 46n 27e
Moldavian SSR: USSR 31; 47n 29e
Molde: Norway . 34; 63n 7e
Molfetta: Italy . 30; 41n 17e
Molières: France . 29; 44n 1e
Mollendo: Peru . 86; 17s 72w
Molndal: Sweden . 35; 58n 12e
Molodechno: USSR . 35; 54n 27e
Molopo: r., S. Africa 69; 26s 22e
Moluccas: i., Indonesia 51; 1n 128e
Molucca Sea . 51; 1s 125e
Mombasa: Kenya . 68; 4s 40e

Page; Lat. Long.

Mombetsu: Japan . 55; 44n 143e
MONACO . 29; 44n 7e
Mona Passage: W. Indies 83; 18n 68w
Monastir: Yugoslavia 27; 41n 21e
Monchegorsk: USSR 34; 68n 33e
Mönchen-gladbach: Germany . 32; 51n 7e
Moncton: Canada . 85; 46n 65w
Mondego, C.: Portugal 25; 40n 9w
Mondovi: Italy . 33; 44n 8e
Monessen: USA . 84; 40n 80w
Monfalcone: Italy . 33; 46n 14e
*Mongu: N. Rhodesia 69; 15s 23e
Monroe: USA . 81; 32n 92w
Monrovia: Liberia . 66; 6n 11w
Mons: Belgium . 28; 50n 4e
Montague I.: USA . 78; 60n 148w
Montana: State, USA 80; 47n 110w
Montargis: France . 28; 48n 3e
Montauban: France . 29; 44n 1e
Montbéliard: France 29; 48n 7e
Mont Blanc: Fr./It. . 29; 46n 7e
Mont Cenis P.: Fr./It. 29; 45n 7e
Montdidier: France . 28; 50n 3e
Montego Bay: Jamaica 83; 18n 78w
Monte Bello Is.: Aust. 58; 21s 116e
Monte Carlo: Monaco 29; 44n 7e
Monte Cristo: i., Italy 30; 42n 10e
Montélimar: France . 29; 45n 5e
Montenegro: Yugoslavia 27; 43n 19e
Monterey: USA . 80; 37n 122w
Monterrey: Mexico . 82; 26n 100w
Montes Claros: Brazil 87; 17s 44w
Montevideo: Uruguay 88; 35s 56w
Montgomery: USA . 81; 32n 86w
Mont Joli: Canada . 85; 48n 68w
Mont Laurier: Canada 85; 46n 75w
Montluçon: France . 29; 46n 3e
Montmédy: France . 28; 49n 5e
Montmirail: France . 28; 49n 4e
Montpelier: USA . 85; 44n 73w
Montreal: Canada . 85; 45n 74w
Montreuil: France . 28; 50n 2e
Montreuil Bellay: Fr. 29; 47n 0
Montreux: Switzerland 33; 46n 7e
Mont St. Michel: France 28; 49n 2w
Monts du Charollais: Fr. 29; 47n 4e
Montserrat: i., W. Ind. 83; 17n 62w
Mont Tremblant, Parc de: Canada . 85; 47n 74w
Montvalier, Pic de: Fr. 29; 43n 1e
Monza: Italy . 33; 46n 9e
Moosehead L.: USA . 85; 46n 70w
Moose Jaw: Canada . 80; 50n 106w
Moose Lake: USA . 84; 46n 93w
Moosonee: Canada . 81; 51n 81w
Moradabad: India . 52; 28n 78e
Moravia: Czech. . 27; 49n 17e
Moravian Gate: Czech. 27; 50n 18e
Moravská Ostrava: Czechoslovakia . 27; 50n 18e
Morea: Australia . 61; 37s 141e
Morea: Greece . 31; 38n 22e
Moree: Australia . 61; 29s 150e
Moreton B.: Australia 60; 27s 153e
Morgantown: USA . 84; 40n 80w
Morhiban: France . 28; 48n 3w
Morioka: Japan . 54; 40n 141e
Morjärv: Sweden . 34; 66n 23e
Morkalla: Australia . 61; 34s 141e
Morlaix: France . 28; 49n 4w
MOROCCO . 66; — —
*Morogoro: Tanganyika 68; 7s 38e
Morona: r., S. Amer. 86; 3s 77w
Morotai: i., Indonesia 51; 2n 128e
Morreesburg: S. Africa 69; 33s 18e
Morristown: USA . 84; 36n 83w
Mortara: Italy . 33; 45n 9e
Morvan: France . 29; 47n 4e
Mosbach: Germany . 32; 49n 9e
Moscow: USSR . 44; 56n 38e
Mosel: r., Germany . 32; 50n 7e
Moselle: r., France . 28; 49n 6e
Moselle, Côtes de: Fr. 28; 49n 6e
*Moshi: Tanganyika . 68; 3s 37e
Moss: Norway . 35; 60n 11e
Mossel Bay: S. Africa 69; 34s 22e
Mossgiel: Australia . 61; 33s 145e
Most: Czechoslovakia 32; 51n 14e
Mostaganem: Algeria 25; 36n 0
Mostar: Yugoslavia . 27; 43n 18e
Mosul: 'Iraq . 49; 36n 43e
Motala: Sweden . 35; 59n 15e
Motueka: NZ . 55; 41s 173e
Moulins: France . 29; 47n 3e
Moulmein: Burma . 51; 16n 98e
Mount Desert I.: USA 85; 44n 68w
Mount Eba: Australia 58; 30s 136e
Mount Gambier: Aust. 61; 38s 141e
Mount Isa: Australia 58; 21s 139e
Mount Magnet: Aust. 60; 28s 118e
Mount Morgan: Aust. 60; 23s 150e
Mount Vernon: USA 84; 38n 88w
Moyale: Kenya . 68; 4n 39e
MOZAMBIQUE . 69; 20s 35e
Mozambique: Moz. . 69; 15s 40e
*Mpanda: Tanganyika 68; 6s 31e
*Mporokoso: N. Rhod. 68; 9s 30e
*Mtwara: Tanganyika 68; 10s 40e
Mubi: Nigeria . 68; 10n 13e
*Muchinga Mts.: N. Rhod. 68; 12s 32e
Mudgee: Australia . 61; 33s 150e
Mudros: Lemnos . 31; 40n 25e
Muret: France . 29; 43n 1e
Muğla: Turkey . 31; 37n 28e
Muhammad Qol: Sudan 48; 21n 37e
Mühlhausen: Germany 32; 51n 11e
Mukachevo: USSR . 31; 49n 23e
*Mukalla: Aden. Prot. 49; 14n 49e
Mukden: see Shenyang 53; 42n 123e
Mulberry: USA . 81; 28n 82w
Mulhacen: mt., Spain 25; 37n 3w
Mülheim: Germany . 32; 51n 7e
Mulhouse: France . 28; 48n 7e
Mulingchen: China . 54; 44n 130e
Müller Mts.: Borneo 51; 1n 113e
Mullewa: Australia . 60; 28s 116e
*Mulobezi: N. Rhod. 69; 17s 25e
Multan: W. Pakistan 52; 30n 72e
Muna: i., Indon. . 51; 5s 122e

Page; Lat. Long.

München: Germany . 33; 48n 12e
Muncie: USA . 84; 40n 85w
*Mungbere: Congo Rep. 70; 3n 28e
Munich: Germany . 33; 48n 12e
Munro-Kerr Mts.: Antarctica . 91; 69s 68e
Münster: Germany . 32; 52n 8e
Muonio: r., Swed. Fin. 34; 68n 23e
Mur: France . 28; 48n 3w
Mur: r., Austria . 33; 47n 14e
Murat: France . 29; 45n 3e
Murchison: r., Aust. 58; 26s 116e
Murchison Falls: Uganda . 68; 2n 31e
Murcia: Spain . 25; 38n 1w
Murfreesboro: USA . 84; 36n 86w
Murghab: r., USSR . 49; 37n 62e
Murgon: Australia . 60; 26s 152e
Murmansk: USSR . 34; 69n 33e
Murom: USSR . 44; 56n 42e
Muroran: Japan . 54; 42n 141e
Muroto: C.: Japan . 54; 33n 134e
Murray: r. Australia 61; 35s 139e
Murray Bridge: Aust. 61; 35s 139e
Murree: W. Pakistan 52; 34n 73e
Murrumbidgee: r., Australia . 61; 35s 146e
Murupara: NZ . 55; 38s 177e
Murwillumbah: Aust. 60; 28s 153e
Murzuch: Libya . 48; 26n 14e
Muş: Turkey . 49; 38n 42e
Muscat: Muscat & 'Oman 49; 23n 58e
MUSCAT & 'OMAN . 49; 20n 57e
Muskegon: USA . 84; 43n 86w
Muskogee: USA . 81; 36n 95w
*Musoma: Tanganyika 68; 2s 34e
Mussoorie: India . 52; 30n 78e
Mustafa Kemalpasa: Turkey . 31; 40n 28e
Muswellbrook: Aust. 61; 32s 151e
Mutankiang: China . 50; 45n 130e
Mutano: Angola . 69; 17s 15e
Muyun-Kum: USSR . 45; 44n 70e
Muzaffarpur: India . 52; 27n 85e
*Mwanza: Tanganyika 68; 3s 33e
Mweru, L.: Africa . 68; 9s 29e
*Mwinilunga: N. Rhod. 68; 12s 24e
Mycenae: Greece . 31; 38n 23e
Myitkyina: Burma . 50; 25n 97e
*Mymensingh: E. Pak. 52; 25n 90e
Mysore: India . 52; 12n 77e

Nacala: Mozambique . 69; 15s 41e
*Nachingwea: Tangan. 68; 10s 39e
Nacozari: Mexico . 80; 31n 110w
Næstved: Denmark . 35; 55n 12e
Naft-e Shāh: Iran . 49; 34n 46e
Nafud: Sa'udi Arabia 49; 28n 41e
Naga Hills: Ind. Burma 53; 26n 95e
Nagano: Japan . 54; 37n 138e
Nagaoka: Japan . 54; 37n 139e
Nagapattinam: India 52; 11n 80e
Nagasaki: Japan . 54; 33n 130e
Nagoorin: Australia 60; 24s 151e
Nagoya: Japan . 54; 35n 137e
Nagpur: India . 52; 21n 79e
Nagykanizsa: Hungary 27; 46n 17e
Naha: Okinawa . 50; 26n 128e
Nain: Canada . 79; 57n 62w
Nain: Holy Land . 48; Inset
Naini Tal: India . 52; 29n 79e
Nairobi: Kenya . 68; 1s 37e
Naivasha: Kenya . 68; 1s 36e
Najaf: 'Iraq . 49; 32n 44e
Najd: Sa'udi Arabia 49; 25n 43e
Najran: Sa'udi Arabia 49; 17n 44e
Nakhichevan: USSR 44; 39n 45e
Nakhodka: USSR . 50; 43n 133e
Nakhon Ratchasima: Thailand . 51; 15n 102e
Nakina: Canada . 81; 50n 87w
Nakuru: Kenya . 68; 1s 36e
Nal: r., W. Pakistan 52; Inset
Namangan: USSR . 45; 41n 72e
Nambour: Australia 60; 27s 153e
Namib Desert: SW. Afr. 69; 22s 15e
Namoi: r., Australia 61; 31s 150e
Nampula: Mozambique 69; 15s 39e
Namsos: Norway . 34; 65n 11e
Namur: Belgium . 28; 50n 5e
Nanaimo: Canada . 80; 49n 124w
Nanango: Australia 60; 27s 152e
Nanao: Japan . 54; 37n 137e
Nanchang: China . 53; 28n 116e
Nancheng: China . 53; 33n 107e
Nanchung: China . 53; 31n 106e
Nancy: France . 28; 49n 6e
Nanda Devi: India . 52; 30n 80e
Nangchen Japo: mt., China . 47; 33n 94e
Nanking: China . 53; 32n 118e
Nan Ling: China . 53; 26n 112e
Nanning: China . 53; 23n 108e
Nanping: China . 53; 27n 118e
Nansei Is.: Japan . 50; 27n 127e
Nan Shan: China . 50; 38n 100e
Nantes: France . 29; 47n 2w
Nanticoke: USA . 85; 41n 76w
Nantucket: i., USA . 85; 41n 70w
Nantucket Inlet: Antarctica . 91; 75s 62w
Nantung: China . 53; 32n 121e
Nanumea: i., Pac. O. 92; 5s 176e
Nao, C. de la: Spain 25; 39n 0
Napanee: Canada . 85; 44n 77w
Napier: NZ . 55; 39s 177e
Naples (Napoli): Italy 30; 41n 14e
Nara: Japan . 54; 35n 136e
Naracoorte: Australia 61; 37s 141e
Narbada: r., India . 52; 22n 75e
Narbonne: France . 29; 43n 3e
Narrabri: Australia 61; 30s 150e
Narrandera: Australia 61; 35s 147e
Narrogin: Australia 60; 33s 117e
Narva: USSR . 35; 59n 28e
Narvik: Norway . 34; 68n 17e
Nar'yan Mar: USSR. 42; 68n 53e
Nashua: USA . 85; 43n 71w
Nashville: USA . 84; 36n 87w
Nasik: India . 52; 20n 74e

* See Page 131

Page; Lat. Long.

Naşiriyah: 'Iraq 49; 31n 46e
Nassau: Bahamas 83; 25n 77w
*Nassau Mts.:
West New Guinea 58; 4s 136e
Nässjö: Sweden 35; 58n 15e
Natal: Brazil 87; 6s 35w
Natal: S. Africa 69; 28s 32e
Natchez: USA 81; 32n 91w
*Natron, L.: Tanganyika 68; 2s 36e
Natuna Is.: Indonesia 51; 4n 108e
Naturaliste, C.: Aust. 60; 33s 115e
Nauplia: Greece 31; 37n 23e
Nauru: i., Pac. O. 92; 1s 167e
Navarino, B. of: Grc. 31; 37n 22e
Navarra: Spain 25; 42n 2w
Navoro: Japan 54; 44n 142e
Navrongo: Ghana 68; 11n 1w
Naxos: i., Greece 31; 37n 25e
Nazaré: Brazil 87; 13s 39w
Nazareth: Holy Land 48; Inset
Ndola: N. Rhodesia 68; 13s 28e
Nebit-Dag: USSR 44; 39n 55e
Nebraska: State, USA 80; 42n 100w
Neckar: Germany 32; 49n 9e
Negeb, The: Holy Land 48 Inset
Negro: r., Argentina 88; 40s 65w
Negro: r., Brazil 86; 1s 63w
Negros: i., Philippines 51; 10n 123e
Nehbandān: Iran 49; 32n 60e
Neikiang: China 53; 29n 105e
Neisse: r., Ger./Poland 32; 51n 15e
Neiva: Colombia 86; 3n 75w
Nellore: India 52; 14n 80e
Nelson: NZ 55; 41s 173e
Nelson: r., Canada 79; 56n 94w
Neman: r., USSR 35; 54n 25e
Nemours: France 28; 48n 3e
Nemuro: Japan 55; 43n 146e
Nenana: USA 78; 64n 149w
NEPAL 52; 28n 85e
Nerchinsk: USSR 43; 52n 117e
Neskaupstadhur: Ice. 34; 65n 13w
Nestos: r., Grc./Bulg. 31; 41n 24e
NETHERLANDS 32; 52n 6e
NETH. ANTILLES 86; 12n 69w
Neubrandenburg: Ger. 32; 54n 13e
Neuchâtel: & L., Switz. 33; 47n 7e
Neufchâteau: Belgium 28; 50n 5e
Neufchâteau: France 28; 48n 6e
Neumünster: Germany 32; 54n 10e
Neunkirchen: Germany 32; 49n 7e
Neuquén: Argentina 88; 39s 68w
Neuss: Germany 32; 51n 7e
Neustadt: Germany 32; 49n 8e
Neustrelitz: Germany 35; 53n 13e
Nevada: State, USA 80; 39n 117w
Never: USSR 43; 54n 124e
Nevers: France 29; 47n 4e
Nevis: i., W. Indies 83; 17n 62w
New Albany: USA 84; 38n 86w
New Amsterdam:
British Guiana 87; 6n 57w
*New Amsterdam: i.,
Indian Ocean 92; 38s 78e
Newark: N.J., USA 85; 41n 74w
Newark: Ohio, USA 84; 40n 82w
New Bedford: USA 85; 42n 71w
New Bedford Inlet:
Antarctica 91; 73s 61w
New Bern: USA 81; 35n 77w
*New Britain: i., Aust. 92; 6s 150e
New Brunswick: Can. 85; 47n 67w
New Brunswick: USA 85; 40n 74w
Newburgh: USA 85; 41n 74w
New Caledonia: i.,
Pacific Ocean 92; 21s 165e
New Castile: Spain 25; 39n 3w
Newcastle: Australia 61; 33s 152e
Newcastle: Canada 85; 47n 66w
Newcastle: S. Africa 69; 28s 30e
New Castle: USA 84; 41n 80w
Newdegate: Australia 60; 33s 119e
New Delhi: India 52; 28n 77e
New England: USA 81; 43n 71w
New England Ra.: Aust. 61; 30s 152e
Newenham, C.: USA 78; 58n 162w
Newfoundland: Canada 79; 49n 55w
New Georgia: i., Pac. O. 91; 8s 157e
New Guinea 58/59; — —
New Hampshire: State,
USA 85; 44n 72w
New Haven: USA 85; 41n 73w
New Hebrides: is.,
Pacific Ocean 92; 15s 168e
*New Ireland: i., Aust. 92; 3s 153e
New Jersey: State, USA 85; 40n 75w
New Kensington: USA 84; 41n 80w
New London: USA 85; 41n 72w
New Mexico: State,
USA 80; 35n 105w
New Orleans: USA 81; 30n 90w
New Plymouth: NZ 55; 39s 174e
Newport: Ky., USA 84; 39n 84w
Newport: R.I., USA 85; 41n 71w
Newport News: USA 85; 37n 76w
New South Wales:
Australia 59; 32s 145e
New Westminster: Can. 80; 49n 123w
New York: USA 85; 41n 74w
New York: State, USA 85; 43n 75w
NEW ZEALAND 55; — —
Ngami, L.: Bech. 69; 20s 23e
Ngauruhoe: mt., NZ 55; 39s 176e
Nguru: Nigeria 68; 13n 10e
Nhill: Australia 61; 36s 142e
Niagara Falls: Can./USA 85; 43n 79w
Niamey: Niger 66; 13n 2e
Nias: i., Sumatra 51; 2n 98e
NICARAGUA 83; 13n 85w
Nicaragua, L.: Nic. 83; 11n 85w
Nice: France 29; 44n 7e
Nicobar Is.: India 47; 8n 93e
Nicosia: Cyprus 48; 35n 33e
Niedere Tauern: Aust. 33; 47n 14e
Nienburg: Germany 32; 53n 9e
Nieuwpoort: Belgium 28; 51n 3e
Nieuwveld Ra.: S. Afr. 69; 32s 21e
NIGER 66; 17n 10e
Niger: r., Africa 66; 8n 7e
NIGERIA 68; 10n 10e
Nihau: i., Pac. O. 93; 22n 162w
Nihoa: i., Pac. O. 93; 22n 162w
Niigata: Japan 54; 38n 139e
Nijmegen: Netherlands 32; 52n 6e
Nikko: Japan 54; 37n 140e
Nikolayev: USSR 44; 47n 32e
Nikolayevsk: USSR 43; 53n 140e
Nikopol': USSR 44; 48n 35e
Nile: r., Africa 67; 21n 31e
Niles: USA 84; 42n 86w
Nilgiri Hills: India 52; 11n 77e
Nîmes: France 29; 44n 4e
Nimmitabel: Australia 61; 36s 149e
Nimule: Sudan 67; 4n 32e
Ninety Mile Beach:
Australia 61; 38s 147e
Nineveh: 'Iraq 49; 37n 43e
Ningan: China 54; 44n 130e
Ninghsia: China 53; 38n 106e
Ninghsia Auton. Reg.:
China 53; 37n 106e
Ningpo: China 53; 30n 122e
Ninnis Glac.: Antarc. 91; 68s 147e
Niort: France 29; 46n 0
Nipigon: & L., Canada 81; 49n 88w
Nipissing, L.: Canada 85; 46n 79w
Niš: Yugoslavia 27; 43n 22e
Nisiros: i., Greece 31; 37n 27e
Niterói: Brazil 88; 23s 43w
Nivelles: Belgium 28; 51n 4e
Nivernais: France 29; 47n 4e
Nizhniy-Tagil: USSR 45; 58n 60e
*Nkana: N. Rhodesia 69; 13s 18e
Nobeoka: Japan 54; 33n 132e
Noccundra: Australia 60; 28s 143e
Nogales: Mexico 80; 31n 111w
Nogata: Japan 54; 34n 131e
Nogaysk: USSR 44; 47n 36e
Nogent-sur-Seine: Fr. 28; 48n 3e
Noirmoutier, Î. de: Fr. 28; 47n 2w
Nome: USA 78; 65n 165w
Nonacho L.: Canada 78; 62n 110w
Nootka Sd.: Canada 80; 49n 127w
Noranda: Canada 85; 48n 79w
Norden: Germany 32; 54n 7e
Nordenham: Germany 32; 54n 8e
Norderney: i., Ger. 32; 54n 7e
Nordhausen: Germany 32; 52n 11e
Nordhorn: Germany 32; 52n 7e
Nördlingen: Germany 33; 49n 11e
Nordvik: USSR 43; 74n 111e
Norfolk: USA 85; 37n 76w
Norfolk I.: Pac. O. 92; 29s 168e
Noril'sk: USSR 43; 69n 88e
Norman: r., Australia 59; 19s 142e
Normandie, Collines de:
France 28; 49n 1w
Normandy: France 28; 49n 0
Normanton: Australia 59; 18s 141e
Norman Wells: Can. 78; 65n 127w
Nornalup: Australia 60; 35s 117e
Norris Dam: USA 84; 36n 84w
Norrköping: Sweden 35; 59n 16e
Norseman: Australia 60; 32s 122e
North Adams: USA 85; 43n 73w
Northam: Australia 60; 32s 117e
Northampton: Aust. 60; 28s 115e
North Battleford: Can. 80; 53n 108w
North Bay: Canada 85; 46n 79w
*NORTH BORNEO 51; 5n 117e
North Carolina: USA 85; 36n 79w
Northcliffe: Aust. 60; 35s 116e
North Dakota: USA 80; 48n 100w
North Dvina: r., USSR 44; 62n 45e
Northern: Prov., Sudan 48; 20n 30e
Northern: Reg., Nigeria 68; 10n 7e
*NORTHERN
RHODESIA 69; 15s 30e
Northern Sporades:
Greece 31; 39n 24e
Northern Territory:
Australia 58; 20s 135e
Northern Territory:
Ghana 68; 10n 1w
North Frisian Is.: Ger. 35; 55n 8e
North Island: NZ 55; — —
NORTH KOREA 50; 40n 127e
Northland: NZ 55; 36s 174e
North Magnetic
Pole 1962 78; 75n 100w
North Platte: USA 80; 41n 101w
North Sea 26; — —
North Sos'va: r., USSR 42; 63n 63e
North Stradbroke I.:
Australia 60; 28s 153e
North Tonawanda: USA 85; 43n 79w
Northumberland Is.:
Australia 60; 21s 150e
Northumberland Str.:
Canada 85; 46n 63w
*NORTH VIET NAM 53; 22n 105e
Northwest Territories:
Canada 78/79; — —
Norton Sd.: USA 78; 64n 163w
Norvegia, C.: Antarc. 91; 71s 12w
NORWAY 34/35; — —
Norwood: USA 84; 39n 84w
Noshiro: Japan 54; 40n 140e
Nossi Bé: Madag. 71; 13s 48e
Nossob: r., S. Africa 69; 26s 21e
Noto Penin.: Japan 54; 37n 137e
Notre Dame Mts.: Can. 85; 48n 67w
Nouakchott: Mauritania 66; 18n 16w
Nouméa: N. Caledonia 92; 22s 167e
*Nova Lisboa: Angola 71; 13s 16e
Novara: Italy 33; 45n 9e
Nova Scotia: Canada 85; Inset
Novaya Zemlya: USSR 42; 74n 60e
Novgorod: USSR 44; 58n 31e
Novi Ligure: Italy 33; 45n 9e
Novi Pazar: Yugo. 27; 43n 20e
Novi Sad: Yugoslavia 27; 45n 20e
Novocherkassk: USSR 44; 47n 40e
Novograd Volynskiy:
USSR 35; 51n 28e
Novogrudok: USSR 35; 54n 26e
Novokuznetsk: USSR 45; 53n 87e
Novomoskovsk: USSR 44; 54n 38e
Novonazyvayevka:
USSR 45; 56n 72e
Novo Redondo: Angola 68; 11s 14e
Novorossiysk: USSR 44; 45n 38e
Novosibirsk: USSR 45; 55n 83e
Novosibirskiye Ostrova:
USSR 43; 75n 140e
Novouzensk: USSR 44; 51n 48e
Novyy Port: USSR 42; 68n 72e
Nowa Huta: Poland 27; 50n 20e
Nowy Sącz: Poland 27; 49n 21e
Nsuta: Ghana 68; 5n 2w
Nubian Desert: Sudan 67; 21n 33e
Nučice: Czechoslavia 27; 50n 14e
Nueva Rosita: Mexico 80; 28n 101w
Nuits-St. Georges: Fr. 29; 47n 5e
Nuku Hiva: i., Pac. O. 93; 10s 140w
Nullarbor Plain: Aust. 58; 30s 128e
Numazu: Japan 54; 35n 139e
Nundle: Australia 61; 31s 151e
Nunivak: i., USA 78; 60n 166w
Nunkiang: China 50; 49n 125e
Nuoro: Sardinia 30; 40n 9e
Nuremberg (Nürnberg):
Germany 32; 49n 11e
Nuseybin: Turkey 49; 37n 41e
Nushki: W. Pakistan 52; Inset
*Nuwara Eliya: Ceylon 52; 7n 81e
Nyahwest: Australia 61; 35s 144e
Nyala: Sudan 67; 12n 25e
*Nyasa, L.: Africa 68; 12s 34e
*NYASALAND 69; 13s 34e
Nyenchen Tanglha Ra.:
China 47; 30n 90e
Nyeri: Kenya 68; 1s 32e
Nykøbing: Denmark 35; 55n 12e
Nyköping: Sweden 35; 59n 17e
Nymburk: Czech. 27; 50n 15e
Nyngan: Australia 61; 31s 147e
Nyon: Switzerland 33; 46n 6e
Nyíregyháza: Hungary 27; 48n 22e
Nysa: Poland 27; 50n 17e

Oahu: i., Pacific Ocean 93; 21n 158w
Oakland: USA 80; 38n 122w
Oak Ridge: USA 84; 36n 84w
Oamaru: NZ 55; 45s 171e
Oates Coast: Antarctica 91; 70s 160e
Ob': r., USSR 43; 58n 82e
Oba: Canada 84; 49n 84w
Obbia: Somalia 70; 5n 48e
Oberammergau: Ger. 33; 48n 11e
Oberhausen: Germany 32; 52n 7e
Obidos: Brazil 87; 2s 56w
Obihiro: Japan 55; 43n 143e
Obi Is.: Indonesia 51; 2s 128e
Ocean I.: Pacific Ocean 92; 1s 170e
Ochakov: USSR 31; 46n 31e
Odda: Norway 35; 60n 7e
Ödemis: Turkey 31; 38n 28e
Odense: Denmark 35; 55n 10e
Odenwald: Germany 32; 50n 9e
Oder: r., Ger./Poland 32; 53n 15e
Odessa: USSR 44; 46n 31e
Odorhei: Romania 31; 46n 25e
Odra: r., Ger./Poland 32; 53n 15e
Oeno I.: Pacific Ocean 93; 24s 130w
Offenburg: Germany 33; 48n 8e
Ofot Fiord: Norway 34; 68n 16e
Ogaden: Ethiopia 67; 7n 43e
Ogaki: Japan 54; 35n 137e
Ogden: USA 80; 41n 112w
Oglio: r., Italy 33; 45n 10e
Ogoja: Nigeria 68; 6n 9e
Ohai: NZ 55; 46s 168e
Ohakune: NZ 55; 39s 175e
Ohata: Japan 54; 41n 141e
Ohio: r., USA 84; 37n 89w
Ohio: State, USA 84; 40n 83w
Ohře: r., Czech. 32; 50n 14e
Oil City: USA 84; 41n 80w
Oise: r., France 28; 49n 2e
Oita: Japan 54; 33n 132e
Ojos del Salado: mt.,
Chile/Argentina 88; 27s 68w
Oka: r., USSR 44; 55n 42e
Okanogan: r., Can./USA 80; 49n 120w
Okayama: Japan 54; 35n 134e
Okazaki: Japan 54; 35n 137e
Okeechobee, L.: USA 81; 27n 81w
Okha: India 52; 22n 68e
Okhotsk: USSR 43; 59n 143e
Okhotsk, Sea of: USSR 43; 55n 150e
Oki Is.: Japan 54; 36n 133e
Okinawa: i., Japan 50; 26n 128e
Oklahoma: State, USA 80; 36n 98w
Oklahoma City: USA 80; 36n 98w
Okovango: r., Africa 69; 18s 21e
*Okovango Basin: Bech. 69; 20s 23e
Okuma B.: Antarctica 91; 78s 159w
Okushiri I.: Japan 54; 42n 139e
Öland: i., Sweden 35; 57n 17e
Olbia: Sardinia 30; 41n 10e
Old Castile: Spain 25; 42n 4w
Oldenburg: Germany 32; 53n 8e
Oldenzaal: Neth. 32; 52n 7e
Olean: USA 85; 42n 78w
Olekminsk: USSR 43; 60n 120e
Olenek: r., USSR 43; 72n 123e
Oléron, Î. d': France 29; 46n 1w
Ol'ga: USSR 54; 44n 135e
Olomouc: Czech. 27; 50n 17e
Olonzac: France 29; 43n 3e
Oloron-Ste-Marie: Fr. 29; 43n 1w
Olsztyn: Poland 35; 54n 21e
Olten: Switzerland 33; 47n 8e
Olympia: Greece 31; 38n 22e
Olympia: USA 80; 47n 123w
Olympus: mt., Greece 31; 40n 22e
Omaha: USA 81; 41n 96w
'OMAN 49; 26n 56e
'Oman, G. of 49; 24n 60e
Omaruru: S. Africa 69; 21s 16e
Omdurman: Sudan 67; 16n 32e
Omiya: Japan 54; 35n 138e
Omsk: USSR 45; 55n 73e
Omuta: Japan 54; 33n 130e
Omutinskoye: USSR 45; 56n 68e
Onega, L.: USSR 44; 62n 35e
Oneida L.: USA 85; 43n 76w
Onitsha: Nigeria 68; 6n 7e
Onstwedde: Neth. 32; 53n 7e
Ontario: Prov., Canada 79; 50n 85w
Ontario, L.: Can./USA 85; 43n 78w
Oodnadatta: Australia 58; 27s 136e
O'Okiep: S. Africa 69; 30s 18e
Ooldea: Australia 58; 31s 131e
Oosterhesselen: Neth. 32; 53n 7e
Oosterhout: Neth. 32; 52n 5e
Ootacamund: India 52; 12n 77e
Opava: Czechoslovakia 27; 50n 18e
Opeongo L.: Canada 85; 46n 78w
Opobo: Nigeria 68; 5n 7e
Opole: Poland 27; 51n 18e
Oporto: Portugal 25; 41n 9w
Opotiki: NZ 55; 38s 177e
Opunake: NZ 55; 39s 174e
Oradea: Romania 31; 47n 22e
Oraison: France 29; 44n 6e
Oran: Algeria 66; 36n 1e
Orange: Australia 61; 33s 149e
Orange: France 29; 44n 5e
Orange: r., S. Africa 69; 29s 18e
Orange Free State:
S. Africa 69; 28s 27e
Oranienburg: Germany 32; 53n 13e
Orasul Stalin: see Braşov
Orbost: Australia 61; 38s 149e
Ord: r., Australia 58; 16s 129e
Ordos Plat.: China 53; 39n 108e
Ordzhonikidze: USSR 44; 43n 45e
Örebro: Sweden 35; 59n 15e
Oregon: State, USA 80; 44n 120w
Oregon City: USA 80; 46n 123w
Orekhovo-Zuyevo:
USSR 44; 56n 38e
Orel': USSR 44; 53n 36e
Orenburg: USSR 44; 52n 55e
Orense: Spain 25; 42n 8w
Orgeyev: USSR 31; 47n 29e
Orihuela: Spain 25; 38n 1w
Orillia: Canada 85; 45n 79w
Orinoco: r., Venez. 86; 8n 64w
Orissa: State, India 52; 20n 84e
Oristano: Sardinia 30; 40n 9e
Orizaba: Mexico 82; 19n 97w
Orlando: USA 81; 28n 82w
Orléanais: France 28; 48n 2e
Orléans: France 28; 48n 2e
*Orléansville: Algeria 25; 36n 1e
Ornain: r., France 28; 49n 5e
Orne: r., France 28; 49n 1w
Orsk: USSR 45; 51n 59e
Orthez: France 29; 43n 1w
Ortler: mt., Italy 33; 47n 11e
Oruro: Bolivia 86; 18s 67w
Oryakhovo: Bulgaria 31; 44n 24e
Osaka: & B., Japan 54; 35n 135e
Osh: USSR 45; 41n 73e
Oshawa: Canada 85; 44n 79w
Oshkosh: USA 84; 44n 88w
Oshogbo: Nigeria 68; 8n 5e
Osijek: Yugoslavia 27; 45n 19e
Oskarshamn: Sweden 35; 57n 16e
Oslo: & Fd., Norway 35; 60n 11e
Osmanabad: India 52; 18n 76e
Osnabrück: Germany 32; 52n 8e
Osorno: Chile 88; 41s 73w
Ostend: Belgium 28; 51n 3e
Öster Dal: r., Sweden 34; 62n 14e
Östersund: Sweden 34; 63n 15e
Ostia: Italy 30; 42n 12e
Ostrovnoye: USSR 43; 68n 164e
Ostrów Mazowiecki:
Poland 35; 53n 22e
Ostrów Wielkopolski:
Poland 35; 52n 18e
Osumi Is.: Japan 50; 30n 131e
Oswego: USA 85; 43n 76w
Otago: NZ 55; 46s 169e
Otago Penin.: NZ 55; 46s 171e
Otaru: Japan 54; 43n 141e
Othe, Fôret d': Fr. 28; 48n 4e
Otira Tunnel: NZ 55; 43s 172e
Otranto: Italy 31; 40n 19e
Otsu: Japan 54; 35n 136e
Ottawa: & r., Canada 85; 45n 76w
Ottawa: USA 84; 41n 89w
Ottingen: Germany 32; 49n 11e
Ottumwa: USA 84; 41n 92w
Oturkpo: Nigeria 68; 7n 8e
Otway, C.: Australia 61; 39s 144e
Ötztal Alps: Austria 33; 47n 11e
*Ouagadougou: Volta 66; 12n 2w
Ouargla: Algeria 66; 32n 5e
Oubangui: r., Africa 67; 4n 21e
Oudenaarde: Belgium 28; 51n 4e
Oudtshoorn: S. Africa 69; 34s 22e
Ouessant, Î. d': Fr. 28; 48n 5w
Ouidah: Dahomey 68; 6n 2e
Oujda: Morocco 25; 35n 2w
Oulu: & L., Finland 34; 65n 26e
Ou Mts.: Japan 54; 39n 141e
Ourthe: r., Belgium 28; 50n 6e
Oust: r., France 28; 48n 2w
Outjo: SW. Africa 69; 20s 16e
Ouyen: Australia 61; 35s 142e
Ovens: r., Australia 61; 36s 146e
Oviedo: Spain 25; 43n 6w
Owen Falls: Uganda 68; 0 33e
Owen, Mt.: NZ 55; 41s 173e
Owensboro: USA 84; 38n 87w
Owens Creek: Aust. 60; 21s 149e
Owen Sound: Canada 84; 45n 81w
*Owen Stanley Range:
Papua 59; 8s 147e
Owosso: USA 84; 43n 84w
Oxus: r., USSR 45; 38n 64e
Oyo: Nigeria 60; 8n 4e
Oyonnax: France 29; 46n 6e
Ozark Plateau: USA 81; 37n 93w
Özd: Hungary 27; 48n 20e

Paan: China 50; 30n 99e
Paarl: S. Africa 69; 34s 18e
Padang: Sumatra 51; 1s 100e
Paderborn: Germany 32; 52n 9e
Padua (Padova): Italy 33; 45n 12e
Paducah: USA 84; 37n 89w
Paeroa: NZ 55; 37s 176e
Pafuri: Mozambique 69; 22s 32e
Pagoda Pt.: Burma 47; 16n 94e
Paimboeuf: France 29; 47n 2w
Paimpol: France 28; 49n 3w
Pakanbaru: Sumatra 51; 1n 102e
Pakokku: Burma 50; 21n 95e
*Palapye Road: Bech. 69; 23s 27e
Palau Is.: Philippine Sea 51; 7n 134e
Palawan: i., Phil. 51; 10n 118e
Palembang: Sumatra 51; 3s 105e
Palencia: Spain 25; 42n 5w
Palermo: Sicily 30; 38n 13e
Palghat: India 52; 11n 76e
Palk Str.: Ind./Ceylon 52; 10n 80e
Palliser, C.: NZ 55; 42s 175e
Palma: Majorca 25; 40n 3e
Palmas, C.: Liberia 66; 4n 8w
Palm Beach: USA 81; 27n 80w
Palmer Arch.: Antarc. 91; 64s 63w
Palmerston North: NZ 55; 40s 175e
Palm Is.: Australia 60; 19s 147e
Palmyra: Syria 44; 34n 38e
Palmyra I.: Pac. O. 93; 6n 162w
Palos, C. de: Spain 25; 38n 1w
Paltamo: Finland 34; 64n 28e
Pamiers: France 29; 43n 2e
Pamirs: USSR 45; 38n 73e
Pamlico Sd.: USA 85; 35n 76w
Pampas de la Plata:
Argentina 88; 32s 64w
Pamplona: Spain 25; 43n 2w
PANAMÁ 83; 9n 80w
Panamá: Panamá 83; 9n 80w
Panama Canal 83; Inset
Panay: Philippines 51; 11n 122e
Pangong Ra.: China 52; 34n 80e
Panjim: Goa 52; 15n 74e
Pantar: i., Indonesia 51; 8s 124e
Pantelleria: i., Italy 30; 37n 12e
Paoki: China 53; 34n 107e
Paoting: China 53; 38n 115e
Paotow: China 53; 41n 110e
Papakura: NZ 55; 37s 175e
*PAPUA 59; 7s 144e
Para: Brazil 87; 2s 48w
Pará: r., Brazil 87; 2s 50w
Paracel Is.: China 51; 17n 112e
PARAGUAY 88; 23s 60w
Paraguay: r., S. Amer. 88; 21s 58w
Parakou: Dahomey 68; 9n 3e
*Paramaribo: Br. Guiana 87; 6n 55w
Paraná: & r., Argentina 88; 32s 60w
Paraná: r., Brazil 88; 22s 52w
Paraná Plat.: Brazil 88; 25s 53w
Parbati: r., India 52; 23n 77e
Parbhani: India 52; 19n 77e
Parchim: Germany 32; 53n 12e
Pardubice: Czech. 27; 50n 16e
Parece Vela: i., Pac. O. 92; 20n 135e
Parentis: France 29; 44n 1w
Paris: France 28; 49n 2e
Parkersburg: USA 84; 39n 82w
Parkes: Australia 61; 33s 148e
Parma: Italy 33; 45n 10e
Parnaíba: Brazil 87; 3s 42w
Parnassus: mt., Greece 31; 38n 22e
Paros: i., Greece 31; 37n 25e
Parramatta: Australia 61; 34s 151e
Parry, C.: Canada 78; 70n 125w
Parry Is.: Canada 78; 76n 110w
Parry Sd.: Canada 84; 45n 80w
Parthenay: France 29; 47n 0
Pasadena: USA 80; 34n 118w
Pas de Calais: str.,
England/France 28; 51n 1e
Pasni: W. Pakistan 52; * Inset
Passau: Germany 33; 49n 13e
Passchendaele: Belg. 28; 51n 3e
Passero, C.: Sicily 30; 37n 15e
Pasto: Colombia 86; 1n 77w
Patagonia: Argentina 89; 45s 70w
Patay: France 28; 48n 2e
Paterson: USA 85; 41n 74w
Pathankot: India 52; 32n 76e
Pathfinder Dam: USA 80; 42n 107w
Patiala: India 52; 30n 76e
Patmos: i., Greece 31; 37n 26e
Patna: India 52; 26n 85e
Patras: & G., Greece 31; 38n 22e
Pau: France 29; 43n 0
Pauillac: France 29; 45n 1w
Paul Block B.: Antarc. 91; 76s 146w
*Paulis: Congo Rep. 70; 3n 28e
Paulistana: Brazil 87; 8s 41w
Paulo Afonso Falls:
Brazil 87; 9s 39w
Paulsboro: USA 85; 40n 75w
Pavia: Italy 33; 45n 9e
Pavlodar: USSR 45; 52n 77e
Pawtucket: USA 85; 42n 71w
Paysandú: Uruguay 88; 32s 58w
Pays de Caux: France 28; 50n 1e
Pazardzhik: Bulgaria 31; 42n 24e
Peace: r., Canada 78; 59n 114w
Peace River: Canada 78; 56n 117w
Peary Channel: Canada 79; 79n 95w
Pechenga: USSR 34; 70n 31e
Pechora: r., USSR 44; 63n 56e
Pecos: r., USA 80; 31n 102w
Pécs: Hungary 27; 46n 18e
Pedro, Pt.: Ceylon 52; 10n 80e
Pedro Miguel Locks:
Panamá 83; Inset
Peebinga: Australia 61; 35s 141e
Pegasus Bay: NZ 55; 43s 173e
Pegu: Burma 51; 17n 97e
Peh: r., China 53; 24n 113e
Pehpei: China 53; 30n 106e
Peian: China 50; 48n 127e
Peine: Germany 32; 52n 10e
Peiping: China 53; 40n 117e
Peipus, L.: USSR 44; 58n 28e
Pekin: USA 84; 41n 90w
Peking: China 53; 40n 117e
Pelican L.: USA 84; 48n 93w
Pelican Pt.: SW. Africa 69; 23s 15e
Peloponnese: Greece 31; 38n 22e
Pelotas: Brazil 88; 32s 52w
Pelusium, B. of: Egypt 67; Inset
Pelvoux, M.: France 29; 45n 6e
*Pemba: N. Rhodesia 69; 17s 27e

*See Page 131

Page; Lat. Long.
*Pemba: i., Zanzibar . 68; 5s 40e
Pembroke: Canada . 85; 46n 77w
Penang: Malaya . 51; 5n 100e
Penchi: China . 53; 42n 123e
Pendembu: Sierra Leone 66; 8n 11w
Penganga: r., India . 52; 20n 77e
Pengpu: China . 53; 33n 117e
Penmarch, Pte. de: Fr. 28; 48n 4w
Pennar: r., India . 52; 14n 77e
Pennine Alps:
Switz./Italy . 33; 46n 7e
Pennsylvania: USA . 85; 41n 78w
Penobscot: r., USA . 85; 45n 69w
Penrith: Australia . 61; 34s 151e
Pensacola: USA . 81; 30n 88w
Penza: USSR . 44; 53n 45e
Peoria: USA . 84; 41n 89w
Perche, Collines de: Fr. 28; 49n 1e
Percy Is.: Australia . 60; 21s 150e
Perdu, Mt.: Sp./France . 29; 42n 0
Pergamino: Argentina . 88; 34s 60w
Périgord: France . 29; 45n 1e
Périgueux: France . 29; 45n 1e
Perim: i., G. of Aden . 49; 13n 43e
Perm: USSR . 44; 58n 56e
Pernambuco: Brazil . 87; 8s 35w
Pernik: Bulgaria . 31; 43n 23e
Péronne: France . 28; 50n 3e
Perpignan: France . 29; 43n 3e
PERSIA (IRAN) . 49; 32n 55e
Persian Gulf . 49; 28n 50e
Perth: Australia . 60; 32s 116e
PERU . 86; — —
Peru: USA . 84; 41n 86w
Perugia: Italy . 30; 44n 12e
Pervomaysk: USSR . 31; 48n 31e
Pesaro: Italy . 33; 44n 13e
Pescadores Is.: Formosa 53; 24n 120e
Pescara: Italy . 30; 42n 14e
Peshawar: W. Pakistan . 52; 34n 72e
Pessac: France . 29; 45n 1w
Petange: Luxembourg . 32; 50n 6e
Peterborough: Aust. 61; 33s 139e
Peterborough: Canada . 85; 44n 78w
Petersburg: USA . 85; 37n 77w
Petone: NZ . 55; 41s 175e
Petrich: Bulgaria . 31; 41n 23e
Petrópolis: Brazil . 88; 23s 43w
Petropavlovsk: USSR . 45; 55n 69e
Petropavlovsk-Kamchatski:
USSR . 43; 53n 159e
Petroşani: Romania . 31; 45n 23e
Petrovgrad: Yugo. . 27; 45n 20e
Petrozavodsk: USSR . 44; 62n 35e
Petsamo: USSR . 34; 70n 31e
Petukhovo: USSR . 45; 55n 68e
Pfälzer Wald: Ger. . 32; 49n 8e
Pforzheim: Germany . 32; 49n 9e
Phanom Dongrak: Thai. 51; 14n 103e
Phanrang: S. Viet Nam . 51; 11n 109e
Philadelphia: USA . 85; 40n 75w
*Philippeville: Algeria . 25; 37n 7e
PHILIPPINE IS. . 51; — —
Philippine Sea . 51; — —
Philippopolis: Bulgaria . 31; 42n 25e
Philistia: Holy Land . 48; Inset
Phillips Glac.: Antarc. . 91; 86s 150w
Phnom Penh: Cambodia 51; 11n 105e
Phoenicia: Holy Land . 48; Inset
Phoenix: USA . 80; 34n 112w
Phoenix Is.: Pac. O. . 92; 3s 175w
Phuket I.: Thailand . 51; 8n 98e
Piacenza: Italy . 33; 45n 10e
Piatra-Neamt: Rom. 31; 47n 26e
Piave: r., Italy . 33; 46n 12e
Picardy: France . 28; 50n 3e
Picola: Australia . 61; 36s 145e
Picton: NZ . 55; 41s 174e
Pictou: Canada . 85; 46n 63w
Piedmont: Italy . 33; 45n 8e
Pierre: USA . 80; 44n 100w
Pietarssari: Finland . 34; 64n 23e
Pietermaritzburg: S. Afr. 69; 30s 30e
Piet Relief: S. Africa . 69; 27s 31e
Pilcomayo: r., S. Amer. 88; 23s 62w
Pilsen: Czechoslovakia . 27; 50n 14e
Pindus Mts.: Greece . 31; 40n 21e
Pinerolo: Italy . 33; 45n 7e
Piney River: USA . 85; 38n 79w
Pinkiang: China . 53; 46n 126e
Pinnaroo: Australia . 61; 35s 141e
Pinsk: USSR . 44; 52n 26e
Piotrków: Poland . 35; 51n 20e
Piqua: USA . 84; 40n 84w
*Piraeus: Greece . 31; 38n 24e
Pirgos: Greece . 31; 38n 21e
Pirin Mts.: Bulgaria . 31; 42n 23e
Pirmasens: Germany . 32; 49n 8e
Pisa: Italy . 33; 44n 10e
Pisagua: Chile . 86; 20s 70w
Pisco: Peru . 86; 14s 77w
Písek: Czechoslovakia . 27; 49n 14e
Pistoia: Italy . 33; 44n 11e
Pitcairn I.: Pac. O. . 93; 25s 130w
Piteşti: Romania . 31; 45n 25e
Pittsburgh: USA . 84; 40n 80w
Pittsfield: USA . 85; 42n 73w
Piura: Peru . 86; 5s 81w
Placentia Bay: Can. . 79; 47n 55w
Plantaurel, M. du: Fr. 29; 43n 2e
Plassey: India . 52; 24n 88e
Plate: r., Arg./Urug. 88; 35s 57w
Platte: r., USA . 80; 41n 99w
Plauen: Germany . 32; 50n 12e
Plenty, B. of: NZ . 55; 38s 177e
Pleven: Bulgaria . 31; 43n 25e
Ploeşti: Romania . 31; 45n 26e
Plomb du Cantal: Fr. 29; 45n 3e
Plombières: France . 28; 48n 6e
Plön: Germany . 32; 54n 10e
Plovdiv: Bulgaria . 31; 42n 25e
*Plumtree: S. Rhod. . 69; 21s 28e
Plymouth: USA . 85; 42n 71w
Plzeň: Czechoslovakia . 27; 50n 14e
Po: r., Italy . 33; 45n 10e
Pobé: Dahomey . 68; 7n 3e
Pocatello: USA . 80; 43n 112w
Poções: Brazil . 87; 15s 40w
Po Hai Gulf: China . 53; 38n 118e
Pohang: S. Korea . 54; 36n 130e

Page; Lat. Long.
Pointe Noire: Congo . 71; 5s 12e
Poissy: France . 28; 49n 2e
Poitiers: France . 29; 47n 0
Poitou: France . 29; 47n 1w
Poix: France . 28; 50n 2e
Pokaran: India . 52; 27n 72e
Pola: Yugoslavia . 27; 45n 14e
POLAND . 27; — —
Polatlı: Turkey . 31; 40n 32e
Poliyiros: Greece . 31; 40n 23e
Polotsk: USSR . 35; 55n 29e
Poltava: USSR . 44; 50n 34e
Polunochnoye: USSR . 45; 62n 60e
Polynesia: Pac. O. . 92/93; — —
Pomeranian B.: Ger. . 32; 54n 14e
Pomona: SW. Africa . 69; 27s 15e
Pompeii: Italy . 30; 41n 14e
Ponapé: i., Pac. O. . 92; 8n 159e
Pondicherry: India . 52; 12n 80e
Pond Inlet: Canada . 79; 73n 78w
Pontivy: France . 28; 48n 3w
Pont-à-Mousson: Fr. . 28; 49n 6e
Ponta Porã: Brazil . 88; 22s 56w
Pontarlier: France . 29; 47n 6e
Pontevedra: Spain . 25; 42n 9w
Ponthierville:
Congo Rep. . 70; 0 25e
Pontiac: USA . 84; 43n 83w
Pontianak: Borneo . 51; 0 109e
Pontic Mts.: Turkey . 48; 35n 42e
Pontoise: France . 28; 49n 2e
Pontresina: Switz. . 33; 46n 10e
Poona: India . 52; 18n 73e
Pooncarie: Australia . 61; 33s 143e
Poopó, L.: Bolivia . 86; 19s 67w
Popocatepetl: Mexico . 82; 19n 99w
Poperinghe: Belgium . 28; 51n 3e
Poplar Bluff: USA . 84; 37n 90w
Porbandar: India . 52; 22n 70e
Pori: Finland . 34; 62n 22e
Porkkala: Finland . 35; 60n 24e
Port Adelaide: Aust. . 61; 35s 138e
Portalegre: Portugal . 25; 39n 7w
Port Alfred: Canada . 85; 48n 71w
Port Alfred: S. Africa . 69; 34s 27e
Port Arthur: Canada . 84; 48n 89w
*Port Arthur: China . 53; 38n 121e
Port Arthur: USA . 81; 30n 94w
Port Augusta: Aust. . 61; 32s 138e
Port-au-Prince: Haiti . 83; 18n 72w
Port-aux-Basques: Can. 79; 47n 59w
Port Bou: Spain . 25; 42n 3e
Port Chalmers: NZ . 55; 46s 171e
Port Clinton: Australia . 60; 22s 151e
Port Colborne Canada . 85; 43n 79w
Port Elizabeth: S. Afr. . 69; 34s 25e
*Port Étienne: Mauritania 66; 21n 17w
*Port Francqui:
Congo Rep. . 71; 4s 21e
Port Fuad: Egypt . 67; Inset
Port Gentil: Gabon . 68; 1s 9e
Port Harcourt: Nigeria 68; 5n 7e
Port Hedland: Aust. . 58; 21s 119e
Port Huron: USA . 84; 43n 82w
Port Jackson: Aust. . 61; 34s 151e
Port Kembla: Australia 61; 34s 151e
Portland: Australia . 61; 38s 142e
Portland: Maine, USA . 85; 44n 70w
Portland: Oreg., USA . 80; 46n 123w
Port Lincoln: Aust. . 58; 35s 136e
Port Lockroy: Antarc. . 91; 65s 64w
Port Lyautey: Morocco . 66; 34n 7w
Port Macquarie: Aust. . 61; 31s 153e
Port Martin: Antarc. . 91; 67s 142e
*Port Moresby: Papua . 59; 9s 147e
Port Nolloth: S. Africa . 69; 30s 17e
Pôrto Alegre: Brazil . 88; 30s 51w
Pôrto Alexandre: Ang. . 69; 16s 12e
Pôrto Amélia: Moz. . 69; 13s 40e
Portobello: Panamá . 83; 9n 80w
Port of Spain: Trinidad . 86; 10n 62w
Portogruaro: Italy . 33; 46n 13e
Porto Novo: India . 52; 12n 80e
Porto Nuovo: Dahomey 68; 6n 2e
Pôrto Velho: Brazil . 86; 9s 64w
Port Philip B.: Aust. . 61; 38s 145e
Port Pirie: Australia . 61; 33s 138e
Port Radium: Canada . 78; 66n 118w
Port Safaga: Egypt . 48; 27n 34e
Port Said: Egypt . 67; 31n 32e
Port Shepstone: S. Afr. 69; 31s 30e
Portsmouth: N. H., USA 85; 43n 71w
Portsmouth: Ohio, USA 84; 39n 83w
Portsmouth: Va., USA . 85; 37n 76w
Port Stanley: Falk. Is. . 89; 52s 58w
Port Sudan: Sudan . 67; 20n 37e
Port Sulphur: USA . 81; 29n 90w
Port Taufiq: Egypt . 67; Inset
PORTUGAL . 25; — —
*PORTUGUESE
GUINEA . 66; 12n 15w
Port Vendres: France . 29; 43n 3e
Posadas: Argentina . 88; 27s 56w
Possession Is.: Antarc. . 91; 72s 171e
Postmasburg: S. Africa . 69; 28s 23e
Posyet: USSR . 54; 43n 131e
Potenza: Italy . 30; 41n 16e
Potgietersrus: S. Africa 69; 24s 29e
Poti: USSR . 44; 42n 42e
Potiskum: Nigeria . 68; 12n 11e
Potomac: r., USA . 85; 39n 77w
Potosí: Bolivia . 86; 20s 66w
Potrerillos: Chile . 88; 27s 69w
Potsdam: Germany . 32; 52n 13e
Pottsville: USA . 85; 41n 76w
Poughkeepsie: USA . 85; 42n 74w
Poverty Bay: NZ . 55; 39s 178e
Powder: r., USA . 80; 44n 106w
Poyang, L.: China . 53; 29n 117e
Požarevac: Yugoslavia . 27; 44n 21e
Poznań: Poland . 35; 52n 17e
Prades: France . 29; 43n 2e
Prague: Czechoslovakia 27; 50n 14e
Prato: Italy . 33; 44n 11e
Prescott: Canada . 85; 45n 76w
Presque Isle: USA . 85; 47n 68w
Pretoria: S. Africa . 69; 26s 28e
Preveza: Greece . 31; 39n 21e
Pribilof Is.: USA . 93; 57n 170w
Prieska: S. Africa . 69; 30s 23e

Page; Lat. Long.
Prilep: Yugoslavia . 27; 41n 21e
Prince Albert: Canada . 80; 54n 106w
Prince Edward I.: Can. . 85; Inset
Prince George: Canada . 78; 54n 123w
Prince of Wales I.: Can. 79; 73n 100w
Prince of Wales I.: USA 78; 56n 133w
Prince Patrick I.: Canada 78; 77n 120w
Prince Rupert: Canada . 78; 54n 130w
Princess Elizabeth Land:
Antarctica . 91; 70s 80e
Princess Martha Coast:
Antarctica . 91; 72s 4w
Princeton: N.J., USA . 85; 40n 75w
Princeton: Canada . 80; 49n 120w
Principe: i., G. of Guinea 68; 2n 7e
Prinsesse Ragnhild
Coast: Antarctica . 91; 73s 25e
Prins Harald Coast:
Antarctica . 91; 74s 38e
Pripet: r., USSR . 44; 52n 30e
Pripet Marshes: USSR . 44; 52n 28e
Priština: Yugoslavia . 27; 43n 21e
Privas: France . 29; 45n 5e
Prizren: Yugoslavia . 27; 42n 20e
Proclamation I.: Antarc. 91; 66s 54e
Progreso: Mexico . 82; 21n 90w
Prokop'yevsk USSR . 45; 54n 87e
Prome: Burma . 50; 18n 95e
Proserpine: Australia . 60; 20s 149e
Prostějov: Czech. . 27; 49n 17e
Provence: & Alps, Fr. . 29; 44n 6e
Providence: USA . 85; 42n 71w
Providence, C.: NZ . 55; 46s 167e
Provincetown: USA . 85; 42n 70w
Provo: USA . 80; 40n 112w
Pskov: USSR . 35; 58n 28e
Prut: r., Romania/USSR 31; 46n 28e
Prydz Bay: Antarc. . 91; 69s 76e
Przemyśl: Poland . 27; 50n 23e
Puebla: Mexico . 82; 19n 98w
Pueblo: USA . 80; 38n 105w
Puerto Ayacucho:
Venezuela . 86; 6n 67w
Puerto Cabello: Venez. 86; 10n 68w
Puerto Deseado: Arg. . 89; 48s 66w
Puerto Limón: C. Rica . 83; 10n 83w
Puerto Montt: Chile . 89; 42s 73w
PUERTO RICO . 83; 18n 67w
Pukekohe: NZ . 55; 37s 175e
Pula: Yugoslavia . 27; 45n 14e
Pulaski: USA . 84; 37n 81w
Punakha: Bhutan . 52; 28n 90e
Punjab: State, India . 52; 30n 76e
Punjab: W.Pak./Ind. . 52; 31n 75e
Puno: Peru . 86; 16s 70w
Punta Arenas: Chile . 80; 53s 71w
Pur: r., USSR . 43; 65n 78e
Puri: India . 52; 20n 86e
Purnamoota: Aust. . 61; 32s 141e
Purnea: India . 52; 26n 87e
Purús: r., Brazil . 86; 6s 64w
Pusan: S. Korea . 50; 35n 129e
Pushkin: USSR . 35; 60n 30e
Putoran Mts.: USSR . 43; 69n 95e
Putumayo: r., S. Amer. . 86; 2s 77w
Puy de Sancy: France . 29; 46n 3e
Pyatigorsk: USSR . 44; 44n 43e
Pyongyang: N. Korea . 50; 39n 126e
Pyramids: Egypt . 67; 30n 31e
Pyrenees: Fr./Sp. . 29; — —

Qasr Farafra: Egypt . 67; 27n 28e
QATAR . 49; 26n 51e
Qattara Depression:
Egypt . 67; 30n 27e
Qazvin: Iran . 49; 36n 50e
Qena: Egypt . 48; 26n 33e
Qila Saifullah: W. Pak. . 52; 31n 68e
Qom: Iran . 49; 35n 51e
Qomul: China . 47; 43n 93e
Queanbeyan: Aust. . 61; 35s 149e
Quebec: & Prov., Can. . 85; 47n 71w
Quedlinburg: Ger. . 32; 52n 11e
Queen Adelaide Arch.:
Chile . 89; 52s 75w
Queen Charlotte Is.:
Canada . 78; 53n 132w
Queen Elizabeth Is.:
Canada . 78; 77n 110w
Queen Mary Land:
Antarctica . 91; 71s 98e
Queen Maud Land:
Antarctica . 91; 75s 10e
Queen Maud Ra.:
Antarctica . 91; 88s 90w
Queensland: Australia . 59; 20s 145e
Queenstown: NZ . 55; 45s 169e
*Quelimane: Moz. . 69; 18s 37e
Quelpart I.: S. Korea . 50; 33n 127e
Quemoy: i., Formosa . 50; 24n 118e
*Que Que: S. Rhod. . 69; 19s 30e
Quesnel: Canada . 80; 53n 122w
Quetta: W. Pakistan . 52; 30n 67e
Quiberon: & B., France . 28; 47n 3w
Quilpie: Australia . 60; 26s 145e
Quimper: France . 28; 48n 4w
Quimperlé: France . 28; 48n 4w
Quincy: USA . 84; 40n 91w
Quinze, L. des: Can. . 85; 48n 79w
Quito: Ecuador . 86; 0 79w
Qumran: Holy Land . 48; Inset
Qunfidha: Sau. Arab. . 46; 19n 41e
Quorn: Australia . 61; 32s 138e

Rabat: Gozo . 30; 36n 14e
Rabat: Morocco . 66; 34n 7w
*Rabaul: New Guinea . 59; 4s 152e
Race, C.: Canada . 79; 46n 53w
Racine: USA . 84; 43n 88w
Radenthein: Austria . 33; 47n 14e
Ragusa: Sicily . 30; 37n 15e
Raheng: Thailand . 51; 17n 99e
Raichur: India . 52; 16n 77e
Rainier, Mt.: USA . 80; 47n 122w
Raipur: India . 52; 22n 82e
Rajahmundry: India . 52; 17n 82e
Rajasthan: India . 52; 27n 70e
Rajkot: India . 52; 22n 71e
Rajshahi: E. Pakistan . 52; 24n 88e
Rakahanga: i., Pac. O. . 93; 10s 161w

Page; Lat. Long.
Rakaia: r., NZ . 55; 43s 172e
Raleigh: USA . 85; 36n 79w
Rambouillet: France . 28; 49n 2e
Ramillies: Belgium . 28; 51n 5e
Râmnicu Sărat: Rom. . 31; 45n 27e
Râmnicu Vâlcea: Rom. . 31; 45n 24e
Rampur: India . 52; 28n 79e
Rancagua: Chile . 88; 34s 71w
Ranchi: India . 52; 23n 85e
Randers: Denmark . 35; 56n 10e
Rangitaiki: r., NZ . 55; 38s 177e
Rangoon: Burma . 51; 17n 96e
*Rangpur: E. Pakistan . 52; 26n 89e
Raniganj: India . 52; 24n 87e
Rankovićevo: Yugo. . 27; 44n 21e
Rapallo: Italy . 33; 44n 9e
Rapolano: Italy . 30; 43n 12e
Rappahannock: r., USA . 85; 38n 77w
Rarotonga: i., Pac. O. . 93; 20s 160w
Ras al Hadd:
Muscat & 'Oman . 49; 22n 60e
Ras al Madraka:
Muscat & 'Oman . 49; 19n 58e
*Ras Fartak: Aden Prot. . 49; 16n 52e
Ras Gharib: Egypt . 48; 28n 33e
Rasht: Iran . 49; 37n 50e
Rastatt: Germany . 32; 49n 8e
Rathenow: Germany . 32; 53n 12e
Ratlam: India . 52; 23n 75e
Ratnagiri: India . 52; 17n 73e
Raton: USA . 80; 37n 105w
Raukumara Ra.: NZ . 55; 38s 178e
Ravenna: Italy . 33; 44n 12e
Ravenswood: Australia . 60; 20s 147e
Ravi: r., W. Pakistan . 52; 31n 73e
Rawalpindi: W. Pak. . 52; 33n 73e
Rawson: Argentina . 89; 43s 65w
Razdel'naya: USSR . 31; 47n 30e
Raz, Pte du: France . 26; 48n 5w
Reading: USA . 85; 40n 76w
Rebiana: Libya . 48; 24n 22e
Recherche Arch.: Aust. 58; 34s 122e
Recife: Brazil . 87; 8s 35w
Recklinghausen: Ger. . 32; 52n 7e
Red: r., Canada/USA . 80; 49n 97w
Red: r., USA . 81; 34n 95w
Red: r., N. Viet Nam . 53; 21n 105e
Red Basin: China . 50; 30n 105e
Red Bluff: USA . 80; 40n 122w
Redcliffe: Australia . 60; 27s 153e
Red Cliffs: Australia . 61; 34s 142e
Redon: France . 28; 48n 2w
Red Sea . 67; — —
Red Sea Hills: Egypt . 67; 27n 33e
Redwater: Canada . 80; 54n 113w
Reefton: NZ . 55; 42s 172e
Regensburg: Germany . 32; 49n 12e
Reggio di Calabria: It. . 30; 38n 16e
Reggio nell' Emilia: It. . 33; 45n 11e
Regina: Canada . 80; 50n 105w
Ré, I. de: France . 29; 46n 1w
Reims (Rheims): France 28; 49n 4e
Reindeer L.: Canada . 78; 57n 102w
Remoulins: France . 29; 44n 5e
Remscheid: Germany . 32; 51n 7e
Renkum: Netherlands . 32; 52n 6e
Renmark: Australia . 61; 34s 141e
Rennell I.: Pac. O. . 59; 12s 160e
Rennes: France . 28; 48n 2w
Rennick B.: Antarctica . 91; 70s 162e
Reno: USA . 80; 39n 120w
REPUBLIC OF SOUTH
AFRICA . 69; 30s 25e
Repulse B.: Australia . 60; 21s 149e
Resistencia: Argentina . 88; 27s 59w
Reşiţa: Romania . 31; 45n 22e
Resolution I.: Canada . 79; 62n 65w
Rethimnon: Crete . 31; 35n 24e
Reus: Spain . 25; 41n 1e
Reuss: r., Switzerland . 33; 47n 8e
Reutlingen: Germany . 33; 48n 9e
Revelstoke: Canada . 80; 51n 118w
Revermont: France . 29; 46n 5e
Revilla Gigedo Is.: Mex. 93; 19n 112w
Rewari: India . 52; 28n 77e
Reykjavik: Iceland . 34; 64n 22w
Rezā'iyeh: Iran . 49; 38n 45e
Rezekne: USSR . 35; 57n 27e
Rhaetian Alps: Switz. . 33; 47n 10e
Rheden: Netherlands . 32; 52n 6e
Rheims (Reims): France 28; 49n 4e
Rheine: Germany . 32; 52n 7e
Rheydt: Germany . 32; 51n 6e
Rhine: r., Germany . 32; 52n 6e
Rhode Island: USA . 85; 42n 71w
Rhodes: i., Greece . 31; 36n 28e
Rhodope Mts.: Bulgaria 31; 41n 24e
Rhône: r., Europe . 29; 45n 5e
Riau Arch.: Indonesia . 51; 0 105e
Ribeirão Prêto: Brazil . 88; 21s 48w
Riberalta: Bolivia . 86; 11s 66w
Riccarton: NZ . 55; 43s 173e
Richelieu: Canada . 85; 46n 73w
Richmond: Calif., USA . 80; 38n 122w
Richmond: Ind., USA . 84; 40n 85w
Richmond: Va., USA . 85; 37n 77w
Rideau L.: Canada . 85; 45n 76w
Riga: & G., USSR . 44; 57n 24e
Rijeka: Yugoslavia . 27; 45n 14e
Rijswijk: Netherlands . 32; 52n 4e
Rimini: Italy . 33; 44n 13e
Rimutaka Tunnel: NZ . 55; 41s 175e
Ringsted: Denmark . 35; 55n 12e
Riobamba: Ecuador . 86; 2s 78w
Rio Branco: Brazil . 86; 10s 68w
Rio de Janeiro: Brazil . 88; 23s 43w
Rio de Oro: Sp. Sahara . 66; 24n 13w
Río Gallegos: Argentina 89; 52s 70w
Rio Grande: Brazil . 88; 32s 52w
Rio Grande: USA/Mex. 80; 30n 104w
Rio Grande do Sul:
Brazil . 88; 30s 53w
Riom: France . 29; 46n 3e
*Rio Muni: Sp. Guinea . 68; 2n 11e
Rishiri: i., Japan . 54; 45n 141e
Rive-de-Gier: France . 29; 46n 5e
Rivera: Uruguay . 88; 31s 56w
Riverina: Australia . 61; 35s 145e
Riviera di Levante: Italy 33; 44n 9e
Riviera di Ponente: Italy 33; 44n 8e

Page; Lat. Long.
Rivière du Loup: Can. . 85; 48n 70w
Riyadh: Sa'udi Arabia . 49; 24n 47e
Roanne: France . 29; 46n 4e
Roanoke: & r., USA . 84; 37n 80w
Robertson B.: Antarc. . 91; 71s 170e
Robertson I.: Antarc. . 91; 65s 60w
Robson, Mt.: Canada . 78; 53n 119w
Rochechouart: France . 29; 46n 1e
Rochefort-sur-Mer: Fr. . 29; 46n 1w
Rochester: Minn., USA . 84; 44n 92w
Rochester: N.Y., USA . 85; 43n 78w
Rockall: i., Atl. O. . 90; 58s 14w
Rockefeller Plateau:
Antarctica . 91; 79s 126w
Rockford: USA . 84; 42n 89w
Rockhampton: Aust. . 60; 23s 150e
Rock Island: USA . 84; 42n 91w
Rock Springs: USA . 80; 42n 109w
Rocky Mount: USA . 85; 36n 78w
Rocky Mts.: Can./USA . 78; — —
Rocroi: France . 28; 50n 5e
Rødberg: Norway . 35; 60n 9e
Rodez: France . 29; 44n 3e
Roermond: Netherlands 32; 51n 6e
Roeselare: Belgium . 28; 51n 3e
Rogers City: USA . 84; 45n 85w
Roma: Australia . 60; 26s 149e
Roman: Romania . 31; 47n 27e
ROMANIA . 31; 46n 25e
Romans: France . 29; 45n 5e
Rome: Ga., USA . 81; 34n 85w
Rome: N.Y., USA . 85; 43n 75w
Rome (Roma): Italy . 30; 42n 12e
Romilly-sur-Seine: Fr. . 28; 48n 4e
Roncesvalles: Spain . 25; 43n 2w
Ronda: Spain . 25; 37n 5w
Rønne: Denmark . 35; 55n 15e
Roosendaal: Neth. . 32; 52n 5e
Roosevelt I.: Antarc. . 91; 80s 162w
Roquefort: France . 29; 44n 0
Roquefort: France . 29; 44n 3e
Roraima: mt., Venez. . 86; 5n 61w
Rorschach: Switzerland 33; 48n 9e
Rørvik: Norway . 34; 65n 11e
Rosario: Argentina . 88; 33s 60w
Roscoff: France . 28; 49n 4w
Roseires: Sudan . 67; 12n 34e
Rosendaël: France . 28; 51n 2e
Rosenheim: Germany . 33; 48n 12e
Rose Pt.: Canada . 85; 44n 64w
Rosetta: Egypt . 67; 31n 30e
Roswell: USA . 80; 36n 104w
*Ross Dependency:
Antarctica . 91; 68s 175w
Ross Ice Shelf: Antarc. . 91; 80s 180
Rossignol, L.: Canada . 85; 44n 65w
Ross I.: Antarctica . 91; 78s 168e
Ross Sea: Antarctica . 91; 75s 175w
Rostock: Germany . 32; 54n 12e
Rostov: USSR . 44; 47n 40e
Rothenburg: Germany . 32; 49n 10e
Roti: i., Indonesia . 51; 11s 123e
Roto: Australia . 61; 33s 145e
Rotorua: NZ . 55; 38s 176e
Rotterdam: Neth. . 32; 52n 5e
Rottnest I.: Australia . 60; 32s 115e
Rottweil: Germany . 33; 48n 9e
Roubaix: France . 28; 51n 3e
Rouen: France . 28; 49n 1e
Round L.: Canada . 85; 46n 78w
Roussillon: France . 29; 43n 3e
Rouyn: Canada . 85; 48n 79w
Rovaniemi: Finland . 34; 67n 26e
Rovereto: Italy . 33; 46n 11e
Rovigo: Italy . 33; 45n 12e
Rovno: USSR . 44; 51n 26e
Roxburgh: NZ . 55; 46s 169e
Roxo, C.: Mali . 66; 12n 17w
Royan: France . 29; 46n 1w
Ruahine Range: NZ . 55; 40s 176e
Ruapehu: mt., NZ . 55; 39s 175e
Rub' al Khali:
Sa'udi Arabia . 49; 20n 50e
Rubtsovsk: USSR . 45; 52n 82e
Rudnichnyy: USSR . 44; 60n 52e
Rudok: China . 52; 33n 80e
*Rudolf, L.: Kenya . 68; 4n 36e
Ruffec: France . 29; 46n 0
Rügen: i., Germany . 35; 54n 13e
Ruhr: Germany . 32; 51n 7e
*Rukwa, L.: Tanganyika . 68; 8s 33e
Ruma: Yugoslavia . 27; 45n 20e
Rumaylah: 'Iraq . 49; 30n 47e
Rum Jungle: Aust. . 58; 13s 131e
Rupert Coast: Antarc. 91; 76s 144w
Ruschuk (Ruse): Bulg. . 31; 44n 26e
Russell: NZ . 55; 35s 174e
Russian Soviet Federated
Socialist Rep.: USSR . 44/45; — —
Rutland: USA . 85; 44n 73w
Ruvuma: r., Africa . 68; 11s 37e
Ruwenzori, Mt.: Uganda 68; 0 30e
RWANDA . 68; 2s 30e
Ryazan': USSR . 44; 55n 40e
Rybachiy Penin.: USSR . 34; 70n 33e
Rybach'ye: USSR . 45; 43n 76e
Rybinsk: & res., USSR . 44; 58n 38e
Rybnitsa: USSR . 31; 48n 29e
Ryukyu Is.: Japan . 50; 27n 127e
Rzeszów: Poland . 27; 50n 22e
Rzhev: USSR . 44; 56n 34e

Saale: r., Germany . 32; 52n 12e
Saalfeld: Germany . 32; 51n 11e
Saar: & r., Germany . 32; 49n 7e
Saarbrücken: Ger. . 32; 49n 7e
Saaremaa: i., USSR . 35; 58n 23e
Sabadell: Spain . 25; 42n 2e
Sabaloka Gorge: Sudan . 48; 16n 33e
Sabine, Mt.: Antarc. . 91; 72s 169e
Sabkhat Minjora:
Sa'udi Arabia . 49; 19n 53e
Sable I.: Canada . 90; 44n 60w
Sable, C.: Canada . 85; 43n 66w
Sabrina Coast: Antarc. . 91; 67s 118e
Sacramento: & r., USA . 80; 38n 122w
Sá da Bandeira: Ang. . 69; 15s 13e
Sado: i., Japan . 54; 38n 138e
Sadowa: Czech. . 27; 50n 16e
Safi: Morocco . 66; 32n 9w

* See Page 131

Page; Lat. Long.
Sagami G.: Japan 54; 35n 139e
Saginaw: & B., USA 84; 44n 84w
Saguenay: r., Canada 85; 48n 70w
Sahara Desert: Africa 66 67; —
Saharan Atlas: Algeria 66; 33n 2e
Saharanpur: India 52; 30n 78e
Sai: r., India 52; 26n 82e
*Saigon: S. Viet Nam 51; 10n 107e
Sain Shanda: Mongolia 50; 45n 110e
St. Affrique: France 29; 44n 3e
St. Amand: France 28; 50n 3e
St. Amand Mont-Rond: France 29; 47n 2e
St. André, Plaine de: France 28; 49n 1e
St. Anton: Austria 33; 47n 10e
St. Brieuc: France 28; 48n 3w
St. Chamond: France 29; 45n 5e
St. Christophers: i., West Indies 83; 17n 63w
St. Clair: r., Can./USA 84; 43n 82w
St. Clair, L.: Canada 84; 42n 83w
St. Claude: France 29; 46n 6e
St. Cloud: USA 84; 46n 94w
St. Croix: i., W. Indies 83; 18n 65w
St. Croix: r., USA 84; 46n 93w
St. Denis: France 28; 49n 2e
St. Dié: France 28; 48n 7e
St. Dizier: France 28; 49n 5e
St. Elias: mts., Canada 78; 60n 140w
Saintes: France 29; 46n 1w
St. Étienne: France 29; 45n 4e
St. Flour: France 29; 45n 3e
St. Francis, C.: S. Afr. 69; 34s 25e
St. Francis, L.: Canada 85; 46n 71w
St. Gallen: Switzerland 33; 47n 9e
St. George: USA 80; 37n 113w
St. Germain: France 28; 49n 2e
St. Gotthard P.: Switz. 33; 47n 9e
St. Helena: i., Atl. O. 90; 16s 8w
St. Helena B.: S. Afr. 69; 33s 18e
St. Hyacinthe: Canada 85; 46n 73w
St. Ingbert: Germany 32; 49n 7e
St. Jean: Canada 85; 45n 73w
St. Jean-de-Luz, Fr. 29; 43n 2w
St. Jean de Maurienne: France 29; 45n 6e
St. Jean-Pied-de-Port: France 29; 43n 1w
Saint John: & r., Can. 85; 45n 66w
St. John, L.: Canada 85; 49n 72w
St. John's: Canada 79; 47n 53w
St. Joseph: USA 81; 40n 95w
St. Julien: France 29; 46n 6e
St. Junien: France 29; 46n 1e
St. Kitts: i., W. Indies 83; 17n 63w
St. Lawrence: i., USA 78; 63n 170w
St. Lawrence: r., North America 85; — —
St. Lawrence, G. of: Canada 79; 48n 62w
St. Lô: France 28; 49n 1w
St. Louis: Senegal 66; 16n 16w
St. Louis: USA 84; 39n 90w
St. Lucia: i., W. Indies 83; 14n 61w
St. Malo: France 28; 49n 2w
*Ste. Marie, C.: Madag. 71; 26s 45e
St. Martin: i., W. Indies 82; 18n 63w
St. Matthew: i., USA 78; 60n 172w
St. Maurice: Switz. 33; 46n 7e
Ste. Menehould: Fr. 28; 49n 5e
St. Moritz: Switz. 33; 46n 10e
St. Nazaire: France 28; 47n 2w
St. Omer: France 28; 51n 2e
Saintonge: France 29; 45n 1w
St. Paul: USA 84; 45n 93w
St. Paul: i., Ind. O. 92; 39s 78e
St. Paul, C.: Ghana 68; 6n 1e
St. Paul Rocks: Atl. O. 87; 1n 29w
St. Peter, L.: Canada 85; 46n 73w
St. Petersburg: USA 81; 28n 83w
St. Pierre Quilbignon: France 28; 48n 4w
St. Pol: France 28; 50n 2e
St. Pons: France 29; 43n 4e
St. Quentin: France 28; 50n 3e
St. Raphaël: France 29; 43n 7e
Ste. Savine: France 28; 48n 4e
St. Servan: France 28; 49n 2w
St. Stephen: Canada 85; 45n 67w
St. Thomas: Canada 84; 43n 81w
St. Thomas: i., W. Ind. 83; 18n 65w
St. Tropez: France 29; 43n 7e
St. Valéry-en-Caux: Fr. 28; 50n 1e
St. Vincent: i., W. Ind. 83; 13n 62w
St. Vincent, C.: Port. 25; 37n 9w
St. Vincent, G. of: Aust. 61; 35s 138e
Saipan: i., Pac. O. 92; 15n 145e
*Saiwūn: Aden Prot. 49; 16n 49e
Sakaka: Sa'udi Arabia 49; 30n 40e
*Sakania: Congo Rep. 69; 13s 29e
Sakarya: r., Turkey 31; 40n 31e
Sakata: Japan 54; 39n 140e
Sakawa: Japan 54; 33n 133e
Sakhalin: USSR 43; 50n 143e
Salado: r., Argentina 88; 30s 61w
Salala: Muscat & 'Oman 49; 17n 54e
Salamanca: Spain 25; 41n 6w
Sala-y-Gomez: i., Pac. O. 93; 26s 105w
Sale: Australia 61; 38s 147e
Salekhard: USSR 42; 66n 66e
Salem: India 52; 12n 78e
Salem: USA 80; 45n 123w
Salerno: Italy 30; 41n 15e
*Salima: Nyasaland 69; 14s 34e
Salinas, C.: Majorca 25; 39n 3e
Salisbury: Australia 61; 35s 139e
*Salisbury: S. Rhodesia 69; 18s 31e
Salisbury: USA 85; 38n 75w
Salmon: r. & mts., USA 80; 46n 115w
Salon de Provence: Fr. 29; 44n 5e
Salonica: Greece 31; 41n 23e
Salonta: Romania 31; 47n 22e
Salpausselka: Finland 35; 61n 26e
Sal'sk: USSR 44; 42n 42e
Salta: Argentina 88; 25s 66w
Saltillo: Mexico 82; 25n 101w
Salt Lake City: USA 80; 41n 112w
Salto: Uruguay 88; 31s 58w
Salt Range: W. Pakistan 52; 33n 72e

Page; Lat. Long.
Salûm: Egypt 48; 32n 25e
Saluzzo: Italy 33; 45n 7e
Salvador: Brazil 87; 13s 38w
Salween: r., China 50; 31n 96e
Salzach: r., Austria 33; 47n 13e
Salzburg: Austria 33; 48n 13e
Salzgitter: Germany 32; 52n 10e
Samah: China 51; 18n 109e
Samar: i., Philippines 51; 12n 125e
Samara: r., USSR 44; 53n 52e
Samaria: Holy Land 48; Inset
Samarinda: Borneo 51; 1s 117e
Samarkand: USSR 45; 40n 67e
Samarra: 'Iraq 49; 34n 44e
Sambalpur: India 52; 22n 84e
Sambre: r., France 28; 50n 4e
Samnua: Laos 53; 20n 104e
Samoa Is.: Pac. O. 92; 12s 172w
Samos: i., Greece 31; 38n 27e
Samothrace: Greece 31; 40n 26e
Samsun: Turkey 48; 42n 36e
San'a: Yemen 49; 15n 44e
Sanandaj: Iran 48; 36n 47e
San Angelo: USA 80; 32n 100w
San Antonio: USA 80; 29n 98w
San Bernardino: USA 80; 34n 117w
San Carlos de Bariloche: Argentina 89; 41s 71w
Sancerre: France 29; 47n 3e
San Cristóbal: Venez. 86; 8n 72w
San Cristobal: i., Pac. O. 59; 11s 162e
San Cristobal: i., Pac. O. 86; 1s 81w
*Sandakan: N. Borneo 51; 6n 118e
Sandane: Norway 34; 62n 6e
San Diego: USA 80; 33n 117w
Sandgate: Australia 60; 27s 153e
Sandusky: USA 84; 41n 83w
Sandy C.: Australia 60; 25s 153e
San Félix: i., Chile 93; 26s 80w
San Fernando: Chile 88; 34s 72w
San Fernando: Phil. 51; 17n 120e
San Francisco: USA 80; 38n 122w
Sangar: USSR 43; 64n 127e
Sanjo: Japan 54; 38n 139e
San Joaquin: r., USA 80; 37n 120w
San José: Costa Rica 83; 10n 84w
San Juan: Argentina 88; 32s 69w
San Juan: Puerto Rico 83; 18n 67w
Sakishima Gp.: Japan 53; 24n 124e
San Luis: Argentina 88; 33s 66w
San Luis Potosí: Mexico 82; 22n 101w
SAN MARINO 33; 44n 12e
Sanmen Gorge: China 53; 35n 111e
Sanok: Poland 27; 49n 22e
San Rafael: Argentina 88; 35s 68w
San Remo: Italy 33; 44n 8e
San Salvador: El Sal. 87; 14n 89w
San Salvador: i., Bahamas 83; 24n 74w
San Sebastián: Spain 25; 43n 2w
San Severo: Italy 30; 42n 15e
Santa Barbara: USA 80; 35n 120w
Santa Cruz: Bolivia 86; 18s 63w
Santa Cruz de Tenerife: Canary Is. 66; 28n 17w
Santa Cruz Is.: Pac. O. 59; 11s 167e
Santa Fé: Argentina 88; 32s 61w
Santa Fe: USA 80; 36n 106w
Santa Maria: Brazil 88; 30s 54w
Santa Marta: Colombia 86; 11n 74w
Santander: Spain 25; 43n 4w
Santarém: Portugal 25; 39n 9w
Santa Rosa: Argentina 88; 37s 64w
Santa Ysabel: i., Pac. O. 59; 8s 159e
Santiago: Chile 88; 34s 71w
Santiago: Dom. Repub. 83; 19n 71w
Santiago: Spain 25; 43n 8w
Santiago: r., Mexico 82; 21n 104w
Santiago de Cuba: Cuba 83; 20n 76w
Santiago del Estero: Arg. 88; 28s 64w
Santo Antônio: Brazil 86; 9s 64w
Santo Domingo: Dominican Rep. 83; 18n 70w
Santos: Brazil 88; 24s 47w
São Domingos: Port. 25; 38n 7w
São Francisco: r., Brazil 87; 11s 43w
São Leopoldo: Brazil 88; 30s 51w
São Luis: Brazil 87; 3s 44w
Saône: r., France 29; 46n 5e
São Paulo: Brazil 88; 24s 47w
São Roque, C. de: Brazil 87; 6s 35w
São Tomé: i., G. of Guinea 68; 5n 7e
Sapporo: Japan 54; 43n 141e
Saquenay: r., Canada 79; 48n 70w
Saragossa: Spain 25; 42n 1w
Sarajevo: Yugoslavia 27; 44n 18e
Saransk: USSR 44; 54n 45e
Saratoga Springs: USA 85; 43n 74w
Saratov: USSR 44; 52n 46e
SARAWAK 51; 3n 113e
SARDINIA 30; 40n 9e
Sarnia: Canada 84; 43n 82w
Sarny: USSR 44; 51n 27e
Sarpsborg: Norway 35; 59n 11e
Sarra: Libya 48; 22n 22e
Sarrebourg: France 28; 49n 7e
Sarreguemines: France 28; 49n 7e
Sarthe: r., France 28; 48n 0
Sasebo: Japan 54; 33n 130e
Saskatchewan: Prov., Canada 78; 55n 105w
Saskatchewan: r., Can. 80; 53n 103w
Saskatoon: Canada 80; 52n 107w
Sassari: Sardinia 30; 41n 8e
Sassnitz: Germany 35; 55n 14e
Satara: India 52; 18n 74e
Satpura Range: India 52; 22n 77e
Satu-Mare: Romania 31; 48n 23e
SA'UDI ARABIA 49; — —
Sauerland: Germany 32; 51n 8e
Saugor: India 52; 24n 78e
Sault Ste. Marie: Can. 84; 46n 84w
Saumur: France 29; 47n 0
Sauternes: France 29; 45n 0
Sava: r., Yugoslavia 27; 45n 19e
Savannah: USA 81; 32n 81w
Savannakhet: Laos 51; 17n 105e
Savaştepe: Turkey 31; 39n 28e
Saverne: France 28; 49n 7e

Page; Lat. Long.
Savigliano: Italy 33; 45n 8e
Savona: Italy 33; 44n 8e
Savonlinna: Finland 34; 62n 29e
Savoy: & Alps, France 29; 46n 6e
Sawu: i., Indonesia 51; 11s 122e
Scania: Sweden 35; 56n 14e
Schaerbeek: Belgium 28; 51n 4e
Schaffhausen: Switz. 33; 48n 9e
Schefferville: Canada 79; 55n 67w
Scheldt: r., Belg. Neth. 32; 51n 4e
Schenectady: USA 85; 43n 74w
Schiedam: Netherlands 32; 52n 4e
Schio: Italy 33; 46n 11e
Schleswig: Germany 35; 54n 10e
Schmalkalden: Germany 32; 51n 10e
Schoonebeek: Neth. 32; 53n 7e
Schouwen-Duiveland: i., Netherlands 32; 52n 4e
Schwäbisch-Gmünd: Germany 33; 49n 10e
Schwandorf: Germany 32; 49n 12e
Schweinfurt: Germany 32; 50n 10e
Schwerin: Germany 32; 54n 11e
Schwyz: Switzerland 33; 47n 9e
Scoresby Sd.: Grnld. 79; 71n 24w
Scotia Sea 89; 50s 57w
Scott I.: Antarctica 91; 68s 180
Scottsbluff: USA 80; 42n 104w
Scranton: USA 85; 41n 76w
Scugog, L.: Canada 85; 44n 79w
Scutari: Albania 31; 42n 19e
Scutari: Turkey 31; 41n 29e
Seal, C.: S. Africa 69; 34s 23e
Seattle: USA 80; 48n 122w
*Sebakwe: S. Rhodesia 69; 19s 30e
Sebcha di Tauorga: Libya 48; 32n 16e
Sebeş: Romania 31; 46n 24e
Sebha Oasis: Libya 66; 27n 14e
Sechura Desert: Peru 86; 6s 80w
Second Baku: USSR 44; 53n 52e
Sedalia: USA 84; 39n 93w
Sedan: France 28; 50n 5e
Seeheim: SW. Africa 69; 27s 18e
Segovia: Spain 25; 41n 4w
Segovia: r., Cen. Amer. 83; 15n 84w
Ségre: r., Spain 25; 42n 1e
Segura: r., Spain 25; 38n 2w
Seine: r., France 28; 49n 1e
Sekondi: Ghana 68; 5n 2w
Selenga: r., Mong./USSR 50; 49n 103e
Sélestat: France 28; 48n 7e
Selety-Tengiz, L.: USSR 45; 53n 73e
Selima Oasis: Sudan 48; 21n 29e
Selkirk Mts.: Canada 80; 52n 117w
*Selukwe: S. Rhodesia 69; 20s 30e
Selvas: Brazil 86; 6s 65w
Semarang: Java 51; 7s 110e
Seminoe Dam: USA 80; 42n 107w
Semiozernoye: USSR 45; 52n 64e
Semipalatinsk: USSR 45; 50n 80e
Semliki: r., Africa 68; 1n 30e
Semmering P.: Austria 27; 47n 16e
Semnān: Iran 49; 35n 53e
*Senanga: N. Rhodesia 69; 16s 23e
Sendai: Japan 54; 38n 141e
SENEGAL 66; 15n 15w
Senegal: r., Africa 66; 16n 14w
Senja: i., Norway 34; 69n 17e
Senlis: France 28; 49n 3e
Sennar: & dam, Sudan 48; 14n 34e
Sens: France 28; 48n 3e
Seoul: S. Korea 50; 38n 127e
Sept Îles: Canada 79; 50n 67w
Seram: i., Indonesia 51; 3s 129e
Serbia: Yugoslavia 27; 43n 22e
*Seremban: Malaya 51; 3n 102e
Seria: Brunei 51; 4n 114e
*Serian: Sarawak 51; 1n 111e
Serio: r., Italy 33; 45n 10e
Serir of Kalanshu: Libya 48; 28n 22e
Serov: USSR 45; 60n 60e
*Serowe: Bechuanaland 6[?]; 23s 27e
Serra dos Aimorés: Brazil 87; 18s 41w
Serra dos Parecis: Braz. 86; 13s 60w
Serra Geral: Brazil 87; 17s 43w
Serra Geral de Goiás: Brazil 87; 13s 45w
Serrai: Greece 31; 41n 24e
Cète: France 29; 43n 4e
Sétif: Algeria 25; 36n 5e
Setúbal: & B., Port. 25; 39n 9w
Sevastopol': USSR 44; 45n 34e
Severn: r., Australia 61; 29s 151e
Severnaya Zemlya: USSR 43; 80n 95e
Severoural'sk: USSR 45; 60n 60e
Seville (Sevilla): Spain 25; 37n 6w
Sèvre Nantaise: r., Fr. 29; 47n 1w
Sèvre Niortaise: r., Fr. 29; 46n 1w
Sèvres: France 28; 49n 2e
Seward: USA 78; 60n 150w
Seward Penin.: USA 78; 65n 165w
Seydisfjördhur: Iceland 34; 65n 14w
Sézanne: France 28; 49n 4e
Sfântu Gheorghe: Rom. 31; 46n 26e
Sfax: Tunisia 66; 35n 11e
's-Gravenhage: Neth. 32; 52n 4e
*Shabwah: Aden Prot. 49; 16n 47e
Shackleton Ice Shelf: Antarctica 91; 66s 99e
Shahjahanpur: India 52; 28n 80e
*Shahrezā: Iran 49; 32n 52e
Shahrūd: Iran 49; 37n 55e
Shakhty: USSR 44; 48n 40e
Shalym: USSR 45; 53n 88e
Shamokin: USA 85; 41n 77w
*Shamva: S. Rhodesia 69; 17s 32e
*Shangani: r., S. Rhod. 69; 19s 28e
Shanghai: China 53; 31n 122e
Shangjao: China 53; 28n 118e
Shangkiu: China 53; 34n 116e
Shansi: China 53; 38n 113e
Shan States: Burma 50; 22n 97e
Shantung: Prov., China 53; 36n 118e
Shantung Penin.: China 50; 37n 120e
Shaohing: China 53; 30n 121e
Shaowu: China 53; 27n 117e
Shaoyang: China 53; 27n 112e
Sharjah: Trucial 'Oman 49; 25n 55e

Page; Lat. Long.
Sharon: USA 84; 41n 80w
Sharon, Plain of: Holy Land 48; Inset
Shasi: China 53; 30n 112e
Shasta, Mt.: USA 80; 42n 122w
Shasta Dam: USA 80; 41n 122w
Shaw: i., Australia 60; 20s 149e
Shawinigan Falls: Can. 85; 46n 73w
Sheboygan: USA 84; 44n 88w
Shechem: Holy Land 48; Inset
Shelby: USA 80; 49n 112w
Shelbyville: USA 84; 39n 86w
Shelekov Bay: USSR 43; 60n 158e
Shenandoah: Pa., USA 85; 41n 76w
Shenandoah: Va., USA 85; 38n 79w
Shensi: Prov.: China 53; 35n 109e
Shenyang: China 53; 42n 123e
Shepparton: Australia 61; 36s 145e
Sherbrooke: Canada 85; 45n 72w
Sherlovaya Gora: USSR 43; 51n 116e
Sherridon: Canada 80; 55n 101w
's-Hertogenbosch: Netherlands 32; 52n 5e
Shibata: Japan 54; 38n 139e
Shibeli: r., Eth. Som. 67; 6n 43e
Shibetsu: Japan 55; 44n 145e
Shickshock Mts.: Can. 85; 49n 67w
Shigatse: China 47; 29n 88e
Shihchan: China 43; 52n 125e
Shihkiachwang: China 53; 38n 115e
Shikoku: i., Japan 54; 34n 134e
Shikotan: i., Japan 55; 44n 147e
Shilka: r., USSR 43; 53n 118e
Shillong: India 53; 26n 92e
Shimabara: Japan 54; 33n 130e
Shimoga: India 52; 14n 76e
Shimonoseki: Japan 54; 34n 131e
Shimano: r., Japan 54; 37n 139e
Shingu: Japan 54; 33n 136e
Shinjo: Japan 54; 39n 140e
*Shinyanga: Tanganyika 68; 4s 33e
Shipka P.: Bulgaria 31; 43n 25e
Shipki P.: Ind. China 52; 32n 78e
Shirakawa: Japan 54; 37n 140e
Shiraz: Iran 49; 29n 53e
Shire: r., Africa 69; 16s 35e
Shiretoko, C.: Japan 55; 44n 145e
Shizuoka: Japan 54; 35n 138e
Shkoder: Albania 31; 42n 19e
Shoalhaven: r., Aust. 61; 35s 151e
Sholapur: India 52; 18n 76e
Shortland Is.: Pac. O. 59; 7s 156e
Shreveport: USA 81; 32n 94w
Shufu: China 45; 40n 76e
Shumen: Bulgaria 31; 43n 27e
Shwangliao: China 53; 43n 123e
Shwebo: Burma 50; 22n 96e
Si: r., China 53; 23n 112e
Sialkot: W. Pakistan 42; 32n 74e
SIAM (THAILAND) 51; 15n 100e
Sian: China 53; 34n 109e
Siang: r., China 53; 27n 113e
Siangtan: China 53; 28n 113e
Siaulia: USSR 35; 56n 23e
Sibenik: Yugoslavia 27; 44n 16e
Sibi: W. Pakistan 52; 29n 68e
Sibiu: Romania 31; 46n 24e
*Sibu: Sarawak 51; 2n 112e
Sicily: i., Italy 30; 37n 14e
Sidi-bel-Abbès: Alg. 25; 35n 1w
Sidra, G. of: Libya 67; 31n 18e
Sieg: r., Germany 32; 51n 8e
Siegburg: Germany 32; 51n 7e
Siegen: Germany 32; 51n 7e
Siena: Italy 30; 43n 11e
Sierra de Gata: Spain 25; 40n 7w
Sierra de Gredos: Sp. 25; 40n 5w
Sierra de Guadarrama: Spain 25; 41n 4w
SIERRA LEONE 66; 8n 12w
Sierra Morena: Spain 25; 38n 5w
Sierra Nevada: Spain 25; 37n 3w
Sierra Nevada: USA 80; 38n 120w
Sighişoara: Romania 31; 46n 25e
Siglufjördhur: Iceland 34; 66n 19w
Siirt: Turkey 49; 38n 42e
Sikhote: Alin' Ra.: USSR 43; 47n 137e
SIKKIM 52; 28n 88e
*Sil: r., Spain 25; 42n 7w
Silchar: India 53; 25n 93e
Silesia: Poland 27; 51n 17e
Silistra: Bulgaria 31; 44n 27e
Silva Porto: Angola 69; 13s 17e
Silvares: Portugal 25; 40n 8w
Silver Bay: USA 84; 47n 91w
Silverton: Australia 61; 32s 141e
*Simanggang: Sarawak 51; 1n 111e
Simcoe, L.: Canada 84; 44n 79w
Simferopol': USSR 44; 45n 34e
Simla: India 52; 31n 77e
Simonstown: S. Africa 69; 34s 18e
Simplon P.: Switz. 33; 46n 8e
Simpson Desert: Aust. 60; 26s 139e
Sinai: penin., Egypt 67; 29n 34e
Sind: W. Pakistan 52; 26n 68e
Singapore: Malaya 51; 2n 104e
Singaradja: Bali 51; 8s 115e
Singkep: Indonesia 51; 1s 104e
Singleton: Australia 61; 32s 151e
Singora: Thailand 51; 7n 100e
Sinhsien: China 53; 38n 113e
Sining: China 50; 37n 102e
Sin Kiang Uighur Auton. Region: China 47; 40n 85e
Sinop: Turkey 48; 42n 35e
Sinuiju: N. Korea 50; 40n 125e
Sion: Switzerland 33; 46n 7e
Sioux City: USA 81; 42n 96w
Sioux Falls: USA 80; 44n 97w
Siracusa: Sicily 30; 37n 15e
Siret: r., Romania 31; 46n 27e
Sirte: Libya 66; 31n 17e
Sisak: Yugoslavia 27; 45n 16e
Sishen: S. Africa 69; 27s 23e
Sistan: Iran Afghan. 49; 30n 61e
Sisteron: France 29; 44n 6e
Sitapur: India 52; 27n 81e
Sittang: r., Burma 51; 17n 97e
Sivas: Turkey 48; 40n 37e
Siwa: Egypt 67; 29n 26e

Page; Lat. Long.
Skadovsk: USSR 31; 46n 33e
Skagerrak: Nor., Den. 35; 58n 8e
Skagway: USA 78; 59n 135w
Skeena: r., Canada 78; 54n 129w
Skellefte: r., Sweden 34; 65n 19e
Skellefteå: Sweden 34; 65n 21e
Skien: Norway 35; 59n 10e
Skiros: i., Greece 31; 39n 25e
Skive: Denmark 35; 57n 9e
Skjold: Norway 35; 60n 6e
Skaw, The: Swed. Den. 35; 58n 11e
Skierniewice: Poland 35; 52n 20e
Skopelos: i., Greece 31; 39n 24e
Skopje: Yugoslavia 27; 42n 21e
Skövde: Sweden 35; 58n 14e
Slatina: Romania 31; 44n 24e
Slave: r., Canada 78; 60n 113w
Slave Coast: Africa 68; 5n 3e
Sliven: Bulgaria 31; 43n 26e
Slonim: USSR 35; 53n 25e
Slovakia: Czech. 27; 48n 19e
Slovenia: Yugoslavia 27; 46n 15e
Smiths Falls: Canada 85; 45n 76w
Smoky Mts.: USA 84; 36n 83w
Smolensk: USSR 44; 55n 32e
Smyrna: Turkey 31; 38n 27e
Snake: r., USA 80; 47n 118w
Snowy Mts.: & r., Aust. 61; 36s 148e
Sochi: USSR 44; 44n 40e
Society Is.: Pac. O. 93; 17s 150w
Socotra: i., Arab. Sea 49; 12n 54e
Soda Mts.: Libya 66; 29n 15e
Sodawater B.: Aust. 60; 22s 150e
Söderhamn: Sweden 35; 61n 17e
Sodom: Holy Land 48; Inset
Soest: Germany 32; 52n 8e
Soest: Netherlands 32; 52n 5e
Sofala: Mozambique 69; 20s 35e
Sofia (Sofiya): Bulgaria 31; 43n 23e
Sogne Fiord: Norway 35; 61n 6e
Sögut, L.: Turkey 31; 37n 30e
Soissons: France 28; 49n 3e
Solikamsk: USSR 44; 60n 57e
Sol'-Iletsk: USSR 44; 51n 55e
Solimoes: r., S. Amer. 86; 4s 69w
Solingen: Germany 32; 51n 7e
Sologne: France 28; 48n 2e
Solomon Is.: Pac. O. 92; 10s 160e
Solothurn: Switz. 33; 47n 8e
Solta: i., Yugoslavia 27; 43n 16e
Sokoto: Nigeria 68; 13n 5e
*SOMALIA 70; 5n 45w
*SOMALILAND PROT. 67; 10n 45e
Sombor: Yugoslavia 27; 46n 19e
Sombrero: i. W. Indies 83; 18n 63w
Somerset I.: Canada 79; 73n 93w
Somme: r., France 28; 50n 2e
Sommières: France 29; 44n 4e
Son: r., India 52; 24n 81e
Søndre Strømfjord: Greenland 79; 67n 52w
Sondrio: Italy 33; 46n 10e
*Songea: Tanganyika 68; 11s 36e
Songjin: N. Korea 54; 41n 129e
Songkhla: Thailand 51; 7n 100e
Sonora: Mexico 80; 30n 110w
Sorel: Canada 85; 46n 73w
Soria: Spain 25; 42n 2w
Sosnowiec: Poland 27; 50n 19e
Sos'va: USSR 45; 59n 62e
Soochow: China 53; 32n 121e
Soonwald: Germany 32; 50n 8e
Sopron: Hungary 27; 48n 17e
Souk Ahras: Algeria 25; 36n 8e
Sound, The: Swed. Den. 35; 56n 13e
Sounds, The: NZ 55; 41s 174e
Souris: Manitoba, Can. 80; 50n 100w
Souris: P.E. I., Canada 85; 46n 62w
Sousse: Tunisia 66; 36n 10e
South Australia 60; 30s 139e
South Bend: USA 84; 42n 86w
South Carolina: USA 81; 34n 80w
South China Sea 53; — —
South Dakota: USA 80; 45n 100w
Southern Alps: NZ 55; 44s 170e
Southern Cross: Aust. 60; 31s 119e
Southern Ocean 90; — —
*SOUTHERN RHODESIA 69; 20s 30e
Southern Sierra Madre: Mexico 82; 17n 100w
South Georgia: Atl. O. 89; 54s 37w
South Island: NZ 55; — —
SOUTH KOREA 50; 37n 128e
Southland: NZ 55; 46s 168e
South Orkney Is.: Antarctica 91; 60s 45w
South Magnetic Pole: Antarctica 91; 67s 143e
South Pole: Antarc. 91; 90 180
South Porcupine: Can. 84; 48n 81w
South Sandwich Is.: Southern Ocean 90; 58s 27w
South Shetland Is.: Antarctica 91; 62s 60w
*SOUTH VIET NAM 51; 12n 108e
*SOUTH-WEST AFRICA 69; 22s 17e
Sovetsk: USSR 35; 55n 22e
Soviet Harbour: USSR 43; 49n 140e
SPAIN 25; — —
Spandau: Germany 32; 52n 13e
*SPANISH GUINEA 68; 3n 10e
*SPANISH SAHARA 66; 25n 13w
Spanish Town: Jamaica 83; 18n 77w
Sparrows Point: USA 85; 39n 76w
Sparta: Greece 31; 37n 22e
Spartanburg: USA 81; 35n 82w
Spartel, C.: Morocco 25; 36n 5w
Spatha, C.: Crete 31; 36n 24e
Spartivento, C.: Italy 30; 38n 16e
Spassk Dal'niy: USSR 54; 44n 133e
Spasskoye: USSR 45; 52n 68e
Spencer, C.: Australia 61; 35s 137e
Spenser Mts.: NZ 55; 42s 173e
Spessart: Germany 32; 50n 9e
Spetsai: i., Greece 31; 37n 23e
Speyer: Germany 32; 49n 8e
Spiekeroog: i., Germany 32; 54n 8e
Spis: Czechoslovakia 27; 49n 21e
Spitsbergen: Norway 42; 78n 15e

* See Page 131

Page; Lat. Long.
Split: Yugoslavia 27; 43n 16e
Splügen P.: Switz./Italy. 33; 47n 9e
Spokane: USA 80; 48n 117w
Sporades: is., Greece 31; 36n 27e
Spree: r., Germany 32; 52n 14e
Springbok: S. Africa 69; 30s 18e
Springfield: Ill., USA 84; 40n 90w
Springfield: Mass., USA 85; 42n 73w
Springfield: Mo., USA 81; 37n 93w
Springfield: Ohio, USA. 84; 40n 84w
Springsure: Australia 60; 24s 148e
Spruce Pine: USA 84; 36n 82w
Spungabera: Moz. 69; 21s 33e
Squamish: Canada 80; 50n 123w
Sretensk: USSR 43; 52n 118e
Srinagar: Kashmir 52; 34n 75e
Stalinabad: see Dyushambe
Stalingrad: see Volgograd
Stalino: see Donetsk
Stalinogorsk: see Novomoskovsk
Stalin Pk.: see Mt. Communism
Stalinsk: see Novokuznetsk
Stalinstadt: see Eisenhüttenstadt
Stallworthy, C.: Canada 79; 81n 93w
*Stanislav: USSR 44; 49n 25e
*Stanley Falls: Congo Rep. 70; 0 25e
*Stanley Pool: Congo Rep. 71; 4s 15e
*Stanleyville: Congo Rep. 70; 1n 25e
Stanthorpe: Australia 61; 29s 152e
Starke: USA 81; 30n 82w
Stara Zagora: Bulgaria 31; 42n 26e
Stassfurt: Germany 32; 52n 12e
Staten I.: Argentina 89; 55s 64w
Staten I.: USA 85; 40n 74w
Staunton: USA 85; 38n 79w
Stavanger: Norway 35; 59n 6e
Stavelot: Belgium 28; 50n 6e
Stavropol': USSR 44; 45n 42e
Steep Rock L.: Canada 84; 49n 91w
Steigerwald: Germany 32; 50n 11e
Steinkjer: Norway 34; 64n 11e
Stellenbosch: S. Africa 69; 34s 18e
Stelvio P.: Switz./Italy 33; 47n 10e
Stendal: Germany 32; 52n 12e
Steppes: USSR 45; — —
Sterling: USA 84; 42n 90w
Sterlitamak: USSR 44; 54n 56e
Stettin: Poland 35; 53n 15e
Steubenville: USA 84; 40n 80w
Stewart I.: NZ 55; 47s 168e
Stewart Is.: Pac. O. 59; 8s 163e
Steyr: Austria 33; 48n 14e
Stillwell I.: Antarc. 91; 66s 144e
Stip: Yugoslavia 27; 42n 22e
Stirling Range: Aust. 60; 34s 118e
Stjernøy: i., Norway 34; 70n 23e
Stockholm: Sweden 35; 59n 18e
Stockton: USA 80; 38n 121w
Stony Tunguska: r., USSR 43; 61n 95e
Stor L.: Sweden 34; 63n 14e
Storuman: Sweden 34; 65n 17e
Stralsund: Germany 35; 54n 13e
Stranca Mts.: Turkey 31; 41n 28e
Strasbourg: France 28; 49n 8e
Stratford: Canada 84; 43n 81w
Stratford: NZ 55; 39s 174e
Straubing: Germany 32; 49n 13e
Streator: USA 84; 41n 89w
Stresa: Italy 33; 46n 9e
Stromboli: i., Italy 30; 39n 15e
Strömstad: Sweden 35; 59n 11e
Struma: r., Bulgaria 31; 42n 23e
Strumica: Yugoslavia 27; 41n 23e
Stuart Highway: Aust. 58; 20s 134e
Sturt Desert: Aust. 60; 28s 141e
Stuttgart: Germany 33; 49n 9e
Styria: Austria 33; 47n 14e
Suakin: Sudan 67; 19n 37e
Suanhwa: China 53; 41n 115e
Subotica: Yugoslavia 27; 46n 20e
Succoth: Holy Land 48; Inset
Suceava: Romania 31; 48n 26e
Suchan: USSR 43; 43n 133e
Suchiate: Mexico 82; 15n 92w
Suchow: China 53; 34n 117e
Sucre: Bolivia 86; 19s 65w
SUDAN 67; 15n 30e
Sudbury: Canada 84; 46n 81w
Sudd: Sudan 67; 9n 30e
Sudeten Mts.: Czech. 27; 51n 16e
Suez: & canal, Egypt 67 Inset
Sugarloaf Pt.: Aust. 61; 32s 152e
Sui: W. Pakistan 52; 28n 69e
Sukhona: r., USSR 44; 60n 43e
Sukhumi: USSR 44; 43n 41e
Sukkur: W. Pakistan 52; 28n 69e
Sula: is., Indonesia 51; 2s 125e
Sulaiman Ra.: W. Pak. 52; 31n 69e
Sulawesi: i., Indon. 51; 2s 120e
Sulina: Romania 44; 45n 30e
Sulmona: Italy 30; 42n 14e
Sultan Mts.: Turkey 31; 38n 31e
Suluq: Libya 48; 32n 20e
Sulu Sea: Indonesia 51; 8n 120e
Sumbawa: i., Indon. 51; 8s 118e
Sumatra: i., Indon. 51; 0 100e
Sumba: i., Indonesia 51; 10s 120e
Sumgait: USSR 44; 40n 50e
Summan: Sa'udi Arabia 49; 26n 48e
Summit: USA 78; 63n 149w
Sumoto: Japan 54; 34n 135e
Šumperk: Czech. 27; 50n 17e
Sumy: USSR 44; 51n 35e
Sunagawa: Japan 54; 44n 142e
Sundarbans: Ind./Pak. 52; 22n 89e
Sunda Str.: Indonesia 51; 6s 106e
Sundsvall: Sweden 34; 62n 17e
Sungari: r., China 53; 45n 126e
Sungari Res.: China 53; 43n 127e
Sunyani: Ghana 68; 7n 3w
Suo Gulf: Japan 54; 34n 131e
Superior: USA 84; 47n 92w
Superior, L.: Can./USA. 84; 48n 88w
Surabaja: Java 51; 7s 113e
Surakarta: Java 51; 7s 111e
Surat: Australia 60; 27s 149e
Surat: India 52; 22n 73e
Surgut: USSR 45; 61n 73e
SURINAM 87; 5n 55w

Page; Lat. Long.
Susa: Italy 33; 45n 7e
Susquehanna: r., USA 85; 40n 77w
Susuman: USSR 43; 63n 148e
Sutlej: r., Ind./W. Pak. 52; 30n 73e
Suttor: r., Australia 60; 22s 147e
Suttsu: Japan 54; 43n 140e
Suva: Fiji Is. 92; 18s 179e
Suzak: USSR 45; 44n 68e
Svalbard: Norway 42; 78n 15e
Svendborg: Denmark 35; 55n 11e
Sverdlovsk: USSR 45; 57n 61e
Sverdrup Is.: Canada 79; 79n 100w
Svir': r., USSR 44; 61n 34e
Svishtov: Bulgaria 31; 44n 25e
Swabian Jura: Ger. 33; 48n 10e
Swain Reefs: Australia 60; 22s 152e
Swakopmund: SW. Afr. 69; 23s 15e
Swan: r., Australia 60; 32s 116e
Swan Hill: Australia 61; 35s 144e
Swanland: Australia 60; 33s 116e
Swatow: China 53; 23n 117e
SWAZILAND 69; 27s 32e
SWEDEN 34/35; — —
Sweetwater Canal: Eg. 67; Inset
Swellendam: S. Africa 69; 34s 20e
Świnoujście: Poland 35; 54n 14e
SWITZERLAND 33; — —
Sydney: Australia 61; 34s 151e
Sydney: Canada 85; 46n 60w
Sydney Mines: Canada 85; 46n 60w
Syktyvkar: USSR 44; 62n 51e
*Sylhet: E. Pakistan 53; 25n 92e
Syracuse: Sicily 30; 37n 15e
Syracuse: USA 85; 43n 76w
Syr Dar'ya: r., USSR 45; 44n 66e
SYRIA 49; 35n 40e
Syzran': USSR 44; 53n 48e
Szczecin: Poland 35; 53n 15e
Szczecinek: Poland 35; 54n 17e
Szechwan: Prov., China 53; 30n 105e
Szeged: Hungary 27; 46n 20e
Szeping: China 53; 43n 124e
Szolnok: Hungary 27; 47n 20e
Szombathely: Hungary 27; 47n 17e
Sztálinváros: see Dunaujvaros

Tabor, Mt.: Holy Land 48; Inset
*Tabora: Tanganyika 68; 5s 33e
Tabriz: Iran 49; 38n 46e
Tacna: Peru 86; 18s 70w
Tacoma: USA 80; 47n 123w
Taconic Ra.: USA 85; 42n 74w
Taconite Harb.: USA 84; 47n 91w
Tadoussac: Canada 85; 48n 70w
Tadzhik SSR: USSR 45; 38n 71e
Taegu: S. Korea 50; 36n 128e
Taejon: S. Korea 50; 37n 127e
Tafersit: Morocco 25; 35n 4w
Tafilalet Oasis: Mor. 66; 31n 4w
Taganrog: USSR 44; 47n 39e
Tagliamento: r., Italy 33; 46n 13e
Tagus: r., Spain/Port. 25; 39n 8w
Tahawus: USA 85; 44n 74w
Tahiti: i., Pac. O. 93; 18s 150w
Tahsien: China 53; 32n 107e
Tai, L.: China 53; 31n 121e
T'ai-chung: Formosa 50; 24n 121e
Taif: Sa'udi Arabia 49; 21n 40e
Taihape: NZ 55; 40s 176e
T'ai-nan: Formosa 50; 23n 120e
Taipeh: Formosa 53; 25n 122e
Taiping: Malaya 51; 5n 100e
*Taira: Japan 54; 37n 141e
Taitao Penin.: Chile 89; 47s 76w
T'ai-tung: Formosa 53; 23n 121e
TAIWAN (FORMOSA) 53; 24n 122e
Taiyüan: China 50; 38n 112e
Ta'iz: Yemen 49; 13n 44e
Tak: Thailand 51; 17n 99e
Takada: Japan 54; 37n 138e
Takaka: NZ 55; 41s 173e
Takamatsu: Japan 54; 34n 134e
Takaoka: Japan 54; 37n 137e
Takasaki: Japan 54; 36n 139e
Takawa: Japan 54; 34n 131e
Takazze: r., Ethiopia 49; 14n 38e
Take Is.: Sea of Japan 54; 37n 132e
Takla Makan: China 47; 39n 83e
Takoradi: Ghana 68; 5n 2w
Taku: China 53; 39n 118e
Talara: Ecuador 86; 5s 81w
Talaud Is.: Indonesia 51; 4n 127e
Talavera: Spain 25; 40n 5w
Talbot, C.: Australia 58; 14s 127e
Tallahassee: USA 81; 30n 84w
Tallinn: USSR 35; 59n 25e
Taltal: Chile 88; 25s 70w
Tamale: Ghana 68; 9n 1w
*Tamatave: Madag. 71; 18s 50e
Tambo: Australia 60; 25s 147e
Tambov: USSR 44; 53n 42e
Tammisaari: Finland 35; 60n 23e
Tampa: USA 81; 28n 82w
Tampere: Finland 34; 62n 24e
Tampico: Mexico 82; 22n 98w
Tamridah: Socotra 49; 13n 54e
Tamtsak Bulak: Mong. 50; 47n 118e
Tamworth: Australia 61; 31s 151e
Tana: & fiord, Norway 34; 71n 28e
Tana: r., Kenya 68; 1s 40e
Tana, L.: Ethiopia 67; 12n 37e
Tanabe: Japan 54; 34n 135e
Tanana: USA 78; 65n 152w
*Tananarive: Madag. 71; 19s 48e
Tandil: Argentina 88; 37s 59w
Tandou, L.: Australia 61; 33s 142e
Tanezrouft: Algeria 66; 23n 0
*Tanga: Tanganyika 68; 5s 39e
*TANGANYIKA 68; 5s 35e
Tanganyika, L.: Africa 68; 6s 30e
Tangier: Morocco 66; 36n 6w
Tangshan: China 53; 40n 118e
Tanimbar Is.: Indonesia 51; 8s 132e
Tannenberg: Poland 35; 54n 20e
*Tanta: Egypt 48; 31n 31e
Tao: r., China 53; 26n 112e
Tapajos: r., Brazil 87; 6s 57w
Tapa Shan: China 53; 32n 108e
Tapti: r., India 52; 21n 76e
Tapuaenuku: mt., NZ 55; 42s 174e

Page; Lat. Long.
Tara: USSR 45; 57n 75e
Tarakan: Borneo 51; 3n 118e
Taranaki: NZ 55; 39s 174e
Taranto: & G., Italy 30; 40n 17e
Tarare: France 29; 46n 4e
Tararua Range: NZ 55; 41s 175e
Tarascon: France 29; 44n 5e
Tarawa: i., Pac. O. 92; 1n 173e
Tarbes: France 29; 43n 0
Tardenois: France 28; 49n 4e
Taree: Australia 61; 32s 152e
Târgu Jiu: Romania 31; 45n 23e
Târgu Mureș: Romania 31; 47n 25e
Tarija: Bolivia 88; 22s 65w
Tarim: r., China 47; 41n 82e
Tarkhankut, C.: USSR 31; 45n 32e
Tarko-Sale: USSR 43; 65n 78e
Tarn: r., France 29; 44n 2e
Taroom: Australia 60; 26s 150e
Tarragona: Spain 25; 41n 1e
Tarsus: Turkey 48; 37n 35e
Tartary, G. of: USSR 43; 50n 141e
Tartu: USSR 35; 58n 27e
Tarviso: Italy 33; 47n 14e
Taschereau: Canada 85; 49n 79w
Tashkent: USSR 45; 42n 69e
Tasman B.: NZ 55; 41s 173e
Tasmania: Aust. 59; 42s 147e
Tasman Mts.: NZ 55; 41s 172e
Tassili-n-Ajjer: Algeria 66; 26n 8e
Tatar Pass: USSR 31; 48n 24e
Tatarsk: USSR 45; 55n 76e
Tateyama: Japan 54; 35n 140e
Tatry: Czechoslovakia 27; 49n 20e
Tatung: China 53; 40n 113e
Taumarunui: NZ 55; 39s 175e
Taunus: mts., Germany 32; 50n 8e
Taupo: & L., NZ 55; 39s 176e
Tauranga: NZ 55; 38s 176e
Taurus Mts.: Turkey 48; 37n 35e
Tavda: & r., USSR 45; 58n 65e
Taveta: Kenya 68; 3s 38e
Tavira: Portugal 25; 37n 7w
Tavoy: Burma 51; 14n 98e
Tawitawi: i., Philippines 51; 5n 120e
Tayeh: China 53; 30n 115e
Taymyr, L.: USSR 43; 75n 102e
Taymyr Penin.: USSR 43; 75n 105e
Tayshet: USSR 45; 56n 97e
Taz: r., USSR 43; 65n 82e
Tbilisi: USSR 44; 42n 45e
Te Anau, L.: NZ 55; 45s 168e
Te Awamutu: NZ 55; 38s 175e
Tébessa: Algeria 25; 35n 8e
Tebuk: Sa'udi Arabia 48; 28n 37e
Tedzhen: r., USSR 49; 37n 61e
Tegucigalpa: Honduras 83; 14n 87w
Tehrān: Iran 49; 36n 51e
Tehuantepec: Mexico 82; 17n 95w
Tekely: USSR 45; 45n 78e
Tekirdağ: Turkey 31; 41n 27e
Te Kuiti: NZ 55; 38s 175e
Tell Atlas: mts., Algeria 25; 37n 7e
*Tell el Kebir: Egypt. 67; Inset
Telukbetung: Sumatra 51; 5s 105e
Tema: Ghana 68; 6n 0
Temerin: Yugoslavia 27; 45n 20e
Temir-Tau: USSR 45; 50n 72e
Temora: Australia 61; 34s 148e
Temuco: Chile 88; 39s 73w
Tenda P.: France/Italy 29; 44n 8e
Tende: France 29; 44n 8e
Tenerife: i., Canary Is. 66; 28n 17w
Tengchung: China 50; 25n 98e
Tengiz, L.: USSR 45; 51n 69e
Tennant Creek: Aust. 58; 20s 135e
Tennessee: r., USA 84; 36n 88w
Tennessee: State, USA 84; 36n 87w
Tennessee Valley: USA 81; 36n 87w
Tenterfield: Aust. 61; 29s 152e
Teramo: Italy 30; 44n 14e
Teresina: Brazil 87; 5s 43w
Terme di Valdieri: It. 33; 44n 7e
Termez: USSR 45; 38n 67e
Termoli: Italy 30; 42n 15e
Ternate: i., Indon. 51; 1n 127e
Terneuzen: Neth. 32; 51n 4e
Terni: Italy 30; 44n 13e
Terra Nova B.: Antarc. 91; 75s 164e
Terre Haute: USA 84; 39n 87w
Terror, Mt.: Antarc. 91; 78s 169e
Terschelling: i., Neth. 32; 53n 5e
Teruel: Spain 25; 40n 1w
Tessenei: Ethiopia 67; 15n 37e
Tete: Mozambique 69; 16s 33e
Tetuán: Morocco 66; 36n 5w
Tetyukhe: USSR 54; 44n 136e
Tetyukhe-Pristan': USSR 54; 44n 136e
Teutoburger Wald: Germany 32; 52n 8e
Texarkana: USA 81; 33n 94w
Texas: State, USA 80; 32n 100w
Texas City: USA 81; 29n 95w
Texel: i., Netherlands 32; 53n 5e
Tezpur: India 53; 27n 93e
Thabazimbi: S. Africa 69; 25s 27e
THAILAND (SIAM) 51; 15n 100e
Thal: W. Pakistan 52; 32n 72e
Thalwil: Switzerland 33; 47n 9e
Thames: NZ 55; 37s 176e
Thanjavur: India 52; 11n 79e
Thar Desert: India 42; 27n 72e
Thasos: i., Greece 31; 41n 25e
Thayetmyo: Burma 50; 19n 95e
Thebes: Egypt 67; 26n 33e
Thermai, G. of: Greece 31; 40n 23e
Thermia: i., Greece 31; 37n 24e
Thermopylae: Greece 31; 39n 22e
Thessaloniki: Greece 31; 41n 23e
Thessaly: Greece 31; 39n 22e
Thetford Mines: Can. 85; 46n 71w
Thiérache: France 28; 50n 3e
Thiers: France 29; 46n 4e
Thionville: France 28; 49n 6e
Thira: i., Greece 31; 36n 25e
*Thomson's Falls: Kenya 68; 0 36e
Thonon: France 29; 46n 6e
Thore, r.: France 29; 44n 2e
Thouars: France 29; 47n 0

Page; Lat. Long.
Thousand Is.: Canada 85; 44n 76w
Thrace: Greece 31; 41n 25e
Three Kings Is., NZ 55; 34s 173e
Three Points, C.: Ghana 68; 5n 2w
Three Springs: Aust. 60; 29s 116e
Thule: Greenland 79; 76n 70w
Thun: & L., Switz. 33; 47n 8e
Thur: r., Switzerland 33; 48n 9e
Thüringer Wald: Ger. 32; 51n 11e
Thuringia: Germany 32; 51n 11e
Thursday I.: Aust. 59; 11s 143e
Tiaret: Algeria 25; 35n 1e
Tiber: r., Italy 30; 43n 12e
Tiberias: Holy Land 48; Inset
Tibet: China 47; 32n 85e
Ticino: r., Italy 33; 45n 9e
Ticonderoga: USA 85; 44n 73w
Tien Shan: USSR/China 45; 42n 80e
Tientsin: China 53; 39n 117e
Tierra del Fuego: Arg. 89; 54s 67w
Tiffin: USA 84; 41n 83w
Tignes Res.: France 29; 45n 7e
Tignish: Canada 85; 47n 64w
Tigris: r., Asia 49; 34n 43e
Tihama: Sa'udi Arabia 49; 20n 41e
Tihwa: China 47; 43n 88e
Tijuana: Mexico 80; 32n 117w
Tiksi: USSR 43; 72n 129e
Tilburg: Netherlands 32; 52n 5e
Tillabéry: Niger 66; 14n 2e
Tilos: i., Greece 31; 36n 27e
Tilsit: USSR 35; 55n 22e
Timaru: NZ 55; 44s 171e
Timbuktu: Mali 66; 17n 3w
Timiskaming, L.: Can. 85; 47n 79w
Timiskaming Stn.: Can. 85; 47n 79w
Timișoara: Romania 31; 46n 21e
Timmins: Canada 84; 48n 81w
Timor: i., Indon. 51; 10s 125e
Timsah, L.: Egypt 67; Inset
Tintic: USA 80; 40n 112w
Tiranë (Tirana): Alb. 31; 41n 20e
Tiraspol': USSR 31; 47n 30e
Tire: Turkey 31; 38n 28e
Tiruchirapalli: India 52; 11n 78e
Tirunelveli: India 52; 8n 78e
Tista: r., India 52; 27n 88e
Tisza: r., Europe 27; 46n 20e
Titicaca, L.: S. Amer. 86; 16s 69w
Titograd: Yugoslavia 27; 42n 19e
Titovo Užice: Yugo. 27; 44n 20e
Titov Veles: Yugo. 27; 42n 22e
Tivoli: Italy 30; 42n 13e
Tlemcen: Algeria 25; 35n 1w
Tobol': r., USSR 45; 57n 67e
Tobol'sk: USSR 45; 58n 68e
Tobruk: Libya 67; 32n 24e
Tocantins: r., Brazil 87; 4s 49w
Tocumwal: Australia 61; 36s 146e
TOGO 68; 8n 1e
*Togoland: Ghana 68; 7n 1e
Tokaj: Hungary 27; 48n 21e
Tokelau: is., Pac. O. 92; 9s 171w
Tokushima: Japan 54; 34n 135e
Tokyo: Japan 54; 36n 140e
Tolbukhin: Bulgaria 31; 44n 28e
Toledo: Spain 25; 40n 4w
Toledo: USA 84; 42n 83w
Toledo, Mts. de: Spain 25; 39n 5w
Tolo, G. of: Indonesia 51; 2s 122e
Tolosa: Spain 25; 43n 2w
Tolstoy, C.: USSR 43; 59n 155e
Tomakomai: Japan 54; 43n 141e
Tomatlán: Mexico 82; 20n 105w
Tomini, G. of: Indonesia 51; 1s 121e
Tomsk: USSR 45; 57n 85e
Tone: r., Japan 54; 36n 140e
Tonga Is.: Pacific Ocean 92; 20s 175w
Tongatapu: i., Pac. O. 92; 20s 175w
Tonkin, G. of 53; 21n 108e
Tonle L.: Cambodia 51; 13n 104e
Tønsberg: Norway 35; 59n 10e
Toowoomba: Australia 60; 28s 152e
Topeka: USA 81; 39n 96w
Topozero: L., USSR 34; 66n 32e
Torgau: Germany 32; 52n 13e
Torhout: Belgium 28; 51n 3e
Torino: Italy 33; 45n 8e
Torne L.: & r., Sweden 34; 68n 20e
Tornio: Finland 34; 66n 24e
Toronto: Canada 85; 44n 79w
Tororo: Uganda 68; 1n 34e
Toros Mts.: Turkey 48; 37n 35e
Torrens, L.: Australia 61; 31s 138e
Torreón: Mexico 82; 26n 103w
Torres Str.: Australia 59; 10s 143e
Torres Vedras: Port. 25; 39n 9w
Tortona: Italy 33; 45n 9e
Tortosa, C.: Spain 25; 41n 1e
Toruń: Poland 35; 53n 19e
Tosa Bay: Japan 54; 33n 134e
Totomi G.: Japan 54; 34n 137e
Tottori: Japan 54; 35n 134e
Touba: Senegal 66; 15n 16w
Touggourt: Algeria 66; 33n 6e
Toul: France 28; 49n 6e
Toulon: France 29; 43n 6e
Toulouse: France 29; 44n 1e
Toungo: Nigeria 68; 8n 12e
Toungoo: Burma 50; 18n 96e
Touraine: France 29; 47n 1e
*Tourane: S. Viet Nam 51; 16n 108e
Tourcoing: France 28; 51n 3e
Tournai: Belgium 28; 51n 3e
Tours: France 29; 47n 1e
Townshend I.: Aust. 60; 22s 150e
Townsville: Australia 60; 19s 147e
Toyama: Japan 54; 37n 137e
Toyohashi: Japan 54; 35n 137e
Trabzon: Turkey 49; 41n 40e
Trail: Canada 80; 49n 118w
Trafalgar, C.: Spain 25; 36n 6w
Tranås: Sweden 35; 58n 15e
Transvaal: S. Africa 69; 25s 30e
Transylvania: Romania 31; 46n 23e
Trapani: Sicily 30; 38n 13e
Trasimeno, L.: Italy 30; 43n 12e
Traveller's L.: Australia 61; 33s 142e
Traverse City: USA 84; 45n 86w
Traunstein: Germany 33; 48n 13e

Page; Lat. Long.
Trelleborg: Sweden 35; 55n 13e
Trentino: Italy 33; 46n 11e
Trento: Italy 33; 46n 11e
Trenton: Canada 85; 44n 78w
Trenton: USA 85; 40n 75w
Trepča: Yugoslavia 27; 43n 21e
Treviso: Italy 33; 46n 12e
Trier: Germany 32; 50n 7e
Trieste: Italy 33; 46n 14e
Trikkala: Greece 31; 39n 22e
*Trincomalee: Ceylon 52; 8n 82e
Trinidad: i., Brazil 90; 20s 30w
Trinidad: i., S. Amer. 86; 10n 62w
Tripoli: Lebanon 48; 34n 36e
Tripoli: Libya 66; 33n 13e
Tripolis: Greece 31; 37n 22e
Tripolitania: Libya 48; 30n 15e
Tripura: State, India 53; — —
Tristan da Cunha: i., Atlantic Ocean 90; 38s 12w
Trivandrum: India 52; 8n 77e
Trois Rivières: Canada 85; 46n 73w
Troitsk: USSR 45; 54n 61e
Trollhättan: Sweden 35; 58n 12e
Tromsø: Norway 34; 70n 19e
Trondheim: & Fd., Nor. 34; 63n 10e
Trout Lake: Canada 78; 60n 121w
Troy: Turkey 31; 40n 26e
Troyes: France 28; 48n 4e
TRUCIAL OMAN 49; 24n 54e
Trujillo: Honduras 83; 16n 86w
Trujillo: Peru 86; 8s 79w
Truk Is.: Pacific Ocean 92; 8n 151e
Truro: Canada 85; 45n 63w
Tsai: r., China 53; 35n 108e
Tsaidam Swamps: China 47; 37n 94e
Tsangpo: r., China 47; 29n 86e
Tselinograd: USSR 45; 51n 72e
Tsimlyansk Res.: USSR 44; 48n 43e
Tsinan: China 53; 37n 117e
Tsing Hai: China 50; 37n 100e
Tsingtao: China 53; 36n 120e
Tsining: China 53; 41n 118e
Tsinling Shan: China 53; 34n 107e
Tsitsihar: China 50; 48n 124e
Tsu: Japan 54; 35n 136e
Tsugaru Chan.: Japan 54; 41n 140e
Tsu Is.: Japan 54; 34n 129e
Tsumeb: SW. Africa 69; 19s 18e
Tsuni: China 53; 28n 107e
Tsuruga: Japan 54; 36n 136e
Tsuruoka: Japan 54; 39n 140e
Tsuyama: Japan 54; 35n 134e
Tsyurupinsk: USSR 31; 46n 33e
Tuamotu Arch.: Pac. O. 93; 18s 145w
Tuapse: USSR 44; 44n 39e
Tuatapere: NZ 55; 46s 168e
Tübingen: Germany 33; 49n 9e
Tubuai Is.: Pac. O. 93; 22s 150w
Tucson: USA 80; 32n 111w
Tucumán: Argentina 88; 27s 65w
Tucupita: Venezuela 86; 9n 62w
Tudela: Spain 25; 42n 1w
Tugssâq: Greenland 79; 73n 55w
Tula: USSR 44; 54n 38e
Tulare: USA 80; 36n 119w
Tul'chin: USSR 31; 49n 29e
*Tulear: Madagascar 71; 23s 43e
Tulle: France 29; 45n 2e
Tulsa: USA 81; 36n 96w
Tumaco: Colombia 86; 2n 79w
Tumkur: India 52; 13n 77e
Tumut: r., Australia 61; 35s 148e
Tungabhadra: r., India 52; 16n 77e
Tunghwa: China 53; 42n 126e
Tungkwan: China 53; 35n 110e
Tungning: China 54; 44n 131e
Tungshan: China 53; 34n 117e
Tung Ting, L.: China 53; 29n 112e
Tunis: Tunisia 66; 37n 10e
TUNISIA 66; 35n 10e
Tunja: Colombia 86; 6n 73w
Tura: r., USSR 45; 58n 63e
Turanian Plain: USSR 45; 43n 60e
Turbat: W. Pakistan 52; Inset
Turbo: Colombia 86; 8n 77w
Turda: Romania 31; 47n 24e
Turfan: China 47; 43n 89e
Turgay: & r., USSR 45; 50n 64e
Turgutlu: Turkey 31; 38n 28e
Turin: Italy 33; 45n 8e
Turkestan: USSR 45; 43n 68e
TURKEY 48/49; — —
Turkmen SSR: USSR 45; 40n 60e
Turks Is.: W. Indies 83; 21n 71w
Turku: Finland 35; 61n 22e
Turnagain, C.: NZ 55; 40s 177e
Turner Valley: Canada 80; 51n 114w
Turnhout: Belgium 28; 51n 5e
*Tŭrnovo: Bulgaria 31; 43n 26e
Turnu Măgurele: Rom. 31; 44n 25e
Turnu Severin: Rom. 31; 45n 23e
Tuscany: Italy 33; 44n 11e
Tuttlingen: Germany 33; 48n 9e
Tuxpan: Mexico 82; 21n 97w
Tuyün: China 53; 26n 107e
Tuz, L.: Turkey 48; 39n 33e
Two Harbors: USA 84; 47n 92w
Tygda: USSR 43; 53n 127e
Tyre: Holy Land 48; Inset
Tyrol: Austria 33; 47n 11e
Tyrrhenian Sea 30; 40n 12e
Tyumen': USSR 45; 57n 65e
Tzekung: China 53; 29n 105e

Ube: Japan 54; 34n 131e
Uberaba: Brazil 87; 20s 48w
Ubon: Thailand 51; 15n 105e
Ubsa Nor: Mongolia 50; 50n 93e
Ucayali: r., Peru 86; 7s 75w
Uchiura Bay: Japan 54; 42n 141e
Udaipur: India 52; 24n 73e
Uddevalla: Sweden 35; 58n 12e
Udd L.: Sweden 34; 66n 18e
Udine: Italy 33; 46n 13e
Udon Thani: Thailand 51; 17n 102e
*Uele: r., Congo Rep. 70; 4n 28e
Ueno: Japan 54; 35n 136e
Ufa: & r., USSR 44; 55n 56e
UGANDA 68; 0 32e

*See Page 131

Page; Lat. Long.
Uitenhage: S. Africa 69; 33s 25e
*Ujiji: Tanganyika 68; 5s 30e
*Uji-Yamada: Japan 54; 34n 137e
Ujjain: India 52; 23n 76e
Ukhta: USSR 44; 64n 54e
*Ukhta: USSR 34; 65n 31e
Ukrainian SSR: USSR 44; 50n 30e
Ulan Bator: Mongolia 50; 48n 107e
Ulangom: Mongolia 50; 50n 92e
Ulanhoto: China 53; 46n 122e
Ulan-Ude: USSR 43; 52n 108e
Ulawa: i., Pac. O. 59; 10s 162e
Ulchin: S. Korea 54; 37n 130e
Uldza: Mongolia 50; 49n 112e
Ullung Do: i., S. Korea 54; 37n 131e
Ulm: Germany 33; 48n 10e
Ulundi: S. Africa 69; 28s 32e
Ulu-Tau: USSR 45; 48n 67e
Ul'yanovsk: USSR 44; 54n 48e
Ulyungur Nor: China 47; 47n 87e
Ülzen: Germany 32; 53n 10e
Umarkot: W. Pakistan 52; 25n 70e
Umbria: Italy 30; 44n 13e
Umeå: Sweden 34; 64n 20e
Umm Samim:
Muscat & 'Oman 49; 22n 56e
*Umtali: S. Rhodesia 69; 19s 33e
Umtata: S. Africa 69; 31s 29e
Ungava B.: Canada 79; 60n 67w
Ungava Penin.: Can. 79; 62n 75w
Uniondale: S. Africa 69; 34s 23e
UNION OF SOVIET SOCIALIST
REPUBLICS 42/43; — —
Uniontown: USA 84; 40n 80w
UNITED ARAB REPUBLIC
(EGYPT) 67; 25n 30e
*UNITED ARAB REPUBLIC
(SYRIA) 49; 35n 40e
UNITED STATES OF
AMERICA 80/81; — —
United States Range:
Canada 79; 82n 80w
Upper Red Lake: USA 84; 48n 95w
Uppsala: Sweden 35; 60n 18e
Ur: 'Iraq 49; 31n 46e
Ural: r., USSR 44; 52n 55e
Ural Mts.: USSR 42; — —
Ural'sk: USSR 44; 51n 52e
Uranium City: Canada 78; 60n 109w
Urawa: Japan 54; 36n 140e
Urbana: USA 84; 40n 88w
Urdos: France 29; 43n 1w
Urfa: Turkey 49; 37n 39e
Urisino: Australia 61; 30s 144e
Ürküt: Hungary 27; 47n 18e
Urmia: L.: Iran 44; 38n 46e
Uruguaiana: Brazil 88; 30s 57w
URUGUAY 88; 33s 55w
Uruguay: r., S. Amer. 88; 29s 56w
Urumchi: China 47; 43n 88e
Usa: r., USSR 42; 66n 61e
Uşak: Turkey 31; 39n 30e
Usakos: SW. Africa 69; 22s 15e
Ushant: i., France 28; 48n 5w
Ushuaia: Argentina 89; 55s 68w
Üsküdar: Turkey 31; 41n 29e
Usol'ye: USSR 43; 53n 104e
Uspallata P.: Chile/Arg. 88; 33s 70w
Uspenskiy: USSR 45; 48n 73e
Ussuri: r., USSR/China 43; 47n 134e
Ussuriisk: USSR 43; 44n 132e
Ustí nad Labem: Czech. 32; 51n 14e
Ust'-Kamenogorsk:
USSR 45; 50n 83e
Ust'-Kut: USSR 43; 57n 105e
Ust'-Urt Plateau: USSR 45; 44n 57e
Ust'-Uyskoye: USSR 45; 54n 65e
Usuki: Japan 54; 33n 132e
*Usumbura: Burundi 68; 3s 29e
Utah: State, USA 80; 39n 112w
Utica: USA 85; 43n 75w
Utrecht: Netherlands 32; 52n 5e
Utsunomiya: Japan 54; 36n 140e
Uttar Pradesh: India 52; 28n 80e
Uwajima: Japan 54; 33n 133e
Uweinat: mt., Libya 48; 22n 25e
Uxmal: Mexico 82; 21n 90w
Uyuni: Bolivia 88; 21s 67w
Uzbek SSR: USSR 45; 40n 65e
Uzhgorod: USSR 31; 49n 22e

Vaal: r., S. Africa 69; 27s 27e
Vaasa (Vasa): Finland 34; 63n 22e
Vaccarès, Étang de: Fr. 29; 44n 5e
Vaduz: Liechtenstein 33; 47n 10e
Vahsel Bay: Antarc. 91; 78s 35w
Vakh: r., USSR 45; 61n 79e
Valdai Hills: USSR 44; 57n 35e
Valdepeñas: Spain 25; 39n 3w
Valdés Penin.: Arg. 89; 43s 64w
Valdez: USA 78; 61n 146w
Valdivia: Chile 88; 40s 74w
Valence: France 29; 45n 5e
Valencia: Spain 25; 39n 0
Valencia: Venezuela 86; 10n 68w
Valenciennes: France 28; 50n 4e
Valga: USSR 35; 58n 26e
Valladolid: Spain 25; 42n 5w
Valletta: Malta 30; 36n 14e
Valleyfield: Canada 85; 45n 74w
Valmiera: USSR 35; 58n 26e
Valona (Vlonë): Albania 31; 40n 20e
Valparaiso: Chile 88; 33s 72w
Val Tellina: Italy 33; 46n 10e
Val Venosta: Italy 33; 47n 11e
Van: Turkey 49; 38n 43e
Van, L.: Turkey 44; 39n 43e
Vancouver: Canada 80; 49n 123w
Vancouver: USA 80; 46n 123w
Vancouver I.: Canada 80; 50n 125w
Vancouver, Mt.:
USA/Canada 78; 60n 140w
Väner, L.: Sweden 35; 59n 13e
Vänersborg: Sweden 35; 58n 12e
Vangunu: i., Pac. O. 59; 9s 158e
Vannes: France 28; 48n 3w
Vannøy: i., Norway 34; 70n 20e
Vansbro: Sweden 35; 61n 14e
Vanua Levu: i., Pac. O. 92; 16s 179e
Varanasi: India 52; 25n 83e
Varanger Penin.: Nor. 34; 70n 30e
Varaždin: Yugoslavia 27; 46n 16e
Vardø: Norway 34; 70n 31e
Varese: Italy 33; 46n 9e
Varna: Bulgaria 31; 43n 28e
Värnamo: Sweden 35; 57n 14e
Vaslui: Romania 31; 47n 28e
Västerås: Sweden 35; 60n 17e
Väster Dal: r., Sweden 35; 61n 13e
Västervik: Sweden 35; 58n 17e
Vasyugan: USSR 45; 59n 78e
Vatnajökull: Iceland 34; 65n 17w
Vätter, L.: Sweden 35; 58n 14e
Vaupés: r., Colombia 86; 1n 72w
Växjö: Sweden 35; 57n 15e
Vaygach I.: USSR 42; 70n 60e
Veendam: Netherlands 32; 53n 7e
Vega: Norway 34; 66n 12e
Velay, M. du: France 29; 45n 4e
Velikiye Luki: USSR 44; 56n 31e
Vellore: India 52; 13n 79e
Velmandois: France 28; 50n 3e
Velp: Netherlands 32; 52n 6e
Venado Tuerto: Arg. 88; 34s 62w
Vendée: France 29; 47n 1w
Vendôme: France 28; 48n 1e
Venetian Alps: Italy 33; 46n 13e
Veneto: Italy 33; 45n 12e
VENEZUELA 86; 5n 65w
Venezuela, G. of 86; 12n 71w
Venice: & G., Italy 33; 45n 12e
Venlo: Netherlands 32; 51n 6e
Ventimiglia: Italy 33; 44n 8e
Ventspils: USSR 35; 57n 22e
Veracruz: Mexico 82; 19n 96w
Vercelli: Italy 33; 45n 8e
Verde, C.: Senegal 66; 15n 17w
Verdun: France 28; 49n 5e
Vereeniging: S. Africa 69; 27s 28e
Veretski Pass: USSR 31; 49n 23e
Verkhoyansk: USSR 43; 67n 134e
Vermilion: Canada 80; 53n 111w
Vermilion L.: USA 84; 48n 92w
Vermont: State, USA 85; 44n 73w
Verona: Italy 33; 45n 11e
Versailles: France 28; 49n 2e
Verviers: Belgium 28; 51n 6e
Vesle: r., France 28; 49n 4e
Vesterålen: is., Norway 34; 69n 15e
Vest Fiord: Norway 34; 68n 14e
Vesuvius: volc., Italy 30; 41n 14e
Veszprém: Hungary 27; 47n 18e
Vevey: Switzerland 33; 46n 7e
Viareggio: Italy 33; 44n 10e
Viborg: Denmark 35; 56n 9e
Vicenza: Italy 33; 46n 12e
Vichy: France 29; 46n 3e
Vicksburg: USA 81; 32n 91w
Victoria: Canada 80; 48n 123w
Victoria: Hong Kong 53; 22n 114e
Victoria: Nigeria 68; 4n 9e
Victoria: r., Australia 58; 15s 130e
Victoria: State, Aust. 59; 37s 145e
Victoria, L.: Africa 68; 1s 33e
*Victoria Falls: Rhodesia 69; 18s 26e
Victoria I.: Canada 78; 70n 110w
Victoriaville: Canada 85; 46n 72w
Victoria West: S. Africa 69; 32s 23e
Vidin: Bulgaria 31; 44n 23e
Viella: Spain 29; 43n 1e
Vienna: Austria 27; 48n 16e
Vienne: France 29; 46n 5e
Vienne: r., France 29; 47n 1e
Vientiane: Laos 51; 18n 103e
Vierzon-Ville: France 29; 47n 2e
Vigevano: Italy 33; 45n 9e
Vigo: Spain 25; 42n 9w
Vijayavada: India 52; 17n 81e
Vikna: i., Norway 34; 65n 11e
Vila: New Hebrides 59; 17s 168e
Vila Cabral: Moz. 69; 13s 35e
Vila de João Bela: Moz. 69; 25s 34e
Vilaine: r., France 28; 48n 2w
Vileyka: USSR 35; 54n 27e
Villach: Austria 33; 47n 14e
*Villa Cisneros:
Sp. Sahara 66; 24n 16w
Villefranche-sur-Saône:
France 29; 46n 5e
Villeneuve-sur-Lot: Fr. 29; 44n 1e
Villeurbanne: France 29; 46n 5e
Vilnius: USSR 35; 55n 25e
Vilyuy: r., USSR 43; 64n 122e
Viña de Mar: Chile 88; 33s 72w
Vincennes: USA 84; 39n 87w
Vindel: r., Sweden 34; 65n 19e
Vindhya Range: India 52; 23n 77e
Vinh: N. Viet Nam 51; 18n 105e
Vinnitsa: USSR 44; 49n 28e
Vire: France 28; 49n 1w
Virginia: State, USA 85; 37n 79w
Virgin Is.: W. Indies 83; 18n 64w
Virovitica: Yugoslavia 27; 46n 17e
Visby: Gotland 35; 58n 18e
Viscount Melville Sd.:
Canada 78; 74n 110w
Viseu: Portugal 25; 41n 8w
Vishakhapatnam: India 52; 18n 83e
Vistula: r., Poland 35; 53n 19e
Vitebsk: USSR 44; 55n 30e
Viti Levu: i., Pac. O. 92; 18s 178e
Vitim: & r., USSR 43; 59n 113e
Vitória: Brazil 88; 20s 40w
Vitoria: Spain 25; 43n 3w
Vitry-en-Artois: Fr. 28; 50n 3e
Vitry-le-François: Fr. 28; 49n 5e
Vittoria Veneto: Italy 33; 46n 12e
Vize I.: USSR 43; 79n 77e
Vizianagaram: India 52; 18n 83e
Vladimir: USSR 44; 56n 40e
Vladimir Volynskiy:
USSR 35; 51n 23e
Vladivostok: USSR 50; 43n 132e
Vlonë (Valona): Alb. 31; 40n 20e
Vltava: r., Czech. 32; 50n 14e
*Vogelkop Penin.: Neth.
New Guinea 58; 1s 132e
Voi: Kenya 68; 3s 39e
Voiron: France 29; 45n 6e
Volcanic Plat.: NZ 55; 38s 176e
Volga: r. & hills, USSR 44; 50n 45e
Volgograd: USSR 44; 49n 44e
Vologda: USSR 44; 59n 40e
Volos: Greece 31; 39n 23e
Vol'sk: USSR 44; 52n 47e
VOLTA (UPPER) 66; 12n 0
Volta Redonda: Brazil 88; 23s 44w
Vorarlberg: Austria 33; 47n 10e
Vorkuta: USSR 42; 67n 64e
Voronezh: USSR 44; 52n 39e
Vosges: mts., France 28; 48n 7e
Voss: Norway 35; 61n 7e
Voznesensk: USSR 31; 47n 31e
Vranje: Yugoslavia 27; 43n 22e
Vratsa: Bulgaria 31; 43n 24e
Vryburg: S. Africa 69; 27s 25e
Vulcano: i., Sicily 30; 38n 15e
Vyaz'ma: USSR 44; 55n 35e
Vyborg: USSR 35; 61n 29e
Vychegda: r., USSR 44; 62n 52e
Vyshniy Volochek:
USSR 44; 58n 35e

Waal: r., Netherlands 32; 52n 5e
Wabana: Canada 79; 48n 53w
Wabash: r., USA 84; 39n 87w
Waco: USA 80; 32n 97w
Wadden Zee: Neth. 32; 53n 5e
Waddington, Mt.: Can. 78; 51n 125w
Wadi Halfa: Sudan 67; 22n 31e
Wad Medani: Sudan 67; 14n 33e
Wagga Wagga: Aust. 61; 35s 147e
Wagin: Australia 60; 33s 118e
Waiau: & r., NZ 55; 43s 173e
Waikaremoana, L.: NZ 55; 39s 177e
Waikerie: Australia 61; 34s 140e
Waikato: & r., NZ 55; 28s 175e
Waikabubak: Sumba 51; 10s 120e
Waipara: NZ 55; 43s 173e
Waipawa: NZ 55; 40s 177e
Wairakei: NZ 55; 39s 176e
Wairau: r., NZ 55; 41s 174e
Wairoa: NZ 55; 39s 177e
Waitangi: NZ 55; 35s 174e
Waitaki: r., NZ 55; 45s 170e
Waitara: NZ 55; 39s 174e
Wajima: Japan 54; 37n 137e
Wakamatsu: Japan 54; 37n 140e
Wakasa Bay: Japan 54; 36n 136e
Wakatipu, L.: NZ 55; 45s 169e
Wakayama: Japan 54; 34n 130e
Wakefield Mt.: Antarc. 91; 70s 64w
Wake I.: Pac. O. 92; 20n 167e
Wakkanai: Japan 50; 45n 142e
Walcheren: i., Neth. 32; 52n 4e
Walgett: Australia 61; 30s 148e
Wallachia: Romania 31; 44n 25e
Wallaroo: Australia 61; 34s 137e
Wallis Is.: Pac. O. 92; 13s 176w
Walvis Bay: SW. Africa 69; 23s 15e
Wanaaring: Australia 61; 30s 144e
Wanaka, L.: NZ 55; 44s 169e
Wanapitei L.: Canada 84; 47n 81w
Wandiwash: India 52; 13n 80e
Wanganui: & r., NZ 55; 40s 175e
Wangaratta: Australia 61; 36s 146e
Wangching: China 54; 43n 130e
Wangeroog: i., Ger. 32; 54n 8e
Wanhsien: China 53; 31n 108e
*Wankie: S. Rhodesia 69; 18s 27e
Warangal: India 52; 18n 79e
Warburg: Germany 32; 52n 9e
Warmbad: SW. Africa 69; 28s 18e
Warracknabeal: Aust. 61; 36s 142e
Warragul: Australia 61; 38s 146e
Warrego: r., Australia 60; 28s 146e
Warren: Idaho, USA 80; 45n 116w
Warren: Ohio, USA 84; 41n 81w
Warren: Pa., USA 85; 42n 79w
Warri: Nigeria 68; 5n 6e
Warrnambool: Aust. 61; 38s 143e
Warsaw (Warszawa):
Poland 35; 52n 21e
Warwick: Australia 60; 28s 152e
Washington: State, USA 80; 47n 120w
Washington, Mt.: USA 85; 44n 71w
Washington, D.C.: USA 85; 39n 77w
Waterbury: USA 85; 42n 73w
Waterloo: Belgium 28; 51n 4e
Waterloo: USA 84; 42n 92w
Watertown: USA 85; 44n 76w
Watling: i., Bahamas 83; 24n 74w
Watson L.: Canada 78; 60n 129w
Wau: Sudan 67; 8n 28e
Waukegan: USA 84; 42n 88w
Waukesha: USA 84; 43n 88w
Wausau: USA 84; 45n 90w
Wauwatosa: USA 84; 43n 88w
Waynesboro: USA 85; 38n 79w
Webster Groves: USA 84; 44n 90w
Weddell Sea: Antarc. 91; 70s 40w
Wei: r., China 53; 34n 108e
Weiden: Germany 32; 50n 12e
Weifang: China 53; 37n 118e
Weihaiwei: China 53; 37n 122e
Weimar: Germany 32; 51n 11e
Weisshorn: mt., Switz. 33; 46n 8e
Welkom: S. Africa 69; 28s 27e
Welland Canal: Canada 85; 43n 79w
Wellesley Is.: Aust. 58; 17s 137e
Wellington: Australia 61; 32s 149e
Wellington: NZ 55; 41s 175e
Wenchi: Ghana 68; 8n 2w
Wenchow: China 53; 28n 121e
Wentworth: Australia 61; 34s 142e
Wernigerode: Germany 32; 52n 11e
Weser: r., Germany 32; 53n 9e
Wesergebirge: Ger. 32; 52n 9e
West Bengal: India 52; 23n 87e
West Dvina: r., USSR 35; 57n 26e
Western Australia 58; 25s 122e
*Western Desert: Egypt 48; 27n 27e
Western Ghats: India 52; — —
Western Reg.: Ghana 68; 5n 2w
Western Reg.: Nigeria 68; 7n 5e
Western Sayan Mts.:
USSR 45; 52n 90e
Western Sierra Madre:
Mexico 82; 25n 105w
Westerwald: Germany 32; 51n 8e
WEST INDIES, FED. 83; — —
WEST IRIAN 58; 5s 137e
Westland: NZ 55; 43s 171e
*West Nicholson:
S. Rhodesia 69; 21s 29e
*Weston: N. Borneo 51; 5n 116e
WEST PAKISTAN 52; 30n 70e
Westphalia: Germany 32; 52n 8e
West Point: USA 85; 41n 74w
Westport: NZ 55; 42s 172e
West Rift Valley: Africa 68; — 30e
West Siberian Plain:
USSR 45; 60n 72e
West Virginia: USA 84; 39n 80w
Wetar: i., Indonesia 51; 8s 126e
Wetzlar: Germany 32; 51n 9e
*Wewak: New Guinea 59; 3s 143e
Whakatane: NZ 55; 38s 177e
Whangarei: NZ 55; 36s 174e
Wheeling: USA 84; 40n 80w
Whitehorse: Canada 78; 61n 135w
White Mts.: USA 85; 44n 71w
White Nile: r. & dam,
Sudan 67; 13n 32e
White Sea: USSR 42; 65n 37e
White Volta: r., Africa 68; 13n 1w
Whitfield: Australia 61; 37s 146e
Whitney, Mt.: USA 80; 37n 118w
Whitsunday I.: Aust. 60; 20s 149e
Whyalla: Australia 61; 33s 137e
Wichita: USA 80; 38n 98w
Wichita Falls: USA 80; 34n 98w
Wien: Austria 27; 48n 16e
Wiener-Neustadt: Aus. 27; 48n 16e
Wiesbaden: Germany 32; 50n 8e
Wiese I.: USSR 43; 79n 77e
Wilcannia: Australia 61; 31s 143e
Wilhelmshaven: Ger. 32; 54n 8e
Wilkes-Barre: USA 85; 41n 76w
Wilkes Land: Antarc. 91; 70s 120e
Willamette: r., USA 80; 44n 123w
Williamsburg: USA 85; 37n 77w
Williamson Hd.: Antarc. 91; 69s 158e
Williamsport: USA 85; 41n 77w
Williston: USA 80; 48n 104w
Willoughby, C.: Aust. 61; 36s 138e
Willow Run: USA 84; 42n 84w
Wilmington: N.C., USA 81; 34n 73w
Wilmington: N.J., USA 85; 40n 76w
Wilson: r., Australia 60; 28s 142e
Wilson Dam: USA 81; 35n 87w
Wiluna: Australia 58; 22s 120e
Winchester: USA 85; 39n 78w
Windhoek: SW. Africa 69; 22s 17e
Windsor: N.Sc., Can. 85; 45n 64w
Windsor: Ont., Canada 84; 42n 83w
Windward Is.: W. Indies 83; 13n 61w
Windward Passage:
W. Indies 83; 20n 74w
Winibigoshish L.: USA 84; 47n 94w
Winnipeg: Canada 80; 50n 97w
Winnipeg, L.: Canada 80; 53n 97w
Winnipegosis: & L., Can. 80; 52n 100w
Winona: USA 84; 44n 92w
Winston-Salem: USA 84; 36n 80w
Winterthur: Switz. 33; 48n 9e
Winton: Australia 59; 22s 143e
Wisconsin: r., USA 84; 43n 91w
Wisconsin: State, USA 84; 45n 90w
Wisła: r., Poland 35; 53n 19e
Wismar: Germany 32; 54n 12e
Witbank: S. Africa 69; 26s 29e
Wittenberge: Germany 32; 53n 12e
Włocławek: Poland 35; 53n 19e
Wolfenbüttel: Germany 32; 52n 11e
Wolfsburg: Germany 32; 52n 11e
Wollaston L.: Canada 78; 58n 103w
Wollongong: Australia 61; 34s 151e
Wonsan: N. Korea 50; 39n 127e
Wonthaggi: Australia 61; 39s 146e
Woodville: NZ 55; 40s 176e
Woomera: Australia 58; 31s 137e
Woonsocket: USA 85; 42n 71w
Worcester: S. Africa 69; 34s 19e
Worcester: USA 85; 42n 72w
Worms: Germany 32; 50n 8e
Wrangel I.: USSR 43; 71n 180
Wrocław: Poland 35; 51n 17e
Wu: r., China 53; 29n 108e
Wuchang: China 53; 30n 114e
Wuching: China 53; 38n 106e
Wuchow: China 53; 23n 112e
Wuhan: China 53; 30n 114e
Wuhsi: China 53; 32n 120e
Wuhu: China 53; 32n 118e
Wuppertal: Germany 32; 51n 7e
Würzburg: Germany 32; 50n 10e
Wutungkiao: China 53; 29n 104e
Wuyi Shan: China 53; 27n 116e
Wyalong: Australia 61; 34s 147e
Wyangala Res.: Aust. 61; 34s 149e
Wyndham: Australia 58; 16s 128e
Wyoming: State, USA 80; 43n 107w

Xanthi: Greece 31; 41n 25e
Xauen: Morocco 25; 35n 5w
Xingu: r., Brazil 87; 8s 53w

Yaan: China 53; 30n 103e
Yabassi: Cameroon 68; 4n 10e
Yakima: USA 80; 47n 120w
Yakutsk: USSR 43; 62n 130e
Yallourn: Australia 61; 38s 146e
Yalta: USSR 44; 45n 34e
Yamagata: Japan 54; 38n 140e
Yamaguchi: Japan 54; 34n 131e
Yamal Penin.: USSR 42; 70n 70e
Yamatu: China 45; 46n 84e
Yambol: Bulgaria 31; 42n 26e
Yamma Yamma, L.:
Australia 60; 26s 141e
Yampi Sd.: Australia 58; 17s 123e
Yamuna: r., India 52; 25n 81e
Yanbu': Sa'udi Arabia 49; 24n 38e
Yangchuan: China 53; 38n 113e
Yangku: China 50; 38n 112e
Yangtze: r., China 53; 31n 117e
Yangtze (Kinsha): r.,
China 50; 32n 98e
Yannina: Greece 31; 39n 21e
Yantabulla: Australia 61; 29s 145e
Yaoundé: Cameroon 66; 4n 11e
Yap: i., Pac. O. 92; 10n 138e
Yaqui: r., Mexico 80; 28n 110w
Yaraka: Australia 59; 25s 144e
Yarkand: & r., China 47; 38n 77e
Yarmouth: Canada 85; 44n 66w
Yaroslavl': USSR 44; 58n 40e
Yarra: r., Australia 61; 38s 145e
Yass: Australia 61; 35s 149e
Yatsushiro B.: Japan 54; 32n 130e
*Yawata: Japan 54; 34n 131e
Yawatahama: Japan 54; 33n 132e
Yazd: Iran 49; 32n 54e
Yellow: r., China 53; 37n 117e
Yellowhead P.: Can. 78; 53n 118w
Yellowknife: Canada 78; 62n 114w
Yellow Sea 53; 35n 123e
Yellowstone: r., USA 80; 46n 107w
Yel'nya: USSR 44; 55n 32e
Yelwa: Nigeria 68; 11n 5e
YEMEN 49; 15n 45e
Yenakiyevo: USSR 44; 48n 38e
Yenan: China 53; 37n 110e
Yenangyaung: Burma 50; 20n 95e
Yencheng: China 53; 34n 120e
Yendi: Ghana 68; 10n 0
Yenisey: r., USSR 45; 58n 91e
Yenisey, G. of: USSR 43; 72n 80e
Yeniseysk: USSR 45; 58n 92e
Yenki: China 54; 43n 130e
Yerevan: USSR 44; 40n 45e
Yermolayevo: USSR 44; 53n 56e
Yeu, I. d': France 26; 47n 2w
Yevpatoriya: USSR 31; 45n 33e
Yeysk: USSR 44; 47n 38e
Yinchwan: China 53; 38n 106e
Yingkow: China 53; 41n 122e
Yin Shan: China 50; 42n 107e
Yiyang: China 53; 28n 112e
Yokkaichi: Japan 54; 35n 137e
Yokohama: Japan 54; 35n 140e
Yokosuka: Japan 54; 35n 140e
Yokote: Japan 54; 39n 140e
Yola: Nigeria 68; 9n 12e
Yonezawa: Japan 54; 38n 140e
Yongdok: S. Korea 54; 36n 130e
Yonkers: USA 85; 41n 74w
Yonne: r., France 28; 48n 3e
York: USA 85; 40n 77w
York, C.: Australia 59; 11s 143e
Yorke Penin.: Aust. 61; 35s 137e
Yorkton: Canada 80; 51n 102w
Yorktown: USA 85; 37n 77w
Yoshkar-Ola: USSR 44; 57n 48e
Young: Australia 61; 34s 148e
Youngstown: USA 84; 41n 81w
Ypres: Belgium 28; 51n 3e
Yuan: r., China 53; 28n 110e
Yubari: Japan 54; 43n 142e
Yucatan: Mexico 82; 20n 89w
Yucatan Chan.: Mexico 83; 21n 85w
YUGOSLAVIA 26/27; — —
Yukagir Plat.: USSR 43; 66n 155e
Yukon: Canada 78; 63n 135w
Yukon: r., Canada USA 78; 63n 160w
Yulin: China 53; 38n 110e
Yuma: USA 80; 33n 115w
Yungera: Australia 61; 35s 143e
Yungning: China 53; 23n 108e
Yunkwei Plat.: China 53; 27n 107e
Yunnan: Prov., China 50; 25n 103e
Yunnanfu: China 50; 25n 103e
Yverdon: Switzerland 33; 47n 7e

Zābol: Iran 49; 31n 61e
Zabrze: Poland 27; 50n 19e
Zacatecas: Mexico 82; 23n 103w
Zadar: Yugoslavia 27; 44n 15e
Zagreb: Yugoslavia 27; 46n 16e
Zagros Mts.: Iran 49; 32n 50e
Zāhedān: Iran 49; 29n 61e
Zakinthos: i., Greece 31; 38n 21e
Zălău: Romania 27; 47n 23e
Zama: Tunisia 30; 36n 9e
Zambezi: r., Africa 69; 16s 32e
Zamboanga: Philippines 51; 7n 122e
Zamość: Poland 27; 51n 23e
Zanesville: USA 84; 40n 82w
Zante: & i., Greece 31; 38n 21e
Zanthus: Australia 58; 31s 124e
ZANZIBAR 68; 6s 39e
Zapala: Argentina 88; 39s 70w
Zaporozh'ye: USSR 44; 48n 35e
Zaragoza: Spain 25; 42n 1w
Zaria: Nigeria 68; 11n 8e
Zawiercie: Poland 27; 50n 19e
Zaysan, L.: USSR 45; 48n 84e
Zealand: i., Denmark 35; 55n 12e
Zeebrugge: Belgium 28; 51n 3e
Zeerust: S. Africa 69; 26s 26e
*Zeila: Som. Prot. 67; 11n 43e
Zeitz: Germany 32; 51n 12e
Zermatt: Switzerland 33; 46n 8e
Zeya: USSR 43; 54n 127e
Zezere: r., Portugal 25; 40n 8w
Zharma: USSR 45; 49n 81e
Zhdanov: USSR 44; 47n 37e
Zhigalovo: USSR 43; 55n 105e
Zhitomir: USSR 44; 50n 28e
Zielona Góra: Poland 35; 52n 16e
*Zimbabwe: S. Rhodesia 69; 20s 31e
Zinder: Niger 68; 9n 9e
Zittau: Germany 32; 51n 15e
Zlatibor: Yugoslavia 27; 43n 20e
Zlatograd: Bulgaria 31; 41n 25e
Zlatoust: USSR 45; 55n 60e
Znojmo: Czech. 27; 49n 16e
*Zomba: Nyasaland 69; 15s 35e
*Zongo: Congo Rep. 70; 4n 18e
Zonguldak: Turkey 31; 41n 32e
Zrenjanin: Yugoslavia 27; 45n 20e
Zuara: Libya 66; 33n 12e
Zürich: & L., Switz. 33; 47n 9e
Zwickau: Germany 32; 51n 13e
Zwolle: Netherlands 32; 53n 6e
Zyryanovsk: USSR 45; 50n 84e

* See Page 131

APPENDIX TO THE GAZETTEER

Corrections to the gazetteer have been divided into country name changes, other name changes and names which have been added to or deleted from the maps.

An asterisk alongside a gazetteer entry indicates either that the name itself has been changed or deleted, or that the country in which it is located has changed its name.

COUNTRY NAME CHANGES (New names first)

Bangladesh *see* East Pakistan
Belize *see* British Honduras
Benin *see* Dahomey
Botswana *see* Bechuanaland
Burkina Faso *see* Volta (Upper)
Cameroun *see* Cameroon
Comoro Islands *see* Comoro Archipelego
Djibouti *see* French Somaliland
Equatorial Guinea *see* Spanish Guinea
Guinea-Bissau *see* Portuguese Guinea
Guyana *see* British Guiana
Kampuchea *see* Cambodia
Kiribati *see* Gilbert Islands
Lesotho *see* Basutoland
Malawi *see* Nyasaland
Malaysia *see* British Borneo, British North Borneo, Malaya, Sarawak
Namibia *see* South West Africa
Oman *see* Muscat and 'Oman
Pakistan *see* West Pakistan
Sabah *see* British North Borneo
Sabah, Sarawak *see* British Borneo
Sikkim *incorp. into* India
Somali Republic *see* Somalia and Somaliland Protectorate
Sri Lanka *see* Ceylon
Taiwan *see* Formosa
Tanzania *see* Tanganyika and Zanzibar
Tuvalu *see* Ellice Islands
United Arab Emirates *see* Trucial 'Oman
Vanuatu *see* New Hebrides
Vietnam *see* N. & S. Vietnam
Western Sahara *see* Spanish Sahara
Yemen P.D.R. *see* Aden Protectorate
Zaïre *see* Republic of the Congo (Léopoldville)
Zambia *see* Northern Rhodesia
Zimbabwe *see* Southern Rhodesia

OTHER NAME CHANGES (New names first)

Aberdyfi *see* Aberdovy: Wales
Abruzzi *see* Abruzzi-Molise: Italy
Annaba *see* Bône: Algeria
Antananarivo *see* Tananarive: Madagascar
As Shaab *see* Ittihad: Aden
Bandar *see* Masulipatnam: India
Bandar Khomeini *see* Bandar e Shahpur: Iran
Bandar Seri Begawan *see* Brunei
Banjul *see* Bathurst: The Gambia
Béchar *see* Colomb Béchar: Algeria
Bejaïa *see* Bougie: Algeria
Berhampur *see* Chatrapur: India
Bight of Bonny *see* Bight of Biafra
Binzert *see* Bizerta: Tunisia
Boyoma Falls *see* Stanley Falls: Zaïre
Bremerhaven *see* Bremerhaven-Wesermünde: Germany
Bujumbura *see* Usumbura: Burundi
Byrd Land *see* Marie Byrd Land: Antarctica
Caernarfon *see* Caernarvon: Wales
Cape Kennedy *see* Canaveral, Cape: USA
Chipata *see* Fort Jameson: N. Rhod.
Conwy *see* Conway: Wales
Da Nang *see* Tourane: S. Viet Nam
Dakhla *see* Villa Cisneros: W. Sahara
Djaya Pura *see* West Irian: Indonesia
Doberai Penin. *see* Vogelkap Penin.: Indonesia
El Asnam *see* Orléansville: Algeria
El Bayadh *see* Geryville: Algeria
El Dar el Beida *see* Casablanca: Morocco
El Kef *see* Le Kef: Tunisia
Enfida *see* Enfidaville: Tunisia
Faradofay *see* Port Dauphin: Madagascar
F'Derik *see* Ft. Gouraud: Mauritania
Flora *see* Florø: Norway
Ford Range *see* Edsel Ford Range: Antarctica
Gaberone *see* Gaberones: Botswana
Gaza *now in* Israel
George VI Sound *see* King George VI Sound: Antarctica
Goldfields *see* Beaverlodge: Canada
Gombe Falls *see* Livingstone Falls: Zaïre
Gulf, The *see* Persian Gulf
Halq el Oued *see* La Goulette: Tunisia
Hartlepool *see* West Hartlepool: Dur. England
Ho Chih Minh City *see* Saigon-Cholon: Vietnam
Hokang *see* Hingshan: China
Huambo *see* Nova Lisboa: Angola
Ilebo *see* Port Franqui: Zaïre
Ise *see* Uji-Yamada: Japan
Isiro *see* Paulis: Zaïre
Ivano-Frankovsk *see* Stanislav: USSR
Iwaki *see* Taira: Japan
Kabwe *see* Broken Hill: Zambia
Kalevala *see* Ukhta: USSR
Kalemi *see* Albertville: Zaïre
Kananga *see* Luluabourg: Zaïre
Kinshasa *see* Léopoldville: Zaïre
Kisangani *see* Stanleyville: Zaïre
Kitakyushu *see* Kokura: Japan
Moji: Japan
Yawata: Japan
Kota Kinabalu *see* Sabah
L. Eildon *see* Eildon Res.: Aust.
L. Hume *see* Hume Res.: Aust.
Lakshadweep I. *see* Laccadive Is.: India
Likasi *see* Jadotville: Zaïre
Llanelli *see* Llanelly: Carm. Wales
Lubango *see* Sá da Bandeira: Angola
Lubumbashi *see* Elisabethville: Zaïre
Lü-ta *see* Dairen: China
Port Arthur: China
Mafeking *see* Makifeng: South Africa
Maiskhal *see* Cox's Bazaar: Bangladesh
Mahajunga *see* Majunga: Madagascar
Malawi, L. *see* Nayasa, L.: Africa
Mansa *see* Fort Rosebery: Zambia
Maputo *see* Lourenço Marques: Mozambique
Maramba *see* Livingstone: Zimbabwe
Mbala *see* Abercorn: Zambia
Mbandaka *see* Coquilhatville: Zaïre
Menzel Bourguiba *see* Ferryville: Tunisia
Mina Hassan Tani *see* Kenitra, Port Lyautey: Morocco
Molise *see* Abruzzi-Molise: Italy
Mosioa-Joenga *see* Victoria Falls: Zambia
N'djamena *see* Fort Lamy: Chad
Nouadhibou *see* Port Etienne: Mauritania
Nova Sofala *see* Sofala: Mozambique
Nyahuru *see* Thompson's Falls: Kenya
Pool Malebo *see* Stanley Pool: Zaïre
Pune *see* Poona: India
Qomisheh *see* Shahreza: Iran
Ras El Ma *see* Bedeau: Algeria
Ringerike *see* Hønefoss: Norway
Shah Faisalabad *see* Lyallpur: Pakistan
Shumen *see* Kolarovgrad: Bulgaria
Skikda *see* Philippeville: Algeria
Sofala *see* Beira: Mozambique
Sukarnapura *see* Hollandia: Indonesia
Tamil Nadu *see* Madras (State)
Tarabulus *see* Tripoli: Libya
Thunder Bay *see* Fort William: Canada
Port Arthur: Canada
Thurso *see* Strathmore: Scotland
Toamasina *see* Tamatave: Madagascar
Toliary *see* Tuléar: Madagascar
Turkana L. *see* Rudolf L.: Kenya
Ubundi *see* Ponthierville: Zaïre
Uhuru *see* Kilimanjaro: Tanzania
Vadodara *see* Baroda: India
Veliko Turnovo *see* Turnovo: Bulgaria
Voroshilovgrad *see* Lugansk
Xai Xai *see* Quelimane: Mozambique

ADDENDA: changes in Zimbabwe, Gweru see Gwelo, Harare see Salisbury, Hwange see Wankie, Kadoma see Gatooma, Kwekwe see Que Que, Mutare see Umtali, Shurugwi see Selukwe.

ADDITIONS

	Page	
Cumbernauld: Dunbarton	15	NS77
Livingston: W. Lothian	15	NT06
Newton Aycliffe: Durham	13	NZ22
Skelmersdale: Lancs.	12	SD40
Sullom Voe: *sd.*, Shet. Is.	17	HU57
Teeside: Yorks.	13	TA02

	Page	*Lat.*	*Long.*
Akademgorodok: USSR	45	55n	83e
Antarctic Peninsula	91	70s	65w
Azizia: Libya	48	33n	13e
Beida: Libya	48	33n	22e
Bethel: USA	78	61n	162w
Brong-Ahafo: Reg., Ghana	68	7n	2w
Caoma: Austl.	61	36s	49e
Cedar Lake	80	54n	100w
Central: Reg., Ghana	68	5n	1w
Chilung: Taiwan	53	25n	122e
Concepción: Paraguay	88	23s	57w
Dampier: Aust.	58	21s	117e
Elizabeth: Australia	61	35s	139e
Ethiopian Plateau	67	8n	38e
Europoort: Netherlands	32	52n	4e
Fouliang: China	53	29n	117e
Hariana: India	52	29n	75e
Islamabad: W. Pak.	52	34n	73e
Ketchikan: USA	78	55n	132w
Koolyanobbing: Aust.	60	31s	120e
Kotsebue: USA	78	67n	163w
Kwinana: Aust.	60	32s	116e
La Paz: Mexico	82	24n	110w
Las Plumas: Argentina	89	44s	67w
Lendery: USSR	34	63n	31e
McGrath: USA	78	63n	156w
Maharashtra: India	52	19n	76e
MALAYSIA	51	—	—
Malegaon: India	52	12n	74e
Mbale: Uganda	68	1n	34e
Mid-Western: Reg., Nigeria	68	6n	6e
Moura: Aust.	60	25s	150e
Mujezerskij: USSR	34	64n	32e
Nanomea: i., Pacific Ocean	92	5s	176e
Nanyuki: Kenya	68	0	37e
Nasser: Lake	48	23n	33e
Northern: Reg., Ghana	68	9n	0
Palmer Land: Antarctica	91	72s	65w
Pintung: Taiwan	53	23n	121e
Porto Franco: Brazil	87	5s	37w
Quezon City: Phil.	51	15n	121e
Quseir: UAR	48	26n	34e
Ras Lanuf: Libya	67	30n	18e
San Lorenzo: Ecuador	86	1n	79w
Sangli: India	52	17n	74e
Serpa Pinto: Angola	69	15s	18e
Sevan, L.: USSR	44	40n	45e
Shevchenko: USSR	44	44n	50e
Sidra: Libya	67	30n	18e
Sihanoukville: Camb.	51	11n	104e
Socarbo: Brazil	88	23s	48w
Sovetskaya: Antarc.	91	79s	93e
Tarrasa: Spain	26	42n	2e
Tobago: i.	86	11n	61w
Topolobampo: Mexico	80	26s	109w
Upper: Reg., Ghana	68	10n	2w
Vinh Loi: Vietnam	51	10n	106e
Volta: Reg., Ghana	68	7n	0
Willow: South Alaska	78	62n	150w
Ye: Burma	51	15n	98e
Yeniseysk: USSR	37	58n	93e
Yushkozero: USSR	34	65n	32e
Yuzhno-Sakhalinsk: USSR	43	46n	143e

DELETIONS

Names omitted from the maps because they no longer apply.

Isle of Ely: Cambs.
Middlesex: Co., England
Soke of Peterborough: Admin. Co., Northants.

Ajena: Ghana
Atshan: Libya
Australian Antarctic Territory
British Antarctic Territiory
Bugunda: Uganda
Chiengi: N. Rhodesia
Cochin China: Vietnam
Cyrenaica: Libya
Falkland Is. Dependencies
Fezzan: Libya
Hankow: China
Ifni (SP.)
Korsakov: USSR
Lahej: Aden
Pint Stoup, The: Angus
Piraeus: Greece
Ross Dependency: Antarctica
Togoland: Ghana
Tripolitania: Libya
United Arab Republic (Syria)

ABBREVIATIONS

used on the Maps and in the Gazetteers

Aber. . Aberdeenshire
A.C.T. . Australian Capital Territory
Admin. . Administrative
Afghan. . Afghanistan
Afr. . . Africa
Alb. . . Albania
Alg. . . Algeria
Ang.. . Angola
Ann.. . Annual
Antarc. . Antarctica
Arch. . Archipelago
Arg. . . Argentina
Ariz.. . Arizona
Ark. . . Arkansas
Atl. O. . Atlantic Ocean
Aus. . . Austria
Aust. . Australia
Auton. . Autonomous
Ayr. . . Ayrshire

B. . . Bay
Basuto. . Basutoland
Bech. . Bechuanaland
Beds . . Bedfordshire
Belg.. . Belgium, Belgian
Ber. . . Berwickshire
Berks . Berkshire
Bol. . . Bolivia
Br. . . British
Braz.. . Brazil
Breck. . Brecknockshire
Bucks . Buckinghamshire
Bulg.. . Bulgaria
Bur. . . Burundi
Bute. . Buteshire

C., c. . Cape
Caer. . Caernarvonshire
Caith. . Caithness
Camb. . Cambodia
Cambs. . Cambridgeshire
Can. . Canada
Card. . Cardiganshire
Carm. . Carmarthenshire
Cen. Amer. Central America
Chan. . Channel
Ches. . Cheshire
Clack. . Clackmannanshire
Co. . . County
Col. . . Colombia
Corn. . Cornwall
C.R. . . Costa Rica
Cumb. . Cumberland
Czech. . Czechoslovakia

D.C.. . District of Columbia
Del. . . Delaware
Den. . Denmark, Danish
Denb. . Denbighshire
Depr. . Depression
Dept. . Department
Derby. . Derbyshire
Devon. . Devonshire
Dist. . District
Dom. Repub. Dominican Republic
Don.. . Donegal
Dumf. . Dumfriesshire
Dunb. . Dunbartonshire
Dur. . Durham

E. . . East(ern)
E. Loth. East Lothian
Ec. . . Ecuador
Eg. . . Egypt
El Sal. . El Salvador
Eng. . . England

Eq. . . Equatorial
Etg. . . Etang (lagoon)
Eth. . . Ethiopia

Falk. Is. . Falkland Islands
Fd. . . Fjord
Fed. . . Federation
Ferm. . Fermanagh
Fin. . . Finland
Flint. . Flintshire
Fla. . . Florida
For. . . Forest
Fr. . . France, French
Ft. . . Fort

Ga. . . Georgia
Gal. . . Galway
G.B. . . Great Britain
Gd. . . Grand
Ger. . . Germany
Glac. . Glacier
Glam. . Glamorgan
Glos . . Gloucestershire
Gp. . . Group
Grc. . . Greece
Grnld. . Greenland
Gt. . . Great
Gu. . . Guiana
Guin. . Guinea

Hants. . Hampshire
Harb. . Harbour
Hd. . . Head
Hebr. . Hebrides
Here. . Herefordshire
Herts . Hertfordshire
Hond. . Honduras
Hung. . Hungary
Hunts . Huntingdonshire

I. . . Ile (island)
I.(s) i.(s) Isle Island(s) island(s)
Ice. . . Iceland
Ill. . . Illinois
Ind. . . India
Ind. . . Indiana (U.S.A.)
Indon. . Indonesia
Inv. . . Inverness-shire
Irel. . . Ireland
Isr. . . Israel
It. . . Italy

Jap. . . Japan(ese)
Jor. . . Jordan
Junc. . Junction

Kans. . Kansas
Kash. . Kashmir
Kild.. . Kildare
Kilk. . Kilkenny
Kinc. . Kincardineshire
Kinr. . Kinross
Kirkc. . Kirkcudbrightshire
Ky. . . Kentucky

L. . . Lake, Loch, Lough, Lac, Lago
Lan. . . Lanarkshire
Lancs. . Lancashire
Ld. . . Land
Leb. . . Lebanon
Leics. . Leicestershire
Leit. . . Leitrim
Lim. . . Limerick
Lincs. . Lincolnshire
Lit. . . Little
Lon. . . Londonderry
Long. . Longford
Lr. . . Lower

Lux. . . Luxembourg
Madag. . Madagascar
Mal. . . Malaya
Mass. . Massachusetts
Md. . . Maryland
Medit. . Mediterranean
Mer. . Merionethshire
Mex.. . Mexico
Mich. . Michigan
Middx. . Middlesex
Midloth.. Midlothian
Minn. . Minnesota
Miss.. . Mississippi
Mo. . . Missouri
Mon.. . Monmouthshire
Mor. . Morocco
Montg. . Montgomeryshire
Moray. . Morayshire
Moz. . Mozambique
M. Mt. (n) Mount(ain)

N. . . North(ern)
N. Guin. New Guinea
Nairn. . Nairnshire
Nat. . . National
Nat. Mon. National Monument
N.C.. . North Carolina
Neth. . Netherlands
N.H.. . New Hampshire
Nic. . . Nicaragua
N.J. . . New Jersey
Nor.. . Norway, Norwegian
Norf. . Norfolk
Northants Northamptonshire
Northumb. Northumberland
Notts . Nottinghamshire
N.Sc. . Nova Scotia
N.Y.. . New York State
Nyasa. . Nyasaland
N.Z.. . New Zealand

O. . . Ocean
Ont.. . Ontario
Oreg. . Oregon
Ork. Is. . Orkney Is.
Oxon. . Oxfordshire

Pa. . . Pennsylvania
Pac. O. . Pacific Ocean
Pan. . . Panama
Peeb. . Peeblesshire
Pak. . . Pakistan
P.E.I. . Prince Edward I.
Pemb. . Pembrokeshire
Penin. . Peninsula
Perth. . Perthshire
Phil. . Phillipines
Pk. . . Peak
Plat. . . Plateau
Pol. . . Poland
Port. . Portugal, Portuguese
P.R. . . Puerto Rico
Prot.. . Protectorate
Prov. . Province
Pt(e). . Point(e)

Queens.. Queensland

R. r. . River
Ra. . . Range
Rad. . . Radnorshire
Reg. . . Region
Renf. . Renfrewshire
Rep.(ub.) Republic
R. of Irel. Republic of Ireland

Res. . . Reservoir
Rhod. . Rhodesia
R.I. . . Rhode Island
Rom. . Romania
R. & Crom. Ross & Cromarty
Rox.. . Roxburgh
Rut. . . Rutland
Rwa.. . Rwanda

S. . . South(ern)
Salop. . Shropshire
S. Amer. South America
Sau. Arab. Sa'udi Arabia
S.C. . . South Carolina
Sd. . . Sound
Selk.. . Selkirkshire
Shet. Is. . Shetland Is.
Som.. . Somerset
Sp. . . Spain, Spanish
S.S.R. . Soviet Socialist Republic
St. . . Saint
Staffs . Staffordshire
Stirl.. . Stirlingshire
Stn. . . Station
Str. . . Strait
Suff. . . Suffolk
Suther. . Sutherland
Swazi. . Swaziland
Swed. . Sweden, Swedish
Switz. . Switzerland
Syr. . . Syria

Tangan. . Tanganyika
Tenn. . Tennessee
Territ. . Territory
Thai.. . Thailand
Tip. . . Tipperary
Trin.. . Trinidad
Trust. . Trusteeship
Tun. . . Tunisia
Tur. . . Turkey
Tyr. . . Tyrone

U.A.R. . United Arab Republic
U.N.. . United Nations
Up. . . Upper
U.S.A. . United States of America
U.S.S.R.. Union of Soviet Socialist Republics

V. . . Vulcan (volcano)
Va. . . Virginia
Val. . . Valley
Venez. . Venezuela
Vict.. . Victoria
V. Nam . Viet Nam
Volc.. . Volcano
Vt. . . Vermont

W. . . West(ern)
W. Ind. . West Indies
War . Warwickshire
Wat.. . Waterford
Westmor. Westmorland
Wex. . Wexford
Wick. . Wicklow
Wig.. . Wigtownshire
Wilts. . Wiltshire
Wis.. . Wisconsin
W. Loth. West Lothian
Worcs . Worcestershire

Yorks . Yorkshire
Yugo. . Yugoslavia